**Think Twice!**

D1304258

SECOND EDITION

THINK TWICE!

Sociology Looks at Current Social Issues

Lorne Tepperman

University of Toronto

Jenny Blain

Sheffield Hallam University

With the assistance of
  Jenny Hugh
  Maja Jovanovic
  Albert Kwan
  Erik Landriault

PEARSON

Prentice Hall

UPPER SADDLE RIVER, NEW JERSEY 07458

Library of Congress Cataloging-in-Publication Data

Tepperman, Lorne
   Think twice!: sociology looks at current social issues/Lorne Tepperman, Jenny Blain; with the assistance
of Jenny Hugh . . . [et al.].—2nd ed.
      p. cm.
   Includes bibliographical references.
   ISBN 0-13-099528-2
   1. Sociology.   2. Social problems.   3. United States—Social conditions—1980– .   I. Blain, Jenny.
II. Hugh, Jenny.   III. Title.
   HM586.T46 2006
   301—dc22

                                                                                    2005014953

Editorial Director: Leah Jewell
Executive Editor: Christopher DeJohn
Editorial Assistant: Kristin Haegele
Senior Marketing Manager: Marissa Feliberty
Marketing Assistant: Anthony DeCosta
Assistant Manufacturing Manager: Mary Ann Gloriande
Cover Art Director: Jayne Conte
Interior Design: John P. Mazzola
Composition/Full-Service Project Management: Kari Callaghan Mazzola and John P. Mazzola
Printer/Binder: Hamilton Printing Company
Cover Printer: Phoenix Color Corp.

This book was set in 10/12 Times.

Pearson Education LTD.   Pearson Education North Asia Ltd
Pearson Education Singapore, Pte. Ltd   Pearson Educación de Mexico, S.A. de C.V.
Pearson Education, Canada, Ltd   Pearson Education Malaysia, Pte. Ltd
Pearson Education–Japan   Pearson Education, Upper Saddle River, NJ
Pearson Education Australia PTY, Limited

10 9 8 7 6 5 4 3 2 1
ISBN 0-13-099528-2

This book is dedicated to a friend and leading Canadian sociologist,
James (Jim) E. Curtis, who passed away on May 27, 2005.
Jim was convinced that good sociology can improve our lives and our societies.
This book is written in the hope that Jim was right.

CONTENTS

PREFACE

The second edition of *Think Twice!* covers a large number of pressing social issues. As before, our goal is to provoke debate and discussion.

The world has changed a lot since we published the first edition in 1998. Too many people—even young people—have already made up their minds on many of the most pressing public issues of our day. That's because the mass media and other sources present us with information that is one-sided, over-simplified, erroneous, and sometimes even intentionally misleading. Some feel that the Party in power since 2000 has adopted a black-and-white moralistic approach to pressing social issues like war, terrorism, abortion, stem cell research, poverty, religion in the schools, affirmative action, and cooperation with foreign allies. Sociology's job is to encourage skepticism about such rigid views, to get students to "think twice" (or more) about what they take for granted, and to think in sociological ways, using the sociological imagination. It is with the aim of encouraging second thoughts, sociological debate, and informed reasoning that we have written this book.

Think Twice! wants to help teach critical thinking skills to introductory sociology students. (In fact, the material in this book has been classroom-tested on thousands of introductory students, and it works!) As a teaching tool, the book can be used as a supplement to a mainstream textbook. *Think Twice!* is useful as a supplementary text in social problems, social issues, and applied sociology courses. *Think Twice!* is made up of fifteen chapters, corresponding to the most common topics in an introductory sociology course. Each chapter contains three sections, or "debates." Each section, or debate, contains an essay and assorted learning aids: discussion questions, writing exercises, and research activities.

In each debate, the discussion is as fair and even-handed as we can manage. After a brief introduction, we look at the best arguments supporting each side; and finally, we draw our own conclusions from the evidence. This approach helps to launch student papers and to promote classroom and tutorial discussion.

In preparing this book, we have read scores of books, papers, and reports on each topic, but we have kept in-text citations to a bare minimum. We are not suggesting that students write their own essays without appropriate in-text citation. We have done it to ensure the flow of the argument: In-text citations distract undergraduate readers and we want, above all, to have the logic of each debate well understood. Sources that have informed our arguments are found at the end of each chapter. Students are advised to seek out and read any references that seem intriguing. These selected references can provide a starting point for student essays and literature reviews.

It is not the goal of this book to replace the basic textbook, with its definition of concepts, discussion of founding figures, and comparison of sociological paradigms. Nor does it try to provide a comprehensive review of the literature. Any attempt to do this in so short a space would inevitably prove incomplete, quickly out-of-date, and therefore misleading. Nor is it the goal of this book to present the way sociologists actually go about their research, either as individuals or, collectively, as a discipline. There is no attempt to represent the sequencing or give-and-take of arguments as they normally evolve in the research literature. Space

PREFACE

does not permit such an approach, and this book has another, equally important goal.

Our goal is to present students with compelling debates showing two (or more) sides of public issues, in this way helping them to "think twice." We show the underlying logic of debates about public issues: the main points that are being made by opposing sides, and (by implication) the kinds of sociological evidence that are relevant to a complete discussion of any issue. What students can learn from this approach is how sociologists try to move away from normative, common sense, or moralistic stances to an approach that emphasizes the usefulness of research and empirical evidence.

Each debate in this book ends by taking a stand. This is to show that sociological reasoning and evidence can take us beyond a mere clash of views on controversial issues. *Think Twice!* is saying, "There are social problems to be solved. In solving them, social science evidence and reasoning are superior to common sense. That is why students should study sociology." This approach to social issues is what the "founding figures" of sociology stood for. Moreover, this approach connects introductory sociology to applied sociology. It hints at the ways sociology can be used in the real world and encourages students to look for other applications.

We hope that instructors find this book helpful and students find it thought-provoking—the beginning of a series of fruitful debates, though certainly not the end. We look forward to comments and suggestions for improvement.

ACKNOWLEDGMENTS

This book has benefited from the help and criticism of many students and colleagues. We built this second edition on the successful first edition, published in 1998, which has been classroom tested. In preparing to revise it, we relied on the advice of three reviewers and the encouragement of our editor, Chris DeJohn.

Following this advice and encouragement, we added fifteen new pieces to reflect new public debates, and updated the rest to reflect new research findings. Undergraduate assistants Albert Kwan and Erik Landriault drafted eight new pieces for the new edition—specifically, Sections 1.3, 2.3, 10.2, and 12.3 (Albert) and Sections 4.2, 9.2, 10.3, and 14.2 (Erik), respectively. Additionally, Albert, Erik, and other talented undergraduate assistants at the University of Toronto—Monica Beron, Maygan Jorge, Aileen Lin, Athena Maikantis, Ruxandra Popescu, Kara Serebrin, and Joseph Tesoro—helped Lorne Tepperman update the original pieces and revise the new ones. On the other side of the Atlantic, Jenny Hugh helped Jenny Blain write seven new pieces and revise the old ones. Maja Jovanovic gave the manuscript a final critical reading, and Emily Glazer proofread the page proofs during the final pre-press stage.

The final product that you are about to read is the result of many thoughts and second thoughts, and we are grateful to all of the students who were so generous with their time. Thanks also go to Chris DeJohn of Pearson Education/Prentice Hall, who strongly encouraged us to revise our book; to our reviewers—Michael T. Ryan, Dodge City Community College; Randall MacIntosh, California State University, Sacramento; and Debra Welkley, California State University, Sacramento—for their very helpful suggestions; and to instructors over the years who have used and enjoyed this book. Finally, our thanks go to Kari Callaghan Mazzola, who provided cheerful and thorough management of the production of this somewhat unwieldy book. It was great working with her.

Lorne Tepperman
Jenny Blain

 THINK TWICE!

CHAPTER 1  CULTURE

Culture is our uniquely human environment. It includes all of the objects, artifacts, institutions, organizations, ideas, and beliefs that make up the social environment of human life. This social environment is *symbolic* as well as material, in the sense that every human group produces *meanings* that remain in a society's memory.

People who share a culture experience the world similarly. Culture structures a person's perception of the world and shapes his or her behavior. As a result, a common culture helps to hold a society together. On the other hand, differences in cultural values within a society can lead to significant conflict—as was evident in the recent presidential elections. There, it became clear that America is split in two, with one half adhering to traditional, conservative values inspired by religion; and another half adhering to modern, liberal values inspired by science.

In this chapter we discuss three issues connected with culture. First, we consider whether multiculturalism is a good thing for society, or whether it divides people. Second, we examine the debate over the *culture of poverty* and whether some people are poor because of faulty cultural values. Third, we discuss a new social preoccupation—organized gambling—and ask what it says about our culture and whether gambling activity has positive or negative effects on our society.

1.1 Shouldn't Everybody in This Country Think Just Like Me?

The issue: Should our social institutions accept more than one way of thinking and behaving as "legitimate"? This question continues to be important in respect to religious beliefs and their conflict with natural science. The issue has gained greater intensity with fears about terrorism and religious militancy after 9/11.

Since 9/11, Americans have become much more interested in the cultural differences between their own country and the rest of the world. Friction has developed between America and Europe over foreign intervention in Iraq. More dramatically still, there has been talk about a "clash of civilizations" between America—the Christian West, more generally—and Islamic societies of the East.

A similar clash of values was evident in America during the elections of 2004. Then, religion-inspired conservative values personified by the Republican Party battled against (somewhat more) liberal secular values personified by the Democratic Party, and the country was split culturally in half. The country's coastal regions and the north-Midwestern states (Illinois, Michigan, and Wisconsin) largely endorsed Democratic liberalism, while the rest of the country—especially the South, the Plains, and the Southwest—endorsed President Bush's faith-driven agenda.

Often, cultural differences are related to geography, class, ethnic, and racial differences. In the recent U.S. election, for example, the country was split by race. Blacks and Puerto Ricans, urban people and especially the urban poor, were much more likely than whites and small-town people to support the Democrats. Age and marital status also played a part. Young people—especially single young people—were much more likely to support the Democrats, while older and married people were more likely to support the Republican moral agenda.

This problem of moral and cultural differences is new to Americans. Until recently, a strong sense of *Americanism* has united people of widely varying backgrounds by blurring their cultural differences. By contrast, in many other societies, cultural variety has always posed a problem that could not be ignored. Sometimes the difference has divided people and set them against one another. Consider the recent civil wars in the former Yugoslavia, the former Soviet Union, the Congo, and Rwanda. Or, consider the recent debate in France over Muslim schoolgirls wearing head-scarves. This custom has caused much more furor in France than in any other part of the world, precisely because the French consider themselves to be rationalists, democrats, and secularists. They see the head-scarves as an affront to their own cultural tradition, which demands a separation between religion and state activities (such as schooling).

In culturally mixed societies people are forced to debate the issue of multiculturalism. Some communities, for example, have to decide which language(s) are appropriate for schools, government offices, and other public institutions. Then people are likely to ask themselves: Does *multiculturalism* bring us together or pull us apart? Do multicultural policies weaken our sense of identity and unity?

In some countries—for example, in many parts of the European Union—people don't know how to deal with large numbers of culturally different immigrants. Sometimes violence erupts. Some politicians call for an end to immigration. A high rate of childbearing by some cultural groups shifts the balance, too. This change has been apparent in large American cities like New York, Los Angeles, and Miami, and in southwestern states like California and Texas, as well as in a variety of cities in Europe.

Americans need to think about these issues more, because multiculturalism is becoming a problem in America as it is elsewhere. Some communities welcome, and make room for, the new cultural mix. *Multicultural strategies* for inclusion vary widely. Some community leaders arrange events to show public interest in and respect for minority cultures. Others help pay for ethnic arts, dance, theatre, or mass media productions. Some communities make public services, including education, more accessible by offering them in minority languages. In some countries, there have even been efforts to reimburse minority groups for past losses or damages—for example, for the internment of Japanese citizens during WWII.

But do these various forms of multiculturalism divide people? Some say they do.

MULTICULTURALISM IS DIVISIVE

Identity and Standards   Many societies—like the United States, Germany, and France—have a strong *national identity* or *national character*. Members of these societies believe that, as a group, they share certain characteristics—whether cultural, moral, or temperamental. Often citizens of other countries also share this belief. Of course, national identities are stereotypes. The French sociologist Durkheim said that they are "secular totems," meaning that they are ritualistic, simplified, and idealized. However, like all stereotypes, they have a grain of truth to them. And true or not, members of the society believe in their national identity. They are proud of their identity and don't want to lose it.

In some societies, multicultural policies cause people to fear for the survival of the nation's identity. Fearfulness is particularly likely among people who feel that their identity, or the respect shown that identity, is already threatened. Such fears may arise because of foreign competition, the influence of foreign media on the local culture, or for other reasons.

Critics may also be concerned that multiculturalism causes cultural "standards" to fall—that multiculturalism dilutes educational standards and encourages mediocrity. In the United States, for example, some believe that universities are becoming intellectual and cultural disaster zones laid waste by racial and cultural differences among the students. Such views pose a problem for liberal universities and for liberal societies generally.

Many feel it is reasonable to expect schools to provide students with the *Western canon* and *cultural literacy*—a basic familiarity with (Anglo-) American culture. In the eyes of many commentators, this is the key to social and economic success. They argue that we do minority-group students no favor by failing to teach them the ideas, terms, facts, and idioms that people commonly use in our society. So, it is both practical and sensible to force minority students to learn the majority culture.

To do otherwise—to bow to demands that the schools give more attention to minority cultures—means changing traditional standards of excellence. In the short term, this may benefit minority students, but in the long term it fails to prepare them in basic skills.

Multiculturalism Fosters Discrimination A second criticism of multiculturalism is that it fosters discrimination. This is paradoxical because the intent behind multiculturalism is to strengthen and validate minority cultures. Yet occasionally, in practice, the effect of an official multicultural policy has been a weakening rather than enhancement of the status and cohesion of minority groups.

There are several reasons for this. First, discrimination and multiculturalism both encourage people to make ethnic distinctions. Without ethnic distinctions—identifying ancestral differences between people—neither multiculturalism nor discrimination can flourish. So paying attention to group differences may divide us. Making distinctions may invite hatred rather than an appreciation of cultural differences. It certainly offers a visible basis for inequality and discrimination.

In short, multiculturalism risks churning up unwanted negative sentiments. So, if we want to minimize prejudice, discrimination, and ethnic conflict, it may be best to celebrate our shared humanity rather than call attention to our ethnic differences.

A second, related concern is that multiculturalism promotes reverse discrimination. When multiculturalism means making restitution for harm done in the past, it punishes people for something their great-grandparents may (or may not) have done decades earlier.

Finally, multiculturalism, by attempting to remedy past injustices and inequalities, puts some groups on the offensive and others on the defensive. Instead of pointing to people's common interests, it points to their differences. Instead of promoting activities that people of different backgrounds can share, it calls for a redistribution of wealth, power, and prestige on ethnic grounds. In a variety of ways, multiculturalism promotes expressions of envy and hostility. It encourages a "victim mentality"—too much concern with wrongs done in the past—a strategy that does not guarantee the empowerment of former victims.

Multiculturalism Slows Full Social Equality
Many people support multiculturalism in the belief that it brings more equality for minority people. However, multiculturalism may have the opposite effect, for two reasons.

First, multiculturalism discourages assimilation into the mainstream of society. In effect, it encourages people to remain part of that little island of activity that they, or their parents or grandparents, created after immigrating. By strengthening traditional ties, loyalties, and values, multiculturalism makes people less suited to get along with others of different ethnic, linguistic, or religious backgrounds. Insulated and isolated, people may get less education than they need (and can handle), thinking that they can earn a living from the crafts and trades available within their own community. Because of too little education they may not be upwardly mobile. And because of that, traditional elites from an Anglo-American background will continue to be able to dominate society.

Second, by exaggerating the importance of ethnic or cultural ancestry, multiculturalism draws people away from activities that could help to establish more equality. People who focus their interest and effort on their own ethnic group are less likely to join with others of the same social class (but a different ethnic group) to protest unfair working conditions or bad governmental policies. Then the powerlessness of class is hidden by ethnic differences. Mobilizing people around class issues might do more than multicultural policies to equalize society and benefit minority groups.

For these reasons some people oppose multiculturalism, saying it is divisive. However, as we noted earlier, other people take an opposite view, arguing that multiculturalism is not divisive.

MULTICULTURALISM IS NOT DIVISIVE

Diversity Already Exists   The United States *is* ethnically and culturally diverse and it is becoming more so. Thus, we really have only two choices. We cannot eliminate the diversity: We can only grudgingly tolerate it or embrace and promote it.

Many believe that, in truth, the United States is only a collection of regional and local cultures. By this reasoning, the "American national identity" is artificial, a piece of national propaganda and part of the country's civil religion. It is an article of faith, not a fact, that all Americans share a common set of values, norms, or interests. In truth, America was never a melting pot. The U.S. civic culture has traditionally allowed ethnic minorities to maintain their uniqueness and diversity.

If so, multiculturalism is valuable because it recognizes the country's historic variety and continues to encourage a healthy variety in people's thinking. Cultural variety is not only normal and inevitable; it is fundamental to an open, democratic society and firmly rooted in American history. So the idea that there is a single national identity (or national culture) that must be protected against any encroachment needs rethinking. For similar reasons, the concern over cultural and educational

standards also needs closer examination. We should not view minority demands for varied educational materials as an attempt to evade Anglo-American content. We cannot suppose that students are trying to "get off easy" just because they want to speak in their own language or read stories set in a country where their ancestors were born.

On the contrary, minority standards are just fine. At school, other things (such as social class) being equal, immigrants generally outperform native-borns and non-Anglos outperform Anglos. This difference in achievement is more marked for certain ethnic minorities—for example, Chinese-Americans—than it is for others. Yet in general, to insist that immigrants and non-Anglos meet the prevailing (native-born, Anglo) academic standards means asking them to perform worse, not better.

Would the education of students in their own language and cultural context make already high-performing minorities perform better? Or would it have no effect on educational performance levels? We don't know, though it is likely that teaching minorities in their own language would improve their educational attainment and raise their self-esteem as well. All we can say with certainty is that multicultural policies are not intrinsically a strategy to evade tough academic requirements.

Multiculturalism Integrates   Much has been written suggesting that the United States is an atomized, overly individualistic society. Many Americans—especially those who live in large cities—feel isolated and lacking in community. They also feel little obligation to their neighbors and fear victimization by strangers. What holds people together in this society and gives their lives meaning?

Ethnic culture is one of several important sources of community linkage, which also include associational ties, unions, and families. Ethnic ancestry gives minority people a deep sense of community. (For this reason, even a Celtic Revival—emphasizing Irish and Scottish culture—has recently enjoyed success among Anglo-Saxons in North America.) Thus, ethnic identities are actually unifying, not divisive. A plurality of groups and group memberships can reverse the destructive dissociation of individuals from society.

Like it or not, ethnic sentiments and loyalties often exist far below the threshold of reason. They have a deep meaning for people and won't go away. This is not what rational philosophers (like Voltaire and Marx) had expected, nonetheless it is so. Ethnic identity's survival—generation after generation, century after century—tells us something important. The most recent revivals of ethnic and linguistic identity are responses to a need for collective identity in societies that are unable to provide other forms of membership and identification. They help people to satisfy their need for self-realization, communicative interaction, and recognition.

Organic Solidarity Multiculturalism does something else that Emile Durkheim said was necessary in modern societies: It provides *organic solidarity*—social cohesion or connectedness that is based (paradoxically) on differences between people.

Common sense might tell you that it is similarity that ties people together, and this is often true. Other situations, however, call for diversity. In those cases, we gain an advantage by making use of our differences. It is mutual dependency that underlies organic solidarity.

In small, technologically simple societies, people have similar skills and similar ideas. Their similarity ties them together and they can tolerate little variation in beliefs and actions. By contrast, modern societies are large, fluid, and technologically complex. We cannot expect sameness and cannot bring about total uniformity, even by force. In the end, even crushingly authoritarian societies have failed to do so. Therefore, Durkheim wrote, modern people must learn to tolerate, encourage, and benefit from differences.

There is value in our differences, since differences encourage us to enter into exchange with one another, and exchange helps us all. The Korean-American retailer, Portuguese-American construction worker, and Polish-American school psychologist all need each other. Exchanges tie people together in a modern, differentiated society. By

showing respect and encouragement for diversity, multiculturalism honors this principle of strength through difference. Multiculturalism broadens our understanding of different ethnic groups and cultures, thereby fostering awareness and acceptance, rather than ignorance and fear.

Multiculturalism Meets Society's Needs Today, most minorities participate fully in the country's social and economic life. What influences participation most is not a person's ancestry but how much education that person received. Typically, highly educated people are better informed and more involved in public affairs. Membership in unions, churches, and other voluntary associations is also important. Holding constant these factors, minority people are as well-informed and politically active as any other Americans.

People can belong to an ethnic group and to the larger community at the same time—involvement in one need not hinder involvement in the other. In short, ethnic survival and multicultural policies do no harm—indeed, they offer great benefits—to society.

SUMMING UP

Shouldn't everyone be just like me (or you)? Not necessarily. In fact, for most purposes, it's best if there are lots of differences.

Of course, multiculturalism may be integrative up to a point and then become divisive. This is suggested by historical instances of cultural distinctiveness leading to secession: Belgium separating from the Netherlands, Norway from Sweden, and Slovakia from the Czech Republic, for example. Today, many in Catalonia want to secede from Spain, many in Quebec to secede from Canada, and so on. Real problems can arise when ethnic differences reflect differences in power, so that conflict over ethnicity is really a conflict over power and independence.

Yet, in the long run, even these conflicts are steps to a larger integration. Successful multiculturalism will involve sharing power as much as creative cultural diversity. From a global perspective, multiculturalism is a realistic and gracious way to take part in the modern world order. It is, as Durkheim said, recognition that we humans are now all connected by our differences as well as our similarities. The differences between people—cultural, racial, or physical—are problematic only if they are used to justify prejudice and discrimination.

We are just learning to live with one another as neighbors in the same town and residents of the same globe. Public education should include the teaching of multicultural knowledge about the rights and duties of national and global citizenship. Universities and colleges should help to heal a world torn apart by racial and ethnic conflicts, by ensuring the educational curriculum reflects a diversity of cultural traditions.

Is multiculturalism a divisive policy? The research available provides little evidence that it is. Eventually, multiculturalism may become a heated issue in the United States, too, as it has in many other countries. It may be useful, then, to study the experience of other multiethnic societies and draw the appropriate conclusions.

REVIEW EXERCISES

For Discussion and Debate

1. Should all primary and secondary school students be forced to learn at least two languages and demonstrate familiarity with the history and customs of at least two ethnic cultures?
2. Should all new immigrants be forced to take a six-week full-time course in the English language and American customs and history before they can get permission to work?
3. Is it a good thing for a country to have a strong *national identity*? Does it matter what that national identity is?
4. Would the United States have fairer or more progressive social policies if there were fewer cultural differences among Americans?

Writing Exercises

Write a brief (500-word) essay on one of the following topics:

1. The American national identity: its most attractive and unattractive features.
2. How American customs (or values) vary from one part of the country to another (e.g., between the Northeast and the South or Southwest, or between the East Coast and the West Coast, or between large cities and small towns).
3. "How important my ethnic ancestry is to my personal identity and sense of self."
4. "Cultural differences strengthen (or weaken) my relationship with my best friend."

Research Activities

1. Examine published survey data to find out how much the views on an important social issue (you choose the issue) vary from one minority group to another among people with the same level of education.
2. Make a small questionnaire or interview schedule and use it to find out the attitudes of at least a dozen people toward issues of multiculturalism discussed in this section.
3. Carefully observe (and record) the interaction between two culturally different people. What problems, if any, are caused by these cultural differences?

4. Observe and record interactions within a group in which there is clear evidence of the benefits connected with organic solidarity, that is, cohesion based on differences. What do you learn from doing this?

SELECTED REFERENCES

Amin, Ash. 2004. "Multi-Ethnicity and the Idea of Europe." *Theory, Culture & Society* 21, 2 (Apr.): 1–24.

Calabrese, Andrew and Barbara Ruth Burke. 1992. "American Identities: Nationalism, the Media, and the Public Sphere." *Journal of Communication Enquiry* 16, 2 (Summer): 52–73.

Cesareo, Vincenzo. 2004. "Lights and Shadows of Multiculturalism." *Cambridge Review of International Affairs* 17, 1 (Apr.): 105–117.

Charon Cardona, Euridice T. 2004. "Re-Encountering Cuban Tastes in Australia." *The Australian Journal of Anthropology* 15, 1 (Apr.): 40–53.

Connor, Walker. 1993. "Beyond Reason: The Nature of the Ethnonational Bond." *Ethnic and Racial Studies* 16, 3 (July): 373–389.

Duster, Troy. 1993. "They're Taking Over! and Other Myths about Race on Campus." *Philosophy and Social Action* 19, 1–2 (Jan.–June): 30–37.

Fuchs, Lawrence H. 1990. *The American Kaleidoscope: Race, Ethnicity, and the Civic Culture.* Hanover, NH: University Press of New England.

George, Douglas and George Yancey. 2004. "Taking Stock of America's Attitudes on Cultural Diversity: An Analysis of Public Deliberation on Multiculturalism, Assimilation, and Intermarriage." *Journal of Comparative Family Studies* 35, 1 (Winter): 1–19.

Gitlin, Todd. 1993. "The Rise of 'Identity Politics': An Examination and a Critique." *Dissent* 40, 2 (171) (Spring): 172–177.

Graham, Sandra. 1994. "Motivation in African Americans." *Review of Educational Research* 64, 1 (Spring): 55–117.

Horwath, Peter. 1994. "The 'Dead White Male's Canon' under Attack at American Universities: Traditionalist Perceptions." *History of European Ideas* 19, 1–3 (July): 553–560.

Husbands, Christopher T. 1994. "Crises of National Identity as the 'New Moral Panics': Political Agenda Setting about Definitions of Nationhood." *New Community* 20, 2 (Jan.): 191–206.

Kent, Tara Elizabeth. 2004. "Sexual Harassment in a Multicultural Workplace." *Dissertation Abstracts International, A: The Humanities and Social Sciences* 64, 8 (Feb.): 3091-A.

Melucci, Alberto. 1990. "The Voice of the Roots: Ethno-National Mobilizations in a Global World." *Innovation* 3, 3:351–363.

Patterson, Orlando. 1994. "Ecumenical America: Global Culture and the American Cosmos." *World Policy Journal* 11, 2 (Summer): 103–117.

Phillips, Sharia Kim. 2004. "Racial Identity and Rural Schools: A Qualitative Study of White Teachers' Multicultural Perceptions, Understandings, and Teaching Practices." *Dissertation Abstracts International, A: The Humanities and Social Sciences* 64, 7 (June): 2659-A.

Portes, Alejando and Min Zhou. "Should Immigrants Assimilate?" *The Public Interest* (Summer): 18–33.

Schlesinger, Arthur M., Jr. 1991. *The Disuniting of America: Reflections on a Multicultural Society.* Knoxville, TN: Whittle Direct Books.

Schnapper, Dominique. 1994. "The Debate on Immigration and the Crisis of National Identity." *West European Politics* 17, 2 (Apr.): 127–139.

Smelser, Neil J. 1993. "The Politics of Ambivalence: Diversity in Research Universities." *Daedalus* 122, 4 (Fall): 37–53.

Solarzano, Daniel G. 1991. "Mobility Aspirations among Racial Minorities, Controlling for SES." *Sociology and Social Research* 75, 4 (July): 182–188.

Stahl, Abraham. 1993. "Cultural Literacy: A Positive View." *Interchange* 24, 3:287–297.

Tatla, Darshan S. 2004. "Sikhs in Multicultural Societies." *International Journal on Multicultural Societies* 5, 2 (Dec.): 181–196.

Trueba, Henry T. 1993. "Race and Ethnicity: The Role of Universities in Healing Multicultural America." *Educational Theory* 43, 1 (Winter): 41–54.

Verkuyten, Maykel. 2004. "Everyday Ways of Thinking about Multiculturalism." *Ethnicities* 4, 1 (Mar.): 53–74.

Walzer, Michael. "Multiculturalism and Individualism." *Dissent* 41, 2 (175) (Spring): 185–191.

Wax, Murray L. 1993. "How Culture Misdirects Multiculturalism." *Anthropology and Education Quarterly* 24, 2 (June): 99–115.

Wilterdink, Nico. 1994. "Images of National Character." *Society* 32, 1 (211) (Nov.–Dec.): 43–51.

1.2   Do Poor People Have Bad Values?

The issue: Are the poor to blame for their own poverty? Could, and should, the poor learn different values and, in that way, become self-reliant? Or are faulty values beside the point?

In America, there has been a long-running argument, carried over into the political field, about the origins of poverty. For much of the eighteenth and nineteenth centuries, many viewed the poor as having flawed or even depraved characters. Many considered poverty a result of (or punishment for) sinfulness, laziness, or lack of a proper work ethic; therefore the poor were ostracized, avoided, stigmatized, and even thrown in jail.

Sociologists started to study poverty systematically in the late 1800s and they quickly concluded that poverty was also caused by social and economic factors beyond people's own control. Gradually, in the United States, public attitudes toward the poor started changing. In the 1930s, due to the Great Depression, large numbers of people had to struggle to make a living. It became clear that they were not to blame for their joblessness and poverty. Under President Roosevelt's leadership, the public came to realize that the poor needed government assistance. They deserved help and they would get it.

Further discussions about the social causes of poverty in the 1960s helped eliminate a lot of negative thinking about the character of the poor. At that time, under the heading of "The War on Poverty," programs were devised to combat poverty and its harmful effects. However, the results were not what people hoped for. According to recent studies, enthusiasm for the War on Poverty faded in the late 1970s and 1980s. Once again, stereotypes of "welfare queens" and "welfare bums" became common, and support for programs devised to help the poor waned significantly. The War on Poverty was not so much lost as abandoned. Today, attitudes toward the poor are ambivalent. Many people feel that the government should strive to combat poverty. However, many others hold the view that government assistance for the poor is undeserved because they judge poor people to be naturally lazy or incapable.

Genetic explanations of poverty, which attributed poverty to inborn and inherited defects, used to be popular. Today, however, genetic explanations have fallen out of favor and the dominant explanations are cultural and sociological. But what are the links between culture and poverty, and the direction of these relationships? In this section, we first consider the argument known as the *culture of poverty* thesis: that certain types of culture restrict people, prevent them from achieving their potential, and hence act to keep their members—groups, or even whole societies—in poverty. The counterargument reverses the direction of causation: It says that people who are poor learn to act in ways that are adaptations to their poverty.

Whether either of these arguments fully describes or explains the situation of people facing poverty today is something we assess at the end of this section.

What is "poverty"? Entrapment by the welfare state? A lack of food and shelter? Being unable to bring in enough money to live on?

Definitions of poverty vary from one location to another, depending on what people do in their daily lives. In some areas, a few individuals are poor; in others there are entire groups living in mass poverty. In the United States in 2002, 34.6 million people lived below the official poverty line. Mississippi holds the doubtful distinction of being the state with the highest percentage of the population (18.9 percent) living below the poverty line. Likewise, in Canada, approximately 4.9 million lived in poverty in 1999, representing fully 16.2 percent of the population. Other countries also give figures for poverty rates, with a *poverty line* calculated so that it represents a minimal standard of living, generally higher in cities and lower in rural areas, reflecting the cost of living in these areas. In India, for example, 19 percent of the population lives below the poverty line. (Note, however, that governments define "the poverty line," and where that line gets drawn varies over time and from one society to another.)

In the United States, some people are more likely to be poor than others: Thus, 24.1 percent of African Americans live in poverty, compared with only 8 percent of non-Hispanic Whites. A high proportion of children in female lone-parent households—more than fifty percent—live below the poverty line. Issues of poverty are often tied to racial discrimination and gender discrimination, resulting in racial ghettoes and the "feminization of poverty."

CULTURE IS A CAUSE OF POVERTY

Examining who is poor, whether in North America or abroad, is illuminating. Poor families are unduly common among Black North Americans, among Native North Americans, or in households headed by female single parents. There are of course many poor families and individuals that fall into different categories. Generally, women, racial minorities, rural people, and people with less education are more likely to be poor in any given society.

Some anthropologists researching other parts of the world have come up with the answer that culture and poverty are linked, that some people are perpetually economically disadvantaged because, somewhere along the way, they assimilated poor values that handicap their ability to improve their lives. Their work partly echoes that of Max Weber, who showed in his book, *The Protestant Ethic and the Rise of Capitalism,* the connections between the development of capitalist economies in north-western Europe, and religious attitudes influencing people's thoughts and behavior. Weber distinguished between the Calvinist Protestantism of the rising capitalist classes in Britain and Germany and the Netherlands, and the Catholicism of the working class.

According to Weber, Calvinism and Catholicism emphasized different values: Work was essential for Calvinists; giving alms or charity was essential for Catholics. Within Calvinism, earning interest (and achieving prosperity by other means as well) became marks of those who were "chosen." Work was a duty, and not working—or having no work—was viewed as immoral. Weber's Protestant Ethic implies a reliance on hard work, rationalism, and individualism—especially, distinguishing oneself from the masses of other people. Cultural goals here include success, and the cultural means to achieving success include individual hard work. This strong individualism leads to the belief that the poor are themselves to blame for their situation due to their individual failures and flaws.

Yet, these individualistic assumptions do not adequately describe present-day poor people. If we look at who is poor in America, first we can see individuals who have become poor through accidents or bad luck, or perhaps due to old age. Not all of these stay poor—many do recover. However, others have always been poor. They come from poor families, or poor neighborhoods.

They have grown up in poverty. Often, as in the case of Black or Native Americans, the initial poverty arose out of very unequal treatment, due to racist attitudes. However, people have grown used to living in poverty, and it is now very hard for them to extricate themselves from it. Children born into poverty are more likely to grow up to be poor adults, due to a lack of family connections, social capital, and education.

The scientific concept of a "culture of poverty" arose first in the work of anthropologist Oscar Lewis. Lewis described how people can become trapped by their culture. Capitalism could not have arisen without hard work and the concept of investment, but, said Lewis, not all cultures espouse views that are in line with these values. For instance, where people learn to think of themselves as members of a family or community first, and as individuals second, they do not act for themselves and may not try to rise above other family members. This is part of the concept of familism, referred to above; another part is the belief that it is necessary to have many children.

Lewis considered that the people he studied—Mexican peasants, among others—held values that were not consistent with the need to change their farming practices to more profitable ones. They were not innovative; they valued the family over the individual; they were unwilling to place trust in people outside the family; and they viewed anybody who did get ahead as unfairly taking other people's shares of the village economic pie. They were both dependent on and hostile to government policies. All of these traits Lewis saw as handicapping the ability of the villagers to adopt modern farming methods and raise their standard of living.

To repeat, Lewis saw these traits as cultural rather than individual. People learned them as children when they were socialized into the culture. The only hopes for change and for prosperity came from programs initiated outside the villages, and government workers since Lewis's time have commented on the reluctance of peasant farmers to innovate. The major problems of underdevelopment, Lewis concluded, were cultural ones.

Turning again to North America, we can see how the concept of a culture of poverty can explain many of the problems facing individuals, families, and groups today. Where people are willing to innovate and to work hard, they can often remove themselves from poverty. The chronically impoverished members of society are neither necessarily born lazy nor inherently lacking in innovation and enterprise. Instead, it is the culture in which they were raised—a culture that promotes learned helplessness, pessimism, and a lack of faith in the system—that prevents them from amassing the tools and skills necessary to escape their situations.

Modern society requires work *and* initiative, the same values that were instrumental in the development of capitalism. Unfortunately, whole sectors of society have become caught in a series of poverty traps (including the welfare trap, examined in another chapter). Today, those who support the culture of poverty arguments cite evidence drawn from studies of the urban underclass.

Specifically these are studies of communities experiencing concentrated poverty, such as urban *ghettos*. Indeed studies show that these are high poverty areas characterized by a large number of unemployed residents. This high rate of unemployment is said to lead to loss of organization, social capital, and meaning, and to social isolation. Some well-documented characteristics of the ghettos are endemic poverty, high crime rates, high rates of teen pregnancies and female headed households, and widespread welfare dependency. The characteristics that make up a successful community are the same characteristics that are missing in so-called "urban ghettos," namely; a mobilization of social support, religiosity or spirituality, extended family cooperation and cooperation between community organizations.

This view of the *urban underclass* as having a distinct culture and distinct values is enforced by the media, which often portrays ghetto residents as delinquent, dangerous, lazy, sexually promiscuous, uneducated, irresponsible, suffering from addictions, dependent on government assistance, and generally deviant. The findings of numerous studies conducted in urban ghettos actually seem to support the thesis of a vicious cycle of poverty. Most of the children in these areas grow up in poor households. Where children grow up seeing their parents dependent and ineffectual, they will absorb the culture of fatalism.

But in an area of concentrated poverty and joblessness, these children might encounter other negative role models aside from their parents. In the end they might assimilate a lot of the antisocial values that many people in their neighborhood hold and lose faith in established authority and institutions, attachment to mainstream social values, conventions, and norms. Furthermore, educational theorists speak of cultural deficit: When children come to school without an orientation to books, or reading, or work, they may fall further and further behind. In a study of children's aspirations in a low income neighborhood, for example, Jay MacLeod found that children as young as eleven in such areas no longer believe in the benefits of higher education. Overall the statistics for poor children inhabiting poor neighborhoods are grim. No wonder children who grow up poor are six times more likely than average to lead poor adult lives; fully 24 percent of them do so. Timing is crucial. Poverty during the early years of a child's life is the most harmful in causing low school completion rates.

Supporters of the culture of poverty argument also cite the effects of teen pregnancy and single motherhood, phenomena that are also known to be common in impoverished urban neighborhoods. Children of teen mothers and single mothers are usually poor; they also benefit from less parental attention and time, and teen mothers in particular might be less educated. It is difficult for money-stressed parents, especially lone parents, to provide good parenting. Children of single and teen mothers are also said to be more likely to drop out of school, be poor as adults, engage in criminal activities, and girls might become teen mothers in their turn.

Some studies suggest that poverty is perpetuated from generation to generation within the urban underclass. Traits that constitute a lower-class lifestyle are consequences of the extreme present-orientation of that class. According to this theory, the lower-class person lives from moment to moment, and is either unable or unwilling to take account of the future or control his impulses. Daniel Patrick Moynihan and other liberal leaders have long pointed to the high poverty rates within the African American community and associated this with features of the culture of poverty such as absent fathers, unwillingness to defer gratification, and spending for its own sake. Some initiatives have attempted to remedy this situation.

For example, educational programs (such as Head Start) have helped many African American and European American children to break out of the culture of poverty. If we are truly seeing a decline in the poverty statistics today, it may be due to programs such as these, which aim to show children that hard work can pay off.

CULTURE IS NOT A CAUSE OF POVERTY

Don't Forget about Agency The above argument is a classic example of functionalist sociology. In this paradigm, culture is seen as something above and beyond the individual, or even the groups or societies formed by individuals. People are socialized at an early age into the norms, values and beliefs of their cultures, and the socialization affects them for life—at least, according to functionalists.

As people engage in activities, they make plans, form intentions, and foresee circumstances. Actions have unintended consequences. As people engage in their actions and practices, they interact with others who may assist their plans, subvert them, or take up some aspects and ignore others. People have their own agendas. If we regard culture not as a system of norms, values, and beliefs that is fixed and internalized, but as something more fluid, we may see how people in their everyday activities create *culture* and pass it on to their children. Socialization theory depends on the idea that people internalize their parents' values and beliefs as children, and then act on the basis of these. However, it is easy to find people who question the values that have been handed down to them.

What about social structure? A further strand to this argument is that, while people act with intent, they are constrained in what they can do by social structures and processes. These structures and processes become evident through what other people do and the assumptions they make. The culture of poverty theory ignores the structural elements—laws, social policies, institutionalized discrimination—that contribute to the maintenance of a marginalized sector of the population.

Poor people and their cultures are being compared to others and being judged by these others. Their culture is found to be lacking, and critics apply the epithets of lazy, not innovative, uncaring, improvident, or impractical. This judgment occurs without regard to either the processes that made the people poor, or what they themselves think about the situation.

Alice O'Connor, in her book *Poverty Knowledge*, warns us about the biases in poverty research in America. Most research is done by white, upper- or middle-class individuals who will inevitably have an "us" versus "them" perspective on poverty since they did not experience it first hand. We must also be aware that poverty is an ideologically charged issue, one of the main contention points between the liberal and the conservative political traditions and that therefore a lot of the conclusions about poverty might purposefully lack certain explanations that could contradict the particular ideology.

Aside from a cultural explanation, one cannot overlook the social and economic realities that lead to impoverishment. First of all, we already discussed the fact that the poverty of racial and ethnic groups is a legacy of a racist past; by the same token female-headed households are poorer due to the earning gap between genders. Another reason that many blue collar workers became poor was the moving of manufacturing jobs outside of the country, which left them unskilled, untrained for the service sector, and thus unemployed with no end in sight to their poverty.

What if we view poverty instead as a result of the uneven distribution of resources within society? Through taxation and social programs, some societies attempt to distribute resources in a relatively even manner. When money is scarce and not guaranteed in the future, it makes little sense to speak of "improvidence." For example, in her book *All Our Kin*, Stack reveals that households led by single mothers are not a deviant family form, but rather an adaptation to poverty that allows women to interact with an extended kin network and benefit from a lot of help from other females. This allows them to survive their financial situation.

Studies also show that many single mothers choose to remain unmarried in order to qualify for much needed welfare benefits, since men are usually unemployed or have very low paying jobs and would be unable to support them and their children. Many poor children realize that they cannot afford college, they might desperately need a source of income and, therefore, see dropping out of high school as necessary.

Generally, when thinking of a poor neighborhood, one can enumerate many causes for people's inability to rise out of poverty, causes that are unrelated to culture. For example, poor people might not be able to work because they are sick, and this illness might be due to lack of sanitation, improper nutrition, pests, lack of heating, or lead poisoning (lead paint is common in old, low-rental units). Rather than saying that children from poor families have internalized norms of laziness, we can point out that they have to deal with conditions that their wealthier peers do not face: under-equipped classrooms, crowded home conditions, the lack of a place to study, or even hunger during the day, all of which prevent children from giving full attention to their class work. The poverty cycle of low food quality, low income, poor health, malnutrition, poor environmental sanitation, and infectious diseases greatly undermines the ability of children to concentrate and do well in school. Saying that a culture of poverty and the people who share it are responsible for this uneven distribution of physical resources is simply blaming the victims.

The history of victim-blaming in Western society goes back a long way. Some of the ideologies that formed the current concept of welfare arose around the time of the Poor Law in Elizabethan England—nearly five hundred years ago. Victim-blaming originates in the ideas expressed by the Protestant Ethic that Weber described. The idea that people who are not at work are sinful or immoral is a counterpart to the concept of worldly success marking out those who are "God's elect." The notion that a culture of poverty is responsible for keeping people poor fits with our society's dominant ideology. It says that poor people deserve to be poor because they have bad values.

Blaming the poor for their poverty relieves others of the guilt of being on the winning side of an unequal system.

Who Are the Poor? The culture of poverty theory implies that people in poverty remain there and that the children of poor families themselves stay poor. Of those who were poor as children, nearly half do not remain poor in adulthood. It is revealing to look at people who are poor today in North America. Some are unemployed and some of these are not seeking employment: the stereotypical people on welfare. Many others, however, are in the workforce and U.S. figures for 1996 show a rise in the numbers of the "working poor."

It may also be instructive to look at social barriers that prevent poor people from escaping their poverty, such as the poor quality of schooling in low income neighborhoods, the lack of money for college education, racism and discrimination that place certain individuals at a disadvantage compared to others. Such barriers are especially significant in a competitive winner-take-all society such as the American society that financially rewards the best qualified, best trained individuals. Because the poor start the job market competition on an unequal footing their achievements and thus their income will be lower. Lower social, cultural and educational capital continue to impede the poor.

Some live in areas where there is little work to seek. Moving may not be an option that appears to make much sense, particularly where people can contribute to their family economies in ways other than by directly earning a wage (such as by taking care of other family members, children, or elderly relatives). If the only jobs to be found pay a minimum wage, earnings may actually fall below the poverty line for a household with one or more children to support, especially in an expensive city. If you're just able to survive living pay check to pay check, with little money coming in, it is near impossible to save money for emergency purposes, or upgrading to a better neighborhood. Some may have sought work so many times already that they are burnt out, dispirited, incapacitated by the experience.

Many still have commitments to family. It seems odd that culture of poverty theorists stress familism as a problem when, throughout North American society, women are constantly being told that their first commitment should be to their children and other family members. However, many women on welfare say that they would welcome a chance to work—provided they can find reliable, affordable childcare. What of the other components of the culture of poverty: the ideas that the poor are frivolous spenders, concerned only with instant gratification? Middle-class, relatively well-off people often consider that poverty means simply being a bit short of cash and having to do some budgeting. However, for many people in the impoverished areas of Los Angeles or Toronto or Chicago, being poor means not having enough money to pay the rent or power bills on a regular basis. Going into debt in order to feed and house oneself or one's family means that any money earned is already spoken for, and debt and the interest on it accumulate fast.

Poverty-line calculations include only money for basic housing and food, and minimal clothing.

Summing Up

Do poor people have bad values? Like rich people, some poor people have bad values and some don't. But there is only a weak fit between values (or worthiness) and rewards in our society.

Poverty is created by society and maintained by society. Rather than look to individuals for a solution, we can look to the interaction between individuals and their society: how they are treated by officials and authorities, what rules are made concerning their employment and how much they can earn before deduction of benefits, what labels are applied to them by officialdom, what barriers specific groups or people encounter in trying to pursue their goals (e.g., racist attitudes). Rather than blaming the victim, it makes sense for sociologists to ask how labeling comes about and how society is involved in it, how society constructs dependency in people so labeled, and how some groups have managed to break free of it.

Only by looking at the processes by which people struggle to make sense of and overcome their everyday obstacles can we hope to understand the experience of poverty. And only by changing the conditions of that struggle can we hope to reduce the poverty rates. Blaming "bad values" won't do the job.

Review Exercises

For Discussion and Debate

1. "Given the opportunities available to every person in North America today, there is no need for anyone to be poor."
2. Does a strong attachment to family help or hinder individual success? (Does it depend what that "family" is?)
3. Members of a religious order used to say: "Give me a child for the first seven years, and he (sic) will be mine for life." True or not?
4. Are early intervention programs worth the effort and expense?

Writing Exercises

Write a brief (500-word) essay on one of the following topics:

1. How do people learn to be poor?
2. You are the unemployed single parent of a two-year-old child. Describe your chief strategies for avoiding poverty.
3. How and why are culture and poverty associated in the popular press?
4. Discuss poverty and the political debate on its causes.

Research Activities

1. Collect media items (such as press clippings) about relationships between culture and poverty. What views are expressed in these items? Do you agree with these views?
2. Survey your friends or neighbors. How many different views of relationships between culture and poverty can you find?
3. Study speeches of political figures on this topic. Do you find any relationships between the views expressed and the cultural, religious, or ethnic-group membership of the politician?
4. Collect recent poverty statistics. What trends can you observe? Is poverty increasing or decreasing? What groups are becoming more, or less, poor? (Hint: the Internet is a good source of recent official statistics. Some starting URLs are http://www.marketingtools.com/Publications/ NN/96-NN/9606-NN/9606NN03.html and http://www.heritage.org/heritage/cd-ranking/ 44pover.html.)

SELECTED REFERENCES

Ambert, Anne-Marie. 1998. *The Web of Poverty: Psychosocial Perspectives.* Binghamton, NY: Haworth Press.

Asen, Robert. 2002. *Visions of Poverty: Welfare Policy and Political Imagination.* East Lansing, MI: Michigan State University Press.

Banfield, Edward C. 1974. *The Unheavenly City Revisited.* Boston, MA: Little, Brown and Company.

Banton, Michael 1990. "The Culture of Poverty." *Social Studies Review* 5, 3 (Jan.): 112–114.

Boxill, Bernard. 1994. "The Culture of Poverty." *Social Philosophy and Policy* 11, 1 (Winter): 249–280.

Bradley, Schiller. 2004. *The Economics of Poverty and Discrimination.* 9th ed. Upper Saddle River, NJ: Prentice Hall.

Danziger, Sheldon and Robert Haveman. 2001. *Understanding Poverty.* Cambridge, MA: Harvard University Press.

Frank, Robert and Philip Cook. 2003. "Winner-Take-All Markets." In *Wealth and Poverty in America: A Reader,* edited by Dalton Conley. Malden, MA: Blackwell Publishing.

Friedrichs, Jurgen and Jorg Blasius. 2003. "Social Norms in Distressed Neighbourhoods: Testing the Wilson Hypothesis." *Housing Studies* 18, 6 (Nov.): 807–826.

Gans, Herbert J. 1992. "The War against the Poor: Instead of Programs to End Poverty." *Dissent* 39, 4 (169) (Fall): 461–465.

Giddens, Anthony. 1984. *The Constitution of Society: Outline of the Theory of Structuration.* Berkeley and Los Angeles, CA: University of California Press.

Iceland, John. 2003. *Poverty in America: A Handbook.* Los Angeles, CA: University of California Press.

Jencks, Christopher. 1992. *Rethinking Social Policy: Race, Poverty, and the Underclass.* Cambridge, MA: Harvard University Press.

Jones, Delmos J. 1993. "The Culture of Achievement among the Poor: The Case of Mothers and Children in a Head Start Program." *Critique of Anthropology* 13, 3 (Sept.): 247–266.

Jones, Jacqueline. 1992. *The Dispossessed: America's Underclasses from the Civil War to the Present.* New York: Basic Books.

Katz, Michael B., ed. 1993. *The "Underclass" Debate: Views from History.* Princeton, NJ: Princeton University Press.

Kaya, Yunus. 2003. *The Culture of Poverty.* Southern Sociological Society (SSS).

Kelly, Susan E. 2002. "'New' Genetics Meets the Old Underclass: Findings from a Study of Genetic Outreach Services in Rural Kentucky." *Critical Public Health* 12, 2 (June): 169–186.

Lawson, Bill E., ed. 1992. *The Underclass Question.* Philadelphia, PA: Temple University Press.

Lewis, Oscar. 1959. *Four Families: Mexican Case Studies in the Culture of Poverty.* New York: Basic Books.

Lundy, Garvey F. 2003. "The Myths of Oppositional Culture." *Journal of Black Studies* 33, 4 (Mar.): 450–467.

MacLeod, Jay. 2003. "Ain't No Making It: Aspirations and Attainment in a Low-Income Neighborhood." In *Wealth and Poverty in America: A Reader,* edited by Dalton Conley. Malden, NY: Blackwell Publishing.

Mangum, Garth et al. 2003. *The Persistence of Poverty in the United States.* Baltimore, MD: John Hopkins University Press.

Marklund, Steffan. 1990. "Structures of Modern Poverty." *Acta Sociologica* 33, 2:125–140.

Massey, Douglas S. and Nancy A. Denton. 1993. *American Apartheid: Segregation and the Making of an Underclass.* Cambridge, MA: Harvard University Press.

Matza, David. 1966. "The Disreputable Poor," in *Class, Status and Power: Social Stratification in Comparative Perspective.* 2d ed. Edited by Reinhard Bendix and Seymour Martin Lipset. New York: Free Press.

Mayer, Susan. 2003. "What Money Can't Buy: Family Income and Children's Life Chances," in *Wealth and Poverty in America: A Reader,* edited by Dalton Conley. Malden, NY: Blackwell Publishing.

Morris, Michael. 1989. "From the Culture of Poverty to the Underclass: An Analysis of a Shift in Public Language." *American Sociologist* 20, 2 (Summer): 123–133.

Moynihan, Daniel P. 1965. *The Negro Family Case for National Action.* Washington, D.C.: Labor Department Office and Policy Planning and Research.

O'Connor, Alice. 2001. *Poverty Knowledge: Social Change, Social Policy and the Poor in the Twentieth-Century.* Princeton, NJ: Princeton University Press.

Ortiz, Ana Teresa and Laura Briggs. 2003. "The Culture of Poverty, Crack Babies, and Welfare Cheats: The Making of the 'Healthy White Baby Crisis.'" *Social Text* 21, 3 (76) (Fall): 39–57.

Quillian, Lincoln. 2003. "How Long Are Exposures to Poor Neighborhoods? The Long-Term Dynamics of Entry and Exit from Poor Neighborhoods." *Population Research and Policy Review* 22, 3 (June): 221–249.

Ryan, William. 1976. *Blaming the Victim.* New York: Vintage Books.

Sawhill, Isabel V. 2003. "The Behavioral Aspects of Poverty." *The Public Interest* 153 (Fall): 79–93.

Stack, Carol. 2003. "Swapping." In *Wealth and Poverty in America: A Reader,* edited by Dalton Conley. Malden, NY: Blackwell Publishing.

Tropman, John. 1998. *Does America Hate the Poor? The Other American Dilemma.* Westport, CT: Greenwood Publishing Group.

Weber, Max. [1904] 1930. *The Protestant Ethic and the Spirit of Capitalism.* London: Unwin University Books.

Wilson, Jacqueline Zara. 2002. "Invisible Racism: The Language and Ontology of 'White Trash.'" *Critique of Anthropology* 22, 4 (Dec.): 387–401.

Wilson, William Julius. 1987. *The Truly Disadvantaged.* Chicago, IL: University of Chicago Press.

Zundel, Alan. 2000. *Declarations of Dependency: Civic Republican Tradition in U.S. Poverty."* Albany, NY: State University of New York Press.

1.3   What's Wrong with Gambling?

The Issue: Some say that buying a lottery ticket or gambling at a casino is harmless fun. Others argue that the gaming industry disrupts family life and degrades community standards. Who's right and how right are they?

The element of chance is a natural part of any gambling venture, whether the gamble is provided by a casino slot machine, a weekly poker night between friends, or a day at the racetrack. Risk and the possibility of unpredicted payoffs underlie the thrill recreational gamblers and other fans of games experience, and expect to experience.

Anthropologists who study recreation cross-culturally classify games into three groups: games of (1) physical skill, (2) chance, and (3) strategy. In games of pure chance, physical skill and strategy (by definition) play no role in determining the outcome—winning or losing. Dice games, roulette, and bingo are three games whose outcomes rely solely on the random game play—the "roll of the dice." They may appeal to people because the game's uncertain outcome mirrors the uncertainty of life itself. As Roberts and Sutton-Smith note, only certain types of cultural group possess games of pure chance. Their popularity varies from one culture to another.

Gerda Reith, an expert gambling researcher, concludes that the love of gambling grows out of a permanent sense of uncertainty. This fits in with her observation that games of chance are particularly appealing in insecure, complex societies such as our own. By voluntarily engaging in games of chance, modern players try to gain a small measure of influence by controlling the arena in which their chances play out.

The result of a cultural shift in our society toward financial risk-taking is the growth of a massive gambling industry, allied with other massive industries: entertainment, hospitality, sex. Legalized gambling is big business in the United States. According to the final report of the 1999 National Gambling Impact Study Commission (NGISC), the industry has grown tenfold since the mid-1970s. In

1973, only seven states operated lotteries, with sales of roughly $2 billion. By 1997, lotteries were available in 37 states, with total sales of $34 billion. During that same period, per capita annual lottery spending increased from $35 to $150. More generally, gross revenues from gambling increased from $10.4 billion in 1982 to $54.3 billion in 1998, according to statistics from the U.S. General Accounting Office.

Casinos have also enjoyed a remarkable surge in popularity. Today, in addition to the 400-plus resort-style destination casinos of Las Vegas, Reno, and Atlantic City, over 100 riverboat and dockside casinos, and roughly 330 Indian-run casinos, are currently in operation around the country. Today, gambling in some form is legal in all states except Hawaii and Utah.

Money spent on gambling, as a percentage of personal income, has doubled since 1973: The average adult in the United States now spends $238 annually on gambling, approximately one-tenth of their yearly leisure budget. Legal (and illegal) bookmaking on sporting events and retail gambling devices (e.g., video poker terminals, stand-alone slot machines) in bars, convenience stores, and truck stops are also enjoying healthy growth. Meanwhile, pari-mutuel wagering on horse races, dog races, and jai alai have declined in recent years, although racetrack betting remains a popular form of sports gambling.

Growth in the gaming industry has been fueled by a growing acceptance of gambling as a legitimate form of recreation. Those who continue to criticize gambling as a moral sin or violation of America's work ethic are being drowned out by an ever-growing chorus of public support for casino and lottery entertainment. However, the growth of gambling represents a major shift in American culture away from a Protestant work ethic toward a "culture of luck." This, in addition to its social and economic consequences, causes many to wonder whether gambling has become too common, especially among vulnerable populations (i.e., children, elderly people, and poor people).

As gambling becomes increasingly widespread in American culture, policymakers have begun to ask whether unrestricted growth should be permitted to continue, or whether a freeze should be put on future gaming developments while researchers determine the full extent of gambling's effects. The industry's advocates concede that there are social costs to the introduction, maintenance, and expansion of gambling opportunities in a region.

GAMBLING: THE BENEFITS OUTWEIGH THE COSTS

Gambling Is Good for Local Economies   When asked to defend their claim that casinos help out troubled local economies, advocates invariably make reference to the conclusions of the federally appointed National Gambling Impact Study Commission, the most comprehensive study of the gaming industry in the United States conducted to date. The short- and long-term social benefits—increased work, health care, training and education—are undeniable. Some have argued that quality entertainment, in and of itself, is a social benefit to communities and individuals.

Once considered one of the most economically depressed counties in America, Tunica has undergone a dramatic reversal of fortune since casino gambling first appeared in 1992. Within a decade, it had become the third largest gaming town in the country ("The South's Casino Capital"), boasting nine casinos, an expanded regional airport, a national golf and tennis center, a 168-acre eco-park, and over 10 million visitors per year. Tax revenues from the casinos have made possible public investments in education, health care, recreation, law enforcement and fire protection, housing for the elderly and disabled, and road and sewer improvements.

Legalized gambling operations are also often claimed to be the solution to the economic troubles of North America's Indian populations. Since the passing of the Indian Gaming Regulation Act in 1988, which permitted First Nations to operate casinos and bingo parlors, numerous tribal communities have used gambling to revive their otherwise economically and socially depressed communities. Tribal gambling revenues increased from $212 million in 1988 to $14.4 billion in 2002, a nearly seventy-fold increase.

The Foxwoods Casino complex, operated by the Connecticut Mashantucket Pequot Tribal Nation, is currently the largest in the world, with 320,000 square feet of gaming space, 11,500 employees, and over 40,000 visitors per day. Supporters point out that the gambling revenues are used to help advance the welfare of native communities. The establishment of such programs and facilities generate more employment, leading to a reduction in unemployment rates in these native communities.

Similarly, many state governments have begun to use lottery revenues to fund important public projects and services. Of the 38 states currently operating lotteries, 16 have earmarked all or part of the revenues for education. Georgia, for instance, uses lottery money to finance kindergarten programs for 65,000 children as well as the HOPE Scholarship Program for college and university-bound students.

Some believe that state governments risk becoming dependent on gambling revenues. However, gaming advocates note that lottery money typically accounts for little of any state's annual budget (ranging from 0.41 percent in New Mexico to 4.07 percent in Georgia). State income and sales taxes, by comparison, each comprise approximately 25 percent of all revenue collected by states. So, gaming revenues contribute significantly to, but do not overwhelm, the balance of government revenues.

Responsible Gambling Is Harmless Fun
Casinos and racetracks often bill themselves as being a part of the "gaming and leisure industry," and for good reason: Gambling is a popular form of adult recreation. Gambling gives people the experiences of lift and escape: Gambling gives people a sense of lift—sensory, physical, and/or emotional—as the result of the adrenaline rush, and gambling gives people a temporary escape from reality. Gambling gives them an opportunity to leave home and engage in a social activity.

A positive self-concept, in turn, improves the health of these individuals.

Gambling Is Well-Regulated   Given the potential for fraud and greed in commercial gambling, responsibility is demanded of both its suppliers and consumers. The corporate nature of today's casino companies—many of which are traded publicly on stock exchanges—virtually ensures an industry free of organized crime influence.

A variety of procedures—extensive monitoring and strict accounting requirements from the federal Securities and Exchange Commission; the trend toward consolidating casinos into national chains; an executive structure comprising boards of directors, CEOs, attorneys, and lobbyists; strict background checks and constant surveillance of casino floor employees; and hatred of negative publicity—work against the penetration by illegal or unscrupulous elements. Further regulation is conducted at the state level, typically by an independent gaming and/or lottery commission. Strict regulations and security measures are also enforced at a community level, to prevent and deter crime.

Most Gamblers Are Responsible   The vast majority of gamblers are responsible adults who go to casinos for sociability or entertainment, wager only what they can comfortably afford to lose, and stop gambling long before their losses begin to threaten the stability of family relationships, employment status, and community standing.

As with any activity involving risk, a small minority of gamblers lose control when gambling and develop problems that, if left unchecked, lead to financial and social ruin. Hence, even the American Gaming Association, a national trade organization representing the interests of the casino industry in Washington, D.C., funds research into problem gambling and facilitates access to treatment for gambling addiction, as do many casino companies, state-level casino trade organizations, and state-appointed lottery commissions. But to ban gambling in order to prevent social harm to a small segment of the population is unthinkable.

There Is No Persuasive Evidence of Danger
Opponents of legalized gambling raise concerns about the increasing influence gambling has on divorce, bankruptcy, and unemployment rates caused by an addiction to gambling. In some cases, the relationship could be merely correlational where the introduction of casino gambling happens to coincide with a period where an increase in bankruptcy rate is observed. Casinos were built to shore up a declining economy, in which bankruptcies were already imminent. Likewise, growing unemployment was a result of an increase of bankruptcies filed, not a result of the casinos.

Similarly, it is unfair to criticize gambling as being the sole cause of the negative social trends seen in gaming communities. Typically, gambling is promoted in communities that already have significant economic (e.g., poverty) or social (e.g., addiction) problems, to raise revenue to solve these problems. Difficulties in conceptualizing and categorizing social costs make the relationship between gambling and the negative impacts ambiguous. Problems in the reliability and accuracy of the measurement of social costs also hinder demonstrating the impact gambling has over various social trends. That said, many believe that the costs of gambling outweigh the benefits and, for this reason, gambling needs close attention.

GAMBLING: THE COSTS OUTWEIGH THE BENEFITS

The Economic Benefits Are Overblown
Opponents of casino growth think that economic benefits claimed by the gambling industry are misleading and exaggerated, partly because lottery profits amount to only a small part of the total costs of maintaining vital social institutions like education and health care. Contrary to the optimistic claims of gaming industry advocates, gambling expansion also often results in a *transfer* rather than an *increase* in community wealth.

The exception is Las Vegas, where gambling created something out of nothing. Las Vegas arose thanks to a unique meeting of favorable historical and geographic circumstances. A remote, otherwise unremarkable rail-stop town, Las Vegas just happened to have a mild climate and a decades-long national monopoly on casino gambling. By the time casinos opened in Atlantic City and eventually in other jurisdictions, Las Vegas had successfully built itself up into the undisputed king of gambling towns.

Gambling and Cannibalization Few cities with gambling facilities are like Las Vegas. Most of the visitors to their facilities are local residents or daytrippers from surrounding regions (so-called "brownbag gamblers," who pack lunches on their daytrips to the casinos). In these communities that have a clientele consisting of mostly local people, a relationship between bankruptcy and the introduction of casino has been found. In one piece of research, the largest increase in bankruptcy rate was found in Madison County, Illinois, where casinos had been in operation for the longest time of all the communities used in the study. Communities with the second longest period of casino operation ranked second in the increase of bankruptcy rate.

Economic benefits only come to a town when visitors bring in new money. When local people occupy the card tables and slot machines, little economic growth results. Residents are simply spending their money on gambling and related activities—the roulette wheel and the casino buffet—at the expense of older consumer items (e.g., the sporting goods store, the car dealership).

Benefits and Costs for Native Americans
Gambling has been a valuable source of revenue for many Native Americans, helping them to make vast improvements in their health care, education, and social services. Only one-third of Native tribes currently operate gambling facilities, and not all of those tribes benefit equally. The twenty largest casinos account for over half of total Native revenues. Also, analyses measured in purely economic terms continue to leave out the unquantifiable social costs associated with gambling.

The Social Costs of Problem Gambling Are Enormous Accurate population estimates of problem gambling prevalence rates are difficult to calculate. They are even more difficult to compare across studies, for reasons that are both methodological (e.g., reluctance to report a stigmatized behavior) and ideological (e.g., what constitutes "problem gambling" and "pathological gambling"?). Based on a review of existing research and results gathered from their own commissioned national surveys, the NGISC concluded that in a given year, pathological gambling directly affects at least 1.2 to 2 million people, while problem gambling directly affects another 1.4 to 4 million people. A meta-analysis by Harvard scholars of 120 North American pathological and problem gambling prevalence studies found even higher numbers—2.3 million and 5.6 million people, respectively. Many more people—family, friends, and co-workers of problem gamblers—are indirectly affected.

The increase in youth gambling is another area of concern. Rates of adolescent problem gambling on available games (e.g., lotteries and slot machines) are even higher than those for the general population. With an early introduction to gambling and the increasing tolerance of gambling, adolescents may switch to other gambling activities (e.g., casino visits when they become of age). Those who have gambled more than their peers have reported more social and emotional problems.

Although scholars continue to debate the extent of problem gambling in the United States, virtually all agree that gambling addiction is a problem that affects all levels of society. Pro- and anti-gambling advocates continue to dispute the actual effects of gambling at the community level, however. Those opposed to gaming expansion claim that crime rates and traffic problems increase when casinos are introduced into a region. They also point to opinion surveys showing that, while most Americans believe that casinos generally benefit the local economy and are uncomfortable with the idea of gaming prohibition, most also believe that commercial gambling is harmful to family and community life.

Secondary Effects of Problem Gambling   Not surprisingly, problem gamblers and pathological gamblers make poor employees. One recent survey of a Wisconsin chapter of GA found that respondents

lost, on average, seven hours of work per month as a consequence of their gambling problems.

The National Research Council, in their NGISC-commissioned review of pathological gambling in the United States, noted that one-quarter to one-third of the members of Gamblers Anonymous had reported losing their jobs due to gambling addiction. According to a 1999 study of gambling behaviors and consequences by the National Opinion Research Center, problem gamblers are much more likely than nonproblem gamblers to have lost their jobs, declared bankruptcy, required unemployment benefits, been on welfare, and/or been arrested or incarcerated.

Consequences for Families   The intense, consuming nature of gambling addiction inflicts great harm on relationships with family and friends. A recent study in Ontario (Canada), where gambling is available at casinos, racetracks, bingo halls, and elsewhere, reports that of $4 billion spent on gambling in Ontario in 2003, 36 percent ($1.4 billion) was spent by only 5 percent of all gamblers. These turn out to have moderate to severe gambling problems. The inescapable conclusion is that state revenues benefit significantly from the problems of a few.

Many gamblers have high levels of depression, anxiety, stress-related headaches, and respiratory ailments. Separation and divorce rates are significantly higher in problem-gambling households. And teenaged children of problem gamblers currently in treatment report higher rates of drug abuse, eating disorders, unhappy childhoods, depression, suicidal ideation, and gambling problems of their own.

Health Consequences   Problem gambling even harms people's health. Comorbidity—the coexistence of problem/pathological gambling with other disorders—is a common occurrence. Many of those enrolled in problem gambling treatment programs have also been, or are being, treated for alcohol or drug dependence, or mental health problems.

Gamblers often drink and smoke while gambling. Casinos and gambling sites provide an environment where players can drink at atypical times (e.g., early afternoon). The emotions and physiological states (stress, anticipation, excitement, and anger) experienced during gambling serve as cues and temptations to smoke. Furthermore, gambling is a sedentary activity. Gamblers usually sit for long periods of time. If players are frequent visitors to the gambling sites, then the lack of exercise will contribute to negative health consequences of some sort.

The Net Cost of Gambling In a 1999 report to the NGISC, the National Opinion Research Center estimated that, based on their higher rates of job loss and unemployment, welfare dependency, divorce, health problems, and criminal conduct, the actual cost of problem and pathological gambling is $560 and $1,050 per gambler per year, respectively. Multiplied by the NORC's estimate of gambling problem prevalence rates in the United States, the total annual cost exceeds $4 billion.

A similar calculation by University of Illinois economics professor Earl Grinols, which considered both the estimated benefits (including net increases to business profits and tax collections) and costs (including crime, lost workplace productivity, bankruptcy, and social service dependency) associated with casinos, concluded that "an economy that includes casino gambling is worse off by $156 per capita compared to the same economy when casino gambling is prohibited." So with the economic, social, and health risks associated with excessive gambling, the costs definitely outweigh the benefits.

SUMMING UP

Despite many differences of opinion, both sides of the debate generally agree that legalized gambling has both benefits *and* costs for the community. For instance, the tremendous economic and recreational potential of commercial casinos and lotteries, where realized, must be balanced with the sometimes devastating costs to individuals, families, and communities.

Acknowledging that our current understanding of gambling's costs and benefits is "extremely limited," the NGISC made numerous calls in its final report for more high-quality research into this area. Among its many recommendations, the commission encouraged the National Institutes of Health to convene a panel of experts that would provide a guiding framework for future gambling research. It urged the involvement of agencies as diverse as the NIH, the Substance Abuse and Mental Health Services Administration, the National Science Foundation, the National Institute of Justice, the Bureau of Justice Statistics, and the Department of Labor, as well as state and tribal governments, to collect data and assist in research on gambling's positive and negative impacts on society. It acknowledged that we need to know more about gambling prevalence, with a focus on highly vulnerable subgroups such as women, adolescent, elderly, and minority group gamblers.

The greatest danger is that we may close our eyes to obvious health and social costs because, on the one hand, many of us crave the thrill of gambling (as many crave the thrill of drinking, drugs, or fast driving), and governments have found gambling provides a good, easy source of funds without the need to levy unpopular taxes. We may have turned too readily from a culture of thrift and personal responsibility to a culture of chance and risk-taking.

REVIEW EXERCISES

For Discussion and Debate

1. Discuss the underlying factors you think might contribute to the relationship between bankruptcy rates and introduction of gambling.
2. Do you think gambling is fairly controlled in our society? Why or why not?
3. What kinds of activities would you consider "gambling"? For example, does gambling include the purchase and sale of stocks, bonds, real estate, or works of art? And does money always need to be involved for something to be considered gambling?
4. Is gambling making the world a worse place to live?

Writing Exercises

Write a brief (500-word) essay on one of the following topics:

1. "Controlling gambling means eliminating gambling altogether."
2. "More tolerance toward gambling will lead to a higher gambling prevalence and more experiences of gambling at younger ages."
3. "Gambling provides good exercise for the mind."
4. "Laws should be passed to force casinos to impose a maximum limit on what can be spent per visit."

Research Activities

1. Interview two gamblers at the casino, or two purchasers of lottery tickets, and ask for their views about gambling.
2. Choose two communities, one with high rates of gambling (e.g., Las Vegas) and another with little or no gambling, and compare their statistics for one of the following: divorce, suicide, crime, or bankruptcy. Discuss your findings.
3. Devise a research proposal to study gambling and its negative or positive consequences. Be sure to include discussions of the variables you plan to use (what they are and why you chose them), your hypothesis, and methodology.
4. Approach ten of your family, friends, or peers that you know have had gambling experiences and ask them the following questions:
   a. What kind of gambling activity did they engage in (e.g., purchasing lottery tickets, playing cards with friends, etc.)?
   b. How old were they when they first gambled?
   c. Was money involved?
   d. When gambling, do they always think "the next hand might be my lucky hand"?
   e. Have they ever lost control during gambling, thinking they would win all their money back, yet, in the end, losing it all?

   What patterns emerge from the answers? Can you draw a general conclusion about people's gambling behaviors?

Selected References

Albanese, J. 1985. "The Effect of Casino Gambling on Crime." *Federal Probation* 48:39–44.
Bland, R. C. et al. 1993. "Epidemiology of Pathological Gambling in Edmonton." *Canadian Journal of Psychiatry* 38:108–112.
Chang, S. 1996. "Impact of Casinos on Crime: The Case of Biloxi, Mississippi." *Journal of Criminal Justice* 5:431–436.
Clotfelter, C. T. and P. J. Cook. 1999. *State Lotteries at the Turn of the Century: Report to the National Gambling Impact Study Commission* (Apr.).
Collins, P. 2003. *Gambling and the Public Interest.* Westport, CT: Praeger.
Crockford, D. N. and N. el-Guebaly. 1998. "Psychiatric Co-Morbidity in Pathological Gambling: A Critical Review." *Canadian Journal of Psychiatry* 43:43–50.
Curran, D. and F. Scarpitti. 1991. "Crime in Atlantic City: Do Casinos Make a Difference?" *Deviant Behavior* 12:431–449.
Eadington, W. R. 2003. "Values and Choices: The Struggle to Find Balance with Permitted Gambling in Modern Society. Pp. 31–48 in *Gambling: Who Wins? Who Loses?* edited by G. Reith. Amherst, NY: Prometheus Books.
Gallup Organization. 1999. *Gambling in America: Topline and Trends.* Princeton, NJ: Gallup Organization.

Goodman, R. 1995. *The Luck Business: The Devastating Consequences and Broken Promises of America's Gambling Expansion.* New York: Free Press.

Goodman, R. 2003. "Grand Illusions." Pp. 88–95 in *Gambling: Who Wins? Who Loses?* edited by G. Reith. Amherst, NY: Prometheus Books.

Griffiths, M. 1996. "Pathological Gambling: A Review of the Literature." *Journal of Psychiatric and Mental Health Nursing* 3 (6): 347–353.

Grinols, E. L. 1996. "Incentives Explain Gambling's Growth." *Forum for Applied Research and Public Policy* 11:119–124.

Grinols, E. L. 2003. "Cutting the Cards and Craps: Right Thinking about Gambling Economics." Pp. 67–87 in *Gambling: Who Wins? Who Loses?* edited by G. Reith. Amherst, NY: Prometheus Books.

Grinols, E. L. and D. B. Mustard. 2001. "Business Profitability versus Social Profitability: Evaluating Industries with Externalities—the Case of Casinos." *Managerial and Decision Economics* 22 (1–3): 143–162.

Jacobs, D. F. 1989. "Illegal and Undocumented: A Review of Teenage Gambling and the Plight of Children of Problem Gamblers in America." Pp. 275–278 in *Compulsive Gambling: Theory, Research, and Practice,* edited by H. J. Schaffer et al. Boston, MA: Lexington Books.

Lesieur, H. R. 1998. "Costs and Treatment of Pathological Gambling." *Annals of the American Academy of Political and Social Science* 556:154–155.

Lesieur, H. R. and R. Klein. 1987. "Pathological Gambling among High School Students." *Addictive Behaviors* 12:129–135.

Lesieur, H. R. et al. 1991. "Gambling and Pathological Gambling among University Students." *Addictive Behavior* 16:517–527.

Lorenz, V. C. and R. A. Yaffee. 1986. "Pathological Gambling: Psychosomatic, Emotional, and Marital Difficulties as Reported by the Gambler." *Journal of Gambling Behavior* 2 (1): 40–49.

Lorenz, V. C. and R. A. Yaffee. 1988. "Pathological Gambling: Psychosomatic, Emotional, and Marital Difficulties as Reported by the Spouse." *Journal of Gambling Behavior* 4 (2): 13–26.

National Gambling Impact Study Commission (NGISC). 1999. *Final Report.* Washington, D.C.: Government Printing Office.

National Opinion Research Center. 1999a. *Gambling Impact and Behavior Study: Report to the National Gambling Impact Study Commission* (Apr.). Chicago, IL: University of Chicago Press.

National Opinion Research Center. 1999b. *Overview of National Survey and Community Database Research on Gambling Behavior.* Chicago, IL: University of Chicago Press.

National Research Council. 1999. *Pathological Gambling: A Critical Review* (Apr.). Washington, D.C.: National Academy Press.

Reith, G. 2003. "Pathology and Profit: Controversies in the Expansion of Legal Gambling." Pp. 9–28 in *Gambling: Who Wins? Who Loses?* edited by G. Reith. Amherst, NY: Prometheus Books.

Schaffer, H. J. 2003. "A Critical View of Pathological Gambling and Addiction: Comorbidity Makes for Syndromes and Other Strange Bedfellows." Pp. 175–190 in *Gambling: Who Wins? Who Loses?* edited by G. Reith. Amherst, NY: Prometheus Books.

Schaffer, H. J., M. N. Hall and J. Vander Bilt. 1999. "Estimating the Prevalence of Disordered Gambling Behavior in the United States and Canada: A Research Synthesis." *American Journal of Public Health* 89 (9): 1369–1376.

Spunt, B. et al. 1996. "Pathological Gamblers in Methadone Treatment: A Comparison between Men and Women." *Journal of Gambling Studies* 12 (4): 431–449.

Thompson, W. N., W. Gazel and D. Rickman. 1996. "The Social Costs of Gambling in Wisconsin." *Wisconsin Policy Research Institute Report* 9 (6): 1–44.

Tunica Convention and Visitors Bureau (TCVB). 2003. *The Tunica Miracle: 2002 Annual Report.*

Volberg, R. A. 1994. "The Prevalence and Demographics of Pathological Gamblers: Implications for Public Health." *American Journal of Public Health* 84 (2): 237–241.

Volberg, R. A. 1996. "Prevalence Studies of Problem Gambling in the United States." *Journal of Gambling Studies* 12 (2): 111–128.

Volberg, R. A. 2001. *When the Chips Are Down: Problem Gambling in America.* New York: The Century Foundation Press.

CHAPTER 2 ⟫ SOCIALIZATION

Socialization is the social learning process a person goes through to become a capable member of society. The process is "social" because it is through interaction with others and in response to social pressures that people acquire the *culture*—the language, perspective and skills, the likes and dislikes, the cluster of norms, values and beliefs—that characterizes the group to which they belong. As a result, socialization is one of the most important processes by which social structure constrains and transforms us.

Primary socialization is learning that takes place in the early years of a person's life. It is extremely important in forming an individual's personality and charting the course of future development. Very often, primary socialization takes place within the context of a family. Here a young child learns many of the social skills needed to participate in a wide variety of social institutions.

In this chapter we discuss three issues associated with socialization. The first is about primary socialization—specifically, how parents can provide what their children really need. Second, we consider whether corporal punishment—in its most common form, spanking—is a good way to exercise discipline over children. Third, we consider what we should be teaching our children about money and the importance of material success as a means to happiness.

2.1   Is *Father Knows Best* Best for Children?

The issue: What kind of family—especially, what kind of parenting—will help children grow up happy, secure, and competent? Is the so-called traditional family really better than any other kind? Or does family structure make no difference whatsoever?

The end of WWII in 1945 brought servicemen home to start new lives and new families. Growth in the American economy was matched by a sky-high birth rate, lending the name "Baby Boomers" to those born in this era. As years changed to decades, new views on family life also emerged. Alternative family structures appeared, such as nonmarital child-bearing and same-sex parenting. Arrangements that were not thought practical or proper during the times of "Leave It to Beaver" have now become widespread. Ideas about the family, what it is and what function it serves, are some of the hot topics that surround the debate of whether family values are in decline when compared with the idealized family of the first half of the twentieth century.

The debate surrounding the modern family essentially creates two parties: those who believe that families of today lack the structure and values that were celebrated years ago, and those who acknowledge that social change has brought about a change in families. Even people who believe the modern family is *not* in decline argue sometimes that recent changes may not be best for raising children. They note that, compared with the past, children today are more often delinquent, do poorly at school, or have low self-esteem. Today's children are said to be more unhappy than in the past, resulting in high rates of adolescent drug use, depression, and even suicide.

The question remains whether family structures of the 1950s are better able to provide supports that today's modern families cannot. Do children really need two heterosexual opposite-sex parents in the household to grow up healthy and well-balanced?

ONE TYPE OF FAMILY IS BEST

In recent years, heated debates concerning the definition and roles of the family have transformed it into an important platform for politicians. For example, the phrase *family values* was a *motherhood issue* in the 1992 presidential campaign. Everyone who sought election was in favor of good family life and each portrayed the opposing candidate as falling on the wrong side of the issue. In reality, there are many ideas about what a "good family life" is. Today that phrase is used less often, but candidates for political office still take pains to portray themselves as good spouses and good parents.

Some traditionalists take an extreme position when describing the ideal family structure. They claim that mothers working outside the home harm their children, that single-parent households are a result of people not bothering to get married or not taking their marriage seriously, and that abortion is wrong in almost all circumstances. In short, supporters of these extreme family values are confident that problems surrounding family life will be eliminated if society adopts one kind of family, with father as the main (or only) wage earner and mother devoting herself to raising the children and doing housework. This is the *Father Knows Best* image of the American family with which many of the American Baby Boomers grew up.

Family values as a societal issue strikes a responsive chord in many. There is a continuum of family values positions, with many less-extreme versions. It is this nostalgic evidence of an earlier kind of family life that leads us to wonder whether there are grains of truth in this way of thinking.

Sociological support for the view that one type of family is best comes mainly from sociologists who hold a traditional *functional* view of the family. They claim that marriage provides children with the greatest developmental stability. Cohabiting couples, and couples who had children before marriage, have higher levels of marital instability, and provide less stability for their children. The consequences of unstable development, or poor parenting, are deviant childhoods.

But the alternative—a sentimental image of the 1950s family—was never more than just an ideal. The "traditional" family of the 1950s is nothing more than a mythologized reality, many argue. Although the 1950s saw a revival of nuclear family values, there were very real problems coexisting with this ideal family myth. Family structures were never the cocoon that protected people from inequalities based on class, race, and gender. If anything, women's position in society worsened. As fertility rates exploded, the gap between men's and women's job and educational opportunities widened. As the age of marriage fell, middle-class women were forced to marry and depend on marriage for sustenance. Teenage births in the idealized 1950s were almost double what they are today—many of them unplanned and unwanted.

Despite all the evidence of dysfunctional nuclear families in the "Golden Age," sentimentalists still believe that the ideal family of father as breadwinner and mother as bread maker can and should be put into universal practice. They point to research showing the negative effects of a broken marriage as proof that, even at their worst, two-parent families are better than any other.

For example, children who grow up in single-parent households are more likely to engage in delinquent behavior, and are more likely to do poorly in school and at work. Children of divorced parents date earlier and engage in more premarital sex than other children. These same children from alternative family structures are also less committed to marriage and more readily accept divorce as a solution to marital problems. As a result, these children are socialized to accept relationships that result in divorce, dissolution, and single parenthood.

Traditional marriages have other benefits as well. Studies show that the benefits of being part of a traditional family lie in the satisfaction of marital certainty and that more housework and parenting gets done in traditional families when compared to alternative forms of family. A strong and healthy partnership between two spouses means that financial, emotional, and social resources can be pooled, creating a sense of comfort and security that allows children to grow up in a household where all their needs are met by a caregiver.

The Value of Certainty   The idealized traditional family is nothing if not certain. It is this certainty that often reduces friction between family members. The benefits of acquiring certainty are two-fold.

Firstly, clearly defined roles and expectations accompany certainty in households. Husbands and wives know what the culture expects of them, as do parents and children. So long as people live up to these expectations, there is certainty within the family and between the family and its social environment.

Secondly, this certainty is continuous with the past. People who value tradition and justify their behavior on traditional grounds find family life satisfying and comfortable. Especially when the fabric of society is fragile during times of social, economic, and cultural transition does the continuity with families of the past give people a sense that they are anchored in something solid.

Thirdly, a commitment to certainty increases familial stability. Dissatisfied spouses do not divorce because they fear or dislike the uncertainty that would follow. Children who are dissatisfied with their parents do not leave or disobey because they want to avoid feelings of guilt and uncertainty.

THERE IS NO "BEST" TYPE OF FAMILY STRUCTURE

A trade-off that critics of the modern family rarely discuss is the cost of boredom, anger, and frustration that often accompany certainty. For many people, this cost may be too high to endure in the family.

The Value of Caretaking   The numbers of stay-at-home mothers have been reduced because stay-at-home mothers spend more hours per week on unpaid housework and parenting than mothers who work for pay. (Fathers who work for pay spend the same amount of time on these activities, whether their wives stay at home or work for pay.) Most people like a tidy home, clean clothes to wear, and good meals. Most children value the attention a parent gives them. There is no dispute as to the worthiness of housework and parenting.

However, the value of a full-time stay-at-home mom is questionable. For example, does the time a woman spends on housework and parenting yield a diminishing rate of return? Twice as much time spent on these activities rarely brings twice as many benefits. Another family member can cook or delegate chores to be done, and so on. Some would say that we approach a 2005 workplace saddled with a 1950s division of labor.

Costs to the family members providing these services to the family are psychological as well as financial. Nothing is cost-free. Many people—male and female—do not want to work and parent all the time. These attitudes are very similar for younger men and women. Both prefer working outside the home, whether part-time or full-time. Some families agree to these terms because they simply cannot afford a stay-at-home parent: They need a second earner.

Some parents feel guilty about depriving their family of full-time housework and parenting services. Should they feel guilty? Are their families harmed if they go out to work? Researchers who believe there is *not* one "best" kind of family would tell these parents not to worry. It is more important to focus on how the family functions and what purpose it serves its members rather than being preoccupied with how the family is structured.

Many researchers have studied what makes some families more "successful" than others. "Success" in these sociological terms includes an absence of marital conflict, a high degree of marital satisfaction, and avoidance of divorce. Research consistently shows that successful marriages are distinguished from unsuccessful ones by a few important processes that, when followed, lead to marital success. In successful marriages, we commonly find the following:

Expressions of love   Spouses show their mates affection, support, and empathy.

Cooperation   Spouses cooperate with one another and act in a considerate manner.

Communication   Spouses communicate openly and solve their problems together.

Commitment   Spouses express a commitment to their mates and act faithfully toward them.

Agreement   Spouses seek agreement on important issues, like how to spend money and how to raise the children.

Successful marriages, not surprisingly, are more egalitarian and report higher degrees of sexual satisfaction. In these partnerships, neither spouse tries to dominate the other. What critics of divorce rarely admit is that many marriages oppress women and children. Some husbands (and fathers) put a high premium on obedience at the expense of mutual respect and self-expression. Husbands that dominate produce marriages based on unequal partnerships; this in turn creates less happy marriages.

The success-producing processes named above (cooperation, communication, etc.) are possible in every kind of marriage: new or old, legal or common law, same-sex or opposite-sex, first or remarriages, marriages with and without children, and so on. Nothing prevents people from having successful marriages if they act in certain ways.

Similarly, successful parenting produces children that are healthy, happy, and stable. Nothing *structural*—that is, inherent and immutable within the family organization—prevents people from raising their children successfully. In that sense, there is no one best type of family structure. Though the children of single parent families run a higher risk of problems in school, work and marriage, these problems are largely due to poverty or lack of social supports. With adequate income and social supports, these families work as well as any others granted the adequate family processes are sound.

The sociological evidence is clear: Family processes matter more than family structures. If the family processes are sound, a happy family will be the result regardless of the family structure. Poor family processes will ultimately harm the child, whatever the family structure.

Which family processes matter, according to the research literature? The answer is so obvious you may feel embarrassed that we had to tell you. The answer is also similar to what makes for a successful relationship between spouses. Children turn out fine if their parent(s):

Love them   Too little love hurts a child's self-esteem, makes the child less assertive, leads to behavior problems, and increases the risk of delinquency. There can't be too much love.

Supervise them moderately   Too little discipline harms a child's psychosocial development, lowers school achievement, and leads to behavior problems. Too severe discipline also leads to behavior problems, hostility, and antisocial attitudes. Moderate discipline with both parents agreeing is best.

Cooperate with each other   Conflict between the parents harms the children. If there is a lot of conflict, children develop psychosomatic illnesses, psychiatric problems, low self-esteem, and delinquent behavior.

Provide stability   Parents should play a regular, predictable role in the child's life. If both parents work for pay, they should keep a stable day care arrangement. If the parents are divorced, the non-custodial parent should visit the child regularly. Joint custody is best for the child's self-esteem. (Remember: successful couples solve problems together!)

Keep stress under control   When parents are under severe stress, they may become depressed. This increases the risk of domestic conflict, impatience with the children, child abuse, or neglect. The children feel anxious, unhappy and insecure. Often they, too, become depressed and develop behavior problems.

Seek social support   The children of parents who receive social support from relatives, friends, or neighbors are less likely to suffer these problems. Even under difficult conditions, social support helps parents to cope with stress: This benefit is passed along to children as better parenting.

Family Rituals are important processes that help keep family members attached to one another and create a flexibility that allows family members to change their ideas/roles as the situation demands. In the long run, this simplifies family life and makes it more enjoyable.

SUMMING UP

Is *Father Knows Best* really best? What type of family is ideal, and can sociology help answer that seemingly personal question? Yes, it can. Research shows that the "best" family is characterized by certain *processes* (e.g., love and supervision) and not by certain *structures*.

If children are to have the best possible upbringing, not all the attention should be focused on maintaining intact marriages and stay-at-home moms. Parents need to ensure they (1) know how to control domestic conflict and how to cope with stress, (2) get enough social support, and (3) supervise their children properly.

Furthermore, the government needs to implement more social support programs for financially marginalized families in order for them to provide high-quality parenting. Some family structures (e.g., single-parent families) need more support than others. A high demand for reliable, low-cost day care is another issue that needs resolution. Insufficient income is a common source of stress and conflict, and single mothers are most likely to lack a sufficient income. Some two-parent families also require social support for various reasons.

In summary, even the research on same-sex versus opposite-sex parents is consistent in pointing out that *not* one type of family structure is favorable over all others. Other things being equal, gay and lesbian parents raise their children as well as heterosexual parents do. There is no evidence that children need opposite sex parents to serve as role models. Nor is there evidence that a child's sexual orientation is shaped by his or her custodial parent(s).

All intimate or close relations—family relations among them—follow a logic that determines the important outcomes. As we have seen, the important social processes include interaction, communication, cooperation, and empathy. They operate similarly in families of different kinds, ranging from childless traditional heterosexual marriages to same-sex marriages with children. Families give their members similar kinds of experience, whatever the family form or composition.

An issue in family life is the interplay between family, school, and work roles. One important concern is the spillover of energy and emotion from family life to work life and vice versa. Problems in one domain often cause problems in another. Families today are scrambling to invent ways of dealing with role overload: the double burden of work and childcare, eldercare, and often conflicting demands, as work, school, and family demands all change at once.

The best families are the ones that work hardest to find solutions to these problems. Family life is constantly being constructed, and every family bears the unique stamp of its members. No two families enact love, marriage, parenthood, or domestic work in precisely the same way. If anything, the study of families makes clear that social life is a process of continued uncertainty, variety, and negotiation. We get the families we struggle for, although some family members have more power than others in the struggle.

Families *have* changed dramatically in the last 30 years. Accepted ways of thinking, speaking, and behaving have changed because dozens, then thousands, then millions of family members have changed their way of relating closely. We should not conclude that we are in the midst of a breakdown of the family, in which a mate is no more than erotic property, and a child no more than a consumer durable. The way most people continue to struggle and sacrifice for their spouses, children, parents, and siblings suggests that the family means a great deal more.

There can be no doubt that people worldwide are redefining what it means to be an intimate couple. The family remains the arena in which emotional and psychological growth can take place; however, more than ever, couple relationships have come to be voluntary acts—choices that are made freely by individuals. Also, there is a sense that what's done can be undone. Intimate partners are not as economically dependent on each other as they once were, and they can opt out of couple relationships that do not meet their personal expectations.

In Western countries, people are less inclined to marry legally than in the past; more people view singlehood positively. Cohabitation offers many of the benefits of marriage, without the same social and religious constraints.

Yet, where marriage and divorce are concerned, variations persist among industrialized countries. It appears that all Western countries are moving in the same direction, toward diversity of ways to form intimate couple unions. Will the institution of marriage die from a lack of interest? From the data sociologists have examined, we see a continued increase in the acceptance of varied intimate partner forms. We see no decrease in the strength of commitment overall toward exclusive intimacy within a spousal relationship.

Around the world, cohabitation is losing its negative image and becoming much more accepted, and couples are redefining what they mean by a "close relationship." Now, more than ever before, the decision to be a couple and the decisions of what kind of couple to be, are left to the individuals. Additionally, there is an increasing sense that one can separate from one's partner and start again. Legal marriage is less popular and singlehood is seen as more respectable and positive. When we look at marriage as an exclusive contract of intimacy between two people, we see that marriage in all its forms is still a popular arrangement.

What remains is for couples, families, communities, and societies to work out all the social, economic, and legal changes needed to accommodate all of these changes in the practice of people's private lives. Where necessary, we need to provide more support for the children of broken marriages. It seems unlikely we will ever (again) see one single ideal type of family, in practice or theory.

REVIEW EXERCISES

For Discussion and Debate

1. "There are as many types of family as there are actual families."
2. "Certainty in family relationships is far more valuable than any chance of freedom."
3. "It doesn't matter how you raise your children, so long as you are sincere in your beliefs."
4. "The community has no business telling parents how to raise their children."

Writing Exercises

Write a brief (500-word) essay on one of the following topics:

1. "Politicians have no business using family issues to get votes."
2. "Children are captives, no matter how loving the prison."
3. "Parents ought to feel guilty about neglecting their children for paid work."
4. "Poverty is no excuse for raising your children badly."

Research Activities

1. Watch three episodes of at least one "family show" on television. How is the depiction of family life different from the family shows of the 1950s and 1960s mentioned in this section?
2. Devise a way to measure family processes in your own family—for example, how much love, supervision, communication, or stress there is. Then try out the measure on your own family and one other family.
3. Examine the data in three published studies that relate family processes to successful marriage or successful parenting. Do the results agree with each other?

4. Examine the findings of three studies on same-sex marriages. Do you find any differences from opposite-sex marriages in what makes the family work?

SELECTED REFERENCES

Amato, Paul R. 2000. "The Consequences of Divorce for Adults and Children." *Journal of Marriage and the Family* 62, 4 (Nov.): 1269–1287.

Amato, Paul R. and Joan G. Gilbreth. 1999. "Nonresident Fathers and Children's Well-Being: A Meta-Analysis." *Journal of Marriage and the Family* 61, 3 (Aug.): 557–573.

Amato, Paul R. and Sandra J. Rezac. 1994. "Contact with Nonresident Parents, Interparental Conflict, and Children's Behavior." *Journal of Family Issues* 15, 2 (June): 191–207.

Barber, Brian K., Joseph E. Olsen and Shobha C. Shagle. 1994. "Associations between Parental Psychological and Behavioral Control and Youth Internalized and Externalized Behaviors." *Child Development* 65, 4 (Aug.): 1120–1136.

Chao, Ruth K. 1994. "Beyond Parental Control and Authoritarian Parenting Style: Understanding Chinese Parenting through the Cultural Notion of Training." *Child Development* 65 (4): 1111–1119.

Conger, Rand D., Katherine Jewsbury Conger, Lisa S. Matthews and Glen H. Elder, Jr. 1999. "Pathways of Economic Influence on Adolescent Adjustment." *American Journal of Community Psychology* 27 (4): 519–541.

Conger, Rand D., Xiaojia Ge, Glen H. Elder, Jr., Frederick O. Lorenz and Ronald L. Simons. 1994. "Economic Stress, Coercive Family Process, and Developmental Problems of Adolescents." *Child Development* 65, 2 (Apr.): 541–561.

Cornfield, Daniel B. and Toby L. Parcel. 2000. *Work & Family: Research Informing Policy.* Thousand Oaks, CA: Sage Publications.

Dozier, Brenda S., Donna L. Sollie, Steven J. Stack and Thomas A. Smith. 1993. "The Effects of Postdivorce Attachment on Co-Parenting Relationships." *Journal of Divorce and Remarriage* 19 (3–4): 109–123.

Ellis, Godfrey J. and Larry R. Petersen. 1992. "Socialization Values and Parental Control Techniques: A Cross-Cultural Analysis of Child Rearing." *Journal of Comparative Family Studies* 23, 1 (Spring): 39–54.

Foxcroft, David R. and Geoff Lowe. 1991. "Adolescent Drinking Behaviour and Family Socialization Factors: A Meta-analysis." *Journal of Adolescence* 14, 3 (Sept.): 255–273.

Gieve, Katherine, ed. 1989. *Balancing Acts: On Being a Mother.* London: Virago.

Goetting, Ann. 1994. "The Parenting-Crime Connection." *Journal of Primary Prevention* 14, 3 (Spring): 169–186.

Goetting, Ann. 1999. *Getting Out: Life Stories of Women Who Left Abusive Men.* New York: Columbia University Press.

Gringlas, Marcy and Marsha Weinraub. 1995. "The More Things Change . . . Single Parenting Revisited." *Journal of Family Issues* 16, 1 (Jan.): 29–52.

Heuveline, Patrick, Jeffrey M. Timberlake and Frank F. Furstenberg, Jr. 2003. "Shifting Childrearing to Single Mothers: Results from 17 Western Countries." *Population and Development Review* 29, 1 (Mar.): 47–71.

Kurdek, Lawrence A. 2001. "Differences between Heterosexual-Nonparent Couples and Gay, Lesbian, and Heterosexual-Parent Couples." *Journal of Family Issues* 22, 6 (Sept.): 728–755.

Kurdek, Lawrence and Mark A. Fine. 1993. "The Relation between Family Structure and Young Adolescents' Appraisals of Family Climate and Parenting Behavior." *Journal of Family Issues* 14, 2 (June): 279–290.

Lamb, Kathleen A. and Wendy D. Manning. 2003. "Adolescent Well-Being in Cohabiting, Married, and Single-Parent Families." *Journal of Marriage and Family* 65, 4 (Nov.): 876–893.

Lamb, Michael E., ed. 1987. *The Father's Role: Cross-Cultural Perspectives.* Hillsdale, NJ: Lawrence Erlbaum Associates.

Lamb, Michael E., ed. 2004. *The Role of the Father in Child Development,* 4th ed. Hoboken, NJ: Wiley.

McLeod, Jane D. and James M. Nonnemaker. 2000. "Poverty and Child Emotional and Behavioral Problems: Racial/Ethnic Differences in Processes and Effects." *Journal of Health and Social Behavior* 41, 2 (June): 137–161.

McLeod, Jane D. and Michael J. Shanahan. 1993. "Poverty, Parenting, and Children's Mental Health." *American Sociological Review* 58, 3 (June): 351–366.

McLoyd, Vonnie C. and Leon Wilson. 1992. "Telling Them Like It Is: The Role of Economic and Environmental Factors in Single Mothers' Discussions with Their Children." *American Journal of Community Psychiatry* 20, 4 (Aug.): 419–444.

Metzler, Carol W., John Noell, Anthony Biglan, Dennis Ary and Keith Smolkowski. 1994. "The Social Context for Risky Sexual Behavior among Adolescents." *Journal of Behavioral Medicine* 17, 4 (Aug.): 419–438.

Mitchell, Barbara A. 1994. "Family Structure and Leaving the Nest: A Social Resource Perspective." *Sociological Perspectives* 37, 4 (Winter): 651–671.

Olson, Myrna and Judith A. Haynes. 1993. "Successful Single Parents." *Families in Society* 74, 5 (May): 259–267.

Parcel, Toby L. and Elizabeth G. Menaghan. 1994. "Early Parental Work, Family Social Capital, and Early Childhood Outcomes." *American Journal of Sociology* 99, 4 (Jan.): 972–1009.

Raley, R. Kelly and Elizabeth Wildsmith. 2004. "Cohabitation and Children's Family Instability." *Journal of Marriage and Family* 66, 1 (Feb.): 210–219.

Seltzer, Judith. 1994. "Consequences of Marital Dissolution for Children." *Annual Review of Sociology* 20:235–266.

2.2   Should Jamie Be Spanked?

The issue: Should parents hit their children as a means of disciplining them? And if hitting and other corporal punishment is harmful or ineffective, does the State have a right to interfere in parents' rights to discipline their children this way?

Parents and caregivers do all sorts of things to try to socialize and control their children. This can include spanking.

In this section we treat spanking as one (fairly mild) form of corporal punishment and combine the research findings on spanking with the research findings on corporal punishment more generally. Spanking, the mildest form of corporal punishment, can sometimes predict more severe forms of corporal punishment. The fact remains that the most severe use of physical violence against children starts with spanking. There may be a continuum of child abuses that ranges from spanking to physical violence and even homicide. Is spanking a warm-up for more dangerous and even life-threatening practices? Experts disagree on this point. Most believe that physical abuses of children, with different degrees of severity, call for different types of management and treatment. The abuse may or may not have different root causes.

That said, spanking remains a common practice in North America and most seem to approve of physical punishment. However, many critics view spanking as a kind of child abuse. Certainly, distinctions between normal and deviant punishments are often hard to make. There is little wonder that strangers feel uncomfortable about intervening when they see a child being physically punished in public.

A lot of violence against children is never reported, though many parents who admit to their violent acts may do so in the belief that such behavior is both acceptable and effective. At this point in time we do not know the full extent of spanking in North America, nor of people's acceptance of spanking. Researchers get different results when they study spanking using different methods—for example, by asking about recent behaviors, attitudes toward spanking, or responses to vignettes in which spanking is one possible way of dealing with a fictional child's misbehavior.

It has been shown that spanking can be a successful means to get children to pay attention to parental reasoning. Children who have reasoning backed up by spanking often become well-mannered children who have little need for punishment. The research on spanking and attitudes toward spanking provide some fairly consistent patterns. However, popular views range widely about this topic, along with cultural differences, with a significant portion of the population believing that spanking is a good thing to do.

Some people believe that parents have a right to raise their children as they see fit, in keeping with their own cultural and religious beliefs, and that their parenting styles should be free of governmental intrusion.

PARENTS SHOULD SPANK THEIR CHILDREN

Views about spanking vary with the age of the child involved. Most people would feel it is more acceptable to spank a two-year old than an eight-year old, since the younger child has less developed thinking skills and poorer judgment. It is harder for the parent to reason with a two-year old about running onto the road, for example. Parents of toddlers are more likely to support spanking than parents of older children. Consequently, research shows that as children get older they are spanked less frequently and become less aggressive with age (Wissow 2001).

Half of surveyed American parents report using corporal punishment on their adolescent child in the past year; the evidence shows they did so an average of 6–8 times.

As with most things, moderation is key. In the Commonwealth Fund Survey of Parents with Young Children, 2,017 parents with children under three were asked to report on their use of spanking, other disciplinary practices, and nurturing interactions. Data from the parent reports were analyzed and researchers found the following: Parents who used average levels of spanking used nonphysical discipline (e.g., threats, promises, bribes) more than both above-average and below-average spankers and also had higher levels of nurturing interactions than either above- or below-average spanking parents (Wissow 2001). Thus, we would be wrong to assume that all parents who use spanking progress to abusive forms of physical punishment, fail to nurture their children, or fail to use nonphysical discipline as well.

In fact, there is no concrete evidence that a little spanking hurts anyone. The research has focused on physical abusers who obviously go to extremes, far beyond mere spanking. Spanking does not usually lead to more serious forms of physical abuse. Spankers are no more likely to become abusers than drinkers are to become alcoholics.

Support for spanking appears to come from three views. First, some cultures view spanking and other forms of corporal punishment as appropriate social control. Children are perceived as mere human "becomings" . . . "helplessly dependent, unreasonable and selfish" in comparison to adults who are fully human. This conceptualization of children supports parents' rights over children's human rights (Phillips and Alderson 2003). This view is also captured by the old adage "Spare the rod and spoil the child." Second, some religions and cultures also view spanking as moral. This provides the practice with a moral and even supernatural legitimacy. Third, people who were themselves spanked as children tend to support spanking.

Some Cultures Condone Spanking   Most research shows that cultures do vary in their acceptance of spanking. Indeed, many cultures currently support spanking—and more generally, corporal punishment—for child misbehavior. Some even support state-sponsored corporal punishment as a deterrent for crime. This brings up the issue of acceptance of nonparental secondary socialization agents' use of corporal punishment, including nonrelated caregivers and teachers. For example, there was a tremendous amount of international controversy over the American child who was flogged naked in Singapore for doing minor property damage. The reaction reminds us that, even though parents justify spanking their own children, they don't always approve of other people doing it for them.

In the United Kingdom, a recent poll on whether or not parents would support the reimplementation of caning in English schools showed that 51 percent of all parents thought that this would solve educational disciplinary problems within schools (Green et al. 2002). This suggests that at least half of parents from the United Kingdom would support physical discipline of their own child by someone else.

According to studies, spanking is accepted in Indonesia, South Korea, Barbados, and Nigeria, as well as among immigrants to the United States from China, Guyana, and the West Indies. Many unindustrialized societies appear on this list; yet there is no simple pattern of tolerance for spanking. For example, parents in India generally oppose corporal punishment while parents in the more economically developed United States generally tolerate it; so economic development (or literacy or higher education) does not inevitably make spanking unacceptable. However, we will later see that some social factors are indeed correlated with spanking.

Physical punishment appeals to many parents who do not have the time, patience, or inclination to teach rules of behavior inductively. It is often a thoughtless response to irritation, not a reasoned strategy for child-rearing.

Popular acceptance of spanking as a form of child control appears to vary from one culture to another. As with everything that is culturally variable, spanking raises the ethnocentrism issue: Should members of one culture judge another culture's practices, declaring them to be barbaric, inhumane, or foolish? We will consider this further into the section.

Some Religions Support Spanking Like cultures, religions vary in their support for spanking. As we noted earlier, religious support for spanking—and more generally for corporal punishment—serves as an influential information source with which parents gage their decisions against abusive behavior. For example, more parents spank their children if they know that religious leaders condone the practice than if religious leaders ignore or even oppose it.

Survey evidence shows that in the United States, Protestant fundamentalists are the strongest (religious) supporters of corporal punishment. Most fundamentalists support spanking and other forms of corporal punishment both at home and school. Less fundamentalist religious people, whether Protestant, Catholic, or Jewish, are less supportive.

One explanation is that fundamentalist Protestantism (or fundamentalism) is based on a literal reading of the Bible. Fundamentalists interpret the Bible to say that human nature is inherently sinful, that sin demands punishment, and that parents have an obligation to break a child's (sinful) will—to bring it under God's control. From this perspective, corporal punishment is not only a tool by which loving and devoted parents try to lead a sinful child to goodness; it also shows a dedication to God's work of fighting sin. Despite Protestants heavy reliance on corporal punishment, studies suggest that Protestant parents yell at their children less than parents who do not spank. Researchers have even hypothesized that this lack of yelling may moderate the effects of physical discipline.

Related to this fundamentalist interpretation of the Bible is a belief in absolute right and wrong. Fundamentalism is not a relativistic or situational morality in which the same behaviors are sometimes right and sometimes wrong, depending on the situation. According to fundamentalists of any religious denomination, bad behavior is always bad and must always be punished. Good behavior should be approved and emulated.

Thus, spanking often follows from a particular view of good and evil and a particular notion of parents' responsibility to control their children's evil. Indeed, empirical research indicates that, perhaps counter intuitively, physical punishment succeeds in leading a child to view God as loving and omnipotent.

Parents' actions are guided by other information sources as well. A survey conducted found that 33 percent of mothers rated workshops, pediatricians, newspapers, magazines, and books as "very important" and less than 15 percent of mothers gave the same importance rating to parents, relatives, and friends. This research also found that a mother's perception as to whether the source promoted or discouraged spanking influenced whether or not they spanked.

The current trend of a society is often reflected in its publications. In 1994 Straus examined ten widely used textbooks on child development and only one argued against the use of corporal punishment, suggesting potential acceptance for corporal punishment if more information including textbooks support its use.

People Who Were Spanked Support Spanking
One survey of American college students found
that 93 percent had been spanked as children. The
vast majority of "spankees" accept corporal punishment as a legitimate way to control misbehavior and they plan to spank their own children. So,
contrary to what we might expect, people who
were spanked as children do not generally oppose
spanking.

Another survey helps us understand why: It
found that adults who had been spanked as children judge corporal punishment less harshly and
critically than adults who did not experience it.
Critics may be exaggerating the practice's harmfulness out of ignorance and a lack of firsthand experience. However, there are several other possible
ways to explain the support for spanking among
Americans who have themselves been spanked.
First, spanking teaches a view of personal responsibility similar to what we noted among fundamentalists. Thus, spanking is part of learning a
black-and-white moral worldview.

Second, misbehaving boys receive more corporal punishment than misbehaving girls. Thus,
spanking becomes part of the macho male culture,
which demands physical pain as the price for independence and masculinity. From this standpoint,
corporal punishment is normal and even normative: an early test of manliness. Some fathers may
think that spanking their sons initiates them into
manhood.

However, not all Americans support the practice of spanking. And, throughout the world, many
non-Americans oppose it as well.

PARENTS SHOULD NOT SPANK THEIR CHILDREN

Some cultures oppose spanking, and view corporal punishment more generally as an inappropriate
form of child discipline. They recognize that physical violence or suffering intended to modify behavior does indeed shade into abuse, which is
motivated more by a desire to inflict pain. Thus,
what begins as spanking may become corporal
punishment and child abuse. There are reasons why

societies oppose or condone spanking, as we shall
see. In our own society, we find evidence that corporal punishment—including spanking—indicates
family disorganization. Fewer well-functioning
families use corporal punishment to control behavior. And as we shall see, there is evidence that
corporal punishment has harmful consequences
and negative outcomes.

**More Industrialized Societies Reject Corporal
Punishment** We noted earlier that many societies condone corporal punishment. Most societies
that accept corporal punishment are less economically developed, but the United States is an exception to the rule. Societies that place a strong
emphasis on self-reliance versus conformity typically oppose corporal punishment. Americans employ "softer" language when dealing with the
punishment of children. Many are pushing for the
inclusion of corporal punishment under the heading of domestic violence. Why is it unacceptable if
two adults inflict pain on each other, but acceptable for a larger and stronger individual to inflict
pain on a more defenseless child? Children are
spanked only because they are defenseless to resist it. A comparable attack on an adult could result
in criminal charges being laid.

Indeed, most industrial societies oppose corporal punishment. This shows up clearly when we
compare the United States with Sweden, a country
well-known for its concern for society's vulnerable
members, and a trendsetter in European social
practices.

In 1979, Sweden outlawed corporal punishment
at home and in the schools. Since then, survey results show that only 26 percent of Swedish parents
use corporal punishment, compared with 81 percent of American parents. Swedes believe that the
state should intervene in families that abuse their
members physically or otherwise. It puts this belief
into practice through laws prohibiting child abuse.
Beyond that, Sweden provides families at risk—
families in which one or more members are likely
to suffer harm—with shelters, counseling, and economic support.

The evidence suggests that legislation does succeed in reducing spanking and corporal punishment

more generally. Like other progressive beliefs about sex, marriage, parenting, social welfare, and taxation that started in Sweden, these views about spanking have spread throughout northern Europe. Eventually they will prevail in the industrial world as well—including the United States.

Family Disorganization and Poverty We saw earlier that people who were spanked in childhood usually condone spanking. People spanked as children who grew up with friends who were spanked and who live (as adults) among people who spank their own children are unlikely to find anything wrong with corporal punishment. The result: Parents tend to use the disciplinary techniques they experienced firsthand when they were growing up. Unless they are taught to do otherwise, people accept their own childhood experiences as normal. They don't evaluate their own behavior unless they can imagine an alternative.

But what conditions lead people who haven't been spanked to begin spanking their own children? Surely this is the key to understanding the origins of spanking, when it is something other than blind habit. One researcher studied these conditions and found that people used to nonviolent parenting adopt spanking and other corporal punishment techniques when stress becomes extreme—for example, when the husband/father is unemployed, family income is low, or surrounding social norms support violence. Characteristics of neighborhoods related to higher rates of parent-to-child violence include highly disadvantaged neighborhoods with many residents living below the poverty line and/or on public assistance, single-mother families, unemployed parents, and lower levels of immigrants within the neighborhood.

According to this research, the best predictors of corporal punishment—after controlling for whether the parents have been spanked or not—are too many siblings born too soon, delayed child development, stressful living conditions, and inadequate social support for over-stressed or inexperienced parents. Mothers are most often the spankers, and sons more often spanked than daughters. Children of single mothers are less often spanked than children who live with both parents. Most important, perhaps, is the finding that parents usually spank their children in desperation, not as a conscious plan.

Spanking is part of a repertoire of disciplinary techniques that are primitive, punitive, and unreasoning. This means that parents who generally control their children by reasoning or withholding rewards rarely spank their children. Conversely, parents who neither reason nor withhold rewards from misbehaving children are likely to resort to spanking and other corporal punishment.

Research has found that inductive discipline—teaching good behaviour by setting a good example, then rewarding imitation—is better for the child than power assertions. Feelings of guilt, unlike feelings of fear, exercise an internal moral control over the children's behaviour. Adolescents taught using inductive techniques make decisions more independently, for they have learned how to make moral judgements. Parental affection and inductive discipline foster moral internalization, while power assertions (like spanking) diminish moral learning.

Negative Consequences of Corporal Punishment We might condone spanking—even spanking carried out for the wrong reasons—if we could show that it improved children's behavior. But there is no evidence that spanking or other corporal punishment does so. It often has the short-term effect of stopping a particular behaviour while the parent is present, but the long-term effect of increasing the child's likelihood of bad behaviour when the parent is absent.

A question arises as well as to whether a child's behavior is the cause or the effect of corporal punishment: For example, do aggression and other behavioral problems of the child lead parents to spank or does the use of corporal punishment cause the behavioral problems?

Research finds that boys who receive frequent corporal punishment often become more aggressive, girls more withdrawn. The practice backfires in other respects, too. Parents who administer corporal punishment are also more likely to receive it. This is true especially for mothers, who are at greater risk of receiving violence from their children than are fathers. Research has also found that parents are more likely to punish older siblings than younger siblings for fighting, especially boys when they fight with their sisters. This punishment of the more powerful sibling results in more frequent aggression.

Other risk factors of corporal punishment are linked to partner violence. Partner violence increases the risk of corporal punishment within a family for multiple members, including parents. In households where the mother was abused, teenagers (especially boys) are at greater risk of abuse, especially when they intervene during a violent session to protect their mother. Other times, rather than protecting their mother, children (again, most often sons) will model the behavior of the abusive parent (most often their father) and hit their mother. Experiencing a great amount of corporal punishment as a child also increases the probability of being abusive as an adult (wife or husband).

Corporal punishment is most dangerous and probably more likely when the parent or caregiver is under major stress. Parents who believe in the value of corporal punishment are more likely to physically abuse their children when dealing with increasing levels of stress. Caregivers of elderly or dependent family members are known to undergo tremendous amounts of stress. Research comparing children of caregivers and children of noncaregivers found that the incidence of spanking was higher for children of caregivers. However, comparing only those who spanked, caregivers did so less frequently.

Individual risk factors associated with corporal punishment include depression, anxiety, lower grades in school, aggression, delinquency, and slower physical development. Not surprisingly, many children who receive corporal punishment come to feel they have little control over their own lives. They are less likely to be ambitious, confident, optimistic, or happy.

The harm caused by corporal punishment merely begins in childhood; it does not end there. Research shows that among adults who were spanked as children, there are more instances of crime and racism, a sense of personal injustice, general tolerance for violence and aggression, and belief in the value of extreme solutions to social problems—for example, belief in the death penalty. Corporal punishment in childhood is an even better predictor of violence in adulthood than either social class or the viewing of violent TV shows!

Of course, not *everyone* who is spanked will grow up into a violent predator. After all, the vast majority of Americans are spanked, but only a few become violently or criminally abusive. The negative effects of spanking on (later) child and adult behavior result from a complex interaction with other conditions or predisposing factors. Corporal punishment does not always produce negative side-effects; only under certain aggravating circumstances.

For example, corporal punishment mainly causes delinquency when parental discipline is inconsistent, parents' demands are changeable, or discipline is intermittent. Likewise, corporal punishment mainly causes delinquency when a parent relies nearly exclusively on spanking and rarely tries to reason with his or her child.

Summing Up

Most economically developed, literate, and prosperous societies have rejected spanking and other corporal punishment as acceptable methods of child discipline. They tolerate more deviant behavior and punish rule-breakers less harshly. Whether this indicates a moral development away from "repressive justice" or merely slack moral standards as the fundamentalists might charge, is something we cannot answer, for that is a value judgment.

Parents may be under the misconception that they are better parents because they do not spank their children. It is important to realize that the absence of physical discipline does not guarantee that parents have necessarily mastered nonphysical discipline nor does this ensure that parents are engaging in more positive and nurturing interactions. That said, spanking always runs the risk of becoming abusive.

What is the best way to discipline a child and reduce misbehavior? Perhaps neither extreme is beneficial. What may be needed is a combination of nonphysical discipline—like withholding rewards, time-outs, and reasoning with the child—along with occasional physical discipline as a last resort. The State has an obligation to ensure that spanking does not become child abuse; vulnerable members of society, such as children, deserve protection against abuse even by their own parents.

REVIEW EXERCISES

For Discussion and Debate

1. "Capital punishment is a good way to punish serious wrongdoing."
2. "Corporal punishment is more appropriate to use on adult offenders than on children."
3. "Children respond to reasoning better than they respond to threats."
4. "Religion is the source of much of the violence in our society."

Writing Exercises

Write a brief (500-word) essay on one of the following topics:

1. "Spare the rod and spoil the child."
2. The circumstances leading up to the last occasion on which your parents spanked you.
3. Three situations in which torture would be an appropriate form of social control.
4. "What children need most from their parents."

Research Activities

1. Interview at least six people who have witnessed a young child being spanked in public. How did they react?
2. Compare a society in which spanking is widely tolerated with a society in which it is prohibited. How do these societies differ socially or culturally? Collect some published data to illustrate these differences.
3. Make yourself comfortable in a busy public place—for example, a shopping mall—and spend the afternoon watching how parents control and discipline their children. Record your observations. What patterns do you note?
4. Interview a sample of ten people, using two or more different methods to determine their acceptance of spanking as a method of child discipline. How well do the results of these methods agree?

SELECTED REFERENCES

Agnew, Robert. 1983. "Physical Punishment and Delinquency: A Research Note." *Youth and Society* 15, 2:225–236.

Alderson, Priscilla and Ben Phillips. 2003. "Beyond 'Anti-Smacking': Challenging Parental Violence and Coercion." *Child Abuse Review* 12, 5:282–291.

Amato, Paul R. and Alan Booth. 1997. *A Generation at Risk: Growing Up in an Era of Family Upheaval.* Cambridge, MA: Harvard University Press.

Bartkowski, John. 2000. "The Case of Parental Yelling." *Social Forces* 79, 1 (Sept.): 265–290.

Capps, Donald. 1992. "Religion and Child Abuse: Perfect Together." *Journal for the Scientific Study of Religion* 31, 1 (Mar.): 1–14.

Capps, Donald. 1995. *The Child's Song: The Religious Abuse of Children.* Louisville, KY: Westminster John Knox Press.

Crouch, Julie and Leah Behl. 2001. "Relationships among Parental Beliefs in Corporal Punishment, Reported Stress, and Physical Child Abuse Potential." *Child Abuse and Neglect* 25:413–419.

Day, Ronald D., Peterson, Gary W. and Coleen McCracken. 1998. "Predicting Spanking of Younger and Older Children by Mothers and Fathers." *Journal of Marriage and the Family* 60, 1:79–94.

Deley, Warren W. 1988. "Physical Punishment of Children: Sweden and the U.S.A." *Journal of Comparative Family Studies* 19, 3 (Autumn): 419–431.

Deyoung, Yolanda and Edward F. Zigler. 1994. "Machismo Is Two Cultures: Relation to Punitive Child-Rearing Practices." *American Journal of Orthopsychiatry* 64, 3 (July): 386–395.

Dietz, Tracy L. 2000. "Disciplining Children: Characteristics Associated with the Use of Corporal Punishment." *Child Abuse and Neglect* 24, 12:1529–1542.

Duvall, Donna and Alan Booth. 1979. "Social Class, Stress and Physical Punishment." *International Review of Modern Sociology* 9, 1 (Jan.–June): 103–117.

Ellis, Godfrey J. and Larry R. Petersen. 1992. "Socialization Values and Parental Control Techniques: A Cross-Cultural Analysis of Child Rearing." *Journal of Comparative Family Studies* 23, 1 (Spring): 39–54.

Ellison, Christopher G. and Darren E. Sherkat. 1993. "Conservative Protestantism and Support for Corporal Punishment." *American Sociological Review* 58, 1 (Feb.): 131–144.

Ellison, Christopher G. and John P. Bartkowski. 1999. "Are There Religious Variations in Domestic Violence?" *Journal of Family Issues* 20, 1 (Jan.): 87–113.

Felson, Richard B. and Natalie Russo. 1988. "Parental Punishment and Sibling Aggression." *Social Psychology Quarterly* 51, 1 (Mar.): 11–18.

Ferrari, Anne M. 2002. "The Impact of Culture upon Child Rearing Practices and Definitions of Maltreatment." *Child Abuse & Neglect* 26, 8:793–813.

Gelles, Richard J. 1991. "Physical Violence, Child Abuse, and Child Homicide: A Continuum of Violence, or Distinct Behaviors?" *Human Nature* 2, 1:59–72.

Grasmick, Harold G., Robert J. Bursik, Jr. and M'lou Kimpel. 1991. "Protestant Fundamentalism and Attitudes toward Corporal Punishment of Children." *Violence and Victims* 6, 4 (Winter): 283–298.

Graziano, Anthony M. and Karen A. Namaste. 1990. "Parental Use of Physical Force in Child Discipline: A Survey of 679 College Students." *Journal of Interpersonal Violence* 5, 4 (Dec.): 449–463.

Holden, George, Pamela Miller and Susan D. Harris. 1999. "The Instrumental Side of Corporal Punishment: Parents' Reported Practices and Outcome Expectancies." *Journal of Marriage and the Family* 6 (Nov.): 908–919.

Landown, Gerison. 2000. "Children's Rights and Domestic Violence." *Child Abuse* 9:416–426.

Larzelere, Robert E. 1986. "Moderate Spanking: Model or Deterrent of Children's Aggression in the Family?" *Journal of Family Violence* 1, 1 (Mar.): 27–36.

Lenton, Rhonda L. 1990. "Techniques of Child Discipline and Abuse by Parents." *Canadian Review of Sociology and Anthropology* 27, 2 (May): 157–185.

Lienesch, Michael. 1991. "'Train Up a Child': Conceptions of Child-rearing in Christian Conservative Social Thought." *Comparative Social Research* 13:203–224.

Molnar, Beth E., Stephen L. Buka, John K. Holton and Felton Earls. 2003. "A Multilevel Study of Neighborhoods and Parent-to-Child Physical Aggression: Results from the Project on Human Development in Chicago Neighborhoods." *Child Maltreatment* 8, 2:84–97.

Newson, John, Elizabeth Newson and Mary Adams. 1993. "The Social Origins of Delinquency." *Criminal Behaviour and Mental Health* 3, 1:19–29.

Ruane, Janet M. 1993. "Tolerating Force: A Contextual Analysis of the Meaning of Tolerance." *Sociological Inquiry* 63, 3 (Summer): 293–304.

Shepherd, Stolley and Maximiliane Szinovacz. 1997. "Caregiving Responsibilities and Child Spanking." *Journal of Family Violence* 12, 1:99–112.

Straus, Murray A. and Denise A Donnelly. 1993. "Corporal Punishment of Adolescents by American Parents." *Youth and Society* 24, 4 (June): 419–442.

Straus, Murray A. 2001. "Social Science and Public Policy." *Society* 38, 6:52–60.

Swinford, Steven. 2000. "Harsh Physical Discipline in Childhood and Violence in Later Romantic Involvement." *Journal of Marriage and the Family* 62, 2:508–519.

Tajima, Emiko, A. 2002. "Risk Factors for Violence against Children: Comparing Homes with and without Wife Abuse." *Journal of Interpersonal Violence* 17, 2:122–149.

Ulman, Arina and Murray A. Straus. 2003. "Violence by Children against Mothers in Relation to Violence between Parents." *Journal of Comparative Family Studies* 31, 1:41–61.

Walsh, Wendy. 2002. "Spankers and Nonspankers: Where They Get Information on Spanking." *Family Relations* 51, 1:81–88.

Weller, Susan C., A. Kimball Romney and Donald P. Orr. 1987. "The Myth of a Subculture of Corporal Punishment." *Human Organization* 46, 1 (Spring): 39–47.

Wissow, Lawrence S. 2001. "Ethnicity, Income, and Parenting Contexts of Physical Punishment in a National Sample of Families with Young Children." *Child Maltreatment* 6, 2 (Spring): 118–129.

Wolfner, Glenn D. and Richard J. Gelles. 1993. "A Profile of Violence toward Children: A National Study." *Child Abuse and Neglect* 17, 2 (Mar.–Apr.): 197–212.

2.3   Should We Teach That Money Buys Happiness?

The issue: Does money lead to happiness? Media advertisers and popular opinion seem to think so. But is there a connection between one's income and level of life satisfaction? What should we raise children to believe about this matter?

Parents differ in what they teach their children, because they differ in what they believe. Differences in their educational attainment, occupation, class status, and age—as well as personal life experiences—affect the views parents hold about the connections between wealth and happiness, for example. These views will undoubtedly influence what they teach their children about the pursuit of wealth and the importance of money.

For example, different generations may hold different views about the importance of money. Members of older generations (pre-Baby Boomers)—as well as new immigrants and other disadvantaged members of society—have often experienced financial insecurity and instability. Therefore, they are likely to define happiness in terms of achieving a certain level of financial security; and they are likely to encourage their children to earn as much money as possible, to ensure their own comfort and security.

By contrast, Baby Boomers grew up at a time when established traditional institutions were questioned and criticized, and people expressed open concern about social justice, equality, and fairness. Compared to previous generations, many of them are well-educated and occupy very high positions, as a result of their own hard work. This Baby Boom generation has a love-hate relationship with money: They love the opportunities that money affords them, but are concerned about the loss of meaning and spirituality in a consumerist society. And they are particularly worried about their children's fate. Because their children grew up in comfortable circumstances, they are in danger of becoming arrogant, spoiled, and lazy. Generation Xers, the next generation after Boomers, have a very different set of values. What then should we teach our children? Of course money matters, to some degree. This profit motive is at work, consciously or otherwise, in our choice of wardrobe, diet, residence, car, education, occupation, holiday destination, friendships, and lovers.

The philosopher Aristotle, for example, thought happiness was a consequence of living virtuously. Epicurus and his followers found happiness in a life of humble desires and restrained pleasures.

Others have characterized the state of happiness as mental tranquility, civic engagement, good health, being loved and being in love—things that people can find without a lot of money or talent. The American Declaration of Independence, without defining what "happiness" is, affirms that the pursuit of it is an inalienable right. For their part, social scientists typically measure "happiness" using a range of variables that together comprise indicators such as "subjective quality of life" (SQOL) and "subjective well-being" (SWB). By their reckoning, happiness is measurable, understandable, and—perhaps in the end—open to social engineering.

Most people want to maximize their satisfaction with life. "Satisfaction" is related to, but different from, "happiness"—at least in the eyes of people who study this problem seriously. Happiness is a visceral thing: Your guts tell you if you are happy. According to research, happiness increases a person's life expectancy, improves the quality of a marriage, increases the likelihood of finding and keeping a job, and raises a person's self-esteem and satisfaction with personal achievements.

Happiness and satisfaction are connected, and overall life satisfaction is connected to our satisfaction with particular parts of life. There's a complicated relationship between how satisfied we feel with life as a whole and with particular parts (or *domains*) of our lives. Sometimes we are satisfied with life as a whole and with particular domains of life (e.g., with our social activities). Conversely, when we feel dissatisfied with a particular domain of life (e.g., with marriage), we come to feel dissatisfied with life as a whole.

For example, marital happiness, or satisfaction with work, makes our life more satisfying as a whole; and overall life satisfaction makes work and marriage much more enjoyable, too. Studies have also found varying degrees of correlation between happiness and satisfaction. Often, people who are happy with life are satisfied, too, and vice versa. However, you can be satisfied without being happy and happy without being satisfied. It is probably easier to increase your satisfaction than your happiness.

Some people, of course, are not trying to maximize or even increase their satisfaction. Real life tells us that many people—especially people who are poor, insecure, or unhealthy—are less concerned with maximizing satisfaction than they are with minimizing dissatisfaction. When people are very unhappy or unsafe, they are content if they can simply keep their lives from getting any worse. They have little hope of making life dramatically better. As a result, their life strategies are more cautious than those of people who are trying to increase or maximize their satisfaction. They avoid taking risks.

Happiness has long been associated with material comforts, with the pleasures afforded by a life of luxury and wealth. North American culture has been transformed into what social scientists define as a *consumerist culture*—a culture in which money is ascribed great importance, people are defined by what and how they consume, and from which those unable to consume are excluded. As a consequence, when trying to instill their own values about wealth and happiness, parents may find themselves in competition and even conflict with these other sources. Marketers now have the ability to reach children in isolation from their parents, and much of the new "marketing of cool" involves preaching "anti-adult" attitudes: presenting the adult world as generally boring, laughable, and most of all "un-cool," and encouraging "us versus them" attitudes.

In the end, parents who try to criticize materialistic values or limit their children's consumerism are seen as unskilled in the art of being cool, old fashioned, and nonunderstanding. Young people, like their parents, strive for happiness and, more often than not, link it to material well-being. Similarly, "developing a meaningful philosophy of life," which 86 percent considered an important life goal in 1967, had declined to less than 40 percent by 2003, its lowest point in the 38-year history of the study. Another national survey asked Americans what would most improve their quality of life. The most frequent response: "more money."

What's wrong with wanting a six-figure income, if one is willing to put in the hard work to achieve it? Before we buy into the message that money equals happiness, let us first consider whether its claims have merit.

MONEY LEADS TO HAPPINESS

In a world governed by market principles, money is a fundamental need, and it is naive to think otherwise. Research supports the common-sense notion that having money relieves a large portion of the daily worries over finances and cushions the occasional bumps in the road of life. Studies have consistently shown that the lowest income earners—that is, the unemployed and the working poor—score lower on SQOL than those in higher income categories.

Compared to the well-off, those below the poverty level also score lower on physical and mental health measures, educational and employment success, and subjective well-being, and higher on levels of delinquency, drug and alcohol abuse, and criminal activity. Being poor in America can also severely limit one's educational as well as career opportunities. Usually, being wealthy enables one to prepare for obtaining jobs in this competitive job market. From the early childhood of their offspring, parents are concerned with choosing the right schools and right kind of training. Those who can afford it invest large amounts of money in providing the needed education.

Poor people have less cultural, social, and educational capital, and this hinders their ability to get access to those special networks that open up opportunities for career advancement and social acceptance.

Relative poverty—the type of poverty in which one experiences psychological distress rather than bodily distress (hunger)—tends to be more representative of affluent societies. This poverty results from not being able to live up to what our society defines as the "normal, happy life." The results of relative poverty are undoubtedly resentment, self-deprecation, depression, and aggravation.

Happiness and Self-Actualization Psychologist Abraham Maslow put forward a central theory in the study of life satisfactions. The most distinctive feature of Maslow's theory is that it is a *stage theory*. It proposes that people must pass through successive stages of fulfillment. People must successively meet needs for survival, security, belonging, and esteem before being able to reach, or even to want, total fulfillment in the form of *self-actualization*. People must pass through the stages in order, and all lower-level needs must be satisfied before self-actualization is possible.

Researchers since Maslow have found that a failure to satisfy sustenance needs leads people to fixate on these needs. However, satisfaction of sustenance needs reduces their importance. That is, people with a low income or poor health are particularly likely to focus on improving their income or health, while other people are not. Stage-one and stage-two values seem to operate by different rules and have different potentials for influencing a person's life satisfaction. Poverty and poor health can reduce the quality of a person's life; however, high incomes and good physical condition seem to have limited potential for directly increasing well-being. In turn, stage-two domains—for example, work, family, and leisure satisfactions have the potential to make life genuinely enjoyable or genuinely miserable.

People cope differently with the failure to fulfill early-stage needs. People failing to fulfill any of their secondary needs, for example, can substitute other domains as sources of gratification. Thus, unmarried people with good jobs and high incomes place more than average value on their work, while unmarried people with lower incomes place more than average value on leisure. Atkinson and Murray, who studied this problem, conclude that "the substitutability of second-stage values offers some relief from frustrations encountered in particular domains," if other sources of reward are available.

In short, survival and security needs must be satisfied before people can look to other domains for more satisfaction. For most people in our society who are able to meet their basic sustenance needs, higher-level needs can be satisfied in a variety of ways. In general, people make do with what they have at hand.

The factors that influence people's life satisfaction are pretty similar for everyone, despite their different life goals. Three variables seem to characterize the adults who are most satisfied with life: (1) control over their own lives—for example, they have autonomy at work, good health, free time, and a secure income; (2) social integration—for example, they live in a family, have intimate relations, and have friends; and (3) a commitment to something larger than themselves—for example, to religion or family, *not* career or personal development. In short, we could say that the three ingredients of satisfaction are work, love, and hope. Money has only a small role to play in this story.

However, life is not simply about getting by with the basics. It is a reasonable expectation to want to live in comfort, to have sufficient disposable income to afford the pursuit of personal hobbies, interests, and recreational activities—in short, the things that provide a life with depth and substance. Wealth opens doors, removes obstacles, and creates opportunities—in short, money talks. A good example of the opportunities created by wealth is career choice.

MONEY DOES NOT LEAD TO HAPPINESS

Money Doesn't Buy Happiness   As most people instinctively know, there is no linear, one-to-one relationship between money and happiness. While it is true that among the poorest segments of society, happiness increases proportionately as income increases, once a threshold enabling a comfortable life has been reached, the correlation no longer holds true. Other evidence dispelling the "money equals happiness" myth comes from interviews and surveys of the rich. One study found that the overall levels of happiness among *Forbes'* 100 richest Americans were only slightly higher than those of the average person. And within that select group, individual happiness levels varied considerably—some interviewees were gleefully happy; others were consistently miserable. Similarly, lottery winners typically experience a temporary spike in happiness and SQOL, but return to pre-winning levels within a year or two, as reality sets in and prior routines (along with long-lost relatives and ex-boyfriends or girlfriends) resurface.

The abundance of low-priced imported items has made it possible for Americans to buy more material goods. But for ethical consumers this abundance of low-priced imported items is not a reason for happiness but for distress at realizing that this merchandise was produced with the use of child labor and with the cost of human rights abuses and environmental destruction. In countries with an impoverished standard of living, where the ability to meet basic human needs is persistently undermined by a lack of income, increases in productivity and gross national product per capita do indeed give rise to increases in the relative well-being of their citizens.

Cross-cultural surveys show that the average level of subjective well-being (SWB) is consistently higher in, say, Sweden and Australia, than it is in, say, India or Belarus. From an economic standpoint, the average American is more prosperous than the average Australian and less prosperous than the average Swede, but all three are similar on measures of SWB. This suggests that, above a certain level of average national income, increments do not have much effect on happiness or subjective well-being.

It's Human Nature   The irony is that, when asked, most North Americans reject materialistic values. If a materialistic orientation is viewed negatively by the majority, why are so many still falling into the trap of make-money-spend-money?

The hamster wheel of make-money-spend-money, driven by hedonistic adaptation and social comparison, further debunks the argument that having lots of money is a liberating condition that creates more opportunities for indulging in pricey hobbies and diversions. Money might be a necessary component of many recreational pursuits, but so is free time. Indeed studies show that the more materialistic the child, the more likely he or she is to engage in self-destructive, risky behaviors.

Happiness Equals Lowered Expectations   To reiterate, Maslow argues that everyone wants the same things in life—essential or universal wants. He believes that people must attain them in the same sequence in order to maximize life satisfaction. Data support this theory in part, but the theory suffers from serious weaknesses. Rather, people's wants (their concerns, hopes, and desires) vary by age, period, country, and social class.

Second, as we have seen, people can deal with frustrated desires by substituting one satisfaction for another—for example, substituting work pleasures for family pleasures, or vice versa. Once people have satisfied their most basic needs for food and shelter, they can increase their life satisfaction with a wide variety of material, social, and cultural "goods." There is no need for people to attain these goods in stages.

People have a built-in tendency toward moderation and caution. By expecting little out of life, people learn to lower their expectations and, in this way, lower their dissatisfaction when they end up getting little. That's partly why there is so little protest by the poor, the jobless, and other disadvantaged people in our society. A second explanation suggested by this theory may apply, as well. The result is social conservatism, especially among adults. People tend to know most about people much like themselves; therefore, they set low standards for their own futures. It is no wonder that most people in our society are moderately satisfied with life.

The Best Things in Life Are Free   If having more money does not lead to greater happiness, then what, if anything, does? People need to have enough financial resources to meet their basic requirements, but beyond a modest absolute threshold, money and happiness fail to correlate.

Research has shown that equally essential to promoting a high level of subjective quality of life are companionship, an encompassing term that includes strong connections with friends, family, and lovers; a level of health and fitness that permits a full range of activity; involvement in personally meaningful social projects, whether they take the form of stimulating paid employment or challenging private endeavors; an examined system of personally held values and beliefs, either explicitly religious or idiosyncratic in nature; and involvement in something greater than

oneself, which can be anything from accepting the existence of a higher spiritual power (God, nature, Tao, etc.) to volunteering at the local children's hospital.

The well-off individuals can afford to look at "life beyond money" because they already enjoy some of the benefits offered by money, such as time and comfort. Economist Richard Easterlin points out that while hedonistic adaptation and social comparison work to prevent individuals from remaining forever content with what they have, neither mechanism operates equally across all life domains.

Under normal conditions, aspirations in the areas of interpersonal relationships and personal well-being tend to be realistic and remain consistent over time. In these domains at least, people are usually happy with what they have. Easterlin's suggestion, then, is a simple one: Devote more time to improving those areas of one's life—namely, family, friends, and individual well-being—that are less vulnerable to the fickle winds of desire, and the attainment of those goals will lead to a more lasting happiness.

SUMMING UP

In the final analysis, the social science literature confirms empirically what many of us already know instinctively: that money does not buy happiness. Knowing what truly makes (and does not make) people happy is important not least because happiness is associated with better health. Research shows that people with "highly central financial success aspirations" are more likely to experience depression, anxiety, and lower vitality than those who aspire to the goals of community affiliation and self-acceptance. According to another survey, business students who score high on measures of materialism also report "lower self-actualization, vitality, and general happiness, and higher anxiety, physical symptoms and time spent unhappy."

Happiness may indeed be the most elusive of goals, but research shows that the obstacles to attaining it are not primarily financial. This is what we ought to be teaching our children.

REVIEW EXERCISES

For Discussion and Debate

1. Should parents restrict as much as possible their children's access to media sources that promote consumerism, brand attachments, and materialism?
2. "Even if outcomes are not equal, in the United States all citizens enjoy the equal opportunity to rise to the top."
3. "If one works hard enough he can always increase his wealth."
4. "Encouraging people to pursue materialistic goals has led to selfishness, greed, loss of community involvement, and ultimately the isolation of the individual and the erosion of social institutions."
5. "Does consumerism reduce the general level of happiness in society?"

Writing Exercises

Write a brief (500-word) essay on one of the following topics:

1. "Money makes the world go round."
2. "The best things in life are free."
3. What is the balance between too little and too much money? Is this balance the key to happiness?
4. Describe how the lack of money may have robbed you (personally) of opportunities to reach some desired goal(s).
5. List three things that can lead to happiness but are in no way related to money.

Research Activities

1. Ask twenty people which one they would prefer: "a well paid job" or "a fulfilling job." Look at the positive versus negative answers and realize how much importance people truly ascribe to money.
2. Ask ten people you know whether the best things in life are free. Then ask them whether family and companionship are more important than financial rewards. Finally, ask them which type of evening they would enjoy most: one spent at home with family or friends or one spent on an outing to a movie theater or dinner. Observe the possible contradictions between their answers to these different questions.
3. Ask twenty people whether material possessions are important for their happiness or whether they place more importance on nonmaterial things such as love, companionship, spirituality. Then ask them what they would do if they won a million dollars and give them the choices: "Donate it all to charity or a cause I believe in (e.g., help a starving child)," "Divide it with my family," or "Buy all I have ever longed for." Again look at similarities and differences between the answers to the first question and the second one.
4. Using published materials (e.g., magazines and newspapers) from different societies, study the similarities and dissimilarities between popular attitudes toward money, wealth, and the definition of happiness in a consumerist versus a traditionalist or nonconsumerist society.
5. In a shopping center, note the characteristics of the shoppers, such as age, gender, race, ethnic background. Try to determine which demographic groups are overrepresented in this context and which severely underrepresented. Try to create some generalization about how much people shop and what they shop for according to group characteristics.

SELECTED REFERENCES

Adams, Michael. 2001. *Better Happy Than Rich? Canadians, Money and the Meaning of Life.* Toronto: Penguin Canada.

Bauman, Zygmunt. 1998. *Work, Consumerism and the New Poor.* Philadelphia, PA: Open University Press.

Brooks, David. 2003. "Bobos in Paradise: The New Upper Class and How They Got There." In *Wealth and Poverty in America: A Reader,* edited by Dalton Conley. Malden, NY: Blackwell Publishing.

Campbell, A. 1981. *The Sense of Well-Being in America.* New York: McGraw-Hill.

Childs, James, Jr. 2000. *Greed: Economics and Ethics in Conflict.* Minneapolis, MN: Fortress Press.

D'Souza, Dinesh. 2000. *The Virtue of Prosperity: Finding Values in an Age of Techno-Affluence.* New York: The Free Press.

Davis, K. and W. E. Moore. 1945. "Some Principles of Stratification." *American Sociological Review* 10:242–249.

Diener, E., J. Horwitz and R. A. Emmons. 1985. "Happiness of the Very Wealthy." *Social Indicators* 16:263–274.

Easterlin, R. A. 1995. "Will Raising the Incomes of All Increase the Happiness of All?" *Journal of Economic Behavior and Organization* 27 (1): 35–47.

Easterlin, R. A. 2003. "Explaining Happiness." *Proceedings of the National Academy of Sciences* 100 (19): 1176–1183.

Goff, Brian and Arthur Fleisher. 1999. *Spoiled Rotten.* Colorado: Westview Press.

Hearn, Jeff and Sasha Roseneil. 1999. *Consuming Cultures: Power and Resistance.* New York: Macmillan.

Kasser, T. and A. C. Ahuvia. 2002. "Materialistic Values and Well-Being in Business Students." *European Journal of Social Psychology* 32:137–146.

Kasser, T. and R. C. Ryan. 1993. "A Dark Side of the American Dream: Correlates of Financial Success as a Life Aspiration." *Journal of Personality and Social Psychology* 65 (2): 410–422.

Kingwell, M. 1999. *Better Living: In Pursuit of Happiness from Plato to Prozac.* Toronto: Penguin.

Kingwell, M. 2000. *The World We Want: Virtue, Vice, and the Good Citizen.* Toronto: Penguin.

Klein, Naomi. 2000. *No Logo, No Space, No Choice, No Jobs.* Toronto: Vintage Canada.

Mayor, Susan. 2003. "What Money Can't Buy: Family Income and Children's Life Chances." In *Wealth and Poverty in America: A Reader,* edited by Dalton Conley. Malden, NY: Blackwell Publishing.

Myers, D. G. 2000. *The American Paradox: Spiritual Hunger in an Age of Plenty.* New Haven, CT: Yale University Press.

Myers, D. G. 2000. "The Funds, Friends, and Faith of Happy People." *American Psychologist* 55 (1): 56–67.

Sax, L. J., A. W. Astin, J. A. Lindholm, W. S. Korn, V. B. Saenz and K. M. Mahoney. 2003. *The American Freshman: National Norms for Fall 2003.* Los Angeles, CA: Higher Education Research Institute.

Schiller, Bradley. 2004. *The Economics of Poverty and Discrimination.* Upper Saddle River, NJ: Pearson/Prentice Hall.

Schor, J. B. 1998. *The Overspent American: Upscaling, Downshifting, and the New Consumer.* New York: Basic Books.

Schor, Juliet. 2004. *Born to Buy: The Commercialized Child and the New Consumer Culture.* New York: Scribner.

CHAPTER 3 ▶ DEVIANCE AND CONTROL

To sociologists, deviance refers to any behavior that leads to a negative reaction by some part of the community. When no one feels threatened by an uncommon behavior—for example, by the wearing of a polka-dot bow tie—people are likely to see it as simply an expression of individuality. But when people do feel threatened, they react in various ways.

Reactions depend largely on how the behavior is perceived. But perception by itself is not enough; for an act to be deviant, perception must be turned into action. How much weight that action carries will depend on how much power people have to enforce their own views of acceptable behavior. Social control refers to the institutions and procedures that make sure members of society conform to rules of expected and approved behavior. The operation of social control is most obvious when it is formal, especially when laws are enforced through the police and the courts. Formal social control gives specific people (such as police officers) the responsibility of enforcing specific rules or laws, while following specific control methods. And formal control varies widely across countries.

In this chapter we look at deviance and control of various types. First, we consider whether more poverty in a society translates into higher rates of crime. Second, we look at evidence as to whether (formal) efforts to control deviance by imprisoning criminals are effective or desirable. Third, we consider the pros and cons of legalizing recreational drugs like marijuana, focusing on the likely consequences of this for both deviance and control.

3.1 Does More Poverty Equal More Crime?

The issue: Is the "crime problem" a result of poverty, so that increasing poverty increases the danger in our everyday lives? And if so, should we take steps to deal with poverty in order to deal with crime?

Fear of crime is widespread in North America and in some communities the fear is increasing. Research has shown that some groups—for example, older people and heavy television viewers—are even more fearful of criminal victimization than others, and there is little correlation between actual victimization and the fear of it. In fact, the fear of crime has become a problem almost as grave as crime itself.

Nonetheless, the fear remains; and as we learned from the research of the early sociologist W. I. Thomas, a thing that is believed to be real is real in

its consequences. Consequences of this increased fearfulness include public support for more police, stiffer penalties for convicted criminals, and more imprisonment of convicts. Politicians play on this fearfulness to increase their own popularity, even though their actions further increase fearfulness and a willingness to explore extreme solutions.

The media also play a role in increasing the fear of crime by choosing to report the most sensational of crimes and exploiting these stories by showing only the most severe and shocking aspects, in order to increase their ratings.

Less imaginary is the increase, among urban poor people, of unemployment and desperate economic conditions. Common sense suggests a connection between unemployment (or poverty) and crime. If such a connection exists, will a worsening economic situation and the growth of an urban underclass lead to more crime and a more justified fearfulness about crime? Sociologists have researched and debated this question almost as long as the discipline has existed. Yet strangely, given all the research, there are conflicting points of view on this question. Let's look at them and form our own judgment.

MORE POVERTY DOES NOT MEAN MORE CRIME

Several different kinds of arguments are put forward to explain why we cannot be certain that more poverty means more crime. First, even if more poverty increases the motivation to commit crimes, other factors may have an opposing influence—among them legal deterrence and a lack of opportunity to commit certain kinds of crimes. Second, even if poverty appears to cause crime—therefore, more poverty should cause more crime—there may be other factors that explain this relationship. Third, research that shows poverty and crime are correlated doesn't prove that poverty causes crime, or that more poverty will cause more crime.

Motivation Isn't Everything The reason why poverty may cause crime is best presented by Robert Merton in his famous "anomie theory." There, Merton argues that people who experience a gap between what the culture has taught them to value (i.e., society's cultural goals) and the approved method (or "institutionalized means") of pursuing these goals will suffer from *anomie*. In other words, deviance is driven by a basic conflict or paradox: a discrepancy between culturally defined goals and socially approved means for attaining those goals. One way out of anomie—a way with a long tradition in America—is what

Merton calls "innovation," and one form of innovation is crime—the use of illegitimate means to attain wealth and success.

What crime does, in Merton's eyes, is allow disadvantaged people to pursue the culture's goals by unconventional, often disapproved means. Merton claims innovation is the form of adaptation most likely to be found among the lower class. While all classes share the same goals, Merton sees the lower class as most lacking in access to the approved means necessary for achieving these goals. Seen from this perspective, crime is as American as apple pie—a way that disadvantaged groups can pursue their ambitions and thus keep faith with the mythologized American Dream.

However, Merton also points out that people in a state of anomie have other options open to them. For example, some will conform, but really they've given up all hope of personal success. Merton calls this ritualism, where people no longer have any expectations for themselves. Secondly, some people will deal with anomie by simply giving up, they in fact become retreatists—such as alcoholics, drug addicts or suicides. Lastly, some people will rebel against inequality and reject the norms and values upon which it is based.

In short, research tells us that people actually do handle their anomie in each of these ways, so crime is not an inevitable consequence of poverty.

Therefore, we should not be surprised that some research finds only a weak relationship between poverty and crime. Moreover, other factors enter in. The likelihood of committing criminal (or delinquent) acts also depends on one's opportunities. Many types of crime (e.g., embezzlement and other white collar crimes) are not possible for poor people. Close policing also makes it difficult to commit some crimes undetected, and the high risk of arrest and punishment makes crime less likely in some communities than in other, poorly policed communities. Also, as sociologist Howard Becker points out in *Outsiders*, rule-breaking behavior must be noticed and labeled to become crime, and poverty might produce rule-breaking action that is not perceived as such.

Appearance May Not Be Reality   Second, the relationship between poverty and crime may be only apparent. It depends on how well we have managed to measure the true extent of crime in a given community or group, for example.

On the one hand, there is ample evidence of official bias against poor or working-class people—a bias observed in policing, arrest, bail-setting, conviction, and punishment patterns. Some researchers have viewed it, instead, as a bias in favor of middle-class and wealthy people; but either way we view it, the result is a higher rate of recorded criminality by lower-class people. More poverty appears to cause more crime because the formal system of justice criminalizes more poor people, and it is this bias—captured in the official statistics—that leads sociological researchers to conclude that poverty causes crime.

As a result of such biases, many researchers have turned to using self-reports of crime or delinquency. These self-reports typically show less difference in class-based rates of crime (or other deviance) than do the official statistics. However, some claim that this difference shrinks because people misreport their own crime and the data they provide cannot be believed. And if the data cannot be believed, we cannot assume that they are any better than the official statistics, or reasonably conclude that poverty has little effect on crime.

In the end, we are stuck with two kinds of defective data. It would be foolhardy to draw any conclusion whatsoever about the link between poverty and crime.

What Causes What?   Assume for a moment that the data—whether official or self-reported—are not as flawed as we have been saying; then, suppose that these data show a correlation, or association, between poverty-type variables and crime-type variables. There are now additional problems to handle.

First, in studying the poverty-crime link, researchers have used a variety of different measures. On one side of the equation, some have focused on poverty (whether absolute or relative), others on class or status level, others on unemployment, and others still on social inequality. These variables are

related to one another by anomie theory: Feelings of anomie may be equally intense among poor people, lower class people, unemployed people, and people in the bottom half of a highly unequal society. However, these measures are not all the same, and research using different measures is not strictly comparable. The same holds true on the other side of the equation: Some researchers have studied crime, others delinquency. Of those studying crime, some have focused on crimes of violence, others on property crime, and so on.

Given these variations, how would we reconcile the following three hypothetical findings?: (1) Poor people are more likely to commit burglary than rich people; (2) There is somewhat more delinquency in highly unequal societies than in less unequal societies; and (3) Unemployed people are no more likely to commit murder than employed people. Do these findings show that the poverty-crime linkage is strong or weak, or that we are comparing apples and oranges?

That problem aside, what does a consistent correlation between the poverty measures and the crime measures really mean? It may mean that poverty causes crime; or that criminal activity causes poverty; or that poverty and crime reciprocally cause each other. It may even mean that something else is causing both poverty and crime, so that the relationship between poverty and crime is spurious. For example, past imprisonment, a poor school record, or a concentration of urban young people would each increase both poverty and crime.

So, given all these problems, it is risky to conclude that poverty definitely causes crime, and that an increase in poverty will surely increase crime. Before such a conclusion is possible, it is necessary to solve the logical and methodological problems we have just reviewed.

But not every researcher would take this position.

MORE POVERTY MEANS SOMEWHAT MORE CRIME

Another, larger group of researchers would argue there is little doubt that poverty is strongly and consistently linked with crime. A majority of studies, however flawed, come to this very conclusion and that cannot be accidental.

However, the same researchers would disagree amongst themselves about what importance to attach to this finding, for two reasons. The first has to do with the relative importance of poverty, as compared with other causes of crime. The second has to do with competing theories about the reason poverty is linked to crime.

Competing Variables   A common problem in sociology is what is called *overdetermination.* That is, there are too many good, plausible causes for every effect, and usually these causes are related to one another in complicated ways.

There are many good theories about the causes of crime or delinquency. Some stress the importance of early experiences: abusive or neglectful parenting, family conflict, family criminality, or early institutionalization. Other theories focus on the effects of antisocial peers, or gang pressures to participate in crime. Still others refer to social or community disorganization or, on the other hand, to deviant subcultures. Other theories focus more on the ways labeling (stigmatization) creates a criminal or deviant career. Some theories claim that racial discrimination has a stronger effect on crime than poverty does, while others deny it. Others focus less on criminal motivations and more on differential opportunities to commit crimes, or on the deterrent effects of policing and stiff sentences for convicts.

All of these are good variables that have been shown, many times, to influence the likelihood of criminal behavior. But theorists would disagree on the relative importance of poverty compared to any or all of these other influences. Few would argue that poverty is surely the most important of the lot.

Competing Theories   Not only are there too many variables, there are also too many different theories linking these variables—individually or collectively—to crime. In fact, some of these theories are incompatible with one another. For example, a theory stressing the role of criminal subcultures is not always compatible with a theory stressing social or community disorganization.

Likewise, a theory that emphasizes faulty socialization is not always compatible with a theory that emphasizes stigmatization or police bias.

These different theories, with their different, important variables often grow out of different sociological paradigms: structural functionalism, conflict theory, symbolic interactionism and so on. Some day they may all fit together in a unified theory of crime causation, but so far no one has managed to do that. And part of the reason for this failure is that different paradigms ask different questions and collect different kinds of data. So, for example, some theories seem to call for real (community-level) measures of crime and poverty, while others call for individual-level measures. For the most part, there has been little success in linking together the findings obtained from these different kinds of studies.

Given our profusion of variables and theories, once again it seems foolhardy to draw any final conclusion about the link between poverty and crime. All we can say with some certainty is that there is a nontrivial relationship.

MORE POVERTY SOMETIMES MEANS MUCH MORE CRIME

If you are thinking that this section title is the same as the previous section's title, read them both again. They're not the same. The previous section noted that some sociologists would willingly accept the premise that poverty always has an effect on crime, but it may be a small effect. Indeed, they might say that any attempt to predict crime would have to take dozens of variables into account, only one of which would be poverty.

The sociologists we want to talk about now would take a different position: namely, that under some circumstances poverty has little or no influence; but under other circumstances, poverty would have a powerful, overwhelming effect.

This difference in outlooks is not unique to the study of crime. Throughout sociology, some theories assume that a lot of small influences add up to a big influence: Call these *additive theories.* Others, however—call them *interactive theories*—

assume that any given variable or group of variables will have a big effect only when it interacts with, or varies under, specified conditions. Holding a lit match in one hand and a firecracker three feet away in the other hand does not give you an explosion. For an explosion, the two items have to come together: That's an interactive relationship.

But what *are* the conditions under which poverty (or unemployment, or inequality, or lower social class) likely has its greatest impact? Poverty in a poor, stable country produces less crime than poverty in a poor, rapidly developing country, or in a rich country. And poverty seems to have a different effect on boys and girls. Why?

Sociologist John Hagan has tried to explain why there is more difference in the criminality of boys and girls at the bottom of the class structure than there is at the top. He argues that to answer this question we need to know about more than class or poverty. We need to also understand the interaction between class experiences and gender experiences. The result is what Hagan calls a *power-control theory* of crime.

Here's a simplification of the argument: As you go down the class structure, from richest to poorest, two-parent families tend to be more "patriarchal," in the sense that wives have little power relative to husbands, daughters have little freedom relative to sons, and daughters are less delinquent than sons. Gender differences of every kind are diminished in egalitarian families, which are more common further up the class structure (where the spouses are also, typically, more highly educated). Power-control theory explains this variation in terms of gender divisions in domestic social control.

Typically, in the more patriarchal families, interpersonal relations featuring shared intimacy, mutual understanding, and caring (among others) are more characteristic of women than men. Mothers in these patriarchal families control their daughters more closely than their sons. This leads daughters to prefer risk-taking less than sons; as a result, they are less likely to engage in delinquency. Daughters are also under more pressure to take their schooling and job responsibilities seriously; in turn, early employment contacts increase their prospects of getting a job and advancing occupationally. By contrast, early involvement in crime isolates boys from schooling and employment that would improve their chances of legitimate adult employment.

This interpretation argues that delinquency results (at least in part) from a lack of familial control and embeddedness in structures leading to economic success. It predicts that any conditions that reduce school or familial control—whether child neglect or poor supervision—or increase the control of nonconforming influences (e.g., delinquent peers) will increase crime and delinquency. Thus, homeless people and street kids get involved in more crime than other people both because they need money and because they are relatively uncontrolled. Paradoxically, children of unemployed parents—though often suffering more poverty than their peers—are more likely to be closely controlled—hence, less delinquent. (Note, however, that the cost of reducing delinquency, according to this scenario, is a domestication of mothers who forego careers and work in order to tame their children and cater to their husband.)

So in the end, there are factors associated with poverty that motivate delinquency and crime. But to produce criminal behavior, these factors must interact with social conditions such as lax supervision (or for adults, lack of family responsibilities), criminal peers, and/or a lack of legitimate employment opportunities. The effect of poverty on crime is conditional. Therefore, more poverty means more crime only when the social constraints of civil society—family, community, job—break down or disappear.

SUMMING UP

More poverty does produce more crime under some conditions. For example, more poverty produces more crime under conditions of anomie—a gap between goals and means; also, under conditions of great inequality or rapid change. All of these conditions excite feelings of uncertainty, frustration, and envy. As a result, they excite the desire to take shortcuts to culturally valued goals, or to relieve frustration through aggressive acts.

Poverty also produces more crime when people's behavior is less effectively regulated, whether because of lax law enforcement or lax parenting. Even under conditions of frustration, people are likely to restrain their desires if doing otherwise will carry great costs. In this respect, bringing shame to one's family may seem as "costly" to some people as years spent behind bars.

Poverty, while increasing frustration and a desire for shortcuts, may also cut social bonds, thus releasing people from effective control. Take homeless people or "street kids": They are certainly poor and often this poverty leads them to petty crime, out of the need to survive. But equally poor people living at home would be less likely to resort to crime, because their family would limit their behavior. So, poverty under conditions of relative social isolation will have different effects on crime than poverty under conditions of social integration.

Poverty leads to crime in another sense, one that classical conflict theory would illuminate: It is privilege and advantage that constructs the legal system and pays for its enforcement. The very issue of what is "crime" is thus decided by those at a distance from poverty. Some would put it more bluntly, saying that when wealth *takes,* we call it an "investment strategy"; when poverty *takes,* we call it theft.

If worsening economic conditions produce poverty and also family (or community) breakdown, then more poverty will mean more crime. This suggests that government policies aimed at preventing crime need to fight both poverty and family (or community) breakdown. Equally important, it argues the importance of taking steps to promote civil society as an informal buffer against the effects of poverty. We will further discuss the importance of civil society in a later chapter.

REVIEW EXERCISES

For Discussion and Debate

1. If more poverty equals more crime, why is there much less crime in China or Costa Rica than in the much wealthier United States?
2. How would you account for large differences in the crime rates of the United States, Canada, Japan and Sweden—all of which have roughly similar levels of per capita income?
3. If you had to choose between official statistics and self-reports on criminal behavior, which kind would you choose? Do you think the data provided by this source would be more reliable for one kind of crime than for another? Explain.
4. Think of a sociological problem besides poverty-and-crime that requires an interactive or conditional explanation. (For example, how about the effects of divorce on children's well-being?)

Writing Exercises

Write a brief (500-word) essay on one of the following topics:

1. "Eliminating crime means first eliminating poverty."
2. "Stricter parenting is the answer to the delinquency problem in North America."
3. "Differences in the crime rate from one group to another reflect differences in what should be considered a crime."
4. "More gender equality equals more crime."

Research Activities

1. Interview at least two police officers to find out how they decide whether to arrest or merely caution a juvenile who has gotten into trouble.

2. Examine published crime statistics for your community and see how, and by how much, they have changed in the last ten years. What categories of criminal behavior have changed most?

3. Construct a brief questionnaire to measure opinions about the "crime problem" in your community—especially, how serious it is perceived to be and what should be done about it; then administer the questionnaire to at least six students in your college and interpret the results.

4. View ten hours of prime-time television or five recent movies that are about crime or delinquency. What are the implied causes of crime? What kinds of people are the criminals, and what kinds of crime (e.g., street crime versus white collar crime) are depicted?

SELECTED REFERENCES

Ajzenstadt, Mimi. 2002. "Crime, Social Control, and the Process of Social Classification: Juvenile Delinquency/Justice Discourse in Israel, 1948–1970." *Social Problems* 49, 4 (Nov.): 585–604.

Allan, Emilie Andersen and Darrell J. Steffensmeier. 1989. "Youth, Underemployment, and Property Crime: Differential Effects of Job Availability and Job Quality on Juvenile and Young Adult Arrest Rates." *American Sociological Review* 54, 1 (Feb.): 107–123.

Broe, Dennis. 2003. "Class, Crime, and Film Noir: Labor, the Fugitive Outsider, and the Anti-Authoritarian Tradition." *Social Justice* 30, 1 (91): 22–41.

Carreras, Steven Andrew. 2002 "Multiple Risk Factors for Academic and Behavior Problems at the Beginning of School." *Dissertation Abstracts International, A: The Humanities and Social Sciences* 63, 5 (Nov.): 2015-A.

Chiricos, Theodore G. 1987. "Rates of Crime and Unemployment: An Analysis of Aggregate Research Evidence," *Social Problems* 34, 2 (Apr.): 187–212.

Cromer, Gerald. 2004. "'Children from Good Homes': Moral Panics about Middle-Class." *British Journal of Criminology* 44, 3 (May): 391–400.

De Welde, Kristine M. 2003. "Women Warriors Fight Back: Resistance and White Femininity in Self-Defense." *Dissertation Abstracts International, A: The Humanities and Social Sciences* 64, 4 (Oct.): 1412-A.

Duster, Troy. 1987. "Crime, Youth Unemployment, and the Black Urban Underclass." *Crime and Delinquency* 33, 2 (Apr.): 300–316.

Farnsworth, Margaret, Terence P. Thornberry, Marvin D. Crohn and Alan J. Lizotte. 1994. "Measurement in the Study of Class and Delinquency: Integrating Theory and Research." *Journal of Research in Crime and Delinquency* 31, 1 (Feb.): 32–61.

Field, Simon. 1990. *Trends in Crime and Their Interpretation: A Study of Recorded Crime in Post-War England and Wales.* London: HMSO.

Hagan, John. 1993. "The Social Embeddedness of Crime and Unemployment." *Criminology* 31, 4 (Nov.): 465–491.

Hagan, John, A. R. Gillis and John Simpson. 1985. "The Class Structure of Gender and Delinquency: Toward a Power-Control Theory of Common Delinquent Behavior." *American Journal of Sociology* 90, 6 (May): 1151–1178.

Hagan, John, John Simpson and A. R. Gillis. 1988. "Feminist Scholarship, Relational and Instrumental Control, and Power-Control Theory of Gender and Delinquency." *British Journal of Sociology* 3 (Sept.): 301–336.

Harer, Miles D. and Darrel Steffensmeier. 1992. "The Differing Effects of Economic Inequality on Black and White Rates of Violence." *Social Forces* 70, 4 (June): 1035–1054.

Hogeveen, Bryan Richard. 2003. "'Can't You Be a Man?' Rebuilding Wayward Masculinities and Regulating Juvenile Deviance in Ontario 1860–1930." *Dissertation Abstracts International, A: The Humanities and Social Sciences* 64, 4 (Oct.): 1416-A–1417-A.

Hsieh, Ching Chi and M. D. Pugh. 1993. "Poverty, Income Inequality, and Violent Crime: A Meta-Analysis of Recent Aggregate Data Studies." *Criminal Justice Review* 18, 2 (Autumn): 182–202.

Inderbitzin, Michelle. 2003. "Outsiders and Justice Consciousness." *Contemporary Justice Review* 6, 4 (Dec.): 357–362.

Kleck, Gary, Travis Hirschi, Michael J. Hindelang and Joseph Weis. 1982. "On the Use of Self-Report Data to Determine the Class Distribution of Criminal and Delinquent Behavior." *American Sociological Review* 47, 3 (June): 427–433.

Kroll, Katherine Marie. 2003. *Cracking the Cocaine Culture.* Southern Sociological Society (SSS).

Lee, Matthew R. and Graham C. Ousey. 2003. *The Civically Engaged Middle-Class and Urban Crime: A Race-Disaggregated Analysis.* Southern Sociological Society (SSS).

Long-Scott, Austin. 2004. "Understanding Race, Class and Urban Violence: Why Journalists Can't Do More to Help Us Understand." *Race, Gender & Class* 11, 1:6–22.

Mauer, Marc. 2004. "Race, Class, and the Development of Criminal Justice Policy." *The Review of Policy Research* 21, 1 (Jan.): 79–92.

McCarthy, Bill and John Hagan. 1987. "Gender, Delinquency, and the Great Depression: A Test of Power-Control Theory." *Canadian Review of Sociology and Anthropology* 24, 2 (May): 153–177.

Reinarman, Craig and Jeffrey Fagan. 1988. "Social Organization and Differential Association: A Research Note from a Longitudinal Study of Violent Juvenile Offenders." *Crime and Delinquency* 34, 3 (July): 307–327.

Sampson, Robert J. and John H. Laub. 1994. "Urban Poverty and the Family Context of Delinquency: A New Look at Structure and Process in a Classic Study." *Child Development* 65, 2 (Apr.): 523–540.

Short, James F. 1991. "Poverty, Ethnicity, and Crime: Change and Continuity in U.S. Cities." *Journal of Research in Crime and Delinquency* 28, 4 (Nov.): 501–518.

Smith, M. Dwayne, Joel A. Devine and Joseph F. Sheley. 1992. "Crime and Unemployment: Effects across Age and Race Categories." *Sociological Perspectives* 35, 4 (Winter): 551–572.

Thornberry, Terence P. and R. L. Christenson. 1982. "Unemployment and Criminal Involvement: An Investigation of Reciprocal Causal Structures." *American Sociological Review* 49, 3 (June): 398–411.

Tittle, Charles. 1983. "Social Class and Criminal Behavior: A Critique of the Theoretical Foundation." *Social Forces* 62, 2 (Dec.): 334–358.

Whiteford, Scott W. 2003. *Classifying Adolescent Drug Use: Predicting Crime and Delinquency.* Southern Sociological Society (SSS).

Wortley, Scot. 2003. "Hidden Intersections: Research on Race, Crime, and Criminal Justice in Canada." *Canadian Ethnic Studies/Etudes Ethniques au Canada* 35, 3:99–117.

3.2   Do We Have Enough Jails?

The issue: How to deal with the "crime problem." Will building more jails reduce the crime problem, leave it untouched, or make it even worse?

Every time we read a newspaper or watch a TV news program, stories and statistics about crime jump out at us. There seems to be a "crime problem" in America. But will more prisons solve this apparent crime problem?

The research on this question dates back over a century. Yet only in the twentieth century did researchers begin to study prisons and prisoners systematically. One researcher, Donald Clemmer, developed his *prisonization* theory out of such careful work. Clemmer stated that, by their nature,

prisons degrade people, coerce them, and take away their rights.

This treatment is inevitable. Without it, prison officials cannot keep order in such a large community of (usually) young men. Yet this treatment, which keeps peace in the prison, also has unintended and undesirable effects. It alienates prisoners from the outside world, and unites them against the prison administration. A prison subculture, growing out of everyday prison life, reflects and hardens this alienation. For example, offenders who were serving sentences in the United States correctional system were asked about the undesirable effects of incarceration, and the majority stated that they developed a more hostile attitude toward society and abiding legal regulation.

Prisoners learn the prison subculture and anti-administration normative code. Through contact with more experienced inmates they acquire new criminal skills, often learning to behave in undesirable and violent ways. When 36 inmates were questioned about their interaction with other offenders in the prison, 90 percent referred to the prison as a "criminal university." They end up with an identity that is more deviant than before they were imprisoned. Thus, *prisonization,* as Clemmer calls it, produces well-socialized prisoners: people who fit perfectly into the inmate society. This, however, is detrimental to the societal reintegration of the offender once their sentence has been served.

What works well in a prison subculture works poorly in society. The prisoners have not been taught how to adapt to life in the "real world." In fact, through prisonization, they learn how to alienate themselves from the normal functions of society. The feeling of being deviant in society is reinforced within the prison. As their release from prison approaches, they feel great stress. After release, they commit even more crimes—indeed, even more violent crimes, and many end up back in prison. This process is called recidivism, or "the revolving door." The prison system lacks programs emphasizing successful reintegration into society. Upon release back into the community, the offenders are all too often without employment, financial, residential, or social support, and so they return to a life of crime.

A sociological classic by Erving Goffman, *Asylums,* took this argument further. Goffman wrote that all residential facilities that try to shape inmate behavior—including prisons, mental hospitals, concentration camps, military barracks, monasteries, convents, and even boarding schools—are *total institutions.* As such, they share many characteristics that Clemmer attributed to prisons alone. For example, they all degrade people, strip away old identities, impose uniformity on dress and behavior,

limit personal freedom, and in these ways create new identities. The process stamps an inmate with the institution's character and makes him or her less prepared for the outside world.

If this description of total institutions and inmate socialization is correct, we have to ask whether prisons are really a solution to the crime problem or, instead, largely the cause of this problem.

PRISONS CAN SOLVE THE CRIME PROBLEM

Criminals Are Special   Some have claimed that people who wind up in prison are not ordinary, average people. After all, small minorities of people produce the vast majority of offenses. They fit easily into the prison subculture and, upon release, commit more crimes because they were crime-prone before they ever went to prison.

Said another way, there are stable, unmeasured differences in the potential for crime within a population. The propensity to commit crime is established early and persists throughout the lifespan. Prisons may fail to reform crime-prone people, but neither are they to blame for a prisoner's commitment to a life of crime. This belief that criminals are a "different breed" of people leads in several directions. First, it justifies using special, coercive treatment. Anything less fails to keep order among poorly socialized people. Second, it argues that more coercion—not less—is needed.

Some prisoners are what we might call *rational calculators:* They commit gainful crimes because the chance of big rewards outweighs the chance of even bigger punishments. Only by increasing the certainty and severity of punishment can we hope to deter these criminals from pursuing a profitable life in crime. To deter would-be burglars, for example, it is more important to increase the probability of imprisonment than the length of a prison sentence. Both the risk of being caught and the prospect of increased gain have a significant impact on burglars' decision making. The threat of legal sanctions, fear of arrest, and conscience all inhibit the commission of illegal acts—especially where past accomplishments or future goals may be jeopardized by such an arrest. Where people have a stake in conformity—something to lose by deviance and something to gain by conformity—they are most likely to obey the law.

One of the expressed goals of imprisonment is rehabilitation—resocialization into a new, orderly, law-abiding lifestyle. And prisons do provide order, rules, and rule enforcement. In this way, they model a new, orderly, law-abiding lifestyle, which prisoners can carry to the outside world after release. Unlike other agents of socialization (e.g., schools or the mass media), prisons can forcibly rehabilitate people. They hold up the prospect of early release through parole as a "carrot"—an inducement to cooperate. And as a "stick" there is the threat of punishment for noncompliance. Obviously, forced rehabilitation does not work for everyone. Yet many administrators believe that the right treatment works for the right people.

What the Community Wants Fear of victimization, crime, and criminals is widespread in America. Though the precise numbers vary over time and from one community to another, a majority of citizens want criminals—especially dangerous or repeat criminals—behind bars. They feel safer knowing that prisons are handling the problem.

To some degree, the "crime problem" is a perception problem: People feel there is a crime problem and need to feel that it is being handled. Thus, getting criminals into prisons helps to solve the problem (in their minds). Few harbor the illusion that prisons either deter crime or rehabilitate criminals. However, prisons at least get criminals off the streets for a while. If prisons don't solve the problem in the long run, they buy time and a sense of greater safety for law-abiding citizens.

Perhaps this is an out-of-sight = out-of-mind way of handling the problem: If the prisons are taking care of the criminals, then the public doesn't have to think about it.

Alternatives Don't Work Reliably Many believe that privatizing prisons—putting their administration into private contractors' hands—increases efficiency and lowers the cost. This makes prisons affordable, despite a rising imprisonment

rate. Indeed, many governments both in the United States and abroad are considering and/or trying private prisons.

Even if they grant that prisons are unable to deter crime, rehabilitate convicts, or keep criminals off the street for long, advocates may still believe that prisons—public or private—are needed because we have no reliable alternative. They point out that other efforts to prevent criminal behavior have failed. Many methods have already been tried. And in some quarters, there is skepticism about the effectiveness of alternatives such as intensive probation. Community alternatives to custody—which we discuss shortly—do not necessarily guarantee better results. Some studies even find higher rates of recidivism with noninstitutionalized offenders.

Furthermore, even if it were possible to prevent crime through efforts of these kinds, many citizens would oppose them. They view crime as immoral behavior. Accordingly, they believe that the criminal (and his or her family)—not society—should take responsibility and pay the cost. By this reasoning, crimes should be prevented by moral training at home, not by spending public money on costly remedies after the fact.

In the end, many feel that there is no acceptable alternative to prisons. The success of prison alternatives is unknown. Until we can be certain that alternative methods deter and rehabilitate criminals, we may have to continue relying on prisons.

PRISONS CANNOT SOLVE THE CRIME PROBLEM

Other researchers and administrators oppose using prisons to punish routine or nonviolent offenses. People holding this view believe that few criminals are dangerous or unchangeable. On the contrary, a great many people pass through periods of life, or circumstances, when criminal behavior is quite likely.

Criminals Are Like Everyone Else Most criminals are young and male. As they age, they become less likely to commit crimes. Likewise, as the general population ages, a falling proportion of young men will lead to a decrease in the general crime rate. Crime and imprisonment rates will decline naturally.

Demographic factors aside, the view that criminals are just like everyone else is supported by labeling theories of deviance. They argue that, at one time or another, most people commit deviant or criminal acts and few are caught and punished. Most give up their rule-breaking behavior voluntarily, for a variety of reasons: maturation, a change of views or opportunities, or a stronger stake in conformity due to marriage and employment.

But because of the way laws are enforced, some people are more likely to get caught and punished for their rule-breaking. Other factors (such as offense seriousness) being equal, race has a strong effect on the chance of incarceration, with African Americans and Latinos running the highest risk. Gender also affects correctional practice, with women experiencing closer rule-enforcement and more severe punishment in some prisons. Moreover, gender stereotypes also shape the nature of work and vocational training.

As for repeat offenders, an explanation is offered by the labeling theory, which comes out of the symbolic interactionist school of sociology. Conviction and imprisonment stigmatizes people, giving them a deviant identity, reducing their legitimate opportunities, and increasing their tendency to break rules. Sociologists have called this behavior secondary deviation—further deviant activity that results from having been given the label of *deviant* or *criminal*. Placing a label on a person only serves to increase the chance that person will internalize the deviant identity and act accordingly. Being labeled a deviant or criminal may also promote further deviancy because the labeled person is unable to escape stigmatization. This, in turn, results in a greater reliance on illegitimate means for survival. Also, the labeled person begins to internalize and live out the identity of "deviant." Prison also costs society much more than probation, due to the combined costs of attempted rehabilitation and increased recidivism. Given the risk of secondary deviation, some researchers believe it may be best to put almost no one into prison, and, once in, let almost no one out.

What the Community Doesn't Know   Average North Americans want as many criminals as possible kept in prison for as long as possible. However, much of the support for imprisonment is based on ignorance of prison conditions and on short-term thinking—a desire for revenge or immediate psychological comfort rather than long-term safety. The social benefits of imprisonment are only temporary. Eventually, most prisoners are back on the streets.

Although there is a great support for the use of prisons, consideration needs to be given to the effects of imprisonment. Prisons break up families. Imprisonment therefore has important unintended consequences for the next generation. Family separation may produce a new generation of criminals. Also, imprisonment contributes to child poverty—already a widely recognized social problem.

Prisons increase health risks, too. Most American prisons are overcrowded, even by their own reckoning. As a result, prisoners are at greater risk of contracting communicable, often lethal diseases than are nonincarcerated people. Violence and its effects—both mental and physical—is an ever-present feature of prison life (as in other "total institutions"). This may result from drug use and drug trafficking, ineffective mechanisms of social control and conflict resolution, or new gang subcultures. Rates of HIV and AIDS are high because of drug injection and because many inmates are raped or otherwise forced into sex.

The high risks of abuse and violence translate into stress reactions like sleeplessness, high blood pressure, respiratory problems, and high suicide rates. In many prisons, conditions are unconstitutionally awful. They represent a cruel and unusual punishment, regardless of the crime a prisoner is originally labeled as having committed.

Alternatives to Prison Do Work   For certain types of criminals, community-based alternatives work better than prison: They are cheaper, more humane, and more effective. When questioned about the success of imprisonment on rehabilitation and reintegration, a great majority of offenders expressed that "community work" was the most effective and appropriate punishment for nonviolent offenses. These alternatives are also less intrusive and disruptive, and do not create a dangerous inmate culture. Some, like probation and parole, carry a low risk to public safety. Other alternatives include paying fines, making restitution, and performing community services.

Another alternative to prison is electronically monitored home detention. A recent study, carried out in Cleveland as part of an effort to keep people out of jail, illustrates the potential of this alternative. There, people awaiting trial for misdemeanors (minor offenses) or nonviolent felonies (serious offenses) were allowed to remain in detention at home for ninety days.

Each participant wore a coded wristlet that matched a base unit attached to their home telephone. Participants were expected to stay at home. To verify their presence, a computer telephoned them at random moments during the day. They had several seconds to make a contact between their coded wristlet and the telephone receiver. Doing so informed the computer that they were indeed at home. A repeated failure to wear the wristlet or make contact with the ringing telephone violated detention conditions and resulted in jail detention until their trial.

Evaluating the experimental results, researchers found that three-quarters of the participants finished the detention period without any trouble and showed up for their trial as expected. Another 13 percent were jailed for violating the rules of home detention (e.g., failing to answer the phone regularly). Finally, 14 percent ran away; a few were still at large when the program ended. These results demonstrate two important factors with regards to prison alternatives.

First, money can be saved. For three in every four accused people, jail or prison is unnecessary. A cheaper, healthier alternative—home detention—works just as well. In fact, it may work better: In one study, house arrestees had lower rates of recidivism and higher rates of social and economic reintegration than community treatment center residents. Savings from the use of this program are enormous. In contrast to imprisonment, monetary savings arise from lower recidivism, lower medical expenses, and a lower overall crime rate. Also, the overall cost to savings ratio is projected at "1 to 10," with the savings division being a 46 percent savings for the correctional system, and 54 percent for the society and taxpayers. This translates to a total savings of approximately $32 billion dollars over five years for every 1,000 offenders who are not imprisoned and fewer prison staff employed.

Second, we know which offenders to choose for this treatment. In the Cleveland study, most people who had previously committed only minor offenses finished the 90-day detention without difficulty. And most people who lived with their family also finished well. Socially integrated people with little or no previous record of criminal activity are good candidates for home detention. Conversely, people who are socially isolated, or have offended many times in the past, are relatively poor prospects for this program.

SUMMING UP

Do we have enough jails? We sure do, and then some.

Can prisons be relied on to solve the crime problem? The argument on this issue goes back and forth; right now, there is a readiness to believe that something can be done about crime and delinquency. However, the evidence we have examined leads us to doubt that prisons will play an important part. At best, researchers are pessimistic about the effects of prison experience, which often induce what sociologist David Matza called "drift"— a denial of responsibility. But this is only the beginning of the problem.

First, we have trouble believing that people who end up in prisons are impossible to help and impossible to change. Just as important, prisons cannot be shown to make people better. They probably make them worse, for all the reasons we have noted above. Second, the community's desire to imprison convicted criminals—to use capital punishment, too—is real enough. However, it grows out of ignorance, a desire for revenge, and, often, an excessive fear of victimization. Prison building is an intervention of last resort when people lose faith in the social welfare enterprise. Third, there are alternatives to prison. We have to study them carefully, one at a time, before making final decisions.

However, the early findings are clear enough: For socially integrated people who have been accused and/or convicted of minor crimes, alternative methods work satisfactorily. In any event, people receiving these treatments are not made worse by prison and they and their families may even bear the costs of detention.

REVIEW EXERCISES

For Discussion and Debate

1. "Most offenders should never go to prison; the rest should never get out." Discuss.
2. The similarities between prisons and other *total institutions* are more apparent than real.
3. "People don't want prisons to solve the crime problem; they want prisons to punish wrongdoers—something they do very well."
4. "There are good reasons why some social, racial, and ethnic groups are overrepresented in prisons and others are underrepresented. We have no reason for concern on that account." Do you agree or disagree?

Writing Exercises

Write a brief (500-word) essay on one of the following topics:

1. The three most frightening things about being locked up in a prison are . . .
2. "Probably, most convicts would prefer corrective brain surgery (if possible) to a year in prison."
3. How I would organize an electronic, home-detention program for serious criminal offenders (or, for socially isolated offenders).
4. "Prisons of the future": Design your own imaginary prison to avoid the problems discussed in this section.

Research Activities

1. Collect some historical information to find out how one particular society (your choice) dealt with lawbreakers before the development of the modern prison system.
2. Using biographies and other published accounts of prison life, find out some of the main elements—the values, norms, rules, and roles—of the "prison subculture." (e.g., the role of tattoos).
3. Collect statistical data on at least a dozen countries, indicating the fraction of the population that is imprisoned at any given time. Then, collect other statistical data about the same countries that would help to explain why some countries have higher rates of imprisonment than others.
4. Collect statistical data to find out whether countries with high rates of imprisonment have low rates of crime. If so, does this prove that prisons solve the crime problem?

SELECTED REFERENCES

Brown, Michelle S. 2003. "Penological Crisis in America: Finding Meaning in Imprisonment Post-Rehabilitation." *Dissertation Abstracts International, A: The Humanities and Social Sciences* 64, 6 (Dec.): 2263-A.

Cohen, Thomas Henry. 2003. "The New Penology: How Court Sentencing Practices Have Been Influenced by the Growing Emphasis on Actuarialism and Managerialism." *Dissertation Abstracts International, A: The Humanities and Social Sciences* 64, 4 (Oct.): 1416-A.

Decker, Scott, Richard Wright and Robert Logie. 1993. "Perceptual Deterrence among Active Residential Burglars: A Research Note." *Criminology* 31, 1 (Feb.): 135–147.

Dressel, P. L. 1994. ". . . And We Keep on Building Prisons: Racism, Poverty, and Challenges to the Welfare State." *Journal of Sociology and Social Welfare* 21, 3 (Sept.): 7–30.

Farrington, Keith. 1992. "The Modern Prison as Total Institution? Public Perception versus Objective Reality." *Crime and Delinquency* 38, 1 (Jan.): 6–26.

Geerken, Michael R. and Hennessey D. Hayes. 1993. "Probation and Parole: Public Risk and the Future of Incarceration Alternatives." *Criminology* 31, 4 (Nov.): 549–564.

Gilfoyle, Timothy J. 2003. "'America's Greatest Criminal Barracks': The Tombs and the Experience of Criminal Justice in New York City, 1838–1897." *Journal of Urban History* 29, 5 (July): 525–554.

Gottfredson, Denise C. and William H. Barton. 1993. "Deinstitutionalization of Juvenile Offenders." *Criminology* 31, 4 (Nov.): 591–611.

Gottschalk, Marie. 2002. "Black Flower: Prisons and the Future of Incarceration." *The Annals of the American Academy of Political and Social Science* 582 (July): 195–227.

Grasmick, Harold G. and Robert J. Bursik, Jr. 1990. "Conscience, Significant Others, and Rational Choice: Extending the Deterrence Model." *Law and Society Review* 24, 3:837–861.

Hartwell, Stephanie. 2003. "Prison, Hospital or Community: Community Re-Entry and Mentally Ill Offenders." *Research in Community and Mental Health* 12:199–220.

Hunt, Geoffrey, Stephanie Riegel, Tomas Morales and Dan Waldorf. 1993. "Changes in Prison Culture: Prison Gangs and the Case of the 'Pepsi Generation.'" *Social Problems* 40, 3 (Aug.): 398–409.

Kolstad, Arnulf. 1996. "Imprisonment as Rehabilitation: Offenders' Assessment of Why It Does Not Work." *Journal of Criminal Justice* 24, 4:323–335.

Krebs, Christopher P. and Melanie Simmons. 2002. "Intraprison HIV Transmission: An Assessment of Whether It Occurs, How It Occurs, and Who Is at Risk." *AIDS Education and Prevention* 14, supplement B (Oct.): 53–64.

Magill, David L. 2003. "Cost Savings from Teaching the Transcendental Meditation Program in Prisons." *Journal of Offender Rehabilitation* 36, 1–4:319.

Mahone, Melvin. 2002. "What Are the Economic Feasibility and Social Impact of Privatized Prisons in America?" *Dissertation Abstracts International, A: The Humanities and Social Sciences* 63, 3 (Sept.): 1139-A.

Mathiesen, Thomas. 1990. *Prison on Trial.* Beverly Hills, CA: Sage Publications.

McCorkle, Richard C. 1993. "Living on the Edge: Fear in a Maximum Security Prison." *Journal of Offender Rehabilitation* 20, 1–2:73–91.

McDonald, Douglas C. 1994. "Public Imprisonment by Private Means: The Re-Emergence of Private Prisons and Jails in the United States, the United Kingdom, and Australia." *British Journal of Criminology* 34, 1 (special issue): 29–48.

McLennan, Rebecca. 2003. "Punishment's 'Square Deal': Prisoners and Their Keepers in 1920s New York." *Journal of Urban History* 29, 5 (July): 597–619.

Morris, Norval and Michael Tonry. 1993. *Between Prison and Probation: Intermediate Punishments in a Rational Sentencing System.* New York: Oxford University Press.

Nagin, Daniel S. and David P. Farrington. 1992. "The Stability of Criminal Potential from Childhood to Adulthood." *Criminology* 30, 2 (May): 235–260.

Patrick, Steven and Robert Marsh. 2001. "Perceptions of Punishment and Rehabilitation among Inmates in a Medium Security Prison: A Consumers' Report." *Journal of Offender Rehabilitation* 33, 3:47.

Richards, Stephen C., James Austin and Richard S. Jones. 2004. "Kentucky's Perpetual Prisoner Machine: It's about Money." *The Review of Policy Research* 21, 1 (Jan.): 93–106.

Roberts, Julian V. 2003. "Evaluating the Pluses and Minuses of Custody: Sentencing Reform in England and Wales." *Howard Journal of Criminal Justice* 42, 3 (July): 229–247.

Russo-Lleras, Marion. 2003. "A Non-Statistical Meta-Evaluation of Adult Prison Boot Camps: An Analysis of Program Components of Efficacious Programs." *Dissertation Abstracts International, A: The Humanities and Social Sciences* 64, 5 (Nov.): 1856-A.

Sandhu, Harjit S., Richard A. Dodder and Minu Mathur. 1993. "House Arrest: Success and Failure Rates in Residential and Nonresidential Community-Based Programs." *Journal of Offender Rehabilitation* 19, 1–2:131–144.

Shelden, Randall G. 2004. "The Imprisonment Crisis in America: Introduction." *The Review of Policy Research* 21, 1 (Jan.): 5–12.

Sherman, Lawrence W., Douglas A. Smith, Janell D. Schmidt and Dennis P. Rogan. 1992. "Crime, Punishment, and Stake in Conformity: Legal and Informal Control of Domestic Violence." *American Sociological Review* 57, 5 (Oct.): 680–690.

Shichor, David. 1993. "The Corporate Context of Private Prisons." *Crime, Law and Social Change* 20, 2 (Sept.): 113–138.

Smith, Linda G. and Ronald L. Akers. 1993. "A Comparison of Recidivism of Florida's Community Control and Prison: A Five-Year Survival Analysis." *Journal of Research in Crime and Delinquency* 30, 3 (Aug.): 267–292.

Stevens, Dennis J. 1994. "The Depth of Imprisonment and Prisonization: Levels of Security and Prisoners' Anticipation of Future Violence." *Howard Journal of Criminal Justice* 33, 2 (May): 137–157.

Sturr, Christopher. 2004. "Philosophical Theories of Punishment and the History of Prison." *Studies in Law, Politics, and Society* 30:85–104.

Sullivan, Mercer L. 2004. "Youth Perspectives on the Experience of Reentry." *Youth Violence and Juvenile Justice* 2, 1 (Jan.): 56–71.

Ubah, Charles B. A. 2003. "Reaffirming the Limits of Offender Rehabilitation but with Caution." *Criminal Justice Studies: A Critical Journal of Crime, Law and Society* 16, 3:197–203.

Useem, Bert and Jack A. Goldstone. 2002. "Forging Social Order and Its Breakdown: Riot and Reform in U.S. Prisons." *American Sociological Review* 67, 4 (Aug.): 499–525.

Useem, Bert, Raymond V. Liedka and Anne Morrison Piehl. 2003. "Popular Support for the Prison Build-Up." *Punishment & Society* 5, 1 (Jan.): 5–32.

Walker, Nigel. 1983. "Side-effects of Incarceration." *British Journal of Criminology* 23, 1 (Jan.): 61–71.

Ward, David A. and Thomas G. Werlich. 2003. "Alcatraz and Marion: Evaluating Super-Maximum Custody." *Punishment & Society* 5, 1 (Jan.): 53–75.

3.3   Should Getting High Be Legal?

The issue: The nation's "drug problem"—is it really a problem, and if so, what kind of problem is it: a crime problem or a health problem? What, if anything, should be done about people's perception that there is a "drug problem"?

When people ask questions that begin with the word "should," as this question does, they may be asking an efficiency question. In sociology, *efficiency questions* ask whether or how we can solve a social problem by changing our present laws or practices. In the present case, sociologists want to know things like these: "Should recreational drugs (like marijuana, hashish, and maybe even cocaine) be legalized to reduce the costs of arresting and imprisoning drug offenders? Or, to reduce health risks? Or, to control the quality of drugs sold on the street?"

Other times when people ask questions that begin with the word "should" they are asking a moral question, such as the following: "Is it right (or proper) for society to legalize recreational drugs?" Sociologists research moral issues by taking a social constructionist approach to the question itself. Social constructionists study the ways people "negotiate" meanings for everyday life, given competing interpretations of reality.

Here, constructionists ask, "Why do some people want to legalize recreational drugs while others do not?" Why does the problem in question seem particularly pressing right now? Is a "moral panic" taking place, and if so why? What kinds of people think that there is a pressing drug problem to be solved? What current ideologies—religious, political, economic, or otherwise—fit well with this idea? And whose political interests are served by promoting the idea that there is a drug problem that needs solving?

With these ideas in mind, consider the debate about legalizing the sale and use of "recreational drugs." Chemicals like THC—found abundantly in marijuana and hashish—are used mainly for pleasure. Unlike alcohol, nicotine, and caffeine—addictive legal substances that many people with high status frequently use—these recreational drugs are currently outlawed, therefore making society's response to drugs irrational.

WE SHOULD LEGALIZE RECREATIONAL DRUGS

Most arguments that support legalizing recreational drugs are efficiency arguments. They support the decriminalization of recreational drugs by emphasizing the practical benefits of legalization or the harm done by failing to permit these drugs.

Current Laws Don't Work We should legalize drug use because laws aimed at preventing it have no effect. Drug use is widespread. There are few signs that use is declining, or that stiff penalties control people's behavior. No consensus exists among drug enforcement critics except that criminal sanctions have little effect on drug use and attempts to control illegal drug use by law enforcement strategies will fail. Thus, a great deal of money spent on drug law enforcement is wasted. When, in the 1920s, laws prohibiting alcohol use and sales failed to have an effect, they were repealed. Many argue that the same should be done today with drug laws.

Prevention Works Better Than Arrests Sociologists know that it is usually easier to prevent people from starting a deviant career than to cure or rehabilitate them afterwards. So, instead of spending money to arrest and convict drug users, we should work at learning how to reduce people's need or desire to use drugs, and educate people about the social, economic, and health costs of using recreational drugs. In short, we must approach this problem as we do cigarette smoking and excessive drinking: as a health problem with economic and social consequences. From a medical perspective, U.S. drug policy should try to reduce harm, increase safety, provide care for those who need it, and foster norms of self-regulation of risky behavior. Furthermore, legalizing these "soft drugs" would allow the government to take on an active role in dealing with certain health effects of these substances. Consequently, this would initiate the development of programming and support groups to help individuals who are suffering from severe health problems due to drug abuse.

Crime Is the Problem to Solve At present, neither the medical nor criminal justice approach adequately deals with the problems of crime associated with dangerous drug use. The public concern about drugs is really a concern about crimes. Do drugs, drug laws, or the production, sale, purchase, and possession of illegal drugs raise the number of crimes to purchase illegal drugs, the commission of crimes while under the influence of drugs, or the violent and corrupt behavior of drug traffickers, to such an extent that decriminalizing illicit drugs would render a more effective response?

The decriminalization of illicit substances would lower criminal activity associated with drug trafficking, purchasing and selling. By eliminating drug laws, the vast majority of drug crime would cease to exist. If illicit substances such as marijuana and hashish were legalized, this would eliminate the need for "black markets," by destroying the criminal world of dealers and purchasers. Also, the decriminalization of "soft drugs" would allow for the resources previously used to target drug dealers and drug users to be put toward the enforcement against exploitative criminal activity between competitors.

A related problem is drug addiction. Some recreational drugs, like marijuana and hashish, are not physically addictive. Unlike heroin and cocaine, these soft drugs do not directly drive people to commit crimes. There is little evidence that decriminalizing the use of soft drugs (e.g., marijuana) will result in dramatic increases in substance abuse. Approximately 80 to 90 million people have used illicit drugs at some point in their lives, which accounts for close to 40 percent of the American population over the age of twelve. This highlights the lack of compelling evidence that these recreational drugs lead people to use addictive drugs like heroin or cocaine.

Some people fear that drug use will explode if people are no longer punished for use of illicit substances; however, this fear has proven unfounded. When individuals were questioned as to their decision to refrain from the use of drugs, very few said that it was because they feared legal sanction. This suggests that the removal of penalties is unlikely to cause drug use to skyrocket. Despite changing drug laws and enforcement practices over the past thirty years, drug use has remained relatively steady. Statistics show that states that adopted "frequent and severe" sanctions for drug offenders have not experienced a decline in drug use over the past ten years.

A second theory explaining the lack of explosive drug use despite the virtual decriminalization of substances such as marijuana and hashish is the "forbidden-fruit" phenomenon. Adolescents are more likely to engage in experimental, illegal behavior when it is perceived as risky or prohibited. The experience in itself is compounded by the thrill of sharing in a deviant activity. By removing the illegality and the stigma from the experience, the state reduces the use of illicit drugs for the purpose of rebelling.

A third problem to be solved is the costliness of addictive drugs. If addictive drugs were cheap (or free), addicts would not have to commit crimes to get them. Most of the criminal behavior associated with drugs is focused on financing the habit of addiction. Robberies, burglaries, and other theft serve as money-making activities to raise funds for the purchase of drugs. Just like alcohol prohibition in the 1920s, drug prohibition has produced a large and lucrative criminal industry. A regulated repeal of prohibition would limit overall consumption and put a dent in the revenues of organized crime. Though a radical change in drug

policy may not be politically feasible right now, many drug-related crimes would decrease if public health agencies provided free drugs or drug substitutes (like Methadone). This has been tried in various countries (e.g., the Netherlands, the United Kingdom), resulting in a predicted reduction in crime.

Research also shows that decriminalization of the possession of marijuana since the early 1970s has resulted in decreased costs of enforcement and prosecution of marijuana-related offenses.

Illegal Drug Use Is a Health Hazard   So long as drug use is illegal, we can do little to monitor the quality of drugs available to users, or the conditions under which people use these drugs. Where alcohol and caffeine are concerned, food and drug regulations ensure that we don't consume dangerous or poor quality substances. (The same cannot be said of cigarettes, which contain known carcinogens as well as nicotine.) Similarly, health-protective rules should apply to recreational drugs. If government regulation was in place for the decriminalization of "soft drugs," standards of quality and purity of the purchased drug would be enforced, limiting many of the toxic and dangerous substances that are frequently added to both marijuana and hashish.

One reason for repealing Prohibition was the recognition that, when quality-controlled alcoholic beverages are unavailable, people will drink just about anything. In the 1920s and 1930s, people died or went blind from drinking beverages that contained dangerous impurities or the wrong kind of alcohol (i.e., methanol instead of ethanol). More recently, some users have died from drug overdoses because they had no way of knowing the strength of the drug. Legalization could prevent this by regulating strength and quality.

When drugs are illegal, users also take fewer health precautions. For example, needles shared among heroin users spread HIV and AIDs. By driving the drug-user culture underground, the law works against safety, good hygiene, and disease prevention. With the decriminalization of soft drugs, healthier alternatives and environments would be made available to drug users. Programs in other countries have reduced the sharing of contaminated equipment without increasing drug use.

Penalties Make Things Worse What happens to drug users and sellers when they are arrested and convicted? Some are sent to overflowing, underfunded prisons where, to alleviate their horror, they take drugs. Decriminalization of soft illicit substances would help to remove multiple minor offenses from the legal systems. Given the limited capacity of the state and federal prisons, it becomes evident that funding needs to go to incarcerating the most dangerous offenders instead of nonviolent drug users. Statistics show that incarcerating such a large percentage of offenders for drug charges costs the American government three times the amount it would to introduce every individual with a drug problem into a national rehabilitation program. Furthermore, for women drug users, the punitive American policy has resulted in gender-biased or inaccessible treatment programs, the prosecution of pregnant drug users, and a rising population of female prisoners.

A second problem is the stigma that comes with an arrest and conviction for a drug offense. Having a record for a drug offense may ruin a person's chances to get a good job or enter a profession. Depressed and desperate, such people turn again to drugs, perpetuating the cycle. The emphasis on punishment is too expensive in terms of the human costs of jailing many people for relatively minor offenses.

If our goal is to draw people into law-abiding activity, we want to avoid handing out criminal records. Criminal records exclude people from normal life by restricting legitimate market opportunities, and in this way increase their chances of committing crimes. By decriminalizing the buying and selling of illicit substances, the government will be able to intervene and control the drug market, consequently severing the cycle of illegitimate jobs, criminal charges and records, and blocked access to legitimate careers. By legalizing the drug market, the state can put in place laws to enforce traceable business relations between dealers and customers, promoting safe and reputable substance transactions, and the protection of both parties from violence and "sour merchandise."

The "War on Drugs" Hurts Foreign Relations
The War on Drugs has focused on two main enemies. At home, it has targeted local users and sellers, in hopes that stiffer penalties and more policing would reduce the demand for drugs. It has not.

At the same time, American governments have tried to reduce the drug supply reaching the United States. They have used various means—for example, cooperating with international police efforts to capture large drug producers and traffickers. They have also tried to get the governments of other countries (e.g., Colombia, Panama, Mexico) to control the growth and transport of drugs that otherwise end up in the United States.

However, such efforts have had undesirable side-effects. They jeopardize the peace and economic well-being of countries like Peru and Colombia, which largely depend on producing drugs for the U.S. market. Another side-effect is the establishment of friendly relations with corrupt or dangerous rulers (like Manuel Noriega of Panama) just because they cooperate, or appear to cooperate, in the War on Drugs. In this way, the United States risks being viewed as a country that is "soft" on dictators and tyrants.

Moreover, some of the money the American government provides to tyrants who promise help in the War on Drugs ends up in Swiss bank accounts. Militarization of the drug war in Latin America means increasing economic hardship, repression, and radicalization of the peasantry, as well as the further corruption of the military, historically part of the drug problem rather than its solution. Finally, the attempt to repress drug trafficking by war tactics is contrary to democratic ideals.

Much Public Support for Legalization Survey evidence shows that many still oppose drug use and sales and some oppose legalization. However, most Americans are indifferent to legalizing nonaddictive recreational drugs: They just don't care. Many feel that engaging in such particular behaviors as drug use is an individual preference, and to each their own. They oppose efforts to construct a "war on drugs" that they consider unwarranted. Some strongly favor legalization, for the reasons given previously. Others actively support the use of marijuana for the treatment of people suffering from terminal illness (for example, AIDS). Many researchers claim the drug has medicinal properties in certain situations.

There is no "war on drugs" aimed at cigarettes because cigarette smoking, for generations a mainstream cultural habit, supports a legal billion-dollar industry. Cigarette smoke is a lethal drug that our society has decided to regulate rather than ban, despite the very real and widespread harm that it does to North Americans every year. It's finally time for society to look at the issue rationally instead of morally and realize that drugs and alcohol do more harm to people than legalizing marijuana ever will.

WE SHOULD NOT LEGALIZE DRUG USE AND SALE

People usually oppose legalizing drug use and sales on moral grounds, or because they disagree with the "efficiency" evidence provided by the other side.

Drug Use Is Immoral   Some communities consider drug use immoral, and therefore consider drug sales immoral, too. The law sometimes uses community standards—for example what the community considers pornographic—to decide what deviant or marginal behavior to allow. In this case, courts might be reluctant to legalize drug use if they felt this violated the community's moral standard.

People who oppose drug use on moral grounds believe that there is a drug problem. There is a belief that decriminalizing the use of drugs for recreational pleasure would greatly increase the percentage of people who take drugs. Individuals supporting the existing ban of illicit substances fear that if drug use was to be made commonplace, the results would be a huge increase in users, dealers, and addicts. Also, a concern is raised regarding the availability and distribution of drugs. They support moral and political solutions that include

stiffer penalties for wrongdoing and attaching personal blame to wrongdoers, through the enforcement of penalties. On the other hand, they oppose "medicalizing" the drug problem by viewing it as a health problem requiring medical treatment. They also oppose legalizing immoral behavior merely because it is hard to control.

Others oppose legalization for a different moral reason: They believe that, by legalizing drug use, we ignore the plight of drug users. We also ignore the social problems that lead people to use drugs in the first place. In other words, legalization lets us forget about the poor and the ill-treated in our society.

Efficiency Arguments   Many people opposing legalization claim that drug use—especially the use of hard drugs like heroin, cocaine, and speed—is physically and mentally harmful. Drugs cause health problems for users. They also cause social, psychological, and financial problems for the users' family and friends. Drug dependent people experience increases in drug tolerance. There will be no way to prevent an escalation in the frequency or severity of drug abuse if everything is legalized. At its worst, drug abuse can also lead to domestic violence, marriage dissolution, job loss, and bankruptcy.

Though soft drugs like marijuana and hashish are less directly harmful, they are said to lead to the use of hard drugs. Most hard-drug users have used soft drugs at one time or another. Some opponents to the legalization of soft drugs are concerned that legalizing these drugs eases the way for the legalization of hard drugs.

Current Efforts Are Working   Some believe that the current policy of zero tolerance is working in the military. For this reason, efforts to eliminate drug and alcohol abuse should be intensified by continuing programs in assessment, deterrence and detection, treatment and rehabilitation, and education and training. The downward trend in marijuana use in high schools also suggests progress in prevention among adolescents. It is argued that a "get tough" policy—including efforts to control cigarette and alcohol consumption at school—offers more promise than legalization.

Market Problems Remain Some people claim that legalizing drugs will not solve the problems associated with illegal marketing. Judging from past experience with narcotics, alcohol, and tobacco, some illegal markets in drugs will persist. If decriminalization of specific "soft drugs" occurs, than the hard drugs will continue to be sold within an illegal market. Moreover, if individuals have access to soft drugs accessible through cheaper means, the drug market will continue underground. People will continue to buy drugs from unlicensed or unregulated sources if the prices are lower (as they are if there are no sales taxes to pay). They will also continue to buy from illegal sources that offer more varied brands through the illegal production of "designer drugs." Also, if the evidence suggests that softer drug use leads to the use of more dangerous substances, then legalizing marijuana and hashish will only perpetuate addiction to minor drugs, which will lead to the illegal purchasing of more dangerous, illicit substances.

Controlling a legal market may be even harder than controlling an illegal one. Look how hard it has been to control cigarette manufacturers. Testimony shows they have increased the addictiveness of cigarettes through nicotine additives, and worked at addicting children to cigarettes at even younger ages than before. Legal drug-sellers like these not only have power, wealth, and social respectability, but they also have access to lawyers and legal rights that continually protect their active marketing. Thus, legalization might make controlling recreational drugs even more difficult than it already is.

SUMMING UP

Should getting high be legal? Yes; but we have to take some steps to make sure that this recreation of choice does not become a fulltime lifestyle.

A compromise solution is needed, since the two sides are talking past each other. Start by admitting that the War on Drugs has failed, for the same reasons Prohibition failed: Too many people want to do what the law forbids. At the same time, many people, especially poor young people in the inner-cities, are being destroyed by hard (though not by soft) drugs. We need to find out why this group appears to be engaged in the drug lifestyle, and do something about it. Prevention and harm reduction, with minimal application of criminal law, may be the most effective public health policy toward drugs.

A compromise includes decriminalizing soft drug use and finding alternatives to criminalization. Inevitably, psychoactive drugs will be available. So, license the production and sales of soft drugs to regulate their quality, distribution, and use. Explore the possibilities of a free market versus a government monopoly versus medical control over access to drugs. Tax the profits on legalized drug sales and use the taxes for drug education. At the same time, reduce the penalties for using hard drugs. Treat unlicensed drug-selling as a regulatory or tax offense, punishable by huge fines.

Develop a comprehensive public health approach to addressing illegal drug problems. Educate the public against excessive drug use and the use of harmful, illegal drugs. In short, shift the emphasis of drug education to consideration of irresponsible versus responsible drug use. And learn more about the relationship between drug use and socially adaptive or harmful behavior.

Most importantly, carry out research on ways to reduce the desire to use soft drugs excessively or hard drugs at all. This research may show that people with optimism, a belief in the future, and a stake in conformity usually stay sober. What is needed is "grudging toleration," which has fewer disadvantages than either absolute prohibition or uncontrolled legalization. Prohibition cannot substitute for an integrated and well-coordinated approach that includes prevention, treatment, and enforcement and is supported by an educated public.

REVIEW EXERCISES

For Discussion and Debate

1. Should alcohol be made illegal or its use limited to people who need it for medical purposes?
2. "Addiction is a moral problem, not a social or medical problem." Discuss.
3. The harmfulness of drugs is shown by its connection to other risky or antisocial behaviors, such as drinking, smoking, gambling, dangerous driving, and violent behavior.
4. "It makes perfect sense to continue the War on Drugs, even though it has had no success whatever."

Writing Exercises

Write a brief (500-word) essay on one of the following topics:

1. "The State has no business regulating how people seek their pleasure, so long as no one else is hurt."
2. "The kind of society in which recreational drugs would pose no problem."
3. Why organized crime loves to see the State prohibiting pleasure.
4. How we might more effectively discourage young people from getting addicted to drugs.

Research Activities

1. Collect information on a program designed to discourage young people from using drugs. How successful has the program been? (Note: Specify how you are measuring "success.")
2. Review published evidence on the likelihood that a user of recreational drugs will "graduate" to regular use of heroin, cocaine, or other hard drugs.
3. Interview a dozen students to find out their knowledge of, attitude toward, and use of recreational drugs. What is the connection between their (past or present) use of recreational drugs and their support for legalization of these drugs?
4. Collect published information about the effect of drug production on the economy and politics of any major drug-producing country (e.g., Colombia, Afghanistan).

SELECTED REFERENCES

Boekhout von Solinge, Tim. 1999. "Dutch Drug Policy in a European Context." *Journal of Drug Issues* 29, 3 (Summer): 511–528.

Boyum, David and Mark A. R. Kleiman. 2003. "Breaking the Drug-Crime Link." *The Public Interest* 152 (Summer): 19–38.

Brownstein, Henry H. 1991. "The Media and the Construction of Random Drug Violence." *Social Justice* 18, 4 (Winter): 85–103.

Currie, Elliott. 1993. "Toward a Policy on Drugs. Decriminalization? Legalization?" *Dissent* 40, 1 (170) (Winter): 65–71.

De Leon, George. 1994. "Some Problems with the Antiprohibitionist Position on the Legalization of Drugs." *Journal of Addictive Diseases* 13, 2:35–57.

DiChiara, Albert and John F. Galliher. 1994. "Dissonance and the Contradictions in the Origins of Marihuana Decriminalization." *Law and Society Review* 28, 1 (Feb.): 41–77.

Duncan, David F. 1992. "Drug Abuse Prevention in Post-Legalization America: What Could It Be Like?" *Journal of Primary Prevention* 12, 4 (Summer): 317–322.

Economist. 2001. "The Case for Legalization." London: July 28, Vol. 360, 8232: S15.

Erickson, Patricia. 1993. "The Law, Social Control, and Drug Policy: Models, Factors, and Processes." *International Journal of the Addictions* 28, 12 (Oct.): 1155–1176.

Farr, Kathryn Ann. 1990. "Revitalizing the Drug Decriminalization Debate." *Crime and Delinquency* 36, 2 (Apr.): 223–237.

Goode, Erich. 1990. "The American Drug Panic of the 1980s: Social Construction or Objective Threat?" *International Journal of the Addictions* 25, 9 (Sept.): 1083–1098.

Goode, Erich. 1999. "Thinking about the Drug Policy Debate." Pp. 111–124 in *The Drug Legalization Debate,* 2d ed., edited by James A. Inciardi. Thousand Oaks, CA: Sage.

Heath, Dwight B. [1921] 1992. "U.S. Drug Control Policy: A Cultural Perspective." *Daedalus* 3 (Summer): 269–291.

Husak, Douglas. 2003. "Four Points about Drug Decriminalization." *Criminal Justice Ethics* 22, 1 (Winter): 21.

Inciardi, James, ed. 1990. *Handbook of Drug Control in the United States.* New York: Greenwood Press.

Jacobs, James B. 1990. "Imagining Drug Legalization." *Public Interest* 101 (Fall): 28–42.

Jensen, Eric L. and Jurg Gerber. 1993. "State Efforts to Construct a Social Problem: The 1986 War on Drugs in Canada." *Canadian Journal of Sociology* 18, 4 (Fall): 453–462.

Kleiman, Mark A. R. 1992. "Neither Prohibition nor Legalization: Grudging Toleration in Drug Control Policy." *Daedalus* 121, 3 (Summer): 53–83.

Levine, Harry G. and Craig Reinarman. 1991. "From Prohibition to Regulation: Lessons from Alcohol Policy for Drug Policy." *Milbank Quarterly* 69, 3:461–494.

Miron, Jeffrey A. 2001. "The Economics of Drug Prohibition and Drug Legalization." *Social Research* 68, 3 (Fall): 835–855.

Nadelmann, Ethan A. 1989. "Drug Prohibition in the United States: Costs, Consequences, and Alternatives." *Science* 245, 4921, 1 (Sept.): 939–947.

Newcomb, Michael D. 1992. "Substance Abuse and Control in the United States: Ethical and Legal Issues." *Social Science and Medicine* 35, 4 (Aug.): 471–479.

Reuter, Peter 1988. "Quantity Illusions and Paradoxes of Drug Interdiction: Federal Intervention into Vice Policy." *Law and Contemporary Problems* 51, 1 (Winter): 233–252.

Sher, George. 2003. "On the Decriminalization of Drugs." *Criminal Justice Ethics* 22, 1 (Winter): 30.

Single, Eric W. 1989. "The Impact of Marijuana Decriminalization: An Update." *Journal of Public Health Policy* 10, 4 (Winter): 456–466.

Skolnick, Jerome H. 1992. "Rethinking the Drug Problem." *Daedalus* 121, 3 (Summer): 133–159.

Tonry, Michael and James Q. Wilson, eds. 1990. *Drugs and Crime, Crime and Justice: A Review of Research* 13. Chicago, IL: University of Chicago Press.

Trevino, Roberto A. and Alan J. Richard. 2002. "Attitudes toward Drug Legalization among Drug Users." *The American Journal of Drug and Alcohol Abuse* 28, 1 (Feb.): 91–108.

Winick, Charles. 1991. "Social Behavior, Public Policy, and Nonharmful Drug Use." *Milbank Quarterly* 69, 3:437–459.

Yacoubian, George S., Jr. 2001. "Beyond the Theoretical Rhetoric: A Proposal to Study the Consequences of Drug Legalization." *Journal of Drug Education* 31, 4:319–328.

CHAPTER 4  CLASS AND STRATIFICATION

By *class,* sociologists mean a group of people who share similar "life chances"—opportunities to attain what they need and want in life. According to theorists who follow the Marxist paradigm, these life chances are structured mainly by people's control over the means of production, by which we earn a living. According to theorists who follow the Weberian paradigm, life chances are also structured by people's position in the hierarchies of status and power that are not directly connected with economic domination.

Stratification, then, refers to the layering of society that results when people have different life chances. Within each layer, people often come to share a common awareness of their condition and a willingness to act in terms of their common problems and common interests. This may reveal itself in voting patterns, lifestyle choices, and acts of resistance or protest.

In this chapter we examine three issues associated with class and stratification. First, we consider the functional theory of stratification, which argues that inequality and stratification are not only inevitable but also socially beneficial. Second, we consider whether everyone in America really does have an equal opportunity to rise to the top. Third, we return to an earlier theme: the poverty problem, and whether social welfare makes the problem worse.

4.1   Shouldn't Poor People Be Happy That Others Are Rich?

The issue: A wide inequality between the poor and the rich. Is it natural and inevitable, or can it be decreased? And if it can be decreased, would it improve the society to decrease inequality, or would doing so stifle people's ambition?

Many people are accustomed to economic inequality and accept it as normal and natural. We seem to assume that, just as people differ in their musical ability or sports ability, they differ in their ability to succeed economically. These differences in natural ability, in turn, are assumed to produce economic inequality—some classes that are much richer or poorer than others.

This raises the interesting question: if inequality is natural, why does it vary socially? Why are small, technologically simple societies much more egalitarian than large, technologically complex societies?

Why are some industrial societies more equal than agricultural societies, while others are less so? And why are some industrial societies, like Sweden, more egalitarian than other industrial societies, like the United States?

Likewise, economic opportunity varies over time. For several decades after the Second World War, economic growth meant that almost everyone was doing better financially. People paid less attention to inequality, though it didn't go away. But in the closing decades of the last century, economic growth declined, wages stagnated or fell, and unemployment grew. Many middle-class people lost ground financially. The rich got richer while the poor got poorer, so inequality increased.

Under such conditions of changing inequality, people—sociologists among them—look for explanations. Some proceed from very strong theories about the reasons for inequality—for example, attributing it to ownership of the means of production. Others proceed more cautiously, looking at the matter case by case without a strong theory. Likewise, some people view inequality as a good thing—something that benefits society—while others look at it as something that hurts society. Let's look at the matter from both sides now.

ECONOMIC INEQUALITY BENEFITS SOCIETY

A sociological theory proposed by sociologists Kingsley Davis and Wilbert Moore over 50 years ago provides one explanation of why people are unequal economically. It also suggests reasons why inequality varies from one society to another and implies that inequality is necessary. In short, it argues that economic inequality benefits society.

Briefly, the theory runs as follows: In any society, people largely agree on which social roles contribute the most to society's survival and are, therefore, the most valuable roles. Valuable talents and abilities are always in short supply. It is necessary, then, to motivate people to train for and commit themselves to the most valuable—and usually the most demanding—roles (e.g., cardiac surgeons, cancer researchers, chief executive officers). We must pay them large amounts of money and prestige (or respect) to provide the necessary motivation; wide inequalities of income and prestige result from doing so. In the end, society prospers because economic inequality draws out the talent that society needs.

Inequality varies over time or from one society to another because (1) societies differ in the degree to which people view some roles as more valuable than other roles, and (2) societies vary in the scarcity of talent needed to perform the most valuable roles.

As a result, military leadership is valued more highly in wartime than in peacetime. Societies with a warlike culture or societies that prosper mainly by warring on other societies, reward military leaders more highly than peace-loving societies. According to the same theory, societies that place a high value on artistic performance will reward concert pianists more highly than less artistically inclined societies. But when highly talented concert pianists become numerous, the rewards paid to individual pianists will start to decline (unless they have a "union" as doctors, lawyers, and many other professionals do).

This functional theory is like the economist's theory that prices reflect the supply and demand for particular goods and services. It differs in proposing that there is a social consensus about which goods and services are most highly valued. You may be able to think of reasons why the functional theory often makes wrong predictions and think that these wrong predictions tell us that functional theory, if not completely wrong, at least needs modification. But let's begin by considering why its predictions are sometimes right and why one could therefore believe that economic inequality benefits society.

Inequality Motivates Effort Poverty and inequality are necessary functional aspects of capitalism, according to this theory. They help to persuade workers to perform alienating work for pay, warn workers of the consequences of labor militancy, maintain a reserve army of unemployed workers who depress the wages of employed workers, keep down the prices of goods and services supplied by underpaid workers, and keep marginal enterprises afloat.

Too little inequality or poverty is unprofitable for capitalists; though too much undermines work incentives or provokes the poor into militant action. The trick is to find the right balance between work incentives and low-wage labor markets, and between the preservation of order and the amelioration of discontent. If people experience too much inequality, or view it as too unfair, they will rebel, or, at least, retreat into self-destructive, unproductive behavior.

Inequality Reveals Talent The drive for upward mobility on a long ladder of opportunities produces a competition in which everyone tries hard to win. Only the most talented succeed. Thus, the most valuable positions in society are filled with the most talented, hard-working people. Merit is rewarded and the most meritorious hold positions of the greatest importance to society. This is good for society and good for the meritorious, hard-working individuals.

Inequality Promotes Investment If America's wealth were shared equally, everyone would be comfortable but no one would have enough money to invest heavily. Large enterprises, however, need large amounts of capital. A high degree of income inequality produces personal fortunes and company profits that can be invested in new technologies or to build new factories. This investment creates thousands of new jobs for people lower down the ladder. Even conspicuous consumption by the rich creates work for many millions of people employed in the luxury goods and services market. Thus, inequality benefits the many by benefiting the few.

Inequality Promotes Philanthropy The same principle applies to philanthropy. Since the Middle Ages, the wealthiest citizens have patronized the arts, the church, colleges and universities, and other deserving public institutions (e.g., hospitals, orphanages, etc.). Without this patronage, society would be worse off. More inequality creates more millionaires and, in this way, creates more philanthropy. This, in turn, builds colleges, hospitals, symphonies, libraries, and other public institutions.

Inequality Maintains Labor Supply A rapidly changing economy requires *some* poverty and unemployment, what Marx called a "reserve army" of labor. A high degree of inequality produces lots of highly motivated poor people who are willing to enter new jobs as they become available. In this way inequality contributes to rapid, even explosive, economic growth and flexible supplies of labor power.

Inequality Produces Economic Development In the long run, everyone benefits from economic inequality and from capitalism, which increases

economic inequality. The poor struggle to escape poverty. Middle-class people struggle to move up the economic ladder, year by year and generation by generation. The wealthy demonstrate the rewards of hard work and invest in the economy. The net result is economic development. It is because of economic development—which helps everyone—that people put up with economic inequality. In fact, more inequality is better. Inequality and economic development tend to increase together in industrial and postindustrial societies.

Under capitalism, business is motivated by self-interest and confidence in progress. It relies on the anticipation, though not sure knowledge, of a future return. Capitalism's confidence, optimism, and faith are positive qualities that produce altruism as well as economic growth, wealth as well as inequality and poverty. In short, we have to take the bad with the good where inequality is concerned.

However, many challenge these arguments. Critics of this approach hold the view that economic inequality may not be natural or inevitable. Even if it is, less inequality is better than more equality, for moral as well as social reasons. Researchers raise many questions about the validity of arguments made earlier. Let's consider these counter-arguments in roughly the same sequence as before.

ECONOMIC INEQUALITY DOES NOT BENEFIT SOCIETY

Inequality Motivates Effort Up to a point, increases in inequality may increase people's motivation to escape the bottom rungs and reach the top rungs. However, there are limits to this principle; too much inequality may deaden people's motivation, not stimulate it.

Think of this from a life course perspective. Some people's problems start early in life, when they begin their formal education or even before. Formal education determines a person's chances in life—for example, their job possibilities, which help to determine their adult quality of life. Given this, students from poor homes are stuck in a trap. They are likely to have a worse educational experience than students from wealthy or middle-class homes.

Their schools, in under-funded school districts, have the fewest extra-curricular programs and the least effective, most demoralized teachers. One researcher found that students who received ineffective teachers for three years in a row scored in the 45th percentile on a math test, while those who received good teachers scored in the 85th percentile.

In this case, then, inequality doesn't create talented individuals; it does the opposite. Some people with great potential never have their talent developed; their schools don't have the facilities and their teachers don't have the skills.

Now, let's think about the other end of the economic continuum and ask whether inequality ensures talented individuals at the top end. It is widely argued that high pay is needed to attract competent managers, for example. However, extravagant incentives are not needed to attract talented people to serve in utilities, government positions, universities, or other public sector institutions. Many of these managers and professionals come from the same class that traditionally has managed U.S. big businesses; little incentive is needed to recruit them.

We all know that top performers in a variety of fields—entertainment and sports, but also law, journalism, fashion, and academia—reap a disproportionate share of financial rewards for their work. Is that because their talent merits such high wages, and inequality is a result of competition between the "titans" within every field? No, the disparity in salaries is due to market imperfections that reduce competition at the top, and a culture of greed that has marked American capitalism for much of the last 25 years.

Does inequality increase motivation at the lower end of the income distribution? The answer is no: People far down the economic ladder become demoralized and stop trying. As sociologist Robert Merton argued, they are likely to adapt to an experience of "anomie" by retreating into drugs, alcohol, or suicide. They become preoccupied with the day-to-day problems of mere survival. Without opportunities for education and entry into good jobs, they have little chance to move upward as far as their talent and energy warrant. However, what Karl Marx called *false consciousness*—a delusional picture of

reality disseminated by an apparatus of ideology—surely holds many to the belief that one can move easily from rags to riches if only one is lucky enough. For most, however, their thwarted ambitions soon die, turning them over to bitterness or laziness—to what Merton called ritualism, empty conformity, or even crime.

Inequality Reveals Talent   According to this theory, only the most talented succeed in such a system; but is this true? In a system of equal opportunity, the most talented would indeed profit most. However, there is plenty of evidence showing barriers to the education, hiring, and promotion of certain subgroups of intelligent and ambitious people—among them, women, racial minorities, people with handicaps, and people from impoverished backgrounds. As a result, we find a weak fit between success and the usual signs of talent or merit: namely, intelligence, drive for success, aptitude, or commitment to the job.

If talent is not the only way—or perhaps even the best way—to explain success in America, what is? The answer is probably a combination of influences that include high social class origin (i.e., one's parents' position), good social contacts, a good education, and location in a thriving country, industry, organization, or line of work.

Inequality Promotes Investment   Does a high degree of income inequality produce personal fortunes and jobs for people lower down the ladder, by increasing economic growth?

In principle, this should happen. Indeed, this idea underlies "supply side economics," which became popular in the 1980s under Republican governments and has resurfaced in the government of George W. Bush. Supply side economics justifies cutting government in order to cut taxes. What monies the rich had earlier paid in taxes, they could now invest, thus creating jobs for the poor.

However, evidence from the past twenty years does not support the theory's predictions. Throughout the twentieth century, the top 1 percent owned approximately 25–30 percent of all the wealth in the United States and 55–65 percent of the wealth that matters most (i.e., corporate stocks). Further, a mere 0.1 percent of Americans own 19 percent of all the wealth. Wealth concentration levels like this cannot possibly help the common American; most of the benefits of economic development will inevitably go to those who are already rich.

Some so-called economic development is illusory and doesn't benefit more than a very few rich people. For common people to benefit, new, better-paying jobs must be created. However, much personal wealth is invested in financial activities—acquisitions and mergers, buy-outs and sell-offs, stock market, currency and land speculations—all of which earn profits for the investor but create no new jobs. They often actually destroy businesses and jobs, and wipe out other people's savings. Thus, these activities merely redistribute wealth upwards from the poor and middle classes to the (already) rich.

Likewise, most investment in new jobs is "offshore," in low-wage developing countries. Investment produces new jobs, but not in America. As well, many wealthy people use tax loopholes and "tax havens" (off-shore residence) to avoid paying taxes on their earnings. So, investments that build the economy profit the wealthy shareholders but bring fewer benefits—either as jobs or taxes—to ordinary Americans. Thus, the benefits of economic growth are limited to the already rich.

Inequality Promotes Philanthropy   Does more inequality mean more philanthropy—more benevolent gift-giving by the very rich?

The evidence raises doubts about this assertion, too. Some wealthy people contribute lavishly to cultural, educational, and other institutions. They also receive tax breaks for doing so; their philanthropy costs them little or nothing. But what *percentage* of their personal wealth do they give away in socially beneficial ways? The amount is small and the percentage they donate varies little, even when economic inequality increases. In comparison, the poor give proportionately more through their taxes.

Corporate philanthropy, like many other corporate activities, is best explained as a form of imitation or contagion—not as a selfless or humane activity. Corporate giving serves to create and maintain businessmen's positions within the business

elite, or improve their public image. Further, philanthropic foundations (such as the Rockefeller Foundation) work to maintain the social order rather than change it. This has been visible in the effects of philanthropic foundations on the development of the social sciences.

Since the degree of inequality has little impact on the amount of philanthropy, there is no justification for a high degree of inequality, at least on philanthropic grounds.

Inequality Maintains Labor Supply   How about the claim that inequality produces highly motivated poor people willing to enter new jobs, thus contributing to economic growth?

A "reserve army of labor" may have been useful a century, or even a half-century ago. Today, however, there is little industrial advantage to having many poor and/or unemployed people in America. They often lack the skills that are needed by a postindustrial economy. And given the cost of living, they can't work as cheaply as Third World people, where labor is cheaper than it may ever be again in America. Other new jobs disappear through automation, which substitutes machines for people, to lower production costs. (In the long run, machines are even cheaper and easier to control than Third World workers.)

Thus, maintaining extreme economic inequality in America means reproducing a large impoverished underclass. The poor lack spending power—hence, they contribute little to the economy—and they need public support merely to survive. The middle-class pays to support this underclass while the rich invest overseas. In this case, too, inequality produces no social benefit.

Inequality Produces Economic Development Does inequality give rise to more economic development? As we have seen, more inequality does not automatically produce more economic development—at least not in America. The wealthy profit from their investments and on the surface these profits look a lot like economic growth, but in truth, the average American's income is dropping. It would drop faster if not for the payment of public moneys—social security, welfare, and

AFDC, among others—to the neediest. Likewise, middle-class household incomes would drop, too, if not for the ever-increasing contribution by second-income earners (typically, wives) and longer working hours for people who have jobs at all.

In recent years, there has been rapid economic development in Europe and Japan—countries with less economic inequality than the United States. Even the Pacific Rim countries such as Korea, Taiwan and Hong Kong—which began with higher levels of economic inequality—have reduced inequality in order to promote development. Low inequality stimulates growth in four ways: by inducing large increases in the savings and investments of the poor, by contributing to political and macro-economic stability, by increasing the morale and efficiency of low income workers and, with higher rural incomes, by increasing market demand for domestic products. The Asian success story should hold some lessons for America.

SUMMING UP

Shouldn't poor people be happy that others are rich? Well, if you believe that extreme inequality is an incentive to try harder, we guess they should be happy.

But in the end, the functional theory of stratification leaves many unanswered questions. Worst of all, it justifies a status quo in which large numbers of people are left destitute while a few live in luxury.

As we said in an earlier section, inequality is not primarily a result of differential merit: Mainly it is caused by the capitalist economy that determines the precise amount of poverty and degree of inequality. The state, controlled by America's richest and most influential business leaders, reinforces unequal power relations emerging from the interaction of class and labor market operations. Are high incomes and loads of prestige needed to motivate hard work? Not really. Lots of people work very hard for other reasons: for example, service to their community or to humanity, or duty to their family. More inequality doesn't yield more devotion—often the opposite.

How much economic inequality is too much? There is no evidence that an income ratio of 100 to 1—where the top boss earns 100 times what the average worker does—produces more economic growth or social well-being than a ratio of 20 to 1, which is more typical of other industrial societies. If the same social benefits can be achieved with less social inequality, then more inequality is too much.

REVIEW EXERCISES

For Discussion and Debate

1. Do inequalities of power benefit society? How are they related to economic inequalities?
2. "Fear of loss is a stronger motivator than the promise of gain." Discuss.
3. Does the functional theory of stratification account for economic inequalities among nations of the world? Why or why not?
4. What kind of evidence would prove that equality—economic or otherwise—is better for societies than inequality?

Writing Exercises

Write a brief (500-word) essay on one of the following topics:

1. What is a "fair" system of economic inequality?
2. Why are hunter-gatherer societies economically equal?
3. Why is greed more socially useful than unselfishness?
4. Is economic inequality becoming more or less important?

Research Activities

1. Collect data to determine whether the most functionally important players on a professional sports team (you choose the sport) earn the highest wages.
2. Collect data from at least six industrial societies to determine whether economic inequality (use the Gini index to measure inequality, if possible) is correlated with high or low rates of annual growth in productivity (use the GNP per capita to measure this).
3. Collect data on wages within an industry (you choose the industry) to find out whether labor conflict (e.g., strikes) increases with an increase in economic inequality.
4. What role, if any, did economic inequality play in the downfall of a major society or civilization? Use historical sources to find the data you need.

SELECTED REFERENCES

Abrahamson, Mark. 1979. "A Functional Theory of Organizational Stratification." *Social Forces* 58, 1 (Sept.): 128–145.

Abrahamson, Mark. 1973. "Functionalism and the Functional Theory of Stratification: An Empirical Assessment." *American Journal of Sociology* 78, 5 (Mar.): 1236–1246.

Allen, Michael Patrick. 1981. "Power and Privilege in the Large Corporation: Corporate Control and Managerial Compensation." *American Journal of Sociology* 86, 5 (Mar.): 1112–1123.

Betz, Michael, Kemp Davis and Patrick Miller. 1978. "Scarcity, Income Advantage, and Mobility: More Evidence on the Functional Theory of Stratification." *Sociological Quarterly* 19, 3 (Summer): 399–413.

Blumberg, Paul. 1978. "Another Day, Another $3,000: Executive Salaries in America." *Dissent* 25, 2 (111) (Spring): 157–168.

Bok, Derek. 1993. *The Cost of Talent: How Executives and Professionals Are Paid and How It Affects America.* New York: Free Press.

Broom, Leonard and Robert G. Cushing. 1977. "A Modest Test of an Immodest Theory: The Functional Theory of Stratification." *American Sociological Review* 42, 1 (Feb.): 157–169.

Cullen, John B. and Shelley M. Novick. 1979. "The Davis-Moore Theory of Stratification: A Further Examination and Extension." *American Journal of Sociology* 84, 6 (May): 1424–1437.

Domhoff, William G. 1999. "State and Ruling Class in Corporate America." *Critical Sociology* 25, 2/3:266–277.

Ehrenreich, Barbara. 2001. *Nickel and Dimed: On (Not) Getting By in America.* New York: Metropolitan Books.

Ehrenreich, John and Barbara Ehrenreich. 1973. "Hospital Workers: A Case Study in the 'New Working Class.'" *Monthly Review* 24, 8 (Jan.): 12–27.

Fisher, Donald. 1980. "American Philanthropy and the Social Sciences in Britain, 1919–1939: The Reproduction of a Conservative Ideology." *Sociological Review* 28, 2 (May): 277–315.

Fisher, Donald. 1983. "The Role of Philanthropic Foundations in the Reproduction and Production of Hegemony: Rockefeller Foundations and the Social Sciences." *Sociology* 17, 2 (May): 206–233.

Galaskiewicz, Joseph. 1985. *Social Organization of an Urban Grants Economy: A Study of Business Philanthropy and Nonprofit Organizations.* Orlando, FL: Academic Press.

Galaskiewicz, Joseph and Ronald S. Burt. 1991. "Interorganization Contagion in Corporate Philanthropy." *Administrative Science Quarterly* 36, 1 (Mar.): 88–105.

Gilder, George. 1981. "Moral Sources of Capitalism." *Society* 18, 6 (134) (Sept.–Oct.): 24–27.

Gordon, David M. 1972. "American Poverty: Functions, Mechanisms and Contradictions." *Monthly Review* 24, 2 (June): 72–79.

Harris, William T. 1992. "Rule Changes and the Earnings of National Football League Field Goal Kickers." *Sociology of Sport Journal* 9, 4 (Dec.): 397–402.

Hochschild, Jennifer L. 2003. "Social Class in Public Schools." *Journal of Social Issues* 59, 4:821–840.

Lageman, Ellen Condliffe, ed. 1999. *Philanthropic Foundations: New Scholarship, New Possibilities.* Bloomington, IN: Indiana University Press.

Mason, Patrick L. 2000. "Understanding Recent Empirical Evidence on Race and Labor Market Outcomes in the USA." *Review of Social Economy* 58, 3 (Sept.): 319–338.

Ostrower, Francie. 1995. *Why the Wealthy Give: The Culture of Elite Philanthropy.* Princeton, NJ: Princeton University Press.

Richards, Donald G. 2003. "A (Utopian?) Socialist Proposal for the Reform of Major League Baseball." *Journal of Sport & Social Issues* 27, 3 (Aug.): 308–324.

Simpson, Miles. 1990. "Political Rights and Income Inequality: A Cross-National Test." *American Sociological Review* 55, 5 (Oct.): 682, 693.

Wachtel, Howard. 1972. "Capitalism and Poverty in America: Paradox or Contradiction?" *Monthly Review* 24, 2 (June): 51–64.

4.2   Who Gets Ahead in the "Land of Opportunity"?

The issue: The United States has arguably the strongest economy in the world, owing to an educated population and an abundance of natural resources. But is the wealth shared fairly? Does everyone really have a good chance to get ahead in America?

Equal opportunity and the ability to better oneself are foundations of the American Dream. The historical key to success is hard work. Accordingly, the working poor strive toward self-sufficiency, working to support themselves and move up in the world. By accepting employment rather than relying on welfare and social support, the working poor also show a strong work ethic and lots of personal ambition. Yet, of the 32.9 million Americans below the poverty line in 2001, 6.8 million were members of the working poor.

Is there a shortage of opportunity in America, or are the working poor to blame for not taking better advantage of the opportunities provided? Is there unequal opportunity in America? As always there are competing views on this matter. On the one side, some people argue that the working poor have plenty of opportunity to get ahead.

ECONOMIC DEVELOPMENT PROVIDES LOTS OF OPPORTUNITY

Equal opportunity means that all positions in society are equally open to everyone, regardless of age, race, gender, religion, or class of origin. *Unequal* opportunity means there are differences in the chance that people will get to enjoy an improved social condition: more wealth, authority, and prestige; better health; more happiness.

Life, sociology tells us, is often an unequal contest. Because of early advantages, some people will (almost) always win and others will (almost) always lose in society's contests for wealth, power, and social standing. If you are born a "Jones" you will win, but if you are born a "Smith" you will lose. As in sporting contests, so, too, in social contests for better life chances, poorer starts produce poorer finishes because unequal social origins—origins in environments with unequal resources—mean unequal prospects in the contest for better life chances.

Here's some evidence that life chances are unequal, from a study (Corak and Heisz 1996) of the incomes of fathers and their sons. The study looks at 440,000 father-son pairs, examines father's income group when the son is a teenager, then asks what income group the son is in roughly fifteen years later. Fathers are compared with fathers in 1978 and sons with sons in 1993, using constant dollars. The data show that teenage sons of fathers who were in the top income decile (i.e., 10 percent) in 1978–1982 grow up twice as likely to be in the top income decile (when they are earning an income of their own) as they are to be in the bottom income decile. Sons of poor fathers grow up three times as likely to be in the lowest income decile themselves as to be in the top income decile. This means that, at the top and bottom of society, sons tend to inherit their father's wealth, or poverty. (The data would be similar for daughters, but not exactly the same.)

However, in the middle of the income hierarchy—among "middle class" people—there is a great deal of upward and downward social mobility—sons moving one, two or more income deciles higher or lower than their fathers. When studying these processes of change, sociologists routinely find out what fraction of upward mobility is structural and what fraction is exchange mobility. Most upward mobility is *structural mobility*—a result of growth in the number of "good" jobs available in the economy. Only a small amount of upward mobility is *exchange* mobility—a result of some people vacating their social positions so that others can enter them. What determines the overall amount of social mobility is economic growth. During an economic recession almost no one gets ahead, regardless of education, hard work, or good values. During a period of economic expansion, many people get ahead who would not have had much chance to do so before.

Many observers note that the U.S. economy has been working at a very high level of profitability in the past decade. By this reckoning, any failures to get ahead are not likely due to the economy but to the individuals themselves.

THE WORKING POOR ARE TO BLAME

It seems cruel to hold people responsible for their misfortune, but in a system that (supposedly) rewards the best people for their merit, what else are we to do? Since most upward mobility is due to economic growth or structural expansion, and there has been plenty of growth and expansion in the past decade, we cannot blame the economy or the stratification system per se. We must praise those who benefited from growth and hold the rest responsible for their own failure.

Just Lazy   Perhaps, some people—the people who don't get ahead—just don't work as hard as others, and not hard enough to get ahead. The United States was built upon the hard work of generations of immigrants, most of whom got ahead. Traditionally, many people have been the working poor and through hard work, they or their families have been able to rise. Immigrants have historically done very well in America. The people who come here from other countries believe in the American dream and work hard to achieve it. The experiences of Asian immigrants from China, Hong Kong, Taiwan, Singapore, and Korea, for example, show that hard work does pay off in higher incomes and better lives.

According to some, the working poor simply lack initiative. They work too few hours and that is why they are poor. For example, on average, the working poor person only works two-thirds of the year, meaning that one-third of the year consists of forgone income. How can a person who only works part-time hope to get ahead?

In recent years, blacks as well as whites have been profiting from the economic growth. Originally, the American dream only applied to white property-owning men. However, recent measures of white versus black socioeconomic mobility show that the mobility of blacks has increased at a much faster rate than that of whites, translating into increased access to opportunities. Increasingly, black people *see* their access to opportunity to be similar to that of white people. In a similar survey asking about opportunities for advancement, 34 percent of blacks compared to 35 percent of whites foresaw these opportunities (Hochschild 1995:58). There was no difference in the perception of opportunities by blacks and whites.

Not Enough Jobs   Some have claimed that the working poor are poor because they receive wages that are too low. However, according to Deere, Murphy, and Welch, the problem of low-wage workers is not that there are too many low-wage jobs, but that there are not enough. People need more jobs to augment their income, and some of America's jobs have moved overseas to countries where the wages are even lower.

In keeping with this argument, if there were more low-wage jobs, individuals would have more access to opportunity. They wouldn't have to work part-time, but could work full time in these low-wage and low-skill jobs. This is what a great many immigrant families have done: strung together as many jobs as they needed, to make ends meet.

Who Are the Working Poor?   Others have raised the possibility that our estimates of the working poor are exaggerated by the inclusion of temporarily low-income young people. Many in the reported statistics on society's "working poor" combine the genuine working poor with young graduates just entering the workforce, as well as elderly workers with alternative sources of income. So, the supposed evidence of immobility may be incorrect.

If so, if we had data only on the chronically poor workers, we would conclude that they are relatively few in numbers. The vast majority of poor workers move in and out of poverty over their lifetimes—indeed, within a period of five years or less. The working poor who are chronically—that is, permanently—poor are few and different in many respects from the temporarily poor workers.

However, others argue that for the most part the figures on immobility are believable: There is a problem with opportunity and mobility at the lower end of the stratification system.

THE WORKING POOR ARE NOT TO BLAME

Much of the economic growth in the past decade has been an increase in low-wage jobs. Low-wage jobs do not open up opportunities; they lock people into a cycle of poverty. Raising the federal minimum wage to a livable wage would ensure that all have the opportunity to cover their expenses, establish some savings, and pursue their dreams.

According to the Organization for Economic Co-operation and Development (OECD), the United States has one of the lowest rates of mobility for low-pay jobs. Compared to France, Italy, and the UK, as well as centralized countries like Germany, Denmark, Finland, and Sweden, the United States has lower levels of mobility for all of its low-wage

earners. Compared to laborers in these nations, the average member of the working poor in the United States will spend more time stuck in the same dead-end occupations with little hope or opportunity for upward advancement.

The 24/7 Economy   Low wage jobs operate in a 24/7 economy, in which workers are most often hired on a part-time basis without benefits. Since the 1970s, the nature of the economy has changed drastically, such that the American economy has more or less adopted nonstandard work hours for much of the low-wage jobs.

A 24/7 economy poses unique challenges for these marginalized workers, since it is conducive to part-time work and puts many families in a bind for childcare. Gone are the days when stable firms would hire and protect its workers. Today, firms are more likely to "hire the labor *without* hiring the people." Most industries want to hire part-time workers, because doing so allows flexibility in scheduling and costs the company much less.

For many workers, however, part-time employment is often an involuntary compromise. Part-time jobs do not offer healthcare, unemployment, disability, sick/parental/maternity leave, or pension plans. As such, they help to perpetuate a system in which the children of these working poor will also become disadvantaged: They will get a poor start in the contest for success. Also, part-time work contributes to poverty because it disqualifies many individuals for social assistance, which could help them rise out of poverty. Finally, due to the variability in scheduling, many working poor find that they cannot take up another part-time job to supplement their meager incomes.

The decline in full-time low-wage work has also been parallel to the decline of union membership. The absence of unions increases the likelihood that workers will receive low wages, few benefits, and little security. Even if most of the working poor worked 40 hours a week and 52 weeks a year, they would remain poor.

Residential Location   Working poor families are also stuck in a system of disadvantage based on their neighborhoods. Wealthier workers can afford to buy property in "good" neighborhoods and indirectly buy their children a better education. The working poor are most often relegated to poorer neighborhoods where the quality of education is much lower, due to a shortage of school supplies, crumbling infrastructure, demoralized teaching staff, and so on. When children receive few educational opportunities, their chances of improving their life conditions are much worse.

Family Arrangements   The rise of the working poor and their limited access to the American Dream has much to do with changing family structures. Increasingly, families have come to rely on two income-earners, and employers have assumed as much. However, the expected increase in the average family income due to women's widespread entry into the workforce has been offset by the rise in single motherhood. Children with two employed parents have fared the best of any children. Many children, however, grow up with only one parent in the household and one family income.

Working mothers also face numerous stresses that impede their upward mobility. Often, working mothers end up in part-time jobs, with irregular hours and few (if any) benefits or opportunities for advancement. A 1996 amendment to the Temporary Assistance to Needy Families (TANF) named families on welfare as a priority, making it more difficult for working poor families to receive government support. A similar perversion of the American Dream (i.e., work hard and you will succeed) is found in healthcare coverage. Social assistance regulations are such that families who work longer hours are actually *more* likely to have a member of the family who is uninsured.

For many people, welfare makes better economic and familial sense than a low-paying job. Amy Burke puts it well when she says, "forcing individuals into the only jobs they can find does not strengthen families, foster economic mobility, or protect children."

Careers and Their Entry Points   Over extended periods, people in careers—even in good jobs—remain in the same industries and occupations. Careers—highly predictable and protected job sequences—however are becoming the exception in mature industrial societies. Where these careers do exist, they are hard to get into because of internal labor markets.

Careers are highly patterned largely because of the workings of *internal labor markets,* of which we say more shortly. These markets impose a high degree of control over who enters, at what level, through what stages people will move, and at what rate. The result is that, even today, society sorts people into different types of careers, and their children into different neighborhoods, schools, and marriages.

Careers Structure People's Opportunities
Career lines have five elementary properties: age, composition, continuity, channeling, ports of entry and exit, and career development. People enter the given career at similar ages and advance at similar (though not identical) rates. Over the ages 18–30, their chances are structured, first, by differences in human capital and social psychological orientation. These greatly determine people's educational aspirations and achievements, and occupational aspirations. Gender also affects the access to career lines. Communities of origin and residence are the local opportunity structures within which people seek and find their first real jobs. Finally, life course events—in education, work, family and otherwise—interact with contingencies to sort people into jobs with better and worse prospects.

All of this begins early in life. People who miss some of the key entry points are likely to remain on the outside looking in. Different occupational groups and labor market segments have different career patterns (e.g., stages, ports of entry and exit). This is due in large part to the organization's need to control labor—especially scarce and highly skilled labor—by promising future rewards, a practice we sometimes call "bureaucratic control."

The Importance of Schooling and "Headstarts"
Mobility early in one's career has a strong relationship with promotion and demotion probabilities in each successive period. This becomes amply clear in studies of the "internal labor markets" of schools that practice tracking.

In many schools, children are "streamed" or "tracked" into nonacademic programs. In subtle and complex ways, this reduces their postgraduate opportunities. For example, tracking tends to differentiate the IQ scores of students in the higher track and homogenize scores in the lower one. Graduates from the "higher" streams are more likely to be hired into good jobs than graduates from the "lower" streams. The positions into which they are hired are more likely to lead to upward mobility within the organization.

Moreover, students from "good schools" are more likely to get hired than students with equal grades from "bad" schools, or unknown schools. The high school, college, and labor market are linked over the life-course, and together shape the lifetime career. Employers look for information about job candidates in the school records: where they went to school, what they did there, and how they did.

Such institutional linkages are valuable to societies, employers, and employees. Though economic theory warns about the inefficiencies of institutional linkages, school-employer linkages can enhance incentives, the flow of information, and employment outcomes. At best, the school-workplace linkage can efficiently supply needed workers with the needed skills and verify their quality. In this way they support a reward system at work that is based on merit. However, they also support a reward system that is based on parental social class.

Internal Markets Exclude Outsiders Careers take place within submarkets or economic sectors, in which a segmentation of jobs and careers has occurred. Primary and secondary labor markets coexist within every region, province, and size of community. The *primary labor market* consists of jobs that offer good wages, chances to get ahead, and job security: It includes jobs like lawyer, plumber, and teacher. The *secondary (or marginal) labor market* consists of jobs that pay low wages, offer little chance to get ahead, and promise little job security: jobs like taxi driver, secretary, or bank teller.

People with different social traits, backgrounds, and skills often locate in different markets. For example, far more women and visible minorities have moved to the secondary labor market, and far more white men, in the primary labor market, than could have occurred by chance. Within markets, we find submarkets that also contain different kinds of jobs and different kinds of people. The big difference between primary and secondary markets tends to blur important differences among jobs in the *same* market. Within submarkets, we even find internal labor markets within occupations. Jobs within the core of this market are more stable and individuals have greater chances for mobility. At the periphery of the market, individuals merely hold a job. From one standpoint, an *internal labor market* is an organizational process for allocating people with particular training and experiences to a particular sequence of positions. Employees who are part of an internal labor market are generally more committed to their work and their organization than employees who are not.

Research suggests that the greatest concentration of such internal labor markets is found among male-dominated middle-management positions. Within such internal labor markets, experience counts for a great deal: sometimes, even more than education or expertise. Employers particularly value on-the-job training and the acquisition of job-specific skills, and organizational loyalty. Other things being equal, *internal* markets gain and lose importance for careers inversely as *external* markets decrease and increase job creation.

Internal labor markets are like what Ralph Turner called a *sponsored mobility* system in which people, once selected, are helped and almost guaranteed to get ahead. Sponsored mobility works against "outsiders" such as women, racial minorities, and the poor. Much of the exclusiveness and inequality we associate with class relations can be derived from the theory of internal labor markets. Likewise, much of what we call discrimination is due to the working of internal labor markets.

Ethnicity and Protected Markets Job markets that have perfected the exclusion of certain kinds of people will sometimes exclude people on the grounds of race, ethnicity, or gender. The process of job-based racial inequality (or race-based employment) works like a hiring queue in which minorities usually occupy the lower positions among workers ranked according to their desirability to employers. The larger the minority, the greater is the oversupply of workers. So, employers easily relegate a large minority to lower occupational standing.

Throughout the United States, the larger the number of black men in the work force, the higher are the wages for whites (male and female) and black women. Racial queuing concentrates whites in better jobs. As increases in population increase the size of the job market, the best new jobs go disproportionately to white men. Often, excluded minorities respond by creating protected markets. A protected market exists when consumers from an ethnic group uniformly obtain their goods and services from co-ethnics. As the topmost ethnic groups move up the labor queue, lower-ranking ethnic groups struggle to fill their place. The continuous recourse to new ethnic immigrants to fill the lowest-paying jobs has made ethnicity the crucial mechanism for ordering groups of people into distinct sets of jobs.

SUMMING UP

The evidence indicates that the benefits of economic growth are not allocated equally. As a result, there is not equal opportunity to benefit from economic growth—not equal opportunity to get ahead. People with an early lead tend to win the race for success.

As we have seen, this is because wealth earned through economic growth is not shared equally; it is not true that everyone benefits equally. Nor is it true that the working poor have enough job opportunity: When the wages are low enough, even working 24 hours a day—an impossibility—would not earn enough to support a family. More important still, people who start out poor or otherwise disadvantaged are limited by the structure of labor markets and the peculiarities of career structuring. These favor "insiders," people who are selected early, trained well, and protected. The working poor and their children rarely find themselves in this situation.

Culturally determined preferences for, and perceptions of, certain kinds of people shape people's life chances. As a result, different kinds of people—men and women, whites and nonwhites, immigrants and native-borns—have different work histories and more or less likelihood to rise out of the working poor. Careers tell us at least as much about the culture, politics, and structuring of our society as they do about the individual people who are living these careers. That's why it's unreasonable to suggest that the working poor are to blame if they can't get ahead.

Recent years have seen growing income disparities in the population, with a growing class of wealthy people and a growing class of poor. The number of homeless people has increased. Emergency food assistance alone grew 18 percent between 1998 and 2000, fueled by the needs of working people. In this context, people have had to struggle harder to stay afloat—to pay the bills and send their children to school. The working poor have had to struggle hardest.

REVIEW EXERCISES

For Discussion and Debate

1. Is it still true that America is a land of opportunity for everyone, or only for white able-bodied heterosexual males?
2. What social policies would, if enacted, go furthest in making opportunity more widely available for everyone?
3. Why can't immigrants and racial minorities today use the same strategies to get ahead as immigrants used 50 or 100 years ago?
4. How have changes in the organization of work in America made it more difficult to get ahead simply through education and hard work?

Writing Exercises

Write a brief (500-word) essay on one of the following topics:

1. "America never was a land of opportunity for most people—it was a land of mythology and tall tales."
2. "The part of America that provides the most opportunity today is . . ."
3. "Women have a different story to tell about 'getting ahead' than men do, and they always have."
4. "Today, China is the 'land of opportunity,' not America."

Research Activities

1. Talk to some of the older people you know—family members, or people in the neighborhood—and find out whether they would agree that America used to be a land of opportunity but isn't any more.
2. Collect data from at least three industrial nations (e.g., the United States, Canada, France) and determine whether they are all "lands of opportunity" when economic growth is taking place.
3. Collect detailed information on the occupation histories of at least three people over the age of 45 and find out what factors they believe account for particular occupational successes or failures (e.g., jobs lost or gained, pay raises, promotions).
4. Make a map of the country showing where jobs were gained and lost between 1981 and 2001. What do you notice about the location of these gains and losses? How can you explain this pattern?

SELECTED REFERENCES

Blau, Joel. 1999. *Illusions of Prosperity: America's Working Families in an Age of Economic Insecurity.* Oxford: Oxford University Press.

Bok, Derek. 1995. "Expanding Opportunity in America." In *Opportunity in the United States: Social and Individual Responsibility.* Report of the Domestic Strategy Group Meeting, August 19–23. Aspen: The Aspen Institute.

Burke, Amy D. 2001. "Ending Welfare, Continuing Poverty." *Dissent* 48, 4:90–95.

Casper, Lynne M. and Rosalind B. King. 2004. "Changing Families, Shifting Economic Fortunes, and Meeting Basic Needs." In *Work-Family Challenges for Low-Income Parents and Their Children,* edited by Ann C. Crouter and Alan Booth. Mahwah, NJ: Lawrence Erlbaum Associates.

Ehrenreich, Barbara and Thomas Geoghegan. 2002. "Lighting Labor's Fire." *The Nation* 275, 22:11–16.

England, Paula. 2004. "Labor Market and Family Trends and Public Policy Responses." In *Work-Family Challenges for Low-Income Parents and Their Children,* edited by Ann C. Crouter and Alan Booth. Mahwah, NJ: Lawrence Erlbaum Associates.

Furstenberg, Frank F. 2003. "Growing Up in American Society: Income, Opportunities, and Outcomes." In *Social Dynamics of the Life Course: Transitions, Institutions, and Interrelations,* edited by Walter R. Heinz and Victor W. Marshall. New York: Aldine de Gruyter.

Hawkins, Daniel N. and Shaun D. Whiteman. 2004. In *Work-Family Challenges for Low-Income Parents and Their Children,* edited by Ann C. Crouter and Alan Booth. Mahwah, NJ: Lawrence Erlbaum Associates.

Hochschild, Jennifer L. 1995. *Facing Up to the American Dream: Race, Class, and the Soul of the Nation.* Princeton, NJ: Princeton University Press.

Huston, Aletha C. 2004. "Childcare for Low-Income Families: Problems and Promises." In *Work-Family Challenges for Low-Income Parents and Their Children,* edited by Ann C. Crouter and Alan Booth. Mahwah, NJ: Lawrence Erlbaum Associates.

Jencks, Christopher. 2004. "The Low Wage Job Puzzle: Why Is America Generating So Many Bad Jobs?" *American Prospect* 15, 1:35–37.

Johnson, Margaret. 2000. "Race, Self Employment and Upward Mobility: An Illusive American Dream." *Contemporary Sociology* 29, 4:628.

Kim, Marlene. 1998. "Are the Working Poor Lazy?" *Challenge* 41, 3:85–99.

Kuttner, Robert. 2004. "High-Wage America: How We Can Reclaim a Middle-Class Society." *American Prospect* 15, 1:60–62.

Lee, Judy M. and Marcia K. Meyers. 2003. "Working but Poor: How Are Families Faring?" *Children and Youth Services Review* 25, 3:177–201.

Levitan, Sar. A, Frank Gallo and Isaac Shapiro. 1993. *Working but Poor: America's Contradiction,* rev. ed. Baltimore, MD: John Hopkins University Press.

Schiller, Bradley R. 2004. *The Economics of Poverty and Discrimination,* 9th ed. Upper Saddle River, NJ: Pearson Education.

Sheryll, Cashin. 2004. *The Failures of Integration: How Race and Class Are Undermining the American Dream.* New York: Public Affairs.

Shulman, Beth. 2003. *The Betrayal of Work: How Low-Wage Jobs Fail 30 Million Americans and Their Families.* New York: The New Press.

Smith, Michael R. 2002. "Income Inequality and Economic Growth in Rich Countries: A Reconsideration of the Evidence." *Current Sociology* 50, 4:573–593.

Starks, Brian. 2003. "The New Economy and the American Dream: Examining the Effect of Work Conditions on Beliefs about Economic Opportunity." *The Sociological Quarterly* 44, 2:205–225.

U.S. Department of Labor, Bureau of Labor Statistics. 2003. "A Profile of the Working Poor, 2001." (http://www.bls.gov/cps/cpswp2001.pdf, accessed on May 16, 2004).

4.3   Isn't Welfare Dangerous?

The issue: Have attempts to help the poor with welfare benefits created new problems that are worse than the poverty itself? Has the institution of welfare become an economic, social, and political nightmare?

Since 1970, the conditions of the poor—even the conditions of poor children—have gotten worse, despite the efforts of public assistance or welfare to improve the situation. Is welfare likely to solve the problem of poverty, or is it part of the problem?

Answering this question takes us into the domain of such concepts as the feminization of poverty, the marginalization of the poor, the poor underclass, and the culture of poverty. In explaining poverty, many continue to search for *cultural deficiency,* whether in the form of flawed values, family relations, or welfare rules. The poor couldn't be poor, in other words, unless something were wrong with them.

The argument against welfare and other forms of assistance arises from the fact that, for various reasons, many people who are not poor believe the poor are very different from themselves. In a society based on the idea (if not the fact) that merit is rewarded, some in more affluent classes believe that the poor have not tried hard enough to succeed, are in some sense undeserving, or are, at the very least, lazy.

Alternatively, supporters of welfare argue that the poor are not on welfare by choice—if ample opportunities existed, they would choose to work rather than struggle on welfare. Supporters concede that the system is expensive although it is a necessary one, since it helps people in times of need. The absence of welfare would likely be as detrimental as it was in the days of the depression. It would create unrest and amplify the downward spin in the economy.

Before we begin to examine both sides of the issue, we must examine the idea of the underclass, since it is central to our discussion of welfare.

The Underclass

According to the notion of *underclass,* the poor do not just lack money, they lack the social and moral virtue that helps people to get money. Besides poverty, the underclass is characterized by long-term unemployment, a high proportion of one-parent households (typically, a mother), and intergenerational dependence on welfare. Concentrated in rundown sections of towns and cities, the underclass produces crime and delinquency, drug-dealing and drug-use, low educational achievement, and teenage pregnancy.

Some believe this occurs principally because the underclass does not share societal norms of achievement. This underclass is located below the working poor and middle class, both financially and morally. It is also seen as an underachieving and under-conforming social group. For example, the concept of the "black" underclass—like that of the culture of poverty—places much of the responsibility for their poverty on themselves, asserting that social reform has failed.

Does welfare create or perpetuate the underclass? If so, it does harm—perhaps more harm than good. Let's look at the evidence on both sides.

Welfare Does More Harm Than Good

Those who believe that welfare perpetuates an underclass make various arguments to support their view. Their arguments fall into three main categories: a concern with the harmful effects of welfare dependence, concern with the economic costs of welfare programs, and concern that welfare is ineffective in dealing with poverty.

Dependence on Welfare   Those who believe welfare does more harm than good claim that welfare is a disincentive to work. They also argue that the welfare state, in expanding its responsibility for public needs, thereby lessens individual responsibility. This system of paternalism or "government knows best" erodes individual morality.

It is argued that the welfare system has created behavioral disincentives that trap generations of recipients in poverty by fostering dependence and a culture of poverty. The process also reduces work effort and diminishes the sense of work ethic. Increased dependence also has strong negative effects on children's intellectual abilities and life prospects. Children raised by families on welfare are more likely to fail in school, be engaged in criminal activities, and end up on welfare themselves than those raised with more privileges. By this reasoning, part of the long-term solution to get rid of this culture of poverty is to get rid of the welfare program.

Since many people on welfare have little education and few skills, their chances of earning a satisfactory wage are slight. The jobs that many can hope to get may pay minimum wage or lower. Though welfare pays less than the minimum wage, a rational person would still choose welfare over a week's hard work for just a few dollars more.

It is in this context that we can understand the recent wave of *workfare* programs. With some local variations, they all require welfare recipients to spend a fraction of their week at unfamiliar jobs from which they gain no marketable job skills. Supporters argue workfare programs ensure that valuable public work gets done and welfare recipients maintain a routine of doing productive work.

Available evidence suggests that various workfare approaches rapidly increase earnings, lower unemployment rates, and reduce welfare benefits. These workfare programs use welfare workers like contingent workers. This reduces the amount of good jobs with health benefits, fair compensation, and vacation time. Such jobs also encourage relatively little development of skills. The long-term effectiveness of such programs is questionable and programs emphasizing job search appear to fare better.

A second aspect of this concern about welfare dependence is the perception of recipients as poorly socialized. The underclass is seen as lacking in personal responsibility. In short, paying welfare encourages laziness, sexual promiscuity, and reckless procreation. No wonder, critics say, that cities and states with higher welfare payments draw large numbers of poor migrants from other cities and states.

The Cost of Welfare   Other critics focus less on the worthiness of recipients and more on the cost of welfare programs.

First, they argue that welfare and associated programs for the poor are too expensive to sustain. They may have been warranted in earlier times, when the economy was growing and there was less public indebtedness. Today, the middle class cannot afford to pay high taxes to service debts for earlier welfare programs, while also paying welfare to growing numbers of current recipients. Welfare and other public programs must be put on the back burner until government balance sheets are in order.

Second, critics argue that welfare and related programs require a huge, costly bureaucracy to administer. Money transfers are ineffective because money is always lost in the bureaucracy from the taxpayer to the welfare recipient. This monetary loss can effectively be seen as waste since it does not help to combat poverty. Until we can figure out how to deliver programs more efficiently, we may have to cut (or cut back) the programs themselves.

Third, welfare and other social programs are so costly in many cities and states that they impose heavy tax burdens on business to pay for these programs. High taxes reduce business profits, so many businesses are forced to move to less-taxed municipalities—often entirely out of the country—in order to survive. By increasing taxes, welfare drives out business and reduces new job creation. Essentially, the tax burden puts new people on welfare and perpetuates the system by limiting opportunity for those currently on welfare.

Effectiveness   Finally, critics point out that, despite its cost and longevity, welfare has not succeeded in reducing the number of poor or improved their chances of escaping poverty. For fifty years, public welfare has promised too much, failed to separate effective from ineffective programs, and hidden its setbacks.

As it stands, welfare is only supposed to provide people with short-term (emergency) assistance, although it often provides long-term assistance. It should be possible, critics say, to devise a program for the poor that does more than provide temporary support on a long-term basis. To become viable again, social welfare policy should emphasize specific themes: productivity (getting people back to work), reciprocity (something given for something taken), community (a sense of responsibility for others), and privatization (the competitive contracting of social services to third parties). These are indeed the themes emphasized in the welfare reform bill signed into law by President Bill Clinton in his first term in office.

WELFARE DOES MORE GOOD THAN HARM

Those who support welfare see it as an essential social institution, since it acts as a safeguard that prevents most Americans from reaching levels of absolute poverty. Supporters argue that people do not choose to go on welfare, that the cost is high but necessary, and that it is an effective means of sustaining individuals.

Dependence on Welfare   First, those who take the opposing view emphasize that few people are on welfare by choice. They are not to blame for being poor, nor is there much they can do to escape poverty.

In a society with high unemployment rates, due mainly to globalization and the growth in contingent work, many people are bound to be out of work at any given time. With low minimum wages, prevalent part-time work, and little job security, many people are unable to save up money for the times when they are out of work. As such, welfare recipients should not be characterized as lacking in moral responsibility or a desire to work.

The Cost of Welfare   One cannot deny that welfare and related programs carry huge costs. Nor can we deny the need to deal with the public debt—in small part a result of past spending on social services and fiscal mismanagement.

However, it is unfair to focus on welfare as the chief source of present financial problems and unreasonable to imagine these problems are remedied by reducing (even eliminating) public welfare. In fact, most public spending benefits the middle-class and wealthy—not the poor. Consider higher education. The working poor pay taxes to support college education, yet their children are unlikely to get much of it. The main beneficiaries are middle-class children. Likewise, investors, business people, and self-employed professionals have many legal opportunities to reduce their taxes, depriving the state of needed revenues. Unlike the rich, the working poor have virtually no tax loopholes to exploit, nor are many of the public spending programs aimed at them.

To look at the issue of public spending on welfare, we can turn to the European example. Research shows that welfare does not necessarily have a negative impact on economic growth. Researchers found no trade-off between the two. In fact, the United States did not have higher growth than the Dutch or the Germans, who effectively reduce poverty with public funds.

To solve society's financial problems, we must take into account benefits paid to the nonpoor and see to it that everyone contributes a fair share. More than 90 percent of the trillion U.S. dollars spent on welfare every year are spent benefiting middle- and upper-income individuals and corporations, in the form of social security, Medicare, and wealth redistribution to U.S. business. Other examples include farm subsidies, below-market government loans, tax breaks for the wealthy, corporate bailouts, and subsidized government insurance. Cutting poverty programs while maintaining this "upside-down welfare" program seems hypocritical at best.

Effectiveness Just as welfare critics say, current welfare programs are ineffective. They neither prevent nor eliminate the conditions that drive people to welfare. Nor do they help people to get off welfare. They simply keep people alive from one month to another. Though the system does not help create dependent individuals, it does sustain them, which is better than the alternative.

However, research shows that spells on welfare are shorter, inheritance of dependency is less common, and welfare fraud is rarer than most people believe. The welfare abuses that become public are not typical and, like most "news" in the media, are interesting precisely because they are atypical.

The media play on people's fear, and many people fear welfare fraud the way they fear crime and drug use. They perceive they are being taken advantage of—while they work hard for their money at jobs they hate, others are sitting at home waiting for the welfare check to arrive. This fear of being made a sucker, alongside the belief that everyone on welfare is taking advantage of the system, produces fear and contempt for people on welfare.

Moreover, welfare—a plan designed to deal with short gaps of need—becomes a way of life. Public welfare professionals need to educate political leaders and the public that welfare is not a subsidy of people but of the economic system. The key to making welfare more effective is not in reducing welfare entitlements but in increasing the reward of work and opportunities for work.

Until the system changes, the best that can be said for welfare is that it does what people thought it would when they invented it. Welfare provides a moderating influence on the economy—and on social life—during an economic depression. Remember that modern welfare took its present form during the Great Depression of the 1930s, when unemployment was even higher than it is today. The purpose of welfare was to keep unemployed people alive and, secondarily, to pump money into the economy. Welfare was created to jumpstart a devastated economy and to bring order and security to a frightening situation. Many feared surges of crime, violence, and political upheaval. Welfare helped to control all these threats to the social order (though it did not—and could not—eliminate them).

The expansion of the welfare state from 1935 to the mid-1970s meshed well with the needs of profitable production, political legitimacy, and patriarchal control. With the economic crisis of the 1970s, the welfare state became too competitive with capital accumulation and too supportive of empowered popular movements. Women, persons of color, and the poor ranked high among the victims of the new economic plans.

Today, it is important to point out that though we have moderate growth, a weak economy is not the cause of problems. The problem lies in the distribution of income: The gap between rich and poor has been growing for the past 40 years. Again, welfare is controlling the threats to order, but it is not—and cannot be—a solution in itself. Since the 1960s, the welfare state has been failing due to a combination of slowed economic growth, lower corporate taxes, greed for high profits, and unreasonably high wages, which have reduced distributable surpluses. Most important of all, the Bush government's delivery of tax cuts to the rich, combined with a foreign war in Iraq, have undermined the possibility of additional funds for greater social spending.

In the past decade we have seen that neither a planned nor a competitive economy works particularly well without substantial modification. In this context, welfare pluralism acts as a form of damage limitation in which the deficiencies of one approach are more or less balanced by the strengths of others.

Response to Recent Changes   Those who view welfare in a more positive light may not agree on the ways to reform current programs in order to solve long-standing problems of poverty and unemployment.

However, they do agree that under the present economic conditions, reducing welfare is especially harmful to women and children, who are among the main recipients. Single mothers with preschool children in particular have the least opportunity to find and keep jobs if welfare is cut. Recent changes to legislation have started to pose additional problems. People, but most notably mothers, are forced to work or be in work-related activities in order to receive aid. With a five-year aid limit and the difficulties imposed by childcare and/or making ends meet on a minimum wage, the welfare system is particularly harsh on these women. The history of the national welfare rights movement has been, and is increasingly, an ongoing revolution for and by women.

Welfare supporters also agree that nothing is to be gained by privatizing welfare and using the voluntary, informal, and commercial sectors. One facet of change to this arrangement in general has been the emergence of user fees and sales as the principal source of nonprofit growth. We see this with hospitals and universities but also with some social services and civil organizations. Although these trends may have positive results, they raise serious questions about the future of the nonprofit sector and about access to care on the part of the disadvantaged.

Contrary to what some welfare critics believe, the problems some associate with welfare may not have such a clear link. They may fail to take in all the relevant factors. Reducing welfare may not lower the teenage pregnancy rate, for example. It might have no effect on the divorce rate. Cutting welfare transfers would fail to usher in a new era of "traditional" and stable family life. To reduce these problems to welfare alone is to be blind to all the other social forces at work. Welfare does not cause any of these problems; therefore they are not resolved by eliminating welfare. Instead, they are part of a large transformation of family life in all social classes and all industrialized countries.

Finally, reducing welfare payments would not reduce poverty. To reduce poverty, we need to make more jobs available. Despite the arguments of supply-side economics, which we discussed in an earlier chapter, there is no evidence that more jobs are created when public spending is reduced.

SUMMING UP

Isn't welfare dangerous? No; the absence of welfare would be far more dangerous.

In the end, the decisive argument against viewing welfare as harmful is a historical argument: Welfare is a stage in the evolution of the idea of *social citizenship.* T. H. Marshall, an English sociologist, pointed out that the concept of citizenship is an evolving concept. The status of citizen, as we mentioned in an earlier chapter, began to develop in medieval cities. The idea was that citizenship makes a person free and, in important respects, equal to everyone else.

With the rise of nation-states, the citizenship idea expanded in three ways. First, in the seventeenth and eighteenth centuries came civil citizenship. It guaranteed liberty of the person; freedom of speech, thought, and faith; the right to own property and to conclude valid contracts; and the right to full justice in the courts. Political citizenship developed next, in the nineteenth and twentieth centuries, with the spread of universal suffrage. This is the right of all adults to vote in elections and run for office.

The concept of social citizenship began to develop only in the present century. It reflected an understanding that economic disadvantages limit people's ability to enjoy full civil and political citizenship. If people are to be full citizens, they need economic security: a minimum wage, the right to unionize, rights to a job, and fair treatment on the job. In all industrial societies, social citizenship has thus become a goal of social development and the mark of a civilized society.

In many respects, the United States is distinctive. For example, in contrast with most liberal democracies, the U.S. Constitution did not establish affirmative welfare rights or obligations. And, the structure of the U.S. welfare system—pensions, health insurance, etc.—is to a large degree privately organized. Economic development produces not only efficiency and growth but also market failures, socioeconomic and political conflict, and general economic insecurity. Social programs are needed to help individuals cope with the problems accruing with economic success. Seen from this perspective, welfare is not a gift to the lazy or unlucky; it is one of the defining characteristics of a modern society.

REVIEW EXERCISES

For Discussion and Debate

1. What would be some likely social consequences of a 50 percent reduction in the welfare payments in your community?
2. What is "workfare" and how does it fit into the Protestant Work Ethic we discussed in an earlier section?
3. Why would someone prefer to depend on welfare, rather than have a job? What evidence would you need to support your argument?
4. How does the payment of welfare, and other social programs to equalize people's life chances, actually help to maintain the existing system of inequality?

Writing Exercises

Write a brief (500-word) essay on one of the following topics:

1. "Welfare handouts kill people's desire to work hard and get ahead."
2. People have a natural desire to work as a means of expressing themselves and making contact with other people.
3. The tax system provides far more "handouts" to rich people than it does to poor people.
4. The development of social responsibility for the poor is a major step in human history.

Research Activities

1. Collect data on how three poor families and three middle-income families budget their income each month. What proportion, in each case, goes to food, shelter and other necessities?
2. Analyze three political speeches about poverty or the poor from the 1930s, showing what has (or hasn't) changed in the way politicians approach the topic.

3. Collect and compare information about the welfare benefits provided to poor families with two children in two American states and two foreign countries (e.g., Sweden, Japan, Nigeria). Explain the differences.
4. How do chronically unemployed people spend their time? Devise a research strategy for collecting data to answer that question. Time permitting, collect some data and analyze them.

SELECTED REFERENCES

Axinn, J. M. and A. E. Hirsch. 1993. "Welfare and the 'Reform' of Women." *Families in Society: The Journal of Contemporary Human Services* 74, 9 (Nov.): 563–572.

Beito, David T. 1993. "Mutual Aid, State Welfare, and Organized Charity: Fraternal Societies and the 'Deserving' and 'Undeserving' Poor, 1900–1930." *Journal of Policy History* 5, 4:419–434.

Beito, David T. 1997. "'This Enormous Army': The Mutual Aid Tradition of American Fraternal Societies before the Twentieth Century." *Social Philosophy and Policy* 14, 2 (Summer): 20–38.

Besharov, Douglas J. 1992. "Beware of Unintended Consequences: Too Many Questions Remain Unanswered." *Public Welfare* 50, 2 (Spring): 18–19.

Beverly, Creigs C. and Howard J. Stanback. 1986. "The Black Underclass: Theory and Reality." *Black Scholar* 17, 5 (Sept.–Oct.): 24–32.

Birdsall, Nancy, Allen C. Kelley and Steve Sinding, eds. 2001. *Population Matters: Demographic Change, Economic Growth, and Poverty in the Developing World.* Oxford: Oxford University Press.

Birdsall, Nancy, David Ross and Richard Sabot. 1995. "Inequality and Growth Reconsidered: Lessons from East Asia." *The World Bank Economic Review* 9, 3:477–508.

Bloom, Leslie Rebecca and Deborah Kilgore. 2003. "The Volunteer Citizen after Welfare Reform in the United States: An Ethnographic Study of Volunteerism in Action." *Voluntas: International Journal of Voluntary and Nonprofit Organizations* 14, 4 (Dec.): 431–454.

Christopher, Karen, Paula England, Timothy M. Smeeding and Katherine Ross Phillips. 2002. "The Gender Gap in Poverty in Modern Nations: Single Motherhood, the Market, and the State." *Sociological Perspectives* 45, 3:219–242.

Cushing, Brian J. 1993. "The Effect of the Social Welfare System on Metropolitan Migration in the U.S., by Income Group, Gender, and Family Structure." *Urban Studies* 30, 2 (Mar.): 325–338.

Dattalo, P. 1992. "The Gentrification of Public Welfare." *Social Work* 37, 5 (Sept.): 446–453.

Glazer, Nathan. 1990. "Is Welfare a Legitimate Government Goal?" *Critical Review* 4, 4 (Fall): 479–491.

Goodin, Robert E. 1993. "Moral Atrophy in the Welfare State." *Policy Sciences* 26, 2 (May): 63–78.

Goodin, Robert E. 2001. "Democratic Wealth, Democratic Welfare: Is Flux Enough?" *New Political Economy* 6, 1:67–79.

Gornick, Janet C. and Marcia K. Meyers. 2004. "Welfare Regimes in Relation to Paid Work and Care." *Advances in Life Course Research* 8:45–67.

Griffen, Sarah. 1992. "Poor Relations: The Backlash against Welfare Recipients." *Dollars and Sense* 176 (May): 6–8.

Gueron, Judith M. 1993. "Work for People on Welfare." *Public Welfare* 51, 1 (Winter): 39–41.

Headey, Bruce, Robert E. Goodin, Ruud Muffels and Henk-Jan Dirven. 2000. "Is There a Trade-Off Between Economic Efficiency and a Generous Welfare State? A Comparison of Best Cases of the Three Worlds of Welfare Capitalism." *Social Indicators Research* 50, 2:115–157.

Headey, Bruce, Stephen Headey, Ruud Muffels and Carla Janssen. 2004. "Who Enjoys the Fruits of Growth? Impact of Governments and Markets on Living Standards in Germany, the Netherlands, and the U.S.A., 1987–1996." *Social Indicators Research* 65, 2 (Jan.): 125–144.

Jensen, Leif, David J. Eggebeen and Daniel T. Lichter. 1993. "Child Poverty and the Ameliorative Effects of Public Assistance." *Social Science Quarterly* 74, 3 (Sept.): 542–559.

Karger, Howard Jacob. 1991. "The Global Economy and the American Welfare State." *Journal of Sociology and Social Welfare* 18, 3 (Sept.): 3–20.

Karger, Howard Jacob. 1999. "U.S. Welfare Reform and Its International Implications." *Social Development Issues* 21, 1:12–18.

Kerlin, A. E. 1993. "From Welfare to Work: Does It Make Sense?" *Journal of Sociology and Social Welfare* 20, 1 (Mar.): 71–85.

Korteweg, Anna C. 2003. "Welfare Reform and the Subject of the Working Mother: 'Get a Job, a Better Job, Then a Career.'" *Theory and Society* 32, 4:445–480.

Kutner, Nancy G. and Michael H. Kutner. 1987. "Ethnic and Residence Differences among Poor Families." *Journal of Comparative Family Studies* 18, 3 (Autumn): 463–470.

Liebmann, George W. 1993. "The AFDC Conundrum: A New Look at an Old Institution." *Social Work* 38, 1 (Jan.): 36–43.

Lobao, Linda and Gregory Hooks. 2003. "Public Employment, Welfare Transfers, and Economic Well-Being across Local Populations: Does a Lean and Mean Government Benefit the Masses?" *Social Forces* 82, 2 (Dec.): 519–556.

Marwell, Nicole P. 2004. "Privatizing the Welfare State: Nonprofit Community Organizations." *American Sociological Review* 69, 2:265–291.

May, Edgar. 1993. "Social Policy and the Poor: Fifty Years of Looking Ahead." *Public Welfare* 51, 1 (Winter): 32–34.

Moynihan, Daniel Patrick. 1989. "Toward a Postindustrial Social Policy." *Public Interest* 96 (Summer): 16–27.

Murray, C. 1992. "Discussing Welfare Dependency Is Irrelevant." *Public Welfare* 50, 2:24–25.

Northrop, Emily M. 1990. "The Feminization of Poverty: The Demographic Factor and the Composition of Economic Growth." *Journal of Economic Issues* 24, 1 (Mar.): 145–160.

Persons, Georgia. 2004. "National Politics and Charitable Choice as Urban Policy for Community Development." *The Annals of the American Academy of Political and Social Science* 594 (July): 65–78.

Rank, Mark R., Hong-Sik Yoon and Thomas A. Hirschl. 2003. "American Poverty as a Structural Failing: Evidence and Arguments." *Journal of Sociology and Social Welfare* 30, 4 (Dec.): 3–29.

Roy, Kevin M., Carolyn Y. Tubbs and Linda M. Burton. 2004. "Don't Have No Time: Daily Rhythms and the Organization of Time for Low-Income Families." *Family Relations* 53, 2 (Mar.): 168–178.

Stoesz, David. 1989. "A New Paradigm for Social Welfare." *Journal of Sociology and Social Welfare* 16, 2 (June): 127–150.

Stoesz, David. 1999. "Unraveling Welfare Reform." *Society* 36, 4 (240) (May/June): 53–61.

Svallforfs, Stefan. 2003. "Welfare Regimes and Welfare Opinions: A Comparison of Eight Western Countries." *Social Indicators Research* 64, 3 (Dec.): 495–520.

Vedder, Richard and Lowell Galloway. 1993. "Declining Black Employment." *Society* 30, 5 (205) (July–Aug.): 57–63.

Vedder, Richard and Lowell Galloway. 1999. "Wages, Profits, and Minority Businesses." *Society* 37, 1 (243) (Nov.): 88–92.

Zinn, Maxine Baca. 1989. "Family, Race, and Poverty in the Eighties." *Signs* 14, 4 (Summer): 856–874.

CHAPTER 5 ◄◄ ►► GLOBAL INEQUALITY

Global inequality—the economic and political inequality between different societies of the world—is signified by what social scientists call *imperialism* and *neoimperialism*—the exercise of political and economic control by one state over the territory of another, often by military means. Imperialism's purpose is to exploit the indigenous population and extract economic and political advantages.

Early European imperialism occurred through colonization, the settlement and administration of foreign lands. However, domination of a foreign land does not always require colonization. In fact, economic domination is far safer, less costly, and more stable. By gaining control of a nation's economy—whether through ownership of lands or industries, the purchase of stocks and bonds, or monopolistic control of key resources (e.g., a long term contract to buy all its oil, or cars, or wheat, or water at a certain price)—it is possible to control the political and social life of the country very effectively.

As colonialism has declined, a more subtle form of imperialism, neocolonialism, has become common. Under neocolonialism, core states exercise economic control over "peripheral" countries that are formally politically independent.

In this chapter we consider three issues associated with global inequality and imperialism. First, we ask whether it is likely, desirable, or even possible that all societies can develop economically in the same way, and hence catch up. Second, we consider the role of foreign aid as an instrument that some believe helps societies develop and others believe serves as a veiled form of imperialism. Third, we look at the need to go beyond economic development to human development and cultural liberties. Is democracy the answer?

5.1   Is Economic Development the Answer?

The issue: Historically, the West held itself up as the only or best model of modernization. All other paths were wrong. However, at the end of the twentieth century, the successes of Japan, Singapore, and China (among others) suggest that we may have to reevaluate our views of history and ourselves.

The arguments on the following pages deal with issues of *modernity* or *development*. We often talk about developed societies versus developing, or under-developed, or less developed, ones. All these terms imply that development is of a particular nature, and that it is good. One aim of this section is to reconsider these terms and their implications.

There are issues here about the structure and organization of government, about the technology available to a society, and about people's daily lives. Here we will be dealing not only with ideas of modernization or technology, but also ideas about bureaucracy, rationalism, and democratic government. The sociologist Max Weber raised the question, at the beginning of the twentieth century, of how religion, social structure, and bureaucracy were related. We are raising some similar points with regard to ideas about *culture* (rather than specifically religion) and *progress*.

A particular kind of development has led to Western society as we know it today. Is it the only possible kind of society, given the level of technology that we have? Has this development been universally "good"? Were other ways of developing equally possible? And, is there a difference between *economic* development and *human* development? To ask these questions is to recognize that however good a lifestyle most of us consider we have, there are always other possibilities. A further implication is that the current North American lifestyle may have disadvantages, and these disadvantages may accrue to different people than do the advantages. So we must ask: "In order for me to live as I do, does someone else have to pay a penalty?"

The three questions in this chapter are linked. First, should the countries of the poorer South develop economically, in the same way as those of the richer North? Or are there other ways to think about the global community?

ECONOMIC DEVELOPMENT IS THE KEY TO EQUALITY

The North-South debate is about tensions between the developed North and the less developed South. Basically in the rich North, people have a more affluent life-style, based on industry and on international trade. The main trading partners of North countries are other North countries. Obviously the terms North and South are a bit misleading—Australia is "North" in the sense of being developed, whereas Afghanistan, as a less developed economy torn apart by strife and war would be "South."

Poverty is both a social issue and a political issue. For all people to have a better standard of living, we need development. That includes economic structures, advanced technology, and western medicine, including reproductive technologies for fertility control. And, thankfully, because we know the history of those countries that went through the Industrial Revolution, we know what to avoid. Fast-track modernization is the answer, according to modernization theory.

The Nature of "Modernization Theory" The argument that all societies should develop in essentially the same way forms part of what is known as *modernization theory*. This theory looks at the technological development of Western societies such as the United States, Canada, Britain, and Germany, and at the history of how this technological development came about. This path of development—modernization—is seen as the way societies should go, or eventually will go, although modernization theorists acknowledge that some aspects of the development will vary. Some processes in Europe and North America took several centuries to evolve, but these same processes can be exported to "third world" countries in finished form. Health improvement through the use of Western medicine is an example here.

Modernization theory assumes that, until about two centuries ago, the entire world was poor. Some people were able to amass wealth, but overall the standards of living and life expectancies were low. Then something happened in the Western World— the Industrial Revolution. In short order, people could produce far more goods, and so live better. Knowledge increased at a vast rate, including knowledge of the human body and of how to treat illnesses, and modern medicine was born. People began to live longer, birth rates dropped, and as families became smaller, people were more able to care for and educate their children. As a result, they could obtain better jobs, create more knowledge, invent more things that people needed, and take their places in a prosperous, industrialized world.

There are large similarities among industrial societies that may or may not be "capitalist" in the traditional sense. For this reason, many sociologists believe that our society is now best described as an industrial society. The term *industrial society* refers not only to a society in which industrial (or mass) production prevails, but to a whole packet of associated features we consider basic to contemporary life. In the shift to an industrial society, subsistence farming disappears, the number of people in farming declines, and people produce for exchange with others—not their own consumption. Alongside mechanization, workers begin to produce goods in large factories, large machines increasingly assist production, jobs and workers become highly specialized, and the number of wage-laborers increases. Mechanization is also associated with urbanization: More people come to live in large cities, more people learn how to read and write, scientific research changes industrial production, and people become more concerned with efficiency.

In these respects, societies as different as the United States and China, Russia and Argentina, are all industrial societies. Whatever the political system or economic ideology, industrialization leads a society to develop the features listed above. Sociologists have spent a lot of time identifying these features of industrial society. The factors that lead societies to industrialize are so many and complex that we can only discuss three main ones here.

One key feature of industrial society is a concern with improving human capital. Human capital theorists are concerned with improving people's general well-being through better health, education, welfare, and public security. After all, they argue, people are key to creating wealth in an industrial order. Money invested in human well-being (that is, in human capital) is money invested in future economic growth.

Investment in human capital is expensive and slow in bringing expected payoffs; and such investment changes many parts of the economy and society in unexpected ways. One such change is the effect on class structure and the class struggle. Generally, an investment in human capital unsettles the population and mobilizes protest.

The rise of an industrial society also changes class relations: The "cash" relations replace customary feudal ties of mutual obligation. New social classes, especially the bourgeoisie and proletariat, emerge as a result. But the class structure changes in other ways, too. For example, industrialization pushes and pulls the rural peasantry into cities and factories. More and more peasants are forced off the land and into wage labor as landholdings become larger and privatized, producing cash crops rather than subsistence crops. Many of these peasants work part-time on the land and part-time in factories.

The contrasts between Canada and India, Brazil, or Nigeria point to differences between industrial societies (as a group) and nonindustrial or developing societies. Generally, industrial societies have (1) a secular culture focused on efficiency, consumerism, and a high standard of living, (2) a highly developed state that provides health, education, and welfare benefits to its citizens, and (3) a class structure dominated (numerically) by the urban, middle class.

As a result, there are important similarities between industrial societies like the United States and Japan, which, a century ago, had almost nothing in common. The growing similarity of industrial societies around the world has produced what sociologists call the *convergence thesis.* Supporters of this thesis argue that, as societies industrialize, their social patterns converge or become more similar, despite differences that existed before.

The convergence thesis is an important part of the theory of industrial society. It rests on the idea that industrialization gives rise to changes—like mass literacy, a nuclear family, and respect for the rule of law—that are linked to economic life. The linkages are easy to understand. For example, as people become literate, they become better informed, more politically active, and more eager to demand political liberties. The result is participatory democracy. Another common feature is the growth of a political rights-seeking middle class that manages large businesses. One emerged in Korea in the 1980s and another in Thailand in the 1990s. Similar changes seem to occur in *every* industrial society, though not always in the same sequence.

What is remarkable about convergence is the certainty of the process. The convergence thesis plays down capitalism as a crucial feature of economic life and puts industrial society in its place. It argues that what is important in world history is industrialism, not capitalism. With exceptions, non-Western experience has provided much support for the convergence thesis. Developing societies differ mainly in whether they merge selected "modern" ideas with their existing culture, as Japan has done, or rearrange their cultures around these ideas, like Singapore. Industrialization everywhere has certain key features, but it is not clear whether industrial societies converge because they must satisfy the same societal needs (e.g., for literacy) or because social practices spread from richer to poorer societies. There is evidence to support both views.

Development, in this paradigm, is a process of using science and technology to help achieve a higher quality of lifestyle, expressed as a higher standard of living. If people don't have enough to eat, or their harvests are at the mercy of extreme weather conditions, such as droughts that occur every few years, modern scientific agriculture can feed them. If life expectancy is low, modern medicine can extend it. If people have large families and cannot support all of their children, scientific birth control can help prevent large families, ensuring greater prosperity for those who are born. Some countries are more developed than others just now, yes, but those others can catch up. Some are catching up fast—India has now become the world's fifth largest economy (after the United States, China, Germany, and Britain).

The idea of *catching up* has been sought or promoted within both countries of the North, and governments of countries of the South, for half a century. In 1949 President Harry Truman, in his inaugural speech to Congress, for the first time defined as "underdeveloped areas" large sections of the world. This speech implied that all countries in the world were on the same track, but some had merely fallen behind in the race.

According to this perspective, technology and industrial advance have given the countries of the North a high, and increasing, standard of living, as measured by Gross Domestic Product (GDP)—that part of a nation's activities for which a monetary value can be compiled. The goods and services of modern life, so measured, contribute toward an enhanced quality of life for people within the society. Within a household, running water on tap, electricity and electrical appliances, and easily available food to cook in the appliances, all make it easier to care for a family. The availability of televisions, books, newspapers, and computer e-mail networks means that family members will be both informed

about their world and entertained. Synthetic fabrics mean that they can be inexpensively clothed to keep them warm in winter; modern building standards, heating devices, and air conditioning help keep them secure and healthy, even in extreme climatic conditions. Surely everyone should have such basic amenities—or should they?

Rostow's Stages of Economic Growth Modernization theory sees "catch-up" development as the goal, and foreign investment, aid, and loans to technological projects as the means to achieve it. Rostow's theory of stages of economic growth toward modernization spells out the stages of the way. Every country, Rostow claims, will necessarily go through the same five stages in the same sequence; these stages are as follows:

Stage 1: Traditional stage. A stagnant economy, with agricultural subsistence and craft industries.
Stage 2: Preconditions for take-off. Development of a market economy, with mining and cash crops for export, and the development of roads and railways. Society run by a political and business elite who have an "achievement orientation"—that is, are motivated toward modernization. Investment is around 5 percent of GNP.
Stage 3: Take-off stage. Investment rises to around 10 percent of GNP. Manufacturing industries start to grow, and social, institutional, and political structures arise that favor development.
Stage 4: Drive to Maturity. This involves urbanization, mass public education, and high investment and growth in all sectors of the economy.
Stage 5: High mass consumption stage. The country now has an economy similar to those of "advanced" nations, with the availability of a wide range of consumer durables (such as kitchen appliances) and services. Its international importance is established.

Some societies have been able to move more quickly along this path than others. Those that were able to emphasize manufacturing have moved faster than those that emphasized the provision of services or exported raw materials. Critics of the theory have pointed, however, to imbalances in modernization as a drawback in many cases, saying that agricultural development must parallel that in manufacturing or the pace is slowed. Many economists have moved away from the absolute lineal stages that Rostow outlined, emphasizing instead that countries show similar (rather than identical) patterns of development—and pointing to ways to shortcut the process to allow for catching up. What Rostow's model does is point to the importance of investment. This is one way that the North has helped the South develop.

ECONOMIC DEVELOPMENT ISN'T THE ONLY STORY

Does an overall emphasis on technology and "catching up" work? Consider an example: In the 1960s, the "Green Revolution" promised food for the world's hungry. Large areas of Pakistan and India (notably the Punjab), and parts of Africa, were planted with Western-developed, high-yield varieties of wheat and rice. These grains were "heavy feeders," requiring the application of chemical fertilizers to the soil, which in turn required machinery to apply them. They also required large-scale irrigation projects to provide steady moisture levels. Because one strain of wheat or rice would be planted over large tracts of land, there was an increased risk that the crop might be wiped out by an attack of insects or diseases, so chemical pesticides and fungicides were also required.

Some farmers did well with this, doubling or tripling yields. However, many small farmers could not afford the chemicals and equipment. Also, over a period of twenty years, the fertility of the soil gradually declined. By the mid-eighties, a number of communities in Bangladesh were attempting to return to the indigenous varieties of grain their ancestors had farmed. While these might yield smaller harvests, they were more reliable, less prone to insect attack, and required fewer chemicals to grow.

At the same time, attempts were being made to encourage the use of western contraceptives and sterilization, to lower birth rates. However, these had only a limited impact: Few people made consistent use of them. Thus, any advantages gained from the use of high-yield crops were cancelled out by population increases.

Modernization theory assumes that changes to the structure and culture of South countries—making them more like so-called North countries—will enrich the countries and their people, after a Western industrial pattern. But in the example we just considered, there was no net gain from modernization. In other cases, change has even resulted in impoverishment. This is most likely to happen when too little attention is paid to cultural or social conditions that limit or pervert the use of Western technology and productive practices. For example, Western models assume individual, or corporate, ownership of land. An assumption of colonists and policy makers has been that this ownership will be by males in a family. But in many peasant societies, extended families or lineage groups "own" land that is worked by women. These women have, therefore, rights to work land and to control their own land parcels. Land reform programs make use of the male "head of family" concept, so that ownership becomes removed from the women—the people who are using land to produce food for their own and their families' consumption.

An example comes from the Gambia. In 1984, village headmen had leased the women's land, along with unused swamp land, to the Gambian government, for a multi-million-dollar rice-growing project. The plan was to make the land productive. However, the headmen had also leased the land on which women grew rice crops to feed their families, and the women were prohibited from growing their rice, being promised food aid while the land was bulldozed and re-apportioned. Fifteen hundred acres of ripened rice crop were bulldozed. In the end, crops were lost but far more important than that, Western aid was used to deprive women of *de facto* control of farming land. In this way it made relations between men and women far less "modern" than they had been before.

The Demographic Transition   We are often told, in America, that the world has a population problem, but that the problem resides in other countries, not the countries of the North (or the industrialized West). Previously we discussed the idea that there is a "population explosion" that is taxing the resources of the earth and must be controlled. In line with this thinking, aid programs of countries of the North are often tied to requirements for underdeveloped countries to promote birth control programs, with, however, limited success, as we have seen.

Demographers who have studied the composition of the population in Europe and North America during the eighteenth and nineteenth centuries, warn that popular thinking on this issue may be upside-down. In Europe 200 years ago, families of nine, eleven, thirteen, and even twenty children were not unknown; however, many of these children would die in childhood or even infancy. Children who survived were the support of their parents in later life, and contributed to the family income as economic producers from their childhood on. In the towns of England and France it was common for working-class townswomen to be engaged in paid jobs when their children were too small to contribute economically, but to leave their jobs to become household managers when the children entered the paid workforce.

Soon, all that was to change. In the nineteenth century, child labor laws and compulsory education meant that children became expensive to raise: net consumers, not net producers. At the same time, better nutrition resulting from a greater availability of food meant that women, children, and men were healthier. Fewer children died in infancy. (This predated, and so should not be attributed to, modern medicine and standards of medical hygiene.) The birth rate dropped even before modern contraceptives were available. And once these became available they were widely used, as they made it possible for people to plan their childbearing. Delays in legalizing contraceptives, such as the diaphragm or the cervical cap, were due to the pro-natalist policies of legislators and governments who saw declining fertility as a problem, not a blessing. However, regardless of the methods of birth control used, the population went through a demographic transition.

History (and demographic transition theory) shows that, in Europe, lower rates of childbearing followed after (and were associated with) more security and a higher likelihood of children's survival. Materialists (that is, Marxists and other conflict theorists) have concluded from this that

when people have enough to eat—so that they are reasonably sure their children will not die—they are motivated to produce fewer children. It is the practicalities of life—having food and security—that come first and influence people's ideas and opinions about how many children to have.

Some believe that this analysis contradicts modernization theory, which urges others to be like people in the West: "Have fewer children and you will prosper." In other words, modern behavior will follow from the adoption of modern values, and an improved standard of living will follow from modern behavior. However, other researchers consider that both demographic transition theory and modernization theory agree on one thing: the importance of technology and industrialization.

Is Technology Really the Key?   Why did people in Europe start to have better levels of nutrition and lower levels of childbearing? Was it really all due to technology?

The eighteenth and nineteenth centuries were centuries of European colonial expansion. People were going out from Europe to other parts of the world, and claiming these for Germany or Britain or France, among others. We think of this, often, in terms of colonial administrators, people with education going to "the colonies" to make a name for themselves. However, many of the people who left Europe were poor, and many of these did not leave of their own volition. Social changes in Europe had created millions of landless people whose ancestors were peasants, but whose land had been claimed by large-scale landowners.

An example is the Highland Clearances in Scotland. Landowners considered it more to their advantage to push out the peasants who had worked small farms for generations, and turn the land over to sheep-grazing. Many of the displaced peasants headed for the cities, where they became workers in the factories emerging under the new system of capitalism. Others headed for the colonies: In the case of the Highland Clearances, they went to what would become Canada and the Eastern United States. Other impoverished immigrants flooded into Australia, Southern Africa, and other parts of the previously non-European world.

Colonial practices were to turn these poverty-stricken immigrants into European-style farmers and miners, providers of resources and raw materials for the "home" countries; but the demographic transition theory does not mention the people they displaced from the lands they came to.

Not all of these colonized indigenous people were farmers. In what is today Bangladesh, colonial administrators found a thriving cotton textile industry, with its own patterns and styles of weaving and embroidery, and its own markets, built up over centuries of trading. The textile industry in Britain was in crisis, and displaced crofters and peasants were flooding into Britain's textile towns looking for work. The British government's solution was to collect textile patterns and send people to learn weaving skills, then to close down the indigenous textile industries while supporting the weaving of these same patterns within factories in Britain. The famous Paisley pattern comes from the Indian sub-continent, but gets its name from the Scottish town whose weavers learned to create its delicate designs and weave them into expensive shawls. These, made for the high-fashion market in Europe and its colonies, were even exported back to the Indian sub-continent for the wives and daughters of colonial administrators to wear.

Part of the prosperity of nineteenth-century Europe, therefore, should be traced to its habit of exporting poverty along with its manufactured products. It was this export of poverty, as much as technological change, which led to the growth of wealth in industrial Europe.

The Politics and Economics of "Catching Up"

So, the wealth of the North, and the relative poverty of the South, can be traced back historically. The branch of social theory that looks at this historical tendency is *dependency theory*, initially put forward by the Argentinian economist Ral Prebisch. It isn't that some societies became developed and others didn't. The economic and political mechanisms of colonialism had already "developed" the countries of the South—that is, developed them as dependencies that were *peripheral* to the countries that made up the *center* of the global economic system. Can these countries catch up now?

Rostow's stages of economic growth model doesn't accommodate this fact. For example, where on Rostow's scale would we place a country that pays out in debt interest more than it takes in through trade and aid—regardless of the motivation of its economic elite? And where in his theory do international agencies such as the World Bank or the IMF enter the picture? Yet in the late twentieth century these concerns were crucial and some countries were so crippled by debt that, for some, the only solution was *debt forgiveness.*

After a half-century of intensive global development, the gap between "front-runners and stragglers" had not been bridged; on the contrary, it had widened. As a result, today the populous Southern countries make only a small contribution to the world's economic productivity, at least as it's reckoned by GNP. But can that contribution increase?

Some countries—prime examples are in southeast Asia and include Japan, China, South Korea, Hong Kong, and Taiwan—have been able to achieve success in the catching-up endeavor. Others—especially in Africa, Latin America, and the Middle East—have either fallen further behind, or become single resource providers, tied into the world economic system by being providers of scarce goods on which the center countries are in turn dependent. The chief of these resources is oil. And if we look within countries to the people who live in them, we often find more extreme changes. Even if economic elites have indeed been "developed," the living conditions of the majority of the people have worsened. (Prime examples of this are to be found in Russia and the formerly communist countries of eastern Europe.) This may go along with an apparent increase in GNP and in the average standard—though not the quality—of living.

To understand these discrepancies and variations, we have to look at ways in which people make their living. A small-scale farmer may be able to grow crops to feed her family for part of the year, while she and other family members also engage in craft industry. However, her farming activities do not count as part of the country's GDP, nor do craft activities provide materials for household use. The GDP tallies only activities that result in items for sale. If the family is forced off the land—for instance by a dam construction project—and moves to the city, it develops greater dependence on being able to buy food and other necessary items. Such transactions (if not conducted on the black market) *do* appear in GDP statistics, but the quality of life of the family may have suffered greatly in the meantime.

Thus the GDP—the so-called standard of living—may be low even if families are secure and doing reasonably well; it may rise even when families are less secure and suffering a decline in their "quality of life."

The question is, does catching up mean increasing the standard of living or the quality of life? And who supports each outcome? Poor farmers and displaced peasants—who would tend to support the latter—have little voice on either a national or a global level; so the call remains from the South, as in the North, for more development, more catching up—a higher nominal standard of living. Development experts and national elites tend to believe that only "the economy" matters, whatever the impact of economic change on actual quality of life.

SUMMING UP

Is economic development, after the model of the North, the answer? Not necessarily.

Many of the development advantages we associate with technology may be linked with advantages due to colonialism. Likewise, many of the disadvantages we associate with less-developed societies may also be due to colonialism and later neo-colonialism. The evidence suggests that there are many different paths to economic development. People adopt new technologies when they can afford to: when the technologies are available and pose little risk to their economic well-being.

Improved material conditions are attractive to everybody—but not all adoptions of new technologies have led to advances in living conditions.

Also, assuming that cultural change is needed before development is possible is a wrong reading of the evidence. Moreover, history shows us that a single development model is culturally destructive, as we have seen with the example of the Gambian women farmers. There is a profound danger in convincing people that they must re-adjust the relations of men to women, old to young, or individuals to families before economies can begin to grow. As we are seeing in Eastern Europe, the risks to social cohesion—even law and order—are very great.

Finally, what are we to learn from the European experience that can be useful in today's developing countries? If Europe "developed" by exporting its poverty, can India do this today? Where is left to colonize? Who, in this age of globally available nuclear weapons, can be safely overrun? The age of imperial solutions to local economic problems is (nearly) at an end. And even if it weren't, none of today's less developed countries would be in a position to exercise these options. Today's less developed countries cannot and will not develop in the very same way that Western Europe and the Untied States did a century ago.

This discussion has pointed to some further questions. If we need different kinds of development, what are these? What about sustainability? What about the problem of having enough oil? What about investment—where can it come from? How can people have more say in what is to happen to them—human rather than only economic development? Some of these issues will be further addressed in the following sections, and others in the chapters on Social Change.

REVIEW EXERCISES

For Discussion and Debate

1. "Technology will always get us out of a fix."
2. "If people in the third world didn't grow so many cash crops, we wouldn't have our coffee."
3. "Some countries can only catch up if others will slow down."
4. "Getting ahead—on a global basis—is the name of the game."

Writing Exercises

Write a brief (500-word) essay on one of the following topics:

1. Are there different meanings of economic "development"?
2. How women farmers in the Gambia could win back their farmlands from a government project.
3. Your description of an ideal development project that would benefit everyone concerned.
4. "How I see links between population and prosperity."

Research Activities

1. Conduct some research on your own family history and background. Find a group of people, in any part of the world, that you are descended from. How did industrialization and/or colonialism affect this group? (Were they benefited, disbenefited, or was there a combination of effects?) From this, how has industrialization and/or colonialism affected who you are today?
2. Work with a group of your friends to list ways in which you are connected with countries of the "South." (Hint: Look at your family histories, but also think of the foods you eat, the clothes you wear, and the music you listen to.)
3. Interview ten people about what *global development* means to them. Analyze their ideas in terms of the competing paradigms presented in this section.
4. Collect media items on development, and examine the ideas presented. Analyze these ideas in terms of the competing paradigms presented in this section. How do they compare with the opinions of the people you interviewed?

SELECTED REFERENCES

Arnould, Eric J. 1989. "Anthropology and West African Development: A Political Economic Critique and Auto-Critique." *Human Organization* 48, 2 (Summer): 135–148.

Barry, Frank. 1991. "Industrialization Strategies for Developing Countries: Lessons from the Irish Experience." *Development Policy Review* 9, 1 (Mar.): 85–98.

Cavanagh, John and Sarah Anderson, eds. 2002. *Alternatives to Economic Globalization: A Better World Is Possible.* International Forum on Globalization.

Chirot, D. 2001. "A Clash of Civilizations or of Paradigms? Theorizing Progress and Social Change." *International Sociology* 16, 3:341–360.

Cole, Sam. 1994. "A Conflict of Visions: Reflections on African Futures Studies." *Futures* 26, 3 (Apr.): 259–274.

Council of Europe. 2004. "North-South Centre." European Centre for Global Interdependence and Solidarity. Available online at http://www.coe.int/T/E/North-South_Centre/. Accessed 6 November.

Crocker, David A. 1991. "Toward Development Ethics." *World Development* 19, 5 (May): 457–483.

Dickens, David R. 1989. "The Relevance of Domestic Traditions in the Development Process: Iran, 1963–1979." *International Journal of Contemporary Sociology* 26, 1–2 (Jan.–Apr.): 55–70.

Evans, Peter B. and Paulo Bastos Tigre. 1989. "Going Beyond Clones in Brazil and Korea: A Comparative Analysis of NIC Strategies in the Computer Industry." *World Development* 17, 11 (Nov.): 1751–1768.

Evers, Hans Dieter and Solvay Gerke. 1992. "The Culture of Planning: Transmigration Area Development in East Kalimantan, Indonesia." *International Sociology* 7, 2 (June): 141–151.

Gordon, April. 1989. "The Myth of Modernization and Development." *Sociological Spectrum* 9, 2 (Spring): 175–195.

Martinelli, Alberto. 2003. "Markets, Governments, Communities and Global Governance." *International Sociology* 18:291–323.

Manzo, Kate. 1991. "Modernist Discourse and the Crisis of Development Theory." *Studies in Comparative International Development* 26, 2 (Summer): 3–36.

Mies, Maria, and Vandana Shiva. 1993. *Ecofeminism.* London: Zed Books.

Mukhopadhyay, Sudhin K. 1994. "Adapting Household Behavior to Agricultural Technology in West Bengal, India: Wage Labor, Fertility, and Child Schooling Determinants." *Economic Development and Cultural Change* 43, 1 (Oct.): 91–115.

Mytelka, Lynn Krieger. 1993. "Rethinking Development: A Role for Innovation Networking in the 'Other Two-thirds.'" *Futures* 25, 6 (July–Aug.): 694–712.

Parsonage, James. 1992. "Southeast Asia's 'Growth Triangle': A Subregional Response to Global Transformation." *International Journal of Urban and Regional Research* 16, 2 (June): 307–317.

Pattnayak, Satya R. 1992. "Integrating Liberal-Pluralist and Dependency Perspectives of Development at Specific Levels of State Capacity." *International Review of Modern Sociology* 22, 2 (Autumn): 87–101.

Philip, George. 1990. "The Political Economy of Development." *Political Studies* 38, 3 (Sept.): 485–501.

Prigoff, Arline. 1991. "Women, Social Development, and the State in Latin America: An Empowerment Model." *Social Development Issues* 14, 1 (Fall): 56–70.

Quaye, Randolph. 1991. "Planning the Health Care System in a Decade of Economic Decline: The Ghanaian Experience." *Crime, Law and Social Change* 16, 3 (Nov.): 303–311.

Schulman, Michael D. and Sheila R. Cotton. 1993. "Adaptations to the Farm Crisis: Macro Level Implications of Micro Level Behaviors." *Applied Behavioral Science Review* 1, 1:93–111.

Shenhaw, Yehouda A. and David H. Kamens. 1991. "The 'Costs' of Institutional Isomorphism: Science in Non-Western Countries." *Social Studies of Science* 21, 3 (Aug.): 527–545.

Sutton, Francis X. et al. 1989. "Development Ideology: Its Emergence and Decline." *Daedalus* 118, 1 (Winter): 35–58.

Tabb, William K. 1999. "Progressive Globalism: Challenging the Audacity of Capital." *Global Policy Forum.* Available online at http://www.globalpolicy.org/globaliz/define/progglob.htm. Accessed 6 November.

Tenbruck, Friedrich H. 1990. "The Dream of a Secular Ecumene: The Meaning and Limits of Policies of Development." *Theory, Culture and Society* 7, 2–3 (June): 193–206.

Tilley, Louise A. and Joan W. Scott. 1978. *Women, Work and Family.* New York: Holt, Rinehart and Winston.

Waring, Marilyn. 1990. *If Women Counted.* San Francisco, CA: HarperCollins.

Weede, Erich. 1993. "The Impact of Military Participation on Economic Growth and Income Inequality: Some New Evidence." *Journal of Political and Military Sociology* 21, 2 (Winter): 241–258.

Wolf, Martin. 2004. "Globalization and Global Economic Governance." *Oxford Review of Economic Policy* 20, 1:72–84.

Woo, Myung Oc. 1993. "Export Promotion in the New Global Division of Labor: The Case of the South Korean Automobile Industry." *Sociological Perspectives* 36, 4 (Winter): 335–357.

Woolsey, R. James. 2004. "Implications of U.S. Dependence on Middle Eastern Oil." *Policywatch Special Policy Forum Report.* Available online at http://www.washingtoninstitute.org/watch/Policywatch/policywatch2004/882.html.

5.2   Does Western "Aid" Actually Help?

The issue: Continued neediness in much of the southern hemisphere has clashed head to head with a growing withdrawal from aid-giving by the Western industrial nations. For the West, is aid-giving still a useful economic tool? Is it still a useful political tool? Is it ever with no strings attached?

There are two main kinds of "aid": public governmental aid and private charity aid. In practice, the two are not completely separate: Charities may work with governments, and are subject to government regulation, in both donor and recipient countries. And governmental aid may be given to projects supervised or organized by charities.

It seems self-evident that aid, whether from a state or from a charity, must make things better. Aid, after all, is aid. If I have no food today and you feed me, I am better off. I am no longer hungry, and perhaps tomorrow I will find work and so be able to feed myself, especially if you can tell me where the likely jobs are to be found.

Modernization theory looks to aid to assist with the modernizing of underdeveloped countries. It is through aid from wealthier states that new projects can be developed and old ones maintained; that work can be created for people; and that the effects of natural disasters, such as drought, can be alleviated. Finally, it is through aid that the recipient countries will become able to "catch up" to the donors in technology and standard of living.

It would seem on the face of it, then, that aid is an altogether good thing, at least from the standpoint of the recipient. Why then do we find criticisms of many aid programs and suspicion about the motives of many donors? Let's begin by considering how and why we think that aid is, generally, a good thing.

AID DOES MAKE THINGS BETTER

We have already considered why aid might be beneficial to countries that receive it. What about the donors? Aid is a cost to the donor nations and has to be justified to taxpayers by the governments that give it. But it has its benefits also. The giving of aid strengthens international links between nations, friendships, and bonds of mutual support. By helping create a prosperous economy in a previously "underdeveloped" state, the donor country creates a trading partner, a market for its own goods and services and a source of other goods and services that its people can purchase. Finally, by helping countries with their problems of poverty, disease, and unemployment, the donor country can prevent strife and conflict. Aid, therefore, helps create a more stable world.

Now, let's turn this picture 180 degrees and look at it again. You know from your own experience that giving gifts establishes a bond between the donor and recipient. At the least, it establishes a need for reciprocity, and reciprocating a gift may be difficult if one of the parties to the transaction is significantly poorer than another. It may be even

more difficult if there are strings attached to the gift—conditions defining when the return gift is expected and, even, roughly what it should be.

Some gifts require very expensive upkeep; imagine we give you a pet leopard and you have to feed it fifty pounds of fresh meat every day. Our gift of a pet pony will force you to find it a stable and space to run around. Other gifts are transparently self-serving: Imagine that we give you tickets for one of a dozen movies to be shown at our theatre. More likely than not, you will end up bringing someone and having to pay for the extra ticket, and that's money in our pockets.

Again, you can look at this in a positive or negative way. It's nice to get gifts: pet leopards, ponies, tickets to movies. On the other hand, it's a bother and a cost to have to pay them back, keep them up, or pay for peripherals. Believe it or not, these are the very same problems that arise when rich countries provide aid to poorer, less developed countries.

AID IS NOT NECESSARILY BENEFICIAL

Who Benefits from Aid?   The giving of aid can be seen as a self-interested behavior that increases the wealth and power of the donor nation. How can that be?

First, the giving of foreign aid creates bonds of dependency. For example, a recipient nation may be obliged to support (i.e., defend) its donor nation in international conflicts, for fear of losing the aid. Second, the donor country creates a *trading partner* that is bound to buy goods from the donor country, and that will serve as a cheap source of raw materials. Third, by helping countries with their problems of poverty, disease, and unemployment, the donor can prevent people within the country from attempting to develop other systems of government that might threaten the existing world order, and prevent the recipient nation from forming loyalties elsewhere.

These are the key tenets of *dependency theory,* a counter to modernization theory proposed by political economists, notably by Andre Gunder Frank from the earlier work of Prebisch and others. These theorists say that modernization theory, with its focus on development aid, ignores the problem of how nonindustrial countries of the South developed historically to become what they are today. Frank argues that these states are neither developed nor undeveloped, but are deliberately *under*developed to create dependency on the capitalist donor nations. The destruction of the textile industry of the Indian subcontinent, discussed in Chapter 14, is an example of this deliberate underdevelopment. Under both mercantile and imperial colonialism, countries or regions were exploited for their raw materials. Their political and economic structures were dismantled. Infrastructures were designed for the convenience of the host county and the administrators. In many parts of Africa, roads lead to the nearest port, to facilitate export of raw materials, instead of to other parts of Africa along the old trade routes.

In the present day, colonial empires have been dismantled but economic dependence, referred to as neo-imperialism, remains. The South remains a source of raw materials for the North. Now, also, the South is becoming a source of cheap labor. Multinational corporations, with their headquarters in the United States, Germany, England, Canada, or Japan, control large sectors of the economies of countries of the South. Through economic links and pressures, they also control many of the economic policies of the North, including aid-granting policies.

Workers in the South are employed by multinationals to make goods for sale in the North—such as computer components or shoes—often at low rates of pay. Call centers are another example. Prime agricultural land is used to grow cash crops such as coffee and sugar cane, which deplete soils.

Against this economic backdrop, foreign aid can be given for several reasons. One is pure philanthropy, and there can be no doubt that many of the people who advocate giving aid are indeed moved by philanthropy. But there are other reasons, as indicated above. Of these, commercial reasons take precedence. Much foreign aid is just a way of creating a market or hooking customers. Much of the aid money is spent within the country of origin on materials to be sent overseas, and on the buying of expert services, creating many jobs.

When this aid reaches its intended recipients, it requires further expertise to administer, operate, and maintain. Provision of tractors for an agricultural project, for example, means that later the recipients will have to buy tractor parts. Provision of seeds through the Green Revolution programs resulted in demands for chemical pesticides and fertilizers. In consequence, the net cost of foreign aid to the donor country may be zero or *less*.

Despite foreign aid programs, the net flow of funds is from South to North, not the other way. Dependencies created through imperial colonialism, mercantile colonialism, and neoimperialism result in a reliance on Northern equipment and expertise. After all, large-scale projects are expensive to run. In theory, loans have to be repaid. But in practice, international North-South loans are not repaid but serviced—that is, the loan-givers continue to collect interest on them. Further loans under the auspices of the World Bank and the International Monetary Fund (IMF) go either toward debt servicing, or for projects designed to further exports, to gain foreign currency to pay that loan interest. The goal of creating communities that are self-sufficient, that grow their own food and manufacture their own textiles from locally grown materials, is not in line with the goals of the IMF, which are to further international trade.

Much of the "aid" sent by countries of the North, therefore, goes to further dependency, including loan-dependency. An example of the movement of funds from South to North is Brazil, which between 1979 and 1985 paid $69 billion in debt repayments, being deeper in debt at the end of the period than at the start. As a result, local conditions often worsen: "In the 1960s, a third of Brazilians suffered from malnutrition; in the 1980s, after 20 years of IMF-inspired development, two thirds did" (Engler 1995:135).

Is Aid Always Wrong?   Almost everyone agrees that there are times—droughts, floods, disasters—when immediate, on-the-spot aid in the form of food, clothing, and other relief supplies may be crucial to saving lives. There have, however, been debates, even here, about how much of the aid reaches its intended recipients. If some is diverted, not only does it not benefit the people most in need, but also it may directly undercut the market sales of small-scale local producers, forcing them into bankruptcy and so out of production, resulting in later food shortages. However, this is not a reason to deny help in a grave crisis situation. It is a reason for countries that provide food aid to attempt to monitor how it is used, to listen to the voices of local people in need, and to work with local distribution networks.

We can regard other situations in the same way. Modernization theory holds that aid is a way countries of the North can assist those of the South in technological development. Dependency theory counters that aid works to maintain dependence and to get countries of the South deeper into debt. Each defines the terms of the argument in different ways. We can try to take another view of this question by asking, "Are there types of aid that work, and, if so, what are they?"

Useful Aid   Here we have to define what we mean by "work." Whose standards are we adopting? Some aid-administering organizations take the view that aid has to make things better on a small-scale, local level, in ways that are not environmentally destructive, and in ways that will last when the aid-granting agency is no longer present. In other words, aid should not encourage debt, though it may encourage local trade. The aid is to help communities become self-sufficient.

However, this may have unforeseen consequences. Previously we mentioned the Green Revolution. Its dependence on expensive chemical fertilizers and imported seeds and machinery meant that agricultural aid was given to owners of medium-sized or large farms. Many small-scale peasant farmers in Bangladesh lost their land. Recently, workers paid by North American charitable agencies have been assisting peasants in founding cooperatives and gaining title to land. They have also assisted in finding seeds of indigenous varieties of grain and helping local communities establish their own seed banks. Workers have assisted in developing composting facilities, so that the dependence on imported fertilizer is lessened. Most important, these workers have been assisting, not as directors,

but as facilitators. A project supervisor states that there is no point in trying to impose ideas from outside. The ideas must come from the local community members, or they will be jettisoned when the charity workers leave.

The aim of such aid is to provide expertise (including political and legal expertise) and cover start-up costs so that communities can develop their own technologies and self-sufficiency. Other examples include small-scale health initiatives that rely on training local people in the provision of basic health services—midwifery, diagnosis of childhood ailments, rehydration techniques, contraceptive techniques. There is an emphasis on "appropriate technology," or working with what is available locally. Rather than nuclear power plants, for example, these projects promote the local building of solar ovens.

A charge often heard against foreign aid is that it takes money from poor people in rich countries, and gives it to rich people in poor ones. Many charitable organizations, such as Oxfam or Inter Pares or the Unitarian Service Committee, attempt to show that this is not so by working directly with peasant farmers. They may find that this is not always easy to do. Governments control access to regions of the country, and peasant farmers generally have little political power. And even established plans can go awry when events such as currency devaluation, dictated by the IMF, intervene.

Here's another example of a plan that went awry: Villages in the Kigoma region of Tanzania were to receive oxen to assist them in ploughing their fields to grow their corn and beans. The oxen would make a tremendous difference to the amount they could grow. Oxfam had budgeted for eight oxen and their necessary veterinary supplies. But between the time the farmers received the grant and went to purchase their oxen, the price of the animals—like the price of just about everything else in Tanzania—had risen. Instead of eight animals, they could afford to buy only six. Worse, some supplies—such as pumps for spraying the oxen to kill deadly ticks, and medicines for protection against the tsetse fly—were not available at all. These medicines are essential to the animals' survival, but like most veterinary supplies, they must be imported. To conserve funds needed to pay its foreign debt, the government imposed restrictions on these and other desperately needed imports. So in the end, the aided villagers received neither enough oxen, nor the medicines needed to keep them alive. Who's to blame?

SUMMING UP

Does Western aid actually help? It depends on the kind of help given and the strings that are attached. Foreign aid, which seems on the face of it such a good idea, does not always have the effect we would wish. Aid for large scale projects—immense river dams or nuclear power plants, for example—often binds the recipient nation into long-running dependencies that result in more, not less, debt. These large-scale projects often leave thousands of people homeless (or destined for "resettlement" on land of doubtful agricultural value). The effectiveness of aid is measured in dollar values or increases to Gross National Product (GNP), which means that aid that results in transnational trade (through growing cash crops) counts as effective, whereas aid that acts to make families more able to feed themselves appears ineffective as these peasants no longer have to buy their food!

When there is a call for emergency aid—for example, for famine relief in the case of floods and droughts—North Americans do respond. Vast amounts of money are collected and sent off. This shows that large numbers of people in North America do believe they should try to help people in other parts of the world. They would like their aid dollars to be effective.

Sociologists can help by making the public aware of the problems associated with aid and its administration. We can draw the public's attention to successful aid programs. We can educate people about the role of the IMF and GATT. We can attempt to ensure that governmental aid programs become accountable not only to the IMF, but to an aware, involved, and educated voting public, who evaluate aid on its effectiveness in human terms, not GNP. Most importantly, we can help to create foreign aid programs that really "make things better."

REVIEW EXERCISES

For Discussion and Debate

1. "Foreign aid workers shouldn't tell people what to do, they should just help them find the means to do it."
2. "The biggest problem faced by countries of the South isn't poverty—it's the countries of the North."
3. Food crops versus cash crops? Debate this by dramatizing a scene of villagers who grow traditional food crops, government representatives who wish them to grow cash crops for export, and aid workers (who may take either side).
4. "Let the politicians look after the global development picture. We're too busy looking after ourselves."

Writing Exercises

Write a brief (500-word) essay on one of the following topics:

1. A week in the life of an overseas aid worker.
2. "Why I give or do not give money to foreign aid charities."
3. A week in the life of a village where a new development program has just been announced.
4. A cooperative textiles project in a country of the South.

Research Activities

1. Examine statistics on foreign aid for the last 40 years. How much aid is sent, and what percentage is this of GNP? Attempt to find the countries that have chiefly benefited from this aid.
2. Conduct a detailed study of one charitable organization that is involved with overseas aid. Find out how money is gathered, what proportion of it is sent to projects, and how a typical project is administered.
3. Locate a movie that describes an aid project, and watch this. Remember that the project will be differently described and analyzed depending on who is making and funding the movie.
4. With a group of four to six other students, plan and conduct a survey of people's attitudes toward foreign aid projects: Do people see these as beneficial to this country and to the recipient countries?

SELECTED REFERENCES

Anderson, Mary B. and Peter J. Woodrow. 1991. "Reducing Vulnerability to Drought and Famine: Developmental Approaches to Relief." *Disasters* 15, 1 (Mar.): 43–54.

Aslund, Anders. 1992. "Russia's Road from Communism." *Daedalus* 121, 2 (Spring): 77–95.

Bohning, W. R. 1994. "Helping Migrants to Stay at Home." *Annals of the American Academy of Political and Social Science* 534 (July): 165–177.

Bradshaw, York W. and Jie Huang. 1991. "Intensifying Global Dependency: Foreign Debt, Structural Adjustment, and Third World Underdevelopment." *Sociological Quarterly* 32, 3 (Fall): 321–342.

Britan, Gerald M. 1991. "The Future of Foreign Assistance." *Studies in Third World Societies* 44 (Apr.): 1–12.

Bryceson, Deborah Fahy. 1994. "Trade Roots in Tanzania: Evolution of Urban Grain Markets under Structural Adjustment." *Sociologia Ruralis* 34, 1:13–25.

Carty, R. 1982. "Giving for Gain: Foreign Aid and CIDA." In *Ties that Bind: Canada and the Third World,* edited by R. Clarke and R. Swift. Toronto: Between the Lines.

Edwards S. 2003. "Debt Relief and the Current Account: An Analysis of the HIPC Initiative." *The World Economy* 26, 4:513–531.

Engler, Allan. 1995. *Apostles of Greed.* London: Pluto Press.

Frank, Andre Gunder. 1972. "Sociology of Development and the Underdevelopment of Sociology." In *Dependence and Underdevelopment: Latin America's Political Economy,* edited by J. D. Cockcroft, A. G. Frank and D. L. Johnson. New York: Doubleday.

Frideres, James S. et al. 1993. "From Peasants to Capitalists." *Community Development Journal* 28, 2 (Apr.): 129–140.

Gaydos, Joel C. and George A. Luz. 1994. "Military Participation in Emergency Humanitarian Assistance." *Disasters* 18, 1 (Mar.): 48–57.

George, Susan. 1989. *A Fate Worse than Debt.* London: Penguin.

Green, Marshall. 1993. "The Evolution of U.S. International Population Policy, 1965–1992: A Chronological Account." *Population and Development Review* 19, 2 (June): 303–321.

Hanlon, Joseph. 1991. *Mozambique: Who Calls the Shots?* Bloomington, IN: Indiana University Press.

Hoogvelt, A. M. 1976. *The Sociology of Developing Societies.* London: Macmillan.

Ihonvbere, Julius O. 1992. "The Military and Political Engineering under Structural Adjustment: The Nigerian Experience since 1985." *Journal of Political and Military Sociology* 20, 1 (Summer): 107–131.

Kelly, Marion and Margaret Buchanan Smith. 1994. "Northern Sudan in 1991: Food Crisis and the International Relief Response." *Disasters* 18, 1 (Mar.): 16–34.

Kingston W. 2004. "Removing Some Harm from the World Trade Organization." *Oxford Development Studies* 32, 2 (June): 309–320.

Knack S. 2004. "Does Foreign Aid Promote Democracy?" *International Studies Quarterly* 48, 1 (Mar.): 251–266.

Mannan, Manzurul. 1996. "Women Targeted and Women Negated: An Aspect of the Environmental Movement in Bangladesh." *Development-in-Practice* 6, 2 (May): 113–120.

Moseley, K. P. 1992. "West African Industry and the Debt Crisis." *Journal of International Development* 4, 1 (Jan.–Feb.): 1–27.

Peterson, Marti. 2004. "Foreign Aid and the Moral Value of Freedom." *Ethical Theory and Moral Practice* 7, 3 (June): 293–307.

Rao, J. Mohan. 1994. "Judging Givers: Equity and Scale in Aid Allocation." *World Development* 22, 10 (Oct.): 1579–1584.

Saxe-Fernandez, John. 1994. "The Chiapas Insurrection: Consequences for Mexico and the United States." *International Journal of Politics, Culture and Society* 8, 2 (Winter): 325–342.

Sharpless, John. 1995. "World Population Growth, Family Planning, and American Foreign Policy." *Journal of Policy History* 7, 1:72–102.

Shiva, Vandana. 1993. "GATT, Agriculture and Third World Women." In *Ecofeminism,* edited by Maria Mies and Vandana Shiva. London: Zed Books.

Smith, Brian H. 1990. *More than Altruism: The Politics of Private Foreign Aid.* Princeton, NJ: Princeton U. Press.

Stewart, Frances. 1991. "The Many Faces of Adjustment." *World Development* 19, 12 (Dec.): 1847–1864.

Tabb, William B. 1999. "Defining Globalisation." *Global Policy Forum.* Online: available at http://www.global policy.org/globaliz/define/progglob.htm.

Vilas, Carlos M. 1994. "Latin America in the 'New World Order': Prospects for Democracy." *International Journal of Politics, Culture and Society* 8, 2 (Winter): 257–282.

Walzer, Michael. 1995. "The Politics of Rescue." *Dissent* 42, 1 (178) (Winter): 35–41.

Wedel, Janine R. 1992. "The Unintended Consequences of Western Aid to Postcommunist Europe." *Telos* 92 (Summer): 131–138.

5.3   Is Democracy the Answer?

The issue: What is the link between global development and the spread of Western-style democracy? Should everyone live in a democracy? And are there other forms of development that take precedence over economic "progress"?

The views presented thus far have dealt with economic development and the consequences of "catching up" for both underdeveloped and developed countries. But aside from the economic standpoint, another important aspect is human development. While everyone can acknowledge the obvious attributes of economic development— as in a greater probability of people being able to make a living, and less likely to live in poverty— a more contentious or debatable issue lies in the development of human rights. Politicians and human rights workers alike, continuously lobby to keep the focus on human rights, and their main assertion is that people should always have a say in what happens to them, what do you think?

Many theorists have put democracy, human rights, culture, and economic development together as inextricable links in the ultimate goal of equality and the equitable sharing of resources. For example, if times are good, does everybody benefit, and if they do, are the benefits equally distributed? Or, if times are rough, do some suffer much more than others? Does it matter where you live, or who's in office?

One of the more popular ideas in the United States today is that the exportation of democracy will inevitably lead to a better world for many to live in—especially for people in developing countries who need a fair share of the resources that their country may possess. Here is the ultimate question: "Is democracy enough, and would one kind of democracy work for everybody regardless of where they lived?"

DEMOCRACY IS THE BEST SAFEGUARD FOR RESOURCES AND RIGHTS

It seems fairly obvious that democracy and rights are linked. If people have a say, then they are able to influence what happens to them. In western-style liberal democracies, people vote for their leadership. Other systems exist around the world, and some have had partial successes in achieving development while others have moved to a democratic framework. For instance, the breakdown of the communist systems in the former Soviet Union and elsewhere occurred partly because they resulted in a distribution of wealth that was more, not less, unfair than in the West. The systems collapsed, and with the establishment of new countries and representative systems, democracy reached all across Eastern Europe and through those parts of Asia that were previously Soviet.

History shows many examples of how culture, industry development, and democracy are connected. We have already looked (in Chapter 1) at cultures of poverty and whether these do or do not exist. Even if culture is not the only factor, as shown there, how we think of ourselves affects the kinds of social relationships that we create and the kinds of political structures that are possible. Some ways of thinking are more likely to promote democracy, and these are also the ones that promote industrial capitalism: independence and interdependence, with a focus on each person doing the best they can for the society and being rewarded according to what they can contribute.

Let's take a couple of examples. The first is from classical sociology. Max Weber looked at the development of capitalism and its link to religion. Why had capitalism developed where it did—in very specific parts of Europe? He came to the conclusion that it was about how people thought about themselves and their destinies, which connected with particular ways of doing things and organizing one's life. Specifically, he found a link between types of Protestantism and the development of capitalism. This is an example of an idealist approach—the way we think makes us more likely to behave in particular ways.

Weber found that particular parts of Europe, the Protestant areas, had developed a capitalist mode of living. Individual employers had considered themselves members of "God's elect," and taken their success as small business people as evidence for this. They plowed the profits from their businesses back into the businesses, enabling these to grow. This is the process of capital investment. Then this generated further profits, these were further invested in the businesses, and the success was further seen as a mark of God's favor.

In Catholic areas, people were equally religious but this took another expression. People would give money to the poor or to the church as an attempt to show their piety and win favor from God. As they didn't develop the same attitude to profits and investment, capitalist economies didn't arise until later.

So, for Weber, the *Protestant Ethic* was directly related to the development of capitalism, and to the industrial revolution and the beginning of those stages of development that we saw in earlier chapters—and indeed to the idea of catch-up development.

If we shift the focus from capitalist economic development to human development, though, what happens?

Part of the idea behind Weber's thinking was that a "good" employer would look after the interest of the workers—and indeed some of the advances in workplace environments came from owners concerned to promote humane work conditions. But for the most part, such considerations were secondary. However, anybody might, given a few resources and their own initiative, succeed on their own. Indeed, this application of the Protestant Ethic is the basis of the American dream—succeed on your own, by means of hard work and perseverance.

North Americans today, for the most part, are highly individualistic. They consider that each person's main goal in life is to work for their own advancement and support their dependent children.

They also believe they are autonomous in that they have, to a large extent, control over their own lives. How often have you heard people say, "She can do anything if she only sets her mind to it," or "Never mind what other people say, just do it!"

By contrast, in many developing countries, people are or have been familistic. They want to do what other members of their group do, and not stand out as being different. They carefully consider the effects of their actions on other family members, even on people that Americans would consider to be distant cousins. And they also appear fatalistic, in that they feel they will have little say in determining the course of their lives. Events happen to them, and they accept their fate.

These ideas about people, their attitudes, and their everyday lives lead us to two conclusions.

The first conclusion is that for less developed countries to share in the prosperity of the advanced industrial nations, people must not only use the technologies of the first world, but also adopt the attitudes that go with them: especially the beliefs that they can control their own destinies (including having fewer children) and aim for personal success. The presumption implied by this theory is that by adopting modern science and modern attitudes, people will become better off. But do such changes actually bring about modernization as predicted, and do they make people better off?

The second conclusion is that social structures have to exist so that people can see that they have a chance to do this. In the European countries that industrialized, the feudal system had been overturned and people began to develop the idea that everybody had a chance of success. Over centuries, democracy developed in North America and Europe, and ideas of human rights emerged. In democratic systems, every adult has a vote and politicians compete for these votes. Because everyone has a vote, no particular section of society—no single family, no small group, and, in multicultural countries, no cultural or religious group—can be assured that things will go unanimously its way. This is a safeguard put in place for everybody. For resources to be shared and people to have an equal chance of making the most of these resources requires a democratic process. Because

everybody has a say, this ensures that each person or family has a chance to make something of their lives and contribute to society.

Today's developing countries are on a road to democracy and progress, and in many countries the democratic process is well established. We have already said that India is one of the largest economies, and it is a democracy. Others that first took another route are now are turning back to democracy. And once started on the road to democracy, there is considerable hope that nations will be more likely to get along with each other.

DEMOCRACY MAY NOT DO EVERYTHING—AND MAY NOT WORK FOR EVERYBODY

Certainly, a number of countries turned to a democratic process after the breakup of the Soviet political and economic system. Others have adopted an electoral process, particularly in response to advocacy and pressure from the United States and Britain. Democracy holds out promises of safeguarding human rights. In countries that have had problems with ethnic nationalism, a democratic system has the potential to help people focus on issues that concern the whole nation or country, not only parts of it: The economy or the education system become something that everybody can discuss and have opinions about. The numbers of democracies—countries using an electoral system—increased from 30 to 58 between 1973 and 1990. But since 1990 they have risen considerably more. In 2002 there were 121 countries using a democratic system. Marc Plattner has described this progress: ". . . the fall of dictators in Indonesia and Nigeria; the ouster of rulers hostile to democracy in Slovakia, Croatia, and Serbia; and the peaceful turnover to opposition leaders for the first time in Korea, Taiwan, Mexico, Senegal, and Ghana" (Plattner 2002:57).

But is democracy really linked with the ideals of economic and human development? And is it the only system that can promote these ideals while working toward global equality? Let's look at two arguments that suggest not. One is people's dissatisfaction with democracy. The other is about globalization and equality—that global equality may have two different strands in it, of which democracy is only one.

It is over a decade since the Soviet Union split up into 15 independent states. The breakup was in response both to economic stagnation resulting in a need for restructuring, and liberalizing influences within the government, notably Glasnost (or freedom of speech). Democratization has been strongly emphasized in many of the republics: Indeed, they account for part of the increases in democratic states since 1990. But in Russia itself (the largest of the states, and itself divided into a number of republics and other regions) not everybody likes what has happened. Indeed a survey reported in PRAVDA in 2003 found that 60 percent of Russians regretted the breakup of the soviet union. In a 2004 survey, only ten percent of Russians considered Russia a democratic nation, and 18 percent thought that Russia never would become democratic.

When we look at some other states of the former Soviet Union, outside observers have blamed so-called Asian values or the importance of religion for a failure of electoral democracy to provide the necessary impetus for modernization. Part of the modernization hypothesis, as we've seen, is that people in North American cultures are individualistic, while people in less developed countries are familistic. People with a familistic orientation do not try to get ahead and be successful, and are slow to adopt new ideas and technologies.

It is not hard to refute this argument. One of the leading, most successful industrial nations—Japan—is well-known for the extent of its people's familism. In Japan, people are viewed as family members, aiding their family in its success. When a child is learning to walk, its first steps are taken, symbolically, with rice cakes bound to its back, to signify that this child, when it emerges from the security in which it is raised, will enter into the responsibilities of caring for its entire family.

Indeed, within North America, some groups of people are more familistic than others. We occasionally see this familism given as a reason for their lack of success, in that they do not want to appear more knowledgeable, skilled, or successful

than other family members. This is often cited as a reason for the assumed failures of Native American groups to become "modern." Yet some Native groups have combined a familistic orientation with successful group enterprise. In other groups, familism is credited with helping them to succeed, as family ties and loyalties strengthen the group as a whole and give support to its members. In a familistic culture, no one goes hungry while another family member has food. Only under particular circumstances does familism become a problem to its members and to the group as a whole. It may be that, historically, these circumstances were created by the colonial administrators who attempted to destroy family ties and loyalties. In its place they put a structure that assumed that the values of white, middle-class colonial bureaucrats were the only values that counted. Likewise, many of the disadvantages we associate with less-developed societies may also be due to colonialism, or in the case of the Russian republics and indeed the non-Russian states of the former Soviet Union, to Russian imperialism, not to familistic values, which—under other circumstances—might work very well.

Be that as it may, it is evident that many non-western states are quite disillusioned with the promise of how democracy is supposed to set everything right. Fairbanks discusses the central Asian republics and how the promise of democracy has failed, on several grounds. These grounds include the development of dependence and a long history of political repression, as the context within which today's move toward democracy is being tested. But they also include a current neglect of the ways that people identify with their families, communities, religion, and history—not nearly as simplistic as *familism* versus *individualism* or even *values*. The 2004 Human Development Report points to democracy's ability to help safeguard people's identities and heritage, but only if these are recognized and if it is further recognized that each situation is unique—that one style of democracy does not necessarily fit all.

And another reason for disillusionment with western-style democracy is its apparent fragility.

Some think that once a democratic process is established, it persists. People keep on voting as individuals, and they elect representatives who then debate issues and vote either as members of established parties or as representatives of their constituencies. But in several nation-states, elected governments have put in place rules that make it difficult for anyone else to be elected, or that even ban opponents. Kazakhstan and Zimbabwe may provide examples. Even in Western countries, allegations of vote-rigging or of engaging in other unacceptable practices periodically surface. And at least one small European state has voted (democratically) to return to a monarchical system, because people felt it was in their interests to do so.

How democratic is a system of elected representatives? In many democratic countries, elections are contested between political parties. In a two- or three-party system, people combine on political causes. But not all viewpoints are incorporated into major parties, so voters don't always have choices in line with their interests. And some ideas are not heard and ultimately disappear because they are not picked up by major parties or by their sponsors. Furthermore, not everybody votes. In the 2004 U.S. elections, the approximately 120 million people who voted were 60 percent of those who could have voted. This was a high turnout. But where were the other 40 percent? International commentators spoke of America as polarized between the major parties—as "two nations that loathe and fear each other." After the election, many people felt that their vote for a losing candidate (in legislature or presidency) did nothing—it had no effect on policy. Is that a recipe, exportable to the developing nations of the world, for harmony and progress?

SUMMING UP

We consider that representative democracy is a good system. It has served many countries well and hopefully will continue to do so. More countries are developing a democratic system, and they are also increasing their commitments to global human rights.

However, democracy and human rights don't always go together. Other forms of representation within government can work, and tribal or even familistic systems can work well to provide care and consideration for the most vulnerable members of a society. One-person-one-vote democracies can be open to exploitation and manipulation, and party systems don't give representation to everybody: For instance, in Britain a long-standing campaign to reform the electoral system is once again being heard.

Some commentators have pointed to a basic contradiction in the idea that democracy and global equality go together. On the one hand, a democratic system does appear the best guarantor of liberties, justice, and human development. The Human Development Report (2004) points to democracy as the best guarantor, not only of individual liberties but of *cultural liberties*—the ability of groups, individuals, and communities to retain and develop their own traditions and heritage within a modern economic system—though it stresses that democracy doesn't always have to take the same form. However, if global equality is about the sharing of resources and giving everybody a say in their own destinies, it isn't clear that democracy based on existing nations is the best way to do this. After all, the structures of neocolonialism or neoimperialism are still there. The vote of a young woman in Kazakhstan may not affect the most important people in determining her future, if these people are outside her own country. And today, when some of the largest economies are those of commercial organizations, not countries at all, it isn't clear what or who are the determining factors in many people's lives.

Plattner comments that global equality has two sides: "a liberal element that limits the scope and reach of government in the name of preserving individual freedom, and an element based on popular sovereignty that calls for majority rule, expressed at the ballot box" (2002:59). He sees a tension between the two, but also sees that we need both. Without the ballot box, rulership is not accountable to the people; and without the liberal element, the majority can ride roughshod over the minority.

Today's Western societies strike an uneasy balance between the two. Societies elsewhere will find their own balances, and cultural and religious aspects will play a part in these. But either way, democracy and global equality will require work and care from many people, indeed all people. Ultimately, democracy must come from the people and cannot be forced upon them.

REVIEW EXERCISES

For Discussion and Debate

1. "Any country could be just as rich as America—it's all a question of attitude."
2. "Democracy gives everyone a right to be heard."
3. "The West isn't concerned about global development because of human rights, it's because of oil."
4. "Electoral democracy is the best protection against the power of multinational corporations."

Writing Exercises

Write a brief (500-word) essay on one of the following topics:

1. Familism and its links with success.
2. Democracy in the postcommunist republics of the former Soviet Union.
3. Exporting democracy and its effects on the economy: the example of Afghanistan.
4. A discussion of "Cultural liberty" in a named country, and how it can be protected by democratic systems.

Research Activities

1. Investigate the recent history of Russia and the postcommunist republics. How have the different republics fared in achieving electoral democracy?
2. With a group of 5 or 6 friends, conduct a survey of approximately 50 people on what democracy means to them. What are the most common responses?
3. Compare different electoral systems in Western countries such as the United States, Canada, France, and Germany. What are the similarities and differences?
4. Use the internet to research *cultural liberty* and its links with democracy.

SELECTED REFERENCES

Arjomand, Saod Amir. 2004. "Social Theory and the Changing World Mass Democracy, Development, Modernization and Globalization." *International Sociology* 19, 3:321–353.

Cooper, F. 2001. "What Is the Concept of Globalization Good For? An African Historian's Perspective. *African Affairs* 100, 399:189–213.

Diamond, Larry. 2003. "Can the Whole World Become Democratic? Democracy, Development, and International Policies." *Center for the Study of Democracy* (Apr. 17), Paper 03–05. Available online at http://repositories. cdlib.org/csd/03-05.

Fairbanks, Charles. H. 2001. "Disillusionment in the Causasus and Central Asia." *Journal of Democracy* 12, 4:49–56.

Fisun, Oleksandr. 2003. "Developing Democracy of Competitie Neopatrimonialism? The Political Regime of Ukraine in Comparative Perspective." Workshop on "Institution Building and Policy Making in Ukraine." University of

Toronto, October 24, 2003. Available online at http://www.utoronto.ca/jacyk/Fisun-CREES-workshop.pdf. Accessed 2 November 2004.

Goulet, D. 1997. "Development Ethics: A New Discipline." *International Journal of Social Economics* 17, 24, 11 (Dec.): 1160–1171.

Human Development Reports. 2004. *Cultural Liberty in Today's Diverse World.* Human Development Report. Available online at http://hdr.undp.org/reports/global/2004.

Mouzells, N. 1999. "Modernity: A Non-European Conceptualization." *British Journal of Sociology* 50, 1:141–159.

Nabudere, D. W. 1997. "Beyond Modernization and Development, or Why the Poor Reject Development." *Geografiska Annaler, Series B, Human Geography* 79, 4:203–215.

Plattner, Marc F. 2002. "Globalization and Self-Development." *Journal of Democracy* 13, 3:54–67.

Rau, William and Dennis W. Roncek. 1987. "Industrialization and World Inequality: The Transformation of the Division of Labor in the World." *American Sociological Review* 52:359–367.

CHAPTER 6

RACE AND ETHNIC RELATIONS

From a sociological point of view, both *ethnicity* and *race* are socially constructed. They are ideas we have about ourselves and others that affect how we perceive and interact with one another. They are similar in that both terms imply some kind of common biological origin that ties people together: People who share a common ethnicity or race are usually considered to be related by "blood" or to have had some common ancestor. They differ in that ethnic identity is likely to form among people with a common culture, language, religion, or national origin. Members feel they are culturally and socially united, and that is how others see them. In contrast to ethnicity, members of a race are identified on the basis of presumed physical traits, especially appearance. A race could include members from many ethnic and social backgrounds and is defined in terms of shared appearance rather than shared history or culture.

Neither race nor ethnicity are objective concepts. Interethnic and interracial contacts have been taking place for thousands of years. As a result, no supposed racial group is genetically pure and racial divisions do not reflect genetic realities. They reflect the assumptions, biases, or stereotypes with which people categorize one another.

The first section in this chapter considers whether problems often associated with race and ethnicity—namely, prejudice and discrimination—are diminishing. The second section examines affirmative action—a set of legislative actions taken to reduce discrimination—and asks whether they are merely another form of discrimination against the majority group. The third section considers whether ethnic nationalism, which is flourishing around the world, is a positive or negative social force.

6.1   Is Love All You Need?

The issue: Is discrimination decreasing, or are ethnic and racial minorities as disadvantaged as they were a generation ago, when today's Baby Boomers were listening to the Beatles sing "Love is all you need"?

The study of ethnic and race relations has its own set of terms and phrases, used at different times variously by minority and majority groups, governments, and social agencies. In this first section, the focus is on discrimination, prejudice, and stereotyping. In the next, it shifts to systemic discrimination, racism, and the process of being racialized. The third section examines the intersection of ethnicity with nationalism.

Discrimination refers to the process of making a selection based on some criteria. For instance, we may discriminate between two pieces of music based on the criteria of style or tonality. Fifty years ago, to say someone was "discriminating" would mean that he or she made fine distinctions regarding quality. In fact, it was paying a compliment, for it suggested that the person chose high-quality products and had "good taste." Later the word became used for making distinctions based on criteria that were not strictly relevant. In particular, it came to refer to making distinctions between people based on *stereotypes* or *prejudices*. So, to discriminate, used popularly, has come to mean looking not at the individual but at images and stereotypes. Thus a Scot or a Norwegian or a Nigerian is judged not on his or her own talents and abilities but on characteristics popularly associated with Scots or Norwegians or Nigerians as a group. For instance, some evaluate individual Scots according to the stereotype that, as a group, they are stingy and penny-pinching, nicely represented by Disney's Scrooge McDuck.

Jokes, cartoons, and common phrases and sayings illustrate this stereotype. If someone believes it and thinks of Scots in that way, we say that person is prejudiced. If she acts on the prejudice by, for instance, not admitting Scottish people to her circle of friendship because she considers them likely to be stingy, she is engaging in discrimination that is unfounded in two ways. First, she is applying a group stereotype to an individual without examining whether the individual is typical of the group. Second, she is assuming that the group label, or stereotype, does hold, though she has not tested that either. If she were to visit Scotland she might meet examples of another tradition, hospitality, that might change her mind. However, it is likely that while she makes assumptions about Scots based on the stereotype, her behavior will not attract many friends. And the Scottish people she meets will also have assumptions about Americans, based on stereotypes that are familiar to them and their own prejudices. So it is easy for a prejudice to be self-fulfilling.

To examine whether discrimination and prejudice are decreasing, we must examine not only how they operate, but how people get their prejudices. Because of limited space, for the most part we will focus on relations between African American and European American groups.

DISCRIMINATION AND PREJUDICE ARE DECREASING

If we look at the situation within the United States today, we can see clearly that race relations have changed. Fifty years ago there were few nonwhite professionals. The important people in a community, the mayor, leading politicians, elected officials, industrialists, doctors, and lawyers, were almost always bound to be white. Television shows were about white, European American people, with people of color shown only in minor supporting roles.

In 1954 came the Montgomery (Alabama) bus boycott and the emerging Civil Rights Movement. By 1964, the call to eliminate racial discrimination was heard loudly. The Civil Rights Act of 1964 removed many unfair hiring practices and guaranteed access to public accommodations and federal organizations. The Voting Rights Act of 1965 made it much more possible for the voices of African Americans to be heard in the political sphere, not only as electors but as those elected. Since then, the numbers of African Americans in the public eye have risen, and almost all major political offices have had African Americans elected to them (the only exceptions being president and vice president). In 1990 there were almost five times as many African American elected officials as in 1970, a mere 20 years before. In 2001 there were 4.5 times as many black male office-holders as in 1970, and an astounding 20 times more black female office-holders!

Along with these pieces of legislation have been public education programs to reduce prejudice by attacking stereotypes. In addition, television presents us with images of successful black Americans, not only in programs such as *Oprah* and *The Bernie Mac Show*, but through advertising that shows African American men and women in many varied roles, including executive positions. Finally, if we look at today's children of all ethnicities and races, their heroes very often include the sport figures they see on television, and many of these are African Americans. The names of basketball stars are household words. Today, it seems, doors are open to people of all ethnicities to work and study and reach their full potential.

There are many reasons why reductions in prejudice and discrimination have occurred. One is simply that people have realized how unfair such discrimination is. Another is that people have realized that we need the contributions of every member of society, to their fullest potential, in order to remain competitive in a global economy. We can look at the changes to advertisements, which now show people of color making important decisions about their futures and daily lives. This development is no more than a recognition by advertisers that African Americans and other minorities hold responsible jobs and merit the same treatment and recognition as anyone else.

A few prejudiced individuals do remain, and they continue to pose a problem. When members of minorities experience problems, generally it is because they have met one of these prejudiced people. Gradually, with education, we can expect their numbers to become fewer and fewer, until prejudice based on race or ethnicity is finally a thing of the past.

PREJUDICE AND DISCRIMINATION ARE NOT DECREASING NOTICEABLY

Christopher Bates Doob makes the case in his book *Racism: An American Cauldron* that racism is very much present today, and that stereotyping, prejudice, and discrimination are still with us. Let us re-examine some of the information given above, starting with the political scene since the 1960s, in the light of what he has to say. In 1964, according to research by Jaynes and Williams, civil rights was seen as the "most important problem facing the country." By 1966 its importance had declined in the popular eye, and it has never since been viewed as so important.

Was this, however, because the problem had been solved? Let us look again at the numbers of black elected officials. In 1970, there were 1,479; in 1985, 6,312; and in 1990, 7,335, was certainly an advance. But the figure for 1985 represented only 1.2 percent of all elected officials. By January 1999 the figure stood at 8,936 nationwide—representing 1.7 percent of all elected officials, according to the Joint Center for Political and Economic Studies: In

2001 the figure reached 9,101. The rate of increase had slowed, said the Joint Center press release, with fewer black men actually elected than in 2000, though more black women. In other words, the slackening of ethnic prejudice may not be the only factor involved here. Further, the Joint Center report points out that the increase since 1990 is more a factor of the Voting Rights Act and changes in district boundaries than the diminishing of racial and ethnic prejudices.

Let us look at another area, that of presentation of black actors and black issues on television. Has there been an advance? Or are African American actors only given work when they have to portray "black" characters? Again, it seems clear that there has been some advance. More black actors are visible, particularly in advertisements, but how far-reaching has this advance been?

Research indicates that, for the most part, black characters are still portrayed in stereotypical situations. We might think there are key exceptions, like the successful middle-class characters typified by the Huxtables on *The Cosby Show*. But these two characters are rarely, if ever, portrayed at their employment (as doctor and lawyer). Nor are issues of race or ethnicity addressed in such shows. The effect, says Doob, is to create the impression that blacks, like whites, can be successful if they choose to and have only themselves to blame if they are not. If commercials showing people of color in many kinds of occupation are an advance—and certainly there are many reasons why they have become prevalent—they would likely not exist without extensive lobbying by African American organizations, and threats to boycott products if African Americans continued to be shown only in a negative light. In this area, as in others, equality has not come without a struggle.

The Public Broadcasting System does air many discussions about issues concerning African Americans, and documentaries such as *Eyes on the Prize* have received high praise. Yet they are watched by a relatively small proportion of the population, as compared with the numbers who watch situation comedies on major networks.

While there have been notable advances in some areas, for many African American people today these advances have little effect on their daily lives. True, now there are some rights that before were denied: rights to equal treatment under the law, rights to receive an education, and rights to vote. However, exercising these rights becomes difficult.

Doob gives examples dealing with education, and interactions with police and the legal system. Let us first look at education.

Black Youths in a White Education System
Sociologist George Dei comments that black youths are encouraged to see themselves as failures. They are surrounded by media portrayals in which they are in trouble with the law, unemployed, or failing at school. Within school, teachers often see their students in terms of the media portrayals. This is prejudice. However, we must ask questions about where this prejudice comes from and how it is constructed, and also about how it affects those young African American men and women.

Many schooling practices have been constructed on the assumption that black youth will not need advanced education. It is still common to find black students disproportionately in vocational classes. Studies of the distribution of students to classes point to decisions taken by administrators, hurriedly, without a knowledge of the individual students, and based on these kinds of assumptions. An academic class has three students too many in it. Who can be dropped? Who will not need it? This is where prejudice enters the decision-making, often unconsciously. Perhaps the administrators are not meaning to be racist but the effect of their actions is to create yet another generation of black youths who do not have the qualifications to move on to more advanced education, or to get good jobs when they leave school.

The effects of such discrimination are compounded. Students see that few African Americans are in the educational fast tracks. They may believe this is because of race. There is still research being conducted that purports to show differences in intelligence between different races, and reports of this are still periodically displayed in the popular media, as part of the discourse of race. Some black students will believe they are simply less intelligent, that they cannot be expected to do academic

work, and drop out of school or take vocational courses. Other black students will see through the workings of the school system and be well aware of the discrimination they face. They may feel it is not worth fighting the system, that regardless of their own abilities or how well they do in school, the cards are stacked against them. Similarly, they will be more likely to drop out or to take less academically challenging courses. Others who attempt to continue with high-level courses report dealing with incredulous administrators and constantly having to prove themselves and their abilities.

Some students have pointed to the culture of the school as a source of discrimination. When they are in the classroom dealing with the textbook material, they are assumed to be "individuals" who are processing material according to their own intelligence. But the material very often is alien, based in European American/Canadian-Centric views of the world. When a student who is not European American enters the classroom, she or he must set aside culture, tradition, personal history, and racism faced in the world outside the school, and even the racism expressed in the graffiti within the school's own washrooms, to deal with this European American bias.

Protests from activist groups have led to some changes in classroom materials, but often schools are short of money and therefore cannot acquire many of the excellent new materials available.

Teachers of course have a part to play here. Some are quite frankly prejudiced. Many others, themselves from a wide variety of ethnicities and cultures, are very open to suggestions about how to make students who are not European American feel at home in their classrooms. Often, however, their solutions rely on the students themselves providing material, giving talks to the class, and so on. While class participation is important and interesting, is it fair to use renowned books and films to present a European American perspective and then expect a grade 10 student to present a different perspective, and call this "giving equal time"? Some school students are highly literate and very knowledgeable, but few could expect to win a debate with the "great thinkers" whose books are routinely used in school systems.

Some schools, however, do attempt to give their students an education that is embedded in their own cultural backgrounds and that enables them to appreciate cultural and ethnic diversity as a strength of their community and society. The Rafael Hernandez School is a "school of choice" in the Boston area to which parents from the African American, Puerto Rican, and European American communities can send their children. This school has two-way bilingual teaching and a strong performing arts focus. It has a waiting list from all three groups, and in 2001 was designated a *Compass School* by the Massachusetts Department of Education.

Interactions with Officialdom   Our second set of examples of present-day discrimination and prejudice comes from interactions of members of visible minorities with officials of the State: notably police officers, judges, and others involved in legal and law enforcement systems. First, however, a short example from Canada, where internationally known journalist Jan Wong, returning from the 1996 Atlanta Olympic Games, found herself separated from other Canadians passing through passport control and detained for several hours for reasons that were never made entirely clear to her. Her long wait ended with an apology from a senior official. She has concluded, however, that the only reason she was detained at all was that she looked different from a junior official's conception of "Canadian." When she published an account of her long wait in *The Globe and Mail* newspaper, a stream of letters to the editor resulted. Many of these gave other examples. A few, written by European Canadians, stated that racism could not be the reason for her detention because such things simply did not happen. Clearly, perceptions of whether racism exists, and of what racism is, differ widely.

Interactions between members of visible minorities and a largely European American officialdom have erupted into violence. Very often, officials will believe that minority group members are more likely to be violent, and more likely to have engaged in criminal behavior: To be black becomes to be suspect. Instances in both the United States and Canada indicate that many police officers, seeing a black, Hispanic, or Native person, will fit that person's appearance to that of a suspect, or make assumptions based only on the person's minority status. In extreme cases this has resulted in the shooting of innocent, law-abiding citizens. More often it results in a beating or an arrest. The "suspect" may be engaging in the ordinary activities of walking down the street, talking to friends, or (as in the case below, cited by Doob from an article in the *New York Times* in 1990) forming part of a crowd.

> In September 1990 John Andrews, a black man, was standing in an otherwise all-white crowd whose members were asking two white police officers to stop a tow truck from hauling off a women's car, which had been parked illegally. According to witnesses, even though Andrews was acting just like everyone else in the crowd, the officers pulled him out, slammed him against the car, and arrested him. One of the witnesses explained that "the younger cop . . . totally lost control. He punched the kid in the stomach and at one point unsnapped his holster. And the kid never laid a hand on the officer.

Human Rights Watch points out that in 2000, 63 percent of people incarcerated in adult facilities in the United States were black or Latino. Marvin Free has discussed how processes of discrimination tend to be displayed in arrest rates or in early court procedures.

Finally, at least one set of prejudices appears to be increasing: Middle Eastern and Asian people are targeted for abuse and discrimination. Elaine Hagopian and her colleagues point to how a "demonization" of Middle-Eastern-looking terrorists, as part of the "war on terror," has affected the daily lives of Arabs and Muslims in the United States and other countries. Here we are dealing not with simple prejudice but with the creation of prejudice through political propaganda, including a constant replaying of negative images in the media. Nancy Murray, director of the American Civil Liberties Union of Massachusetts, believes that constitutional rights have been eroded as prejudice increases.

SUMMING UP

When, in the late sixties, the Beatles sang "Love is all you need," most members of the baby boom generation wanted to believe that war, poverty, strife—also, prejudice and discrimination—could be easily made to disappear. Now, more than thirty years later with the baby boomers in charge, it hasn't turned out to be quite so easy after all.

In some areas of life, it appears that prejudice and discrimination against members of minorities are declining. In others, there is little evidence for a decline, and much to indicate that prejudices and their acting out in discrimination are still very much with us. Talking about prejudice, however, does not give the whole picture. We need to ask why particular, widely shared prejudices have come about, and why some prejudices may recede and some appear to be increasing in today's societies: For instance, many Arabic men and women may be facing increased hostility since 9/11. We need to ask why, in an advanced, multiethnic society such as the United States, the same old prejudices are so widely shared. In the next section, we investigate the social, as opposed to individual, nature of discrimination or oppression, and investigate whether the concept of affirmative action can help in countering some of the social problems associated with *systemic discrimination.*

REVIEW EXERCISES

For Discussion and Debate

1. "Racial violence is everywhere you look in our cities."
2. "Minority groups should learn that their best hope is in the ballot box."
3. "Minority group members are more likely to engage in crime."
4. "Prejudiced people are just ignorant."

Writing Exercises

Write a brief (500-word) essay on one of the following topics:

1. "How I would go about overcoming prejudice."
2. "The role of legislation in preventing discrimination."
3. "White folks don't see the racism in society."
4. "What today's children learn about the Civil Rights Movement."

Research Activities

1. In your favorite television sit-coms or soaps, how are members of majority and minorities shown? Document the number of times minority actors appear, indicating whether or not their character must be played by a minority actor in order to fit the story line. How does this compare with majority actors?
2. Canvass your friends. How many of them can give examples of discrimination they have experienced or witnessed, against members of minorities?
3. List the high school and college or university classes you have participated in, with the approximate proportions of minority and majority students in each. Now, find out the statistics on minority and majority proportions in your geographical area. Is there a difference, and if so, why?
4. Examine one stereotype about an ethnic, racial, cultural, or religious group of which *you* are a member. How is this stereotype shown in popular culture? How do you feel when you think of this stereotype being applied to yourself?

SELECTED REFERENCES

Banton, Michael. 1992. "The Nature and Causes of Racism and Racial Discrimination." *International Sociology* 7, 1 (Mar.): 69–84.

Bositis, David. 2004. "Black Elected Officials: A Statistical Summary." *Joint Center for Political and Economic Studies*. Available online at http://www.jointcenter.org/publications/BEO/BEO-01.html. Accessed 6 October.

Doob, Christopher Bates. 1993. *Racism, an American Cauldron.* New York: HarperCollins.

Dei, George J. Sefa. 1996. *Anti-Racism Education: Theory and Practice.* Halifax, NS: Fernwood.

———. 1999. "Knowledge and Politics of Social Change: The Implication of Anti-Racism." *British Journal of Sociology of Education* 20, 3:395–409.

Eggers, Mitchell L. and Douglas S. Massey. 1992. "A Longitudinal Analysis of Urban Poverty: Blacks in U.S. Metropolitan Areas between 1970 and 1980." *Social Science Research* 21, 2 (June): 175–203.

Free, Marvin D. 1996. *African Americans and the Criminal Justice System.* New York: Jr. Garland Publishing, Inc.

Gonzales, Juan L., Jr. 1993. "Race Relations in the United States." *Humboldt Journal of Social Relations* 19, 2:39–78.

Goza, Franklin. 1990. "Differential Income Attainment among Asians in the United States, 1960 to 1980." *International Review of Modern Sociology* 20, 1 (Spring): 1–31.

Hagopian, Elaine C., ed. 2004. *Civil Rights in Peril—The Targeting of Arabs and Muslims.* Haymarket Books.

Hill, Herbert and James E. Jones. 1993. *Race in America: The Struggle for Equality.* Madison, WI: University of Wisconsin Press.

Human Rights Watch. 2002. "Race and Incarceration in the United States."

Human Rights Watch Press Backgrounder, February 27. Available online at http://www.hrw.org/backgrounder/usa/race. Accessed 16 October 2004.

Joint Center for Political and Economic Studies. Available online at http://www.jointcenter.org/. Accessed 10 October 2004.

Jones, Evonne Parker. 1991. "The Impact of Economic, Political and Social Factors on Recent Overt Black/White Racial Conflict in Higher Education in the United States." *Journal of Negro Education* 60, 4 (Fall): 524–537.

Kellough, J. Edward and Euel Elliott. 1992. "Demographic and Organizational Influences on Racial/Ethnic and Gender Integration in Federal Agencies." *Social Science Quarterly* 73, 1 (Mar.): 1–11.

Kilbourne, Barbara, Paula England and Kurt Beron. 1994. "Effects of Individual, Occupation and Industrial Characteristics on Earnings: Intersections of Race and Gender." *Social Forces* 72, 4 (June): 1149–1176.

Li, Peter. 1992. "Race and Gender as Bases of Class Fractions and Their Effects on Earnings." *Canadian Review of Sociology and Anthropology* 29, 4 (Nov.): 488–510.

Marrow, H. 2003. "To Be or Not to Be (Hispanic or Latino): Brazilian Racial and Ethnic Identity in the United States." *Ethnicities* 3, 4:427–464.

Murty, Komanduri, Julian B. Roebuck and Gloria R. Armstrong. 1994. "The Black Community's Reactions to the 1992 Los Angeles Riot." *Deviant Behavior* 15, 1 (Jan.–Mar.): 85–104.

Paek, H. J. and H. Shah. 2003. "Stereotyping of Asian Americans in U.S. Magazine Advertising." *Howard Journal of Communications* 14, 4:225–243.

Ransford, H. Edward and Bartolomeo J. Palisi. 1992. "Has There Been a Resurgence of Racist Attitudes in the General Population?" *Sociological Spectrum* 12, 3 (July–Sept.): 231–255.

Sandefur, Gary D. and Anup Pahari. 1989. "Racial and Ethnic Inequality in Earnings and Educational Attainment." *Social Service Review* 63, 2 (June): 199–221.

Short, Geoffrey. 1993. "Prejudice Reduction in Schools: The Value of Interracial Contact." *British Journal of Sociology of Education* 14, 2 (June): 159–168.

Thomas, Melvin E. 1993. "Race, Class, and Personal Income: An Empirical Test of the Declining Significance of Race Thesis, 1968–1988." *Social Problems* 40, 3 (Aug.): 328–342.

———, Cedric Herring and Hayward Derrick Horton. 1994. "Discrimination over the Life Course: A Synthetic Cohort Analysis of Earnings Differences between Black and White Males, 1940–1990." *Social Problems* 41, 4 (Nov.): 608–628.

Weitzer R. and S. A. Tuch. 1999. "Race, Class, and Perceptions of Discrimination by the Police." *Crime & Delinquency* 45, 4:494–507.

Yetman, Norman R. and Forrest J. Berghorn. 1993. "Racial Participation and Integration in Intercollegiate Basketball: A Longitudinal Perspective." *Sociology of Sport Journal* 10, 3 (Sept.): 301–314.

Zipp, John F. 1994. "Government Employment and Black-White Earnings Inequality, 1980–1990." *Social Problems* 41, 3 (Aug.): 363–382.

6.2 Are Two Wrongs Trying to Make a Right?

The issue: Affirmative action, which some call "reverse discrimination." Have efforts to discriminate in favor of racial and ethnic minorities (and women) taken a wrong step, creating a white backlash (including rejection of the policy by voters in California)?

Affirmative action has a bad name today in many quarters. The task of this section is to indicate why, and whether this bad reputation is deserved. In the process, we hope to clear up some misconceptions about discrimination, prejudice, and attempts to counter these.

Affirmative action is most often discussed with regard to hiring practices. It can also be found in assigning housing, and in admission to courses at high school and college level. Other forms of affirmative action, not necessarily named as such, may be seen in selection of television programs to be screened, or programs for a community radio station, or texts in a school course.

Often affirmative action is seen as an attempt to right an old wrong. Because it is popularly associated with hiring, we will take an example here. In the past, let us say, members of a particular minority group have been excluded from jobs in a department store (or at least from jobs where they were visible to the consumers). Now the owners of the store wish to remedy this situation, perceiving it as unfair. How should they go about it?

Many options are open, including the following:

- Attempt to ensure that substantial numbers of minority-group members apply for jobs in the store, then give the jobs to the most qualified applicants, irrespective of ethnicity, race, or gender.
- Attempt to ensure that substantial numbers of minority-group members apply for jobs in the store, then apportion the jobs so that highly qualified members of the minority group get at least some of them.
- Select a group of the best-qualified applicants, and award jobs first to the minority-group members among these, then to other members of the best-qualified group.
- Hire only qualified members of the minority, for a period of time, until the minority group becomes represented in reasonable numbers within the store's workforce.

The concept of affirmative action is broad and general, stretching over a long period of time. It goes further than one instance, and implies that the store has made a commitment to a long-term plan based on one or more of the above.

Is this practice unfair, a case of "reverse discrimination"? Or should it be seen as necessary? Is there something going on here that goes beyond the concept of discrimination against the individual? If someone achieves a position through affirmative action, has this compromised the concept of jobs being awarded on merit?

AFFIRMATIVE ACTION IS REVERSE DISCRIMINATION

In the past, many people did not get the jobs they merited because of racism. Today we should be attempting to make sure that the only criterion for hiring is individual merit. Society requires that the best qualified people get the best jobs, regardless of race.

Very often, when you see a member of a visible minority in a professional or managerial job, you wonder how they got there. Often people say they got there as a result of affirmative action. Sometimes you have to wonder just how good people are at their jobs, if they gained them through affirmative action.

It doesn't help anybody to be treated as if they are special, and to have jobs or university places made just for them. People need to be able to stand on their own feet. It does them much more good to be able to compete on equal terms, and if they achieve the positions in an open competition this is much better for their self-esteem. Also, other employees will respect them more. There are minorities in high positions today, in businesses and in government. These are real role models who demonstrate that in today's advanced societies, such as the United States, Canada, Britain, or Australia, it is possible to get ahead based on your own merits. When a black woman can become National Security Advisor and then secretary of state, surely we are past the time when false "action" programs are needed. Race and ethnicity have been shown not to matter anymore. Let people succeed on their own merits so that we can have a truly "color blind" economy.

So-called affirmative action means that well-qualified people may be overlooked in favor of those who are less well-qualified. Surely it would be better to help members of minorities to gain qualifications and become competitive, but not to give them special treatment. After all, the people who are overlooked have to live and make ends meet for their families, too.

There are some jobs now for which white people know they needn't bother applying. This situation is not going to promote harmony between different ethnicities or between minority and majority groups. Affirmative action programs are seen as reverse discrimination and arouse a lot of resentment.

Those who promote affirmative action are well-meaning, but are not taking account of the realities of life today. Affirmative action only encourages hatred and divisiveness, because so many people see it as being unfair more than anything else.

AFFIRMATIVE ACTION IS A NECESSARY ATTEMPT AT FAIRNESS

All the opinions given above have likely been heard by many readers in the past. These are commonly expressed beliefs about affirmative action. In this section we will examine some of them to see whether they hold any truth.

Hiring Should Be on Individual Merit   Individual merit is often given as the ideal criterion for hiring. The implication is that in today's world, other considerations should not matter. However, researchers who have examined hiring indicate that in practice, people are hired for a variety of reasons, not all concerned with individual merit. In general, those people who have responsibility for hiring hire people who are most like themselves or who are recommended by other people like themselves, in terms of culture, behavior, and the ability to make conversation. Those who are seen as "different" have several strikes against them: In an interview situation they may display cultural differences that the hirer finds confusing or worrisome, because he or she does not recognize them; or the hirer may simply assume that they will be different or difficult to get along with.

These assumptions take many forms, as we saw previously. What makes them especially problematic is that they form part of, and reinforce, structures of racism or oppression that persist throughout much of North American society, and that they take place within a framework where members of the majority—the ones doing the hiring—are, for historical and structural reasons, more likely to be in positions of power. Without some kind of affirmative action, despite occasional high-placed examples, there is no guarantee that well-qualified members of minorities will be hired, even when their qualifications are superior to those of other candidates, or that they will gain admittance to educational programs. Even when members of minorities are carrying out the hiring they may be under pressure to not hire other minority members. Doob cites one case in which an African American manager felt unable to hire an African American secretary because of how his department would be viewed: "That's a black operation over there, so it can't be too effective" were the words that he feared.

Hiring to senior positions have been notably few. Advances since 1979 have been so scant as to be negligible. A 1979 survey of 1,708 senior executives (of Fortune 1000 corporations) indicated that 3 were African American, 2 Asian, 2 Hispanic, and 8 women while a 1985 survey of 1,362 senior executives found 4 African Americans, 6 Asians, 3 Hispanics, and 29 women.

It seems that only when large corporations are engaged in affirmative action will they hire people who are minority members, women, or especially minority women to high positions. This barrier to advancement, so subtle as to be almost invisible, is known as the "glass ceiling," and we will examine its operation, with special reference to gender. It operates similarly where race and ethnicity are concerned.

Hiring should be on individual merit. Affirmative action helps level the playing field to make this possible. Perhaps one day in the future we can dispense with the mechanics of affirmative action and focus *only* on merit—but certainly not yet.

People Who Have Benefited from Affirmative Action Cannot Be the Best   This indicates a lack of understanding of most affirmative action programs. In general, these work by first selecting people who meet a standard for the job that is considered adequate-to-high, then choosing from among these, bearing in mind the criteria of the affirmative action program and its long-term goal, which is (often) to eventually have a workforce that reflects the character and diversity of the population of the local area. At times, the "standard" is reconsidered and even adjusted upward or downward. Sometimes, therefore, affirmative action does result in what can be seen as a "lowering of standards" but the original standards were set higher than the content of the job requires.

An example comes from a gas-pipe construction company. They would not hire anybody who did not have a grade 12 education, which was beyond the qualifications of most Native people of the area, for historical and structural reasons.

Federal affirmative action consultants examined the content of the job, and pointed out it did not require a grade 12 education. The company itself admitted there was no good reason for the grade 12 requirement, except that it had always been there. Given the pattern of education in the area, the grade 12 requirement was discriminatory, an example of systemic discrimination. Educational practices and job hiring practices were intersecting to deny jobs to Native peoples. When it was changed many more aboriginal people were hired on the construction project.

However, the charge that people who benefit from affirmative action cannot be "the best" is generally leveled at those who occupy senior positions. We have already mentioned the phenomenon of the "glass ceiling." It would seem more logical to state that if a company has no members of minorities and few women in senior positions, then the senior executives must have reached their position through preference and favoritism, having been protected from the competition that minority members might give them. There are many African Americans, Asian Americans, Native Americans, and women who graduate from universities with high awards, so that we should reasonably expect them to appear among the holders of top-ranked jobs. Affirmative action programs are an attempt to level the playing field, so that the achievements of candidates of all races and ethnicities can be taken into account.

People Need to Be Able to Stand on Their Own Feet   The concept of individualism is very strong within North America. Often, people look only at the individual and individualism, neglecting the social world within which each individual exists. This concept fits in with the "American Dream." Everyone can be successful, get ahead, and achieve a life-style that will support a family in relative comfort, as long as they work hard, study, apply themselves, and be respectful, while at the same time standing up for themselves as individuals; at least, so goes the dream.

When we look at society, however, we see that it is not so simple. Success is far more attainable by people in some sectors of society than others.

Furthermore, some people do not stop at modest achievements, but go on to amass fortunes. Again this can be part of the dream, but in a capitalist society one person's fortune is predicated on the assumption that many others will have relatively little. In other words, as society is currently structured, not everyone can succeed.

Many of the laws, norms, practices, and institutions of society have come from a past in which racism was not only common but legal: in fact, a past in which racism was constructed by leading members of society as a protection of their own privileged position. This "scientific racism" of the eighteenth and nineteenth centuries has been discussed by, among others, Stephen J. Gould in his book *The Mismeasure of Man*. In association with "scientific sexism," its goal was to demonstrate the superiority of one group of people, European males of the scientists' countries of origin and of the middle and upper classes, over all others, using indexes such as brain size (cranial capacity) and head proportions (cephalic index). To many people today this goal makes no sense whatsoever. In the context of eighteenth and nineteenth century colonialism, it did make sense to those people who saw themselves as having a right to control the lives of others. The rulers of the English and French colonial empires saw themselves as superior to the Irish or Scots or East Indians or Ghanaians or Native Americans they were attempting to control. They used terms such as "savage" or "barbarous" to describe these people and to justify their rule. They constructed a scale, from highest (themselves) to lowest (Africans, and people of African descent).

Of course they were not doing something entirely new. Throughout history, people have attempted to vilify those whose land they wanted to invade, or whom they saw as enemies or threats. The persistence of European anti-Semitism indicates how often these eighteenth and nineteenth century rulers drew on anti-Semitism as part of their system. What was new, according to Gould, was the "scientific" nature of the enterprise.

As part of this, many Africans were enslaved, and brought to the United States and Canada. Slavery was not a new phenomenon, but its linking with "scientific" racism was. In the areas where slavery was most economically profitable, a series of laws arose to prohibit the education of slaves. Even after the abolition of slavery, segregation remained strongly in force in many parts of North America, supported by law.

Seen against their historical background, many present-day acts of discrimination fall into place as the everyday outcome of a historic process called racialization. This is the tendency in a community to introduce racial distinctions into situations that can be understood and managed without such distinctions. Thus, race becomes a substitute for distinctions that would be otherwise based on class, education, age, or job experience, for example. In this way, race sometimes becomes the basis for decisions about hiring, purchasing, renting, befriending, and respecting others. Racialization is based on ignorance as much as on fear and indifference to the consequences for those who are treated this way.

To say that people must "stand on their own two feet" implies that an individual person, unaided, can combat the system of racialization and win. But if we look at the very real advances that have been made toward the elimination of racism, we can see that these have taken place through collective, rather than individual, action. Where affirmative action programs have been put into place, they have come about through the action and protests of minorities. Affirmative action is the result of members of minority groups coming together to say, "Enough!"

SUMMING UP

Are two wrongs—prejudice and affirmative action—trying to make a right? The answer is "no," if you accept the notion that affirmative action is a social response to a historically constructed situation of inequality, *not* discrimination against individuals. In the recent challenges to Michigan University's admission procedures, appeals went to the U.S. Supreme Court, which concluded the need to have a student body that reflected the diversity of the population did constitute a "compelling interest" and that flexible affirmative action processes, carefully administered, were justified as essential to this interest.

Problems associated with affirmative action typically relate to its portrayal in the media, and to the current economic situation. Put simply, in many areas jobs are scarce. Many people are unemployed or underemployed. Members of privileged groups in society have grown up with the assumption that they will be able to find a job. When they cannot, it is easy to find a scapegoat. If there is only one job available, and that job goes to a minority group member, other candidates rationalize their disappointment, by saying that they have lost out because of affirmative action. They receive support from the media, which focuses on the ethos of individualism and success.

In actuality, relatively few people have been the beneficiaries of affirmative action. In the United States, affirmative action showed some success in the 1960s and 1970s. In later years, the shortage of jobs has posed a major problem for members of all ethnic groups. In Canada, employment equity, as it is known, is mandatory in the federal public service, but voluntary in the private sector, and federal jobs are currently being downscaled.

Affirmative action can be a useful tool in the attempt to create a more fair and just society. It cannot work in isolation, but requires a population that understands the process and understands the need for it. We advocate antiracism education so that people of all ethnicities can understand how historical processes of racialization and gendering affect North American society. Racism remains one of the major problems of today's North America. Affirmative action programs can help, but cannot do the job alone.

REVIEW EXERCISES

For Discussion and Debate

1. "Racial discrimination is all in the eye of the beholder."
2. "American Democracy is another word for majority rule."
3. Governments and elected assemblies should have the same proportions of minority group members as there are in the community electing them.
4. Nobody could feel proud of getting a job through affirmative action.

Writing Exercises

Write a brief (500-word) essay on one of the following topics:

1. "People should be hired on their own merits."
2. "Popular views of affirmative action, and why these arise."
3. "Today, everybody has the same access to the education system, and so anybody can get the qualifications they need to succeed."
4. "Getting ahead as a minority group member."

Research Activities

1. Find media accounts of a court case involving alleged discrimination in hiring or promotion. Who was involved, and how was the case reported? If you can, find accounts of the same case in media targeted for different audiences, and compare the reports.
2. Examine a copy of a newspaper that gives information about business and finance. Look at the pictures of people selected for executive positions. What do these tell you about race and gender patterns of hiring? Explain your findings.
3. Examine representation of minorities at local government levels in your area, over the past ten years. What changes do you find, and why?

4. What laws regarding hiring discrimination apply in your area? To what jobs do these apply—all, or only some? What groups are protected by these laws, and are there some (e.g., religious minorities) that are not protected?

SELECTED REFERENCES

Barker, Kathleen. 1994. "To Be PC or Not to Be? A Social Psychological Inquiry into Political Correctness." *Journal of Social Behavior and Personality* 9, 2:271–281.

Bobo, Lawrence and James R. Kluegel. 1993. "Opposition to Race Targeting: Self-Interest, Stratification Ideology, or Racial Attitudes?" *American Sociological Review* 58, 4 (Aug.): 443–464.

Brutus, S., L. F. Parr, M. Hunter, B. Perry and F. Ducharme. 1998. "Attitudes toward Affirmative Action in the United States and Canada." *Journal of Business and Psychology* 12, 4:515–533.

Burstein, Paul. 1992. "Affirmative Action, Jobs, and American Democracy. What Has Happened to the Quest for Equal Opportunity?" *Law and Society Review* 26, 4:901–922.

Butler, John Sibley. 1992. "Affirmative Action in the Military." *Annals of the American Academy of Political and Social Science* 523 (Sept.): 196–206.

Calliste, Agnes. 1995. "The Struggle for Employment Equity by Blacks on American and Canadian Railroads." *Journal of Black Studies* 25, 3 (Jan.): 297–317.

Cunningham, Susan. 1992. "The Development of Equal Opportunities Theory and Practice in the European Community." *Policy and Politics* 20, 3 (July): 177–189.

DiTomaso, Nancy and Donna E. Thompson. 1988. "The Advancement of Minorities into Corporate Management: An Overview." *Research in the Sociology of Organizations* 6:281–312.

Doob, Christopher Bates. 1993. *Racism, an American Cauldron.* New York: HarperCollins.

Drake, W. Avon and Robert D. Holsworth. 1994. "Affirmative Action and Elite Racial Reconciliation." *Research in Race and Ethnic Relations* 7:57–82.

Edwards, John. 1994. "Group Rights v. Individual Rights: The Case of Race-Conscious Policies." *Journal of Social Policy* 23, 1 (Jan.): 55–70.

Epstein, Richard. 1992. *Forbidden Grounds.* Cambridge, MA: Harvard University Press.

Fry, F. L. and J. R. D. Burgess. 2003. "The End of the Need for Affirmative Action: Are We There Yet?" *Business Horizons* 46, 6 (Nov.): 7–16.

Gamson, William A. and Andre Modigliani. 1987. "The Changing Culture of Affirmative Action." *Research in Political Sociology* 3:137–177.

Glazer, Nathan. 1975. *Affirmative Discrimination.* New York: Basic Books.

Gould, Stephen J. 1981. *The Mismeasure of Man.* New York: W. W. Norton.

Graham, Hugh Davis. 1994. "Race, History and Policy: African Americans and Civil Rights since 1964." *Journal of Policy History* 6, 1:12–39.

Green, Denise O'Neil. 2004. "Fighting the Battle for Racial Diversity: A Case Study of Michigan's Institutional Responses to Gratz and Grutter." *Educational Policy* 18, 5:733–751.

Henry, Frances and Carol Tator. 1985. "Racism in Canada: Social Myths and Strategies for Change." In *Ethnicity and Ethnic Relations in Canada,* edited by Rita M. Bienvenue and Jay E. Goldstein. Toronto: Butterworths.

Hirschman, Albert. 1991. *The Rhetoric of Reaction.* Boston, MA: Belknap Press.

Killian, Lewis M. 1991. "Gandhi, Frederick Douglass and Affirmative Action." *International Journal of Politics, Culture and Society* 5, 2 (Winter): 167–182.

LeFevre, J. 2003. "The Value of Diversity: A Justification of Affirmative Action." *Journal of Social Philosophy* 34, 1:125–133.

Lipset, Seymour Martin. 1992. "Equal Chances versus Equal Results." *Annals of the American Academy of Political and Social Science* 523 (Sept.): 63–74.

———. 1992. "Two Americas, Two Value Systems: Blacks and Whites." *Tocqueville Review* 13:137–177.

Mentzer, Marc S. and John L. Fizel. 1992. "Affirmative Action and Ethnic Inequality in Canada: The Impact of the Employment Equity Act of 1986." *Ethnic Groups* 9, 4:203–217.

Naylor, L. A. and D. H. Rosenbloom. 2004. "Adarand, Grutter, and Gratz: Does Affirmative Action in Federal Employment Matter?" *Review of Public Personnel Administration* 24, 2:150–174.

Olivas, Michael A. 1993. "The Attack on Affirmative Actions: Lives in Parallel Universes." *Change* 25 (Mar.–Apr.): 16–20.

Skocpol, Theda, Jim Sleeper, Robert S. Browne and Jonathan Rieder. 1992. "Race, Liberalism, and Affirmative Action (II)." *American Prospect* 10 (Summer): 86–97.

Starr, Paul. 1992. "Civil Reconstruction: What to Do without Affirmative Action." *American Prospect* 8 (Winter): 7–14.

6.3   Is Too Much National Spirit a Bad Thing?

The issue: Has nationalism—an extreme love of one's nation or ethnic group—done more harm than good in human history, and will it engulf more of us in wars and genocidal acts until people learn to reject such extreme sentiments?

This topic looks both at the issue of *ethnic nationalism* and at what have been called *hyphenated identities.* Though separate, these issues are interrelated. The phrase *ethnic nationalism* conjures up images of the horrors of war in the former Yugoslavia, or *ethnic cleansing,* of the struggle between Hutu and Tutsi peoples in some central African countries. It can also refer to the longstanding attempts of the Basques of the boundary between France and Spain, or the Kurdish people of the Middle East, to achieve international recognition. Already some readers will think of desperate struggles for autonomy; and others will think of terrorism. In September 2004, the world watched in horror as Chechen terrorists occupied a school in the Russian town of Bezlan. The result was a bloodbath.

Closer to home, we can examine the situation of Native groups in Mexico. What about within the United States and Canada? Does ethnic nationalism occur there, and how should we, as sociologists, view it? What about issues such as *white power*—how does it arise, and to what extent is it related to other forms of extreme political movements, and to the apparent increase in some forms of prejudice in today's society?

But what are both *ethnicity* and *nationalism?* Very often these words are used without definition, in the implicit understanding that everyone knows

what they mean. Yet the word ethnicity may mean something different for different ethnic groups, and its meaning changes as we move from North America to Europe. The concept of ethnicity includes both subjective and objective components. People feel that they belong to an ethnic group. Others perceive them as part of this group. They may claim a common ancestry, or language, or religion, or "race," or some or all of these. They may base their group membership on culture. One useful definition is that ethnicity refers to

> an involuntary group of people who share the same culture or to descendants of such people who identify themselves and/or are identified by others as belonging to the same involuntary group. (Isajiw 1985:16)

Nationalism refers to loyalty to one's nation. Michael Ignatief, in his book *Blood and Belonging: Journeys into the New Nationalism,* outlines two kinds of nationalism, civic and ethnic. In his view, civic nationalism is constituted by a community of citizens who, as equals, express loyalty and patriotic attachment to a shared set of values, both social and political. Ethnic nationalism, however, is loyalty based on inheritance rather than values. In this section we will examine Ignatief's distinction, and its usefulness.

ETHNIC NATIONALISM IS NOT DESTRUCTIVE

People have a deep-seated need to belong. Humans are social beings, who come together to construct communities based on shared cultural values and traditions. In the United States and Canada we can easily see how different cultural groups construct communities that differ from each other. Often, therefore, Italian Americans will identify with other Italian Americans, Vietnamese Canadians with other Vietnamese Canadians.

Here in North America, however, many of these groups meet, at least theoretically, as equals. For a long time, the prevailing ideology in the United States was that of the melting pot, where all cultures would "melt" to create a new society and a new culture. Although in practice some cultures have been more fully represented in the resulting mix than others, North Americans in general share many of the same pursuits, tastes, hobbies, and recreations. Baseball, football, soccer, and hockey are sports enjoyed by a wide variety of people regardless of their background. Pop music is a great example of something that is enjoyed by almost all teenagers worldwide. Just look at the fans in Asia, New Zealand, Norway, and Germany who fill arenas for pop stars such Britney Spears, Hilary Duff, and Sheryl Crow.

Ethnicity and Identity   And yet when we walk down the streets of a city, such as Los Angeles or Toronto, we are amidst the sights, scents, and sounds that indicate multiple ethnicities. We can hear several languages being spoken. People use clothing, hairstyles, and jewelry to proclaim not only their personal style but also their ethnicity. Some will identify themselves as American or Canadian, but others construct their identities as African American, Italian American, or German Canadian.

For some, this is a simple statement of identity, reflecting family ties, language, religion, tradition, and culture. For others, this claiming of group membership is a declaration of resistance, against being treated as an "other," outside the bounds of society, by those who are considered the "mainstream."

We have discussed this so far for North America, and considered people who came as immigrants,

in one way or another. (The situation of Native Peoples of North America will be considered later.) What of the situation in which people see themselves not as immigrants, or as the great-great-grand-daughters and sons of immigrants, but as indigenous inhabitants of their country?

Ethnicity and Nationhood   The term *ethnic group* has been less often used, sociologically, in Europe than in North America. Groups of people that in North America would be considered ethnic groups are in Europe spoken of as nations. This term is often associated with political boundaries.

The words *nation* and *state* do not have the same meaning, but in Europe a nation often controls its own state, or is at least a potential candidate for statehood.

Alternatively, the nation may be a *national minority* within a state. In either case, there is a political dimension to the word *nation* that is lacking in the word *ethnic group*. In many cases, a nation will have its own land base. There are Scots living all over Europe, but they have their own land base in Scotland. It may surprise some North American readers to learn that, although Scots consider themselves a nation, Scotland is not a nation-state.

Ethnic nationalism for such groups is a search for identity, a tracing of roots to a shared cultural past, together with a search for political recognition. To stay with European examples: All over Europe there have been movements seeking national autonomy. Basque, Scottish, and Welsh nationalism are only three examples. When the former Soviet Union split apart, it did so along national lines, and groups with shared cultural links and their own land bases become the new nation-states of Georgia, Belarus, the Ukraine, and others.

In many parts of the world, people are calling for the right to govern themselves as they see fit. They claim this right based on their concept of nationhood, rooted in their culture and history. In making their claims, they speak not only of the traditions and customs they share, but legal, educational and political systems and institutions that they consider are uniquely their own.

Within North America there are groups that claim nationhood rather than ethnic group status:

most notably, the people of Quebec, many of whom consider that they constitute a distinct society, and the many aboriginal nations who point out that they were governed by their own political and legal systems long before Europeans landed on North American soil. Not all Quebecois seek independence from Canada. (Just over half of those who voted in the Quebec Referendum of 1995 voted to remain part of Canada.) Many, however, including many of those who voted against separation, define themselves as Quebecois rather than Canadian. As Ignatief points out, the provincial assembly of Quebec is called L'Assemblée Nationale. Similarly, while many people of Native ancestry consider themselves Native American, or Native Canadian, others see themselves first as Mohawk or Mi'kmaq or Navaho.

Where people with a geographical land base consider themselves a nation, feel strongly loyal to that nation, and form or maintain their own institutions such as political, legal, and educational systems, there seems little reason to insist that they are not a nation. Surely it is more productive to spend time and energy working out how economic and political links can be formed or maintained between the new nation and others around it, than endlessly arguing over whether such a nation has a right to exist.

ETHNIC NATIONALISM IS DESTRUCTIVE

So far, we have considered the case of people with a geographical land base, who consider themselves one nation. But this may rarely be found, or the geographical land base may be very small. Different ethnic groups continue to share areas, either living amongst each other or in small enclaves such as, in the former Yugoslavia, where one village might be predominantly of one ethnicity, the next of another.

In 1990, eyes across Canada were drawn to Kanehsatake, otherwise known as Oka, where many Mohawk people took a stand to protect a wooded area, a burial ground, from being turned into a golf course. In the initial police raid on a small barricade across a little-used road leading to the area, a police officer was shot and killed. People of the nearby reserve of Kahnawake joined in

the dispute, barricading the Mercier bridge leading to Montreal. European-Canadians from a nearby town came to the barriers to protest, and their activities included burning an effigy of "a Mohawk warrior" and throwing rocks at carloads of people—pregnant, sick or elderly—being evacuated from Kahnawake. This resulted in the death of an elderly veteran who was, paradoxically, a European Canadian who had married into a Mohawk family.

In Kanehsatake, Mohawks and European Canadians lived next door to each other. Over the next few weeks, many Europeans left the area. Some of their houses were looted. Some of these residents did not return.

Ethnic nationalism is not the same as simple patriotism or love for one's country or culture. Ethnic groups are found in situations of multiple ethnicities where more than one such group are present. The Kanehsatake Mohawks are "ethnic" only with respect to their French Canadian or English Canadian neighbors who, sociologically speaking, are equally "ethnic." The expressed nationalism of one group arouses fear, distrust, and an equal nationalism in others. Many English Canadians today speak in tones of wounded pride at the idea that Québecois would want to separate, as if it is a personal affront. They perceive it as an attack on the concept of Canada as a tolerant, peaceful, and all-inclusive country, and hence an attack on themselves as good citizens of such a country. They cannot understand why French Canadians (or for that matter Native Canadians) do not share their view of Canada.

Ignatief's distinction between ethnic and civic nationalism has already been mentioned. Ignatief defines himself as a cosmopolitan, a member of a global society, part of a global economy. He speaks several languages and feels at home in the diversity of a big city. But he points out that the ability to be cosmopolitan is fragile. People can only be cosmopolitan if they have their own cosmopolitan state or if they live in states that can guarantee order and peace to their citizens. As Ignatief says:

> Globalism in a post-imperial age only permits a post-nationalist consciousness for those cosmopolitans who are lucky enough to live in the

wealthy West. The Bosnian Muslims are perhaps the most dramatic example of a people who turned in vain to more powerful neighbors to protect them. The people of Sarajevo were true cosmopolitans. (Ignatief: 9)

But the Bosnian Muslims did not live in a strong nation-state that could guarantee peace and tolerance within its bounds.

Ignatief also defines himself as one who favors civic nationalism. In his view, a nation should be a community of equals, held together by law and by respect, not by the ties, real or supposed, of blood. Within a community of equals, each should be free to be herself or himself. The goal of multiculturalism is a community in which people can express themselves through culture, religion, and language, respecting and valuing the cultures, religions, and languages of others. But such respect and value are fragile. It is too easy for a demagogue to gather a following through boosting his or her own culture by denigrating others. Old prejudices compound this, so that it seems not only that another's culture is "inferior," but also that "they," the others, must always create inferior cultures.

Ethnic nationalism is a fantasy constructed out of rhetoric that denies basic humanity to others. The rhetoric is full of contradictions. There are many stories in Bosnia of people who recount the evil of their neighbors, then in the next breath speak longingly of the days when they could live in harmony side by side. This rhetoric feeds the fantasies of power: particularly for those who wield their power through wielding weapons. Ignatieff writes "most nationalist violence is perpetrated by a small minority of young males between the ages of 18 and 25. . . . I met lots of young men who loved the ruins, loved the destruction, loved the power that came from the barrels of their guns" (Ignatief: 187).

It would, however, be a mistake to trace the destructiveness of ethnic nationalism to the power complexes of these young men. They do not invent the rhetoric, or the nationalist fantasy, though they do maintain it. The only real defense against this destructiveness is a political system that prevents the buildup of nationalism by denying the demagogues a platform. If this is so, then ethnic

nationalism, however it arises, should be seen as inherently destructive, and resisted.

Another Look at Ethnic Nationalism   Ignatief speaks of ethnic nationalism as inherently destructive, and he wishes to promote civic nationalism. Yet when he looks at the world, he sees increasing numbers of places in which the strife of ethnic nationalism is occurring, and he sees reasons for its occurrence. Where people are ruled by others, where they live with fear, where they have little say in their own lives, they are easily swayed by a simplistic nationalism that seeks to put others down.

This section has reviewed arguments for seeing ethnic nationalism as positive pride in heritage, or as simplistic and destructive. In our view, these arguments do not give the whole picture. Ethnic nationalism is a complex phenomenon, and it emerges differently under different conditions. The following are some examples.

The war in Chechnya has been brutal. Beginning after the breakup of the Soviet Union, at times it has seemed to die down, only to reemerge. Since 2003, Chechnya has been officially an independent republic within the Russian federation. Chechen people have repeatedly gone to the polls to elect, or give elected legitimacy to, various new governments of independence or dependence. Most recently, a new president was elected in October 2004.

Chechen nationalism is defined in opposition to Russia. Chechnya was occupied by a Czarist regime in the nineteenth century. After Chechnya's declaration of independence in 1917 it was again occupied by the Bolsheviks. During the Second World War the Chechen people were forcibly relocated by Stalin, and attempts were made to suppress their culture and religion. Suppression contained but did not eradicate resistance, and when the iron hand of the Soviet state was removed, resistance to Russian rule became a nationalist uprising.

Whether this resistance—now seen as rebellion against an elected government—should still be seen as nationalist uprising, however, is a difficult point. While some observers see Russian assistance in suppressing internal strife, others see a second Chechen War now of five years duration. The international

Human Rights Watch (http://hrw.org/) has pointed to continued breaches of human rights within this disturbed nation, and names Russian imperialism as the driving force. Russian journalist Anna Politkovskaya—author of *Putin's Russia,* interviewed for the British newspaper *The Guardian* and for *Time*—joins the HRW in pointing out how the West ignores Chechnya. Politkovskaya sees (and reports on) a series of complex phenomena including continued interference (including bombing) and imprisonment and disappearances of ordinary people. She points also to economic interests, notably oil and the weapons trade. In Politkovskaya's eyes, this is not simply a matter of ethnic nationalism, but of abuse of power that is, in turn, becoming a breeding ground for terrorism and revenge. She and other commentators see the only solution being one of political negotiation, not military action.

Consider another example: In Spain, the Basque people had zealously protected the medieval charters that guaranteed them a measure of autonomy and local self-government. During the nineteenth century, these were abolished by Spain. Finally, during the Spanish Civil War, General Franco targeted the Basques with the bombing and partial destruction of the town of Guernica (in which 1,500 died), and the closing of schools, newspapers, and other cultural institutions, and the prohibition of public use of the Basque language. Fifty thousand Basques died during the Civil War. After the war, Basques retaliated with growing underground resistance movements, including the terrorist movement *Euskadi ta Askatasuna* (ETA), which was responsible for a number of attacks.

Franco's death brought political change in its wake, and eventually the granting, or re-granting, of a measure of autonomy to the Basque community. An agreement signed in 1988 stated that Basque government and Basque identity should be sought through negotiation, not violence. Today four areas of the North of Spain form the *Euskadi,* or the Autonomous Community of the Basque Country. An article in *National Geographic* states that "nearly every Basque now agrees on one thing: The future should be decided by negotiations, not violence." Yet violence continues, with the ETA targeting various high-profile politicians

and organizations. Further developments have included proposals in 1998 (and subsequent years) for taking negotiations forward. A stumbling block is the need for a ceasefire to be accepted by both the ETA and the Spanish government. The proposals pointed out that "the nub of the problem is not in a supposed confrontation between Spain and the Basque Country, in which the ETA occupies the role of 'front line' representative of the authentic will of the Basque people, but in the conflicting opinions of Basques over what they are and what they want to be."

SUMMING UP

Is too much national spirit a bad thing? In one sense, the answer is simple: Too much of anything is usually a bad thing. But some would say that, where virtue and justice are concerned, the same rules do not apply. In summing up, let us bring this nearer home, back to those "hyphenated identities" of North America, and one in particular.

Gerald R. Alfred, a Kahnawake Mohawk, writes in *Heeding the Voices of Our Ancestors* of his own nation and its nationalism. This nationalism has arisen in response to conditions over centuries. It draws upon traditional Mohawk symbols and concepts, and Mohawk history to create a distinctive identity. It is a community response, and it changes as ideas arise within the community and people attempt new ways of dealing with the conditions of their lives, including relations between their community and the Canadian government.

Mohawk nationalism cannot be understood unless its historical roots are considered. We can trace three phases in the development of Mohawk nationalism, after a starting point when Mohawks and their institutions were trading partners and allies of Euro-American colonists. Native communities, generally isolated, attempted to maintain their institutions on a piecemeal basis. "Revival nationalism," the second phase, did not arise until the colonists' goal of removing Mohawk institutions and identity became clear. This period was marked by various forms of confrontation, and focused around the reconstruction, on a traditional basis, of Mohawk identity and institutions. Now, in the third phase, "complex nationalism," the community is drawing on both traditional and modern concepts, seeking to develop a Mohawk state based on a modified version of the old institutions of the Iroquoian confederacy.

Mohawk nationalism is a historically-constituted issue for the Canadian state, as presently constituted. The question is whether this can come about peacefully, or whether ethnic nationalism, generating further competing ethnic nationalisms, must result in destruction.

REVIEW EXERCISES

For Discussion and Debate

1. "Can't we all just be American?"
2. "Nationalism is a response to oppression."
3. "Aboriginal people should join the mainstream."
4. "Every group has the right to self-determination."

Writing Exercises

Write a brief (500-word) essay on one of the following topics:

1. "Cultures meeting"—an imaginary reconstruction of the first meeting between aboriginal peoples and Europeans in your area.
2. Ethnicity and identity—can they be separated?
3. "Nationalism is about power."
4. "Who am I? Factors important in my own identity."

Research Activities

1. Trace the "ethnic history" of your geographical area, describing the groups that have settled in the area. Go as far back as you can.
2. Trace your own ethnicity. (Don't just settle for "American.") How does this form part of your identity? If, like most North Americans, you can trace descent from more than one cultural group, which is more important to you, and why?
3. Search the World Wide Web for statements of ethnicity and nationhood from any one group you wish to know more about. (Be specific in your search; name the group you intend to find.) How do you react to the statements? Why?
4. Find media reports of conflict associated with ethnic nationality. What terms are used to describe the participants? Which sides do the media favor, and why?

SELECTED REFERENCES

Abercrombie, Thomas J. 1996. "The Basques." *National Geographic* (Nov.): 74–97.
Alfred, Gerald R. 1995. *Heeding the Voices of our Ancestors.* Toronto: Oxford University Press.
Baumann, Zygmunt. 1989. *Modernity and the Holocaust.* Ithaca, NY: Cornell University Press.
Brown, D. 1998. "Why Is the Nation-State So Vulnerable to Ethnic Nationalism?" *Nations and Nationalism* 4, 1:1–15.
Dadrian, Vahakn. 1988. "The Anticipation and Prevention of Genocide in International Conflicts: Some Lessons from History." *International Journal of Group Tensions* 18, 3 (Fall): 205–214.

———. 1992. "The Role of the Turkish Military in the Destruction of Ottoman Armenians: A Study in Historical Continuities." *Journal of Political and Military Sociology* 20, 2 (Winter): 257–288.

Danforth, Loring M. 1993. "Claims to Macedonian Identity: The Macedonian Question and the Breakup of Yugoslavia." *Anthropology Today* 9, 4 (Aug.): 3–10.

Debeljak, Ales. 1994. "The Disintegration of Yugoslavia: Twilight of the Idols." *International Journal of Politics, Culture and Society* 8, 1 (Fall): 147–116.

Denitch, Bogdan. 1993. "Learning from the Death of Yugoslavia: Nationalism and Democracy." *Social Text* 34:3–16.

Derlugian, Georgi. 1993. "'Ethnic' Violence in the Postcommunist Periphery." *Studies in Political Economy* 41 (Summer): 45–81.

Dietler, Michael. 1994. "'Our Ancestors the Gauls': Archaeology, Ethnic Nationalism, and the Manipulation of Celtic Identity in Modern Europe." *American Anthropologist* 96, 3 (Sept.): 584–605.

Eriksen, Thomas Hylland. 1993. "A Future-Oriented Non-Ethnic Nationalism? Mauritius as an Exemplary Case." *Ethnos* 58, 3–4:197–221.

Fein, Helen. 1990. "Genocide: A Sociological Perspective." *Current Sociology* 38 (Spring): 1–126.

Gheorghe, Nicolae. 1991. "Roma-Gypsy Ethnicity in Eastern Europe." *Social Research* 8, 4 (Winter): 829–844.

Guardian online. 2004. *Special Report: Chechnya.* Available online at http://www.guardian.co.uk/chechnya/ 0,2759,180787,00.html. Accessed 20 October.

Ignatief, Michael. 1993. *Blood and Belonging.* London: Vintage.

Isajiw, Wsevolod W. 1985. "Definitions of Ethnicity." In *Ethnicity and Ethnic Relations in Canada.* 2d ed. Edited by Rita M. Bienvenue and Jay E. Goldstein. Toronto: Butterworths.

James, Carl. 1995. *Seeing Ourselves: Exploring Race, Ethnicity and Culture.* Toronto: Thompson Educational.

Kaufmann E. 2002. "Modern Formation, Ethnic Reformation: The Social Sources of the American Nation." *Geopolitics* 7, 2:99–120.

Lingle, Christopher. 1992. "Collectivism and Collective Choice: Conflicts between Class Formation and Ethnic Nationalism." *Ethnic Groups* 93, 3:191–201.

Lukes, Steven. 1993. "Five Fables about Human Rights: What Would It Be Like If . . . ." *Dissent* 40, 4 (173) (Fall): 427–437.

Ma'iz, R. 2003. "Framing the Nation: Three Rival Versions of Contemporary Nationalist Ideology." *Journal of Political Ideologies* 8, 3 (Oct.): 251–267.

Manz, Beatrice F. 2003. "Multi-Ethnic Empires and the Formulation of Identity." *Ethnic and Racial Studies* 26, 1 (Jan.): 70–101.

Nagel, Joanne. 1993. "Ethnic Nationalism: Politics, Ideology, and the World Order." *International Journal of Comparative Sociology* 34, 1–2 (Jan.–Apr.): 103–112.

Nagi, Saad Z. 1992. "Ethnic Identification and Nationalist Movements." *Human Organization* 51, 4 (Winter): 307–317.

Ryan, Stephen. 1990. "Ethnic Conflict and the United Nations." *Ethnic and Racial Studies* 13, 1 (Jan.): 25–49.

Smyth, Frank. 1994. "Cashing in on Rwanda's Genocide." *New Statesman and Society* 7, 313, 29 (July): 16–17.

Spohn, W. 2003. "Multiple Modernity, Nationalism, and Religion: A Global Perspective." *Current Sociology* 51, 3–4:265–286.

Staub, Ervin. 1989. *The Roots of Evil: The Origins of Genocide and Other Group Violence.* Cambridge: Cambridge University Press.

Van den Berghe, Pierre L. 1992. "The Modern State: Nation-Builder or Nation-Killer?" *International Journal of Group Tensions* 22, 3 (Fall): 191–208.

Zukier, Henri. 1994. "The Twisted Road to Genocide: On the Psychological Development of Evil during the Holocaust." *Social Research* 61, 2 (Summer): 423–455.

CHAPTER 7  RELIGION

Some sociologists define *religion* as "a set of beliefs, symbols, and practices (e.g., rituals), which is based on the idea of the sacred, and which unites believers into a socio-religious community." This approach to religion follows in the steps of Emile Durkheim, who focused on the functions of belief and ritual in binding people together in social groups. Other sociologists, following in the steps of Max Weber, view religion as "any set of coherent answers to human existential dilemmas—birth, sickness, death—which make the world meaningful." Here, the concern is less with social cohesion and more with the role religion plays in interpreting the world for individuals.

In both definitions, religion includes all of the thoughts and practices that put people in touch with what are thought of as supernatural forces, powers, or experiences that "transcend" ordinary life. The followers of some religions believe the supernatural resides in natural objects like the ocean and natural forces like the wind. Others think of distinct supernatural creatures—gods, goddesses, nymphs, and devils. Some religions have many gods, others have only one, while some religions—like Buddhism—have none. Some believe in an afterlife or in reincarnation, while others do not. Differences in ideas of good and evil, and differences in ritual practices, also distinguish the religions of the world.

In this chapter we consider three issues that illustrate the connection of religion to the rest of the social world. First, we ask questions about religion and gender, we look at the role and depiction of women in some of the world's religions, and we ask whether religions are typically hostile to women. Second, we look at what people see as *sacred,* and particularly at who owns or uses (or should own or use) ideas of *sacred heritage*—sacred places, sacred knowledge, and ways of celebrating culture and identity. Third, we consider whether the church–state connection is still important—that is, whether religions should be involved in politics and indeed whether the connection of religion and politics is destructive.

7.1   Are Traditional Religions against Women?

The issue: On one side, many people have a strong need to believe in something beyond themselves—a need traditionally fulfilled by religion. On the other side, many feminists contend that traditional religions teach the wrong kind of ideas about men and women.

Are traditional religions misogynistic—that is, do they show hatred toward women? This question has been hotly contested within and outside "traditional" churches in North America and elsewhere. Proponents of the view that religions are against women say that not only have women been treated badly by conventional religions, but that this treatment is intrinsically part of the religion, not something found in only a few problematic situations. Opponents of this view point out that more women than men are churchgoers: If women were badly treated, presumably they would not attend church as avidly as they do. This section finds that, in important respects, traditional religions are against women, and discusses the ways that people both inside and outside conventional churches are attempting to deal with their misogynistic elements.

TRADITIONAL RELIGIONS ARE NOT NECESSARILY MISOGYNISTIC

Many people within the churches spoken of as traditional in North America—that is, various denominations of Christianity and Judaism—have pointed to inequalities in the treatment of women and men. Here we deal for the most part with Christianity. Some church members and also some sociologists deny that such inequalities exist. Many, however, think that they do, but give conflicting reasons. Some feminist theorists charge that inequalities stem from a basic misogyny within traditional religions. Others, including other feminists, think that religious organizations may merely reflect social inequalities of their times, so that the problems women face within traditional religions are transient and can be expected to disappear with church reforms as women achieve a higher status elsewhere in the public sphere, and as women put pressure on church authorities.

Churches Change with the Times   One hundred years ago, women held no positions of authority within mainstream churches. They were not allowed to be preachers, ministers, priests, deacons, or bishops and they could hold authority only over other women, or children. Today, the picture is changing. Many churches have women in senior positions. The first woman moderator of the United Church of Canada was Lois Wilson, in 1980. Women have also been ordained within Anglican churches, even, recently, within the Church of England. Although many people threatened to leave the church if women were permitted to become priests, and a few did actually leave, the vote to have women as priests was carried by a majority.

If we look to the earliest writings of the Christian church, we find accounts of women as *deacons*—people who were recognized as knowledgeable and respected leaders within the emerging church. Later, these positions have been filled only by men, and it is true that some of the writings and statements of these men do appear misogynistic. However, we have to take these in the context of their times. When society was misogynistic, so were its churches. Moreover, during many periods in European history, churches were organizations within which women had more choice than they did generally in society. Within the church, women who became nuns could have far more access to both scholarship and authority than other women. Senior members of female religious orders were widely respected, even venerated.

The Worst Times for Women   During the period referred to as "the Burning Times," roughly the fifteenth to the seventeenth centuries, large numbers of women were condemned by the church and accused of "witchcraft," often for no other reason than that they were women. Some feminist scholars have said that this indicates misogyny. However, if we examine the evidence from that period, we find that, first, the numbers executed were small (approximately 60,000 rather than the millions that have been suggested) and that men as well as women were accused, although in almost all areas of Europe the numbers of women accused were higher.

It may be by chance that more women were accused. In many areas the "witch" became a convenient scapegoat—all the ills affecting a district could be blamed on her or him. People who did not fit in (e.g., who uttered curses or were seen as bad neighbors) were more likely to be targeted by an untutored peasantry as witches and as the source of local problems. Further, the *witch craze* was conducted by civil authorities as well as by the churches, so the churches alone can't be blamed for this craze.

Important Roles for Women   Since those unhappy times, many aspects of society have changed. The work people do, the distribution of that work, and its value for society, all influence the ways women and men are thought of. Today in many churches women and their roles are once again highly valued. In some churches these roles are different from the roles of men. For instance, in the Catholic church both women and men can be teachers and theologians, though only men can be called to the priesthood. Within Catholicism, priesthood represents a highly specialized position, and because all the first apostles were men, Catholic doctrine holds that their successors must be men also. Many Catholics point out that other positions are open to women, and that women within the church are highly respected, having their own spheres of influence and decision making.

Women have played an important role within religiously inspired movements in the past. Often movements for social change, linked to the churches, have been organized or headed by women, or have taken up causes favored by women: The temperance movement is an outstanding example. Within church congregations, often the work of visiting, helping, and giving counsel and comfort is performed by women. These women are seen as the backbone of the church, central to its processes.

If we look at today's church congregations, we find that in almost all major denominations, the majority of church members and church-goers are women. National U.S. surveys indicate that women are more likely than men to report attending a religious service in the past week (by 46 percent to 35 percent). They are also more likely to report their religious commitment as a positive experience, and to see it as an important factor in their lives.

Major churches are strongly influenced by their memberships, and so women have a strong voice in decision making. If women require change, they have only to ask for it. Churches, therefore, are no more misogynistic than other social institutions, and indeed may be less so than the institutions of politics or business, for instance. There have indeed been examples of church-based misogyny, whether stemming from highly prejudiced individuals, or occurring during times of exceptionally bad social treatment of women. However, churches are not necessarily misogynistic, and indeed, in these more enlightened times, they consciously minister to the needs of both female and male church members.

TRADITIONAL CHURCHES ARE MISOGYNISTIC

A number of feminist scholars and others charge that, since the times of the early church, social processes operating within the church have acted to exclude women from positions of power and decision making, and that both doctrine and practice have reflected this. Although women today have more chance to participate at a higher level, these processes remain in operation to a greater or lesser extent, depending on the religious denomination. In the more conservative churches, exclusionary processes remain in force: In the more liberal churches, their operations are masked and contested, but they remain part of the structure of the church. Movements such as those for inclusive (i.e., nonsexist) language within churches are viewed as secondary or "fringe" interests, not essential to the basic operation of the church, or even to the real challenges and issues facing churches today.

Participating in church, and playing a large part in the organization of the everyday life of churches, from bake sales to visiting charity work and vast amounts of committee work, is not enough: Women remain invisible. In part because of this, increasing numbers of women are looking for and finding their religion outside traditional churches.

Women and Church Hierarchy   Mary Daly, well known as a critic of established churches, indicates that the structure, symbolism, and language of the churches are profoundly antiwoman. Churches promote the concept of hierarchy, with "God" at the apex, followed by men (in some churches, various levels of male priests, then laymen), women, and children. Even Protestant churches, which do not necessarily promote a hierarchy of clergy, have traditionally viewed men as closer to God. This hierarchy is strengthened and promoted by an overwhelming number of male images. Most often, God is still presented as male; images of Jesus abound in many churches; figures of the (male) apostles appear everywhere, from church windows to children's books.

Often the only apparent female image is that of Mary, viewed as mother and described in ways that (as many feminist theologians and sociologists point out) make plain that she is set apart from ordinary women, and so cannot be truly emulated. Besides, she is spoken of as merely an *intercessor.* Even as mother of God, she has no power, and she does not form part of the male Trinity. When, in 1987, the world's first female Catholic theology professor, Uta Ranke-Heinemann, challenged the concept of the Virgin Mary as asexual, untainted, and pure—an impossible model for women—the church revoked her authority to teach theology.

Until recently, women were considered by mainstream churches to be incapable of acting as priests or ministers; and although in many Protestant churches women can now be ministers, this was not achieved without a struggle. The Catholic church recently reiterated its position on the issue of women as priests. Bishop Angelo Scola stated that Christ was male and his apostles were male, and clearly he wanted to have only male priests. "The church does not have the power to modify the practice, uninterrupted for 2,000 years, of calling only men," Scola said, adding that "this was wanted directly by Jesus," and that the all-male priesthood is "objectively linked to the sex of Jesus." Feminists have been quick to point out that what was "wanted by Jesus" has been interpreted and reinterpreted by generations of male clergy.

The concept of women as spiritually different from men, in ways that matter for traditional religions, can be traced through the writings of theologians. According to theologian Joanna Manning, "St. Thomas Aquinas taught that in the natural or earthly order, only men possessed the fullness of humanity and women's defective humanity was derived through men's."

Another Look at the Witchcraze The witchcraze, culminating in the sixteenth and seventeenth centuries, has already been referred to. During that period civil as well as ecclesiastical courts condemned both women and men. The men were most often those associated with the women condemned as witches—their fathers, sons, or husbands, or men who tried to defend them. About 80 percent of those accused were women. It is no coincidence that this was also a period of the growing domestication and restriction of women. At the start of it, women acted in the public sphere, as farmers, traders, craftspeople, midwives, and folk-healers. Some may have been involved in folk-religious practices akin to shamanic techniques of healing and prophesy found in many other parts of the world.

By the end of the period, a woman's place was as an adjunct to her husband, if she had one. Seen in a broader context, the process of accusation, trial, torture, and execution of thousands of "witches" proved to be one method by which men were able to restrict women's lives more in the early 1800s than ever before or since. And in this context, one has to wonder whether the current enthusiasm for Jane Austen's nineteenth century domestic novels represents a backlash against modern feminism and the actual liberation of women from second-class status.

The theology of the times made the witchcraze possible. Women were seen as the carriers of evil: susceptible to the advances of the devil from whom they derived their powers through a pact, sexually insatiable, the greatest danger to Christian society. The most famous witch-hunter's manual, *Malleus Maleficarum,* prepared by two Dominican priests, was published in 1486 and went through six editions before 1500, at least thirteen by 1520, and another sixteen by 1669. It was translated into German, French, Italian, and English, was intensively quoted in later manuals, and soon spread into civil law. There, even enlightened judges, under the influence of church doctrine, sought supernatural explanations for phenomena such as the death of animals or sickness of people.

Today, most analyses of the witchcraze period still do not mention the intense misogyny inculcated by Christian doctrines, or the determined hunting-out of the remnants of folk-religious practices. When it is mentioned, the witchcraze is depicted as something that is in the past, irrelevant to modern society. Many feminist scholars, however, point out that the effects of the witchcraze period are still with us in many popular images of women, especially in the ways that we speak of older women or "troublesome" women as "witches."

SUMMING UP

Are traditional religions against women? To the extent that they were misogynistic in the past and have yet to reform their practices, yes, they are.

The witchcraze provides evidence that standard church doctrines and practices have included a strong strand of misogyny. In some churches, women remain excluded from areas of religious life, and their qualifications to speak as theologians and teachers are under constant review. Harassment of women attending theological colleges is commonly reported, and the images of divinity presented today within Christianity are still overwhelmingly male.

Does this, however, constitute grounds for saying that traditional religions are misogynistic? Some feminist scholars and theologians argue that traditional religions are redeemable, and that a constant pressure for reform will bring change, in time. Others, however, maintain that women can best express their spiritualities outside established churches.

Today, some writers are attempting to construct feminist theologies in which divinity is conceptualized as female, or as both female and male. Many other people within North America and Europe are exploring their spiritualities through reconstructed practices, based on the folk religions of Africa, America, and Europe. Native groups are working to re-establish indigenous North American religions. Others look to their background or ancestry, focusing on African traditions and beliefs or on European, Celtic, and Nordic folklore and mythology.

These practitioners reject the misogyny of the Burning Times. Some conceptualize divinity as both female and male; some follow a Goddess, and some have returned to a polytheist understanding of many deities: female, male, neither, or both. Often, though, these practitioners share a concept of Earth as the mother of all beings, and become advocates for environmental awareness. While misogyny is only one of many reasons for this attempt, many of the people involved with Goddess Spirituality or with goddesses within Pagan religions have "empowerment" of women and men as a specific aim. Unlike much of the so-called "New Age," pagan ideas of deity and community often strongly emphasize the embodiment of religion and identity, valuing body as much as spirit and finding beauty in women and men of all ages. Also, they are working to reclaim words such as *witch* (as a practitioner of magic, female or male, rather than *evil woman*), and *Pagan* and *Heathen* as words used at the times when Christianity came into contact with European pre-Christian religions, before they acquired the highly negative meanings that they hold today in some sections of society.

It is too early to tell what kind of challenge these reconstructed religions will pose to Christian hegemony within North America. It may be that in a postmodern world, with an atmosphere of more religious tolerance, each religion (however small) can hold its own and empower its adherents. Yet women who speak out are still viewed negatively, as "witches," and women and men who are followers of Wicca, Santeria, Paganism, or Heathenry may find that others in their community see them as a threat. The Burning Times may not be totally behind us.

REVIEW EXERCISES

For Discussion and Debate

1. "Using inclusive language in church is just being politically correct."
2. "Women need their own space to reclaim their spirituality."
3. Does organized religion control or oppress men?
4. The Witchcraze—was it an expression of women-hating?

Writing Exercises

Write a brief (500-word) essay on one of the following topics:

1. "The roles of women and men in a religious institution." (Choose your own institution.)
2. "Why women seek the Goddess."
3. "How people seek personal fulfillment in their religions."
4. "My own experience—does religion empower me?"

Research Activities

1. Interview ten women who are members of an established church. What do they see as problems facing women in their church? How can these problems be overcome? Present your findings to a group of students from your class.
2. Survey at least 20 students who are not members of your class on their attitudes toward followers of earth-centered spirituality, including Pagans, Wiccans, Heathens, and Goddess worshippers. (Many of these may be known as "witches.") Discuss your findings with other members of your class.
3. Draw up a short questionnaire on church attendance (including denomination and frequency of attendance) and views on changing roles of women. Using this, survey at least 15 people, and prepare your results for presentation to the class. (Remember that "church" can mean sociologically any religious organization.)
4. Conduct interviews with active religious practitioners (five women and five men) on the use of *inclusive language* within their religions.

SELECTED REFERENCES

Adler, Margot. 1986. *Drawing Down the Moon.* 2d ed. Boston, MA: Beacon.

Aldridge, Alan. 1989. "Men, Women, and Clergymen: Opinion and Authority in a Sacred Organization." *Sociological Review* 37, 1 (Feb.): 43–64.

Bartel, Pauline. 2000. *Spellcasters: Witches and Witchcraft in History, Folklore, and Popular Culture.* Dallas, TX: Taylor Trade.

Blain, Jenny. 2002. *Nine Worlds of Seid-Magic: Ecstasy and Neo-Shamanism in North European Paganism.* London and New York: Routledge.

Blain, Jenny, Douglas Ezzy and Graham Harvey, eds. 2004. *Researching Paganisms.* Walnut Creek, CA: AltaMira.

Choksy, Jamsheed K. 1988. "Women in the Zoroastrian Book of Primal Creation: Images and Functions within a Religious Tradition." *Mankind Quarterly* 29, 1–2:73–82.

Christ, Carol P. 1987. *Laughter of Aphrodite: Reflections on a Journey to the Goddess.* New York: Harper Collins.

———1992. "Why Women Need the Goddess." In *Womanspirit Rising: A Feminist Reader in Religion,* edited by Carol P. Christ and Judith Plaskow. San Francisco, CA: Harper.

Daly, Mary. 1973. *Beyond God the Father: Toward a Philosophy of Women's Liberation.* Boston, MA: Beacon.

Eller, Cynthia. 1993. *Living in the Lap of the Goddess: The Feminist Spirituality Movement in America.* Boston, MA: Beacon Press.

Erturk, Yakin. 1991. "Convergence and Divergence in the Status of Moslem Women: The Cases of Turkey and Saudi Arabia." *International Sociology* 6, 3 (Sept.): 307–320.

Finley, Nancy J. 1991. "Political Activism and Feminist Spirituality." *Sociological Analysis* 52, 4:349–362.

Ghadbian, Najib. 1995. "Islamists and Women in the Arab World: From Reaction to Reform." *American Journal of Islamic Social Sciences* 12, 1 (Spring): 19–35.

Ginzburg, Carlo. 1991. *Ecstasies: Deciphering the Witches' Sabbath.* Translated by Raymond Rosenthal. New York: Pantheon Books.

Goldscheider, Calvin and William D. Mosher. 1991. "Patterns of Contraceptive Use in the United States: The Importance of Religious Factors." *Studies in Family Planning* 22, 2 (Mar.–Apr.): 102–115.

Griffin, Wendy. 1995. "The Embodied Goddess: Feminist Witchcraft and Female Divinity." *Sociology of Religion* 56, 1:35–48.

Griffin, Wendy, ed. 2000. *Daughters of the Goddess: Studies of Healing, Identity and Empowerment.* Walnut Creek, CA: AltaMira Press.

Greek, Cecil E. and William Thompson. 1992. "Antipornography Campaigns: Saving the Family in America and England." *International Journal of Politics, Culture and Society* 5, 4 (Summer): 601–616.

Hoodfar, Homa. "The Veil in Their Minds and on Our Heads: The Persistence of Colonial Images of Muslim Women." *Resources for Feminist Research* 22, 3–4 (Fall–Winter): 5–18.

Hunter, James Davison and Kimon Howland Sargeant. 1993. "Religion, Women, and the Transformation of Public Culture." *Social Research* 60, 3 (Fall): 545–570.

Hutton, Ronald. 2001. *The Triumph of the Moon.* Oxford: Oxford University Press.

Ingersoll, Julie J. 1995. "Which Tradition, Which Values? 'Traditional Family Values' in American Protestant Fundamentalism." *Contention: Debates in Society, Culture and Science* 4, 2 (Winter): 91–103.

Jelen, Ted G. 1988. "Changes in the Attitudinal Correlates of Opposition to Abortion, 1977–1985." *Journal for the Scientific Study of Religion* 27, 2 (June): 211–228.

Kieckhefer, Richard. 1994. "The Holy and the Unholy: Sainthood, Witchcraft, and Magic in Late Medieval Europe." *Journal of Medieval & Renaissance Studies* 24 (Fall): 355–385.

King, Ursula. 1989. "Women and Spirituality: Voices of Protest and Promise." Pp. 91–105 in *Women in Society,* edited by Jo Campling. London: MacMillan Education Ltd.

Kintz, Linda. 1994. "Motherly Advice from the Christian Right: The Construction of Sacred Gender." *Discourse* 17, 1 (Fall): 49–76.

Levack, Brian P. 1987. *The Witch-Hunt in Early Modern Europe.* London: Longman.

Lottes, Ilsa L. and Peter J. Kurloff. 1992. "The Effects of Gender, Race, Religion, and Political Orientation on the Sex Role Attitudes of College Freshmen" *Adolescence* 27, 107 (Fall): 675–688.

Lozano, Wendy G. and Tanice G. Foltz. 1990. "Into the Darkness: An Ethnographic Study of Witchcraft and Death." *Qualitative Sociology* 13, 3:211–234.

Luff, Tracy L. 1990. "Wicce: Adding a Spiritual Dimension to Feminism." *Berkeley Journal of Sociology* 35:91–105.

Luhrmann, Tanya M. 1993. "Resurgence of Romanticism: Contemporary Neo-Paganism, Feminist Spirituality and the Divinity of Nature." Pp. 219–232 in *Environmentalism: The View from Anthropology,* edited by Kay Milton. London: Routledge.

Mernissi, Fatima. 1988. "Muslim Women and Fundamentalism." *Middle East Report* 18, 4 (153) (July–Aug.): 8–11.

Obermeyer, Carla Makhlouf. 1994. "Reproductive Choice in Islam: Gender and State in Iran and Tunisia." *Studies in Family Planning* 25, 1 (Jan.–Feb.): 41–51.

Patterson, Orlando. 1994. "The New Puritanism." *Salmagundi* 101–102 (Winter–Spring): 55–67.

Ralston, Helen. 1991. "Religious Movements and the Status of Women in India." *Social Compass* 38, 1 (Mar.): 43–53.

Russell, Jeffery Burton. 1972. *Witchcraft in the Middle Ages.* Ithaca, NY: Cornell University.

Schüssler Fiorenza, Elisabeth. 1983. *In Memory of Her: A Feminist Theological Reconstruction of Christian Origins.* New York: Crossroad.

Sered, Susan Starr. 1994. "Ideology, Autonomy, and Sisterhood: An Analysis of the Secular Consequences of Women's Religions." *Gender and Society* 8, 4 (Dec.): 486–506.

Staats, Valerie. 1994. "Ritual, Strategy, or Convention: Social Meanings in the Traditional Women's Baths in Morocco." *Frontiers* 14, 3:1–18.

Starhawk. 1982. *Dreaming the Dark: Magic, Sex, & Politics.* Boston, MA: Beacon Press.

Touabi, Noureddine. 1990. "Acculturation, Value Conflicts and the Place of the Sacred in Family Life in Algeria." *International Social Science Journal* 42, 4 (126) (Nov.): 539–545.

Whitney, Elspeth. 1995. "International Trends: The Witch 'She'/The Historian 'He': Gender and the Historiography of the European Witch-Hunts." *Journal of Women's History* 7 (Fall): 77–101.

7.2 Whose Heritage Are We Protecting?

The Issue: Should spiritual heritage be protected, reserved for some people only? Or should it be open to all?

What is *sacred* and what is *secular*? This differs greatly from one culture, or area, to another. Three of the great religions of the world—Judaism, Islam and Christianity—are known for their sacred scriptures. The Qur'an has been translated into many languages and is read around the world, as are the Old and New Testaments. Some other religions likewise have much-translated writings—for instance Hindu scriptures. A *sacred book* also has secular uses: The Bible is used in the United States, Canada, and Western Europe in courts and lawyers' offices. This is a way that religion becomes part of everyday life—even for people who would have very low scores on *religiosity* (engagement with religious practices).

Ideas of sacredness are part of religious and cultural expression. Sociologist Emile Durkheim saw religion as expressing concepts and ideas that were central to any culture. Each culture and society developed its own religious expressions, and these changed as the culture changed. Other sociologists have viewed religion differently, from the functionalist approach of discussing and enumerating the ways religion strengthened social ties and social cohesion, to the Marxist concept of religion as the "opiate of the people," acting to maintain existing power structures. Today, sociologists view religious expressions as acting in complex ways, sometimes as mechanisms of social control, at other times as vehicles of resistance and empowerment. Many sociologists emphasize the need to consider how religion is implicit in people's construction of meaning in their lives, and so are moving away from examining religion merely in terms of its social functions.

In this section we look at arguments about *sacred heritage* and the *spiritual supermarket*. Can or should heritage be shared? The Bible or the Qur'an are translated and read by many people from many different cultural—and religious—backgrounds. Are there other forms of sacred heritage for which this cannot, or does not, occur?

HERITAGE IS FOR SHARING

All over the world, people are interested in sacred places and events. They read about events, watch news stories and documentaries, and focus attention on sacred heritage. They look things up on the Internet. They attend events and go on pilgrimages. Even many who are not themselves religious will show interest in accounts of special events: The great Islamic pilgrimage of The Hadj is one that every Muslim hopes to make, but non-Muslims read and watch with interest. In places such as Walsingham in England, Anglicans and Catholics visit their special shrines, but these are open to others who come as tourists or to learn. People write books, create documentaries, and design Web pages in order to explain their spirituality to others.

Coleman and Elsner (p. 46) quote a priest in Walsingham as saying:

> Walsingham is like a huge icon. It's almost like a Christian theme park, in which we set out the wares and then allow people to make of it what they will. And I think there's something about that which is very therapeutic . . . it's the best kind of spiritual direction, which actually allows a pilgrim to find his or her own way in what God offers. . . . And I think we just make available these resources, and people use them as they find best.

Religion here is something for consumption—part of a "spiritual supermarket." Indeed, Walsingham can be seen as an industry. This form of spiritual tourism benefits everybody—those who organize it, and those whose lives are enriched by the experience. It clearly shows that religion and spirituality are not out of place in today's world.

And this is an important point. Increasingly through the twentieth century, sociologists predicted that religion would decline in importance, often basing their work on the ideas of Durkheim who assumed that religion and religious expression would change as society changed. His work dealt with solidarity, which holds society together, and he defined two types: mechanical and organic. The first referred to societies where everyone did much the same thing so that households were self-sufficient—as among foraging peoples or small-scale agriculturalists. The second referred to societies where people were interdependent: People's work differed greatly, but each person was reliant on many others for the necessities of life—as in present-day industrial societies. Mechanical solidarity was built on similarities of daily life, shared norms, beliefs, and ways of thinking. Organic solidarity consisted of obligations to other people within the society, however different they might be.

Durkheim studied the religions of aboriginal peoples of Australia, and compared them with the religions he saw around him in Europe. He concluded that religions form an expression of central values in society. When people engage in their religious practices they are linking themselves to society. The deities they refer to and worship can be considered essentially personifications of their own society.

In one important respect, Durkheim illustrates a general feature of the sociological study of religion: Social scientists do not question whether "God" or "Gods" or "Goddesses" exist outside of people's social expressions. That is a topic for theology, a different discipline. Instead, like Durkheim, sociologists focus on how people create their understandings of divinity. Durkheim was not asking whether God exists, only how people relate to and worship their gods.

According to Durkheim, different concepts of *deity* are differently suited to mechanical and organic societies. Religious tensions, conflicts, and oppression are common in heterogeneous societies. For a complex organic society, the old ways of relating to divinity may be more destructive than productive. Durkheim hoped that, regardless of people's personal beliefs and encounters with divinity, a form of Humanism would become the religion of industrial societies—a religion in which people see their common humanity, not their specific religious beliefs, as what links them together.

This process is spoken of as *secularization.* Many scholars have pointed to secularization within western societies, noting a steadily diminishing influence of religion in public life. Bryan Wilson, for example, points to three features of life in industrial societies that lead toward secularization: social differentiation, societalization, and rationalization.

Social differentiation forms part of the pattern of societies becoming increasingly complex, changing from little difference in what people do to great specialization and specificity. In the past, religion and its institution (which, following Durkheim, we can call a *church* regardless of the type of religious worship) was central to much of social life. Besides providing for worship and teaching about sacred things, the church taught basic skills, supported those in need, cared for the sick, served as a meeting place, and organized social events. In modern societies, these functions are taken care of by many separate institutions: schools, hospitals, government agencies, and social clubs, among others. This means that the church is no longer central to daily living, but merely one institution among many. It is also one with which many individuals may have little contact as it is no longer necessary to belong to a religious institution in North American or Western European society, though it is seen as necessary for children to attend school, and for sick people to visit a doctor's office.

Societalization   The strength of religion is still its basis in community. But *societalization*—the second aspect of secularization—refers to how people increasingly relate, not to a community in which every person knows everyone else but to *society* in the abstract. In North America and Europe today, most people look to society—a large, amorphous unit with its organizations run on bureaucratic principles—to provide for their needs. People regularly find and work at jobs, read and watch the news, attend school, and vote in elections. All of these activities put them into contact with a society that sustains and regulates their activities. The interaction of people with society leaves little room for religion, which is increasingly viewed as personal, not societal, and indeed marginal to social life. Whether they are Buddhist or Roman Catholic, Protestant or Jewish, Muslim or Hindu or Atheist, for most people religion is not an important part of their dealings with society. They don't talk about it at work.

At its most important, religion helps people form meaning and identity though a community-wide understanding of relations to sacred things. But where people's chief attachment is to the wider society, religion is no longer a central, shared part of community life. Even though many people continue to engage in prayer and worship, and attend synagogue or church, their religion has become a thing they engage in primarily as individuals, a lifestyle choice made out of interest or for personal development—a private matter when compared to the public pursuits of going to work or voting in elections.

The third feature of modern life that undercuts the importance of religion is *rationalization*—a focus on explaining the world and its events by means of ideas that rely on the logical interpretation of empirical evidence. The Judeo-Christian religions of the Western world themselves supported and encouraged the spread of rationalization, in part to reduce reliance on superstition and folk-magic practices. Along with this emphasis on rationality, as Weber observed, modern religion has emphasized theology over myth. In most Christian denominations, the leadership emphasizes philosophical inquiry into the nature of people and their relationship with the divine, instead of the early Bible stories of the creation. (This is, indeed, the basic difference between mainstream and fundamentalist churches.)

However, rationalization eventually acted against the churches. The major western religions are ultimately based in faith, and tenets of faith are never susceptible to empirical testing. "Is there a God?" is not a question one can answer by applying the scientific method. A tendency within modern societies was, it seemed, increasingly to view *all* religion as superstition, and faith as a (possibly useful) psychological crutch to help people deal with problems in their everyday lives.

But how does this relate to the "spiritual supermarket"? Rather than disappear, religions have acted to make themselves relevant in today's society in two main ways—relevant to society and relevant to people's personal identities. First, though Durkheim

thought religion was losing its functions, it was gaining another, thanks to those changes in society and the development of large nation-states. Robertson, an eminent historian of religion, notes that "against a long, drawn-out historical background . . . there crystallized at the end of the eighteenth century a view of religion centered on the place of individual religious commitment in the nationally constituted society" (Robertson: 13).

As strong nation-states arose, together with the concept of the individual there came a need in these nation-states for individuals to show loyalty directly to the nation-state and its society, not to their local community and the practices of their daily life. Religion taught people to be good citizens. Societalization, instead of weakening the functions of religion, changed and strengthened it, making the concept of religion global (or all-encompassing). And with this globalization of religion came the concept of religious toleration, together with a separation of religion from the political workings of society. The church was no longer synonymous with the state. The church should not run the state, but churches would influence the people of that state and strengthen their attachment and loyalty to it.

With today's globalization and the coming of the information society, religion has taken yet a further step. Durkheim and others hoped for the coming of humanism to help people see their common humanity. Humanism has indeed emerged—as another religion—but its tenets are shared. Today's religions teach people to be citizens of the world. New religions are emerging and can compete with the older ones. Within this information society we click a button and access knowledge about different religions. We read teachings from past and present. We find ideas that suit us. Importantly, people can *evaluate* and *choose* their religion. Teachings shared are teachings that can be assessed and that are subject to the competition of the consumer market.

Far from being unimportant, religion, spirituality, and belief are and remain central in how people shape their identities and develop their interests and knowledge. Religions teach us about ourselves, our roots, and our potential, relinking us with other communities and showing us what we have in common with people around the world. Both old and new forms of spiritual heritage will be assessed, in the end, by how useful they are to help people become better humans, members of a global civilization.

TO UNDERSTAND SACRED HERITAGE, YOU MUST LIVE IT

The previous argument makes interesting points about the growth of global communication. However, it does not address issues of how different communities today relate to the *global network* and the *spiritual supermarket.*

Let us return for a moment to Durkheim. He compared religions of aboriginal peoples of Australia with the religions he saw around him in Europe. He saw the differences as part of a change from traditional to modern societies—he termed these *mechanistic* and *organic.* This work has resulted in a modernization thesis that one route to modernity applies to everyone. The assumption is that as societies develop and change, religion changes also.

Indeed, if we look at small, traditional societies such as hunter-gatherer bands, the concept of "religion" as we know it may be absent. That does not mean that people are not religious. Far from it. Instead, it means that religion is closely interwoven with people's daily lives. Rather than being concerned with an afterlife or even with a deity or deities, religion gives meaning to people's relations with their environment, the seasons of the year, the animals and plants that are their life-support. There may not be religious specialists; however, there *are* people who specialize in healing magic and ritual, in hunting magic and ritual, and in telling and enacting the tales that carry the myths of the society—the shared concepts of who people and animals are, how they came to be, and their relations with each other. The work of these shamans and storytellers is an intrinsic part of the cultural life of these traditional societies.

Ideas about modernization assume that as societies change, religion will become more global in its context—more concerned with humanity and less with community and locality. But if we look into small-scale communities within today's nation states, we can still find shamans and storytellers!

The spiritual supermarket, with all its wares on display, assumes that all religions can be so displayed and that people as individuals have the right to make choices and find what suits them. Indeed, since the 1960s Europeans and North Americans have been seeking various kinds of "truth" in all parts of the world. The Beatles' involvement with Maharishi Mahesh Yogi is a well-known example. The New Age movement valued spirituality over the materiality of life, and drew often on ideas from Christianity, Hinduism, and Buddhism, looking particularly to the lives and works of mystics.

Songs and chants such as the music of Hildegard of Bingen, neglected for centuries, have become best-sellers, and many teachers have arisen claiming a link to either ancient or forgotten wisdom. For while Buddhist and Hindu philosophies are much studied, together with the Christian mystics, increasingly it is indigenous religions—such as Native American, African, or Siberian—that are on display. Do these fit with the spiritual supermarket?

Not according to some indigenous leaders and writers, who charge the New Age with *appropriation* and with romanticizing Native knowledge and spirituality as more pure and in touch with the earth.

Appropriation   We are dealing here both with beliefs and practices—what people do in their religion, and places that may be sacred to them. In some cases there are religious traditions that have developed over millennia, in particular locations. Uluru or Ayers Rock in Australia is a huge sandstone rock that rises from the desert floor. During the day the rock appears to change color as the sun strikes it, glowing violet and purple at sunset. There are many aboriginal legends of Uluru, and various parts of the rock are covered with paintings going back approximately 1,000 years (and often renewed). The whole area is a sacred place, and some of its sites—according to the Anangu people, the traditional owners of the rock—should be kept secret. But Ayers Rock is a major tourist attraction and the legends may be told for the benefit of visitors, out of the context of their meaning for people who live in the culture and climate of the Australian desert.

Closer to home, a number of Native North American spiritual leaders have protested against what they see as the theft of culture and spirituality. Classes and workshops, often held by non-natives, claim to teach ceremonies and "medicine." In 1993 a group of Canadian and U.S. Lakota, Nakota, and Dakota leaders produced a "Declaration of War against Exploiters of Lakota Spirituality," saying that "for too long we have suffered the unspeakable indignity of having our most precious Lakota ceremonies and spiritual practices desecrated, mocked, and abused by non-Indian 'wannabes,' hucksters, cultists, commercial profiteers, and self-styled 'New Age shamans' and their followers." The declaration called on Lakota and other Native peoples to protest and campaign against such desecrations, and "to preserve the purity of our precious traditions for our future generations, so that our children and our children's children will survive and prosper in the sacred manner intended for each of our respective peoples by our Creator."

In particular, some non-Native authors have been identified as people who took pieces of Native practice and marketed these, deliberately, as "authentic Native American" spirituality (whereas no group or tribe calls its spirituality "Native American" but rather indicates a particular culture or nation). Native authors have commented on the phenomenon of "wannabes" in articles such as "For All Who Were Indian in a Former Life" by Andy Smith. They object to pieces of their cultural and spiritual heritage being packaged for a New Age audience and sold for profit, and to the art and music of Native artists being used and exploited without the artists themselves being named.

Romanticism   We need to ask what draws non-Native people toward these forms of spirituality. Why does this appropriation exist? We can look for some roots in the arguments about secularization given earlier, particularly ideas about *societalization* and *rationalization*. As societies have developed into nation-states, and "superstitious" folk-magic has been frowned on, people have not lost their desire for community and identity. In the chapter on ethnicity we discussed ideas of civic versus ethnic nationalism, and found these to be too simple.

Similarly here, people find themselves rootless in a modern world, and have gone in search of spiritual identity—whether through mainstream or fundamentalist churches (both of which are emphasizing community, though in different ways) or through seeking a "return" to origins or to a "simpler" mode of life.

Sociologists, like the Native writers pointed to earlier, see indigenous groups around the world as located politically, economically, culturally, and materially as well as spiritually. But many new age seekers see only the spiritual location. And what they see is indigenous groups having something they themselves do not have: magic and identity.

Others may think that they can help the economic and political conditions of indigenous people by adopting or publicizing their spirituality. Indigenous spokespeople point out that this helps no one. Such help is based on seeing indigenous people as a romantic, primitive other, close to nature and yet, paradoxically, unable to function in a modern, advanced world. It is neo-colonialism, patronizing with one hand while taking with the other. In the words of Margo Thunderbird:

> And now, after all that, they've come for the very last of our possessions, now they want our pride, our history, our spiritual traditions. They want to rewrite and remake these things, to claim them for themselves. The lies and theft just never end.

SUMMING UP

Can heritage be shared? Do new age seekers respect the cultures they draw from? Is appropriation always wrong? We have shown two sides of a discussion that includes ideas of appropriation and exploitation, versus sharing and religious tolerance; between people who see themselves and others having not only a right but possibly a duty to learn and share; and those who locate their spirituality within cultural contexts that have been seriously attacked and undermined by colonialism.

One point remains though. Why do people seek a "purer" religion? Poet and anthropologist Wendy

Rose attempts to understand the appropriations from a critical Native American perspective.

> Those of us who have publicly criticized the "whiteshamans" and their cult-followers have tried to find explanations for all this that will make sense to Indian people. It has, for instance, been noted that European-derived Americans face a cultural imperative to cut their own roots to Europe . . . [so] they have flopped around in a cultural vacuum, trying to get a grip on the roots of others. . . . Were the givers to be credited, this would be fine—simple diffusion of ideas and artifacts; however, credit is not placed where credit is due in either case. The roots of colonized people are grasped firmly but blindly by the rootless in order to achieve some kind of stability, however superficial or delusional. The young European American asks "Who am I?" And no one answers.

Some spiritual leaders have advised European-American seekers to look to their own traditions and roots, and this has of course been done: European (and other) paganisms form part of that cultural and spiritual supermarket, and usually these are distinct from the "New Age." In Europe some pagan spiritualities are coming to be seen as *new-indigenous* where people are re-linking pre-Christian lore (both literature and folklore) with observations of landscape, animals, and seasons.

In North America it is harder: The stories that Europeans can access relate to other places—Wales rather than British Columbia, the Hebrides rather than Texas, Gascony rather than Michigan. And just as with appropriation of indigenous North American spiritualities and practices, claims of being a "Celtic Shaman" based on having a great-great-grandmother from Argyll in western Scotland may not sit well with people who have just achieved a Scottish Assembly after half a century of campaigning. But Wendy Rose points out that European Americans can create their own stories of place and spirituality, as long as it is plain that these are *their* stories, new ones, "their own sacred ways," which may be informed by, but are not the same as, somebody else's.

This issue of spiritual appropriation will be with us for some time. Resolutions may be possible but will require an understanding on the part of seekers that cultures are lived, not learned in a weekend workshop or bought in a book; that indigenous religions have developed within particular geographical and cultural settings; and that *shamanism* is not, indeed, a word from any Native American language. In the meantime, many spiritual seekers find identity and meaning through the spiritual supermarket, choosing their religion and learning to live it in their own way, and in doing so create their own communities of choice.

REVIEW EXERCISES

For Discussion and Debate

1. "Countries do best when there is one major religion that most people follow."
2. "How can existence have a meaning if people don't have religion?"
3. "Spirituality is not something that can be bought and sold."
4. "Religion is important, but it isn't part of daily life."

Writing Exercises

Write a brief (500-word) essay on one of the following topics:

1. "Can there be shamans in the city?"
2. "In large cities today, people create their communities based on religion."
3. "My own experience—the importance of religion in my life today compared to when I was a child."
4. "Why people search for religion."

Research Activities

1. Survey students in your class on religious membership. What is the spread of religion? (Note: Remember to include atheism and humanism as religions.)
2. Interview three people, whose religious affiliations are different from your own, about their religious group membership. How did they become members of their religion (through birth or choice) and why is it important to them? What does this exercise tell you about your own choices?
3. Read the Web site *A Line in the Sand* at http://www.hanksville.org/sand/index.shtml. What are the issues raised by this Web site? Why is the inclusion of material on cds, Web sites, and so on, without accreditation of authors, a problem in this context?
4. Collect newspaper articles on Native American religions. What are most of the articles about?

Selected References

Beckford, James A. 1989. *Religion and Advanced Industrial Society.* London: Unwin Hyman.

Blain, Jenny. 2002. *Nine Worlds of Seid-Magic: Ecstasy and Neo-Shamanism in North European Paganism.* London and New York: Routledge.

Blain, Jenny, Douglas Ezzy and Graham Harvey. 2004. *Researching Paganisms.* Walnut Creek, CA: AltaMira.

Blain, Jenny. "Shamans, Stones, Authenticity and Appropriation." In *A Permeability of Boundaries? New Approaches to the Archaeology of Art, Religion and Folklore,* edited by Robert J. Wallis and Kenneth Lymer. BAR International Series 936.

Carmichael, David L., Jane Hubert, Brian Reeves and Audhild Schanche. 1994. *Sacred Sites, Sacred Places.* London: Routledge.

Cheal, David. 1992. "Ritual: Communication in Action." *Sociological Analysis* 53, 4 (Winter): 363–374.

Cole, David E., Jordan Dill, Arlie Neskahi, Tara Prindle and Karen Strom. 2004. "A Line in the Sand." Available online at http://www.hanksville.org/sand/index.shtml. Accessed 27 October 2004.

Coleman, Simon and J. Elsner. 1998. "Performing Pilgrimage: Walsingham and the Ritual Construction of Irony." In *Ritual, Performance, Media,* edited by Felicia Hughes-Freeland. London and New York: Routledge.

"Declaration of War against Exploiters of Lakota Spirituality." Available online at http://www.aics.org/war.html.

Demerath, N. J. III and Rhys H. Williams. 1992. "Secularization in a Community Context: Tensions of Religion and Politics in a New England City." *Journal for the Scientific Study of Religion* 31, 2 (June): 189–206.

Dobbelaere, Karel. 1993. "Church Involvement and Secularization: Making Sense of the European Case." Pp. 19–36 in *Secularization, Rationalism and Sectarianism: Essays in Honour of Bryan R. Wilson,* edited by Eileen Barker, James A. Beckford and Karel Dobbelaere. Oxford: Clarendon Press.

Eisen, Arnold M. 1990. "The Rhetoric of Chosenness." *Society* 28, 1 (89) (Nov.–Dec.): 26–33.

Eisenstadt, Shmuel. 1991. "The Expansion of Religions: Some Comparative Observations on Different Modes." *Comparative Social Research* 13:45–73.

Goody, Jack. 1993. "Knots in May: Continuities, Contradictions and Change in European Rituals." *Journal of Mediterranean Studies* 3, 1:30–45.

Halliday, Fred. 1995. "Fundamentalism and the Contemporary World." *Contention: Debates in Society, Culture and Science* 4, 2 (Winter): 41–58.

Harley, Brian and Glenn Firebaugh. 1993. "Americans' Belief in an Afterlife: Trends over the Past Two Decades." *Journal for the Scientific Study of Religion* 32, 3 (Sept.): 269–278.

Hoover, Dwight W. 1991. "Middletown: A Case Study of Religious Development, 1827–1982." *Social Compass* 38, 3 (Sept.): 273–284.

Jaimes, M. Annette, ed. 1992. *The State of Native America: Genocide, Colonization, and Resistance.* Boston, MA: South End Press.

Jelen, Ted G. and Clyde Wilcox. 1991. "Religious Dogmatism among White Christians: Causes and Effects." *Review of Religious Research* 33, 1 (Sept.): 32–46.

Lindsey, Donald B. and John Heeren. 1992. "Where the Sacred Meets the Profane: Religion in the Comic Pages." *Review of Religious Research* 34, 1 (Sept.): 63–77.

Malone, Kobutsu. 2004. "Narcissism and Spiritual Materialism: The New Age Legacy." The Engaged Zen Foundation. Available online at http://www.engaged-zen.org/articles/Kobutsu-New_Age_Legacy.html. Accessed 26 October 2004.

Martin, David. 1991. "The Secularization Issue: Prospect and Retrospect." *British Journal of Sociology* 42, 3 (Sept.): 465–474.

Meyer, Carter Jones and Diana Royer. 2001. *Selling the Indian: Commercializing and Appropriating American Indian Cultures.* University of Arizona Press.

Robertson, Roland. 1993. "Community, Society, Globality, and the Category of Religion." Pp. 1–18 in *Secularization, Rationalism and Sectarianism: Essays in Honour of Bryan R. Wilson,* edited by Eileen Barker, James A. Beckford and Karel Dobbelaere. Oxford: Clarendon Press, 1993.

Rose, Wendy. 1984. "Just What's All This Fuss about Whiteshamanism Anyway?" In *Coyote Was Here: Essays on Contemporary Native American Literary and Political Mobilization,* edited by Bo Schöler. Aarhus, Denmark: Seklos. Available online at http://www.english.uiuc.edu/maps/poets/m_r/rose/whiteshamanism.htm.

Rose, Wendy. 1992. "The Great Pretenders: Further Reflections on Whiteshamanism." Pp. 403–422 in *The State of Native America: Genocide, Colonization, and Resistance,* edited by M. Annette Jaimes. Boston, MA: South End Press.

Skill, Thomas, James D. Robinson, John S. Lyons and David Larson. 1994. "The Portrayal of Religion and Spirituality on Fictional Network Television." *Review of Religious Research* 35, 3 (Mar.): 251–267.

Smith, Andy. 1993. "For All Those Who Were Indian in a Former Life." Pp. 168–171 in *Ecofeminism and the Sacred,* edited by Carol J. Adams. New York: Continuum.

Stark, Rodney and William Sims Bainbridge, eds. 1985. *The Future of Religion: Secularization, Revival, and Cult Formation.* Berkeley, CA: University of California Press.

Wallis, Robert J. 2003. *Shamans/Neo-Shamans: Ecstasies, Alternative Archaeologies and Contemporary Pagans.* London and New York: Routledge.

Walliss, John and Wayne Spencer. 2003. "The Lost Aisle: Selling Atlantis in the Spiritual Supermarket." *Journal of Religion and Popular Culture* 3 (Spring). Available online at http://www.usask.ca/relst/jrpc/index.html. Accessed 26 October 2004.

Witten, Marsha G. 1993. *All is Forgiven: The Secular Message in American Protestantism.* Princeton, NJ: Princeton University Press.

Wolf, Michael. 1993. *The Hadj: An American's Pilgrimage to Mecca.* New York: Grove Press.

7.3   Should Churches Mix in Politics?

The issue: The concern voiced by some that, in reviving religious enthusiasm, the so-called fundamentalists may have overstepped the line between Church and State—a line that took centuries to draw and may have helped to prevent many religious wars.

Relationships between religion and politics vary greatly around the world. In some countries religion is not separated from the state—for instance, in Islamic states in which religion is intertwined with government. The question of whether such states should run their governments in the ways they do is properly a subject for discussion within these states and within their religions. This section examines the general arguments for and against the involvement of religions in politics within states where separation of church and state has occurred, as in many countries of Africa and Asia, in addition to Europe, North and South America, and Australasia.

For the most part, within these countries, religious organizations do not form political parties or field candidates for election. They may, however, lend support to candidates of particular political parties, and such election support has been increasing. More often, local, national, or international religious leaders speak on political issues in nonpartisan terms, drawing the attention of political leaders and voters to social and political concerns.

Should religions be involved in political matters in these ways? Here we present the arguments both against and for such involvement.

RELIGIONS SHOULD STAY OUT OF POLITICAL MATTERS

There are two main arguments as to why religion should stay out of politics. One focuses on the effect involvement may have on politics; the other, on the likely effect of politics on religion.

If we look at what religion does in modern societies and how it operates, we can see many ways in which religions have adjusted to the modern world. One of these is the emphasis on individual fulfillment and the creation of community feeling—bonds linking members with others within their organization. Within a religious organization, therefore, people are held together by bonds of mutual support, belief, and commitment. The political arena is different. Within a democratic state, we look to individuals for ideas and debates. Every person is considered equal with every other, and may contribute to the political process as she or he chooses.

Thus, the democratic ideology argues that we should not allow religious institutions to become key actors in political affairs. Beyond that, there is evidence that when religions have become key actors in world history, the consequences have sometimes been disastrous. In the extreme, religions have promoted genocide (e.g., the Spanish Inquisition against Jews and Islamic Moors) and the suppression of particular groups (e.g., women, religious minorities, or others with "unacceptable" attributes). In general, the Catholic Church played an antidemocratic role in European history, which is why Napoleon (who was initially democratic)

broke its hold wherever his armies were victorious. Some would say that Catholic and Islamic religions support conservative and/or antidemocratic regimes in much of the world today.

The Effect of Religion on Politics   If a religious organization places support behind one or another political party, or one or another political cause, what are its members to do? Should they follow the dictates of their religious leaders, given that many churches have hierarchical, not democratic, power structures when it comes to making decisions about principles, morals, or right behavior? And if they do so, what happens to democracy?

This issue is particularly important for religions that claim jurisdiction over the actions of their members. If a priest suggests a possible course of action—say, actively supporting a candidate for election, or canvassing for her or his campaign— should the priest then be permitted to check on the actions of the member? What if a parishioner feels obliged to confess that she did not support the candidate, or even voted for someone else? A similar argument can be made for other forms of political behavior, such as lobbying or campaigning for or against policies. Religious organizations often hold strong sway over the minds, hearts, and loyalties of their members, and religious leaders can have great influence. If they wield this influence over political matters, people's political decisions are being made on grounds of belief, emotion, and loyalty, rather than on grounds of practicality and reason.

We all have heard of situations in which people, swayed by emotion and religious fervor, even go to the lengths of committing criminal acts in order to support a cause. Religion should exercise this power over the hearts and minds of people in order to cause people to face their own faults and guide their own lives, not to intervene—in nonrational, nonpolitical ways—in political decisions.

During the 2004 elections in the United States, an interfaith alliance made a call to "keep politics out of churches." Speakers from a variety of religious organizations warned that religions were becoming a tool of political campaigns. They called for the maintenance of the historic separation, in the United States, of church and state. They discussed claims of politicians to speak "for God." In multi-ethnic and multi-religious states such as the United States, Britain, or Canada today, no one religion can claim that it has all the answers for society's needs.

The Effect of Politics on Religion   The separation of politics from religion in the west has been beneficial for religion. Previously there have been long periods in history when religious leaders have become power-brokers, or political leaders. Consequently, they and their followers have been subject to the same temptations and problems as people in the political world. Scandals of political corruption have affected religious leaders in the past. Where religious groups take a direct part in the political sphere, the leaders' ability to provide for the spiritual needs of their parishioners or followers may be severely compromised.

Religions in the present day chiefly serve the function of helping people within them develop and achieve fulfillment by exploring their potential for spirituality. This is not compatible with political involvement. In modern thought, politics deals with the material basis of life and with power and its operation, religion with spiritual life and the relation of people to the divine. If religions are to advocate political courses of action, then they can no longer speak to all their followers but only to those who belong to particular political parties or espouse particular secular causes. If religions enter the political arena, they become merely pressure groups for political causes. If they compete for political favors they lose the right, in the eyes of the general public, to speak to higher moral issues. That's why religions should stay out of politics; or at least, some people think so. But here's the other side.

RELIGIONS SHOULD PARTICIPATE IN POLITICAL MATTERS

If we look around, we can see many examples of religious participation in politics. These include Catholic nuns who campaign for increased status for women and an end to spouse abuse; many leading religious figures who campaign for peace; and outstanding examples where a single individual,

as spokesperson for a religious movement, becomes associated with a civil cause. Anyone who has heard of South Africa's successful move to equality knows the name of Archbishop Tutu. And looking to the recent past, anyone who has heard of the American Civil Rights movement knows about the achievements of Dr. Martin Luther King. Both Tutu and King were, at least originally, religious and not political leaders; they used their religious insights and preaching skills to mobilize people for political causes.

From Durkheim on, social scientists have discussed religion's role in formulating and expressing the moral values of society. Religions do not only form a way for people to develop their spiritualities and their relations with the divine: They are also the custodians of society's moral standards. Some religions express these standards in the form of simple guidelines (such as the Ten Commandments), others as more complex theologizing.

Politics involves making decisions about people and their environments. Accordingly, politicians look to what is possible and, often, to what will be popular with particular constituencies. But if religions are the custodians of morality and ethical behavior, religious leaders and their followers also have an obligation to involve themselves in the workings of society, in an attempt to ensure that society's decisions are made on a moral foundation. In theory, at least, it would be desirable to bring ethics and not mere expediency to bear on decisions about the way society is run, and religious leaders may be better equipped than politicians to do this.

In a society in which one religion or religious organization is dominant, such an association could lead to a merging of church and state. But in North American society no single religious organization dominates. The majority of people follow a form of Christianity (though not all of these are church-goers) but belong to many different churches or denominations. A sizeable number belong to other religions, including Islam, Buddhism, and Judaism. Groups such as Unitarians even draw on the teachings of several religions and philosophies: Unitarians formally acknowledge contributions and teachings from many religions and religious leaders, specifically naming

Christianity, Judaism, Humanism, and Earth-based religions.

For many people, religious expression includes a strong component of social activism. Many churches and other religious organizations promote the concept of all people as equal, regardless of ethnicity or race, and encourage their members to campaign for social equality. Antipoverty issues also provide a focus for action that may include organizing charity events such as food-bank drives. In fact, it can mean anything from lobbying at a local government level, to mobilizing and supporting antigovernment protest, as in the liberation theology of Latin American churches. Indeed, for some groups (e.g., Unitarians), engaging in social activism is more important than adherence to a creed or belief.

Problem Areas: The Example of Same-Sex Marriages A problem results, however, when some religious groups favor one political course of action, others another, particularly when these courses of action stem from different views of moral or right conduct.

An example is the controversy over the legal status of marriage between same-sex couples— currently legal in some areas of the United States but not in others. Within some religious doctrines, marriage is a sacrament that can occur only between a woman and a man. It is often viewed as an institution for the production of children, and groups holding these views may oppose legislation to legalize same-sex marriage. Other religious groups view marriage as a social and religious recognition of love between two individuals, and they may campaign to have same-sex marriages legalized. Still other groups, probably constituting the majority, are divided amongst themselves. Their members are unsure of what course they should take, or whether their faith's teaching on marriage should or could be a part of the public debate. All these groups are part of our society, and in a democratic society have a right to be heard.

Can Religion and Politics Truly Be Separate?
There are other ways in which we can debate the rightful relationship between religion and politics. Religions exist as part of society. Religious opinion

and doctrine thereby become constituents of political ideology, concepts appearing and reappearing in political discourse. Political economy theorists have pointed to multiple links between dominant religion and other social structures. In Max Weber's discussion of the origins of capitalism, in his book *The Protestant Ethic and the Spirit of Capitalism,* religious theory, doctrine, and practice is closely associated with the rise of the capitalist elite, without requiring a conscious and deliberate involvement of religion in politics. The question becomes, not *should* religion and politics be separate, but *can* they ever be separate?

So far we have dealt only with dominant religions and their links with politics. Here conflict theorists argue that the same concepts and discourses influence religious and political thought. Religion, they say, can be a form of social control: Through religion, people are encouraged to act in ways that benefit ruling sectors of society, to be meek, to not cause problems for employers. Instead of seeing this as religion's influence on politics, we could describe it as the influence of politics on religion! However, there are other ways in which religion and politics become linked, notably through the sense of religion as resistance.

The clearest examples come from situations where religion not only fosters identity as a group member, but gives value to traditional ways of life, and gives to both everyday and political events a meaning different from that ascribed to religion by the dominant society. In North America, for example, traditional religions of the aboriginal peoples have recently been experiencing a revival. Native religions interpret the relation of people with the earth and with animals and plants in ways that show Native peoples as caretakers and conservationists, often in opposition to the European American concept of "making use" of land, animals, and plants. Many people discover in these religions ways in which they can not only express themselves and identify with their communities, but reinterpret political events and take political action to protect social and community rights. These religions are attractive to many aboriginal people and, as we have seen previously, to growing numbers of European Americans.

Many campaigners against poverty, racism, or violence in society trace the strength of their commitment to their religious (including humanist) affiliations. Their religion gives them a philosophy and a sense of purpose—also, a feeling that by acting on their principles they can help create a better world to live in. They use their religious commitment to actively oppose trends in society that they feel to be against their beliefs. People come together as religious groups to demonstrate their beliefs through marches, boycotts, political lobbying, or active participation. Often they join with other groups in doing this.

In the mid-1990s, after several black Baptist church buildings in the United States were destroyed by arson, Unitarians and Mennonites joined forces to show their opposition to both racism and intolerance by providing labor to rebuild the churches: When the outrage of these burnings was repeated, many other churches and religions, from Catholicism to Zoroastrianism, added their labor and assisted with funds. Black Baptist churches themselves demonstrate how religious feeling can unite communities in political action.

As already mentioned, Martin Luther King—a Baptist preacher—acted as his community's spokesperson against the injustices he saw. Interfaith groups have arisen in many countries, to call for social justice—particularly in antiracist campaigns. Environmental issues are also targeted by faith organizations: Unitarians and Pagans are known for supporting environmental causes, and a major interfaith campaign to call attention to global climate changes is sponsored by mainstream Jewish and Christian churches.

Summing Up

Should churches (or synagogues or mosques, etc.) mix in politics? Napoleon didn't think so; that's why he took such pains to separate Church and State wherever he took control in his nineteenth century conquest of Europe. (In this sentiment, he was supported by a great many revolution-minded Europeans.) But for many in religious organizations today, prayer and contemplation is not sufficient. Their goals are not all related to speculation about an afterlife, and they feel a moral commitment to social action.

This is not true for *every* person who goes to a church, attends a synagogue, or thinks deeply about humanity and its relationship with its world. People make their own decisions, in today's world, on their religious and political commitment. Some believe that religion and politics can and should be separate. Others see them as inextricably intertwined, with religion indicating political routes that they are obligated to take. For such people, political action, which is not opposed to religion, becomes a necessary corollary to religious belief.

Many of the examples in the previous section, however, showed interfaith attempts to direct attention to social and environmental problems. A different situation may pertain where one group claims to have an exclusive line on "truth" or the morality of what needs to be done. Henry Giroux argued in 2004 that from 2000 to 2004 the divisions between state and religion in the United States were reduced in what he sees as a deliberate attempt to link state policy with evangelical Christianity. This included, says Giroux, considerable funding for faith-based charitable groups, a statement by the Secretary for Education that he believed schools should teach Christian values, and what Giroux describes as a "never-ending rhetoric aimed at undermining church and state distinctions" (Giroux 2004:422). Giroux differentiates such deliberate linking from the more general interfaith or social action campaigns referred to previously.

This section cannot resolve the question of whether religion and politics should be separate. This is a moral question each person must decide for her or himself and sociology cannot resolve problems of what "should" be. What sociology can do, however, is indicate that in many ways, and for many people, religion and politics go hand in hand. From a sociological and historical perspective, the struggle to link, limit, and separate religion and politics is never-ending. And, like any major struggle, it brings out the best and the worst in human beings.

REVIEW EXERCISES

For Discussion and Debate

1. "Because some links between religion and politics are destructive, all political campaigning by religious groups should be banned."
2. Can politics be kept out of religion?
3. "Native religions are an important focus of resistance for Native communities. That's why they were suppressed by Europeans."
4. Pros and cons of religious leaders standing for public office.

Writing Exercises

Write a brief (500-word) essay on one of the following topics:

1. "My own experience: How religion connects with political leanings, in me and in those around me." (Note: Remember to treat humanism and atheism as "religions.")
2. "Politics needs the moral leadership of religion."
3. "Alternative 'earth-based' religions and the environmental movement."
4. "Politics and religion in the 2004 U.S. elections."

Research Activities

1. Observe a demonstration or protest march, or look for newspaper articles of a march. From banners or other signs, what religions or denominations are present? What is the reason for the protest and how does this connect with the philosophy of these religious groups, as far as you are aware of them?
2. Devise a questionnaire on how people's religion influences or connects with their political attitudes. Use this to survey fifteen people, and tabulate results for presentation to your class.
3. Search the World Wide Web for sites linking religion and politics. (Be aware that you may find links that you disapprove of, and remember that any site, on its own, may not speak for all members of the religion.) Discuss your findings with other students from your class.
4. Study popular materials produced by any religious organization (for instance, handouts given door-to-door) looking for information or advice on (a) daily living and (b) political activity. To what extent can these two aspects of life be separated?

SELECTED REFERENCES

Abu-Rabi, I. M. 2003. "Religion and State: The Muslim Approach to Politics." *The Muslim World* 93, 2:327–331.

Ashraf, Ahmad. 1990. "Theocracy and Charisma: New Men of Power in Iran." *International Journal of Politics, Culture and Society* 4, 1 (Fall): 113–152.

Barker, Eileen. 1993. "Behold the New Jerusalems! Catch 22s in the Kingdom-Building Endeavors of New Religious Movements." *Sociology of Religion* 54, 4 (Winter): 3377.

Beyerlein, K. and M. Chaves. 2003. "The Political Activities of Religious Congregations in the United States." *Journal for the Scientific Study of Religion* 42, 2:229–246.

Billings, Dwight B. and Shaunna L. Scott. 1994. "Religion and Political Legitimation." *Annual Review of Sociology* 20:173–202.

Brewer, M. D., R. Kersh and R. E. Petersen. 2003. "Assessing Conventional Wisdom about Religion and Politics: A Preliminary View from the Pews." *Journal for the Scientific Study of Religion* 42, 1:125–136.

Chaves, Mark and Lynn M. Higgins. 1992. "Comparing the Community Involvement of Black and White Congregations." *Journal for the Scientific Study of Religion* 31, 4 (Dec.): 425–440.

Collins, Randall. 1993. "Liberals and Conservatives, Religious and Political: A Conjuncture of Modern History." *Sociology of Religion* 54, 2 (Summer): 127–146.

Davidson, James D. 1994. "Religion among America's Elite: Persistence and Change in the Protestant Establishment." *Sociology of Religion* 55, 4 (Winter): 419–440.

Durham, Martin. 1994. "Abortion and the Politics of Morality in the USA." *Parliamentary Affairs* 47, 2 (Apr.): 280–292.

Giroux, Henry A. 2004. "Beyond Belief: Religious Fundamentalism and Cultural Politics in the Age of George W. Bush." *Cultural Studies/Critical Methodologies* 4, 4:415–425.

Hasenclever, A. and V. Rittberger. 2000. "Does Religion Make a Difference? Theoretical Approaches to the Impact of Faith on Political Conflict." *Millennium: Journal of International Studies* 29, 3:641–674.

Horowitz, Irving Louis. 1991. "The Glass Is Half Full and Half Empty: Religious Conviction and Political Participation." *Society* 28, 5 (193) (July–Aug.): 17–22.

Jaynes, J. 2003. "Religion and Politics: What Is the Impact of September 11?" *Contemporary Politics* 9, 1:7–15.

Kohut, Andrew, John C. Green, Scott Keeter and Robert C. Toth. 2000. *The Diminishing Divide: Religion's Changing Role in American Politics.* Washington, D.C.: Brookings Institute Press.

Maddox, G. 2003. "The 'Crusade' against Evil: Bush's Fundamentalism." *Australian Journal of Politics & History* 49, 3 (Sept.): 398–411.

Marty, M. E. 2000. "Religion and Politics." *The Annals of the American Academy of Political and Social Science* 572, 1:156.

Moen, Matthew C. 1994. "From Revolution to Evolution: The Changing Nature of the Christian Right." *Sociology of Religion* 55, 3 (Fall): 345–357.

Mueller, Carol. 1983. "In Search of a Constituency for the 'New Religious Right.'" *Public Opinion Quarterly* 47, 2 (Summer): 213–229.

Olson, Daniel V. A. and Jackson W. Carroll. 1992. "Religiously Based Politics: Religious Elites and the Public." *Social Forces* 70, 3 (Mar.): 765–786.

Oommen, T. K. 1994. "Religious Nationalism and Democratic Polity: The Indian Case." *Sociology of Religion* 55, 4 (Winter): 455–472.

Raymond, Paul and Barbara Norrander. 1990. "Religion and Attitudes toward Anti-Abortion Protest." *Review of Religious Research* 32, 2 (Dec.): 151–156.

Regan, Daniel. 1993. "Islamic Resurgence: Characteristics, Causes, Consequences and Implications." *Journal of Political and Military Sociology* 21, 2:259–266.

Sanneh, Lamin. 1991. "Religion and Politics: Third World Perspectives on a Comparative Religious Theme." *Daedalus* 120, 3 (Summer): 203–218.

Smith, Christian. 1994. "The Spirit and Democracy." *Sociology of Religion* 55, 2 (Summer): 119–143.

The Interfaith Alliance. Available online at http://www.interfaithalliance.org. Accessed 12 October 2004.

Timmerman, David M. and Larry David Smith. 1994. "The World According to Pat: The Telepolitical Celebrity as Purveyor of Political Medicine." *Political Communication* 11, 3 (July–Sept.): 233–248.

Wilson, John F. 1992. "Religious Movements in the United States." *Journal of Interdisciplinary History* 23, 2 (Autumn): 301–307.

Wuthnow, Robert. 1991. "Understanding Religion and Politics." *Daedalus* 120, 3:1–20.

CHAPTER 8

GENDER RELATIONS

In contrast to biological sex, *gender* refers to culturally learned notions of masculinity and femininity. Sociologists describe *gender roles*—learned patterns of behavior that a society expects of men or women,—as a widespread aspect of social life. By *masculinity,* then, we mean that package of qualities that people in our society expect to find in a typical man. By *femininity* we mean that package of qualities people expect to find in a typical woman. Some sociologists prefer to speak of *gender practices* or of *the performance of gender;* and increasingly people are aware that there may not be only one typical (or hegemonic) set of qualities that make up being female or being male.

Since gender is learned, gender roles or practices vary from one culture to another. In short, beliefs about masculinity and femininity are not linked to sex in the same way in all societies. Like race, gender is a social construction that varies across societies. And, like race, gender is largely an imposed social construction that confers more benefits on some people (in this case, men) than it does on others (namely, women).

In this chapter we examine three issues associated with gender and gender relations. The first section discusses discrimination against women in the workplace, and whether women experience a "glass ceiling" that sets limits on their career possibilities. The second section considers whether ideas about masculinity have changed. Is there a "twenty-first century man," and, if so, have phenomena such as *laddism* reversed all the ideas of the "new man" of the late twentieth century? The third section examines how media, including the Internet, influence our notions of masculinity and femininity, and particularly, whether media have negative effects on both women and men.

8.1   Do Employers Treat Women Like Second-Class Men?

The issue: Do women have an equal opportunity in the workplace, or do they still hit a "glass ceiling" when they take their ambition and talent to the maximum and strive for advancement?

The possibility that there is a "glass ceiling" on women's jobs is a topic that is argued by employers and employees, sometimes through the court system. On the one hand, many claim that all barriers to women's hiring and promotion have been eradicated. On the other, women in many walks of life point to instances when they were denied promotion. Many claim this is because of their gender and the assumptions that were made about them,

that they were asked questions that indicated they were being evaluated in ways differently from men, and against different standards.

The women's movement took as its goal, in the 1960s and 1970s, that women should have the same opportunities as men. Has this goal been met? Is it true that women's career advancement opportunities are—like those of men—determined only by the woman's own ambition and qualifications? On the other hand, can we consider "ambition" and "qualifications" without also wondering why women might be encouraged, during high school years, to set their sights lower, to be less ambitious and so obtain fewer qualifications? What of sexual harassment, which some women have said plays a part in keeping them out of occupations that have traditionally been considered "male"?

This topic ties in with that of affirmative action—as we have seen, often a highly divisive question. If there is no restriction on women's labor force participation, surely there is no need for affirmative action, as women will be hired or promoted according to their merits. Some women find offensive the suggestion that they should be hired because of affirmative action. To them this concept reduces the value of their qualifications. Other women and men point out that where affirmative action schemes are not in place, women are not hired to the extent that their qualifications deserve: They speak of this as systemic discrimination, which is not necessarily based on the personal prejudices of employers but on the accumulated weight of habit, assumptions, and the precedents of past hiring decisions.

Take an example: A number of years ago we became aware that several young female science students had been turned down for summer employment in a field camp. Each was interviewed, and rejected individually, on the basis that, while her qualifications were good, she would be the only woman in the camp, which was considered to be a bad idea. The key word here is *individually:* If all three had been hired, they would clearly have had female company! This kind of summer employment was valuable work experience, so that at the end of their university programs these women would have had fewer qualifications for permanent employment than their male classmates who were hired. An affirmative action program stating that, all other academic qualifications being equal, women should have preference in hiring, would have resulted in the hiring of these women (and some men).

Does a glass ceiling exist? Here is some of the evidence; you decide.

THERE ARE NO LONGER ANY CEILINGS ON WOMEN'S WORK

In the past there were many barriers against the employment or promotion of women. Men were seen as "breadwinners" who had to support a family, so that many people felt that women should not compete for men's jobs. Ideas about different skills and abilities of women and men led also to the idea that there were jobs women could not do, as well as those they should not do. Even as recently as twenty years ago, it was common for women to be paid less than men for doing the same work (because the men had to support families), and for women seeking promotion to be told they were not eligible for high-position employment.

In reality, many women also had to support families, but social assumptions overlooked this. Women, it was thought, would not be able to give the same attention to difficult or complex tasks because of their responsibilities to their spouses and children. And in any case, if women's abilities were different, women would not be capable of the sustained concentration required for high performance jobs. For example, in a letter to John Stuart Mill, Sigmund Freud objected to Mill's championing of women's rights by saying that it would not be right for him to assume that "my own dear child" could or should undertake the intellectual pursuits that he himself engaged in. He was referring to his fiancée. His attitudes were typical of the time and persisted well into the twentieth century.

These barriers, however, have now been removed. As the twentieth century progressed, women demonstrated that their capabilities paralleled those of men, and that they, too, could excel in math, science, and politics, and other "male" fields of endeavor. Further, society showed that it has a need for the skills of talented women as well as men. In many parts of the Western world it is illegal for employers to discriminate against women in their hiring practices, and jobs are commonly advertised as "open to women and men." In today's schools, girls as well as boys study math, sciences, and arts, and barriers to the entry of women in law schools and medical schools have long been gone.

However, if we look at the distribution of occupations, we find that there are fewer women than men in high paying positions, and on average women still earn around 64 cents for every dollar earned by men, calculated on the basis of hourly wages. This need not, however, indicate that women experience barriers to promotion. The highest wages are earned by people in senior positions. The average age of chief executive officers of the leading thousand (most valuable publicly traded) U.S. companies, according to a 1992 *Business Week* analysis, is 56. These senior men (and a few women) commenced their careers over thirty years ago, in the 1950s and 1960s, when the women's movement was just getting underway and while prejudices against women's careers were still in effect. There was indeed a ceiling on women's careers at that time, which has now, thanks to changed attitudes and legislation, been removed. We should therefore look not at the highest earners but at people who are currently working their ways up the corporate and professional ladders. Many women are graduating from universities with degrees in accounting, management and finance, engineering, and economics, and they are the ones we will expect to see at the top of the employment tree in the future.

Many women still seek entry into the traditionally female occupations of stenographers and secretaries, sales clerks, bookkeepers and accounting clerks, cashiers, nurses, elementary teachers, general office clerks, and janitors and charwomen. "Job ghettos" still exist. However, if women do take these jobs, it is because they choose to do so. Many women still enter into occupations that are relatively low-paid, or that do not lead to promotions and career paths. They do so for a variety of reasons. Sometimes they are attracted to the content of the job. Sometimes they consider the job will fit in with their family responsibilities. At more senior levels, women may postpone career plans in order to bear and raise children. If they do so, they will take longer to achieve more senior executive status. The existence of the so-called Mommy track, however, indicates not that a supposed glass ceiling prevents women from reaching the upper levels of management, but that the women themselves make choices about their lives, which obviously affect their career plans. For any given woman, raising a family may take priority at one point in her life, and her career may be highlighted later on. And increasingly, women in professional jobs are delaying childbearing until they have established careers.

In the 1990s, the *Wall Street Journal* reported that "After decades in the trenches, women are finally moving into Madison Avenue's executive suites." Today, we see women reaching into business and government. The contribution of Condoleeza Rice as National Security Advisor and Secretary of State was referred to in the chapter on ethnicity. There is talk about a future presidential election being between women candidates. It takes time to reach the senior positions—that's all.

A GLASS CEILING EXISTS AND SOME WOMEN BREAK THROUGH IT

It is true that the imbalance in salaries at present is caused partly by an overabundance of men in senior positions. But this is only part of the picture. At all levels of age and experience, men continue to earn more than women. Either they are in occupational fields that pay better, or they hold job titles that are seen as "higher." For instance, salaries in engineering are higher than those in nursing, and managers are paid more than secretaries. Some of these job "choices" lead to promotion, while others do not.

Further, U.S. statistics show women earning around 70 cents to the male dollar for full-time employment but only 60 cents at the higher levels; indicating that when women do reach the upper echelons, they are paid less for their contributions.

Many women do go into occupational ghettos, seeking jobs in traditionally female fields. We can raise questions, however, as to whether this is purely by their own choice. What causes women to become secretaries? Also, why should secretaries be seen as less important and less eligible for promotion than other people in their industries? And why, when we open the business section of a newspaper and look at the "new executive appointments," are the photographs almost all of men?

Women seeking employment or promotion in a variety of fields have commented that they still have to prove they can do the job better than men. In discrimination cases appearing before the court, women have brought evidence of being told jobs were not open to women, or being asked for higher education qualifications than were male applicants. Further, women say they are judged by different criteria. In some occupations—such as that of television news anchors—the standards of age and attractiveness applied to women and men differ, with women being removed from public view at—with a few notable exceptions—a much younger age. In other cases, women have to demonstrate not only that they have the required job skills but also that their family, if they have one, will not interfere with their job commitment. If they have no children, they may be asked if they plan to have children.

In some jurisdictions such questions are illegal, but they are still asked. An article in Toronto's *The Globe and Mail* newspaper quoted a senior executive officer as saying that he judged women's performance by stricter criteria than men's. Junior men are still "groomed" for promotion, taken to conventions, and shown the mechanics of decision making, while it is rarer for aspiring women to be groomed in this way.

The U.S. Government's Glass Ceiling Commission worked in the 1990s to produce strategies for women and minority members to break through the glass ceiling. In its time, it produced a series of papers (still online at http://www.ilr.cornell.edu/library/keyWorkplaceDocuments/government/federal/Glass ceilingreport.html) that explain how the glass ceiling operates. Some women were making it through to the top, they said, but they were rare, very determined, and often without families. These women who hold high-level executive positions were often found in staff functions such as personnel, as were women in mid-management positions. They found a similar pattern for male minority-group members. The question becomes not why only a few women are found in high-level positions, but how and why women and minority members continue to be "ghettoized" into the less prestigious areas of staff functions (or in medicine, pediatrics; or in law, family law).

For instance, in a case before the U.S. courts in the 1990s, a woman was denied partnership within a large legal firm in the area of litigation, despite the glowing recommendations of several male partners in the litigation group where she had worked, and despite her excellent track record. Less highly recommended male candidates were successful. The firm did, however, offer her partnership if she would manage the domestic relations department, an area in which she had little interest and less expertise. (She did not accept.)

Another lawyer, commenting on the hiring situation for women generally, said, "They expect perfection of women, but not of men." The Glass Ceiling Commission's report in the mid-1990s stated that, while women make up 45.7 percent of the total U.S. workforce and earn over half of all Master's degrees, 95 percent of senior-level managers in the United States are men. Also, women earned about 72 cents for every dollar earned by men. And René Redwood, previous executive director for the Glass Ceiling Commission, though stating that "we are in motion, and the world has changed," characterized the situation in 1996 as follows:

> We do not yet live in a color blind or gender blind society. Sexism, racism, and xenophobia live side-by-side with unemployment, underemployment and poverty; they feed on one another and perpetuate a cycle of unfulfilled aspirations among women and people of color.
>
> Do not get sidetracked by semantics. For people confronting these barriers, it's discrimination plain and simple. The glass ceiling is one manifestation of the perpetual struggle for equal access and equal opportunity. Glass ceilings are the artificial barriers that deny women and minorities the opportunity to advance within their careers. (http://www.inmotionmagazine.com/glass.html)

The Glass Ceiling Dataline, another fact-finding organization, was created in 1991 as a newsletter that would "report on the 'glass ceiling' in American corporations." Their observations were as follows:

- The rate at which women and minority men were moving up has slowed.

- Ghettoization of women and minority men in areas like human resources and staff jobs has increased.
- Retaliation against anyone who complains of discrimination at management levels is swift and terrible.

This organization gathered data on academia as well as on corporations, and followed and documented the progress of lawsuits brought by people who were discriminated against or who were subjected to sexual harassment at work.

The U.S. Department of Labor's report on "The Glass Ceiling Initiative," focusing on employment practices among nine federal contractors, stated the following:

> The OFCP (Office of Federal Compliance Programs) initially anticipated concentrating on the executive suite and the highest levels of management. As the pilot project progressed, however, the reviewing team discovered that much of the investigative questioning and many areas of prospective analysis became irrelevant because there were no minorities and women at these levels. To put it plainly, the glass ceiling existed at a much lower level than first thought. . . . All of the companies reviewed had a level beyond which few minorities and women had either advanced or been recruited, and minorities tended to be found at lower levels of management than women.

Indeed, a 2004 report for the Annenberg Public Policy Center (of women leaders in communications industries) reported that where companies had more women on boards of directors, they had better maternity leave policies and more women-friendly benefits packages. But only 15 percent of executive leaders, and 12 percent of board members in these companies were women. For these communications industries, the highest rating for women in corporate leadership was in publishing companies—18 percent.

So, those are the figures. But what do they mean? Is it still the case that they result from women's own choice to adopt the "mommy track"? Is it simply that women in professions are choosing to not be like men? Or is it related to the choices that people (men or women) are expected to make? UK writer Mary Ann Stevenson made the following comments:

> Women are still suffering from the assumption that the average employee is a man, with a wife at home to look after his children and arrange his social life so that he doesn't have to worry about losing touch with friends and family. This doesn't work for women, and increasingly it doesn't work for men either. . . . Ultimately, smashing the glass ceiling is about re-thinking the balance between work and home, recognizing that a change in hours is not just better for women, it's better for men, too.

Stevenson points out that the culture of working long hours—particularly, the expectation that ambitious employees will do this and the assumption that women will not do this but their male counterparts will—is not found in countries of continental Europe. But such expectations, from both employers and employees, create a situation in which it is hard to break through the glass ceiling.

SUMMING UP

Do employers treat women like second-class men? Does a glass ceiling exist? If so, is it an artifact of the age structure and demographics of the working population? Is it due to women who choose to take time off from their careers to raise children, or the assumptions of employers that women will *want* to do this? Is it because of expectations on employees to voluntarily work much longer hours? Does it exist in some fields, and not in others? Has progress been made, or has progress ceased? The evidence bearing on these questions is read differently by observers, depending on where they are positioned in the political and social structure within which employment and promotion occurs.

The U.S. Federal Government took the glass ceiling seriously enough to create a commission to study it. However, critics say that the commission was created to placate feminists and minority leaders rather than to study a "real" phenomenon. The work done by this commission, and by other researchers, suggests that a glass ceiling does exist. Though gains have been made by women and minority group members in the past 30 years, these will not automatically persist, and indeed the numbers of women and minority group members being promoted may be decreasing rather than increasing.

In some areas, however, there do seem to be gains. In the field of education, there is still an imbalance in the numbers of women to men who are elementary teachers, and the numbers of men to women who are principals of secondary schools. However, the imbalance is lessening, with more women becoming principals. Whether the same pattern is found in other areas of education—secondary schools, colleges, and universities—is another matter. There remain few female university presidents.

On balance, therefore, we consider that a glass ceiling does exist. Individual women manage to breach it and still others may, too, if legislative initiatives are maintained. But we are unlikely to see large numbers of female top executives while current hiring practices (such as hiring women middle managers predominantly within staff functions) persist. Only when there exists a substantial number of women and minority members in management and executive positions at all levels will we see an automatic hiring of women and minority members to these positions, and until then the work of organizations such as the Glass Ceiling Dataline will be required. We wait in hope for a future in which restrictions on hiring will truly be a thing of the past.

REVIEW EXERCISES

For Discussion and Debate

1. "There are no restrictions on women's employment any longer."
2. "Pressures in the workplace discourage women from competing."
3. "If women choose to take part-time jobs while they're raising their kids, that's not the fault of employers."
4. "Women don't like to be responsible for holding top jobs."

Writing Exercises

Write a brief (500-word) essay on one of the following topics:

1. "Sexual harassment in the workplace, and its effect on the jobs people hold."
2. "Who mentors women in business?"
3. "The Mommy Track."
4. "Pink-collar ghettoes."

Research Activities

1. Examine a newspaper that gives announcements of hirings and promotions of top executives. What proportion of appointments are of women? What kinds of companies are they in?
2. Search the World Wide Web for discussions of the Glass Ceiling in the hiring of women.
3. Interview ten graduates of your college, five women and five men. Who is in full-time employment? Who has achieved promotion, and how long did it take them? Has gender been a factor, and what other factors may have been operational here?
4. Watch your favorite TV sit-coms or soaps. Document the number of female and male characters who are in professional or executive careers. Does the show portray these characters at their work?

SELECTED REFERENCES

Aldridge, Alan. 1992. "Discourse on Women in the Clerical Profession: The Diaconate and Language-Games in the Church of England." *Sociology* 26, 1 (Feb.): 45–57.

Anneberg Public Policy Center. 2003. "The Glass Ceiling Persists: The Third Annual APPC Report on Women Leaders in Communication Companies." *Public Policy Center of the University of Pennsylvania.* Available online at http://www.annenbergpublicpolicycenter.org/02_reports_releases/report_2003.htm.

Anneberg Public Policy Center. 2001. Progress or No Room at the Top? The Role of Women in Telecommunications, Broadcast, Cable and E-Companies." *Public Policy Center of the University of Pennsylvania.* Available online at http://www.annenbergpublicpolicycenter.org/02_reports_releases/report_2001.htm.

Brinton, Mary C., Hang Yue Ngo and Kumiko Shibuya. 1991. "Gendered Mobility Patterns in Industrial Economies: The Case of Japan." *Social Science Quarterly* 72, 4 (Dec.): 807–816.

Burke, Ronald J. and Carol A. McKeen. 1993. "Career Priority Patterns among Managerial and Professional Women." *Applied Psychology: An International Review* 42 (Oct.): 341–352.

Corsun, D. L. and W. M. Costen. 2001. "Is the Glass Ceiling Unbreakable? Habitus, Fields, and the Stalling of Women and Minorities in Management." *Journal of Management Inquiry* 10, 1:16–25.

Dugger, K. 2001. "Women in Higher Education in the United States: Has There Been Progress?" *International Journal of Sociology and Social Policy* 21, 1–2:118–130.

Etzkowitz, Henry, Carol Kemelgor, Michael Neuschatz and Brian Uzzi. 1992. "Athena Unbound: Barriers to Women in Academic Science and Engineering." *Science and Public Policy* 19, 3 (June): 157–179.

Evetts, Julia. 1994. "Women and Career in Engineering: Continuity and Change in the Organisation." *Work, Employment and Society* 8, 1 (Mar.): 101–112.

Foley, S., D. L. Kidder and G. N. Powell. 2002. "The Perceived Glass Ceiling and Justice Perceptions: An Investigation of Hispanic Law Associates." *Journal of Management* 28, 4:471–496.

Gibelman, Margaret and Philip H. Schervish. 1993. "The Glass Ceiling in Social Work: Is It Shatterproof?" *Affilia* 8, 4 (Winter): 442–455.

Glass Ceiling Commission. Key Workplace Documents. Available online at http://www.ilr.cornell.edu/library/keyWorkplaceDocuments/government/federal/Glassceilingreport.html. Accessed 22 October 2004.

Glass, Jennifer. 1990. "The Impact of Occupational Segregation on Working Conditions." *Social Forces* 68, 3 (Mar.): 779–796.

Heward, Christine. 1994. "Academic Snakes and Merit Ladders: Reconceptualising the 'Glass Ceiling.'" *Gender and Education* 6, 3 (Oct.): 249–262.

Hultin, M. 2003. "Some Take the Glass Escalator, Some Hit the Glass Ceiling?: Career Consequences of Occupational Sex Segregation." *Work and Occupations* 30, 1:30–61.

Lopata, Helena Znaniecka. 1993. "Career Commitments of American Women: The Issue of Side Bets." *Sociological Quarterly* 34, 2 (Summer): 257–277.

Mattis, M. C. 2004. "Women Entrepreneurs: Out from Under the Glass Ceiling." *Women in Management Review* 19, 3:154–163.

Mitra, A. 2003. "Breaking the Glass Ceiling: African-American Women in Management Positions." *Equal Opportunities International* 22, 2:67–79.

Spurr, Stephen J. 1990. "Sex Discrimination in the Legal Profession: A Study of Promotion." *Industrial and Labor Relations Review* 43, 4 (Apr.): 406–417.

Stewart, James B. and Juanita M. Firestone. 1992. "Looking for a Few Good Men: Predicting Patterns of Retention, Promotion, and Accession of Minority and Women Officers." *American Journal of Economics and Sociology* 51, 4 (Oct.): 435–458.

Tienda, Marta, Katharine M. Donato and Hector Cordero-Guzman. 1992. "Schooling, Color, and the Labor Force Activity of Women." *Social Forces* 71, 2 (Dec.): 365–395.

Truss, Catherine J. G. 1993. "The Secretarial Ghetto: Myth or Reality? A Study of Secretarial Work in England, France and Germany." *Work, Employment and Society* 7, 4 (Dec.): 561–584.

Waddoups, Jeffrey and Djeto Assane. 1993. "Mobility and Gender in a Segmented Labor Market: A Closer Look." *American Journal of Economics and Sociology* 52, 4 (Oct.): 399–412.

Waring, Marilyn. 1990. *If Women Counted.* San Francisco, CA: HarperCollins.

Wenk, DeeAnn and Rachel A. Rosenfeld. 1992. "Women's Employment Exit and Reentry: Job-Leaving Reasons and Their Consequences." *Research in Social Stratification and Mobility* 11:127–150.

Yoder, Janice D. 1991. "Rethinking Tokenism: Looking beyond Numbers." *Gender and Society* 5, 2 (June): 178–192.

Zane, N. C. 2002. "The Glass Ceiling Is the Floor My Boss Walks On: Leadership Challenges in Managing Diversity." *Journal of Applied Behavioral Science* 38, 3:334–354.

8.2   Whatever Happened to the "New Man"?

The issue: Have men changed? Is there a new form of masculinity that lets men express their emotions and spend time looking after their children? Does "new" masculinity lead to gender equality? In this section we look at heterosexual masculinities and change.

The sight of a man pushing a stroller, rare forty years ago, is now commonplace. Men express interest in issues that were once seen as women's. Men have fashions; clothes have a wide range of styles, and men's hair and looks are the subject of debate. Stores sell hair-care and skin-care products for men as well as women. Twenty years ago we were promised the arrival of a "New Man," promoting gender equality and other social causes and environmental issues: He would be in touch with his "expressive side," more able to deal with feelings, and willing to take responsibility for childcare. Some researchers today have pointed to phenomena such as the Promise Keepers or the Million Man March, and fathers' campaigns for rights to visit children or be custodial parents. They discuss influences of religion and ethnicity in looking at how masculinity is constructed and presented today. Still others return to issues of male violence and resistance to new styles.

So, what affects styles of masculinity more: fashion, religion, economics, or social relationships? Whatever did happen to the "new man"? And should men just behave like, well, men?

TODAY'S MEN ARE DIFFERENT

The old ideas that men have to be at work earning a living and women have to be at home with children have largely gone. Since the 1960s there has been an increasing movement for people to develop their own potential, to follow careers that seem most suited to them, and to express themselves as they choose. We have new styles of art and design being created. We have the huge expansion of the Internet as a place where people talk and debate, make friends, and post their opinions and views. This is the society of the global marketplace, and it doesn't matter whether you are female or male, you do what you can. That includes jobs, parenting, friendships, and leisure. Today's young men and women have friends of both genders. They are not bound by yesterday's conventions. One area where we see this clearly is in people's household arrangements. Today, as the *American Association for Single People* puts it, "Family diversity has become the norm" (http://www.unmarriedamerica. org/Census%202000/households-type-trends-family %20diversity.htm).

U.S. Census reports from 2000 show that people are exercising choice in how they live. There is no "one fits all" pattern here. According to the census, over half (52.8 percent) of households were married couples, with or without children; 6.1 percent were unmarried couples, one third of these being same-sex; and over one quarter (25.5 percent) of households were single-occupant, with a further 8.9 percent representing single parents living with their children. (Other possibilities such as living with friends or with other relatives accounted for the remaining percentages.) And one in six children who live with one parent live with their dad.

Household structures, then, show an increasing diversity. Within these households, there is scope for men to take leading roles in parenting, spending more time with their children than ever before. Fathers are seen with children in many public places, from parks and playgrounds to galleries. While some may take only a minor part in the raising of their children, many look after their children for many days at a time, while mothers are away on work-trips or tours of duty. And an increasing number of fathers, in the eventuality of a separation, expect to spend at least part of each year with their children, caring for them.

Indeed where it's difficult for fathers to spend time with their children, many protest. No longer is it assumed that children are only women's responsibility—fathers who spend their time with their children want to be custodial parents. As increasing numbers of women have been drawn into the workforce (now only a quarter of children in two-parent households have only the father as breadwinner), increasing numbers of men are finding that not only can they spend time looking after their children, but that they both have to and want to do this.

Fathers have come forward, in the United States and other countries, to show how much they care for their children. Men have reacted to the accusations of being "deadbeat dads" through organizations such as the Promise Keepers, a Christian men's movement with the slogan, "If you truly want to change the world, change the men." The public pledges of the Million Man March showed African American men taking responsibility and supporting women.

Parenting, however, is only one dimension. Many of today's young men have grown up with the idea that women and men are, in many ways, very similar. They share likes and dislikes. They listen to the same music, go to the same events. In the 1980s and 1990s, some sociologists heralded the advent of the "New Man," who would be sensitive and caring, antiracist and antisexist. That announcement was decidedly premature, at that time,

and a bit misleading, as many men continued to express sexist attitudes and avoid parental tasks. Some resentment against feminism also ensured that many people—women as well as men—were reluctant to show themselves in a new light, and reluctant to express views that others would dub "PC" ("Politically correct").

But gradually masculinity has changed, and support comes from many places. Younger men today follow fashions and style their hair like David Beckham's. They don't give women special consideration but they treat them as friends or colleagues, even if they sometimes act like *lads*. And men are increasingly entering jobs that were previously seen as women's. Take nursing, for instance. Currently around 6 percent of U.S. nurses are men—a small proportion but growing, and men in nursing are beginning to appear in popular TV, for instance in the NBC "Scrubs" show in which a male nurse was presented in a positive light.

They may not be the "New Man" of the 1980s, but today real men make their choices and deal with a world in which men and women meet as equals—and choices are open to these men that would have seemed very unusual thirty years ago.

THERE ARE CHANGES BUT IT'S NOT ALL ONE WAY

Let's look again at some of the changes. Yes, there have been some, but is it merely that the idea of male responsibility—and women's equality—has now caught on? We'd suggest that there are other issues involved, and that the changes in masculinity are more complex than presented above.

First, the issue of fatherhood: What is going on with men as caregivers, or the Promise Keepers, or the men in the Million Man March of 1996?

As stated above, one response to the increased workforce participation of women has been increased childcare participation by men. Also, many men express a wish to be involved with their children's care; and if marriages or partnerships dissolve some men remain highly involved, either as primary caregivers or taking care of children for part of the time.

Yet Michael Lamb—while seen as an advocate of joint custody and men's continued involvement with their children by the fatherhood movement—points out that often the performance of specific childcare tasks is confused with carrying responsibility for those tasks. In studying childcare and fatherhood, he has looked at three levels of task performance. First comes basic supervision of children, as in "keeping an eye on them" or possibly engaging in a activity like play or sports, and men very often do this. Second is basic physical care: feeding, bathing, diapering, and so forth. Men do some of this, though not to the same extent as activities such as play. Third, however, comes something different. Feeding children is an important task, but who ensures that there is food of a suitable kind for them to eat? Who ensures that there are diapers on the shelf and clean clothes in the closet?

These tasks Lamb categorizes as *taking responsibility* for children, and in his findings they are performed very infrequently by men. Blain's study found some men taking responsibility for some aspects of childcare, which they often attributed to their own personal preferences or choice. But others pointed out that they took responsibility when they had to.

What of the Promise Keepers? This movement of Christian men seems to be based in an ideal of the "New Man" taking responsibility as more sensitive and caring husbands and fathers. Yes, in some sense, says Melanie Heath, in a 2003 study, but in this essentially middle-class, educated and "color blind" (though largely white) masculinist movement, the idea of sensitiveness and responsibility seems strongly linked to the idea of father in charge.

Heath (p. 440) comments: "It appears that these men were willing to make changes in their lives on an interactional and personal level because the movement does not challenge them to grapple with the structural conditions that undergird their privilege. Their worldview follows from a tradition of American Evangelical Christianity that focuses on individuals rather than social structure . . . the lack of attention to structural inequality does, in fact, reinforce existing power relations." The men attended to issues of support for spouse and children in ways that devalued feminist understandings. And because they did not challenge ideas about the social system but attempted to integrate masculinity with support and caring (specifying these as Christian values in the home, although ideas of caring and nurture are found in all religions), their actions tended to support, not question, inequalities of gender, sexuality, and, despite the inclusion of nonwhite men in the movement, even ethnicity.

Anna Gavanas looked at the fatherhood responsibility movement, again investigating ideas of fatherhood and masculinity, and asked, "How do you masculinize domesticity and at the same time domesticate masculinity?" (2004:247). She found that the particularly male versions of "parenthood" identified by the movement emphasized three dimensions: sports, religion, and heterosexuality. Both Gavanas and Heath point to contradictions. One such is the emphasis on heterosexuality, paired with the ethos on personal care. For, while some men have always (throughout history) directly engaged in caring for the children, their parents, or their spouses, the great emphasis on men as empathic caregivers, overturning stereotypes, arose in the 1980s and 1990s, when HIV became prevalent and when many gay men devoted themselves to years of caring for sick partners.

Sport is one of the areas that Gavanas mentions. This has its own contradictions, and researchers point to different forms of masculinities within it. Hockey players interviewed by Pappas et al. talked about links between sport and aggression—on and off the ice. In the subjective experiences of these athletes, violent behavior was linked with alcohol use and objectification of women; they referred to a culture of masculinity that included the "pack mentality" among the players, and that was carried over to aggressive behaviors off the ice.

On the ice this was functional violence, largely ignored by referees unless more than two players were involved, and seen as appropriate (even though breaking rules) by most other players. Off ice it was not functional. Other studies of sports and masculinities have looked at sports figures in different ways. British soccer star David Beckham has been seen as a *feminized* man, and appears as a leader of fashion, setting a style of masculinity that has been copied on both sides of the Atlantic. In sociological terms, new styles of masculinity give opportunity for both accommodation to mainstream or *hegemonic* masculinity, and resistance. *Laddism* is an example.

"Lads" aren't simply "men behaving badly"— young men are reacting against mainstream images, the "new man," and feminism, all at once. McNair states, "New Lad rediscovered the simple pleasures of football, beer, and birds . . . to be pursued henceforth without apology or guilt. 'Glamour' was reintroduced . . . (as) celebrity pin-ups who, if they were exercising their right of self-objectification in a postfeminist world, were nonetheless being put to the service of pre-feminist attitudes" (McNair 159). The phenomenon was largely created by a pop-culture publishing industry, aiming at an audience of younger men, that later expressed amazement at how it turned out. The "new lad," said magazine editors, with his emphasis on sex-talk and consumption of popular culture, was meant to be ironic. Rosalind Gill points out that these labels—new lad, new father, etc— don't describe real individual people, but do describe *interpretive repertoires* or discourses available within today's society; and real people will adjust their behavior, in different circumstances, to what is possible or appropriate.

The fatherhood movement and laddism are opposed at some points—one emphasizing responsibility, the other living for the day. However they have some points in common. The emphasis is on the individual—individual promises and relationships, or individual pleasure. Both are, to some extent, antifeminist; and both rely on an equation of masculinity with heterosexuality. Both may encourage homophobia. The current upsurge in the United States against same-sex marriages, for instance, may be linked not only with the religious right, but with popular styles of masculinity.

We are now told by the media that the "new lad" has had his day. New popular culture magazines are targeting young men whose interests are wider than alcohol, sex, celebrities, the latest gadgets, and clothes. New interpretative repertoires

of masculinities—new ways of "being a man" are emerging—and will continue to do so.

SUMMING UP

Is there a new way to be a man today? Our answer is both "no" and "yes." No, there isn't one single identity that is emerging. Society hasn't been transformed overnight, or even over a decade, nor will it be. But there are always new styles of masculinity or interpretive repertoires that become available for people to take up.

It used to be that if sociologists spoke of gender, people thought they meant something that affected women. Now we see men and masculinities as constructed by society and culture—equally "gendered." Social movements such as the fatherhood movement, or even the laddism fad, are part of that construction today, and the process goes on. Today's society includes a wide range of ways to be a man.

The involvement of the publishing industry with masculinity is an interesting and fast-growing one. Men's magazines used to be mostly about hobbies or pornography. The popular culture magazines that created the "lad" have considerable scope to involve men in a reflexive creation of new interpretive repertoires. They and other media sources such as the Internet may present men with ideas and possibilities. We hope for a more critical awareness, in society, that ways of being a man are not only a matter of individual choice and preference but create possibilities in culture and society. Masculinities are linked to social structures and causes, including social inequality.

The idea of the "New Man" was based on social critique and an awareness of gender, ethnicity, and sexuality as sources of inequality. Today's movements and fads may have largely lost that critique, but there is scope for it to be regained. And the call from other sectors of society, and in particular from critical feminists and from the gay movement, is that mainstream heterosexual men do need to look at how their behaviors and attitudes affect other people.

Review Exercises

For Discussion and Debate

1. "Who should have custody in child care disputes?"
2. "Men who care for their families are more than willing to help out with the childcare."
3. "Where's the problem with being a Lad?"
4. "In all cultures, it's the men who do the hunting."

Writing Exercises

Write a brief (500-word) essay on one of the following topics:

1. "Gendered patterns in my childhood, and how they've affected my life today."
2. "Why the 'New Man' didn't catch on."
3. "Men's clothing and images, and what image says about people."
4. "Single fathers in today's society: Do they get more help than single mothers?"

Research Activities

1. Observe adults with young children in one of the following locations: a doctor's or dentist's waiting room, a playground in a park on a sunny day, a store that sells children's clothes. Observe for one hour, noting which adults accompany children and the interactions between children and their adults.
2. Interview six people in your class about their hobbies or interests, including music. Are there common themes? Are there gendered themes? Why?
3. Observe people in a public setting, such as a bar or a sports activity, watching for differences in male and female behavior, and between groups of women or men.
4. Compare magazines that you read with those an opposite-sex friend reads—at least three magazines each. What are the common themes? What themes are different? How important are music and popular culture in the magazines?

Selected References

Beynon, John. 2002. *Masculinities and Culture.* Buckingham, UK: Open University Press.

Blain, Jenny. 1993. "'I Can't Come in Today; the Baby Has Chickenpox!' Gender and Class Processes in How Parents in the Labour Force Deal with the Problem of Sick Children." *Canadian Journal of Sociology* 18:407–431.

———. 1993. "The Daily Construction of Fatherhood: Men Talk about Their Everyday Lives." In *Canadian Men and Masculinity,* edited by Tony Haddad. Toronto: Canadian Scholar's Press.

Cabrera, N., C. S. Tamis-LeMonda, R. H. Bradley, S. Hofferth and M. E. Lamb. 2000. "Fatherhood in the Twenty-First Century." *Child Development* 71, 1:127–136.

Cashmore, Ellis and Andrew Parker. 2003. "One David Beckham? Celebrity, Masculinity, and the Soccerati." *Sociology of Sport Journal* 20, 3 (Sept.): 214–231.

Dizon, Kristin. 2004. "New Lad Mag Promises 'No Britney and No Snark.'" *Lifestyle, Seattle Post-Intelligencer* 25 (Sept.). Available online at http://seattlepi.nwsource.com/lifestyle/192348_giantmag25.html.

Edwards, Tim. 2003. "Sex, Booze and Fags: Masculinity, Style and Men's Magazines." P. 132 in *Masculinity and Men's Lifestyle Magazines,* edited by Bethan Benwell. Oxford, UK: Blackwell.

Gadsden, V. L., S. E. F. Wortham and H. M. Turner III. 2003. "Situated Identities of Young, African American Fathers in Low-Income Urban Settings: Perspectives on Home, Street, and the System." *Family Court Review* 41, 3:381–399.

Gavanas, Anna. 2004. "Domesticating Masculinity and Masculinizing Domesticity in Contemporary U.S. Father-hood Politics." *Social Politics* 11, 2:247–266.

Gerson, Kathleen. 1994. "A Few Good Men: Overcoming the Barriers to Involved Fatherhood." *American Prospect* 16 (Winter): 78–90.

Gill, Rosalind. "Power and the Production of Subjects: A Genealogy of the New Man and the New Lad." Gender Institute, London School of Economics. Available online at http://www.lse.ac.uk/collections/genderInstitute/pdf/powerAndProduction.pdf.

Heath, Melanie. 2003. "Soft-Boiled Masculinity: Renegotiating Gender and Racial Ideologies in the Promise Keep-er's Movement." *Gender and Society* 17, 3:423–444.

Hochschild, Arlie with Anne Machung. 1989. *The Second Shift: Working Parents and the Revolution at Home.* New York: Viking.

Lamb, Michael E. 1987. "Introduction: The Emergent American Father." In *The Father's Role: Cross-Cultural Perspectives,* edited by Michael E. Lamb. Hillsdale, NJ: Lawrence Erlbaum Associates.

———. 1999. *Parenting and Child Development in "Nontraditional" Families.* Lawrence Erlbaum Associates.

Luxton, Meg. 1986. "Two Hands for the Clock: Changing Patterns in the Gendered Division of Labour in the Home." In *Through the Kitchen Window: The Politics of Home and Family,* edited by Meg Luxton and Har-riet Rosenberg. Toronto: Garamond Press.

Messner, Michael A. 1993. "'Changing Men' and Feminist Politics in the United States." *Theory and Society* 22, 5 (Oct.): 723–727.

McNair, Brian. 2002. *Striptease Culture: Sex, Media and the Democratisation of Desire.* London and New York: Routledge.

Pappas, Nick T., Patrick C. McKenry and Beth Skilken Catlett. 2004. "Athlete Aggression on the Rink and off the Ice: Athlete Violence and Aggression in Hockey and Interpersonal Relationships." *Men and Masculinities* 6, 3:291–312.

Popenoe, David. 1993. "Parental Androgyny." *Society* 30, 6 (206) (Sept.–Oct.): 5–11.

Rost, H. 2002. "Where Are the New Fathers? German Families with a Nontraditional Distribution of Professional and Family Work." *Community, Work & Family* 5, 3:371–376.

Seltzer, Judith A. and Yvonne Brandreth. 1994. "What Fathers Say about Involvement with Children after Separa-tion." *Journal of Family Issues* 15, 1 (Mar.): 49–77.

Silverstein, Louise B., Susan Sperling, Jay Belsky, Vicky Phares and Michael E. Lamb. 1993. "Primate Research, Family Politics, and Social Policy: Transforming 'Cads' into 'Dads.'" *Journal of Family Psychology* 7, 3 (Dec.): 267–282.

Walters, J., F. Tasker and S. Bichard. 2001. "'Too Busy'? Fathers' Attendance for Family Appointments." *Journal of Family Therapy* 23, 1:3–20.

8.3   Do We Imitate the Males and Females We See on TV?

The issue: Whether portrayals of girls and women in the mass media—especially, in television—keep gen-der stereotypes alive and, in this way, keep women from achieving equality with men, at home, or at work.

All around us, in the mass media, are images of women and men, boys and girls. By definition, al-most every time a person is portrayed or described that person's gender is evident. Does this matter? Opinions differ. Some research indicates that pre-sentation of gender does matter, that people often imitate what they see on television or read about in the papers. Others suggest that people do not mere-ly slavishly imitate what they see, and that media can usefully present people with a range of ex-pressions of gender, from which they can choose. More opportunities are available to women, and more to men, than ever before, and media alerts us to these opportunities.

Still other researchers indicate that the effect of media presentations of gender is highly complex. Media images may influence small details of people's lives, by suggesting to them what is culturally approved or possible, and by suggesting a goal to aim for. A further complexity is that different agencies of the media may aim images toward different sectors of the population: Often the media assumes a male reader or viewer, but sometimes images are produced for the "female gaze." Race and sexuality intersect with gender in these arguments.

Who controls media is another issue that relates to content, topic, and presentation. Research by the Annenberg Public Policy Center of the University of Pennsylvania shows that, while companies and their boards are changing constantly to meet the demands of this fast-paced industry, the participation of women at high levels does not seem to change much. Looking in 2001 at the leading media, telecom, and e-commerce companies in the United States, they found that 13 percent of the top executives and 9 percent of the boards of directors were women. A 2003 update, extending the scope to include advertising companies, indicated a small upturn—to 15 and 13 percent—within the 57 companies included, though 7 had no women executives and 10 had no women on the board.

In this section we will indicate some of the complexities of the arguments as to whether gendered media images affect people's daily lives. Inevitably, some of the discussion will lean more toward a *social constructionist* perspective than in other parts of the book. Indeed this topic can provide a useful introduction to some aspects of constructionist approaches to the world, which students may wish to pursue at a later stage in their careers.

MEDIA IMAGES AFFECT OUR DAILY LIVES

When we look around us, we see gendered images: women and men, boys and girls; even animals are presented as gendered. Now *gender,* as used by many social scientists, implies a social component to a distinction between male and female, so let us be clear on what is meant here. Many items that people use (toys, clothes, books, and magazines themselves) are presented as for people of one or the other biological sex to use. As social scientists, we see this presentation as based on social assumptions about what generalized male people and female people do, rather than following directly from the people's biology. We therefore discuss it in terms of socially constructed gender, not biological sex.

For example: I go into a store to buy a birthday present for one of my children's friends, aged eight. I wander around the aisles, my eyes glazing over with the variety of items. An assistant approaches me and offers to help. "I'm looking for a present for an eight year old, maybe around fifteen to twenty dollars worth," say I. The inevitable response is, "Is it for a girl or a boy?"

This can be pursued through several levels of experiment. If I have time, and if the store is not too busy, I may say (for example), "It's for a child who really likes bugs." The response is usually an assumption of gender, whereupon the assistant starts calling the child "he," or the assistant asks again, "Yes, but is it for a boy or a girl?"

Why does the assistant ask this? Is it because she or he assumes that gender is the most salient characteristic a child can have—that being male or female takes precedence over whether they like bugs, when choosing a suitable present? Or is this a marketing technique suggested by representatives or required by store managers? Often this is a required sales technique, but one that fits in with the assistant's own conception of how the world is divided into male and female people, rather than people who do and do not like bugs, even in second grade.

So what is the connection here with media? Take a look at Saturday morning children's television—cartoon shows interspersed with commercials. The commercials are aimed directly at girls or boys, typically matched to the type of show; Barbie dolls or GI Joe figures. The result can be seen in the demands from viewing children for this toy and that toy, usually quite *gender-specific.* Children are not only being entertained but learning which toys are for them, how they as girls or boys are expected to behave, and what they are expected to want in a gendered way.

And the messages from TV are clear. Boys will fight and push aside others whom they don't respect, expecting to make decisions about themselves and their actions. Girls will mostly wait, play with dolls, and expect to be chosen—though the feisty tomboy appears, she is the exception; and it's the same in story books and movies. In the newer media, such as computerized adventure games, the stereotypes remain—though here the feisty fighting woman is more evident, her appeal still depends as much on sexiness as on competence. Perhaps an odd indication of *equality* is appearing; however, with boys and young men also becoming exploited and objectified. Ten years later the stereotypes are acted out, as young women plan to follow the men whom they feel have chosen them, trying to appear not too aggressive, not too successful, in case they are perceived as a threat and thereby rejected. Meanwhile, in the popular media, women are still described in terms of the number of children they have, and men in terms of occupations or political affiliations. A woman who emphasizes politics in her life, or a man whose first priority is his children's care, is pointed out as a curiosity, not as a role model.

Some branches of the media see their role differently, as forerunners and agents of change, and will deliberately show the female engineer, the male nurse or elementary teacher, not as curiosities but as experts in their fields, deliberately chosen as role models. These programs and magazines show awareness of diversity in race and ethnicity as well as gender. But these programs are themselves stereotyped by the rest of the media as "educational" or "feminist," and are watched, read, or listened to by relatively small numbers of people. However, some attempts are being made by socially conscious agencies to use commercial media (e.g., television advertisements) to promote change. Therefore we see male sports stars talking about problems of violence against women, in an attempt to promote models of masculinity that are concerned, caring, and nurturing as well as strong.

These attempts are based on long-standing research that shows the power of imitation in constructing social behavior. Certain kinds of people are more likely to be imitated than others: those who are close to the individual, those who are perceived as warm and caring, those who are perceived as powerful and important. Hence the use of well-known, admired figures, who in advertisements seem to look directly at the viewer and to speak to him or her. These are the people we look up to, and we copy their appearance and behavior.

WE'RE NOT SO SUSCEPTIBLE TO MEDIA

There is much research indicating the importance of imitation. However, the concept of a direct imitative influence of media images on viewers, and hence society, may be rather too simplistic. It is true we can isolate stereotypes of masculinity and femininity, and it is true that these are all around us, and it is true we can present children and adults with models of what seem to be socially acceptable and expected. But the counterargument is that people do not merely imitate. Early socialization theories such as those of Bandura do not give room to human agency. Other, more sociological theories, such as social action accounts of socialization, allow for people to engage in interaction with others. People creatively shape their behavior, and learn from their previous interactions.

Are we saying, then, that media images have no impact?

No indeed. We are saying that it is hard to measure their impact, and that there isn't necessarily a straightforward imitation process at work. What many theorists today look to is how these media images are put together, why they appear as they do, and how people associate themselves with the social relations portrayed in the images, rather than just copying the actions.

There is an argument, often heard, that media portrayals do not shape people's actions. Media's job is to reflect the social world, in news stories, cartoons, and literature. Media's job is also to "give people what they want." If violent masculinity is reflected in TV shows, this is because it is exists in the real world. If women appear indecisive or passive, say proponents, this is because many women want to act like this for at least part of the time. And, as evidence that the media reflects the world, they will point to stories in which women are brave and courageous, or in which people of either gender perform community service such as rescues.

It is not hard to demolish this argument. Though many "real life" actions are portrayed, countless others are not. What are omitted are the ordinary, everyday activities, the ways people spend most of their time. This is when the second argument made on behalf of current media productions is made, the argument that the media gives people what they want. They do not want to see "ordinary" activities, because these are boring.

Media and the Male Gaze   This is where the question of "gaze" arises. What typeset people are movies made for? Who are assumed to be the chief viewers of television material, the chief listeners to radio, the chief readers of newspapers? It is still quite common to discover that newspapers are directed at male readers, perhaps male readers of a particular social class, with incidental pages containing what women are assumed to "want" (fashion, not politics). We still talk of "the man in the street" as meaning the ordinary viewer, the ordinary person, obscuring the fact that just over one half of ordinary people are female. People conducting media studies find that the majority of Hollywood films present women and women's bodies as objects for the male gaze. There may have been some change in the presentation: In the 1950s women appeared as domesticated, passive objects. In the 1990s they were sometimes wild, "liberated," or sexy, but they were still objects. Few films are made for a female gaze, even when the filmmakers include women.

If we turn our attention to other media, we still find the male gaze or male readership predominating. Authors of children's books are still advised by their publishers that girls will read books about boys, but boys will not read books with leading female characters, so that they should make their leading characters male. The majority of newspaper stories remain about males: In Canada in 1991, Media Watch found that fewer than one-fifth of newspaper reports mentioned women. In the United States in 2004, Fairness and Accuracy in Reporting turned its spotlight on the Fox's flagship news program, *Special Report,* looking at the guest list over 25 weeks. The results show that in terms of ethnicity, gender, and political philosophy, the show failed the "fair and balanced" test. Seven percent of guests were women. Perhaps this can be seen as a dictatorship of the market, or of what the market is assumed to be: a largely male readership or viewership. And it is true that adult men have more income, on average, than adult women, to spend not only on books, magazines, and movie-going, but on the products that are advertised in magazines and on television.

When a news story is told from a male point of view, particularly a European-American male point of view, the standpoint of the reporter or editor is not noted. It is assumed to be a general, unbiased, objective point of view. When or if a story is told from the point of view of a Native American woman, it is common for both her Nativeness and her femaleness to be pointed to, in some way. She is deemed to represent a *special interest,* and her standpoint is seen as not objective. Her words are modified to present them to a male, European gaze.

Even when we look at areas deemed to be of interest specifically to women, we can find an objectification. A case in point is the advertising of menstrual products. We see women in these commercials determined to hide any evidence of menstruation and to deny that the physical body changes associated with it need have any effect on their daily lives, particularly in terms of their ability to "have fun" and to "not let it stop you." Rather than being an integral part of women's lives, menstruation becomes both a liability and indeed a disability. In short, these advertisements make plain that to be seen as interesting or important, women must deny any relationship to their own bodies and the cycles of their lives.

And in general, news items deemed of special interest to women often receive scant coverage; an example being the march for women's reproductive rights in Washington, D.C. in April 2004. Over 1,400 organizations signed on for the event, two of the key sponsors being the National Latina Institute for Reproductive Health and the Black

Women's Health Imperative, with attendance estimated at up to 1.15 million. Some of the mainstream news media appeared to ignore the march, while others, with a few notable exceptions, such as Lynette Clemetson's article in the *New York Times* (4/24/04), focused on a single issue: abortion. Issues such as health and family planning were not, apparently, newsworthy.

SUMMING UP

Do we all just imitate what we see on television? No, not in any simple, monkey-see, monkey-do fashion. But don't underestimate the importance of the media!

Media images of gender have a vast impact on women and men in their daily lives. This impact, however, is not simple. It is not merely a question of a girl seeing female children on TV playing with a doll house and copying their actions; or a boy seeing GI Joe and performing an exact imitation, though sometimes this may happen. Both young and old people process the information that is presented to them in the light of what they already know about the world. Some of the girls who watched stereotyped TV shows in the 1950s and 1960s grew up to be the feminist activists of today! Others are now quite antifeminist. Clearly there is more going on here than merely a copying of activities. People engage with the information given them and construct their own ways of behaving, sometimes imitating, sometimes resisting models offered them.

More importantly, the media images present us with ideas of how the world is organized, the social relations that prevail, and the assumptions about men and women, maleness and femaleness, that people use when they construct their own everyday behavior. In this section we have used gendered social relations as the example. Clearly, these are not the only relations within North American society or its mass media.

But whether we focus on gender, race, ethnicity, religion, or social class, the media show us the dominant, or *hegemonic,* social patterns of who is important, whose words are worth more air-time, who has power. Further, critics within media studies debate the extent to which these images are deliberate—to what extent the content and context of television shows is influenced by business and political interests. Ann J. Simonton, founder of Media Watch (and an ex-fashion model) comments from her own experience on "how advertisers and the corporations that hire them dictate every detail of what we perceive as news and media entertainment."

We can challenge this in many ways, by promoting other forms of presentation, by showing that we want news stories told from a female perspective, a Native American perspective, an Asian American perspective, by showing that regardless of our own blackness or whiteness, maleness or femaleness, we find such stories interesting and important to know about. But more important still will be the entry of females and minority persons to powerful jobs in the media industry. In a society that claims all people are individuals, no one group has a monopoly on objectivity, and in order to work toward a society that is truly fair and just to all, we all need to understand how other people perceive the social world.

REVIEW EXERCISES

For Discussion and Debate

1. "Today, women are trying to be just like men."
2. "Women always have to have the last word."
3. "Boys will be boys."
4. "TV is simply entertainment. It shouldn't try to change the world."

Writing Exercises

Write a brief (500-word) essay on one of the following topics:

1. "How gendered stereotypes affect and influence me."
2. "Two people who have been my role models."
3. "Women are encouraged to view themselves through men's eyes."
4. "Violence against women on TV should be censored."

Research Activities

1. View two installments of a TV sit-com. Note the behaviors of women and men. What behaviors are stereotypically male or female? Do any women use stereotypically male behaviors or men use stereotypically female behaviors? What makes the humor in this sit-com?
2. View Saturday morning kids' TV for two hours. Time the commercials, noting gender of participants, product, who the product is aimed at, and the title of the show. Present results as a table. What does this tell you about gender?
3. Draw up a short interview schedule on self-presentation—dress, jewelry, makeup. Include questions on how and where people learn about these things, who they imitate, and what are the chief influences on their appearance. Choose a convenient site such as a shopping mall, or a park; interview four people, and present your findings in the form of a short report.
4. Invite a group of your friends to discuss the latest movie they've seen. Ask them about how women and men are portrayed in the movie—is there any stereotyping? While they are talking, watch the gendered dynamics of their talk—who speaks most, and who interrupts. What have you learned? Did the subject of the conversation influence who spoke?

SELECTED REFERENCES

Bandura, Albert. 1973. *Aggression: A Social Learning Analysis.* Englewood Cliffs, NJ: Prentice Hall.

Bonner, Frances and Paul Du Gay. 1992. "Representing the Enterprising Self: Thirtysomething and Contemporary Consumer Culture." *Theory, Culture and Society* 9, 2 (May): 67–92.

Brinson, Susan L. 1992. "TV Fights: Women and Men in Interpersonal Arguments on Prime-Time Television Dramas." *Argumentation and Advocacy* 29, 2 (Fall): 89–104.

Chaudhuri, M. 2001. "Gender and Advertisements—The Rhetoric of Globalisation." *Women's Studies International Forum* 24, 3:373–385.

Coutts, L. Block and D. H. Berg. 1993. "The Portrayal of the Menstruating Woman in Menstrual Product Advertisements." *Health Care for Women International* 14, 2 (Mar.–Apr.): 179–191.

"Fair: Fairness and Accuracy in Reporting." Available online at http://www.fair.org/.

Furnham, Adrian and Nadine Bitar. 1993. "The Stereotyped Portrayal of Men and Women in British Television Advertisements." *Sex Roles* 29, 3–4:297–310.

Griffin, Michael, K. Viswanath and Dona Schwartz. 1994. "Gender Advertising in the U.S. and India: Exporting Cultural Stereotypes." *Media, Culture and Society* 16, 3 (July): 487–507.

Keller, Kathryn. 1992. "Nurture and Work in the Middle-Class-Imagery from Women's Magazines." *International Journal of Politics, Culture and Society* 5, 4 (Summer): 577–600.

Kissling, E. A. 2002. "On the Rag on Screen: Menarche in Film and Television." *Sex Roles* 46, 1–2:5–12.

Kray, Susan. 1993. "Orientalization of an 'Almost White' Woman: The Interlocking Effects of Race, Class, Gender, and Ethnicity in American Mass Media." *Critical Studies in Mass Communication* 10, 4 (Dec.): 349–366.

Livingstone, Sonia. 1994. "Watching Talk: Gender and Engagement in the Viewing of Audience Discussion Programmes." *Media, Culture and Society* 16, 3 (July): 429–447.

Lotter, Ilsa, Martin Weinberg and Inge Weller. 1993. "Reactions to Pornography on a College Campus: For or Against?" *Sex Roles* 29, 1–2 (July): 69–89.

Mayne, I. 2000. "The Inescapable Images: Gender and Advertising," *Equal Opportunities International* 19, 234:56–61.

McRobbie, Angela. 1993. "Shut Up and Dance: Youth Culture and Changing Modes of Femininity." *Cultural Studies* 7, 3 (Oct.): 406–426.

Media-Watch. 1991. "Two Years of Sexism in Canadian Newspapers: A Study of 15 Newspapers." *Resources for Feminist Research* 20, 1/2 (Spring): 21–22.

Meyers, Marian. 1994. "News of Battering." *Journal of Communication* 44, 2 (Spring): 47–63.

Milburn, S. S., D. R. Carney and A. M. Ramirez. 2001. "Even in Modern Media, the Picture Is Still the Same: A Content Analysis of Clipart Images." *Sex Roles* 44, 5–6:277–294.

Perimenis, Louisa. 1991. "The Ritual of Anorexia Nervosa in Cultural Context." *Journal of American Culture* 14, 4 (Winter): 49–59.

Rohlinger, D. A. 2002. "Eroticizing Men: Cultural Influences on Advertising and Male Objectification." *Sex Roles* 46, 3–4:61–74.

Rudman, William J. and Akiko F. Hagiwara. 1992. "Sexual Exploitation in Advertising Health and Wellness Products." *Women and Health* 18, 4:77–89.

Schleiner, A. M. 2001. "Does Lara Croft Wear Fake Polygons? Gender and Gender-Role Subversion in Computer Adventure Games." *Leonardo* 34, 3 (June): 221–226.

Schooler, D., Ward L. Monique, A. Merriwether and A. Caruthers. 2004. "Who's That Girl: Television's Role in the Body Image Development of Young White and Black Women." *Psychology of Women Quarterly* 28, 1:38–47.

Shaw, Donald L. and Shannon E. Martin. 1992. "The Function of Mass Media Agenda Setting." *Journalism Quarterly* 69 (Winter): 902–920.

Smith, P. 1999. "Sex, Lies, and Hollywood's Administrators." *Journal of Educational Administration* 37, 1:50–66.

Tannen, Deborah. 1990. *You Just Don't Understand: Women and Men in Conversation.* New York: Morrow.

Tiefer, Leonore. 1994. "The Medicalization of Impotence: Normalizing Phallocentrism." *Gender and Society* 8, 3 (Sept.): 363–377.

Treneman, Ann. 1989. "Cashing in on the Curse." In *The Female Gaze,* edited by Lorraine Gamman and Margaret Marshment. Seattle, WA: Real Comet Press.

Turner, G. 1990. *British Cultural Studies: An Introduction.* Boston, MA: Unwin Hyman.

Walters, Suzanna Danuta. 1992. "Material Girls: Feminism and Cultural Studies." *Current Perspectives in Social Theory* 12:59–96.

Williams, T. 2000. "Gender, Media and Democracy." *The Round Table* 357, 1 (Oct.): 577–578.

CHAPTER 9

FAMILY

A family consists of a group of people who are related to one another through marriage, descent, or legal adoption. Family members have institutionalized roles that define what they can expect from one another and what duties they owe each other. The nature of these rights and duties is determined by cultural values. In turn, they are influenced by economic realities and in many cases backed up by the laws of the state.

Adult family members have a legal duty to take care of their dependent children. This means taking care of their basic survival needs, like food and shelter. Ideally, it includes providing love, comfort, and a sense of security. Good families also teach their children the language, customs, beliefs, norms, skills, and values they will need to fit into their society. To a degree, most families do these things. Yet real families fall short of the ideal in many ways, and this can cause problems. Just like the society that it mirrors, a family can display selfishness and cruelty, inequality and violence.

In this chapter we examine three issues that have generated a lot of debate. The first section considers whether, in modern societies, the family is "in decline"—not providing its members with what they expect and need. The second section asks whether same-sex unions are really families. The third section examines evidence on mating to determine whether one "kind" of mate provides more satisfaction or offers a better chance of the marriage's survival than another.

9.1   Do Families Have a Future?

The issue: Are families in decline, as so many critics have said in the last two decades? If so, what's wrong with them and can they be fixed? And if they're not in decline, what can we do about the critics who say they are?

In the past decade, there has been a lot of talk about the supposed "decline of the family." This results in part from a concern about the growth of a single-parent family "underclass," which we discussed earlier. It is also related to concerns about what some have called the sexual revolution and the second demographic transition. Both changes, related but distinct, reflect a separation of sexual activity from marriage and procreation, and the development of contraceptive technology that makes this separation possible.

A third concern is due to problems of parenting, educational quality, and the future of our children. In the past thirty years, rising divorce rates and rates of women's participation in the paid work force—combined with a traditional absence of fathers from active parenthood—have raised the fear that children are not getting the parenting they need. The weak influence of schools (and churches) on young people and the strong media influence prompts concern about delinquency and vocational incompetence.

Given these rapid changes in people's intimate lives and work lives, many fear for the future of the family. They declare that the contemporary family is "in decline" and urge that we return to earlier forms of family life. But is the family in decline?

THE IDEAL(IZED) FAMILY

Most people would agree that the nuclear family is something worth preserving. Families provide people with intimacy—close relations that give them things they need and cannot get elsewhere. People continue to value families because they provide emotional support and economic benefits. In fact studies show that parental trading-off of spousal and personal time for involvement with their children does not go unnoticed, since children do assess their parents rather positively in their ability to manage work and family life. Perhaps most importantly, families give us grounding in an otherwise uncertain and chaotic world. The familiarity of family can be reassuring and, throughout our lives, gives us the confidence to explore new things.

Families have varied in form throughout history, still vary from one society to another, and are very different within societies like Canada and the United States. There is, in this sense, no traditional family. Families now regarded as traditional are themselves a significant departure from earlier traditions. Today, the co-resident heterosexual couple with children cannot be taken for granted as the basic unit of society. The hegemony of the conventional family is experiencing significant challenge not only because of women's growing economic, social, and cultural independence but also by the increase of "out" same-sex relationships.

Definitions of *family* matter a lot. In practice, how family is defined determines whether we get time off from work to attend to a family emergency, who is entitled to benefits under workplace policies, who can immigrate with us, who we can marry, and so on. Debates rage about common-law spouses having the same rights as married spouses, about spousal rights for gays and lesbians, and about the financial responsibilities and the rights

(to custody, access, etc.) of divorced people. Structural definitions of family—in terms of size or composition—have limited value, however, because family structures are so diverse and change so quickly. Much of the research on marriage patterns attributes change over time to structural factors. However, many cite changing values as an increasingly important component shaping both the type of union into which young adults enter and whether to enter into a union at all.

Process definitions may be more helpful. Accordingly, the United Nations (1991) defines family by the important socio-economic functions it performs, such as emotional, financial, and material support to its members, care of each other, transmitting cultural values, and serving as a resource for personal development. In doing so, the UN is defining families in terms of their main shared processes, rather than in terms of structural features that they may not—increasingly, do not—share. Although there is still a lot of discussion about the "traditional family"—glamorized on television in *Leave It to Beaver* and *Ozzie and Harriet* type sitcoms when Baby Boomers were children—the "traditional family" never really existed. This "perfect family" was never more than a myth, continuously propagated by conservatives and dreamers. In every American family form, from the colonial families that existed three centuries ago, to families of the 1950s, and right up to the families that exist today, we can see very real inequalities based on race, sex, and gender. So process, not form, is the best way to think about how we want families to evolve.

The social groups we think of as families typically share many features and that commonality can help us begin to understand the nature of families. Because families are extraordinarily diverse, it is difficult to generalize about them.

- *Dependency and Intimacy* All close relations have in common attachment and some kind of dependency or interdependency. This is not unique to families; most close friendships and work relationships also include some degree of emotional dependency, based on familiarity and expectations of reciprocity. However, family relations are special in that they tend to include long-term commitments, both to each other and to the shared family per se.

- *Sexuality* Adult partners within families typically have, or are expected to have, a long-term, exclusive sexual relationship, whereas among co-workers and among friends, sexual relations are either absent or of short duration. In families, sexual relations are permitted and expected between certain members (e.g., spouses) but prohibited between other members (e.g., parents and children). Norms of sexual propriety are much stronger in families than they are in friendship or work groups. Taboos against sexual exploitation of children exist to prevent sexual relations with a family member other than a spouse. Nevertheless, sexual abuse of children and elders does occur within families.
- *Protection* Effective families keep their members under guard against all kinds of internal and external dangers. There is a clear cultural expectation that families will try to protect their members. Spouses are supposed to protect one another, and adult children are supposed to protect and help their parents. In reality, family members often fail to protect each other sufficiently, and worse, some people neglect, exploit, or abuse family members.
- *Power* Households and families are small social groups whose members spend a lot of time together and depend on each other to fill both economic and social needs. There are large differences in power, strength, age, and social resources among members. Ideally, the more powerful family members protect the less powerful ones.

We have already noted that families are diverse and changing rapidly. Some believe that modern changes to family life make families worse off than before, with the result that families are actually declining rather than just evolving. There is evidence that experiencing a nontraditional family structure in childhood changes young adults' values and attitudes about the importance of marriage and likely union stability.

In light of all this, Morgan (1996) suggests that we should use *family* not as a noun, but as an adjective, and proposes a notion of *family practices*

to counter the reification of the concept. Therefore, some ask if the family is really in decline.

THE FAMILY IS IN DECLINE

Anthropologists and historians know that there are scores if not hundreds of different family types already on record. American families today are not the way they were forty years ago, but neither were families forty years ago the way they were eighty years or two hundred years before that. Many argue that changes away from the more "traditional" two-parent families have created much of the social malaise that Americans experience.

What's more, families existing at a given moment always vary from one society to another, one social class to another, one ethnic group to another, and so on. Thus, variability—not uniformity—is the norm in family life, and it always has been. When people speak about the family, they have in mind an abstraction and an ideal. There is no such thing as "the family," only families. There has always been diversity, but in the past there was a stronger, wider acceptance of the nuclear family as an ideal or optimal type of family.

So when people say that families, or the family, are in decline, they are taking that particular nuclear family type as the reference point. It is against such a backdrop that critics of modern families declare that, today, the family is in decline.

Few families today look like this idealized family, if families ever did. The statistics show us that today fewer people are marrying, staying married, or having many children. First, people are delaying marriage or avoiding it entirely, choosing cohabitation—or common law marriage—instead. Traditionalists argue that cohabitation waters down intimate domestic relationships, resulting in a trend that threatens the well-being of women and children.

However, young adults are more accepting of remaining single and cohabiting, and growing numbers emphasize the restrictions inherent in married life. Interestingly, though the more educated appear to have led the early growth in cohabitation, the acceleration of cohabitation in the 1970s was most rapid for those with less schooling.

Traditionalists have suggested that the growing new option of cohabitation has contributed to the decline of marriage and family.

Second, fewer people are staying married; said another way, the divorce rate is high. Estimates vary, but most researchers predict that 40–50 percent of American marriages will end in divorce. Divorce occurred in the past, too, specifically the late nineteenth century, and occurred more often than assumed in the form of informal divorce or desertion/abandonment. Many husbands and wives who had undergone these informal divorces, used an alias and married others, becoming bigamists, in an attempt to show fundamental respect for the institution of marriage. Just because divorces were relatively rare in the past, when the divorce laws were more rigid, doesn't mean that there weren't any divorces, and it certainly does not mean that marriages were happier. People today simply have more choice to exit unhappy marriages than they did in the past.

This means that divorce and separation was not as uncommon in the past as previously assumed. Still, divorce rates are much higher than a century ago. As a consequence, many people have two or more marriage-like relationships in their lifetime, along with many shorter-lived pairings.

Third, people have fewer children today than in the past. The baby boom period—roughly 1945–1965—was America's last childbearing frenzy, and it interrupted a century-long slide in birth rates. This is when the parents of most of the readers of this book were born. It is not that today's couples have no children whatsoever, but they do have fewer children. Of course, these childbearing patterns vary, too: Poorer people, less educated people, and rural people have always had higher fertility and they still do. But everyone's average childbearing has fallen.

Perhaps the demographic change likely to be brought on by the current "war on terrorism" may similarly affect birthrates, the formation of families, and the rate of divorce. Results from one study revealed that there were lower observed divorce rates following the Oklahoma City bombing than the prevailing 10-year divorce trend would have predicted.

In short, today's family is less likely than its predecessor to contain two married spouses and three or four children. In the Los Angeles suburb of Westwood, for example, many couples who can afford large families in fact have small ones because housekeepers refuse to take jobs where they must care for more than one or two children. Many of the household services formerly provided by wives can now be purchased in the market place and the acceptance of sexual intimacy outside of marriage has removed another incentive for matrimony.

Recent years have seen dramatic increases in the percentage of mothers—even mothers of preschool children—who work for pay. Fewer women stay home during the day, and often these are older women, women without work experience, or women who cannot get suitable daycare. As a result, most families today have at least two income-earners. More than half of all married couples hold the status of dual-earner couples.

Women's large-scale entry into paid work has had important consequences. One, as we see, is that it further reduces the number of families that relied on a single income earner (or "breadwinner"). Women's liberation and/or the conflict of dual-earner couples and work/home spillover may be reasons divorce rates have climbed. When wives' resources were measured in dollars, wives' income showed a positive linear association with the odds of divorce. Since work and family affect each other, these worlds sometimes collide, leading to marital dissatisfaction.

Findings consistently indicate that the presence of children and the greater number of children create more demands on parents and lead to negative spillover. Work and home life appear to be in increasing competition for scarce time and attention.

However, families serve fewer purely economic functions today than they once did. People—especially women—do not need to live in families if they don't want to: They can make it on their own. (Among other things, this change reflects antidiscriminatory hiring laws, more egalitarian views about males and females, and more education for women.) Some studies have found that egalitarian attitudes are linked to the reduction in men's likelihood of getting married. People who live in families today are there, more often than in the past, because they choose to be. This means families are contingent and somewhat unpredictable—not permanent and rooted in tradition, as in past families. Some conservatives believe that these changes are bad for families and bad for individual members of families.

So on virtually every dimension, the idealized family of the past is in decline. Indeed, though idealizations of this family remain, the actual family type is disappearing and just about gone. But is that bad, as critics of modern families believe? Let's take a closer look at these idealized families—characterized by distinct gender expectations and limited opportunities for women in education and the labor force. For example, let us look at family life in nineteenth-century America, before the major changes we have mentioned all took place. That may help us better understand why traditional families died out as quickly as they did.

THE IDEALIZED FAMILIES WERE IMPERFECT

What about the "good old days"? In those days, what were people's prospects for a happy family life? A century or two ago there was little choice of mate, for people had little contact with the world outside their community. Some were deemed "unacceptable" on class or racial grounds. Once married, a woman was dependent financially on her husband.

Women stayed in these marriages because they had no other options. Culturally, legally, and financially, men dominated their wives and children. This meant women and children had little protection against abuse or neglect. With shorter life expectancies than today, many men died leaving their wives widows and single parents. Family life was dominated by the uncertainties of childbearing. Poor birth control technology meant many unexpected or even unwanted children. With birth control pills, the morning after pill, and abortions, sex today does not necessarily lead to birth. This empowers women to seek alternative relationships, concentrate on a career, or to plan.

A century ago, pregnancies and deliveries risked a woman's life. Child raising was a strain that lasted through most of a woman's adult years. Naturally, each child had many brothers and sisters. This limited children's privacy, chances for education, access to parental attention, and other benefits that children take for granted today.

Would you want to take part in this "ideal" family? No wonder people changed their family relations as quickly as opportunities permitted.

A century ago many constraints on family life were economic and demographic (a result of births, deaths, and location). As the economic and demographic factors changed, so did family patterns. Over the last hundred years or so, people's lives have lengthened. We spend less time observing or anticipating death. So, we can focus our thoughts and efforts on the future, and the future has grown longer for everyone. One result is we spend more time planning for the future.

Another is that we spend less time in marriage and more time alone or in cohabiting relationships. By cohabiting, couples get an idea of how marriage with their partner might be and it helps those who intend on marrying to make an informed decision about marriage. More people today plan their families: how many children they want to have, and when they want to have them. A higher proportion of children borne are actually wanted. So, parents today have a stronger emotional attachment to their (fewer, longer-living, wanted) children than in the past. With reduced fertility and generally improved living conditions, wives come to outlive their husbands by wider margins than in the past. This means a longer period of widowhood.

At the same time, there are more parents (even grandparents) living into old age. Consequences include the establishment of retirement communities for both single and married elderly people, emotional dependence on adult children that lasts many decades and, for people without children, financial dependence on the state. Parents are less likely to die in early or middle age and lone female parents aren't discouraged from keeping their children, so there are fewer orphans today. Most children today have living parents, even if those parents do not live with one another or with the child.

Most dramatic of all, since spouses are unlikely to die in early or middle age, unsatisfied husbands and wives face a new dilemma. In the past many unhappy marriages ended when one or the other spouse died. Married people today face many years spent in an "empty nest," alone with their spouse. High current divorce rates reflect this new demographic reality, as much as they reflect women's greater economic independence and fewer young children.

Today, if not ended by divorce, about four marriages in ten reach a fiftieth anniversary (compared with half as many 1851). Today, marriage is not centrally concerned with childbearing and child raising any more than it is centrally concerned with economic production (as it was in farm families of 1851). Marriage is about companionship, affection, and emotional support between spouses.

In every modern family, life is a series of choices: whether to marry, when to marry, whether to have children, when to have children, whether to divorce, when to divorce, whether to remarry, when to remarry, and so on. These choices are never easy, but people like having choices. What's more, people choose differently and the result is a vast variety of intimate relations we call families.

To capture this variety, our definition of family must be broader than in the past. Here's one possible definition of family that reflects the new reality: A family is two or more people in an intimate, meaningful relationship marked by mutual, enduring responsibility. This modern family—immensely variable and based on personal choice—is not in decline. People still form families, though their ideas about family life vary widely.

As noted, people form families for less instrumental reasons today than in the past. They form different kinds of families than in the past. Yet they still use the traditional language of family life, speaking of husbands, wives, parents, children, brothers, and sisters—even when the reality is far more complicated.

The 1950s family—the traditionalist's ideal—was a short-lived historical accident. Briefly, it interrupted the century-long rush toward greater choice: especially, fewer children and more divorce. American families today are no worse than families at any other time or place; they are simply different and appropriate to this moment in history. In that sense, families are not in decline.

SUMMING UP

Are families going bad? As we have seen, families today vary immensely. As never before, people are rethinking what we mean by "family life" and what we can expect from family as a social institution. One wonders whether earlier expectations are still appropriate, and if not, what we can reasonably expect modern families to offer their members.

To determine whether families are getting better or worse, we must explore the various ways that people live in families. In talking about families, we must be careful to consider how earlier expectations of family fit together with times past. We must also draw contrasts between what we expect from families and what families can actually give us. Family life is becoming more, not less, important. For this reason people want families to succeed as much as possible. Success depends on a family's ability to provide its members with security, identity, companionship, and other important resources.

A successful family life produces social, economic, and psychological well-being—even increased longevity and good health. Healthy families are productive families and they benefit society at large as well as the individual family members. Much is known about how healthy and successful families are nourished and what works to make them successful.

However, old expectations and old solutions to family problems—indeed, old-fashioned family forms—do not always work as desired. Romanticizing "traditional" families and gender roles will not produce the changes in job structures, work policies, medical practice, educational preparation, political discourse, and gender inequalities that would permit families to develop moral and ethical systems relevant to the realities of 2005. In many areas, we need to find new solutions to family problems. The deeper we look into the family decline question, the more we realize that for people in modern societies, family is both part of the problem and part of the solution.

REVIEW EXERCISES

For Discussion and Debate

1. What's better about families today than families fifty or one hundred years ago?
2. What are the likely disadvantages in the reduction of childbearing in North America in the last thirty years?
3. "Demographic change explains all the important changes in family life." Agree or disagree?
4. What kinds of data could show that families are becoming more important than they were in the past?

Writing Exercises

Write a brief (500-word) essay on one of the following topics:

1. "Divorce has proved an unmitigated social disaster and should be prevented at all cost."
2. "Only under special circumstances of financial need should women with young children be encouraged to work for pay."
3. "In the good old days, marriage really meant something."
4. "Today, family life is based almost entirely on choice."

Research Activities

1. Collect the most recent statistics you can on cohabitation: who does it, for how long, and why? How often do cohabiting couples marry?
2. Read a published memoir, diary, or biography of a nineteenth century "ordinary" woman. What was her view of family life?
3. Examine old photographs or paintings to see how they express family relationships in the nineteenth or early twentieth century.
4. Develop a short questionnaire measuring what young people expect from their future marriage and parenthood. Try out the questionnaire on at least five people and tabulate the results.

SELECTED REFERENCES

Bernard, L. Diane. 1992. "The Dark Side of Family Preservation." *Affilia* 7, 2 (Summer): 156–159.

Bianchi, Suzanne M. and Lynne M. Casper. 2002. *Continuity & Change in the American Family*. Thousand Oaks, CA: Sage Publications.

Burgess, Robert L. 1994. "The Family in a Changing World: A Prolegomenon to an Evolutionary Analysis." *Human Nature* 5, 2:203–221.

Cherlin, Andrew. 1983. "Changing Family and Household: Contemporary Lessons from Historical Research." *Annual Review of Sociology* 9:51–66.

Cherlin, Andrew J. 2003. "Should the Government Promote Marriage?" *Contexts* 2, 4 (Fall): 22–29.

Coleman, James S. 1993. "The Rational Reconstruction of Society." *American Sociological Review* 58, 1 (Feb.): 1–15.

Currie, Dawn H. 1993. "'Here Comes the Bride': The Making of a 'Modern Traditional' Wedding in Western Culture." *Journal of Comparative Family Studies* 24, 3 (Autumn): 403–421.

Dickson, Lynda. 1993. "The Future of Marriage and Family in Black America." *Journal of Black Studies* 23, 4 (June): 472–491.

Dilworth Long, Jennie E. "Predictors of Negative Spillover from Family to Work." *Journal of Family Issues* 25, 2:241–261.

Dobson, James C. 2004. "Marriage Is the Foundation of the Family." *Notre Dame Journal of Law, Ethics and Public Policy* 18, 1:1–6.

Gillis, John R. 1989. "Ritualization of Middle-Class Family Life in Nineteenth Century Britain." *International Journal of Politics, Culture and Society* 3, 2 (Winter): 213–235.

Gillis, John R. 1999. "'A Triumph of Hope over Experience': Chance and Choice in the History of Marriage." *International Review of Social History* 44, 1:47–54.

Gubrium, Jaber F. and James A. Holstein. 1990. *What Is Family?* Mountain View, CA: Mayfield.

Gubrium, Jay and James A. Holstein. 1999. "What Is Family? Further Thoughts on a Social Constructionist Approach." *Marriage and Family Review* 28, 3–4:3–20.

Halsey, A. H. 1993. "Changes in the Family." *Children and Society* 7, 2:125–136.

Hodson, R. 2004. "Work Life and Social Fulfillment: Does Social Affiliation at Work Reflect a Carrot or a Stick?" *Social Science Quarterly* 85, 2:221–239.

Jallinoja, Ritta. 1994. "Alternative Family Patterns: Their Lot in Family Sociology and in the Life-Worlds of Ordinary People." *Innovation* 7, 1:15–27.

Laslett, Peter. 1983. *The World We Have Lost*. 3d ed. London: Methuen.

Manning, Wendy D. and Pamela J. Smock. 2002. "First Comes Cohabitation and Then Comes Marriage?" *Journal of Family Issues* 23, 8 (Nov.): 1065–1087.

Marchena, Elaine. 2004. "The Interaction of Work and Family Life in Middle Class Dual-Earner Families." *Dissertation Abstracts International, A: The Humanities and Social Sciences* 64, 7 (June): 2662-A.

Okin, Susan Moller. 1989. *Justice, Gender, and the Family*. New York: Basic Books.

Palermo, George B. and Douglas Simpson. 1994. "At the Roots of Violence: The Progressive Decline and Dissolution of the Family." *International Journal of Offender Therapy and Comparative Criminology* 38, 2 (Summer): 105–116.

Popenoe, David. 1991. "Family Decline in the Swedish Welfare State." *Public Interest* 102 (Winter): 65–77.

Popenoe, David. 1999. "Can the Nuclear Family Be Revived?" *Society* 36, 5 (Jul.–Aug.): 28–30.

Ritala-Koskinen, Aino. 1994. "The Family Structures Are Changing—but What about the Idea of the Family?" *Innovation* 7, 1:41–49.

Rosen, David M. 1991. "What Is a Family? Nature, Culture, and the Law." *Marriage and Family Review* 17, 1–2:29–43.

Roseneil and Budgeon. 2004. "The Editors' Introduction: Beyond the Conventional Family." *Current Sociology* 52, 2:127–134.

Roseneil and Budgeon. 2004. "Cultures of Intimacy and Care Beyond the 'Family': Personal Life and Social Change in the Early 21st Century." *Current Sociology* 52, 2:135–159.

Rossi, Alice S. 1993. "The Future in the Making: Recent Trends in the Work-Family Interface." *American Journal of Orthopsychiatry* 63, 2 (Apr.): 166–176.

Rossi, Alice S., ed. 2001. *Caring and Doing for Others: Social Responsibility in the Domains of Family, Work, and Community*. Chicago, IL: University of Chicago Press.

Rubin, Roger H. 2001. "Alternative Lifestyles Revisited, or Whatever Happened to Swingers, Group Marriages, and Communes?" *Journal of Family Issues* 22, 6 (Sept.): 711–727.

Sassler and Goldscheider. 2004. "Revisiting Jane Austen's Theory of Marriage Timing." *Journal of Family Issues* 25, 2:139–166.

Scanzoni, John and William Marsiglio. 1991. "Wider Families as Primary Relationships." *Marriage and Family Review* 17, 1–2:117–133.

Smith, Daniel Scott. "The Curious History of Theorizing about the History of the Western Nuclear Family." *Social Science History* 17, 3 (Fall): 325–353.

Tilley, Louise A. and Joan W. Scott. 1978. *Women, Work and Family*. New York: Holt, Rinehart and Winston.

Vinovskis, Maris A. 1990. "Death and Family Life in the Past." *Human Nature* 1, 2:109–122.

9.2 Are Homosexual Unions *Really* Families?

The Issue: There is no single idea about families, and never has been. Definitions of family and marriage have always been in flux. But should the definition of family now be changed to allow same-sex couples the same rights to marry as heterosexual couples?

Throughout history, state-sanctioned marriages have been contracted between a man and a woman. Today, some people are favoring a new definition of marriage that permits marriage contracts between a man and a man, or a woman and a woman. And, just as definitions of marriage have changed over the years, some believe that the definition needs to change again to include same-sex couples.

However, not everyone supports this view. In fact, in the American elections of 2004, voters in all 11 states that asked the question voted to amend the state constitution to declare that marriage is only the union of a man and a woman. Additionally, no same-sex marriages from other states or jurisdictions would be recognized and no divorces could be granted by a judge in the case of same-sex marriages. Opponents of same-sex marriage argue that same-sex couples should not be recognized as families because they are not biologically capable of having children. Others raise questions about whether same-sex marriage is moral, whether it is healthy for children, and whether the American family could survive such an upheaval as the inclusion of same-sex marriage.

Those who want to maintain the status quo point out that marriage is a sacred union that has existed for thousands of years. It is the method by which most children are raised and given values that help to make America great. Biology makes a difference. Isn't a same-sex couple unnatural and inherently wrong, since the couple cannot reproduce biologically? And, when it comes to parenting, isn't the optimal arrangement for children to have two parents of the opposite sexes, so that they can learn both the male and female viewpoints?

Supporters of same-sex marriage, on the other hand, argue that marriage will remain a central institution in any event, and by including same-sex couples, marriage becomes even more solidly rooted. We disenfranchise same-sex couples and their families by excluding them from legal marriage, which is central to civil society. Supporters also view same-sex marriage and parenting as two different issues, arguing that sexual orientation has no impact on the quality of parenting.

Whether you agree with legalizing same-sex marriages or not, the debate is continuing, as now, more than ever, more gays and lesbians try to marry and create families. So, what are the pros and cons of this issue, and what does social research tell us that could inform a decision on this topic?

SAME-SEX MARRIAGE SHOULD BE LEGAL

Definitions of Marriage and Family Are Constantly Changing Definitions of what constitutes a family and marriage have changed over the course of history. Anthropologists, sociologists, and historians all concede that marriage is a complex phenomenon that is influenced by the cultural, social, political, and economic environment. It was only 1967, less than 50 years ago, when the U.S. Supreme Court, in the case of *Loving vs. Virginia*, abolished the statutes that made black and white marriage illegal. In America today, it seems hard to believe that interracial marriage was *ever* an issue, but it was.

This shows that behaviors or practices that were rejected at a certain point in history become acceptable as time and society changes. Furthermore, it is important to keep in mind that in the past people tended to marry other people not only because of their similar racial background but their religious and ethnic affiliations. These aspects of *homogamy* are far less important today, as people are more inclined to select their partners based on shared educational background, age, interests, and values. It would not be surprising if 50 years from now the rejection of same-sex marriage would seem absurd.

Apart from embracing interracial marriage, society has had to deal with other important changes in family life in the past 50 years, including high rates of divorce and blended families. Part of the argument against same-sex marriage is that every child should grow up in a family with a father and a mother. The reality is that many heterosexual families already lack a father or mother, and this has always been so. Moreover, we should question the assumption that having a male and a female parent is critical. Far more important is having two good parents of whatever sex.

Our current definitions of family and marriage are relatively new and constantly changing. Before 1900, marriage was more an obligation than a voluntary union between lovers. People often entered into marriage out of necessity. A woman married because she needed a man to support her throughout life. A man married because he needed someone to bear his children and keep his house. How different this is from our thinking today, which emphasizes choice, romance, and sexual attraction. This difference clearly shows that the definitions of marriage and family evolve and adapt to the changes that occur in society.

It is true that in the past legal marriages were always between men and women, not same-sex partners. This was likely premised on the assumption that reproduction was the main goal of marriage, as reproduction without marriage was not only undesirable but rejected. Current definitions of marriage and family are changing to reflect new adoption practices and reproductive technologies, as well as drastic declines in voluntary childbearing that lead many families to have no children and most to have very few. Today, little of an adult's married life is spent bearing and raising children, so marriage can scarcely be first and foremost about children.

At the same time, many lesbians and gays are already parents from previous heterosexual marriages. Adoption and in vitro fertilization are other means of becoming parents that permit gays and lesbians to bear children. Though in the past there were no means by which same-sex couples could create a family, these means exist today. These changes merit changes of the definition of marriage.

Opponents of same-sex marriage argue that the purpose of marriage is to have children; yet no one forces a heterosexual couple to procreate. Many heterosexual couples turn out to be infertile and some choose not to have children. At the same time, unplanned pregnancies occurring before and outside of marriage prove that marriage and procreation are not as closely connected as opponents of same-sex marriage lead us to believe.

Same-Sex Couples and Their Families Are Disenfranchised By disallowing same-sex marriage, thousands of families and individuals are *disenfranchised*—that is, treated as less than full members of society. Many institutions see marriage as a legal basis for many of their policies. Take the example of an individual who is denied access to a lover in a hospital because he or she is not related by blood, neither is he or she the patient's legal partner. Also consider that this individual may be the person most indicated to care for the patient because of the emotional bond between them. However, because same-sex marriage is not allowed this person is not only discriminated against but the patient's right to be properly cared for is violated.

The legal inclusion of same-sex marriage would not only prevent the disenfranchisement of these families but it would also help to promote marriage and family life as societal norms. In fact, in proclaiming the National Family Week in November of 2001, President Bush stated that the "government can support families by promoting policies that help strengthen the institution of marriage [to] help parents rear their children" (U.S. Department of Health and Human Services). And a good way for doing this would be to allow same-sex marriage, thus including more people in such a socially central institution.

In today's society, divorce rates are on the rise and single parenting compromises the future opportunities of children. Unfortunately, because of their incapacity to marry, many gay couples cohabit or engage in domestic partnerships, which may include children from previous heterosexual relations. It is documented that married couples have the capacity to build more wealth, which decreases the likelihood that their offspring will grow in poverty. Likewise, research has shown that legal marriages are stronger—less likely to dissolve—than cohabiting partnerships, since they are harder to exit. Research shows that within five years 20 percent of marriages will come to an end, whereas in the same period of time 54 percent of cohabitation unions will come to an end. One of the arguments to support these findings is that in marriage, partners receive more rights to each other's property and they are expected to fulfill obligations to each other. Allowing same-sex marriages would increase the number of married couples, thus there will be more children living and growing in more secure environments.

Marriage for Political Reasons   Many assert that homosexual groups and activists are campaigning for the legalization of same-sex marriages just as a means to change the legal structure and acquire political power. Yet homosexuals have always been marginalized groups that are merely seeking their entrance into American mainstream society, as blacks and other minorities had to do. In fighting for the right to marry, homosexuals are fighting for the right to conform with social institutions and to assimilate. This interest in assimilation into one of society's most fundamental institutions should be encouraged and not the cause of subordination and discrimination. America is an international advocate of human rights and equality among human beings. By legalizing same-sex marriage, gay and lesbian unions would be considered as no different from heterosexual, thus helping to eliminate homophobia and discrimination.

Monogamy   Some have argued that gay men should not be allowed to marry because they are promiscuous and less likely than heterosexual men to be monogamous. Monogamy, however, is not a natural human state but a value that individuals hold. Though it is a value that some gay men do *not* hold, monogamy is also a value that many heterosexuals do *not* hold. In fact, it is a value that many married people do not hold, or practice, as seen by the numbers of extramarital affairs. Therefore, promiscuity should not be a key determinant of the right to marriage, since it is not limited to homosexuals.

Sexual Orientation and Parenting   Some opponents of same-sex marriage fear that gay parents would have or raise gay children. First, this should not be an issue if we accept homosexuality as a fundamental human characteristic like any other. In principle, we should not fear this any more than we fear that parents who play the piano will produce piano-playing offspring. Second, there is no evidence that homosexuals actively recruit or "create" homosexuals. On the contrary, the only sexual identity actively imposed on children is a *hetero*sexual identity. This is done within the family from birth onward, as well as in churches, schools, and the mass media.

If anything, same-sex marriage will help children form healthy identities by teaching them more about sexual equality. Marriage has a history of creating and maintaining gender roles. By getting rid of the traditional notions of marriage, perhaps some of the sexist ways of the past can be eliminated. Egalitarian marriages—some of them homosexual—provide excellent examples for America's youth. By legalizing same-sex unions, marriage will help to endorse equality for both men and women in the institution of marriage

In all, no research finds notable differences between children raised in heterosexual families and those raised in homosexual families. Rather, lesbian, gay, and bisexual parents are equally capable of being good parents. In fact, sexual orientation has no bearing on parenting. One might just as well talk about the relative merits of short parents and tall ones, or blond parents and brunettes, as talk about the merits of gay versus heterosexual parents.

The Importance of Tradition   For some, the case of same-sex marriage is linked to national identity and national tradition. Evidence of this is seen in the Defense of Marriage Act signed by President Clinton on September 21, 1996. Republican statements on the matter explain that "the traditional family has stood for 5,000 years and whatever the eventual fate of this Nation, will continue to stand as the fundamental cornerstone of all successful civilizations" (Westervelt 2001:109).

Many opponents of same-sex marriage invoke the Bible as a source for their ideas about same-sex marriage. Yet the Bible has surprisingly little to say on the topic. Terms such as *homosexual* and *heterosexual* were first used at the end of the 1800s and the term gay was first discovered in the 1900s in prison slang. Only in the 1940s in a revised edition of the Bible was the term homosexual included. It has been human institutions that have interpreted the Bible and accommodated its message. In short, the Bible lacks validity on the argument of same-sex marriages, as it does not clearly reject the notion of homosexuality before being altered in 1940.

MODERATE VIEWS

Some moderate literature on this topic supports same-sex unions but also warns of the problems implementing these marriages now. It recognizes that same-sex marriages can be beneficial since they promote commitment between couples and include more people in the married state that is so fundamental to civil society. Some fear, however, that the United States is not ready for same-sex unions and that such a change would cause upheaval. Same-sex marriage, according to this view, is a notion that millions must get used to and a change that is best done gradually to minimize the effect on Americans.

However, some have argued vigorously against same-sex marriage, for a variety of reasons.

SAME-SEX MARRIAGE SHOULD NOT BE LEGALIZED

Marriage and Same-Sex Couples According to traditionalists, the institution of marriage has endured more or less intact for the past 5,000 years and in 2002, 69 percent of children under 18 years lived with both of their married parents. Americans have been born and raised within this institution since the start of the nation. Marriage has provided America with stability and a sense of morality, which children need. Thanks to the institution of heterosexual marriage, they say, the United States is one of the most successful nations in the world. Altering this means of socialization (the nuclear family) weakens the social fabric of the nation and may lead to greater social problems. Tampering with the traditional family to allow same-sex marriage would bring about the downfall of marriage as we know it, and would shake the foundation of American society.

Opponents recognize that gays and lesbians are already a marginalized group in society. Marriage would not bring them into the mainstream. If the institution of marriage were extended to same-sex couples, it would only serve to marginalize them further. Those lesbian and gay men, especially the poor or those of color, would become prime targets for discrimination if they chose not to marry.

It is well known that in homosexual relationships, partners become more like "best friends" than typical husband and wife. If these unions were legalized, they would be markedly different from most marriages that currently exist. Moreover, the notion of marriage itself may be the opposite of what gay and lesbian identity is all about. Coming out as gay or lesbian means taking on a lifestyle that involves choice—for most, it means choosing a life in which one cannot get married. Part of the point of same-sex relationships is to challenge natural notions of sexuality, marriage, and family. The point of "coming out" is *not* to get married and have children.

The Relationship Promiscuity threatens the stability of society by threatening the stability of families. As such, why should the government allow gays—a group known for its promiscuity—the right to marry? If anything, allowing same-sex couples to marry will only increase the divorce rate and the amount of conflict between these couples. Men, more than women, are naturally promiscuous. Because of this, male-to-male marriages will be doubly promiscuous, since it is not marriage that dulls men's promiscuity, but the presence of women.

Marriage may not bring as much trouble for lesbians, but there would be greater troubles if gay men married. Research shows that women are more aware of relationship problems than men and they are socialized to manage complex networks of individuals. Men, on the other hand, are more likely to withdraw from conflict and take longer to recover from the stress that it causes. As such, having two men in a relationship means that there will be twice the problem of conflict avoidance. Due to the way that men have been socialized, many gay couples have lower quality relationships than heterosexual couples, some assert.

Homosexuality or Gay-Parenting Is Not Natural

Opponents of same-sex marriage assert that homosexuality is a learned pathology. If an individual is anatomically male or female, he or she is also heterosexual. The group "Focus on the Family" has done research on this topic and has successfully helped individuals to come out of homosexuality.

The same group labels homosexuality as a developmental disorder that results from improper gender formation. For example, if a boy is raised without a father or has a distant and unapproachable father, he may reject the building of a normal male identity and as such become a homosexual. According to their theory, since the boy does not identify with his father his desire for closeness with a male model becomes eroticized and manifests itself in homosexuality

Though not all would agree that homosexuality is unnatural, many think that gay parenting is. One philosopher asserts that gay parenting is an unnatural phenomenon and a threat to culture. Sexual difference is the basis of our culture, he claims, and it is impossible to deny the need of a female and male to create a child. It is therefore biologically arranged that a male and female be involved in parenting, whereas it is biologically unnatural for two people of the same-sex to raise a child. The philosopher stresses that both parents do not need to be present during the child rearing process. However, the parents must exist as psychic points of reference so that the child emerges in a proper way.

Further, opponents say that gay and lesbian couples do not make proper role models for children. In "normal" relationships, both a man and a woman exist if not in body, at least in mind; they serve as a point of reference to a child. In same-sex relationships, the dynamics are entirely different. It is evident that same-sex couples do not create the same types

of relationships as heterosexual couples. In same sex couples, you lose one of the key social roles in our culture—male or female. By allowing same-sex marriage, the government would sanction raising children in a culturally confusing environment.

Marriage Is a Private Matter

Many consider that marriage is a private matter as it is based on the personal relationship of two human beings; therefore, the state should not interfere. However, marriage is a social and legal institution and the main socialization agent in children's development. At this point marriage ceases to be a private affair, as it is fundamental to the functioning and the future of American society as a whole. Furthermore, as Dr. Johnson from the group "Focus on the Family" claims, the legalization of same-sex marriage would only open the door for other groups that may advocate for the legalization of marriage between children and adults, or polygamous marriages, among other examples.

Abuse

Lesbian relationships, in theory, are supposed to be less misogynistic than heterosexual relationships. However, research does not support this conclusion. The percentage of lesbians in abusive relationships varies widely, based on definitions of abuse, from 7 percent to 90 percent; Whatever the estimate, abuse is a serious problem amongst lesbians. Some have suggested that lesbians are mutual batterers. Likewise, male-to-male relationships have similar problems. After AIDS and substance abuse, domestic violence is the third largest health problem for gay males.

Same-sex couples should not be allowed to parent, since many homosexuals have problems that would interfere with activities of parenting. One study reports that as many as 90 percent of lesbians have internalized a feeling of shame. Many think of themselves as immoral or evil because of their attraction to people of the same sex. This bodes poorly for parenting: An individual who believes that he or she will be condemned for eternity should not be raising a child. Similarly, feelings of shame contribute to patterns of abuse. For this reason, same-sex couples—who are more likely than heterosexuals to harbor these feelings—should not have children because they may be more likely to abuse them than heterosexual couples.

The problem of gay parenting is compounded by the fact that same-sex couples lack the support of most of society. Many families and religious institutions do not support gay marriage and as such, gay families would have a smaller network of support in difficult times. Children of these same-sex couples might also be abused by others and grow up in a hostile environment.

Gay Parents Make Gay Children   Opponents of same-sex marriage believe that the concept of homosexuality as a learned pathology does have some merit. Children of lesbian and gay couples are more likely to experiment with homosexuality than are the children of heterosexual couples. If legalized, gay marriage would increase the number of homosexuals in American society, further disrupting the foundation of the nation.

The Bible Says That It's Wrong   The argument goes that God made Adam and Eve, not Adam and Steve. Though there is technically a separation between church and state in America, the church has been instrumental in providing U.S. families with guidance and support. The Bible has been central in this endeavor by providing the guidelines by which people live. If people ignore important sections of the Bible, such as the ones that see homosexuality as a sin, it could lessen the message of all other important teachings and cause more social problems.

Summing Up

Research finds stereotypical views about homosexuality even among young, highly educated people. These views include the beliefs that homosexual parents create a dangerous environment for the child, provide a less secure home, and offer less emotional stability. Such views are more common among older, rural, or less-educated respondents, among people who are highly religious, and among people who are fearful about sex.

But research on same-sex couples does not provide any grounds for these concerns. Contrary to popular belief, gay and lesbian parents raise fine, healthy families as often as heterosexual families do. Many studies support the finding that gay and lesbian parents are just as capable in child-rearing as heterosexual parents. Children raised by homosexual parents do not have different behavioral and educational outcomes than children of heterosexual unions, nor do they feel any less loved or accepted by their parents. And there is no more chance of children growing up gay or lesbian in a same-sex family than there is in a heterosexual family.

Some critics of homosexual parenting argue that lesbian unions lack a proper father figure, which could affect the growth of the child. This is not so, as many lesbian mothers include the fathers in the child's life in the cases where they know the donor. However, those who oppose homosexual parenting are often not as concerned about the role of the mother in parenting between two gay men. In addition, many lesbian mothers are challenging the idea that biological fathers should be involved as parents in their children's lives as part of normal development. Besides fighting for their right to raise children, many gay and lesbian parents also wish to dispel the notion that parenting be synonymous with gendered assumptions about mothering and fathering, and that mothers and fathers should share a household with their children.

How do children of same-sex unions feel about their family situations? Many of them view their upbringing positively in the love and attention they received and their preparation to enter the adult world. Many feel they gained important insights into gender relations and broader, more inclusive definitions of family by growing up with same-sex parents.

Although research points to no negative implications for gay parenting, it is important to keep in mind that more information and understanding of the subject must be developed. For both sides of the argument, there is still a lot to discover and debate. It will be in the years to follow that society will be able to evaluate a new generation of children growing up with same-sex parents, either married or unmarried. In the meantime, definitions of family policies will still be changing as they have in the past in one way or the other to accommodate the changes in society.

REVIEW EXERCISES

For Discussion and Debate

1. Some say that gay parades and demonstrations create a false image of the gay community, depicting a promiscuous life style. Do you think this negatively influences people's perception of their capacity to form families?
2. How could the legalization of homosexual unions undermine U.S. international capacity?
3. Statistics show that couples who cohabit before marriage are more likely to divorce than those that do not. If, up to now, gays and lesbians' only chance to live as a couple has been cohabitation, is there any hope for same-sex marriages to be lasting unions?
4. The "men don't cry" approach would have no place in a same-sex household and this is emotionally positive for boys. Agree or disagree?

Writing Exercises.

Write a brief (500-word) essay on one of the following topics:

1. "Countries that legalize same-sex marriage will see a further decrease in their population's capacity to replace itself."
2. "The rise of cohabitation is a trend influenced by the gay lifestyle, and it undermines the institution of marriage."
3. "Parentless children are better off in the State's care than being adopted by a gay couple."
4. "Gay and Lesbian parents would raise emotionally strong children."

Research Activities

1. Prepare a questionnaire that measures what people consider to be the most important challenges faced by gays and lesbians. Try the questionnaire on 25 individuals and find out on what level of priority same-sex marriage is rated.
2. Check the Gay and Lesbian groups and offices at your school. Investigate what programs and resources are out there to help these couples on a personal and legal basis.
3. Try to find a biography of someone who grew up with same-sex parents. Analyze their experiences and how they influenced his or her life.
4. Try to research one or two major legal custody cases involving same-sex couples. Analyze what implications the legalization of same-sex marriage would have had on the case.

SELECTED REFERENCES

Apostolidis, Paul. 2001. "Homosexuality and 'Compassionate' Conservatism in the Discourse of the Post-Reaganite Right." *Constellations* 8, 1:78–105.

Biblarz, Timothy J. and Judith Stacey. 2001. "(How) Does the Sexual Orientation of Parents Matter?" *American Sociological Review* 66, 2:159–183.

Blaise, Fortunata and Carolynn Kohn. 2003. "Demographic, Psychosocial and Personality Characteristics of Lesbian Batterers." *Violence and Victims* 18, 5:557–568.

Bumpass, Larry and Hsien-Hen Lu. 2000. "Trends in Cohabitation and Implications for Children's Family Context in the U.S." *Population Studies* 54, 1:29–41.

Census Bureau. 2004. "America's Families and Living Arrangements, 2003." Available online at http://www.census.gov/population/www/socdemo/hh-fam/cps2003.html.

Clarke, Victoria. 2003. "Lesbian and Gay Marriage: Transformation or Normalization." *Feminism and Psychology* 13, 4:519–529.

———. 2000. "Stereotype, Attack, and Stigmatize Those Who Disagree: Employing Scientific Rhetoric in Debates about Lesbian and Gay Parenting." *Feminism and Psychology* 10, 1:152–159.

———. 2001. "What About the Children? Arguments Against Lesbian and Gay Parenting." *Women's Studies International* 24, 5:555–570.

Corliss, Heather, Susan Cochran and Vickie Mays. 2002. "Reports of Parental Maltreatment during Childhood in a United States Population-Based Survey of Homosexual, Bisexual, and Heterosexual Adults." *Child Abuse and Neglect* 26:1165–1178.

Dobson, James. 2004. "Marriage Is the Foundation of the Family." *Notre Dame Journal of Law, Ethics and Public Policy* 18, 1:1–6.

Donavan, Catherine, Brian Heaphy and Jeffery Weeks. 2001. *Same Sex Intimacies: Families of Choice and Other Life Experiments*. London: Routledge.

Dutton, Donald G. and Monica A. Landolt. 1997. "Power and Personality: An Analysis of Gay Male Intimate Abuse." *Sex Roles* 37, 5/6: 335–359.

Hausknecht, Murray. 2003. "Gay Marriage and the Domestication of Sex." *Dissent* 50, 4:8–11.

Hull, Kathleen E. 2003. "The Cultural Power of Law and the Cultural Enactment of Legality: The Case of Same-Sex Marriage." *Law and Social Inquiry* 28, 3:629–657.

Kerr, Marcee G. and Corey J. Vitello. 2002. "Law Enforcement Officers' Perceptions of Same-Sex Domestic Violence: Reason for Cautious Optimism." *Journal of Interpersonal Violence* 17, 7:760–772.

Kurdek, Lawrence A. 2001. "Differences between Heterosexual-Nonparent Couples and Gay, Lesbian, and Heterosexual-Parent Couples." *Journal of Family Issues* 22, 6:728–755.

Miller et al. 2001. "Domestic Violence in Lesbian Relationships." *Women and Therapy* 23, 3:107–127.

Moss, Kevin. 2002. "Legitimizing Same-Sex Marriages." *Peace Review* 14, 1:101–107.

National Center for Health Statistics. 2002. "Cohabitation, Marriage, Divorce, and Remarriage in the United States." Series Report 23, 22 (July 24): 103. Available online at http://www.cdc.gov/nchs/pressroom/02news/div_mar_cohab.htm.

Stiers, Gretchen A. 1999. *From This Day Forward: Commitment, Marriage, and Family in Lesbian and Gay Relationships*. New York: St. Martin's Press.

Turell, Susan C. 2000. "A Descriptive Analysis of Same-Sex Relationship Violence for a Diverse Sample." *Journal of Family Violence* 15, 3:2000.

U.S. Department of Health and Human Services. 2004. "ACF Healthy Marriage Mission." Administration for Children and Families. Available online at http://www.acf.hhs.gov/healthymarriage/about/mission.html#goals.

Westervelt, Don. 2001. "National Identity and the Defense of Marriage." *Constellations* 8, 1:106–126.

9.3   Does a Happy Marriage Mean Finding "Mr. or Ms. Right"?

The issue: A high and worrisome rate of divorce and, some believe, a rejection of stable marriage in favor of cohabitation, singlehood, or sequential monogamy—none of these believed to be good for children. Can this be prevented by better mating practices?

Our culture puts a huge emphasis on romantic love. We are bombarded by stories and images of love every time we turn on the television, go to the movies, or open a magazine. Our culture also places a lot of importance on the family as a source of personal meaning and happiness. These two themes come together in our culture's mating rituals. According to popular thought, some people search for the best and most perfect mate. In marrying that mate, they are supposed to achieve as much marital bliss as is humanly possible. This romantic marriage is presumably the best place to develop personally and raise children. When this romantic love disappears marriage can end in divorce.

Are these cultural assumptions about mating and marriage sociologically valid? Do people really mate in this way and are successful marriages really based on finding the single best mate—"Mr. or Ms. Right"? If so, what makes one potential mate better than all the others? And how do people go about finding this one best mate? As usual, sociologists disagree about the answers to these interesting and important questions.

Note however that this discussion is somewhat different from others in this book. It isn't really a debate insofar as the two halves don't really oppose each other. The first argues that there is no one "Mr./Ms. Right," while the second argues that most people end up marrying someone similar to themselves. So as long as a similar mate is your ideal, there isn't really a difference of opinion here. This section offers two different ways of looking at the issue of human mating

THERE IS NO MR./MS. RIGHT

In cultures where mate choice is not left to individuals, marriage is arranged. The logic behind this practice is the belief that young people will seek pleasure and be unlikely to find themselves a suitable partner. So parents, relatives, and friends become matchmakers. Successful, satisfying arranged marriages suggest that there is no Mr. or Ms. Right if the two participants love each other, even though they did not have choice.

From a purely mathematical standpoint, taking the world's population into consideration, it seems impossible that there is one best mate. Even if there were, it is statistically unlikely that we would find that person. Demographers understand marriage as a type of market, in which the duration of searches and quality of outcome are determined by the market conditions. And from a sociological standpoint, that is probably why research has not found a correlation between the number of partners dated before marriage and marital satisfaction.

If marital satisfaction were really a "shopping problem" of finding the best bargain among available mates, then people who had shopped more and longer would stand the best chance of finding the bargain. Think about buying a new car: You don't buy the first one you see. You study the cars available, talk to friends, visit different dealers, test-drive a lot of different models: This is aimed at increasing the likelihood you find the car that will (probably) please you the most. We often also do these things before marrying: study possible mates, talk to friends, and date different people, for example. However, survey evidence on mating collected by Martin Whyte finds that extensive shopping (i.e., dating) does not produce a happier marriage than less extensive shopping. This finding suggests that the shopping metaphor is quite inappropriate.

There are other reasons to reject this metaphor. Finding Mr./Ms. Right is statistically improbable. Suppose you made a list of the five most important qualities in a mate: attractive appearance, a good sense of humor, intelligence, honesty, and kindness. Now, suppose that you required your ideal mate scores in the top 20 percent of the population for each of these qualities. Assuming these qualities are uncorrelated and independent of one another, only $(.2)(.2)(.2)(.2)(.2) = .00032$ (or one person in 3,125) would be suitable. If your standards are even higher and you only consider people in the top 10 percent of the population on each of these five qualities, only one person in 100,000 would be suitable.

Assuming that your ideal mate exists, he or she may not rate you in the top 20 percent. Even if he or she did, finding each other is rare, and you are unlikely to find each other by chance. In fact, the likelihood of you wanting and finding each other by chance alone is less than $(.00032)(.00032) =$ approximately 1 in 10 million. The chances are less likely if you're both looking for someone with the same shopping list as your own. The odds of 1 in 10 million are not very. Few of us have time for 10 million dates (though film and television portray a world where this is possible).

How might people increase their odds? One way would be to search systematically (not randomly) by going places and joining groups where people with the desired qualities are most likely to be found. Doing this maximizes the chances of meeting someone with the qualities you are searching for—for example, someone rich, well-educated, or of Italian descent. This is most often seen through marital assimilation. Searches for members of communities are often narrowed because they find people within their communities who share common values and background. However, this process is time-consuming and risky. Sure, we can increase the likelihood of meeting someone rich, but how would we increase our chances of meeting someone honest, kind, intelligent, or funny? Would you know where to go to find many people with these qualities?

Another search strategy is to cast your net as widely as possible. Some people, for example, put advertisements (or answer advertisements) in newspapers or magazines. Internet dating sites, where members post personal ads online and flirt via e-mail and chat, are proliferating. Advertising increases the total number of people who will come to know that you are a potential mate with particular desirable qualities, an improvement on the random mate search. However, many people will feel uncomfortable about advertising in this way; others will have difficulty evaluating the responses they receive. Some may be unpleasantly surprised.

A more realistic strategy may be to lower your standards. Settle for Mr. or Ms. Almost-Right. For example, you might settle for a candidate who is in the top 50 percent of the population on all of your five desired qualities. Doing this improves your chances considerably. Now, the chance of your bumping into each other is $(.5)^5(.5)^5 = 1$ in a thousand (roughly). This could then be improved through systematic searches (i.e., joining groups) and advertising. Even if we get the chances of meeting Mr. or Ms. Almost-Right down to 1 in 500, you are still very unlikely to meet. Based on these calculations one can conclude that *most people do not meet and marry this way*.

It seems much more conceivable that you will meet and marry someone who just happens to be nearby. You don't shop for a mate at all. Instead, often without expecting it, you fall in love with someone you like, get married, and (if lucky) live happily ever after. Let's call this the "potluck" scenario. However plausible this scenario may seem, there is still another way to think about mating.

THERE IS A MR./MS. RIGHT

If the potluck scenario were valid, people would meet their mates by chance and settle down because they were both ready. If that was how people mated, married people would be different from their mates as often as they were similar. In other words, marriages "made in heaven" would look like a blindfolded God (or chance) had randomly selected pairs of people from a big sack of candidates.

This isn't what the literature on mating shows. Research finds that most interpersonal attraction between people, whether for purposes of mating or merely friendship, is based on similarity. People like other people who are like themselves. When applied to marriage, this principle of like attracting like is called *homogamy*.

Concurrent with this idea is that we tend to look for similar qualities in all types of relationships. Consistency was found in research for the most desirable and important qualities for all relationships (i.e., married couples, dating couples, casual sex couples, same sex friends, and opposite sex friends). These qualities included warmth, kindness, expressiveness, openness, and sense of humor. There is one major exception to this rule—men and women differ from each other in a variety of ways, including what they look for in a mate. More often than not, research finds that men are looking for an attractive appearance while women are looking for the ability and willingness to support a family. This aside, research finds that marriages are usually homogamous. How is that possible and why does it happen?

Some research shows that spousal similarity is not due to homogamy or the initial similarity between mates before marriage. Rather, it is due to a convergence, a growing similarity, of spouses' qualities after marriage. The longer people live together the more alike they become, in their interests, activities, views, even their appearance. This may sound dreadful to one who is seeking independence and selfhood and hopes that marriage can be an opportunity for free growth and personal expression.

This, most often, is not how marriage works. But research shows that homogamous marriages are happier and more satisfying than heterogamous marriages (in which the spouses are dissimilar). A possible explanation for the failure of heterogamous marriages is that qualities that initially attract individuals to one another eventually become disliked. These are sometimes known as fatal-attractions. A study of a sample of 125 dating individuals found that roughly 44 percent of the sample had experienced fatal attractions, showing that opposites often do attract. We are not always drawn to others who are similar; but in the long run, "dissimilar or extreme qualities in a partner are significantly more likely to become disliked," yielding less relationship satisfaction.

In turn, the literature shows that marital satisfaction produces life satisfaction. A happy marriage spills over into other domains—how people view their work, for example.

Similar spouses do not have to be similar in every respect; some similarities are more important than others. It used to be said that ethnic or racial differences posed a serious problem for couples who decide to marry outside their own group. However, current research does not support this view. Unless the friends and relatives of the couple create a problem, such differences don't seem to matter much. That is, they have no effect on marital satisfaction or the likelihood the couple will break up.

Educational similarity is much more important for marital satisfaction. The same is true of similarity in ages. This marks a major change in the conditions necessary for an enduring marriage. In the nineteenth and early twentieth century, when divorce was rare, men often married women who were much younger and less educated than they were. We don't know how satisfying these marriages were, but they lasted. Presently, divorce is more accessible and common. As a result, marriages rely a lot more on spouses wanting to be with one another; and increasingly, people are marrying spouses who are similar in age and education. As a

result, the more education one obtains, the longer one waits to get married. This is especially true for women. These qualities seem to draw people together and keep them together, at least more than a common ethnicity or race does. A common religion makes a difference if one or both spouses are seriously committed to their religion, its practices, and beliefs.

Much less is known about the common social, political, or sexual attitudes that draw people and keep people together, or about the personality differences that are tolerable in a successful marriage. Therefore, it is difficult to ascertain whether two insecure mates are better matched than a secure mate and an insecure one. Or whether there is a problem if a Republican marries a Democrat, or if a feminist marries a male chauvinist. There is room for those of you still active in the mating game to do your own research.

Similarity and Marital Satisfaction   Let's allow that some mates are probably better for you than others; in that sense, there *is* a Mr. or Ms. Right. More properly, there may be many Mr. or Ms. Rights, but a vastly larger number of Mr. or Ms. Wrongs. Given the impossible shopping problem we discussed earlier, how do (did) you and your suitable mate manage to find each other? Why are homogamous marriages more likely to be satisfying, and how do they happen far beyond the realm of chance?

The success and satisfaction of homogamous marriages can be explained though geographical, social psychological, and sociological justifications.

Geographical   Most social interactions between single people, especially young single people, take place in relatively homogamous settings. Take your primary school, high school, or college: Though there are many kinds of people in each of these places, they are far more similar to you (in every respect) than a random sample drawn from the world at large. Most important, they are roughly the same age and educational level as you are. Less important but also notable, they represent only a few of the world's ethnicities, races, social class levels, language groups, and cultures. You are far more likely to find someone very much like you sitting at the next seat in the cafeteria than, say, working in a match factory in southern India, or growing yams in a loincloth in the Amazon River valley. (For their part, young tribal yam growers in Brazil don't stand much chance of finding homogamous, or any other, mates in the cafeterias of North American colleges.)

Social Psychological   Research has found that couples with similar identity styles report greater marital satisfaction than couples who are dissimilar. This is especially true for women. The rationalization behind this is "that the changes in an individual's identity that are necessitated by the marital commitment may be easiest for those who have similar styles of problem solving and decision making. . . . Being around people similar to ourselves tends to reinforce existing beliefs and attitudes" (Cook and Jones 2002). So marital partners whose beliefs and attitudes are reinforced are likely to spend more time with their spouses than couples who do not feel as supported. Similar identities, then, have the effect of creating a "sense of closeness," which further contributes to marital satisfaction (Cook and Jones 2002).

Perhaps more-satisfied people consciously and unconsciously manufacture the appearance of homogamy. They don't want to look like or feel like losers. Beyond that, they identify with their spouse, search for and develop similarities, and even exaggerate similarities, all because this strengthens the marital bond and increases marital satisfaction. If the marriage is indeed satisfying, the longer the spouses live together and the more interactions they have, the more similar they will become.

People who are capable of happiness or satisfaction do not spend a lot of time comparing what they have with what they don't have. Those who are capable of settling for a nearby mate with whom they have much in common will be much happier than people who continue to shop for the "perfect mate," an almost unattainable goal. Extensive research backs this up, since those who go into marriage with the highest expectations are most often the ones who feel disappointment with married life. The result: a world split into happy homogamous couples, unhappy "still looking" singles, and late-marrying, never-satisfied heterogamous couples.

Consider a more sociological explanation. Durkheim, in his book *Suicide*, makes a case for what he calls *anomie*, or normlessness, and *egoism*, or lack of integration into social groups. He argues, for example, that single and divorced people (especially men) commit suicide far more often than married people (especially men) because marriage roots people and sets limits to their desires and aspirations. Unlimited desires are dangerous, socially and psychologically—hence, the urge to suicide. If homogamous marriages are easier to achieve and maintain (i.e., lower maintenance relationships) than heterogamous marriages, then they will more readily bring people satisfaction.

Regardless of whether or not you find a suitable match, other factors determine whether your marriage will last. Despite popular belief, divorce in the United States is on the decline. This increase in marital stability has been attributed to increased female education and increasing age at first marriage. The latter suggests that with age couples make more mature decisions about their marital commitment. Consequently, it could be argued that cohabitation promotes marital stability by delaying age at marriage (Heaton 2002).

SUMMING UP

All marriages are homogamous to some degree and heterogamous to some degree. For example, most marriages are between people of different sexes, and men and women tend to be different in some important respects. Therefore, we are referring to differences of degree—differences between more- and less-homogamous marriages.

Additionally, we have really only looked at socially homogamous marriages in this section. Less is known about psychologically homogamous marriages. Possibly the best marriages are homogamous in some important social respects (e.g., similarities in age and education between the spouses) but heterogamous in some important psychological respects (e.g., spousal differences in emotional volatility or expressiveness).

Finally, remember that this section is not aimed at sending people out to shop for people who are clones of themselves, any more than it is aimed at sending people out to shop for mates who are vastly different. In general, we oppose the notion of there being a single Mr. or Ms. Right, and the idea that shopping is a possible, rational, or conscious mating strategy for the majority of people. Our point is not so much that you shouldn't mate by shopping; it is that most people can't mate by shopping, and extensive shopping does not produce better outcomes. Neither are better outcomes apparently produced by settling quickly for a nearby mate and then spending your lifetime struggling to live with that choice. Is lifelong marriage to a single partner a natural thing? Isn't it more natural for people to do otherwise—to be polygamous, or serially monogamous (with one partner after another)? And even if monogamy *is* natural, is it good for people's states of mind? Isn't lifelong marriage too boring? How else can we account for the high rates of infidelity and divorce? Don't they show that people really are not meant to spend the rest of their days with only one person? These are not simple questions but you should try to answer them (if you want to lead a happy life).

It is not at all clear that some marriages work better than others because some people have chosen more suitable mates than others. Ultimately, what makes marriage work is what happens after the wedding, not before it; that is, successful participants *work at* marriage. In particular, working on marital communication is enormously important.

The research shows that marital satisfaction is lower for couples with frequent disagreements and infrequent shows of affection, and this is not surprising. Typically, people who are happily married kiss frequently and fight relatively little—and anyone would rather kiss than fight.

Happily married couples look on themselves as best friends and are very accepting of each other; they work harder on their marriage than other couples. They also confide in each other very often, a habit whose frequency has a positive effect on marital satisfaction. Satisfied spouses understand each other's desires for change, more often than not agree with one another, and believe that they are better understood by their spouse than by anyone else.

The *quality* of communication matters as much as the quantity. Happy marriages are marked by an ability to de-escalate arguments and dispel bad feelings, not simply communicate good feelings. Frequent low-intensity interactions, such as sharing the events of the day, are the key to good marital communication. Happily married couples usually communicate in a friendly, open, relaxed, and attentive way; unhappily married couples communicate in less varied and satisfying ways. Some research suggests that couples increase their marital satisfaction by spending leisure time together. However, shared leisure activity increases marital satisfaction only if the couple communicates satisfactorily in the course of that activity. High stress couples are rarely capable of this.

Spouses who do not like or love each other do not communicate adequately and will not experience what contemporary Western culture defines as a happy marriage. No amount of work on their communication will change the fact that they do not like each other. At the same time, spouses who like each other should be able to develop good communication patterns, if they take the trouble to think about it and do it. Good interaction and communication patterns are what make a marriage work, no matter who you've married. So put away your shopping list and roll up your sleeves.

REVIEW EXERCISES

For Discussion and Debate

1. Do you find the very idea of mating as a "shopping problem" offensive? Why or why not?
2. Do people get jobs by shopping? Is "job search" a typical or useful way of thinking about how most people end up in jobs? What are alternative explanations?
3. Do you find the idea that mating is a "potluck" process offensive? Why or why not?
4. What kinds of differences between mates are likely to make for a happier marriage? Why?

Writing Exercises

Write a brief (500-word) essay on one of the following topics:

1. "When I meet Mr. or Ms. Right, I'll know it right away."
2. "Marriages between similar people are bound to be boring."
3. "I'll never meet someone who's right for me. It's mathematically impossible."
4. "High divorce rates in our society are a direct result of our mating ideology."

Research Activities

1. Interview six males and six females in your college to find out what qualities they are looking for in a mate. How do males and females differ in this regard? How much similarity in desires do you find within each gender group?
2. Make your own list of the qualities you are looking for in a mate. Then collect some data—either published or obtained through interviews—that allow you to calculate how many eligible people with these qualities probably live in your community.
3. Interview six married or cohabiting couples—three who seem to be happy in their relationship and three who seem to be unhappy. By observing them interact during the interview, and by what they say about their relationship, what seems to differentiate one group from the other?
4. If you are in a love relationship, do an experiment. For one week, change your behavior (i.e., improve your communication and interaction style) and see what effect it has on the quality of your relationship. (If you are not in a love relationship, try this experiment on a close friend.)

SELECTED REFERENCES

Amato, Paul R. and Denise Previti. 2003. "Why Stay Married? Rewards, Barriers, and Marital Stability." *Journal of Marriage and Family* 65, 3 (Aug.): 561–573.

Batabyal, Amitrajeet A. 2001. "On the Likelihood of Finding the Right Partner in an Arranged Marriage." *Journal of Socio-Economics* 33:273–280.

Bratter, Jenifer and R. Kelly Raley. "Not Even if You Were the Last Person on Earth! How Marital Search Constraints Affect the Likelihood of Marriage." *Journal of Family Issues* 25, 2 (March): 167–181.

Buss, David M. 2003. *The Evolution of Desire: Strategies of Human Mating.* rev. ed. New York: Basic Books.

Buss, David M., Todd K. Shackelford, Lee A. Kirkpatrick and Randy J. Larsen. 2001. "A Half Century of Mate Preferences: The Cultural Evolution of Values." *Journal of Marriage and Family* 63, 2 (May): 491–503.

Caspi, Avshalom and Ellen S. Herbener. 1990. "Continuity and Change: Assortative Marriage and the Consistency of Personality in Adulthood." *Journal of Personality and Social Psychology* 58, 2 (Feb.): 250–258.

Cook, Jerry and Randall M. Jones. 2002. "Congruency of Identity Style in Married Couples." *Journal of Family Issues* 23, 8:912–926.

Crohan, Susan E. 1992. "Marital Happiness and Spousal Consensus on Beliefs about Marital Conflict: A Longitudinal Investigation." *Journal of Social and Personal Relationships* 9, 1 (Feb.): 89–102.

Deal, James E., Charles F. Halverson, Jr. and Karen Smith Wampler. 1999. "Parental Similarity on Child-Rearing Orientations: Effects of Stereotype Similarity." *Journal of Social and Personal Relationships* 16, 1:87–102.

Deal, James E., Karen S. Wampler and Charles F. Halverson. 1992. "The Importance of Similarity in the Marital Relationship." *Family Process* 31, 4 (Dec.): 369–382.

Dobson, Coretta D. and Sharon K. Houseknecht. 1998. "Black and White Differences in the Effect of Women's Educational Attainment on Age of First Marriage." *Journal of Family Issues* 19, 2 (Mar.): 204–223.

Felmlee, Diane H. 2001. "From Appealing to Appalling: Disenchantment with a Romantic Partner." *Sociological Perspectives* 44, 3:263–280.

Glenn, Norval. 1982. "Interreligious Marriages in the United States: Patterns and Recent Trends." *Journal of Marriage and the Family* 44, 3 (Aug.): 555–566.

Groot, Wim and Henriette M. Van Den Brink. 2002. "Age and Education Differences in Marriages and Their Effects on Life Satisfaction." *Journal of Happiness Studies* 3:153–165.

Haller, Max. 1981. "Marriage, Women, and Social Stratification: A Theoretical Critique." *American Journal of Sociology* 86, 4 (Jan.): 766–795.

Heaton, Tim B. 2002. "Factors Contributing to Increasing Marital Stability in the United States." *Journal of Family Issues* 23, 3 (Apr.): 392–409.

Heaton, Tim B. and Cardell K. Jacobson. 2000. "Intergroup Marriage: An Examination of Opportunity Structures." *Sociological Inquiry* 70, 1 (Winter): 30–41.

Heaton, Tim B. and Edith L. Pratt. 1990. "The Effects of Religious Homogamy on Marital Satisfaction and Stability." *Journal of Family Issues*, 11, 2 (June): 191–207.

Kalmijn, Matthijs. 1991. "Shifting Boundaries: Trends in Religious and Education Homogamy." *American Sociological Review* 56, 6 (Dec.): 786–800.

Kalmijn, Matthijs. 1998. "Intermarriage and Homogamy: Causes, Patterns, Trends." *Annual Review of Sociology* 24:395–421.

Krueger, Robert F. and Avshalom Caspi. 1993. "Personality, Arousal, and Pleasure: A Test of Competing Models of Interpersonal Attraction." *Personality and Individual Differences* 14, 1 (Jan.): 105–111.

Liao, Tim Futing and Gillian Stevens. 1994. "Spouses, Homogamy, and Social Networks." *Social Forces* 73, 2 (Dec.): 693–707.

Lichter, Daniel T. and Zhenchao Qian. 2001. "Measuring Marital Assimilation: Intermarriage among Natives and Immigrants." *Social Science Research* 30, 2:289–312.

Lykken, David T. and Auke Tellegen. 1993. "Is Human Mating Adventitious or the Result of Lawful Choice? A Twin Study of Mate Selection." *Journal of Personality and Social Psychology* 65, 1 (July): 56–68.

Mancie-Taylor, C. G. and S. G. Vandenberg. 1988. "Assortative Mating for IQ and Personality due to Propinquity and Personal Preference." *Behavioral Genetics* 18, 3:339–345.

Mare, Robert D. 1991. "Five Decades of Educational Assortative Mating." *American Sociological Review* 56, 1 (Feb.): 15–32.

McPherson, J. Miller and Lynn Smith-Lovin. 1987. "Homophily in Voluntary Organizations: Status Distance and the Composition of Face-to-Face Groups." *American Sociological Review* 52, 3 (June): 370–379.

Pagnini, Deanna L. and S. Philip Morgan. 1990. "Intermarriage and Social Distance among U.S. Immigrants at the Turn of the Century." *American Journal of Sociology* 96, 2 (Sept.): 405–432.

Qian, Zhenchao and Samuel H. Preston. 1993. "Changes in American Marriage, 1972 to 1987: Availability and Forces of Attraction by Age and Education." *American Sociological Review* 58, 4 (Aug.): 482–495.

Rytina, Stephen, Peter M. Blau, Terry Blum and Joseph Schwartz. 1988. "Inequality and Intermarriage: A Paradox of Motive and Constraint." *Social Forces* 66, 3 (Mar.): 645–675.

South, Scott J. and Katherine Trent. 2003. "Spousal Alternatives and Marital Relations." *Journal of Family Issues* 24, 6 (Sept.): 787–810.

Sprecher, Susan and Pamela C. Regan. 2002. "Liking Some Things (in Some People) More Than Others: Partner Preferences in Romantic Relationships and Friendships." *Journal of Social and Personal Relationships* 19, 4:463–481.

VanLaningham, Jody, David R. Johnson and Paul Amato. 2001. "Marital Happiness, Marital Duration, and the U-Shaped Curve: Evidence from a Five-Wave Panel Study." *Social Forces* 78, 4 (June): 1313–1341.

Weisfeld, G. E., R. G. H. Russell, C. C. Weisfeld and P. A. Wells. 1992. "Correlates of Satisfaction in British Marriages." *Ethology and Sociobiology* 13, 2 (Mar.): 125–145.

White, Lynn K. 1983. "Determinants of Spousal Interaction: Marital Structure or Marital Happiness." *Journal of Marriage and the Family* 45, 3 (Aug.): 511–519.

Whyte, Martin King. 1992. "Choosing Mates—the American Way." *Society* 29, 3 (197) (Mar.–Apr.): 71–77.

Whyte, Martin King, ed. 2000. *Marriage in America: A Communitarian Perspective*. Lanham, MD: Rowman & Littlefield Publishers.

CHAPTER 10

WORK AND THE ECONOMY

We all know something about work, whether from first-hand experience or the accounts others provide to us. Young people work at going to school, then most move on to work at a job or career. Some people work in the home, keeping house or caring for children; normally, they get no pay for doing this. Others work at home and earn an income by selling goods or services outside the home. Most of us work in large organizations—in factories or offices—to earn a living. Working together in large numbers, we create goods and services, earn a wage for ourselves, and produce a profit for the company.

The daily work routine is so common that people who break the pattern seem abnormal. No wonder so many unemployed and retired people feel like outsiders to the "real" business of society. For the same reason, many people have trouble relaxing at night, on the weekend or holidays. For some, stress and sleep disorders have become a constant problem. For many full-time housewives, the problem is boredom and a sense of worthlessness; they look to alcohol or antidepressants for solace. In short, as work has become more and more central to our society, it has also become a main source of stress in our lives.

In this chapter we look at three issues related to work and the economy. First, we examine the role of education in a postindustrial economy and ask whether higher education is still a good investment. Second, we ask what ever happened to the surplus leisure we were all expected to experience. Third, we consider whether the process of de-industrialization is resulting in better jobs for everyone or a loss of the good jobs to overseas workers.

10.1   Is College a Waste of Time?

The issue: Given the problems of finding a job, many young people are coming to doubt the value of a higher education. Would they be better off just getting into the job market right after high school? Or is higher education still worthwhile?

Since you are reading this book, you must be a college student. That means you have already thought about the question, Is higher education a good investment? What's more, you have answered the question with a "Yes." So it may seem pointless to raise this question.

On the other hand, many people have started to doubt the value of a higher education. Some students wonder whether the sacrifices they make for an education are really worth it, especially when they hear about the numbers of unemployed and underemployed graduates. Taxpayers also seem to have doubts about the value of higher education, as it costs more and more. They are much less willing to invest large amounts of public money in schools than they were a generation ago. And employers are often heard to complain about the quality of graduates on the job.

So it's time for another look at this question. Is higher education still a good investment, compared with other ways you could spend your time (e.g., gaining on-the-job experience)? To answer it, we'll do more than rely on personal experience and mass media reports. As in the rest of the book, we'll look at sociological evidence.

As with every topic we discuss, there are arguments on both sides of the issue. We begin by considering the view that, today, higher education is a poor investment of time and effort.

HIGHER EDUCATION IS A POOR INVESTMENT

In 1967, people graduated from college to enter a booming job market. They were the first wave of the so-called baby boom generation or even "preboomers," and because there were so few of them, they didn't need outstanding talent or effort to succeed: Employers were waiting to snap them up. Most industries and professions were growing and they needed highly educated employees. Most graduates quickly got jobs at good starting salaries in the field they had trained for. Their investment in higher education quickly paid large dividends. People who had borrowed money to finance an education were able to pay off their loans. Soon, many were able to buy a home, raise a family, and enjoy the American middle-class way of life.

Today the picture is different. Graduates enter a slow-growing job market, in which organizations have "flattened" to eliminate managerial staff (we discuss flattening later) and many workers are involuntarily self-employed. Few industries or professions are growing, so few need lots of highly educated employees. While there has not been a significant increase in the number of jobs requiring an education, there has been an increase in the number of people getting an education. This means that competition is fierce for jobs and many who do get an education end up in jobs that do not require one. People take longer to find jobs in the field they trained for, and starting salaries are often disappointing. People who borrowed money to finance an education will have trouble paying off their loans. It will be longer until they can buy a home, raise a family, and enjoy the American middle-class way of life.

These two snapshots, taken thirty years apart, describe different worlds of experience with education.

The experiences of American parents and their children—a mere difference of one generation—are worlds apart: a real generation gap! How difficult it is for young people, under these circumstances, to understand the enthusiasm of their parents for higher education. How difficult it is for parents to understand their children's skepticism and doubt.

There are at least four reasons to think that today, higher education is a poorer investment than it used to be or than people believed. One is the cost of higher education; another, the declining financial return on these costs; a third, the low return in job satisfaction; and finally, a low return in the form of upward social mobility.

Costs   Since 1967 the costs of education have risen, with higher tuition fees at most institutions. Yet student loans have not, typically, become more generous or accessible. And, relative to wages, living costs have risen. So many recent graduates have gone into debt—even poverty—to complete their schooling. The cost of education has been high and constantly rising before their eyes.

Financial Returns   In purely financial terms, today's college education returns a lower (percentage) profit on the money invested than it did a generation ago. With more competition for fewer jobs, today's new graduate can expect more unemployment, more (unwanted) part-time work, a lower starting salary and lower lifetime income than graduates in 1967. The graduate in 1997 has no guarantee of work, income, or job security; though never guaranteed, these were all more certain in 1967. Furthermore, it is evident that many students may be wasting their money with a university education. Though enrollment in universities and four-year colleges has increased, the dropout rate has also increased. Of those who enroll, more than half will not complete a degree. It would be to these people's advantage to get a job instead of accumulating debt over an education.

Job Satisfaction Returns   Graduates today are more likely than graduates thirty years ago to have to take work for which they were not trained, or work that makes little use of the graduate's skills, aptitudes, and knowledge, or even work that could be done by a high school dropout. Since employment is, for many people, as much about doing something meaningful as it is about collecting a paycheck, being forced out of economic necessity to perform a role that one neither enjoys nor values can be a demoralizing and stressful experience.

Some people call this "underemployment," since the economy underemploys the graduate's talents. Sociologist Ivar Berg, in his well-titled book *Education and Jobs: The Great Training Robbery,* concludes that many jobs that employ college graduates have little need for such highly educated personnel. Also, this points to a problem with the system: Why is it that policy assumes that everyone wants and should get an education, when the majority of jobs do not require one?

Why, then, are graduates hired? Because bosses value the "credential": College degrees tell them something about the stability and middle-class aspirations of prospective employees, and their ability to learn. Also, large numbers of college graduates give the organization an air of prosperity and respectability. This has nothing to do with the content of the education or the job, however.

Many graduates hired for these reasons feel frustrated. Their morale and productivity suffer as a result. The problem is partly due to inflated expectations and inflamed desires. To see how this works, consider two typical cases—an engineering graduate and a sociology graduate.

The engineering graduate has spent four years solving hard mathematical problems. She has honed her computer skills so that she can write complicated programs in several current languages. She has done great work in graphic representation, built complex (imaginary) bridges or electrical circuits, and simulated complex chemical reactions. She loves engineering.

Upon graduation, she is hired to analyze the flow of inventory at Wal-Mart; this uses (maybe) 1 percent of her knowledge.

The sociology graduate has spent four years reading imaginative, critical analyses of societies past and present, including, five or six times over, the book you are reading right now. Among other things, he knows how to study a small group or a large organization and how to analyze survey data or evaluate historical evidence. He knows the major schools of social thought, can argue both sides of a debate on any social topic, and writes clearly and forcefully. He loves sociology.

But after graduation, he will need "job training" at a graduate school, teacher's college, law school, social work or business school, or he may be hired to sell educational software for a major manufacturer; this uses (maybe) 1 percent of his knowledge.

For both the engineering graduate and the sociology graduate, educational returns (in the form of job satisfaction) are low. Higher education creates expectations and desires that are beyond what most jobs can satisfy. Being a student is often a lot more fun and a lot more challenging than many jobs.

HIGHER EDUCATION IS A GOOD INVESTMENT

You can think about the payoffs of a higher education in at least two ways: in terms of the benefits to you and the benefits to society.

Benefits to Society   Where society is concerned, the benefits of a higher education are clear: More education improves society.

First, the more education people get, the more the civic culture improves. More educated people are better informed and more politically active. Thus, the spread of education—especially higher education—strengthens democracy.

Second, education brings other social changes. For example, highly educated people are more open to changes in family life. They marry later, plan their families more carefully, bear fewer children, raise children more thoughtfully, and live longer and healthier lives. Highly educated men also assume equal status with their wives and children. This makes for more marital satisfaction and better adjusted children. Highly educated women demand, and take, higher status.

Third, some important positions in society—jobs carrying much responsibility and reward—are actually allocated by educational attainment. Greater access to higher education weakens the stratification system by giving poor young people more opportunity. And this means that to some degree talented, hard-working, and well-informed people will gain social positions of the greatest responsibility.

Benefits to You   What about your own well-being? Here, too, the evidence is clear: You will benefit from a higher education.

First, higher education can be very satisfying. School's a challenge—a workout for your brain—and when you're in good mental shape, meeting the challenge feels pretty good. Like physical exercise, mental exercise makes you stronger. When you finish a tough assignment, you know you've accomplished something. As one student said, "School is empowering."

Second, higher education gives you the credentials—sometimes even the contacts—you need to get a job and get ahead. If you were born rich, you don't need this; stop reading and go on to the next chapter. But if you weren't born rich, college education is the best investment you can make. Compared to high school graduates—let alone high school dropouts—college graduates have less unemployment, less underemployment, a higher income, more job security, and a better choice of jobs.

Third, higher education is an opportunity like no other for thought and self-discovery. Admittedly, this benefit often becomes lost amid the hectic juggling of midterms, essay deadlines, seminars, and tutorials that characterizes much of undergraduate life. Yet, for many students, college is also their initial foray into the world as independent persons, free for the first time from parental stricture and support, and hence free to explore for themselves their place in society. It is often during these formative years that one begins to ask—and even to answer—the profound questions: Who am I? What is my purpose? What kind of life do I want to lead? To be sure, the college experience can strengthen the mind and reinforce a resume, but for those willing to seize it, college can also be an opportunity to deepen one's wisdom—and this must surely be, in the final analysis, the most valuable investment of all.

In the postindustrial (or information) society, more jobs demand a college education. There are fewer jobs to be had in manufacturing and few new jobs for people with less than a college degree. This trend will not change direction. In the future, more and more jobs—in the professions, management, service, and sales—will require a college degree or two. Current statistics already show that the number of new jobs going to college graduates has been increasing while the number of new jobs going to less-educated people has been decreasing.

WHAT KIND OF EDUCATION DO YOU NEED?

It often seems that the evolving job market wants new employees to have specialized skills. However, sociologist Daniel Bell, in *The Coming of Post-Industrial Society,* argues otherwise. He claims that jobs of the future will require a combination of general and job-specific skills. Job-specific skills will be gained on the job, in training programs provided by the employer, or in short college courses. General skills, however, will still be available only through a lengthy course of college studies.

Bell believes that in the postindustrial society, knowledge and theory—not capital and labor—are the new sources of value and productivity. Everyone needs to become a good learner to survive in the new world of work, and general skills make learning job-specific skills easier.

What general skills do students gain at college, and how do they facilitate the learning of both theories and job-specific skills? These general skills include literacy, cultural literacy, and learning (or cognitive) skills. Two other products of higher education—cultural capital and interpersonal skills—also fit into this category of general skills.

Literacy   *Literacy* no longer just means the ability to puzzle out a page of text. At the least, it means an ability to master large amounts of written material quickly and accurately. It also means "reading between the lines"—understanding what the writer has left unsaid and why. This also means understanding the writer's ideological bias, and it always means understanding the flow of an argument.

Cultural Literacy   Cultural literacy is a different thing. A term invented by historian E. D. Hirsch, *cultural literacy* means familiarity with a large number of common facts and references. Hirsch shows that this fact-vocabulary changes slowly, and people of all classes and ancestral backgrounds use it. To be unfamiliar with these common facts and references—to be culturally illiterate—means trouble communicating with a large fraction of the population. Colleges all teach cultural literacy. Here's a *very* tiny and quick informal test of your cultural literacy: Who are Lorne Tepperman and Jenny Blain: (a) U.S. figure-skating pairs champions, 1995; (b) O. J. Simpson's accountants; or (c) the authors of this book?

Learning (or Cognitive) Skills   Primary and secondary education are mainly concerned with teaching us facts and how to use those facts. A college education, by contrast, teaches us analysis (the ability to break down arguments), synthesis (the ability to make arguments), and evaluation (the ability to judge the quality of competing arguments). As you can see, we practice all of those skills in this book.

Analysis, synthesis, and evaluation are part of every good essay you write—whether in history, English, science, sociology, or otherwise. The grade you get on an essay depends on how well you demonstrate these skills, far more than on the facts you gather or number of books you cite.

Like good reading, good writing is an essential tool in all learning and communication. Learning to write well helps you think well (and vice versa). Valuable as a medium for communicating with others, good writing is also valuable as a way to communicate with yourself. The process of writing tells you what you think and helps you figure out why.

Cultural Capital   French sociologist Pierre Bourdieu coined the term *cultural capital*. It refers to knowledge that is rarer than the facts and references possessed by the culturally literate. People who have lots of cultural capital think of themselves as *cultured* (or refined) and they value contacts with other people who are cultured. Bourdieu shows that, in France, elites spend a lot of time together showing off their cultural capital. When finished, they

trust each other and can transact their business quickly and smoothly.

Colleges provide cultural capital, though not always intentionally. By watching and talking to others, students learn how to dress, talk, eat, walk, joke, date (and so on) in more "worldly" ways. They can banter about Kierkegaard, or at least about Woody Allen bantering about Kierkegaard. And they can drop Bjork's lyrics into a conversation at McDonald's. But here is an interesting paradox. Knowledge (like this) with no job value—usually acquired for its own sake—often becomes cultural capital. Eventually, it is useful for getting ahead. But knowledge acquired for its immediate usefulness—for example a job-related skill—is rarely cultural capital. In the long run, it is less useful for getting ahead.

Interpersonal Skills   One last benefit of a higher education—interpersonal skills—overlaps with cultural capital.

Understanding people and communicating well (i.e., tactfully, empathetically) is important in all professional, managerial, sales, and service jobs. Since many jobs in the information economy fall into these categories, in the future interpersonal skills will be even more important in getting jobs, keeping them, and doing well. College teaches us to communicate well in various ways. Generally, college programs let us make painless mistakes while learning interpersonal and communication skills. If we made them on the job, the same mistakes might hinder our future.

SUMMING UP

Is college a waste of your time? No way; but you're not surprised to hear us say that, are you? Since the authors of this book are professional educators, it cannot surprise you that we think higher education is a good investment.

We admit that the obvious returns to this investment—cash payoffs immediately after graduation—are lower than they once were. In fact, they are lower than we think they ought to be and lower than Daniel Bell thinks they will be in the future.

We will be able to judge better the quality of Daniel Bell's theory when the postindustrial future arrives and the evidence is in.

For the time being, arguments in favor of a higher education seem more compelling than the arguments against. If you are one of many people born without a "silver spoon in your mouth" (a term that displays a bit of ancient cultural literacy), higher education is the best investment you can make.

But don't think you can simply put your money into this particular account and wait for the interest to accumulate. An investment in higher education has to be active: an ongoing series of choices, efforts, and reformulations. Given who you are and what you hope to accomplish, some educational strategies—some schools, some programs, some courses—are better than others. The best education for you may not be the best education for someone else.

And remember that learning for its own sake often brings the biggest payoffs. (If you've already forgotten why, reread the part on cultural capital.)

REVIEW EXERCISES

For Discussion and Debate

1. "Some kinds of education are more of a waste of time than others."
2. "Financial returns to education are far less important than people make them out to be."
3. "The more educated a society becomes, the better it becomes."
4. "Cultural capital is not something you can learn at school."

Writing Exercises

Write a brief (500-word) essay on one of the following topics:

1. "The interpersonal skills I have gained from going to school."
2. "What ought to be included in a measure of *cultural literacy*."
3. "Anyone with the right credentials can get ahead, whether he or she knows anything or not."
4. "People get far more education than they really need these days."

Research Activities

1. Examine data on the average educational achievements of people in a particular occupation. How do you account for the education "required" for this job?
2. Read the want-ads in your local newspaper, to determine what education is required for the most attractive jobs. Why is educational requirement often unstated?
3. Interview six recent graduates of your college to find out what job(s) they got after graduation, and whether they consider their education a waste of time.
4. Find evidence from one hundred years ago that professional job-holders (e.g., doctors, lawyers, engineers) were worse at their job than people holding the same job today.

SELECTED REFERENCES

Åberg, Rune. 2003. "Unemployment Persistency, Over-Education and the Employment Chances of the Less Educated." *European Sociological Review* 19, 2:199–216.

Berg, Ivar E. 1971. *Education and Jobs: The Great Training Robbery.* Boston, MA: Beacon Press.

Bidwell, Charles E. 1989. "The Meaning of Educational Attainment." *Research in Sociology of Education and Socialization* 8:117–138.

Blau, Peter et al. 1992. "The American Occupation Structure: Reflections after Twenty-Five Years." *Contemporary Sociology* 21, 5 (Sept.): 596–668.

Collins, Randall. 1979. *The Credential Society: An Historical Sociology of Education and Stratification.* New York: Academic Press.

Finkelstein, Marvin S. 1994. "Combining the Liberal and Useful Arts: Sociological Skills in the Global Economy." *American Sociologist* 25 (Fall): 20–36.

Granfield, Robert and Thomas Koenig. 1992. "Learning Collective Eminence: Harvard Law School and the Social Production of Elite Lawyers." *Sociological Quarterly* 33, 4 (Winter): 503–520.

Halaby, Charles. 1994. "Overeducation and Skill Mismatch." *Sociology of Education* 67, 1 (Jan.): 47–59.

Halsey, A. H. 1990. "Educational Systems and the Economy." *Current Sociology* 38, 2–3 (Autumn–Winter): 79–101.

Halsey, A.H. 1997. *Education: Culture, Economy, and Society.* Oxford: Oxford University Press.

Hamilton, Stephen F. and Jane Levine Powers. 1990. "Failed Expectations: Working-Class Girls' Transition from School to Work." *Youth and Society* 22, 2 (Dec.): 241–262.

Hunter, Alfred A. and Jean McKenzie Leiper. 1993. "On Formal Education: Skills and Earnings: The Role of Educational Certificates in Earnings Determination." *Canadian Journal of Sociology* 18, 1 (Winter): 21–42.

Kao, Grace and Jennifer S. Thompson. 2003. "Racial and Ethnic Stratification in Educational Achievement and Attainment." *Annual Review of Sociology* 29:417–442.

Kerkhoff, Alan C. 1990. "Educational Pathways to Early Career Mobility in Great Britain." *Research in Social Stratification and Mobility* 9:131–157.

Kerkhoff, Alan C. and Lorraine Bell. 1998. "Hidden Capital: Vocational Credentials and Attainment in the United States." *Sociology of Education* 71, 2:152–174.

Korupp, Sylvia E., Harry B. G. Ganzeboom and Tanja Van der Lippe. 2002. "Do Mothers Matter? A Comparison of Models of the Influence of Mothers' and Fathers' Educational and Occupational Status on Children's Educational Attainment." *Quality and Quantity* 36, 1:17–42.

Lewis, Darrell R., James C. Hearn and Eric E. Zilbert. 1993. "Efficiency and Equity Effects of Vocationally Focused Postsecondary Education." *Sociology of Education* 66, 3 (July): 188–205.

Mastracci, Sharon H. 2003. "Employment and Training Alternatives for Non-College Women: Do Redistributive Policies Really Redistribute?" *The Policy Studies Journal* 31, 4:585–601.

Monk-Turner, Elizabeth. 1990. "The Occupational Achievements of Community and Four-Year College Entrants." *American Sociological Review* 55, 5 (Oct.): 719–725.

Monk-Turner, Elizabeth. 1998. *Community College Education and Its Impact on Socioeconomic Status Attainment.* Lewiston, NY: Edwin Mellen Press.

Rosenbaum, James E. 2001. *Beyond College for All: Career Paths for the Forgotten Half.* New York: Russell Sage Foundation.

Rosenbaum, James E., Stefanie DeLuca, Shazia R. Miller and Kevin Roy. 1999. "Pathways into Work: Short- and Long-Term Effects of Personal and Institutional Ties." *Sociology of Education* 72, 3 (July): 179–196.

Rosenbaum, James E., Takehiko Kariya, Rick Settersten and Tony Maier. 1990. "Market and Network Theories of the Transition from High School to Work: Their Application to Industrialized Societies." *Annual Review of Sociology* 16:263–299.

Sakamoto, Arthur and Meichu D. Chen. 1991. "Inequality and Attainment in a Dual Labor Market." *American Sociological Review* 56, 3 (June): 295–308.

Smith, Clifton L. and Jay W. Rojewski. 1993. "School-to-Work Transition: Alternatives for Educational Reform." *Youth and Society* 25, 2 (Dec.): 222–250.

Stern, David and Derek Briggs. 2001. "Does Paid Employment Help or Hinder Performance in Secondary School? Insights from U.S. High School Students." *Journal of Education and Work* 14, 3:355–372.

Stern, David, Martin McMillion, Charles Hopkins and James Stone. 1990. "Work Experience for Students in High School and College." *Youth and Society* 21, 3 (Mar.): 355–389.

Stone, James R. and Jeylan T. Mortimer. 1998. "The Effect of Adolescent Employment on Vocational Development: Public and Educational Policy Implications." *Journal of Vocational Behavior* 53, 2:184–214.

Treiman, Donald J. and Harry B. G. Ganzeboom. 1990. "Cross-National Comparative Status-Attainment Research." *Research in Stratification and Mobility* 9:105–127.

10.2   What Happened to Leisure?

The issue: Technology's great promise was that advances in human ingenuity would one day free people from the chains of daily labor, so they could pursue recreations and hobbies. That utopia has failed to materialize.

Not so long ago, politicians and social commentators were heralding the pending arrival of the Age of Leisure, an era in which manual labor would be performed by machines, the workweek would be reduced to a few hours, and people's biggest challenge would be finding pleasant hobbies to fill the free time in their day.

This idea about the soon-to-come leisure revolution is actually an old idea. Over two centuries ago, Benjamin Franklin, reflecting on the technological innovations that would power the Industrial Revolution, claimed that society would soon witness a drastic reduction of work hours to less than one per day. Yet two centuries later, work is, if anything, more important and more present in our lives than at any time in the past. Today the average American spends more time—an additional month per year, according to one estimate—in paid employment than he did thirty years ago, and he works longer hours than everyone else in the industrialized world. While Europeans embrace leisure and legislate holidays, in North America Americans are working ever longer hours per day, more days per year. They are also vacationing less and retiring later in life.

The choice everyone makes between work and leisure is a debate over the appropriate use of time. Since work time often translates into money, while leisure time does not, it is also a choice between more and less money. In a world that values and rewards productive labor, the time devoted to a constructive project is considered "well-spent." "Free time" (i.e., time not taken up by constructive or paid activity) is what we devote to recreation and leisure.

There is a lot to be said for dedicated hard work, and for earning money to pay one's bills and support one's family. But recent commentators, reflecting on our society's seeming obsession with work and productive activity, are beginning to ask whether we have gone too far. They point to a growing percentage of the workforce who now spend part of their weekends holed up in the office. Americans were working an average of 163 more hours per year in 1990 than in 1970. Such findings as these have created a sensation because they show a reversal in the century-long decline in the length of work schedules.

A majority of North Americans feel overworked and time-crunched. Two thirds of Americans desire a shorter paid work schedule. And this is not restricted to adults: Even children's after-school schedules are increasingly frenetic, leaving no time for running around the playground with friends. Is our collective work-life balance in disarray? Some people say it isn't.

IN PRAISE OF WORK

The Protestant Ethic   Americans have an intimate relationship with work. To change their preoccupation with work and achievement would be to change their culture entirely.

The United States was founded, in principle, on the meritocratic notion that a hard day's labor will be rewarded with a fair wage and social esteem. The American Dream was a direct extension of this tradition, promising countless generations of hopeful immigrants that with enough industry, discipline, and talent, anyone could succeed. But although Americans had always been noted by observers for their hard work and self-reliance, it was not until the eighteenth century that this work ethic became the foundation of the American character.

With industrialization, the principle was easier for multitudes to realize. To power the machinery of the emerging factory system of the Industrial Era, employers needed dependable employees willing to work hard under grueling conditions in exchange for relatively little pay. More than just a pool of willing labor, what was needed was an entirely new ideology of work, one that celebrated labor for its own sake.

U.S. Protestant churches, drawing on the teachings of sixteenth-century reformists Martin Luther and John Calvin, emphasized material success as a sign of one's good standing with God. This added a moral twist to mankind's relationship with labor. Toil and sacrifice were seen as natural expressions of one's love for God. As a result, people began throwing themselves into their work, believing that earthly prosperity was a step toward Paradise.

Over time, as society became increasingly industrialized and secularized, this work ethic would become separated from its Protestant roots and find a new home in the system of capitalism. Work became a social and moral, if not spiritual, duty. People came to view hard work as good in its own right, divorced from its spiritual origins.

The Benefits of Work   Today, work continues to be a central part of our lives. In addition to the obvious economic returns, work is an important source of social and psychological well-being. Employment increases self-esteem and self-efficacy—we feel competent when we are being productive—and allows people to be part of a successful group. Whether our work is in the retail service industry, the legal profession, or the cultural production field, it makes up a large part of our identity, giving us direction, purpose, and status.

Work provides people with intrinsic satisfaction in terms of the feeling of a "job well done," and extrinsic rewards such as money, prestige, respect, and social recognition.

A lucky few describe their work as a calling. Indeed, finding the ideal job that combines one's skills, interests, and values—such that one can commit countless hours to one's work—can be immensely rewarding. Psychologist Mihaly Csikszentmihalyi coined the term *flow* to describe the experience of being completely engaged in an activity, where time is suspended and one becomes oblivious to the external world. For people fortunate enough to find this balance, work no longer seems a soul-crushing burden or a financial necessity. Instead, it becomes a daily opportunity for personal growth.

Work for many also has important social benefits. Many friendships and love affairs begin in the workplace, forged by a shared experience of managerial incompetence and bureaucratic inefficiency. Even the rolodex of informal contacts built up during the course of one's daily work can prove to be an invaluable resource. This network is often the source of information about job openings, advancement opportunities, workplace gossip, and office politics.

Sociologist Arlie Hochschild reports that, given the choice, many women work longer hours because they would rather be at work than at home. The fact is, they would be laboring in either place. At "work" at least they are paid, treated with some respect, and able to take the occasional break. For many, "paid work" is more intellectually stimulating and rewarding. In many respects, staying at home is harder work—especially for mothers—than not doing so. Going to work, for them, is positively liberating, almost a vacation from home. Additionally, some Americans may choose to spend more time at work because family strain drives workers back to the office where supportive coworkers and career recognition are found. In other words, for many women work has become home and home has become work.

On the other hand, many people get pleasure from a variety of other things in life, not only work. Most of us rediscover this fact when we go on vacation, take a day off, work for "personal development," or otherwise slack off our duties.

IN PRAISE OF LEISURE

As we have said, many people spend a lot of time at work out of personal ambition, a desire to escape their home life, or economic necessity. But according to surveys, many others feel overworked and stressed for time. Physical inactivity outside the workplace is fairly widespread, perhaps fueling the obesity epidemic in America. National surveys have found that about one in four adults currently has a sedentary lifestyle with no leisure-time physical activity.

A report released by the UN International Labor Organization in 2001 revealed that Americans added almost a full week to their work schedules between 1990 and 2000. On average, Americans work about 6.4 weeks more per year than the British, and a staggering 3 months more per year than the Germans. Even the Japanese, long considered the world's most ardent workaholics, can no longer claim that title: In 1996, the United States surpassed Japan as the most work-intensive nation on the planet, and the gap has only grown with each passing year.

In 1991, Juliet Schor wrote a book entitled *The Overworked American* that sparked a wave of journalistic and scholarly attention. She claimed that the recent rise in work hours could be traced back to the new consumerism introduced during the 1920s, a booming interwar decade that, until the Great Depression began in 1929, saw an explosive growth in national productivity and consumer spending. This consumerist ideal was premised on the notion that material satisfaction would yield emotional fulfillment. Everyone seemed to buy into the idea that more consumer goods meant more fulfillment.

Schor's book built on the work of Swedish sociologist Staffen Linden, who introduced the term *consumption time* to describe free time devoted to spending on consumer products. Increasingly, people were willing to work more hours to have more money for spending on luxury goods. This was a change from traditional working practice.

When working hours first began to drop in the early twentieth century, most people were still too poor to afford the few luxuries available in society, so leisure time was spent primarily with family and friends. The choice then was either more time or more stuff, and, urged on by marketing and social pressures, people tended to choose more stuff. The leisure industry, created to tap into this new market, began offering to willing buyers equipment for expensive recreations like golf and skiing. Increasingly, it provided pricey electronics like radios, televisions, and later, computers and DVD players, cellular phones, and ipods, leading to what Linden called a shift from "time-intensive" to "goods-intensive" leisure.

The funds to finance these consumption habits came from paid employment, and people began working more in order to buy more. With the development of credit cards, people bought even more than they could immediately afford, forcing them to work harder than they had originally planned. Along with credit cards comes credit card debt, which leads to a vicious cycle of minimal credit payments, more purchases, and further debt. A great many Americans spend more than their paycheck on a regular basis, meaning that many are in deep, continuing debt to banks and credit card companies. Once the work-and-spend cycle developed its own momentum, it was difficult to know when or how to stop. And the vicious cycle faced by individual workers was matched by another dilemma faced by their employers.

With people working longer hours, productivity began to grow at a steady clip. As profits rolled in, executives were faced with the choice of raising incomes or reducing working hours. Offering more leisure time might improve worker morale, but it would cause profit rates to plateau. Increasing pay, on the other hand, would fuel the work-and-spend cycle, leading to a stronger commitment from the rank-and-file and the promise of even higher profit margins. The result: Employers provided more pay, but less free time.

Recently, this has started to change. In recent decades more and more companies have downsized, with the result of more work for employees but not necessarily more pay. Under conditions of downsizing, employee turnover tends to rise. Effects on the work force are nasty. Grudge holding, hostility, self-centeredness, blaming, and retribution seeking are common reactions among the survivors of downsizing. These negative reactions lead, in turn, to diminished organizational performance and lower profits.

The Great Escape Those who have been able to hold on to a job are working harder than ever to keep it. Once we consoled ourselves by claiming that we worked for the weekend. Weekends were off-limits to employers. Today, however, time studies reveal that our boundaries have changed. More and more workers, particularly those in the highest and lowest status occupations, are putting in the equivalent of a six-day work week. People who work from home offices also know the difficulties of trying to separate work time from personal time.

They are working longer hours than ever, because they no longer lose work time commuting to and from the office.

The growth of worktime has been accelerated by communications technology that makes it possible—therefore, necessary—for people to respond instantly and remain in touch all the time. Thanks to modern technology like e-mail, cell phones, pagers, and PDAs, and a growing tendency for employers to demand overtime rather than hire extra staff, many salaried white-collar workers are finding themselves obliged to work around-the-clock. You are never farther from your job than you are from your cell phone.

This increase in work time has affected everyone—especially people with the most education and the highest-paid occupations. A 2001 survey of chief financial officers in the United States found that three out of every four did at least five hours of work on the weekend, with 10 percent of those claiming that they did an astounding fifteen hours of work on their days "off."

This prevailing workaholic mentality is also reflected in the average annual vacation time offered by employers. The starting norm for a full-time job offered by most North American companies is a mere two weeks, compared to most Western European nations where four to six weeks of paid vacation time is guaranteed by law and two months is not unheard of for professionals and executives.

What's more, the two weeks off sometimes gets eaten up by the need to catch up with, or avoid, missed work. With 60 percent of workers reporting that they do not have enough time at work to finish "everything that needs to be done" and 88 percent reporting that they have to work "very hard," it is not surprising that many consider taking a full two weeks off, only to return to a mountain of backlog, too stressful to be worthwhile.

Finally, when North Americans do take those long-awaited vacations out-of-town, they are increasingly choosing activities that promise personal growth over frivolous fun and lazing about. A recent trend in the travel industry is "adventure tourism," where, for a fee covering flight, accommodations, meal, and administrative expenses, participants can choose from a long list of worldwide volunteer opportunities, ranging from helping to build a schoolhouse in a rural Peruvian village, to counting whales for marine biologists off the shores of British Columbia, to assisting archeologists in digging up ruins outside of Rome. Other adventurous, out of the way vacation spots may include the Galapagos, Antarctica, Siberia, or New Guinea.

For vacationers accustomed to a fast-paced work environment, where each minute of the day is scheduled and success is measured in terms of productivity and achievement, a week spent on a beach staring at the ocean waves might feel like a waste of time and money. Vacationers often schedule every minute of every day so they can feel they have gotten their money's worth out of their time away—like parents who spend "quality time" with their children by packing innumerable "experiences" into a few hours every weekend.

Such continued stress is hard on individuals and even harder on families. Sometimes occupational stress leads to a decline in family life, and even to divorce, alcohol abuse, or suicide. Children are hit hardest by this work-induced strain, both indirectly and directly.

Childhood Lost   The traditional notion of childhood conjures peaceful images of summers spent mucking around a pond, playing make-believe in a "castle" made of couch cushions, and lying in a field with a best friend, spotting lions and faces in the clouds. It is a carefree time for children to explore the world and themselves, conducted at a leisurely pace of their own choosing.

But in an adult-dominated, competitive, winner-takes-all world, children cannot afford this luxury. Career training is never too early. Expectant mothers pump Mozart into their uteruses, following reports that fetal exposure to classical music may increase intelligence in later life. Golf lessons begin as early as age two, and foreign language classes, age three. Children wander the halls of the Conservatory with miniature violin cases in hand, awaiting their weekly music lesson and the prospect of successful examinations that attest to their talent and industry.

Some children now carry cell phones to school, to coordinate their social lives. Many others struggle under crowded schedules that include soccer practice, hockey practice, ballet class, art camp, music camp, piano lessons, or math tutors, all on top of a growing homework schedule.

The results are not always healthy. Already, children as young as four are landing in doctors' offices and on psychiatrists' couches, with complaints of stress and overburden. Childhood eating disorders, depression, anxiety, and insomnia are all on the rise. Health experts point to the excessive weight of children's backpacks—loaded down with textbooks and gear for after-school activities—as a cause of more frequent spinal abnormalities. Even children's toys are increasingly geared toward intellectual stimulation. No longer can kids just play with toys; now there must an obvious "point" to the playing, or play time is wasted time.

What children are missing is what experts call *unstructured play.* Unlike *quality time,* unstructured play is not scheduled, orderly, or even explicitly productive, but according to many child development specialists, it remains a vital component of childhood. Play has no obvious place on a person's resume, and it doesn't necessarily guarantee admission to Princeton, but some people think it helps children develop.

Some children—especially, the high achievers—never learn to play. In the fall of 2001, Harry Lewis, dean of the undergraduate school at Harvard University, wrote an open letter entitled *Slow Down* to every incoming freshman, pleading for them to decelerate their lives. Rather than blitzing through their degrees living only for the next deadline or exam, Lewis encouraged students to relax and take some time for themselves. University, after all, is a place of maturation and self-discovery, processes that cannot be rushed. To achieve excellence in one's chosen area of study, Lewis suggested, it is best to ensure sufficient time in other areas of one's life for moments of leisure, solitude, and quiet thought. An elegant piece that proved extremely popular with both students and parents, Lewis's words are now sent out to every annual crop of Harvard freshmen.

SUMMING UP

The current debate over work and leisure is neither an attack on industry nor an argument in defense of slackers. One's career can be an opportunity to challenge oneself, make a contribution to society, and provide for one's family—all at the same time. However, there is little point in working to one's limit if doing so leads to the neglect of relationships, community participation, and personal growth.

More leisure time makes sense from many perspectives. The social and health benefits of slowing down are obvious, for example. Less time at work means more time for family, friends, and oneself. In America, overworked parents come home exhausted, too tired to cook, do chores, or spend time with the kids or each other; and their children, worn out from a jam-packed schedule of after-school activities, are too drowsy to pay attention in class the next morning. If the pace of work and school is the culprit, as it is for millions of North Americans, then the solution is to simplify one's schedule and take some time off.

Less obvious are the economic benefits of reduced work schedules. When productivity is measured as value added per hour, both (more leisurely) France and Belgium edge out the United States. Case studies of enlightened corporations show that a well-rested labor force is more creative and productive. A moderate pace of work reduces the margin of human error, increases camaraderie between workers and between staff and management, improves the level of professionalism toward clients, and fosters more creative and effective problem-solving. In light of these findings, many organizations have started to offer free yoga classes or massages, or construct on-site gyms and meditation rooms for their workers' use during work hours. But these efforts by a minority of corporations/companies are few and far between. They are certainly not the norm in the business world, where the bottom dollar is still the overriding concern.

Often, individual workers must choose to shift their priorities, to voluntarily step off the treadmill of working without end. A growing grassroots campaign of downshifters, voluntary simplicity followers, and Slow Movement proponents, with membership in the thousands spanning the globe, is calling for a rethinking of society's relationship with work and leisure. They call for a more balanced lifestyle that favors time over money, relationships over achievements, and quality over quantity. It remains to be seen whether they will succeed.

REVIEW EXERCISES

For Discussion and Debate

1. Can the concept of the "American Dream" still be applied to the social system of the United States today?
2. The imbalance between family commitment and work commitment can be held accountable for the decline of the family. Do you agree or disagree, and why?
3. What kind of data could show a relationship between overworking and suicide?
4. Is the American public's obsession with the rich and famous via the media a contributing factor to their desire to work more and make more money?

Writing Exercises

Write a brief (500-word) essay on one of the following topics:

1. "America's growing epidemic of obesity is heightened by the lack of healthy leisure activities enjoyed by adults and children today."
2. "Human resource practices should be designed to accommodate the needs of a diverse workforce, creating a work environment where all members can perform to the maximum of their potential."
3. "We are a society of overconsumers."
4. "The Capitalist system is ideal for America's economy."

Research Activities

1. Collect data from family and friends about their perception of work and leisure, asking questions such as the following: "Do you feel overworked?" "Do you enjoy any leisure time?"
2. Use published statistics to compare labor in the preindustrial era and the workforce today. What are the similarities and differences?
3. Devise a questionnaire about the kind of leisure people participate in and how often. Include children and adolescents in your participants. Ask 15 people from each category and tabulate your results.
4. Choose another democratic country in the world and research their work ethic. How does it compare to the United States?

SELECTED REFERENCES

Barak, Mor and Levin. 2002. "Outside of the Corporate Mainstream and Excluded from the Work Community: A Study of Diversity, Job Satisfaction and Well-Being." *Community, Work and Family* 5, 2:133–157.

Burke, Ronald, J. 2003. "Length of Shift, Work Outcomes and Psychological Well-Being of Nursing Staff." *International Journal of Public Administration* 26, 14:1637–1646.

Cameron, Bright and Caza. 2004. "Exploring the Relationship between Organizational Virtuousness and Performance." *American Behavioral Scientist* 47, 6:766–790.

Csikszentmihalyi, M. 1990. *Flow: The Psychology of Optimal Experience.* New York: HarperCollins.

De Botton, A. 2004. *Status Anxiety.* London: Penguin.

Granovetter, M. S. 1973. "The Strength of Weak Ties." *American Journal of Sociology* 78, 6:1360–1380.

Honoré, C. 2004. *In Praise of Slow: How a Worldwide Movement Is Challenging the Cult of Speed.* Toronto: Alfred A. Knopf Canada.

Hunnicutt, B. K. 1988. *Work Without End: Abandoning Shorter Hours for the Right to Work.* Philadelphia, PA: Temple University Press.

Jacobs, J. A. and K. Gerson. 2001. "Overworked Individuals or Overworked Families? Explaining Trends in Work, Leisure, and Family Time." *Work and Occupations* 28, 1:40–63.

Linden, S. B. 1970. *The Harried Leisure Class.* New York: Columbia University Press.

Maume and Bellas. 2001. "The Overworked American or the Time Bind?: Assessing Competing Explanations for Time Spent in Paid Labour. *American Behavioral Scientist* 44, 7:1137–1156.

Rybczynski, W. 1991. *Waiting for the Weekend.* New York: Penguin.

Schor, J. B. 1991. *The Overworked American: The Unexpected Decline of Leisure.* New York: Basic Books.

Stack, Steven. 2001. "Occupation and Suicide." *Social Science Quarterly* 82, 2:384–396.

Weber, M. 1946. *The Protestant Ethic and the Spirit of Capitalism.* London: George Allen and Unwin.

Wu and Porrell. 2000. "Job Characteristics and Leisure Physical Activity." *Journal of Aging and Health* 12, 4:538–559.

10.3   Did We Lose the Wrong Jobs?

The Issue: Starting in the late 1960s the process known as de-industrialization began moving manufacturing jobs from the United States to other nations. Are we sending the bad jobs away and keeping the good ones? Or vice versa?

If you're lucky enough to take a road trip across the northeastern part of the United States, you will notice some interesting facts about the country. First, it's large and lovely: packed with cities and towns, mountains, valleys, lakes, and seashore. Even a single state like Pennsylvania offers a vast variety of terrains. There are huge modern cities like Philadelphia and Pittsburgh, the rolling wooded Alleghenies, and tucked here and there, small cities and towns that used to be homes of industry: coal-mining towns, steel towns, and other factory towns.

What you notice then is that the wealth and opportunities found in Philadelphia and Pittsburgh—the high paying jobs, good schools, and excellent facilities—are missing in the smaller, old manufacturing towns. The unemployment rates are higher in those old towns. People in these so-called

rustbelt towns aren't as prosperous-looking, as optimistic, well-fed, or well-dressed. You see less bustle and energy. Many of the smartest young people leave as soon as they are able, for Pittsburgh, Philadelphia, and more often, for cities in the south and west. For the jobs have moved—south and west, and to other countries—and people are following the jobs.

This process of manufacturing job loss is called de-industrialization. In order to understand the pros and cons of de-industrialization, one must know the background. The United States emerged as the world's only large-scale manufacturing economy after World War I. Prior to the 1960s, American companies had few reasons to go abroad to find workers, since they were all making record profits. Going into the 1960s, this era of manufacturing began to decline. In the late 1960s and early 1970s profits began to dip below the 10 percent mark. This meant either that the skills of laborers needed upgrading or that low-skilled workers needed to be displaced to the periphery.

This, in turn, marked the beginning of transnational (or multinational) corporations (TNCs), which made capital truly mobile. American corporations invested their capital, as jobs, in other parts of the world. By relocating jobs, American companies were able to secure profits that sometimes reached 40–60 percent for the Fortune 500. To facilitate this process, international organizations like the United Nations helped to set up free trade zones throughout the world. These were the precursors to organizations like NAFTA, which has profoundly affected the American, Canadian, and Mexican job markets.

These effects on the American job market have become the subject of intense debates among policymakers and the American public. Though research on the topic of de-industrialization was limited at first, after protests like the one in Seattle more attention was paid to the subject.

The debate now is whether de-industrialization hurts or helps the average American. Supporters of de-industrialization will point out that the jobs being sent abroad are low-skill jobs, leaving Americans with the higher-skill jobs to do. They will also argue that de-industrializing ensures that the American economy remains dominant, since American consumers get the best price for the goods they make. On the other hand, people who say that de-industrialization has harmful effects will recall the time when manufacturing jobs were at their peak. Workers received an income that they could live on and unionized companies protected employees throughout their lifetimes. In addition, opponents of de-industrialization show that the decline of manufacturing has brought an absolute decline in wages and working conditions, despite growth in the service sector.

When reading and discussing the following section, it is important to remember that both sides have merits. Think about how capitalism requires the de-industrialization, how the average worker is affected, and how globalization helps the process along.

DE-INDUSTRIALIZATION HELPS AMERICANS

The father of economic theory, Adam Smith, would have supported de-industrialization for the United States. He maintained that products should be produced where there is a local advantage—that is, wherever production is cheapest. According to this theory, it is always better for the United States to import a product at a lower price than it is to produce the product at home for a higher price. This alludes to the notion of competitive advantage. Those who do not support de-industrialization fail to understand this concept, advocates would argue. The American consumer is better off because she can buy her goods at a marginally lower price.

Along similar lines, de-industrialization boosts efficiency. *Efficiency* in economics is defined as the optimal allocation of resources. The efficient use of human capital and natural resources yields the greatest productivity, which means the lowest possible price. If efficiency is taken into account, then each nation produces the goods for which it can allocate the most abundant resources. Countries with the cheapest labor will contribute the most labor in an efficient production process. By this standard, to keep manufacturing jobs in the United States—where labor is relatively expensive—would be to maintain an inefficient economic system.

However, this does not eliminate all manufacturing jobs from the United States—only the least-skilled, worst-paid jobs. Though there has been a decline in the numbers working in manufacturing, the amount of value added (in constant dollars) has remained a similar percentage of the GDP throughout the main years of de-industrialization between 1970 and 1994.

We Do Not Only Help Ourselves Advocates would also say that prosperity is difficult to achieve and some nations must literally start from the bottom, by industrializing through the use of cheap labor. This is a proven way for poor nations to become wealthier nations, as happened in the case of South Korea. When nations like the United States relocate their manufacturing, they do so by moving jobs to the bottom of the wage structure. At the low end, in the world's poorest countries, Export

Processing Zones (EPZs) help poor nations by providing jobs and raising the standard of living for workers. Thus, de-industrialization of the United States is good for the rest of the world.

Thanks to EPZs, firms are attracted by the low wages and, with the growth of production, the nation and its workers benefit. Capital flows into the EPZs and workers' wages rise, either through collective bargaining or through the upgrading of their skills. Labor shortages resulting from the inflow of jobs may also drive up wages.

Currently, about 80 percent of the world's industrial labor is in the *periphery*—that is, in poorer, less-developed countries. By moving industries like manufacturing away from the *core* nations, peripheral nations can gain a foothold in the world's markets. Involving a peripheral nation in world markets is the first step toward industrialization. Through more trade, standards of living rise in peripheral nations, benefiting everyone.

It Sends the Bad Jobs Away   Most of the de-industrialization of America occurred in a way that afforded workers new opportunities, advocates argue. When American manufacturing plants were being relocated to the world's periphery and semi-periphery, job creation in America was strong and unemployment had reached record lows. Relocation did not harm American workers, since they could easily find new jobs. In the past decade, the United States, Canada, and Mexico have all experienced a growth in employment. Even though manufacturing jobs were being relocated, the American economy continued to grow, proving that de-industrialization does not necessarily hurt individuals or the economy.

Moreover, the de-industrialization of America has brought greater opportunity for its citizens. Not only are Americans able to find better jobs, but productivity has improved and the demand for goods and services is rising. It is true that some people enjoy less of this new prosperity than others, due to a skills mismatch. When the economy "switches gears," a few are always left behind. With the disappearance of low-end manufacturing jobs, people with low-end qualifications will face some difficulty. However, this is just a transitional problem that will correct itself as more people seek training for the higher-end jobs that America is increasingly offering. The change benefits everyone in the end.

Promoting Peace   The process of de-industrialization, fueled by globalization, also makes the world a more peaceful place. As companies search for a competitive advantage, they create international networks that span the world. As different nations and companies invest in each other, they develop a greater stake in the conditions existing in other countries. A disruption in one country, then, means a disruption in another. Companies and nations increasingly have to avoid conflict if they want to avoid disrupting their markets. De-industrialization and globalization both reinforce peace through the contribution they make to stable markets.

NEITHER GOOD NOR BAD

According to some economic theories, de-industrialization is neither good nor bad—it is simply part of the natural evolution of economies. Many decades ago, economist Walt Rostow asserted that there are five stages of economic growth: traditional society, preconditions, take-off, the drive to technological maturity, and the age of high mass consumption. In this context, de-industrialization is part of the natural drive to technological maturity, beginning with a decline in main sector manufacturing.

This change also reflects Friedrich Engel's law stating that, as income rises, people substitute away from manufactured goods. For example, once a family has all the basic durable goods (e.g., a refrigerator, an oven, an automobile) new items are not needed for years to come. This leads to a lessened demand for manufactured goods, hence declining production and profits. People save their surplus income or spend it on services. From this standpoint, too, de-industrialization is inevitable, as a society upgrades to a services economy. It is useless to try to turn back the clock, since de-industrialization must occur for the current economic system to succeed.

DE-INDUSTRIALIZATION HURTS AMERICA

However, many disagree with the assertion that de-industrialization is normal or inevitable, or that its results—however normal—are desirable. They claim that de-industrialization should be resisted and its effects remedied, pointing out that even though the United States is experiencing near-full employment and economic growth, its industries face lower labor standards and rising inequality because of de-industrialization.

Downsizing has become common in American industry. For example, a large-scale study of thousands of workers at a computer and networking firm shows that displaced workers were forced to take up temporary work instead. Not only blue-collar workers, but also white-collar workers were being displaced. In fact, most of the workers in this study were found to be downwardly mobile because of their jobs being moved to different nations where labor is cheaper. India is one nation where a lot of computer and networking jobs are moving because the wage rates are lower than in the United States and highly skilled workers are available.

Once downsized American workers find new jobs, often as part-time workers, their livelihoods are hurt further. Companies seldom invest much money in these workers since they turn over quickly. Without investment in their skills, their value (as workers) stagnates. By doing society's poorly paid but necessary work, these displaced workers subsidize the upper and middle classes of America by providing them with cheap labor. This ensures that when wealthy people go to the mall, they will be able to find what they need at low prices. However, the low-wage workers themselves have trouble when it comes to providing for their own families. Some have said that as a result, low-wage workers live to work, whereas others work to live.

Some supporters of de-industrialization point out that *family* incomes have held up despite the closing of factories. What they often fail to mention is that the family income has stayed steady because more family members are out working, for longer hours. Some supporters also fail to take into account *real* incomes—that is, incomes adjusted for inflation. If we adjust for inflation, incomes have not been growing. Average hourly pay for workers has fallen in the United States, Canada, and Mexico over this period of de-industrialization. The evidence shows that de-industrialization does not mean better jobs with higher pay, but jobs with lower pay and less security.

Further, it worries some Americans that the United States has a growing trade deficit. This means that the United States imports more than it exports. American businesses and the American economy are ever more dependent on international funds for domestic investment. Though this may be a symptom of globalization, it *should* worry Americans, critics say. How can America look after its best interests when much of its economic activity is controlled by outsiders?

Good Jobs Are Sent Away Some point out that job losses are a natural part of capitalism and no cause for worry, since progress engendered by capitalism ensures a natural turnover of jobs. However, one characteristic of capitalism is that it tends to produce too few jobs, often substituting machines for people. Without government intervention, the system is set up to produce and maintain unemployment, hence low wages. This is why governments need to intervene against the natural forces of capitalism that create de-industrialization. In effect, governments are obliged to solve the social problems—unemployment, poverty, depression, addiction, violence, and others—that capitalist efficiency helps to produce.

For example, de-industrialization is directly responsible for ruining many of the good jobs that Americans once had. Fifty years ago, many manufacturing jobs (e.g., in the automobile industry) were unionized and, as such, provided families with a living wage, a pension, and a healthcare plan. Today, unions are weaker and fewer workers belong to a union. An example is the large workforce at Wal-Mart. Wal-Mart cannot, and does not, provide workers with the wages and benefits unionized workers received in the past. Most of its workers earn near minimum wage, have no pensions, and receive no benefits.

This has a ripple effect on other industries, since lower pay means less buying by consumers. So, de-industrialization also eliminates jobs and depresses the wages in many other industries. Bosses often respond by threatening workers to close plants if they do not make certain concessions. Experience shows that moving production activities to other countries is easily done; so workers are easily coerced by such threats. Similar strategies are used to suppress union activity or prevent union formation. And, even after companies reduce worker salaries and cut benefits, their jobs are still insecure. American workers must still compete with numerous, poorly paid workers in other nations. This continues to mean an overall lowering of work-standards and absolute salaries.

So, to summarize, America is trading manufacturing jobs for service jobs. The manufacturing industry, known for having higher average wages than the service sector, is disappearing from America. The service industry, with its lower average wages and higher poverty levels, is blossoming.

Consider, as an example, the American apparel industry. The number of clothing manufacture jobs lost in the United States is almost the same as the number of clothing manufacture jobs gained in Mexico over the same period. Critics ask, What good is NAFTA to Americans if it sends American jobs to other nations? Mexico has increased its apparel exports from 1.9 billion dollars in 1994 to 8.1 billion in 2001. Yet this has not benefited Mexican workers as much as expected. Despite increased exports of many goods, the conditions for Mexican workers have worsened. In the period between 1980 and 1996, average compensation for Mexican workers fell by 173 percent. Adjusting for inflation, in the past 20 years the real average income has gone down by 76 percent. So de-industrialization helps neither the Mexican worker nor the American worker. The only winners are American and Mexican capitalists.

As a result, de-industrialization does not reduce conflict or bring the world's people together. Moving jobs to other nations does not ensure cooperation between "us" and "them." Moreover, American consumer culture is incompatible with some of the goals of other cultures. Sometimes, American goods and American jobs intrude on other cultures. Though de-industrialization operates within the framework of globalization, we cannot assume that the entire world wants the same out of life as we do. Modern American consumerist culture is largely secular and materialistic. Wherever it appears, it upsets relations between men and women, parents and children, bosses and workers, rulers and ruled.

Partly because of these upsets, and partly because of perceived imperialism, the United States has experienced antiwestern sentiment in many countries with which it does business.

It Hurts the Most Vulnerable   Nobel prize-winner Nelson Mandela makes an excellent point by asking, "Is globalization only for the powerful? Does it offer nothing to the men, women, and children who are ravaged by the violence of poverty?"

Not only does de-industrialization put people out of jobs, but it has increased the inequality of American society. Since the 1970s, the United States has become a more economically polarized nation. Minority individuals and families are disproportionately hurt by the consequences of de-industrialization. In families that relied on income from a manufacturing job, de-industrialization means the family may lose healthcare and retirement benefits, and may ultimately be forced to live on a lower income. By creating this divide between the rich and poor, de-industrialization helps to perpetuate a system of poverty.

It Creates a Global Hierarchy   Immanuel Wallerstein, the father of World Systems Theory, explains that there is one world system divided into the core, the semi-periphery, and the periphery. Those in the core nations produce capital-intensive objects, whereas those in the periphery nations produce labor-intensive objects. Though people in the periphery produce valuable low-priced goods, they must pay high prices for labor-intensive goods from the core. This inequity maintains an economic hierarchy from which the periphery cannot easily escape. How can a country get wealthy by exporting bananas to a country from which it imports high-precision medical equipment? In the end, the core-periphery relationship creates a world hierarchy maintained by the wealthiest nations to exploit the periphery.

Irrationalities of De-Industrialization In theory, de-industrialization in the United States should help other nations, but in practice this does not occur. In theory, for de-industrialization to work, nations will follow the rules of comparative advantage—that is, work from their areas of greatest strength, whether that be natural resources, location, human capital, large labor force, or otherwise. In practice, this does not occur, as trade zones develop giving favored trading-partner status to some and not to other nations. NAFTA and the EU both promote trade among member countries, but exclude nonmembers who may have a comparative advantage in a good. This is irrational on economic grounds, though rational politically.

Likewise, it would be economically rational to invest profits upgrading the human capital in countries from which you draw your labor force. In practice, this rarely happens under conditions of de-industrialization. Profits made in less-developed countries are most often sent back to company headquarters. Therefore, workers and the region in which they live see little in the form of assistance or improving conditions. It remains to be shown that transnational (or multinational) corporations (TNCs) benefit developing economies; their presence often retards development, since economic benefits flow from cheap, regimented labor. Income inequality in less-developed nations attracts investment from TNCs, and these corporations have no incentive to reduce the inequality.

SUMMING UP

In theory, de-industrialization has the potential to benefit people, but fails to do so in reality. In theory, there is perfect competition and economically efficient use of resources; in reality, politics interferes in the forms of barriers to trade and restricted competition. For these reasons, de-industrialization does not help America or the world.

But there is no indication that de-industrialization will diminish, any more than globalization or the spread of TNCs will diminish. These are all part of a long sweep of history in the direction of ever greater economic integration and ever larger political empires. We cannot see who will dominate these empires of the future, or how the economy of these empires will be organized. But it is safe to assume that, short of a revolution, machines will continue to replace human workers in simple repetitive jobs and low-paid workers will continued to replace high-paid workers in slightly less repetitive jobs.

REVIEW EXERCISES

For Discussion and Debate

1. Discuss people you know who have looked for work in the past year. What were their experiences, and do they demonstrate the effects of de-industrialization?
2. What are the likely effects of de-industrialization on family life and relations between parents and their children?
3. Why does de-industrialization affect members of some racial or ethnic groups more than others?
4. How is de-industrialization affecting the career or job you are choosing to pursue?

Writing Exercises

Write a brief (500-word) essay on one of the following topics:

1. "Globalization has done the human race a lot of good."
2. "Globalization has done Americans a lot of bad."
3. "The cause of de-industrialization in America is consumerism, not capitalism."
4. "Globalization" is just the most recent name for capitalist imperialism."

Research Activities

1. Draw a map of the United States, marking the "Rustbelt" areas in red-brown.
2. Draw a map of the world, using arrows of different sizes to indicate the size (in dollars) of exports and imports flowing between the United States and its ten biggest trading partners.
3. Interview five unemployed people and find out their views of globalization and de-industrialization (as discussed in this section).
4. Interview five business school (MBA) students and find out their views of globalization and de-industrialization (as discussed in this section).

SELECTED REFERENCES

Bair, Jennifer and Gary Gereffi. 2003. "Upgrading, Uneven Development, and Jobs in the North American Apparel Industry." *Global Networks* 3, 2:143–169.

Bluestone, Barry and Bennett Harrison. 1982. *The Deindustrialization of America: Plant Closings.* New York: Basic Books.

Bornschier, Volker and Mark Herkenrath. 2003. "Transnational Corporations in World Development—Still the Same Harmful Effects in an Increasingly Globalized World Economy." *Journal of World-Systems Research* 9, 1:105–139.

Bradley, David, Evelyn Huber, Stephanie Moller, François Nielsen and John D. Stephens. 2003. "Determinants of Relative Poverty in Advanced Capitalist Democracies." *American Sociological Review* 68, 1:22–51.

Brint, Steven. 2001. "Professionals and the 'Knowledge Economy': Rethinking the Theory of Postindustrial Society." *Current Sociology* 49, 4:101–132.

Cormier, David and Charles Craypo. 2000. "The Working Poor and the Working of American Labour Markets." *Cambridge Journal of Economics* 24, 6:691–708.

Cormier, David and Harry Targ. 2001. "Globalization and the North American Worker." *Labor Studies Journal* 26, 1:42–55.

Graeff, Peter and Guido Mehlkop. 2003. "Why Nations Arm in the Age of Globalization." *Comparative Sociology* 2, 4:667–693.

Johnson, Christopher H. 2002. "Introduction: De-Industrialization and Globalization." *International Review of Social History* 47, Supplement 10:3–33.

Kaplinsky, Raphael. 2001. "Is Globalization All It Is Cracked Up to Be?" *Review of International Political Economy* 8, 1:46–65.

Kentor, Jeffrey. 2001. "The Long Term Effects of Globalization on Income Inequality, Population Growth, and Economic Development." *Social Problems* 48, 4:435–455.

Kenworthy, Lane. 2003. "Do Affluent Countries Face an Income-Jobs Trade-Off?" *Comparative Political Studies* 36, 10:1180–1209.

Koeber, Charles. 2002. "Corporate Restructuring, Downsizing, and the Middle Class: The Process and Meaning of Worker Displacement in the 'New' Economy." *Qualitative Sociology* 25, 2:217–246.

Morris, Melissa and Bob Sheak. "The Limits of the Job Supply in U.S. Capitalism: Sub-Employment Measures and Trends." *Critical Sociology* 28, 3:389–414.

Mulder, Nanno. 2002. *Economic Performance in the Americas: The Role of the Service Sector in Brazil, Mexico, and the USA.* Cheltenham: Edward Elger.

Nyahoho, Emmanuel. 2001. "Globalization and Economic Goals." *The Journal of Social, Political, and Economic Studies* 26, 3:543–568.

Palpacuer, Florence and Aurelio Parisotto. 2003. "Global Production and Local Jobs: Can Global Enterprise Networks Be Used as Levers for Local Development." *Global Networks* 3, 2:97–120.

Wood, Adrian. 1994. *North-South Trade, Employment, and Inequality: Changing Fortunes in a Skill Driven World.* Oxford: Clarendon Press.

CHAPTER 11 EDUCATION

In recent years there has been a great deal of debate about the goals and outcome of education. By one definition, the purpose of education is to "draw forth" or "lead out"—to stimulate a love of questioning, promote self-reliance and risk taking. Included in this is the teaching of general skills and knowledge; but since personal growth is the goal, success is to be measured differently for each student. There is no universal norm for judging success.

By another definition, education and schools are to train—to drag, direct, or discipline—their students to function effectively in the real world. This would include familiarizing the students with stock answers, promoting obedience and orderliness, and teaching in skilled activity. By this criterion, the proper outcomes of education are standardized tests and credentials to those who earn them.

Increasingly it is clear that these two ideas of education are different and possibly incompatible. They reflect different conceptions of human nature and lead to different organizational strategies that may produce one outcome but rarely (if ever) both.

In this chapter we examine three issues that are related to this polarization. The first section considers whether the tracking of unequally talented children provides them all with good education and/or perpetuates social inequality. The second section asks about whether religion should be taught in schools. Some say it's necessary—and it may be, though here the need is for teaching *about* religions, not teaching one specific religion. The third section analyzes *home schooling* to determine why some parents don't want their children educated in institutions designed for that purpose.

11.1   Does School Streaming Keep Poor People Poor?

The issue: Whether public schools, which many hoped would reduce inequality in modern societies, actually work to perpetuate and legitimate inequality. Some believe that one way schools may do this is by segregating the so-called better students from the worse ones.

Within public school systems in the United States and Canada, a debate has raged over whether or not students, particularly at secondary levels (junior and senior high schools), should be "streamed" or "tracked" into classes according to their abilities. This is part of a larger debate around *ability grouping*. There are further issues about what students should be learning—the same or different material.

There are three main types of ability grouping. Under the first, very common in elementary classrooms, students may be divided according to differential ability to handle materials, for instance as "slow," "average," and "advanced" readers. Often, especially in elementary school, such groupings are disguised by the use of animal or bird names, on the principle that students should not be discouraged by being told they were in the slow group. However, students who have experienced this during their schooling say that they generally knew which group was which, so that if slow readers picked the name "cheetahs" a ripple of unkind laughter would go around the class.

The second type of grouping is, in Britain, termed *setting*. Different classes exist in each subject, and students are assigned to classes that cover the ground more or less rapidly, according to ability in that particular subject. This system is frequently met with in North American high schools, where classes may be demarcated as "honors," "academic," or "general," the level often indicated by the registration number assigned to the class. This class-by-class grouping is often referred to as *streaming*. So, confusingly, is the third level.

In the third level, referred to as *tracking* or streaming, students move as a block from one class to another, so that they take all classes within a *general,* a *vocational,* or an *academic* level. In parts of Britain, particularly England, until the mid-seventies they not only attended different streams but different schools! Reading the British literature on this subject can be confusing therefore, because sometimes streaming refers to this older system of separate schools rather than to a system of tracks within one school. During the 1970s there was a move to *comprehensive* schooling, whereby students would attend one high school (similar to a North American combined junior and senior high), which might include either several streams, or have classes or sets at different levels within each subject.

The following discussion will focus on the second and third levels of ability grouping, including formal streaming and class-by-class streaming. Today's emphasis is to prepare every student for college, and the most common form of tracking in North American schools is to assign students to advanced, regular, or basic courses, depending on their past performance in each subject, says Maureen Hallinan. On the one hand, proponents of types of ability grouping consider that, when children and young adults are carefully selected for streams or classes, each child can receive instruction at the level she requires. On the other hand, opponents claim that ability grouping, particularly tracking or streaming, perpetuates inequality by disadvantaging a majority of students, particularly those from poor and/or minority backgrounds, by the provision of different materials to different streams, and by labeling students according to their streams.

STREAMING DOES NOT PERPETUATE INEQUALITY

Rather than perpetuating inequality, tracking or streaming and other forms of ability grouping can act to reduce it, by providing children with an education that is suited to their abilities and thus allowing them to achieve their maximum potential. In the past there has been an association between tracking and race, or social class. In the present we can avoid this, by means of a common curriculum throughout much of elementary school and providing remedial education where required to "level the playing field." When students reach secondary school, or the upper elementary grades, they will develop differences of interest, skill, and ability, and it is right that they should have access to a system that will allow them to develop their individual talents to the fullest extent possible.

Results of intelligence and achievement tests and examination scores show clearly that not all children are the same in ability or performance. If all children have to deal with the same curriculum and the same teacher, all will suffer. In untracked classes, bright children become bored with the slow pace of instruction and progress of the class. Less able children will fall behind, often irretrievably, becoming discouraged. Those in the middle will find that the teacher is busy with children requiring instruction to "catch-up," or dealing with "trouble makers" who are discouraged or bored. And most teachers say that, in practice, they have to teach "to the middle" in terms of preparing their curriculum material—both ends of the spectrum suffer, resulting in boredom that turns into trouble. In uniform teaching, there are no winners.

Streaming and provision of enrichment classes in certain subjects means that the bright students get material more suited to retaining their interest. When test scores from streamed and unstreamed classes are compared, controlling for ability or intelligence, bright students in streamed classes do better, according to findings by Kulik and Kulik.

The advantages of streaming have been known for years: Indeed, they were summarized as long ago as 1931, by Turney:

- Streaming permits pupils to make progress commensurate with their abilities.
- It makes possible an adaptation of instructional technique to the needs of the group.
- It reduces failures.
- It helps to maintain interest and incentive, because bright students are not bored by the sluggish participation of the dull.
- Slower pupils participate more when not eclipsed by those much brighter.
- It makes teaching easier.
- It makes possible individual instruction to small slow groups.

All of these points, when investigated by present-day researchers, still hold. Teaching a class of mixed ability students is regarded by many teachers as a nightmare. Bright children from any race or class deserve to be challenged with materials that will broaden their horizons and extend their abilities. This is not possible within mixed ability classrooms. Therefore, not only does tracking not perpetuate inequality, if used properly it will actively reduce it.

Streaming Does Perpetuate Inequality

Not only have the arguments *for* tracking been current for 70 years; so have those *against* it, although recently a few others have been added to the list. Robert Slavin is a thorough opponent of tracking, who lists both sets of arguments as summarized by Turney in 1931. Here are the arguments against.

- Slow pupils need the presence of the able students to stimulate them and encourage them.
- A stigma is attached to low sections or classes, operating to discourage the pupils in these sections.
- Teachers are unable, or do not have time, to differentiate the work for different levels of ability. Often high-ability classes or groups

simply receive more work, rather than a different level of work.
- Teachers object to the slower groups, and do not want to teach them.

Some of these arguments have been borne out, some refuted, by research over the years. All, however, continue to be made. There are two recent additions to the list of disadvantages, and we will come to them shortly. But first, points three and four require examination. Often higher-ability classes or groups simply receive more work, rather than a different level of work; and the dislike of dealing with slow classes may contribute further to a lack of preparation of material for them. Where material for slow classes is available from publishers, it may be of such a level that the students find it insulting and patronizing, further reducing any incentive to study.

The two points Slavin would add are as follows:

- Ability grouping discriminates against minority and lower-class students.
- Low-stream students receive instruction that is slower-paced and of lower quality than that available to higher-track students.

This last point bears expansion. The instruction of low-stream students is not only slower-paced than, but indeed different in kind from, instruction aimed at college-entry-stream students. Students not only cover less material, but do so with less concern for detailed analysis, including social analysis. Low-stream students, who are often disproportionately poor and from minority groups, leave school with fewer skills needed to obtain employment, and with less knowledge of how their society works, and less faith in their ability to effect changes in their own lives.

Students in low streams appear to spend more time "off task," and teachers spend more time trying to maintain order. Less material is covered, and it becomes rare-to-impossible for students to move up into a more academic stream, as they are permanently "behind." Low stream classes lead to other low stream classes, and students who leave school with a *vocational* qualification are likely to find that employers regard this as equivalent to failure.

Conventional wisdom has it that while heterogeneity or homogeneity of grouping may have little effect on average students, nevertheless the ends of the ability spectrum—very high or very low achievers—benefit from homogenous group placement. While the Kuliks did claim a benefit for high-achievers in streaming, other studies do not necessarily bear this out. Slavin found no benefit for high achievers. Neither the Kuliks nor Slavin found that low achievers benefitted in terms of outcome measures. Referring to very low mathematical-ability students, Canadian researcher Lorna Earl found homogeneous low-stream placement a hindrance.

A study by Peterson of heterogeneous grouping considered the premise that students of low ability will achieve better when provided with additional opportunities for learning. The study demonstrated that remedial math students placed in an *accelerated* program made significantly more progress in areas of problem-solving, math concepts, and computational skills compared with students in a remedial class. Perhaps these students had more opportunities for learning, compared with their low-stream counterparts.

There can be many reasons why students find themselves in low-stream classes. Sometimes this is not due to any lack of ability, but rather to lack of interest in school and to active resistance toward it. Students are quite capable of summing up the school system and finding it lacking in what they need. Often working-class and minority youth, if asked, will explain that the school system has little that they want, particularly if it labels them as failures and puts them into low streams, providing them with uninteresting material. Where subjects that are relevant to students' own interests and communities are introduced—such as black history and community studies, labor history, or the math required to plan and operate a community market garden—teachers may report not only that students are more interested, but also that they start to perform at higher ability levels.

Some researchers have examined ways that students are allotted to streams. Their findings are worrying. Low streams are strongly associated with minority or lower-class youth. Gender is less evidently associated with placement overall, but girls

who are not specifically identified as academically gifted may find themselves counseled at high school level to take predominantly vocational, and/or clerical courses. Teachers and counselors make assumptions about the needs of students, and often race, class, and gender are central to these assumptions. Other researchers have been examining the nature of the counseling and choice/selection process operating at the high school level, and its ambiguities and uncertainties. Garet and Delany write of "multiple, loosely connected standard operating procedures at the schools" that may result in discriminatory placement of students, not through deliberate intent but through a myriad of small decisions, adjustments, and tinkerings, driven by the ever-present need to create a manageable school timetable. Students may be assigned to classes in a sort of bureaucratic muddle of administrators and teachers trying to make do, fix schedules, and make ends meet. In the process, assumptions based on gender, race, class, and perceived future needs of the students easily creep into small decisions, small tinkerings, in ways that are difficult to uncover.

The rationale for streaming assumes that students can be divided into different kinds with dramatically different learning needs and learning capabilities. Yet, within a particular stream there may be a very wide range of interests or talents and abilities, or even measured intelligence levels. A junior high "advanced placement" track, for instance, may include students with measured IQs of from around 115 to upward of 160—the measurement reflecting how well each student did on a test on one specific day. Yet tracking tends to encourage a view of these children as essentially similar to each other, and essentially different from the regular children who scored 105 or 110 on the IQ test.

In a 2001 study, George Ansalone shows class, ethnicity, and gender biases still resulting in lower-track assignment. He points to processes within the tracks resulting in students being held back, with ultimate implications for the continuation of poverty within impoverished groups. Other researchers have seen how children who come to believe they cannot deal with more difficult material may even, as adults, never try to read things such as this book—thinking that they simply are not capable of understanding the concepts or of looking up the words in a dictionary.

All in all, it is hard to see how streaming is justified, and easy to see how it can connect with the perpetuation of inequality.

SUMMING UP

We can find little justification for tracking or streaming other than that many teachers like it, and say it helps them with class preparation and management. Hallinan says that many schools find ways to get around providing mixed-ability teaching because tracking is seen as easier to manage. Most teachers prefer to teach high- or middle-stream classes. In much of the literature, low-ability streams are associated with resistance to school, and teachers may avoid such streams because they are discouraging to teach, hard to control, and even physically threatening. In some schools, experienced teachers regularly teach such classes and see their success as an achievement but, in many schools, experienced teachers assign newcomers to deal with problem students. Detracking is seen as beneficial in that "resistors" are no longer grouped together but spread out, one or two to a class. Everyone has to deal with them, and good practice can be shared.

Some think that destreaming can spread out potential troublemakers and reduce the extent to which students' attitudes turn pro- or anti-school. Destreaming has therefore been proposed as a partial antidote to anti-school attitudes, and to their ultimate expression by low-stream students—dropping out. A further component may be an ending of the social promotion of students from one grade to another, so that students would expect either to achieve certain minimum requirements or to repeat a year.

Robert Upshaw, a member of the Black Learners Education Committee in Halifax, Nova Scotia, is strongly opposed to streaming and to social promotion. He sees many black youth going through the school system, which they find inimical to their interests, with the intention of leaving as early as possible, and therefore with minimum qualifications.

Knowing what *detracking* means is necessary to its approval by teachers. Robert Slavin points out a difficulty in reconciling destreaming with traditional teaching if students in a class are perceived as similar to each other in ability and interests. He promotes cooperative teaching, in which students and teachers can draw on the strengths and talents of individual students, to the benefit of all.

Arguments for and against tracking therefore are only part of this important debate about education and equality in our society.

REVIEW EXERCISES

For Discussion and Debate

1. "Athletics is the only way most young black men can get ahead."
2. "Tracking is the only way people can be taught what they need to know for their jobs."
3. "These days, anybody can get a good education if they'll only put their mind to it."
4. "Tracking is the way that schools maintain social class divisions."

Writing Exercises

Write a brief (500-word) essay on one of the following topics:

1. Associations you have observed between streaming and ethnicity.
2. "My own experience: Selecting classes in high school."
3. "When my children are in school, they'll be in the top track."
4. "Enriched programs should be for everyone."

Research Activities

1. Interview six of your friends. How many of them were in tracked classes in high school or junior high? How were their tracks selected? Are they in favor of tracking?
2. Interview six people of the same generation as your parents. How many of them were in tracked classes in high school or junior high? How were their tracks selected? Are they in favor of tracking? Do they give the same reasons as people who were more recently in school?
3. Search the World Wide Web for arguments for or against tracking. What arguments are presented there, and whose views are represented?
4. Working with a group of four to six other students, list the courses you each took in high school, and the decisions represented by these course choices. How many choices were career oriented? What differences in advice were you given? What have you learned from this exercise?

SELECTED REFERENCES

Ansalone, George. 2001. "Schooling, Tracking, and Inequality." *Journal of Children and Poverty* 7, 1:33–47.

———. 2003. "Poverty, Tracking, and the Social Construction of Failure: International Perspectives on Tracking." *Journal of Children and Poverty* 9, 1.

Betts, J. R. and J. L. Shkolnik. 1999. "The Effects of Ability Grouping on Student Achievement and Resource Allocation in Secondary Schools." *Economics of Education Review* 19, 1:1–15.

Contenta, Sandro. 1995. *Rituals of Failure.* Toronto: Between the Lines.

Connell, R. W. et al. 1982. *Making the Difference: Schools, Families and Social Division.* Sydney: George Allen and Unwin.

Dei, George J. Sefa. 1996. *Anti-Racism Education: Theory and Practice.* Halifax, NS: Fernwood.

Delpit, Lisa D. 1988. "The Silenced Dialogue: Power and Pedagogy in Educating Other People's Children." *Harvard Educational Review* 58, 3 (Aug.): 280–298.

Denti, Louis G. 1994. "Walling Students with Disabilities out of the Mainstream: Revealing the Illusions of Inclusion." *International Journal of Group Tensions* 24, 1 (Spring): 69–78.

Earl, Lorna. 1989. *Streaming: Interpreting the Literature.* Scarborough, Ontario: Scarborough Board of Education.

Francis, Kim C., Robert J. Bell and Martha J. Bell. 1994. "Language Diversity in the University: Aspects of Remediation, Open Admissions and Multiculturalism." *Education* 114, 4 (Summer): 525–529.

Fritzberg, G. J. 2001. "Less than Equal: A Former Urban Schoolteacher Examines the Causes of Educational Disadvantagement." *The Urban Review* 33, 2:107–129.

Gamoran, Adam. 1993. "Alternative Uses of Ability Grouping in Secondary Schools: Can We Bring High-Quality Instruction to Low-Ability Classes?" *American Journal of Education* 102, 1 (Nov.): 1–22.

Grey, Mark A. 1990. "Immigrant Students in the Heartland: Ethnic Relations in a Garden City, Kansas, High School." *Urban Anthropology* 19, 4 (Winter): 409–427.

Hallinan, Maureen. 1994. "School Differences in Tracking Effects on Achievement." *Social Forces* 72, 3 (Mar.): 799–820.

———. 2004. "The Detracking Movement." *Education Next* 4, 4. Available online at http://www.educationnext.org/20044/72.htm.

——— and Jeannie Oakes. 1994. "Tracking: From Theory to Practice." *Sociology of Education* 67, 2 (Apr.): 79–84.

Howe, Kenneth R. 1993. "Equality of Educational Opportunity and the Criterion of Equal Educational Worth." *Studies in Philosophy and Education* 11, 4:329–337.

Ireson, J. and S. Hallam. 1999. "Raising Standards: Is Ability Grouping the Answer?" *Oxford Review of Education* 25, 3:343–358.

Kutnick, P., P. Blatchford and E. Baines. 2002. "Pupil Groupings in Primary School Classrooms: Sites for Learning and Social Pedagogy?" *British Educational Research Journal* 28, 2:187–206.

LeTendre, G. K., B. K. Hofer and H. Shimizu. 2003. "What Is Tracking? Cultural Expectations in the United States, Germany and Japan." *American Educational Research Journal* 40, 1:43.

Madaus, George F. 1994. "A Technological and Historical Consideration of Equity Issues Associated with Proposals to Change the Nation's Testing Policy." *Harvard Educational Review* 64, 1 (Spring): 76–95.

Mickelson, Roslyn Arlin. 2003. "When Are Racial Disparities in Education the Result of Racial Discrimination? A Social Science Perspective." *Teachers College Record* 105, 6:1052.

Oakes, Jeannie. 1985. *Keeping Track: How Schools Structure Inequality.* New Haven and London: Yale University Press.

Reynolds, Arthur J., Roger P. Weissberg and Wesley J. Kasprow. 1992. "Prediction of Early Social and Academic Adjustment of Children from the Inner City." *American Journal of Community Psychology* 20, 5 (Oct.): 599–624.

Riddell, Sheila. 1993. "The Politics of Disability: School Experience." *British Journal of Sociology of Education* 14, 4 (Dec.): 445–455.

———, George O. B. Thomson and Sarah Dyer. 1992. "A Key Informant Approach to the Study of Local Policymaking in the Field of Special Educational Needs." *European Journal of Special Needs Education* 7, 1 (Mar.): 47–62.

Rubin, Beth and Pedro Noguera. 2004. "Tracking Detracking: Sorting through the Dilemmas and Possibilities of Detracking in Practice." *Equity & Excellence in Education* 37, 1:92–101.

Slavin, Robert E. 1990. *Achievement Effects of Ability Grouping in Secondary Schools: A Best Evidence Analysis.* National Center on Effective Secondary Schools, Wisconsin Center for Education Research.

Thomson, George O. B., J. Ward and L. Gow. 1988. "The Education of Children with Special Needs: A Cross-Cultural Perspective." *European Journal of Special Needs Education* 3, 3 (Sept.): 125–137.

Tomlinson, Sally. 1988. "Why Johnny Can't Read: Critical Theory and Special Education." *European Journal of Special Needs Education* 3, 1 (Mar.): 45–58.

Wiliam, D. and H. Bartholomew. 2004. "It's Not Which School but Which Set You're in That Matters: The Influence of Ability Grouping Practices on Student Progress in Mathematics." *British Educational Research Journal* 30, 2:279–293.

Yonezawa S., A. Stuart Wells and I. Serna. 2002. "Choosing Tracks: 'Freedom of Choice' in Detracking Schools." *American Educational Research Journal* 39, 1:37.

11.2   Should Religion Be a School Subject?

The issue: While some favor teaching religion in school, others favor separation of public education and religion. Different countries have different rules on this; but is one way best? And what kind of "religion" might be taught?

The first amendment to the U.S. Constitution is about religious freedom and the separation of church and state; yet 78 percent of Americans favor school prayers, and 71 percent feel that the Bible should be used in the classroom (CNN/Gallup Poll 2000).

Elsewhere there are different views: In Britain, religious education is basic to the curriculum. This includes not only some form of teaching, but an assembly of students and staff that includes some form of Christian worship (hymn or prayer). Many people in Britain find this unnecessary, some find it offensive, and others feel that it represents the role of Christianity in the latter part of the development of British heritage. The Church of England is *established* in England and is associated with the state, although relatively few people are churchgoers and Britain includes people of many religions. In Scotland, Religious and Moral Education (the official title) for pupils under 15 is divided between teaching about Christianity, teaching about other World Religions, and "personal search."

Should religion be taught in schools? The debate has been heated. Educators on both sides of the Atlantic are dealing with conflicting demands of groups of parents. Most are attempting to give children a firm basis on which to build tolerance and respect for those of their own faith and of others. How can this best be done? There are also issues about denominational or faith schools, and how these should be financed.

Here are some of the issues. What do you think?

RELIGION SHOULD BE TAUGHT IN SCHOOLS

The first amendment calls for a separation of church and state. This is often given as a reason for religion not to be taught in schools. It can be mentioned, but not promoted. But let's look at why it might be important to teach religion in some schools—maybe in all schools—and to give support to religious schools on the same basis as non-religious or secular schools.

First, there is a strong call from some communities. Particularly in areas of the mid-West, parents and community leaders may consider that their heritage and history is not given sufficient consideration if religion is excluded. Most obviously, understanding of the foundation and settlement of North American communities involves talking about religion. Currently, the extent to which this can be done varies between states and even between school districts.

ʹ In the nineteenth century, most schools in the United States were religious. Indeed, the idea behind the establishment of mass public education was to create good citizens and responsible employees. Religion was strongly part of the fabric of society, and religion was taught then in the school, giving a moral basis for ideas about citizenship and responsibility. Most schools gave an evangelical protestant "spin" on religion, and this became seen as a problem, as it polarized society. During the twentieth century, ideas about religion changed—given increased immigration to North America, teaching one religion (Protestant

Christianity) became less relevant. Because of fairness, the school system became completely secular. In 1962 the Supreme Court ruled that officially mandated prayer in the public schools was unconstitutional—in 1963, further ruling that reading the Bible as religious instruction or a religious exercise should not occur in public schools.

But this causes a further problem—or several. First, by saying that religion should not be taught in this way the school system denies religions (any religions) the right to explain their roles in some processes and decisions from American (or other) history, or indeed in today's political processes and social issues. It isn't enough to simply say that (for instance) there were conflicts between the official religion in England and some of the people who became the early European settlers in eastern North America. Students need to understand the world views of these people. To do so, they need a greater understanding of religion than is given in history lessons. And Protestant Christianity was an integral part of the creation.

Similarly, with Native North American issues much to the fore and controversies over issues of land claims or sacred heritage (see Chapter 7), students need to understand the basics of both Native and mainstream Christian ideas about people and land. Again, this means studying religion—not just as sets of abstract ideas about God (or gods), but finding out what religions mean to the people who follow them. To find out the reasons for the activity of the Black Baptist church in the civil rights movement, students need to learn and understand the beliefs and values of that church.

To understand the grip that some religions in North America have on people's souls and minds, students need a grasp of how these religions relate to their local communities—who belongs to what religion. This means letting local people into the schools to explain. And these people will want to promote their religions, because some of these religions actively engage in evangelism. We can't pretend this doesn't happen.

Different types of religious education are, of course, appropriate to different ages, but in general it is best to start with the local communities and work from there. Students need to know where they are coming from, and this can only be done if we are honest about religion and can show clearly why and how it continues to matter in today's world. This means teaching the basics of appropriate religions and enabling reading and study about them in schools today. In some cases, it means establishing more advanced study, so that students can contribute better to their local communities.

To not teach religion (of any kind) promotes one idea. This idea is that secular humanism is the goal of an educated society. Secular humanism is certainly important to many people, but not to most people in North America today. We need teaching of religions—not only one, but enough to let today's students know something about how important religions are in the world today.

RELIGION SHOULD NOT BE TAUGHT IN SCHOOLS

As mentioned above, increasingly there is a call for religious instruction in the public schools. This often comes from community groups and church groups. While we support the view that community groups should have input into local decisions, including education decisions, there may be dangers in supporting this call. The dangers are those of social exclusion and of intolerance.

In Britain, where religion is taught in schools, the situation is somewhat different. England has an established church that is linked to the state through historical processes—the official head of state (the monarch) is also the head of the Church of England. And yet religious education in both England and Scotland has moved away from the idea of religious instruction in one religion into telling people something about world religions and endeavoring to promote tolerance. And still, this religious education receives a continual critique by students and educators alike.

Fairness and the Curriculum   There are at least two major problems with the first argument above. One is that, to be fair and to achieve its educational objectives, it would need to present all sides in every debate. Sometimes this could be done—but

let's think about how many religions there are in the United States or Canada in the present day.

In looking at the establishment of capitalism in the Eastern Seaboard, we can see that Protestant Christianity was a strong player. It is important to understand how and why people believed as they did. But to teach Protestant Christianity as part of this means . . . what? Teaching at what age? To understand the attachment of capitalists to Protestantism requires an in-depth study, not only of today's Protestant denominations but also of the historic environment and the conditions of work in the mills and factories of the East. Some of this is done on a descriptive and intellectual level, just as religion is now discussed in history, geography, or social studies. To go further takes time from other curriculum subjects. How much time do teachers have for this? What else should be sacrificed?

Religious Intolerance   The second major drawback with the argument above is its reliance on the local environment. There are many religions, sects, and denominations within North America today. But in many areas, one religion and even one denomination predominates, and often that one will not accept other religions' beliefs and views.

What happens if we go with the argument in the first section? In discussions of the European settlement of North America we would have—in fairness—people in the classroom promoting ideas of land, ancestors, and Native traditions, including spiritual beliefs. Parents of some children would dispute this, seeing it as counter to their own ideals. The scene is set for a disastrous confrontation—one likely to be expensive for the school district. Even if students from (for instance) fundamentalist Christian families were withdrawn from lessons, they would miss important parts of their education about historical (and not only religious) issues.

The First Amendment and the 1962 decision taken on the basis of it represent sound common sense. The founders of the United States knew how religious adherence separated people and just how contentious it might be. Events much more recently have shown that these perceptions were accurate. Religious beliefs are deeply held—not only those of people from traditional, mainstream, or fundamentalist religions, but those of people who reject the religions of their background or upbringing, emotionally as well as analytically, and those of people who are members of nontraditional or new religions, sometimes also for several generations. The school system has to stand apart from this emotion and provide a place where all children and students can step outside of religious disputes and gain access to equality of education.

Currently, in some areas of Canada, students (or their parents) can "opt in" to religious instruction; other areas are moving to a "comparative religions" perspective. In the UK, religious education is mandatory, but people are moving away from religious instruction in Christianity (because it is unfair) toward a comparative religion approach. In the United States, religious promotion and official school prayer are not allowed, though prayer by students, individually or in groups, is permitted. Nevertheless, the boundaries between what is permitted and what is not are being constantly challenged by parents' groups and community groups—many pushing for a restoration of school prayer and religious instruction.

In multicultural and multi-ethnic societies, we consider that plurality of belief and religion is a good thing. But teaching these religions in schools is not useful or profitable for a society.

Summing Up

The two views presented here are important to many people. Note that we have not proposed that only one religion be taught—not even where only one community group is calling for the teaching of religion. The authors have considerable sympathy with the first view. The second is more practical, given the contentious nature of religious belief among much of the North American population (and elsewhere) today. Can there be a third way, here?

Religion does matter, and it is very difficult to understand history and society without knowledge of the beliefs of that society at any given time. The most crucial need in our societies today, worldwide, is arguably that for tolerance of difference in religion and belief. This is what we need to

teach—and a view that is only intellectual doesn't do it. But, for all the reasons given, it is impractical (and potentially expensive) to teach religions directly. It is also very difficult to do—and choices have to be made and justified. Teaching one religion within the public school system in any area of North America today seems very problematic.

The example from Britain is instructive. Schools there are attempting to move from a situation of teaching Christianity (usually Protestant or Church of England) to a situation of teaching *religions*. Textbooks therefore may present ideas about "Looking for God" (the name of one actual textbook). But these still adopt what is essentially a Protestant Christian approach to other religions—not all of which have one God. Some teachers are trying to move away from this and to let several religions, of the present-day, history, or prehistory, speak for themselves. But this is hard to do. One obvious alternative is to invite speakers into the classroom. Does this become "promotion" of religion? And what about religions of the past? But, can or should this happen in an American context?

In the British situation, where religious education is expected, individual schools can opt out from the mainstream curriculum if they can demonstrate through a formal application that this makes sense. In one example, a school in a predominantly Muslim area made an application for exemption. The panels that consider exemptions are, in England, one-third Church of England representatives, with the remainder people who have been nominated by a variety of community groups or come forward in the public interest, giving their time as community volunteers. In this case, a small error in the application meant it could easily have been rejected.

The idea that schools should have a (Christian) assembly and religious instruction is what sociologists term *hegemonic*. In the midst of debate and voting, the Jewish representative leaned over to the Pagan representative and commented, "This is why I'm here—to make sure every one of these applications gets through." For these minority religious members, breaking the hegemonic control was important, to let diverse and competing religious traditions have their say about creating something that, in the end, everybody thought was sensible.

Anything that denies a wider community feeling and promotes one religious tradition is not acceptable. But is it possible to develop a comparative religion perspective that allows some debate and gives some students a chance of realizing why religions are so important, without proselytizing or infringing the rights of others? This is the thorny problem that American education is facing. Many students and their parents have been involved, in recent years, with challenges to existing legislation. In such issues as students not being able to bring Bibles or the Book of Mormon into class, specific groups are attempting to redefine boundaries of religion and education. Most of these cases are eventually thrown out by the courts, but they indicate that the situation as it exists is problematic. Communities have different needs—but all communities within North America or Western Europe have a crucial need to include the teaching of tolerance as part of the education of their children.

We think that, on balance, the emphasis of current American policy on an education based in secular humanism is a good one. But there is also a need for more detailed accounts in order to understand the direction and emotionality of history. Detailed examples are good. Yet our educators cannot give examples from all religions. They therefore have to make choices, and educational theory must decide which choices predominate—and these might differ in different areas. But an education that ignores religion ignores too much of human cultural meaning to deal responsibly with today's students, just as an education that gives only an indoctrination into one viewpoint denies fairness and balance to these same students.

How we decide the balance of religious education is a political and pedagogic decision. Given the need for understanding and tolerance between religions of today—whether different Christian denominations or divisions within Islam, Judaism, Paganism, Sikhism, Hinduism, or many others—an education in religion is necessary. But religion has many faces, and it's increasingly necessary that all our children learn about more than one of these.

REVIEW EXERCISES

For Discussion and Debate

1. "Religion has no place in schools today."
2. "Should religious schools be funded by state vouchers—yes or no?"
3. "Does current legislation enable students' religious expression?"
4. "Should the creationism versus evolution debate even matter in today's world?"

Writing Exercises

Write a brief (500-word) essay on one of the following topics:

1. Religious tolerance and how it can be promoted.
2. "My own experience of religion and school."
3. "What religions I'd like to have known more about in school."
4. "How a comparative religions approach would work (or not work) in the school I attended."

Research Activities

1. Interview six of your friends on what they learned about religion in the school system, and present your findings in your discussion group.
2. Interview six people of the same generation as your parents. How do they regard religion in schools? Find their major arguments for and against.

3. Investigate court cases about religious education since 2000. (Use the Internet to do this.) Which groups have brought these? Are they from one religion or denomination? If not, is there a pattern? (Draw on your knowledge of minorities and their feeling of connection to the wider society.)

4. What were your ideas about religion when you were aged 10? Aged 15? And now? How have these changed? How has education (from any source) been a factor?

SELECTED REFERENCES

ACLU press release. 2004. "ACLU Applauds Appeals Court Decision Striking Down Florida School Voucher Program." Available online at http://www.aclu.org/ReligiousLiberty/ReligiousLiberty.cfm?ID=17032&c=140.

Banks, Adelle M. 2000. Religion News Service. *The PEW Forum on Religion and Public Life.* Available online at http://pewforum.org/news/display.php?NewsID=2000.

Black, Susan. 2003. "Teaching About Religion: Where Schools Sometimes Go Wrong Is Ignoring That Little Word 'About.'" *American School Board* 190, 4. Available online at http://www.asbj.com/2003/04/0403research.html.

ECS. 2000. "Religion in Schools." Education Commission of the States. Available online at http://www.ecs.org/clearinghouse/17/13/1713.htm.

Freedom Forum. "A Parents' Guide to Religion in the Public Schools." (n.d.) Available online at http://www.freedomforum.org/publications/first/religioninpublicschools/parentsguidereligion.pdf.

Gilbert, W. A. "Religious Education in the Public Schools: Are Ontario Students Being Shortchanged?" *Ontario Education* (May–June): 10.

"Guidance on Constitutionally Protected Prayer in Public Elementary and Secondary Schools." 2003. Available online at http://www.ed.gov/print/policy/gen/guid/religionandschools/prayer_guidance.html. February 7, 2003.

Lebuis, Pierre. 1996. "Religion in School: An Example of Ambiguous Relations between Churches and the State." *Nouvelles Pratiques Sociales* 9, 1:59–77.

Loconte, Joe. 1996. "One Nation Under God: Making Public Schools Safe for Religion." *Policy Review* 78 (July–Aug.). Available online at http://www.policyreview.org/jul96/1nation.html.

Ministry of Education and Training. 1993. "Ontario, the Common Curriculum, Grades 1–9." Toronto: Ministry of Education and Training, Ontario.

Sorenson, Gail. 1996. "Religion and American Public Education: Conservative Religious Agendas and the U.S. Constitution." *Education and Urban Society* 28, 3:293–307.

11.3   Why Not Stay Home to Learn?

The issue: Widespread dissatisfaction with the public school system and, perhaps, with professional educators as a whole. Some parents feel that they can do a better job of teaching their children than present-day schools can do. This is the impetus behind a small but growing movement to home-schooling.

Home-schooling has been increasing in the United States and Canada over the past decade. The word implies that, rather than attending a state school or registered private school and receiving their schooling there, children remain at home and receive their schooling from a parent or another relative. Many states and provinces have adopted the position that children may legally receive tuition at home as long as they are registered with the school system and as long as their curriculum of study is approved. However, there remains much hostility to home-schooling, and some home-schooling parents report difficulties in having their curricula approved.

Compulsory schooling is a development of the late nineteenth and early twentieth centuries. By 1918, every state of the United States had compulsory education laws in effect: Every child had to attend school. The rationale for compulsory schooling was to give children the skills that they would require in the workforce, and to make them good citizens. The latter was particularly emphasized in areas where immigration made for a mix of cultural values and norms. Many of the nineteenth century reformers who called for mass public education were concerned with producing an obedient workforce that would be suitably deferential to factory owners and management. Conflict theories of education have emphasized this point and it is worth remembering, in the debate that follows, that education has been used as a form of social control.

Home-schoolers often see themselves as resisting this social control. However, this works two ways. Parents say they do not want their children "brainwashed," but want them to "think for themselves." With this sentiment many people, including schoolteachers, would certainly agree. However, what if parents choose home-schooling because they do not wish their children to be exposed to ideas of multiculturalism and the equality of all peoples? Would we still say the child would be brainwashed at school?

This is a complex subject. The two statements following take fairly extreme positions. In practice, many home-schooling parents do not feel that schools are out of date, but simply that, for a variety of reasons, they wish to take responsibility, or take back responsibility, for their children's education.

Some home-schoolers favor the concept of de-schooling or unschooling, the idea that formal education, whether it takes place at school or in a home classroom, is misplaced because it regiments children and stifles their natural creative instincts and motivation. John Holt has suggested that no child should be enrolled in formal school programs below age eight. Other theorists have built on the work of Ivan Illich, who theorized an "education system" in which people would seek out teachers who could teach whatever they felt drawn to pursue at the time. Illich has since revised some of his ideas, and others have critiqued his work on the grounds that social divisions of class, race, and gender make his ideal system currently impossible. Only in a situation where all were truly equal could all take advantage of the opportunities so offered.

Here, then, are some parts of the arguments for and against home-schooling. Does home-schooling render state schools outdated, or vice versa?

"HOME-SCHOOLING" MAKES STATE SCHOOLS OUTDATED

Within North American schooling systems, an increasing number of parents are discontented with state schools, claiming they are outmoded, clumsy, slow to change, and cannot teach children the values and skills they require for life in a complex multicultural society.

Within a multicultural society, each group has its own values. State schools, by definition, must select a particular set of values to teach. This may cause conflict with many families whose culture and beliefs differ from those of the school. Some families or communities perceive the school as teaching values they do not support and neglecting areas they find important. Public schools arose initially to train children in obedience as future workers in the factories of the nineteenth century: They were to obey orders unthinkingly. Today, for many children, public schools encourage alienation and rebellion.

Home-schooling gives the opportunity for families to emphasize areas they consider important, not only in conventional subjects but in values education, and in ideas of what education should include. Some families emphasize concentration and self-discipline, others flexibility and "theme study." With home-schooling, children are not torn between the values and work habits of home and school, but can instead focus on learning.

If we turn to look at outcomes of schooling or home-schooling, the claim is often made that the education of home-schooled children is "spotty." Parents may have expertise in some areas but not in others, and few home-schooling parents have teacher training. Studies have shown that this perception is not accurate. Rakestraw states that "the Tennessee Education Department reported that home-schooled students in Grades 2, 3, 6, and 8 in that state scored higher in every major area of the Stanford Achievement Test than the statewide public school averages for the 1985–1986 school year" (1995:176). Similar findings come from New York, Washington state, and Alabama. In 2004, home-schooling advocate Brian Ray says that home-schooled students average 15 to 30 percentile points above on standardized achievement tests. There may be many reasons for this success of home-schooled students. Children who are in a relaxed home atmosphere, free from the distractions and competitive nature of school, are more able to exercise their natural inclinations to learn what is presented to them. Without the regimentation of a curriculum imposed by others, they can pursue their interests.

State schools are dependent on public funding, and many school boards are facing funding cuts. When a minority of households have children within the public system, governments see education as a target available for cutting, thus depleting the resources available to students and resulting in bigger classes, fewer field trips, and so on.

It is hard to obtain reliable figures for the numbers of students who are home-schooled. Estimates for the United States have varied from around 200,000 (in 1988) to 470,000 (in 1990). By 2003, the U.S. Department of Education said that the number had grown to more than one million home-schooled children. Home-schooling advocates suggest that it is higher, with Brian Ray of the National Home Education Research Institute estimating two million home-schooled children in 2004. Reporting requirements vary for different states, hence the uncertainty. Figures from states that require registration indicate that about 1.7 to 2 percent of children are home-schooled, though even in these states some home-schooled children are not reported. Patricia Lines points to some of the difficulties of estimating numbers, and says that by the

mid-1990s only three states had achieved anything like full registration filing. Registered home-schooled children are seen as exempt from compulsory attendance laws in 31 states. In Canada, home-schooling is legal in all provinces. In Britain, about 15,000 families have home-schooled children. All these figures are increasing rapidly (by 20 or 25 percent per year) according to home-schooling supporters. It may be worthwhile pointing out, however, that a new move to "cyber schools" or online Internet charter schools is causing some confusion. Some parents see these as similar to home-schooling, but real home-school purists do not, as the parents lose control of the educational content of online material.

Many universities will accept home-schooled students, although it remains common for home-schoolers to attend high school for two or three years, precisely to obtain qualifications to gain university admittance.

Although many parents do not have teaching qualifications, they have access to a far wider array of resources than may be available to the classroom teacher. Pre-packaged curriculums can be purchased or educational consulting sought both from departments of education and from private consultants or organizations. Programs such as "Hooked on Phonics" have been popular: Other parents purchase books on whole-language teaching and philosophies. Home-schooling parents have the advantage that they are not forced to follow one educational method or philosophy simply because it is school board policy. Instead they can shop around to find methods and curricula that best suit their child and their own values and beliefs. Home-schooling parents are not isolated, but have contact with other home-schoolers through meetings, newsletters, and the Internet, and they constitute a community in which schooling techniques and philosophies are discussed.

In an era when public schools are underfunded and unwieldy institutions, slow to change, where teachers must attempt to assist children from a wide range of backgrounds and beliefs, home-schooling provides a challenge that indicates just how outdated the state schools are.

"Home-Schooling" Does Not Make State Schools Outdated

Let us consider carefully what is being discussed here. In the preceding discussion many advantages of home-schooling are raised. However, are there also disadvantages? Even if advantages outweigh disadvantages, does this mean public schooling is truly "outdated?" Further, what advantages and disadvantages accrue to the community, rather than to individual families and their children?

Home-Schooling Is Not For Everyone Not all parents can home-school. Not all can have the time or the inclination. Even though advocates of home-schooling state that it is no problem for single parents or for full-time professional parents, realistic assessments of the time budget of parents suggest otherwise. A single parent who works a nine-to-five day, then comes home, tired, to spend time with her child—and make supper, wash clothes, and do all the other things involved in running a household—may certainly still engage in important and meaningful activities; but much of the ability is lost for engaging in the flexible and un-hurried activities mentioned by home-schooling advocates, such as woodland walks and museum visits. Two parents who are each employed full-time are in a position that is not much better. Most people who are employed (whether or not they have a partner) need the salary from their employ-ment to support themselves and their families: Work is not a luxury. Although systems of small alternative schools, with parents from different families sharing the teaching, may be possible for these parents, total home-schooling is not an option for many of them. Around one percent of school-aged children, in U.S. school districts where reg-istration is compulsory, are registered as home-schooled. While this number has been in-creasing and may well increase further with the easing of restrictions on home-schooling and greater understanding of what it is, it seems un-likely that home-schoolers could ever be a major-ity of the population if the structure of employment remains as it currently is.

School Sets the Standards Parents who home-school do so for a variety of reasons. Some feel that they can do a better job than the schools. Often these are parents with university qualifications, including teacher training. They have support from a home-schooling community, through meetings, newslet-ters, and the Internet. Often they *do* a better job if their children's test scores are compared to average scores for state schools. They feel that their chil-dren's love of learning will be stifled in the state schools. Catherine Luke describes them as "the ped-agogues" (following the definition of Jane Van Galen), people with deeply held views and philoso-phies about learning. They generally see their home-schooling as opening possibilities for their children, and encouraging freedom and, indeed, democracy.

Other parents wish their children to receive an education that emphasizes particular beliefs and values. We have seen previously that there is a con-siderable cry for teaching religion—often forms of fundamentalist Christianity. Many home-school-ing parents come from strongly religious groups; they want their own values taught, and they don't want their children exposed to values from secular humanism or indeed from other religions. They, likewise, belong to communities of parents who provide support and, often, materials. Luke terms these parents "The Ideologues."

Another group is parents whose children cannot be in school, for instance for health reasons. Some of these parents receive materials from the school, so that their children are working at the same level and pace as school students. Others use materials found by themselves or by other home-schoolers.

However, the programs of study of most of the children are approved, and the children's progress monitored, by the school board or local education authority. Many jurisdictions have rulings that if a child regularly fails to progress in schoolwork—in other words if the parents cannot demonstrate that they are doing a good job—the authority can re-quire that the child attend school.

It is hard therefore to see how the school sys-tem is outdated—when it is the school system that provides the standards against which progress is evaluated and many of the resource materials for teaching! Most home-schooling parents both rely on, and measure themselves by, the state system.

Time for Teamwork   A claim that is often made is that home-schooling leads to problems with children's *socialization,* meaning their "interaction with peers" rather than the sociological sense of learning how to function in society and become a social being. Home-schooling parents point out, quite correctly, that their children do spend time interacting with other children, including the children of other home-schoolers and school-children who engage in the same community-based pursuits and leisure activities as they do. They see as an advantage that information about living in society comes from the parents, rather than from other children, and that their children do not "run with the herd" (i.e., do not spend most of their time with the same group of peers). This argument returns to the concept of children learning values from their family.

However, children of home-schooling advocates often socialize only with other children who are very much like them. This is particularly the case for children who are home-schooled for reasons of culture or religion: They may meet with children of other home-schooling families within the cultural group, and with neighboring children who have been approved by their parents as belonging to families who share the same or similar values. How are these children to learn to get along with those who are very different from themselves, in terms of culture and belief, if they do not meet them and have no exposure to their beliefs and ideologies?

A reality of life is that as adults they will not only have to get along with others, but to work with them. Few pursuits are totally individual. Most occupations are social—people working in a team with other people. Whether the team is called an office or an orchestra, the work is conducted with other people, usually unrelated and coming from very different backgrounds. Schools, taking account of this reality, are moving more and more in the direction of group learning. Can home-schooling compete?

What Is the School's Job?   We should consider what the school system has to do, and whether this is truly the same as the home-schooling parent's job. Parents tend to evaluate the situation, educationally, in terms of advantages for their particular children. School boards and departments of education have to look to the benefit of the community and of all children. In recent years, school curricula in many jurisdictions of North America have emphasized tolerance and learning about cultures of other students and community members. Thanks to the work of community activists, teachers included, many school districts have adopted antiracist teaching. Teachers are becoming more sensitive to gender issues and cultural diversity.

Schools may be inflexible and slow to change: Many people, including some home-schooling parents, say that the rate of progress toward antiracist teaching has been slow. At the same time, much leadership on issues of social justice and civil rights is coming from within the educational community. Teachers and administrators see themselves as carrying responsibility for a whole population. They do not all agree on how this responsibility is to be handled, and schools vary, one from another, in their methods and their philosophies. But in state-run schools, children are likely to come across a sampling of the diversity of North American culture.

Certainly the values of home and school, or of home and some groups within the school, may conflict, but this gives children a sense of how society is constituted and the social problems they will face. Not much is gained by protecting children, particularly older children, from the realities of society. But much is gained by letting them meet to debate these problems and their solutions, and schools, by their nature, are much better positioned to facilitate this than are those parents who choose to school from the home base.

No, schools are not outdated. Instead, some home-schoolers may have a view of society—and of schools—that is long behind the times.

SUMMING UP

Why not stay home to learn? The idea makes a lot of sense; but we think schools still have a part to play in people's education. Schools are not rendered out of date by home-schooling, but the opposition between state schools and home-schoolers that is frequently expressed by each side calling down the other, as is to some extent found in the discussion above, is hardly productive. Many parents choose to home-school because of deficiencies they see within the school system, or simply because they find pleasure and fulfillment in teaching their children. This is their right, but by exercising it they deprive the school system, and other children, of their expertise, knowledge, and critical thinking.

Parents who cannot send their child to school (for instance because of environmental illness), as well as those for whom home-schooling is a first choice, may find themselves regarded with great suspicion by school authorities and by parents of neighboring schoolchildren. They report being treated as if they are enemies of the school.

Rather than an opposition between home and school, many educators and parents would like to see the development of partnerships. Yes, schools can be inflexible, slow to take up new ideas and methods: Home-schoolers who try out such methods can share with the schools the knowledge and expertise they gain. Yes, schools are places where students can share knowledge, skills, culture, and ideas: So is it possible for home-schooled children to have some access to the schools, to be able to take part in the orchestras and jazz bands, the multicultural evenings, the sports teams, the debates or model parliaments? All in all, is it possible, given partnerships between home and school, to broaden the range of what education is?

Catherine Luke points out that, while home-schooling is by definition outside the state education system, "it is important not to dismiss it as irrelevant to discussions of schools and school reform." Rather, she says, "Home-schooling clearly represents a challenge that reaches beyond debate about curriculum, methods, and objectives to question the very structure of the system."

So, how can today's educators learn to address the critiques of the home-schooling movement, while not forgetting that the children of home-schoolers will join with those educated in the schools as the next generation of workers, thinkers, and policy makers in our society? This is the real challenge posed by the home-schooling movement.

REVIEW EXERCISES

For Discussion and Debate

1. "Teachers are the best people to educate children; parents are too biased."
2. "Values are best learned in the home."
3. "Home-schooled students are isolated from the real world."
4. "Parents should have the right to choose any education they want for their kids."

Writing Exercises

Write a brief (500-word) essay on one of the following topics:

1. Unschooling (also known as deschooling).
2. How values can be taught in the classroom.
3. "The education I would choose for my children."
4. "How I would have benefited (or how I did benefit) from home-schooling."

Research Activities

1. Devise a questionnaire on types of school attended and preferred: state school, private school, boarding school, home-school. Include questions on strengths and weaknesses of each type. Administer this to a sample of 15–20 college students and tabulate your results. What is the range

of diversity in your sample, and what have you learned about attitudes to different types of schooling?

2. Work with a group of four to six other students to draw up a plan for values education within public schools. How do you determine whose values are to be taught? What problems would you foresee in the implementation of such a plan?

3. Conduct an Internet search for home-schooling pages. What arguments are expressed on these pages? Note the religious or other group membership of the proponents, and investigate how the rationale for home-schooling links with group membership.

4. Locate at least one person who either has home-schooled their children or plans to do so. Conduct an extended interview, giving the person the opportunity to state his or her reasons.

SELECTED REFERENCES

Adams, David S. 1994/5. "Home Schooling in Kansas: Friend or Foe." *Children's Legal Rights Journal* 15 (Winter/Spring): 11–21.

Arons, Stephen. 1983. *Compelling Belief: The Culture of American Schooling.* Amherst, MA: University of Massachusetts Press.

Basham, Patrick. 2001. "Home Schooling: From the Extreme to the Mainstream." *Public Policy Sources* 51. Vancouver: Fraser Institute.

Bates, Vernon L. 1991. "Lobbying for the Lord: The New Christian Right Home-Schooling Movement and Grassroots Lobbying." *Review of Religious Research* 33, 1 (Sept.): 3–17.

Beck, Clive. 1990. *Better Schools: A Values Perspective.* New York: Falmer.

Buckman, Peter, ed. 1973. *Education without Schools.* London: Souvenir Press.

Clark, Barbara. 1983. *Growing Up Gifted: Developing the Potential of Children at Home and at School.* 2d ed. Columbus, OH: Merrill.

Cloud, John and Jodie Morse. 2001. "Home Sweet School." *Time* (Aug. 27): 41–48.

Datcher-Loury, Linda. 1988. "Effects of Mother's Home Time on Children's Schooling." *The Review of Economics and Statistics* 70 (Aug.): 367–373.

Dougherty, Kevin J. 1996. "Opportunity to Learn Standards: A Sociological Critique." *Sociology of Education* (special issue): 40–65.

Finn, Chester E. 1996. "Can the Schools Be Saved?" *Commentary* 102 (Sept.): 41–45.

Grolnick, Wendy S. 1994. "Parents' Involvement in Children's Schooling: A Multidimensional Conceptualization and Motivational Model." *Child Development* 65 (Feb.): 237–252.

Holt, John Caldwell. 1989. *How Children Learn,* rev. ed. New York: Delta/Seymour Lawrence.

———. 1981. *Teach Your Own: A Hopeful Path For Education.* New York: Delta/Seymour Lawrence.

Illich, Ivan. 1971. *Deschooling Society.* New York: Harper & Row.

Kinch, Holly. 1995. "A Day in a Home School." *The American Enterprise* 6 (Nov.–Dec.): 82–83.

Klicka, Christopher J. 1998. *Home Schooling in the United States: A Legal Analysis.* Purcellville, VA: Home School Legal Defense Association.

Lines, Patricia. 2000. "Homeschooling Comes of Age." *The Public Interest* 140 (Summer): 74–85.

———. 1999. "Homeschoolers: Estimating Numbers and Growth." *National Institute on Student Achievement, Curriculum, and Assessment.* Office of Educational Research and Improvement, U.S. Department of Education. Web edition available online at http://www.ed.gov/offices/OERI/SAI/homeschool/index.html.

Luke, Catherine. 2003. "Home Schooling: Learning from Dissent." *Canadian Journal of Educational Administration and Policy* 25, April 3. Available online at http://www.umanitoba.ca/publications/cjeap/issuesOnline.html.

McGraw, Jennifer. 1993. "An Exploratory Study of Homeschooling in Kansas." *Psychological Reports* 73 (Aug.): 79–82.

Pitman, Mary-Anne. 1987. "Compulsory Education and Home-Schooling: Truancy or Prophecy?" *Education and Urban Society* 19, 3:280–289.

Rakestraw, Jennie and Donald A. Rakestraw. 1995. "Home Schooling: A Question of Quality, an Issue of Rights." In *Social Problems,* edited by Frank R. Scarpitti and F. Kurt Cylke, Jr. Los Angeles: Roxbury.

Scanlon, M. and D. Buckingham. 2004. "Home Learning and the Educational Marketplace." *Oxford Review of Education* 30, 2:287–303.

Schumm, Walter R. 1994. "Homeschooling in Kansas: A Further Exploratory Study." *Psychological Reports* 74, 1 (June): 923–926.

Smock, Sue Marx. 1995. "Assessing Parents' Involvement in Their Children's Schooling." *Journal of Urban Affairs* 17, 4:395–411.

Stevens, Mitchell. 2001. *Kingdom of Children: Culture and Controversy in the Homeschooling Movement.* Princeton, NJ: Princeton University Press.

Van Galen, Jane A. 1987. "Explaining Home Education: Parents' Authority of Their Decisions to Teach Their Own Children." *The Urban Review* 19:161–177.

———. 1991. *Home Schooling: Political, Historical, and Pedagogical Perspectives.* Norwood, NJ: Ablex Pub.

———. 1988. "Ideology, Curriculum, and Pedagogy in Home Education." *Education and Urban Society* 21, 1:52–68.

Whitehead, John W. and Alexis Irene Crowe. 1993. *Home Education: Rights and Reasons.* Crossway Books.

Williamson, Kerri Bennett. 1989. *Home Schooling: Answering Questions.* Springfield, IL: C. C. Thomas.

CHAPTER 12

POLITICS AND THE STATE

Politics is any activity in which people and groups struggle for control over resources, such as wealth, status, and power. Schools, businesses, and even families are governed by politics and, within these institutions, people vie for control. One of sociology's goals is to reveal the hidden politics of everyday life and develop political theories that apply to all social institutions.

But among social units the state has a special part to play, for it always monitors and attempts to control the ways groups compete. The *state* is that set of public organizations that makes and enforces decisions that are binding upon every member of a society. It includes the elected government, civil service, courts, police, and military. The right to use violence puts muscle behind these state decisions, and only a member of the police or military has the legitimate right to use violence without fear of punishment. In many societies, politics converts the struggle for state power into a competition for electoral votes. Both the need to gain electoral popularity, and constitutional rules, limit the state's use of raw force.

In this chapter we consider several of the many issues that are connected to politics and the state. The first section asks whether a global economy destroys national societies and largely eliminates the need for national governments. The second section considers whether privatization of important social and economic functions previously carried out by the state is good for society. The third section investigates whether the media are too involved in political life.

12.1   Who Needs States When There's MTV, the Internet, and McDonalds?

The issue: Evidence exists that nations are becoming less independent and governments are giving up more of their activities to private industry, within the context of a global economy. Is this something we need to worry about? Will we all end up part of one big world society? And if so, does it really matter?

At various places in the book, we have discussed the effects of globalization. *Globalization* is the trend of increasing interdependence among the economies and societies of the world. It is the highest stage of what Durkheim, discussed earlier, viewed as the growth of organic solidarity or interdependence based on difference. Here we consider the effect of a global economy on the future of nation-states (polities or governments).

Specifically, we ask whether globalization—the creation of a world economy—reduces the importance of nation-states—national societies and cultures. In effect, does it destroy them?

The global economy is a form of world social organization with six defining features. First, as noted, there is global economic interdependence. This means that most societies trade goods and services with one another: People are all buyers and sellers in a single world market. The availability and price of goods and services are determined simultaneously in hundreds of countries. Second, in the global economy a driving force for change is scientific and technological innovation. New methods for producing goods and services develop continuously. New technologies—such as computerized information storage, computer-assisted design, and telecommunication—spread rapidly to all parts of the world.

Third, the key actors in a global economy are "constructed" or corporate entities—especially multinational corporations (e.g., General Motors, Wal-Mart, Mitsubishi, and Exxon). Individuals, small local firms, and even nationwide businesses lose out in the competition for international markets. They usually lack the capital and marketing network to compete effectively. In the end, multinational companies provide a growing fraction of all products and services in the world.

Fourth, in the global economy, cultures and polities are *polycentric*. That is, they are located in and influenced by activities in many nations. More and more cultures today are everywhere, with centers of activity throughout the world. Fifth, an evolving *world culture* homogenizes human aspirations, narrowing the variety of desires and lifestyles. More and more Europeans think and act like the French, English, and Germans—the dominant actors in the European Union.

Sixth, and most relevant to this debate, economic globalization forces nation-states to change. With less influence over the culture and economy, governments have less influence over the people they rule. What, if any, *is* to be the new role of nation-states in a global age? Does globalization entirely do away with the need for nation-states and national societies? Can we expect that by the end of the next century nations will no longer exist?

GLOBALIZATION DESTROYS NATION-STATES

Three arguments support the view that economic globalization destroys nation-states and national societies. First, the presence of global organizations and corporations has eroded sovereignty and increased inequality. Second, as we have noted, a global economy weakens the independence of national economies. Third, it weakens the distinctiveness of national cultures. Finally, when transnational organizations prevail, there is little role for national governments to play.

Globalization Erodes Sovereignty and Increases Inequality Evidence shows that globalization undermines the sovereignty of nations and increases the level of global inequality. At times of numerous trade organizations and transnational corporations, it has become difficult for governments to defend themselves. The right of national self-determination first established at Westphalia (1648) is at risk. The notion is that every nation has a responsibility to its people and that other nations are to respect the internal affairs of others. We erode sovereignty and national self-determination when TNCs and various other trade organizations are able to disrupt government affairs. If the presence and influence of global organizations continues to rise, then the power that nations have over internal affairs will be weakened further.

Moreover, globalization promotes inequality. Globalization's crowning achievement, according to some, is the polarization of the world. Since the 1960s, the gap between the wealthy and poor has doubled. This polarization is connected to the imperialist tendencies of the system. Leading these imperialistic urges is the United States, which has engaged in an almost constant series of wars to promote the tenets of globalization.

At one end, globalization is supposed to promote the free movement of capital, ideas, and people, yet at the same time migration controls are more stringent than they have ever been. Just by flipping through history books, we see how the nineteenth century had greater international migration than present today. For example, millions of Irish came to the United States during the potato famine, yet today people in similar situations are prevented from doing so.

Though the flow of capital between nations and corporations is historically at its highest levels, flows as a percentage of GDP are not historically at their highest levels. Flows as a percentage of GDP were considerably higher in the early 1900s. This points to the fact that globalization doesn't even increase the trade between nations, as it is supposed to do.

Globalization Weakens Economic Autonomy

The key actors in a global economy are multinational corporations. Currently, multinational corporations control half of the world's total economic production. This fraction will continue to increase as more companies "go international" and destroy smaller local competitors with their huge size and competitiveness.

The political significance of multinationals cannot be overstated. Some have budgets larger than most countries. They gather and spend huge amounts of money, create and eliminate huge numbers of jobs. As a result, multinationals are important members of every economic community, yet they are loyal to none. They move their operations wherever they can increase their profits, whatever the consequence for countries in which they do business.

Corporations are also considered persons in the eyes of the courts, legal entities distinct from both those who incorporated it and those who operate it. This system is intended to protect and entice investors—in the event that such a business is sued, for example, laws are in place to protect its owners, managers, and officers from personal liability—but it also accords the corporation a potentially dangerous amount of power. For instance, an incorporated multinational can sue a government—any government—over what it considers to be unfair or unconstitutional laws that impede or limit its profit margin, even if those laws are meant to protect the country's workers, consumers, or national interests.

Because of their capital and control of jobs, multinationals exercise a great deal of political influence. Though never elected to office, they influence national politics by supporting some political candidates against others, or by threatening to take away jobs or investment if a government fails to enact favorable policies. In some cases, simple bribery is enough to gain the desired political results. Poor nations are the most vulnerable to these influences. However, no nation can ignore them: The stakes are too high.

The growth of a global economy in the last two decades has coincided with governments playing a smaller role in the economy. Oftentimes this includes the deregulation of government industries and services such as airlines or healthcare. Through most of the world, governments have deregulated business, reduced taxes, and weakened their labor and occupational health and safety laws. By doing so, they have hoped to persuade multinationals to open up shop and bring in jobs. Thus, nation-states have willingly reduced the scope of government, largely putting themselves out of business.

Globalization Weakens Local Cultures

Like other goods and services in a global economy, culture is traded on the world market. Sooner or later, the cultural products of any society—their music, art, literature, philosophy, foods, and folkways—are available for consumption in every society.

It is important to point out that there is no such thing as a global culture. Experiences from one continent, nation, or city vary so drastically that few people have many common memories. We would be hard-pressed to find a "global" way of thinking or to get everyone to understand his or her "global" history. As such, it is difficult to speak of globalization as a feasible system, since it is faulty to assume that people want to take part in this "global culture," which cannot exist without a common history or memory. Instead, some cultures are exported, as we see in the American case.

As major consumers, Americans enjoy easy access to this cultural smorgasbord: Latin American music, South Asian food, Western European art, and Pacific Rim hardware, for example. But despite their cultural imports, Americans are *net exporters* of culture. The worldwide cultural trade is largely one-sided and one-dimensional "Disneyfication." Most cultural products that travel come from the West—especially the United States.

Mass media are a prime example. The world gobbles up American movies, pop music, and television programs. No sector of the U.S. economy has succeeded in exporting their product worldwide as well as the entertainment industry. This fact supports Daniel Bell's claim that as manufacturing jobs leave America in search of cheaper workers, information-based industries (like entertainment) provide new jobs in the job market.

Some have criticized the export of American culture as a form of cultural imperialism. American media convey a worldview that is nontraditional, secular, competitive, individualistic, and focused on material consumption. In many societies, Hollywood's implied support for capitalism and "the American Dream" promotes non traditional lifestyles. The individualist ethic in American media undermines group loyalties at the level of family, community, tribe, and nation.

Critics lament this spread of American monoculture into the rest of the world. Examples abound of small communities in countries like France and Italy banding together—sometimes successfully, sometimes not—to protest and prevent the opening of a McDonald's or Starbucks in their villages and towns. The fear is that the introduction of these and other American products—which are viewed as representative of a lifestyle that promotes quantity and efficiency over quality and artisanship—will usher in the death of local traditions and practices that cannot compete with the former's "profit-above-all" mentality. "McDonaldization" lowers the overall quality of life with an increase in standardization. Places like McDonalds create a "cult of efficiency," where people become programmed into accepting lower standards of either food (McDonalds) or coffee (Starbucks) or clothing (GAP). The search for maximum efficiency has influenced all aspects of our social culture through an extreme emphasis on efficiency, control, and predictability. The nation-state plays little role in creating or preserving these worldwide cultural shifts. It can hardly withstand them.

Transnational Organizations Prevail   As governments put themselves out of business chasing multinational dollars, and American media erode people's loyalty to their national cultures, civil society—the network of voluntary associations and small-scale local activities—also breaks down.

Countries that have experienced war or authoritarian rule have little civil society to start with. Families, communities, churches, unions, and local service associations are already weak. Globalization

is just the straw that breaks the camel's back. In other countries, globalization weakens a healthy civic culture. Local organizations are no more able to compete with transnational ones, than local businesses with multinationals.

As we have noted, globalization increases the number and influence of transnational organizations. First in importance among these are multinational businesses. Other important transnationals are quasi-governmental, like the European Union, NATO, NAFTA, SEATO, the United Nations, or the World Bank. Others still, like the Red Cross and Amnesty International, are nongovernmental organizations, or even social or religious movements, like Islamic fundamentalism.

All of these organizations satisfy an important need. Many local and national problems are international in their scope and origin. International cooperation is needed to deal with global issues like pollution, genocide, the flow of refugees, the spread of disease, traffic in human beings, and sales of drugs and nuclear weapons (among other items).

Many transnationals—in particular, peace movements, human rights organizations (like Amnesty International), and environmental organizations (like Greenpeace)—reflect a new global outlook. Many new social movements are concerned with worldwide issues like peace, equality, and environmental protection. In time, these movements and organizations may take the place of local organizations and become the roots of a new global civil society.

However, there are arguments on the other side.

GLOBALIZATION DOES NOT DESTROY NATION-STATES

Opposing arguments make three main points: Despite globalization, nation-states are still important, national cultures are alive and well, and signs of change point to a hybridization, not replacement, of national societies.

Nation-States Are Still Important   Throughout the world, governments continue to play an important role. In many countries, they play a key role in the local economy.

Japan and the Asian tigers have been the economic success story of the last thirty years. In many countries, labor, management, and government all plan for the short term, and oppose one another. In Japan, government took the lead in planning for the future. It mediated between capital and labor, and coordinated industrial investment for the best long-term results. Other newly industrial countries—especially those on the Pacific Rim, like South Korea, Singapore, and Taiwan—have followed Japan's example with similar results. Using the state to design and coordinate development pays off, especially for semi-peripheral countries with resources and room to grow economically.

Other states play an administrative role on behalf of foreign multinationals. Big businesses prefer to locate in countries that are stable and have good infrastructure: good communications and transportation, good schools and hospitals, and a peaceful population. In many developed societies, the state ensures peace, order, and good government. It controls the work force, provides welfare to the poor, and educates the middle class. In short, it makes the country attractive to investors.

And a few industrial countries (like the United States) use state power to fight—militarily and diplomatically—for the interests of favorite industries or multinationals. Operation Desert Storm, for example, was fought officially to push the Iraqi army out of Kuwait, which they had invaded illegally with oppressive military force; but many believe that the true impetus for Western coalition troop deployment was the U.S. government's concern with the stability of the global oil industry. With no compelling economic reason for their involvement, fewer U.S. troops were committed to the crises in Bosnia, Rwanda, or Somalia—where threats to democracy (and physical survival) were more pressing.

National Cultures Are Alive and Well   By now, Disney movies and rap videos have smothered the world's entertainment market like a thick fluffy blanket. And there is probably no place on earth where young people couldn't wear Levis, Nike running shoes, and Harvard sweatshirts, if they so choose.

In many parts of the world, cosmopolitanism has taken root. In the highest levels of society, people take part in and drive the world of production and consumption. Researchers have found that a cosmopolitan civil society is emerging in the world's cities. This means that people do not embrace uniformity but diversity. An American urbanite can take delight in living in an ethnic neighborhood, having a taste for Georgian wines, and in appreciating Indian art. Globalization in no way reproduces sameness and superiority of one culture over others, but instead promotes diversity.

Consumer-oriented lifestyles do not hold a meaning for everyone. In many parts of the world, people still require the sense of something in life that is deeper and bigger than a Big Mac. They resist the intrusion of a foreign culture. For example, fundamentalist Islamic groups oppose the homogenizing and secularizing tendencies of Western culture. Their actions keep local and national identities strong.

As a result, cultural differences continue throughout the world and in every area: in religion, sports, the arts, even in sociology. States play a part in stimulating local distinctiveness. It is only in English-speaking countries—where the language barrier to American cultural influence is lowest—that one finds national cultures deteriorating. There, the state must play an even larger role if local culture is to survive. Nothing will prevent the intrusion of foreign culture, nor erase its effects. But nations can play a role in moderating its influence by promoting their own indigenous cultural products.

Even more amazing than an apparently universal desire to watch American sit-coms is an equally universal desire to maintain tribal loyalties that date back thousands of years. Though consumerism is a dominant theme of the twentieth century all around the world, so is tribalism. Every year sees new atrocities committed in the name of racial, ethnic, religious, or national self-determination. This violence is merely the tip of the iceberg. While nobody is recommending civil war as an antidote to global monoculture, the fact that tribal conflicts continue to rage around the world tells us that people everywhere still have a strong commitment to local, traditional identities.

The reception of foreign cultural products is active, not passive. With regularity, new uses are found, and new meanings attributed to foreign culture.

Some believe that the survival of traditional identities and the selective use (or adaptation) of Western culture reflect a continuing need.

Hybridization Is Occurring   As states and local cultures influence the uses made of foreign cultural products, the result is a *hybrid* or cross-breed of the two cultures—something entirely new.

Despite the American media, there will probably never be a single world culture. Running against the trend to homogeneity *across* societies is a trend to heterogeneity *within* societies—a result of mass migrations and individualized lifestyles we have discussed in earlier chapters. These two opposing processes create mega-cultures that spread across geographic units.

For example, we find the Hispanic mega-culture all over the world. The version of it we see in Spain is different from, though related to, Hispanic cultures in Argentina and California. At the same time, the country of Spain contains samples of other mega-cultures. Even food trends are an area in which regional influences have combined with imported cultural goods to create a new and favorable hybrid. Take Asian fusion cuisine, all the rage on the global culinary stage in the latter 1990s. Throughout the world, Western-trained chefs were using Asian ingredients to create gourmet East-meets-West entrees that defied simple classification as Thai or Chinese food. This shows us that the boundaries of cultures and states do not necessarily coincide any more. Fewer cultures survive than in the past but, increasingly, the cultures that survive are bigger than states. In the future, the world may contain fewer than a dozen such worldwide multinational cultures but thousands of local ones.

Hybrid cultures—new mixes of local and international elements—come about through both local resistance and new forms of cooperation. The new transnational organizations are instruments for cultural cross-breeding as much as instruments for domination. Hybrid results feed back and forth, endlessly modifying the world's arts, culture, politics, and even the economy. The world's biggest hybrid culture is developing in the European Union today.

This process is also dialectical, a result of opposing currents. According to political scientist Bernard Barber, on the one hand there is a "McWorld" influence: Western cultural domination and homogenization. This brings uniformity and also cultural detachment from a nation's own history and identity. On the other hand there is a "Jihad" influence: a frustrated cultural imperialism confronted with another cultural imperialism, Euro-Americanism. Named after the Islamic "holy war against infidels," the Jihad influence is a form of exclusionism that brings conflict, even war. Neither influence—McWorld or Jihad—can prevail, because each reflects a genuine, universal desire. The continuing conflict produces new, evolving cultural forms.

SUMMING UP

Who needs countries when there's MTV, the Internet, and McDonalds? It looks like we all do, to some degree.

The evidence we have examined suggests that even these massive global enterprises do not do away with the need for, or existence of, nation-states. Nation-states continue to exist because they perform an important role, even in a global economy. States plan local economic development and provide stability for multinational investors. They protect local cultures and provide a source of identity that is sometimes ideologically close to tribal.

Yet there is no doubt that nation-states will play a smaller role in the future than they have in the past. The age of the nation-state (roughly 1750–1950) is over. In the future, the important actors in history will be either larger than states (e.g., multinational businesses, transnational organizations, and mega-cultures) or smaller than states (e.g., regional or ethnic tribes and social movements). Units larger than states command more capital and international influence, and most comfortably coexist with the other instruments of globalization, such as the Internet, the information economy, and international travel and migration.

The nation-state was a construct, a corporate entity, that served many people well at a particular time in history. (Lest we shed too many tears over the decline of nation-states, we must remember the role they played in world colonialism, imperialism, two World Wars, and the repression of minorities.) Whatever history's verdict, the nation-states we grew up in were just another stage in the movement toward global integration.

Review Exercises

For Discussion and Debate

1. In what sense is *globalization* something new? In what sense is it very old?
2. Do multinationals take the place of nation-states, or do they rely on nation-states to make them work effectively?
3. Why are transnational organizations like the Red Cross becoming more important?
4. What is the evidence that, despite globalization, national cultures still remain distinctive?

Writing Exercises

Write a brief (500-word) essay on one of the following topics:

1. "The jihad cannot prevail over McWorld, nor can McWorld hope to prevail over the jihad."
2. "Tribal identities become more important as the world becomes more impersonal."
3. "National differences were never as distinctive as people made them out to be."
4. "The West, especially the United States, will continue to teach the world how to live."

Research Activities

1. Collect information on which American movies and television programs are most popular outside the Western world. What do you learn from this about cultural change in these societies?
2. Collect information on which foreign movies and television programs are most popular in North America. What do you learn from this about culture change in North America?
3. How has the importation of Western consumer products changed everyday life in one non-Western country (you choose which one). Use published materials to compare life in that country today and thirty years ago.
4. Devise a list of things you might measure to determine whether the world powers of fifty years ago (the United States, Britain, the USSR, France, etc.) have less clout today than they did then. Measure one of these things to see how it has changed over the last fifty years.

Selected References

Alderson, Arthur S. and Jason Beckfield. 2004. "Power and Position in the World City System." *American Journal of Sociology* 109, 4:811–851.

Amin, Samir and Beatrice Wallerstein. 1994. "The Future of Global Polarization." *Review* 17, 3 (Summer): 337–347.

Arditi, Benjamin. 2004. "From Globalism to Globalization: The Politics of Resistance." *New Political Science* 26, 1:5–22.

Bartelson, Jens. 2000. "Three Concepts of Globalization." *International Sociology* 15, 2:180–196.

Boswell, Terry and Christopher Chase-Dunn. 2000. *The Spiral of Capitalism and Socialism: Toward Global Democracy.* Boulder, CO: Lynne Rienner Publishers.

Chase-Dunn, Christopher. 2002. "Globalization from Below: Toward a Collectively Rational and Democratic Global Commonwealth." *The Annals of the American Academy of Political and Social Science* 581 (May): 48–61.

Chase-Dunn, Christopher and Thomas D. Hall. 1992. "World-Systems and Modes of Production: Toward the Comparative Study of Transformations." *Humboldt Journal of Social Relations* 18, 1:81–117.

Frank, Andre Gunder and Barry K. Gills. 1992. "The Five Thousand Year World System: An Interdisciplinary Introduction." *Humboldt Journal of Social Relations* 18, 1:1–79.

Friedman, Jonathan. 1993. "Order and Disorder in Global Systems: A Sketch." *Social Research* 60, 2 (Summer): 205–234.

Fukuyama, Francis. 1992. *The End of History and the Last Man.* New York: Free Press.

Gereffi, Gary. 1989. "Development Strategies and the Global Factory." *Annals of the American Academy of Political and Social Science* 505 (Sept.): 92–104.

Gills, Barry K. 2002. "Democratizing Globalization and Globalizing Democracy." *The Annals of the American Academy of Political and Social Science* 581 (May): 158–171.

Gills, Barry K. 2000. *Globalization and the Politics of Resistance.* New York: St. Martin's Press.

Goldfrank, Walter. 1990. "Current Issues in World-Systems Theory." *Review* 13, 2 (Spring): 251–254.

Hall, Stuart. 2000. "Culture, Community, Nation." *Cultural Studies* 7, 3 (Oct.): 349–363.

Held, David. 1993. "Regulating Globalization? The Reinvention of Politics." *International Sociology* 15, 2:394–408.

Held, David and Anthony McGrew. 1993. "Globalization and the Liberal Democratic State." *Government and Opposition* 28, 2 (Spring): 261–285.

Held, David and Anthony McGrew. 2002. *Globalization/Anti-Globalization.* Oxford: Blackwell Publishers.

Holton, Robert. 2000. "Globalization's Cultural Consequences." *The Annals of the American Academy of Political and Social Science* 570 (July): 140–152.

Karnouh, Claude, Wayne Hayes and Valerie Marchal. 1991. "The End of National Culture in Eastern Europe." *Telos* 89 (Fall): 132–137.

Khondker, Habib Haque and Roland Robertson. 1998. "Discourses of Globalization: Preliminary Considerations." *International Sociology* 13, 1:25–40.

Kumar, Anand and Frank Welz. 2003. "Approaching Cultural Change in the Era of Globalisation: An Interview with T. K. Oommen." *Social Identities* 9, 1:93–115.

Magdoff, Harry. 2003. *Imperialism Without Colonies.* New York: Monthly Review Press.

Melossi, Dario. 1994. "Weak Leviathan and Strong Democracy, or Two Styles of Social Control." *International Journal of Contemporary Sociology* 31, 1 (Apr.): 1–15.

Morse, Elliott R. 1991. "The New Global Players: How They Compete and Collaborate." *World Development* 19, 1 (Jan.): 55–64.

Oommen, T. K. 1992. "Reconciling Pluralism and Equality: The Dilemma of 'Advanced' Societies." *International Review of Sociology* 1:141–172.

Picciotto, Sol. 1991. "The Internationalisation of the State." *Capital and Class* 43 (Spring): 43–63.

Reich, Robert. 1992. *The Work of Nations.* New York: Vintage.

Rieff, David. 1993–4. "A Global Culture?" *World Policy Journal* 10, 4 (Winter): 73–81.

Robertson, Roland. 1990. "Mapping the Global Condition: Globalization as the Central Concept." *Theory, Culture and Society* 7, 2–3 (June): 15–30.

Sklair, Leslie. 2001. *The Transnational Capitalist Class.* Oxford: Blackwell Publishers.

Smith, David A. 1993. "Technology and the Modern World-System: Some Reflections." *Science, Technology, and Human Values* 18, 2 (Spring): 186–195.

Soedjatmoko. 1990. "Toward a World Development Strategy Based on Growth, Sustainability, and Solidarity: Policy Options for the 1990s." *Technological Forecasting and Social Change* 38, 4 (Dec.): 313–322.

Strijbos, S. 2001. "Global Citizenship and the Real World of Technology." *Technology in Society* 23, 4:525–533.

Sweezy, Paul M. and Harry Magdoff. 1992. "Globalization—To What End? Part II." *Monthly Review* 43, 10 (Mar.): 1–19.

Sweezy, Paul M., Harry Magdoff and Leo Huberman. 1992. "Globalization—To What End? Part I." *Monthly Review* 43, 9 (Feb.): 1–18.

Szerszynski, Bronislaw and John Urry. 2002. "Cultures of Cosmopolitanism." *The Sociological Review* 50, 4:461–481.

Wallerstein, Immanuel. 1990. "World-Systems Analysis: The Second Phase." *Review* 13, 2 (Spring): 287–293.

12.2   Does It Really Matter Who Runs the Jails?

The issue: As we noted earlier, governments are reducing their role in society, leaving more to the marketplace and private initiative. Is this a change for the better, heralding a more efficient use of society's resources? Or is it simply a way of turning our backs on society's most vulnerable members? And does private industry really do a better job?

Economic globalization reduces the role of governments in national and international affairs. More and more governments reduce their activities, giving some up entirely, in hopes of reducing public spending. Their goal is to lower taxes and attract jobs. One way to do this is through *privatization*, placing state activities into private hands.

Many services provided by the state today were once provided by private businesses. In some countries, even national defense, which we think of as a task that must belong to the state, was once provided by mercenary forces. Yet, in many countries in the last few years, functions customarily performed by the state have been taken over by the private sector—even in the United States, where public control has never developed as highly as in many European countries or in Canada, for example.

Responsibilities vary from one state to another, so what gets privatized varies from one state to another and one country to another. In formerly communist societies like Hungary and East Germany, heavy industry, transportation, communication, and energy production, once public, may be privatized. In social democratic societies like Sweden and New Zealand, health care, education, public housing, and public broadcasting may be privatized. In capitalist societies like the United States, courts and the building, maintenance, and running of prisons may be privatized. (Jails have already been privatized in some U.S. states, as in the United Kingdom.)

What are the likely consequences of privatization for the state and society?

THE STATE DOES BETTER THAN THE PRIVATE SECTOR

Education   Many argue that the state is better than the private sector at providing its citizens with good education, including college education. As proof, they note that in countries where the government subsidizes postsecondary education, no one misses out on a college education for reasons of financial need. In Germany and France, for example, all students who pass the entrance exams can attend college free. Some of the best colleges in the United States are public, state-funded schools. They are inexpensive for state residents, many of whom could not otherwise afford a higher education, and there are tuition breaks for excellent students who cannot afford a private university education.

Health Care   Many also believe that health care is better taken care of by the government. For example, per capita health care costs are lower in Canada, where health care is universal, than they are in the United States, where a near-majority of individuals have little or no health care insurance.

More people have good health when health care is in the government's hands. Then, people's health improves. Differential access to health care results in huge variations in life expectancy, infant mortality, and illness among communities with different average incomes. If all health care were left to the private sector, only people rich enough to afford quality health care would get it. The health differentials would be even greater.

The Economy   Many argue that without considerable state regulation of the economy, people would be at the mercy of a small business elite. (See the next section for more discussion of this topic.)

Competition and consumer protection are two separate public goods. Self-interested competition is vital to capitalism, and competition between self-interested sellers is supposed to yield lower prices and better products. However, over the twentieth century self-interest has led to a high degree of corporate concentration. This concentration of wealth and economic power stifles competition, leading to higher prices and inferior products. So the government must step in to protect consumers against the self-interest of others more powerful than they. For example, it must ensure safe food and medical products, and safe means of transportation (by airplane, train, bus, and automobile).

Welfare Many believe it is the government's responsibility to ensure that the needy have adequate shelter and enough food. As we saw earlier, people in most modern societies believe the government has an obligation to take care of its poor, elderly, and disabled. This is the meaning of *social citizenship*. Until recently, the state has also had the resources to ensure that people who need help receive it.

Child-Care Most parents have to work for a living. Many—though far fewer in the United States than in other countries—believe that the state has a responsibility to ensure that children are properly cared for while their mothers and fathers are at work.

Publicly funded child-care programs make it possible for parents to continue working when they have small children at home. This saves parents from having to choose between working for pay and having a family. And these programs make fiscal sense. By enabling mothers to work, they free many women from reliance on government unemployment insurance or welfare, and increase employment and national productivity rates.

Infrastructure Many argue that it is the responsibility of the government to maintain the society's infrastructure—its roads, bridges, sanitation, communications systems, garbage disposal, and so on. Without these facilities, people's health suffers and business grinds to a halt. So, even if the state does nothing else, it must maintain the infrastructure.

But must the state actually carry out these tasks, or can they be left to private business? As with the other debates we have examined in this book, there is another side to these arguments.

THE PRIVATE SECTOR DOES BETTER THAN THE STATE

Education On the other side of the debate, some point out that most states already have a dual educational structure: a public school system and a private school system.

They claim that the private system has always been better than the public system. Occasionally this is because the private schools can afford better teachers, better administrators, and more and better facilities. This difference in quality widens as fewer government funds are available for even the most basic public educational expenses. Other times, parents prefer private schools that cater to their specific beliefs or values—a religious school, say, or a school that offers instruction in a non-English language. More often the difference is due to the students: Private schools get the better students, who bring cultural capital and strong parental support for education. But this is no fault of the schools. If private educational institutions offer a more rigorous curriculum, challenging extracurricular activities, a more stimulating learning environment, innovative pedagogical techniques, and a lower student-teacher ratio than the public school system, *and* families are willing to pay to provide their children with these opportunities, then, in a liberal society like the United States, it should be their prerogative to do so.

Health Care Some—especially health insurers and professionals in the United States—argue that private health care is better than public health care. Reliable access to basic, high-quality health care is a universal human right, but it is also an extremely expensive service for a government to provide. In many scenarios involving public health care, economic priorities prohibit the state administration from earmarking the full funding necessary to maintain a reasonable level of service. Waiting times for medical consultations and procedures increase, facilities decline, and health care professionals become overworked, underpaid, and disillusioned. At best, consumers of private health care are treated faster, with newer technologies, by better-qualified doctors. At worst, consumers of public health care are treated in underfunded health centers staffed by overworked, underpaid, and less-qualified medical personnel.

Again, as with education, privatization can also be a solution to a bloated public administration system. When health care is guaranteed perpetual public funding, it can afford redundancy in its practices and a multi-leveled bureaucracy for its structure. Private health care, faced with pressure from the board of directors and stockholders, is forced to maintain top-level service as efficiently as possible. Ultimately the users benefit, since they gain access to excellent medical treatment that has been trimmed of unnecessary or wasteful expenses.

The Economy   Underlying economic liberalism is an assumption that a self-interested pursuit of gain produces the healthiest economy: the best supply of goods at the right price. Thus, open competition is the fairest, most efficient way to organize economic life.

If so, the government has no business regulating the economy. More important, it lacks the ability to do so in a way that satisfies its citizens' best interests. Attempts by communist governments to create *command economies,* which set production goals and prices, proved to be a disaster. Publicly, the most desired consumer goods are always in short supply, but a black market in these goods thrives. For the right price, people can still get anything they want. This shows that markets that supply people's wants must be consumer-driven, not government-driven.

Welfare   As we saw earlier, some people want to get rid of welfare. You will recall at least three reasons for this view: First, government no longer has the resources it requires to take proper care of its needy. Second, government aid fosters dependency among the able poor and saps their initiative to take care of themselves. Third, welfare breaks up families by eroding the sense of family responsibility and obligation. Yet, as we saw earlier, there is no evidence that people retain a "culture of dependence" once they have the chance to earn a decent income. For most, welfare is just a short-term protection and a benefit of social citizenship. The provision of jobs and job-related education gets most people off welfare right away.

Welfare is not likely to disappear from modern nation-states, and the question is who is best equipped to provide it: government or private sources? As with health care, it can be argued that bringing the profit motive into the picture will improve the system's efficiency, since it compels the administration to streamline services, eliminate waste, and ensure that their clients are satisfied.

Child-Care   Some believe that the care of children is, first and foremost, a parental responsibility. According to this view, the state is not responsible for raising children; if it took on that obligation it would be unable to fulfill it.

Further, critics argue that day-care does not give children the kind of love and attention that they need to grow into well-adjusted adults. Moreover, providing free day-care to working parents reinforces the idea that the government will take care of a family's responsibilities if the parents neglect them.

Infrastructure   Some argue that the private sector can build roads and bridges, take care of garbage disposal and so on, far more efficiently than the state. It can hire workers for less money, buy supplies more cheaply, and produce less bureaucratic red tape than governments. Rather than pay for these services out of a universal tax, such products and services should be offered on a per user basis. For example, you use the road, you pay for it; you put garbage out to be picked up, you pay for it; you ride the bus or subway, you pay for it.

THE EFFECTS OF *RAPID* PRIVATIZATION

Despite evidence that the public sector provides many services better and cheaper, privatization is proceeding rapidly in many countries. Privatization can follow either of two patterns: Call them the (faster) economic and (slower) political imperative models. What are the likely consequences for the state of faster versus slower privatization?

Privatization that follows the *economic imperative* model tries to increase economic growth as quickly as possible, whatever the political risk. The rapid privatization of key state activities quickly produces large financial benefits for a few, but lay-offs and unemployment for many others. This increases economic inequality. It also leads to widespread public dissatisfaction and pessimism about the economy. Support for the government, the free market, and liberal democracy all decline.

Governments take this path in hopes that the economy will quickly improve and begin to benefit the majority. Otherwise, the state loses its legitimacy, civil society disintegrates, and political unrest emerges.

On the other hand, a state that follows the *political imperative* model privatizes key sectors of the economy slowly and cautiously. It maintains high employment levels, even if the public debt increases and incomes rise faster than productivity. Here, income equality is unchanged and most people are optimistic about the economy. Public satisfaction is reflected in a high degree of support for the government, the free market, and liberal democracy. However, economic growth is slow.

Governments take this path in hopes that the economy will start to grow before inflation and indebtedness cause a crash. Economic growth takes longer in this scenario, but meanwhile the government remains stable and popular.

For example, two formerly communist countries—Hungary and East Germany—recently began to privatize their economies. Hungary has followed the economic imperative model of rapid privatization. East Germany—now part of a unified Germany—has followed the political imperative model. (Cushioned by help from West Germany, it has been able to change at a more moderate pace.) Survey researchers sampled public opinion in both countries, asking people to evaluate the political and economic systems under communism, at the time of the survey, and (as they imagine it will be) in five years.

The results show that in both countries, people give low ratings to both the economy and the government—past, present, and future. And in both countries, people expect the government and the economy to perform better in five years. But there the similarity between countries ends.

In slow-privatizing East Germany, people have a sense they are making progress. They feel that, both politically and economically, the (capitalist) present is better than the (communist) past, and the future is more promising still. In fast-privatizing Hungary on the other hand, people glorify the (communist) past. To Hungarians, the (political and economic) past looks better than the present or future.

Often, glorification of the past is a warning sign of fascism. It indicates a willingness to look for and accept simple solutions to society's economic and political problems, even at the expense of freedom. This reminds us that faster economic change is riskier change. Unless Hungary's economy improves rapidly, Hungarians may turn their backs on liberal democracy. (This is what Germans did to the liberal Weimar Republic in 1933, when they facilitated Adolf Hitler's rise to power.)

SUMMING UP

Does it really matter who runs the jail? Yes it does, if we view jails (and other social institutions) as having goals other than profit-making. Moreover, the rate at which a society moves in the direction of privatization also matters.

The line dividing the functions under state control from those left to the private sector is drawn differently in different countries. It also varies over time in the same country. Expanding the American welfare state has meant redrawing the line, with the government assuming more responsibilities. The recent and gradual shrinkage of public spending reflects another redrawing of this line.

Evidence suggests that too rapid privatization runs a serious risk of de-stabilizing the state. The amount of risk is proportional to (1) the degree and type, and (2) the speed of privatization. Privatizing government activity in a formerly communist (or social democratic) country is riskier than in a highly privatized society like the United States. Privatizing a government activity closely tied to personal survival (e.g., food, shelter, health care, personal income) is riskier than privatizing other functions (e.g., communication, transportation). And privatizing all state activities at once is extremely risky.

The answer to the original question is: Yes, rapid privatization does weaken the state. Too rapid or too extreme change in one part leads to unpredictable, even violent reactions in other parts. Given the already distressing effects of globalization, too rapid privatization may spell the end for some nation-states. Like the plunge into a cold mountain stream, what is bracing for some is fatal for others.

REVIEW EXERCISES

For Discussion and Debate

1. What reasons are usually given for privatizing public services, and which reasons seem most sensible to you?
2. Why is government regulation of the economy thought likely to have negative effects?
3. Why do some expect health care to improve if it is less regulated by the government?
4. In what respects is fast privatization likely to be better than slow privatization? In what respects is the opposite likely to be true?

Writing Exercises

Write a brief (500-word) essay on one of the following topics:

1. "We learn little about privatization in capitalist countries by studying privatization in formerly communist countries."
2. "Public education is bound to be better than private education, providing the same amount is spent on each student in each case."
3. "Private prisons are even less likely than public prisons to rehabilitate criminals."
4. "Putting welfare in private corporate hands is like asking a wolf to watch the sheep."

Research Activities

1. Collect data from your own country and any Scandinavian country, and compare the degree of privatization in one of the social or health services discussed here.
2. Collect measures of *outcome quality* (e.g., quality of education, quality of health) from your own country and from another country where social or health services are less privatized. What difference do you find?
3. Devise a brief questionnaire to measure public support for public provision of a social or health service that is currently private. Administer this questionnaire to six people and tabulate the results. What kinds of people are most supportive of the change?
4. Do some reading on the former communist countries to learn why they have started to privatize what were once public services.

SELECTED REFERENCES

Aulette, Judy. 1991. "The Privatization of Housing in a Declining Economy: The Case of Stepping Stone Housing." *Journal of Sociology and Social Welfare* 18, 1 (Mar.): 151–164.

Blomqvist, Paula. 2004. "The Choice Revolution: Privatization of Swedish Welfare Services in the 1990s." *Social Policy and Administration* 38, 2 (Apr.): 139–155.

Brotman, Andrew. 1992. "Privatization of Mental Health Services: The Massachusetts Experiment." *Journal of Health Politics, Policy and Law* 17, 3 (Fall): 541–551.

Cremers, Jan. 2004. "The Iron Law of Privatization: Labor Relations in Central and Eastern Europe after the Collapse of the Centrally Planned Economy." *Tijdschrift voor Arbeid en Participatie* 25, 3–4 (Jan.): 207–219.

Estes, Caroll and James H. Swan. 1994. "Privatization, System Membership, and Access to Home Health Care for the Elderly." *Milbank Quarterly* 72, 2 (June): 277–298.

Fairbrother, Peter. 1994. "Privatisation and Local Trade Unionism." *Work, Employment and Society* 8, 3 (Sept.): 339–356.

Fleury-Steiner, Benjamin and Kristian Wiles. 2003. "The Use of Commercial Advertisements on Public Police Cars in the United States, Post-9/11." *Policing & Society* 13, 4 (Dec.): 441–450.

Hogan, Richard Glen. 2004. "Private Prisons: An Evaluation of Cost and Quality." *Dissertation Abstracts International, A: The Humanities and Social Sciences* 64, 10 (Apr.): 3851–A.

Jurik, Nancy C. 2004. "Imagining Justice: Challenging the Privatization of Public Life." *Social Problems* 51, 1 (Feb.): 1–15.

Kalyvas, Stathis N. 1994. "Hegemony Breakdown: The Collapse of Nationalization in Britain and France." *Politics and Society* 22, 3 (Sept.): 316–348.

Lehmann, Susan Goodrich. 1995. "Costs and Opportunities of Marketization: An Analysis of Russian Employment and Unemployment." *Research in the Sociology of Work* 5:205–233.

Lilly, J. Robert and Paul Knepper. 1992. "An International Perspective on the Privatisation of Corrections." *Howard Journal of Criminal Justice* 31, 3 (Aug.): 174–191.

Marwell, Nicole P. 2004. "Privatizing the Welfare State: Nonprofit Community-Based Organizations as Political Actors." *American Sociological Review* 69, 2 (Apr.): 265–291.

McDonald, Douglas C. 1994. "Public Imprisonment by Private Means: The Re-Emergence of Private Prisons and Jails in the United States, United Kingdom, and Australia." *British Journal of Criminology* 34, 1 (special issue): 29–48.

McIntosh, Christopher. 1994. "To Market, to Market: Navigating the Road to Privatization." *Futurist* 28, 1 (Jan.–Feb.): 24–28.

Nelson, Joel I. 1992. "Social Welfare and the Market Economy." *Social Science Quarterly* 73, 4 (Dec.): 815–828.

Odle, Maurice. 1993. "Toward a Stages Theory Approach to Privatization." *Public Administration and Development* 13, 1 (Feb.): 17–35.

O'Looney, John. 1993. "Privatization and Service Integration: Organizational Models for Service Delivery." *Social Service Review* 67, 4 (Dec.): 501–534.

Pedersen, Axel West. 2004. "The Privatization of Retirement Income? Variation and Trends in the Income Packages of Old Age Pensioners." *Journal of European Social Policy* 14, 1 (Feb.): 5–23.

Pickvance, C. G. 1994. "Housing Privatization and Housing Protest in the Transition from State Socialism: A Comparative Study of Budapest and Moscow." *International Journal of Urban and Regional Research* 18, 3:433–450.

Prager, Jonas. 1992. "Is Privatization a Panacea for LDCs? Market Failure versus Public Sector Failure." *Journal of Developing Areas* 26, 3 (Apr.): 301–322.

Relman, Arnold S. 1993. "What Market Values Are Doing to Medicine." *National Forum* 73, 3 (Summer): 17–21.

Ryan, Mick. 1993. "Evaluating and Responding to Private Prisons in the United Kingdom." *International Journal of the Sociology of Law* 21, 4 (Dec.): 319–333.

Smith, Steven Rathgeb and Michael Lipsky. 1992. "Privatization in Health and Human Services: A Critique." *Journal of Health Politics, Policy and Law* 17, 2 (Summer): 233–253.

South, Nigel. 1994. "Privatizing Policing in the European Market: Some Issues for Theory, Policy, and Research." *European Sociological Review* 10, 3 (Dec.): 219–233.

Taylor-Gooby, Peter. 2004. "Open Markets and Welfare Values: Welfare Values, Inequality and Social Change in the Silver Age of the Welfare State." *European Societies* 6, 1:29–48.

Varese, Federico. 1994. "Is Sicily the Future of Russia? Private Protection and the Rise of the Russian Mafia." *Archives Europeenes de Sociologie* 35, 2:224–258.

Vogel, Joachim. 2003. "Toward a Typology of European Welfare Production: Summary and Discussion." *Social Indicators Research* 64, 3 (Dec.): 547–572.

Walter, Jorge. 2004. "The Privatization of Telecommunications and Labor Relations in Latin America." *Sociologie du Travail* 46, 1 (Jan.–Mar.): 99–110.

Wilson, Ernest J. III. 1993. "A Mesolevel Comparative Approach to Maxi and Mini Strategies of Public Enterprise Reform." *Studies in Comparative International Development* 28, 2 (Summer): 22–60.

12.3   Are the Mass Media Too Involved in Politics?

The issue: Are the media too influential in politics today? Do journalists merely report and analyze the daily happenings of Congress and the White House, or are they too often setting the agenda for the politicians themselves? What role should the mass media play in the political process?

Since the first popular radio broadcasts in the early decades of the twentieth century, the mass media have revolutionized the way we communicate political information. Political campaigns just before the introduction of the radio were characterized by "stump oratory," in which candidates addressed up to a few thousand citizens from a bandstand or makeshift podium erected in the town square. Thirty years later, when radios had become a staple of even low-income households, Franklin Delano Roosevelt could reach an audience of over 60 million in one of his famous "fireside chats."

Many today consider the news industry to be essential to the success of the political process. Democracy, after all, rests on an informed citizenry. At least in theory, better media coverage of political dealings and election campaigns, delivered directly to the citizen through mass media (and recently, the Internet) has made the citizenry better informed than ever before.

But the media actively shape their listeners as much as they objectively broadcast the news. Increasingly, we rely on the news industry to provide us not only with the facts but also with an interpretation of the facts. Some commentators have argued that our hunger for instant interpretation is a result of widespread laziness. Others blame a time-crunch that results from too many personal and social responsibilities, or claim that partisan bickering causes many to disengage from political messages that are any more complex than soundbites.

Has the growing influence of the news industry strengthened or weakened the quality of public debate? Further, what should be the media's role in relation to the state and national governments: Calm correspondent? Stubborn watchdog? Determined muckraker? And how large a part should the news industry play in setting the political agenda? Some see the media playing a central, benevolent role in political life; others see the opposite. As usual, there are at least two views about all this.

THE MASS MEDIA KEEPS THE POLITICAL PROCESS IN CHECK

The Fourth Estate   Questions about the proper role of the media go back a long time. An early commentator on this issue was Thomas Carlyle, the famed nineteenth-century British historian and essayist. In *On Heroes and Hero Worship* (1841), Carlyle describes a scene in eighteenth-century Parliament. There, he has statesman Sir Edmund Burke rising to address his fellow politicians. Calling into question their presumed dominance in the hierarchy of political power, he reminds them of the importance of what he calls the Fourth Estate. By "Fourth Estate," Burke means the documenters of parliamentary events, which have since come to refer to the news industry in all its various print, visual, audio, and electronic forms. This Fourth Estate, today, may hold the future of democracy in its hands.

Democracy depends on the existence of an informed citizenry; but this goal is hard to achieve in a large, complex society. The earliest democracy developed in Athens two thousand years ago. There, all eligible men—women and slaves were without political rights—were expected to participate in political events. Humans were deemed "political animals" whose nature it was to connect and engage with others. Accordingly, Athenians held frequent political discussions and exchanged their opinions in an open atmosphere of civility and engagement. But that was Athens, a very small city by current standards.

Today, democratic nation-states are far larger than what the ancient Greeks ever imagined. Citizens of large countries simply cannot come together to ponder every political decision. In recognition of this fact, we ask only that citizens elect political representatives, judge their performances, and vote later to reject or re-elect them. As in Athenian times, democracy still demands citizen participation, however curtailed.

But how does an Alaskan, exercising his right to be an informed U.S. citizen, stay up-to-date with the activities of his government in Washington, D.C., over three thousand miles away? The answer, as Burke suggested, is the press. Ideally, political journalists act as the bridge between the people and their elected officials, asking the questions that people want answered and ensuring that the government remains accountable. The architects of the U.S. Constitution, recognizing the importance of having an independent voice to defend the public's interests, listed first among the Bill of Rights the freedoms of speech and the press.

The Press as Watchdogs The modern press is the observer of every politician and in that sense serves as a watchdog of democracy. When every speech is "on the record" and reported across the nation during the six o'clock news, politicians can no longer make promises to one special interest group without risking the wrath of an opposed group. Gone are the days when a politician could, for instance, court the environmentalists in Washington state by vowing to reduce crude oil subsidies, and then guarantee the opposite the next day to automobile manufacturers in Detroit. Journalists hold elected officials accountable to all their constituents.

Social theorist James Mill (1773–1836) praised the freedom of the press because it "made known

the conduct of the individuals who have chosen to wield the powers of government." Politicians, despite their promises to serve the public interest, cannot be trusted to do so unsupervised once they enter office. The Watergate scandal, arguably the most famous U.S. political scandal of the twentieth century, is a prime example of both the lengths that those in power are willing to go to protect their privilege, and the importance of investigative journalism in uncovering political misconduct. Bob Woodward and Carl Bernstein, the *Washington Post* reporters whose dogged coverage of the initial incident and White House cover-up contributed to the eventual resignation of President Richard Nixon, won the 1973 Pulitzer Prize for their efforts.

Transparency is an essential part of democracy. For this reason, an adversarial relationship between reporters and politicians is desirable, though it may sometimes lead us to wonder about the objectivity of the news reporters themselves.

The Role of the Internet Recently, people have also come to rely on the Internet to provide additional sources of information, beyond what they get from the mass media. Independent Web sites run by grassroots activists are proliferating throughout the Internet, shining spotlights on both Republican and Democratic abuses of power. Trust toward the government builds on information provided by the media. Research has found that, with increasing use of the Internet as a source of political information, trust toward the government has also increased. The political insight offered by the Internet—coupled with users' increasing political knowledge and the belief that they can have an effect over the government (discussed later)—creates a feeling of security that results in greater trust toward politicians and a stronger sense of personal political efficacy.

Independent journalist organizations such as The Center for Public Integrity (www.publicintegrity. org) and watchdog Web sites such as Open Secrets.org work to ensure that information about Political Action Committees, corporate lobbyists, soft money donations, and other potentially compromising activities remain accessible to the public eye.

Cash Flow Problems   Many have expressed concerns over corporations donating large sums of money to a particular political party, arguing that such largesse is merely a form of bribery that ensures the affluent donors preferential treatment later on. At worst, elected officials from both national parties become, conspiratorially, puppets who push forward political initiatives that favor corporations and their wealthy executives at the expense of the middle and working classes.

Few politicians have wanted to take on this problem. Not only do they risk alienating colleagues and their powerful sponsors; they also risk drying up the sources of support they themselves rely on to get elected. As a result, the media have played an important role in keeping politicians honest by publicizing their sources of support and, to a limited degree, the ways in which they use their campaign funds. For example, they may relate a politician's voting pattern in Congress to the individuals and organizations that have funded his election campaign.

Mobilization of Political Participation   The availability of media information does not promote complacency and inaction, as some might imagine. On the contrary, it generates interest and activism. Media messages promote political socialization and individual learning, which increase political participation. Well-informed people are more likely to get together to share views and experiences about recent news and apply their information to the real world. Well-informed people become more engaged in politics and feel they can have an impact on the current political system if they participate. As a result, political participation increases.

Participation is particularly marked among computer-literate people. As we have said, the Internet is another popular medium for political participation, and it combines with mass media coverage of politics to empower the citizenry. Some call it an "electronic town square" that allows people to freely express their political views to one another as well as to elected officials. Research has shown that Internet users are more politically knowledgeable than the average citizen. People can also complete online surveys and polls. That provides feedback on what others think about the issues. Government

officials can use such information as constructive feedback on how they are currently performing, and to determine whether changes need to be implemented if they wish to stay in office.

Grassroots organizations and lobbyists, taking advantage of the low costs involved, use the Internet to spread their messages to the public. This enhances the transparency of political processes and reduces the harmful effects of bias in television and newspaper coverage. The public becomes more informed from these online publications.

All in all, then, it sounds like people have their best interests protected by the mass media. They can get the information they need and, with this information, can make the best political decisions. However, not everyone thinks this is the case. They believe that, in fact, the media tilt and distort our thinking while providing the appearance of unbiased and useful information.

THE MASS MEDIA MANIPULATES THE POLITICAL PROCESS

Soundbite Democracy   As we have said, the mass media today have made the news available to any and all interested consumers. However, the news as it is presented in the morning paper or evening broadcast is not just a neutral assemblage of facts. Increasingly, it is a carefully designed commercial product that promotes a particular political and cultural ideology. In short, it spreads propaganda.

In particular, the mass media help perpetuate the mainstream capitalist ideology. News stories play a role as being "messages in code about the nature of society and the nature of social process." To do this, the news is simplified and slanted. There is too little variety and complexity in the perspectives offered to provide comprehensive information about issues. For example, U.S. foreign policies are presented only from the perspective of the United States.

As this simplifying "media logic" has continued to infiltrate the practice of politics, politicians have learned out of necessity to play by the rules of the news industry. Political strategists, aware that voters respond best to messages delivered in a candidate's own words, advise their nominees to keep statements brief. Short, punchy soundbites are less likely to be edited (and twisted) than extended pronouncements about policy. Statesmen noted for their ease in front of the camera, as Ronald Reagan and Bill Clinton were, are gifted at establishing emotional connections with viewers within the strict time limitations of the prime time news—that is, able to infuse a soundbite with warmth and humor.

During the 1968 presidential election, the candidates' evening news soundbites lasted an average of 42 seconds. By 1996, the average soundbite had been slashed to 8 seconds. And in order to further speed up the pace of the program, candidates' statements are often cut altogether, replaced by terse news-anchor-delivered summaries. In 1968, the candidate's voice accompanied their image 63 percent of the time that they appeared on television. By 1988, politicians' messages were heard in their own words only 16 percent of the time.

Providing the general public with a true picture of current happenings in the political arena has become impossible for the media—true in fantasy but not in fact. In fact, news space and time are limited, forcing editors and reporters to make choices on who and what to cover. Since only the serious candidates are newsworthy, those without winning prospects are cut out from coverage or receive less attention. The opposite is also true, if the media deems a certain story or political candidate "newsworthy," they will play, and replay the soundbites *ad nauseam* to increase the validity of their story. Before you know it, you actually start believing the urgency of the story simply because you've seen it a dozen times on TV. Mentioned before is the importance of coverage to candidates in an election, especially at the beginning of the campaign.

Media Conglomerates Many commentators have expressed concern over the continuing consolidation of today's various media outlets into massive multimedia empires controlled by only a handful of increasingly powerful and influential players.

Time-Warner, for instance, is the largest media company in the world, with interests in the Internet (AOL, Netscape Communications), books (Little, Brown and Company), television (CNN, HBO, TBS, TNT, the WB), and film (Warner Bros. Studio). It also controls Time Inc., the largest magazine publisher in the world, whose 130-plus titles—including *Time, Fortune, People, Parenting,* and *Sports Illustrated*—reach a worldwide audience of over 300 million. Three of the four major television networks, the source of daily news for the majority of Americans, are run by multimedia giants: ABC is owned by the Walt Disney Company (Miramax Films, Hyperion Books); CBS, by Viacom (MTV, Paramount Studios, Insight Broadcasting); and Fox Television, by the News Corporation (*NY Post,* HarperCollins).

As most major media are owned by large business enterprises, the goal of producing revenue for shareholders' parent companies influences what gets published. The nightmare scenario of media consolidation is a news industry in which the entire flow of information passes through a single corporate filter, allowing only the expression of political views corresponding to the dominant ideology of the socioeconomic elite. Dissenting opinions and alternative voices become marginalized, reduced eventually to a decentralized network of activists unable to compete with the massive mainstream news service that, increasingly, condenses the political landscape into a two-party competition and favors punchy soundbites over in-depth coverage.

Free competition between media giants further undermines the democratic system, since commercial interests begin to trump journalistic ones. In the quest for higher profits and market shares, even venerable broadsheets have shown signs of popular tabloid-style trivialization and sensationalism in its stories, as witnessed in the salivating coverage of the Clinton-Lewinsky scandal.

The Biases of Media Coverage Most journalism today is biased in the sense that it supports one political approach over another. For example, newspapers can now be classified as either conservative, neutral, or liberal, based on content analyses of their editorials and commentaries. Biased journalism erodes the quality of political debate because it serves mostly to divide public opinion and force conservatives and liberals to their respective extremes of the political spectrum.

More subtle is *agenda-setting,* decision-making by broadcast journalists about the direction of reporting. By focusing on some issues at the expense of others, news agencies often influence what voters think *about,* if not what they think. What broadcast journalists choose to cover can affect the criteria by which politicians are judged. Views toward candidates in an election can be shaped by the media. Various issues pertaining to candidates in an election receive unequal attention from the press. Some report more on characteristics of the candidate while others focus more on policy issues. Whether positive or negative, coverage of these qualities has been shown to have influenced the views audiences have toward candidates.

The media can also set the tone in which people talk about public issues—whether civilly or not. Public talk radio, for example, has been accused of going out of bounds by tending toward uncivil, racist, homophobic, and chauvinistic tones. After the Oklahoma bombing, for example, President Clinton blamed public talk radio for creating a climate of hatred toward the federal government that could result in terrorism.

Media Provides Incomplete Coverage

Contrary to the theory of democracy, censorship is still exercised over what can be aired. Concerns about the protection of rights, national security, and cultural integrity all have a strong influence over what is and is not published. Most press coverage of the government comes from information supplied by the government itself, giving them control over what is disclosed.

The media, for all its wealth, lacks the power and willingness to exert extra energy to dig out hidden information. Usually, they wait for information to be supplied or leaked to them from insiders. Reporters may be rather passive in this sense. Instead of routinely following and checking on politicians, reporters only investigate political news events if they have been tipped off and the tip is newsworthy. Because of the commercial pressure for the news to appeal to an audience, there is

a focus on entertainment rather than reporting something of political significance.

Coverage Charges   The election process has been seen as corrupted due to the charges from the commercial media. Campaigning becomes very expensive, denying election opportunities to candidates with insufficient resources and allowing the rich, in effect, to "buy" elections. This has also forced campaign ads to be short and uninformative. As a result, messages from ads confuse viewers rather than enlighten them. Candidates are also forced to spend a significant amount of time in fundraising to meet the steep campaigning costs, time better spent attending to actual political issues.

Polling Can Subvert Democracy   The formal surveying of political opinions is not new, dating back to the time of the ancient Greeks. However, only recently has polling become present everywhere. During the nonelection years of 1973, 1975, and 1977, The *New York Times* published a total of 380 polls. During political campaigns, polling data take on much greater importance, with the number of polls reported in newspapers increasing with every successive U.S. election. Furthermore, stories about policy issues during presidential election years declined from 50 percent in 1960 to less than 20 percent in 1992, while stories focusing on the so-called horse race between candidates doubled from 40 percent to 80 percent during that same period.

As to why polling results—which are usually referred to more often by reporters than by politicians themselves—have become a central aspect of modern politics, many experts point to the replacement of live oratory in the early 1900s by impersonal radio and television broadcasts as the primary means for addressing the nation. Politicians give a televised speech; it is instantly "spun" by partisans and analyzed by journalists; and public opinion is instantly polled to determine whether the politician pushed the right buttons in his speech, or the wrong ones.

In *Numbered Voices* (1993), Susan Herbst argues that the increasing use of political polling is also a manifestation of what Max Weber termed the *formal rationalization* of society. This process can be witnessed, Weber argued, in virtually every arena of human activity, including religion, work, law, sexuality, and social norms. In a world where phenomena are most convincingly described in the form of numbers, it follows that public opinion can be extrapolated from the percentage of respondents who agree with a particular statement about a particular issue.

But polling, especially when used to emphasize the horse-race aspect of a political contest subverts the idea of democracy as a deliberative process, in which citizens weigh ideas and elect a representative whose notions of government and the just society most closely align with their own. Instead, studies have found that by devoting most of the coverage to who is leading the race, news agencies increase rates of "bandwagon-ism," where undecided voters simply cast their ballots for whomever is projected to win rather than engage in the political debate. Horse-race coverage also tends to create negative perceptions of candidates as self-interested, concerned only with gaining political power, and hypocritical in their evocations of the public good, ultimately depressing voter turn-out.

SUMMING UP

With too little public involvement, government officials lose their accountability to their constituents, creating a fertile ground for corruption and dishonesty. Long before that, democracy falters, since an uninformed electorate is powerless to protect its own public interests, and social change becomes impossible without access to the media.

We might ask critically, then, whether the "embedded reporters" assigned to specific U.S. military units during the 2003 war in Iraq represent unprecedented media access into a world usually concealed from public scrutiny, or an opportunity for military hawks and politicians to monitor and control what is reported to those watching back at home (such as not airing graphic images of coalition and civilian casualties). We might also ask whether the consolidation of the media industry constitutes a threat to the freedom of the press.

Can a news agency be considered truly independent if its management and editorial staff take their orders from an owner who is well-connected to a particular political party?

The relative dearth of independent voices on newsstands and television screens today, along with the politically slanted reporting and commentary often found in the sources that are available, may tempt one to conclude that the mass media can no longer function as an impartial instrument of the people. The intended purpose of the political press has always been to inform the electorate and facilitate social action when necessary. The press can be made to serve the public good. Ultimately, its proper role in the political arena is whatever best serves the democratic process.

REVIEW EXERCISES

For Discussion and Debate

1. Media are no longer trustworthy sources of news.
2. Along with publications from grassroots organizations and other independent organizations, the Internet is the best source for comprehensive coverage on political issues.
3. Each political party should own one media corporation to ensure that no one political party receives more positive coverage than another party.
4. All reporters should be free-lanced and not part of a major media corporation so there will be no pressures to conform.

Writing Exercises

Write a brief (500-word) essay on one of the following topics:

1. Do the mass media dominate the political arena?
2. Should it be up to the individual viewers to uncover the truths about politics by doing research themselves?
3. Is it critical for the general public to engage in political conversations? State your reasons.
4. Should education training people to treat information presented by the media with a skeptical eye start at a young age?

Research Activities

1. Go through one issue of a newspaper from two major newspaper providers (e.g., *USA Today* and *New York Times*). Read through coverage on two political parties and determine which of the parties receive more positive and negative coverage in each of the newspapers.
2. Engage in a political discussion on a topic of your choice with a group of friends. Does this experience change your views on the issue? Are you more knowledgeable about the topic after the discussion? Is what is covered in the media similar to what you got out of the discussion?
3. Interview Activity: Select six people for this activity—two people falling under the category "very involved in politics," two for "moderate involvement in politics," two for "not involved in politics." Discuss with your participants the listed questions and see if a pattern occurs in each of the above groups:
    a. Do you think by participating in politics (such as voting), you can have an impact on government policies?
    b. When the local government is doing a poor job, do you think it is helpful if you write to them or call them to make suggestions?
    c. Do you think the media are very biased sources?
    d. Does your knowledge toward various political issues come from the media? Or friends and relatives?
4. Pick five ads on each of the candidates from the present or past presidential elections (e.g., Bush and Kerry, Bush and Gore, Clinton and Bush, etc). What characteristics does each of the ads focus on more? Candidates' appearances? Candidates' political platforms? Please discuss your findings.

SELECTED REFERENCES

Adatto, K. 1990. *Sound Bite Democracy: Network Evening News Presidential Campaign Coverage, 1968 and 1988.* Research paper R-2, Joan Shorenstein Barone Center for Press, Politics, and Public Policy, Harvard University.

Ansolabehere, S. and S. Iyengar. 1995. *Going Negative: How Attack Ads Shrink and Polarize the Electorate.* New York: Free Press.

Barnett, S. 2002. "Will a Crisis in Journalism Provoke a Crisis in Democracy? *The Political Quarterly* 73, 4:400–408.

Bennett, W. L. and R. G. Lawrence. 2001. "Rethinking Media Politics and Public Opinion: Reactions to the Clinton-Lewinsky Scandal. *Political Science Quarterly* 116, 3:425–446.

Brooks, R., J. Lewis and K. Wahl-Jorgensen. 2004. The Media Representation of Public Opinion: British Television News Coverage of the 2001 General Election. *Media, Culture and Society* 26, 1:63–80.

Cappella, J. N. and K. H. Jamieson. 1997. *Spiral of Cynicism: The Press and the Public Good.* New York: Oxford University Press.

Diamond, E. and S. Bates. 1992. *The Spot: The Rise of Political Advertising on Television.* 3d ed. Cambridge, MA: The MIT Press.

Donsbach, W. and O. Jandura. 2003. Chances and Effects of Authenticity: Candidates of the German Federal Election in TV News. *Press/Politics* 8, 1:49–65.

Entman, R. M. 1989. *Democracy without Citizens: Media and the Decay of American Politics.* New York: Oxford University Press.

Gallagher, H. G. 1994. *FDR's Splendid Deception.* Arlington, VA: Vandamere Press.

Graber, D. 2003. The Media and Democracy: Beyond Myths and Stereotypes. *Annual Review of Political Science* 6:139–160.

Hart, R. P. 1994. *Seducing America: How Television Charms the Modern Voter.* New York: Oxford University Press.

Haynes, A. A., P. H. Gurian, M. H. Crespin and C. Zorn. 2004. "The Calculus of Concession: Media Coverage and the Dynamics of Winnowing in Presidential Nominations." *American Politics Research* 32, 3:310–337.

Iyengar, S., M. D. Peters and D. R. Kinder. 1982. "Experimental Demonstrations of the 'Not-So-Minimal' Consequences of Television News Programs." *American Political Science Review* 76, 4:848–858.

Jamieson, K. H. 1984. *Packaging the President: A History and Criticism of Presidential Campaign Advertising.* New York: Oxford University Press.

Jamieson, K. H. 1992. *Dirty Politics: Deception, Distraction and Democracy.* New York: Oxford University Press.

Johnson, T. J. and B. K. Kaye. 2003. "A Boost of Bust for Democracy? How the Web Influenced Political Attitudes and Behaviors in the 1996 and 2000 Presidential Elections." *Harvard International Journal of Press/Politics* 8, 3:9–34.

Journalism.org. (n.d.) "The Last Lap: How the Press Covered the Final Stages of the Presidential Campaign." Retrieved October 7, 2004, from http://ca1.csa.com.myaccess.library.utoronto.ca/htbin/ids65/procskel.cgi.

Kellner, D. 2002. "Presidential Politics: The Movie." *American Behavioral Scientist* 46, 4:467–486.

Kingwell, M. 2000. *The World We Want: Virtue, Vice, and the Good Citizen.* Toronto: Penguin.

Lichter, R. and R. E. Noyes. 1995. *Good Intentions Make Bad News: Why Americans Hate Campaign Journalism.* Washington, D.C.: Rowland and Littlefield.

Lichter, R. and T. Smith. 1996. "Why Elections Are Bad News: Media and Candidate Discourse in the 1996 Presidential Primaries." *Press/Politics* 1, 4:15–35.

Paletz, D. L. et al. 1980. "Polls in the Media: Content, Credibility, and Consequences. *Public Opinion Quarterly* 44:495–513.

Patterson, T. E. 1993. *Out of Order.* New York: Alfred E. Knopf.

Patterson, T. E. 1995. *We the People: A Concise Introduction to American Politics.* New York: McGraw-Hill.

Scheufele, D. A. 2002. "Examining Differential Gains from Mass Media and Their Implications for Participatory Behavior." *Communication Research* 29, 1:46–65.

Stempel, G. H. III and J. W. Windhouser. 1991. "Newspaper Coverage of the 1984 and 1988 Campaigns." Pp 13–66 in *The Media and the 1984 and 1988 Presidential Campaigns,* edited by G. H. Stempel III and J. W. Windhouser. New York: Greenwood.

Traugott, M. and R. Rusch. 1989. *Understanding the Proliferation of Medial Polls in Presidential Campaigns.* Paper presented at the annual meeting of the Midwest Association for Public Opinion Research. Chicago, November 17–18.

Weber, M. 1978. *Economy and Society: An Outline of Interpretive Sociology,* edited by G. Roth and C. Wittich. Berkeley, CA: University of California Press.

Wood, D. N. 1996. *Post-Intellectualism and the Decline of Democracy: The Failure of Reason and Responsibility in the Twentieth Century.* Westport, CT: Praeger.

Yanovitzky, I. and J. N. Cappella. 2001. "Effect of Call-in Political Talk Radio Shows on Their Audiences: Evidence from a Multi-Wave Panel Analysis." *International Journal of Public Opinion Research* 13, 4:377–397.

CHAPTER 13  HEALTH

Good health is something we take for granted until we lose it. Research has shown that the absence of good health—especially when it limits our daily activities—has a large impact on our sense of well-being. It also affects our social relations and economic earning power. So good health is extremely important.

But given the importance of the topic, it seems odd that people, groups, and cultures disagree on what constitutes good health, what produces it, and what restores it when it is lost. It is also odd that people appear to have different risks of losing their good health, which is to say that good health is socially variable and, quite possibly, socially structured. The question is not whether this is so: Epidemiologists know it and insurance companies rely on it. The question is why. Finally, given the gradual reduction in public spending discussed in the last chapter, there is a move to make more people responsible for their own health. Nowhere is this more evident than in the gradual de-institutionalization of people with long-term health problems. As sociologists, we have to ask whether this policy has the effect of making people healthier or simply allows us to ignore their sickness.

This chapter addresses all three of these issues. The first section asks whether we can reach any agreement on what constitutes "good health." (If not, we cannot hope to determine whether good health varies from one social group to another, or is improving overall.) In the second section, we ask why poor people appear to lack equal access to good health, and we consider alternative explanations for this phenomenon. In the third section we look at the trend to releasing mental patients from long-term hospitalization and ask why this was done and what was its effect.

13.1   Who's "Sick"?

The issue: Life and death and everything in between. As we shall see, poor health is more common in some social groups than others. But before we can see these patterns and make sense of them, we need to be clear on what constitutes good health and its opposite, illness. Is there much agreement on what sickness actually is?

We all know when we feel healthy and when we feel ill. The trouble is, under similar conditions some people feel healthy and others feel ill. It is difficult to predict people's *feeling* of health or illness. As individuals, people all experience illness differently; and to compound the problem, cultures differ in how they view health and illness, even pain.

Part of the problem originates in the mysterious relationship between the mind and the body. Some cultures (like ours) see a radical distinction between mind and body—even a competition between them for supremacy. Except in the case of mental illnesses, they view sickness as something that happens to the body, which is then reported to the mind.

Good health is, then, an absence of bodily sickness (although, as we shall see, even in our culture some have defined health more comprehensively).

Other cultures make less distinction between the body, mind, and spirit, or soul. They see a continuing subtle interplay among them. A malfunction in one area—body, mind, or spirit—can produce a malfunction in the others. The cure for malfunctions in one domain must be sought in another. The idea of treating bodily symptoms, rather than the underlying mental or spiritual causes, is utterly foreign to this thinking.

If our goal is to improve the health of the world's population—or even our own, for that matter—we must first establish a minimal consensus on what constitutes "health" and "illness." Some believe this is possible—others do not.

THERE IS NO GENERAL AGREEMENT

People who argue that there is no general agreement over what constitutes health and illness point to differences between societies in how each approaches these issues, as well as differences within societies and changes over time. They also note that conceptions of health and illness are socially constructed and constantly being negotiated.

Differences between Societies   Supporters of the view that there is no general agreement about health and illness point out that these concepts can take on different meanings, depending on the cultural context and historical period.

For example, these concepts are defined differently in the East than in the West. They are also defined differently in modern societies than they are in more traditional societies. As we have noted, in the West health is largely defined as an absence of illness. If you are not sick, you are for all intents and purposes considered healthy. But in the East, health is considered to be more than a lack of illness. It is a state of harmonious balance among all the aspects of an individual's life. This includes a person's emotional and psychological states of being, as well as the physical condition of the body.

In the West, an illness is defined by the scientific-medical establishment as a disturbance in the functioning of the body. You are ill when something in your body is not working properly. This may be due to the intrusion of a germ or virus, an internal, genetically based malfunction, a result of insidious physical forces—like the icy road upon the accelerating elbow—or all of these.

We should point out here that the terms East and West are used as convenient descriptive terms for worldviews—in the same way that the terms North and South were used in Chapter 5, on Global Inequality. In general, West refers to North America and the European Union countries, but people living in these areas may well hold traditional worldviews about health and well-being that come closer to so-called Eastern views.

Whatever the cause, an illness is a physical condition that causes some part of the body to malfunction. Only during this century have malfunctions of the mind also come to be defined as illnesses. This has occurred because the increasingly powerful medical profession has concluded—through Freud's ground-breaking work on hysteria—that mental or psychological malfunctions can produce physical symptoms. And today the profession also recognizes that even when there are no physical symptoms, mental anguish can be just as real and painful as physical pain.

In the East, on the other hand, illnesses have long been defined as imbalances in a person's life, brought about by various causes. Many causes may be primarily emotional or psychological in nature. Something considered an illness in the East does not have to affect the physical body primarily, or even at all. Accordingly, diagnosis of the illness is often left to spiritual leaders and not, strictly speaking, to medical practitioners. And the cure may be physical—as in medicine or massage or surgery— or may be spiritual, or perhaps may be something that conventional Western medicine would see as unrelated to either, such as a song.

So, Eastern and Western societies also differ in how illnesses are treated. In the West an illness is a physical problem, to be overcome with the patient's cooperation if possible, or without it if necessary.

The object of scientific attention is the illness, not the patient. The illness is seen as an isolated feature of the patient; thus little attention is paid to the emotional or psychological effect on the patient of the treatment of the physical problem. (Sometimes little attention is paid to how treatment affects other parts of the body!) This outlook fits well with a highly specialized approach to medicine.

As we have noted, in the East an illness, even when it is primarily physical in nature, is viewed as an imbalance that needs correcting. The unit of analysis is always the patient, not the illness. Accordingly, the patient's involvement is central to the treatment process. Though made up of distinct parts, the patient is treated as a whole. Healers could not imagine trying to fix an isolated part, when the problem is an imbalance between the parts. So for treatment to have any success, it must include the emotional and psychological dimensions of the patient, as well as the physical one.

The same dichotomy that marks differences in Eastern and Western approaches to illness also marks differences between more and less developed (or modernized) societies.

Modern societies, dominated as they are by scientific rationality, see illnesses as having empirically measurable symptoms and empirically measurable causes. On the other hand, traditional societies lack scientific rationality and place more emphasis on spiritual (nonempirical) causes. Illnesses for them carry heavy moral and spiritual weight. So it is not surprising if they locate the cause of an individual's pain in a failure to properly worship ancestral shrines. Or in the spells and curses of another group member, believed to possess supernatural powers (such as those of a witch).

To many Westerners, such an approach to illness is the result of superstition and shows an ignorance of scientifically verifiable causes and effects, and cannot possibly provide successful treatment.

Differences within Societies   People who argue that there is no general agreement about health and illness also point out that even in modern Western societies, the scientific-medical establishment defines health and illness differently— some would even say more narrowly—than do

practitioners of *alternative* medicine and public health people. This may be particularly the case when we look at how women's bodies and reproductive systems are defined by the medical establishment. Pregnancy, childbirth, menopause, even menstruation may be discussed within medical literature as "conditions" during which women are in need of "treatment." By contrast, holistic practitioners and women's health advocates say that these should be viewed as part of health, not part of illness.

Increasingly, people dissatisfied by the way the medical establishment treats illness have turned to other ways of achieving good health. Many of these ways are preventive as much as remedial. Alternative approaches vary widely: They include Yoga and other bodily exercises, meditation and other mental exercises, macrobiotic or vegetarian eating, herbal remedies, homeopathy, acupuncture, and an array of spiritual approaches, including forms of shamanic healing.

What they have in common is an emphasis on principles that are key to the Eastern approach we outlined above. They are all holistic perspectives that take into account a person's emotional, psychological, and spiritual needs. Over the last few decades, these alternate approaches have gained popular acceptance—so much so that they have begun to influence the medical profession itself.

Changes over Time   In addition, people who argue that there is no general agreement about health and illness point out that popular thinking about health and illness changes over time.

Some things that were once considered to be illnesses (e.g., homosexuality or PMS) gradually come to be seen as normal or "healthy." Other things that used to be considered normal—for example heavy drinking—become *medicalized* and treated as an illness. We consider certain conditions to be illnesses that were once ignored completely, or treated as crimes. (Eighteenth- and nineteenth-century Western criminal history is full of examples of people being imprisoned for acts that we would now consider to be the result of mental illnesses.)

One condition now recognized as constituting an illness did not even have a name a few years ago. *Post-traumatic stress disorder* is generally accepted by the medical community as a type of suffering caused by the emotional and psychic consequences of a traumatic event. Other examples include PMS and postpartum depression. (The event may even have been forgotten or repressed, with consequences coming long afterward.)

Conceptions Are Socially Constructed Finally, people taking this position note that conceptions of health and illness are socially constructed. What we consider to be health or illness is shaped by society and social relations. They are real enough, but the way people experience and understand them has a subjective dimension that is influenced by the culture in which they live.

Changes in attitudes, social institutions—even economic conditions—affect how people view health and illness. This is equally true of health care practitioners and the public at large. Negotiations and renegotiations of meaning, through repeated interactions among health care practitioners, patients, government bureaucracies, and hospital administrations, affect how people ultimately come to view health and illness in general.

So, for example, people consider some illnesses to be more disreputable, blameworthy, and preventable than others. For many people, AIDS and drug addiction fall into this category. (By contrast, congenital heart weakness or the common cold do not.) However, even here we see changes in public thinking. Such changes reflect a growth in understanding about the causes of different diseases. They also show the effects of *medicalization,* whereby the medical profession re-labels the disease as a health problem, rather than a moral one.

As social constructs, notions of health and illness are largely shaped by cultural factors. For example, Westerners (more than people in the East) tend to somatize distress: They express anxiety, stress, unhappiness, and psychic trauma in physical symptoms. This is perhaps because, as we pointed out above, Western societies view illness as something that takes place in the body and is identifiably wrong with the functioning of the body.

The way in which health and illness are experienced and expressed—the way in which people take on what sociologists have called "the sick role"— also varies by gender, class, ethnicity, and age. This lends further credence to the argument that these are social constructs. Some people are more willing patients than others. It is by willingly taking on the patient role that they escape blame for their inactivity or disability, forcing us to accept medical explanations instead of moral ones.

As usual, however, there is another point of view about the nature of health and illness, with evidence to back it up.

THERE IS A GENERAL AGREEMENT

Most of Us Can Identify "Sick" People Those who argue that there *is* a general consensus about health and illness, point out that most people can distinguish between healthy and sick people.

This is particularly true in respect to physical health. Most people have a basic, intuitive understanding of health as the ability to function in daily life. By this standard, illness is an impairment of that functioning and must be open to redefinition as daily life changes. This basic understanding is what allows the World Health Organization to determine, according to universally agreed upon minimum criteria, who is healthy and who needs care.

Since 1946, the World Health Organization has used a multi-dimensional definition of *health* that runs as follows: "A state of complete physical, mental and social well-being and not merely the absence of disease or infirmity." This definition shows that at least this organization has incorporated both Eastern and Western concepts of health. What remains unclear is how much agreement there is on what counts as "physical, mental and social well-being."

What people usually mean when they say someone is ill (or sick) is that he or she is not acting in ways considered normal or desirable, for reasons beyond personal control. Thus the label *ill* is a way to avoid making moral judgments of non-normative (or deviant) behavior. Since societies differ in the behaviors they consider deviant and the explanations they give for this deviance, they also differ in what they consider to be good or bad health. However these differences are not limitless. And at the extremes—for example, with measures of life expectancy or infant mortality—there is general agreement about the meaning and value of these health outcomes.

Eastern and Western Conceptions Are Similar

A second argument by people on this side of the debate is that differences between Eastern and Western conceptions of health and illness have been exaggerated. And, increasingly, there has been a mutual influence between East and West with respect to how health and illness are understood.

The differences between Eastern and Western conceptions of health and illness have diminished in recent years. Western medical techniques have been adopted throughout the world, but Western medical practice has incorporated many Eastern principles in its approach. Particularly, it has taken non-physical symptoms far more seriously in treating illnesses, and has come closer to viewing the patient from a holistic perspective. Women's health advocates in particular have emphasized the importance of holistic understanding. And, many of today's conventional medical practitioners will accept treatments from alternative therapies based in the principles that we are here calling Eastern. Some will even recommend them.

Further examples of the incorporation of Eastern principles include a greater emphasis on emotional and psychological problems as either sources of illness or as illnesses themselves, and more focus on nonphysical aspects of the patient in the treatment process. Eastern influence is also evident in the growing recognition that stress and other emotional or psychological disturbances can be major contributors to the onset, severity, and duration of illness. This comes close to accepting the Eastern premise that individuals need to achieve inner *harmony* or *balance.*

Health and Illness Are Not Social Constructs

Third, proponents of this view argue that health and illness are not entirely social constructs. Rather, they are objective descriptions of valid, empirically verifiable states of being. Our descriptions may vary over time with advances in scientific knowledge. But this variation shows that

we are gaining an ever more accurate picture of phenomena as they actually are. It does not mean that the concepts health and illness are merely words that can mean whatever we want them to.

Thus, for example, societies may differ in whether they consider recurrent sleeplessness to be a problem. They may even differ in whether they consider it to be a health problem. And they may differ in whether they look for the explanation in a physical, mental, or spiritual source. But in any society that views sleeplessness as a health problem, some treatments will work and others will not. The test is whether the patient can get a good night's sleep. Ultimately, the test of any science is whether it makes valid predictions and provides solutions to acknowledged problems. In the end, it is scientific evidence based on systematic treatment that will settle this debate.

SUMMING UP

Who's sick? Who is well? It's harder to say than one might think.

On one side of this debate are people who argue that there is no general agreement about what constitutes health and illness. They point to broad cultural differences as well as changes over time in how people understand these concepts. They also argue that ideas about health and illness are social constructs and as such are in a constant process of re-definition.

On the other side of the debate are people who argue that in spite of superficial differences in the ways people understand health and illness, there is a basic, underlying agreement about what these concepts mean. Moreover, such agreement is necessary if we, as an international community, are to determine who is healthy, who needs care, and what kind of care to provide. We need to assume agreement about health and illness to be able to determine which health policy objectives to pursue and how to judge their relative effectiveness.

For those who continue to believe that there is no consensus, a worldwide health policy may prove impossible. However, it does not have to result in inaction. Instead it points to a need to tailor health policies to local understandings of health and illness. And, in general, it seems that looking at health problems from several points of view can make a lot of sense. Talking to people from different communities helps in understanding these problems. It may be that we can indeed define health—but that this will need an accepting approach to the idea of body, mind, and spirit components in balance, not simply an absence of illness. If we don't think there is consensus, we can try out different approaches to see what makes most sense in a particular situation. Many people around the world have their own definitions of health, illness, and medicine—and also accept Western medicine, fitting it in with their own folk or magical practices. There isn't necessarily a confrontation. But there is a crucial need for those who seek to improve global health to listen to what people say and try to understand both sickness and health in local terms.

In the end, evidence supports both sides of the debate. Some treatments of some illnesses work well across cultures but many do not. It is in the latter grey area of treatments that do not work, or do not work as well as expected, that all of us—even Americans—must look for culturally variant solutions to health problems, or even for new ways of thinking about whether they are health problems at all.

REVIEW EXERCISES

For Discussion and Debate

1. Which notion of good health—the Eastern or the Western—makes most sense to you? Why?
2. Why has the West paid so much more attention to physical health than it has to spiritual health?
3. "What seems like good health to one person may be bad health to another. It's all relative."
4. Could there be "health professions" as we know them if we adopted Eastern conceptions of health?

Writing Exercises

Write a brief (500-word) essay on one of the following topics:

1. "Chanting and chewing on weeds is not my idea of a cure."
2. "Just because some guy uses equipment that cost $2 million doesn't mean he knows anything about human health."
3. "It took ten thousand years for humanity to reach its present understanding of the human body, and alternate health practitioners want to undo that progress overnight."
4. "The main achievement of Western medicine has been to help people live in pain for decades longer."

Research Activities

1. Read up on the history of one of the alternative health professions. How is it organized as a profession, and how is that organization different from, say, the American Medical Association?
2. See if you can find evidence that, by Western standards of scientific proof, Eastern health practices (e.g., local plants, "medicine men") cure people.
3. See if you can find evidence that, by Eastern standards of knowing, Western health practices (e.g., expensive drugs or technology) cure people.
4. Interview someone who has experienced or participated in a form of shamanic healing. How do they narrate the experience? Is their view of "healing" the same as your own? Why or why not? Report on this to your study group.

Selected References

Amaya, Victor and Maria Black. 1993. "Tradition for Revolution: Traditional Medicine in El Salvador." *Community Development Journal* 28, 3 (July): 228–236.

Atwood, Joan D. and Lawrence Maltin. 1991. "Putting Eastern Philosophies into Western Psychotherapies." *American Journal of Psychotherapy* 45, 3 (July): 368–382.

Bailey, Carol A. 1993. "Equality with a Difference: On Androcentrism and Menstruation." *Teaching Sociology* 21, 2:121–129.

Brien, Sarah, Laurie Lachance and George T. Lewith. 2004. "Are the Therapeutic Effects of Homeopathy Attributed to the Consultation, the Homeopathic Remedy, or Both? A Protocol for a Future Exploratory Feasibility Trial in Patients with Rheumatoid Arthritis." *Journal of Alternative and Complementary Medicine* 10, 3:499–502.

Burdette, Patricia Wells. 2004. "The Power of the Spirit: American Indian Worldview and Successful Community Development among the Oglala Lakota." *Dissertation Abstracts International, A: The Humanities and Social Sciences* 64, 10 (Apr.): 3855–A.

Carr, Gillian and Patricia Anne Baker, eds. 2002. *Practitioners, Practices and Patients: New Approaches to Medical Archaeology and Anthropology.* Oxford: Oxbow Books.

Caspi, Opher and Iris R. Bell. 2004. "One Size Does Not Fit All: Aptitude X Treatment Interaction (ATI) as a Conceptual Framework for Complementary and Alternative Medicine Outcome Research. Part 1—What Is ATI Research?" *Journal of Alternative and Complementary Medicine* 10, 3: 580–586.

Easthope, Gary. 1993. "The Response of Orthodox Medicine to the Challenge of Alternative Medicine in Australia." *Australian and New Zealand Journal of Sociology* 29, 3 (Nov.): 289–301.

Frankish, C. James and Lawrence W. Green. 1994. "Organizational and Community Change as the Social Scientific Basis for Disease Prevention and Health Promotion Policy." *Advances in Medical Sociology* 4: 209–233.

Fraser, J. Dunfield. 1996. "Consumer Perceptions of Health Care Quality and the Utilization of Nonconventional Therapy." *Social Science and Medicine* 43, 2 (July): 149–161.

Gallagher, Eugene B. 1994. "A Typology of Health Rationality Applied to Third World Health." *Advances in Medical Sociology* 4:257–280.

Gillett, Grant. 1994. "Beyond the Orthodox: Heresy in Medicine and Social Science." *Social Science and Medicine* 39, 9 (Nov.): 1125–1131.

Greco, Monica. 1993. "Psychosomatic Subjects and the 'Duty to Be Well': Personal Agency within Medical Rationality." *Economy and Society* 22, 3 (Aug.): 357–372.

Hare, Ravindra S. 1996. "Dava, Daktar and Dua: Anthropology of Practiced Medicine in India." *Social Science and Medicine* 43, 5 (Sept.): 837–848.

Heitzer-Allen, Deborah L., Carl Kendall and Jack J. Wirima. 1993. "The Role of Ethnographic Research in Malaria Control: An Example from Malawi." *Research in the Sociology of Health Care* 10:269–286.

Hsieh, Elaine. 2004. "Stories in Action and the Dialogic Management of Identities: Storytelling in Transplant Support Group Meetings." *Research on Language and Social Interaction* 37, 1:39–70.

Hudson, Terese. 1996. "Measuring the Results of Faith." *Hospitals and Health Networks* 70 (Sept.): 22–24.

Ide, Bette A. and Turkan Sanli. 1992. "Health Beliefs and Behaviors of Saudi Women." *Women and Health* 19, 1:97–113.

Imrie, Rob. 2004. "Demystifying Disability: A Review of the International Classification of Functioning, Disability and Health." *Sociology of Health and Illness* 26, 3 (Apr.): 287–305.

Jenkins, Christopher N. H. 1996. "Health Care Access and Preventive Care among Vietnamese Immigrants: Do Traditional Beliefs and Practices Pose Barriers?" *Social Science and Medicine* 43, 7 (Oct.): 1049–1056.

Johnson, Kirsten K. and Mary Anne Kandrack. 1995. "On the Medico-Legal Appropriation of Menstrual Discourse: The Syndromization of Women's Experiences." *Resources for Feminist Research,* 24, 1–2:23–27.

Kirby, Jon P. 1993. "The Islamic Dialogue with African Traditional Religion: Divination and Health Care." *Social Science and Medicine* 36, 3 (Feb.): 237–247.

Laderman, Carol and Marina Roseman, eds. 1996. *The Performance of Healing.* New York: Routledge.

Lanier, Gina S. 1995. "Constructing Empowerment and Validation in Birth: Direct-Entry Midwives and Home Birth." *Social Problems.*

McLeroy, Kenneth R. and Carolyn E. Crump. 1994. "Health Promotion and Disease Prevention: A Historical Perspective." *Generations* 18, 1 (Spring): 9–17.

Ngokwey, Nodlamb. 1989. "On the Specificity of Healing Functions: A Study of Diagnosis in Three Faith Healing Institutions in Feira (Bahia, Brazil)." *Social Science and Medicine* 29, 4:515–526.

O'Sullivan, Sara and Anne Stakelum. 2004. "Lay Understandings of Health: A Qualitative Study." Pp 26–43 in *Constructions of Health and Illness: European Perspectives,* edited by Ian Shaw and Kaisa Kauppinen. Aldershot, England: Ashgate.

Phillips, Daphne. 1994. "Fatalism and Health in the Brazilian State of Sao Paulo." *International Sociology* 9, 3 (Sept.): 363–375.

Pitts, Marian. 1996. "Lay Beliefs about Diarrhoeal Diseases: Their Role in Health Education in a Developing Country." *Social Science and Medicine* 43, 8 (Oct.): 1223–1228.

Pitts, Victoria. 2004. "Illness and Internet Empowerment: Writing and Reading Breast Cancer in Cyberspace." *Health* 8, 1 (Jan.): 33–59.

Popay, Jennie. 1996. "Public Health Research and Lay Knowledge." *Social Science and Medicine* 42, 5 (Mar.): 759–768.

Senturia, Kirsten D. 1996. "Maternal and Child Health in Albania." *Social Science and Medicine* 43, 7:1097–1107.

Sokoloski, Elizabeth H. 1995. "Canadian First Nations Women's Beliefs about Pregnancy and Prenatal Care." *Canadian Journal of Nursing Research* 27, 1:89–100.

Thorne, Sally. 1993. "Health Belief Systems in Perspective." *Journal of Advanced Nursing* 18, 12:1931.

Tyler, Lawrence. 2000. *Understanding Alternative Medicine: New Health Paths in America.* New York: The Haworth Herbal Press.

Wallerstein, Nina. 1993. "Empowerment and Health: The Theory and Practice of Community Change." *Community Development Journal* 28, 3 (July): 218–227.

Wirth, Daniel P. 1995. "The Significance of Belief and Expectancy within the Spiritual Healing Encounter." *Social Science and Medicine* 41, 2 (July): 249–260.

13.2   Do People Everywhere Have the Same Chance of Good Health?

The issue: What explains the patterns of poor health we mentioned in our introduction to the last section? In particular, are they of sociological interest—that is, do they tell us something about the way our society is organized? And is there anything we—whether as citizens or sociologists—can do to equalize people's chances of good health?

Previously we debated whether people agree on what constitutes *good health.* Ultimately, bad health means pain, frequent illness, activity limitation, and a shortened life span. Do people everywhere have the same chance of good health, or is health socially structured? For example, do poor people have less chance of good health, of a long life and little activity limitation, than wealthy people do?

The answer to this is that class variations in health are clearly evident. Poor people lead shorter lives, on average, and run higher risks of physical and mental illness and limited activity. Can

such variations be avoided? Are poor people "choosing" bad health and could they be healthier if they chose to? As usual, there are debates on both sides of this issue.

POOR PEOPLE HAVE THE SAME CHANCE OF GOOD HEALTH

Although some argue that poor health is a matter of people's *life chances,* that people in different social classes have different opportunities to lead happy, healthy lives precisely because of their position in the social hierarchy, not everyone agrees. Others argue that good health is a matter of choice, not socially defined life chances. This view is based on the belief that all people have a good chance to lead happy, healthy lives. But they have to take advantage of the opportunities that are available to them.

The Poor Cause Their Own Problems In particular, those who argue that good health is a matter of choice, point to social variations in health-enhancing behavior.

For example, they note that poor people are more likely to have a bad diet. Some of this is unavoidable due to a shortage of money, but some of it is not. The poor eat too many carbohydrates and fatty foods. They smoke too many cigarettes and drink too much alcohol. Use of hard drugs is also more common among the poor—especially the urban "underclass" we discussed earlier. And this group—especially young men in this group—are likely to engage in violent or risky behavior, such as fighting, shooting guns, or driving too fast, all of which are bad for one's health in the long run. Finally, poor people are less likely than others to exercise regularly. More exercise would prolong their lives and improve their physical health.

Use of Available Services Along similar lines, the poor are less likely than middle-class people to use available health services.

It is true that many poor people lack health insurance. However, in the United States even poor people who have health insurance and other access to professional health care, are less likely to use these services. Various explanations have been put forward to explain this self-destructive behavior. Some claim that a reluctance to use health professionals is due to discomfort when interacting with middle-class physicians. The poor may feel out of place in doctor's offices, for example. Others claim that poor people are more fatalistic about their health, feeling that they have little control over their lives (including their health). And some claim poverty is bred from irresponsibility and that the poor are likely to be ill because they don't care about health as much as about pleasure

and self-indulgence. In the view of these observers, it is folly for the government to spend money trying to help those who would not help themselves.

Little Illness Prevention More generally, poor people put little emphasis on good health or on preventing illness.

Perhaps poor people have too many other worries—like unemployment, bad jobs, or poor housing—on their minds. Good health may occupy a low position on their list of worries. Or perhaps they have low self-esteem, due to the low regard in which society holds them. This would explain why they give little importance to their own physical health. Unfortunate as this is, no one but the poor can ensure their own health, some would say. People need to take care of themselves.

Too Little Health Information Finally, just as good health varies with income and social class, it also varies with people's education. Generally, well-educated people are wealthier, more secure, have higher social status, *and* are healthier, too. Perhaps education, not income, is the key to good health. Well-educated people get and use more information about health care, and make use of this information in personally beneficial ways.

If true, the key to improving people's health and narrowing the unequal chance of good health is through public education. Governments should ensure that everyone has complete information about their health needs. After that, it is up to individuals to use this information in their own best interest.

These are some of the arguments supporting the view that poor people have an equal chance for good health. However, there are opposing arguments.

POOR PEOPLE HAVE LESS CHANCE OF GOOD HEALTH

Arguments to the contrary address many of the views put forward earlier.

Too Little Income Economic recession and mass layoffs have plunged people of different educational levels into poverty. For women and children, divorce also has economically disastrous consequences. What we find in these instances of sudden disaster is that poverty—and consequences of poverty such as stress and depression—produce many health problems of the poor.

Typically, young and middle-aged people with bad health have one or more of the following characteristics: (1) They live in low-income households, indeed, below the poverty line; (2) if they have a job, they do unpaid or poorly paid work; (3) many live in one-parent families, and of these, many receive welfare and live in subsidized housing.

Beyond Their Control   What is the connection between poverty and ill health?

Researchers have considered this question from various angles and come up with various answers. Some studies find that poverty increases stress and anxiety, with harmful consequences. (Other studies find that stress is associated with higher incomes, but depression is associated with poverty.) Stress weakens the immune system, leaving stressed people more likely to contract infectious diseases. Stressed people are also more likely to suffer long-term, disabling depression that makes it impossible to work or care for their children and themselves.

Poor people with jobs tend to have worse jobs, from a health standpoint. Working conditions are likelier to be unsafe, unhealthy, or stressful. For the poor, food and living conditions are also inferior, so they suffer poor nutrition and too little sleep. At home and work, their environment is also less safe. For this reason, poor people run a higher risk of accidents and violence beyond their own control.

In general, analysts who relate social class to health note that cleanliness, avoidance of infectious environments, sanitation, and care all cost money, so some are less likely to be able to control the environments in which they work and live than others.

Cannot Afford Good Care   Nearly one American in three lacks health insurance. This means that any visit to a hospital, doctor, dentist, or other health professional must be paid for out of pocket. Given the cost of professional services, many people cannot afford to take care of their health, unless illness is directly threatening their lives.

Poor and rich people may differ slightly in their willingness to use insured (or free) health services. However, insured and uninsured people differ far more in their willingness to seek health services. Thus it is income—not motivation (or education)—that accounts for most failures by poor people to seek professional health care.

Fewer Services Available   Furthermore, in many communities health professionals and health facilities are unavailable.

Like most people, doctors, nurses, and other health professionals prefer to work in safe, prosperous communities. Life there is typically more pleasant and earnings for professional work are higher. As a result, there are fewer health professionals and health services (e.g., hospitals, hospital beds, clinics) *per capita* in poor than in rich states, rural than in urban areas, or poor than in wealthy parts of the city. In poor areas, the available services are likely to be crowded and overused, and it may take longer to get a doctor's appointment.

Cannot Take Illness "Seriously"   Poor people are more likely to lack private transportation. To get to a doctor at some distance from home, they may have to take the bus. This means more discomfort, delay, and time lost. Moreover, poor people usually work at jobs where they lose pay if they take time off to see a doctor, or even to recover from illness. (This is not true in most professional jobs. Professional workers have more autonomy—can come and go more easily—and suffer few if any penalties for losing work time due to illness.) In short, poor people cannot afford to be sick, because they cannot afford to lose wages (or risk their job). Many prefer to work while sick for these reasons. They know that taking time off to recover would be healthier, but they can't afford it.

Needs of Poor Ignored   Finally, we noted earlier a reluctance by the poor to use health professionals due to their discomfort when interacting with middle-class physicians.

Most doctors are middle-class people from middle-class backgrounds, accustomed to dealing with middle-class patients, and as long as medical education is very expensive they are likely to remain so. They may have as much difficulty dealing with poor people as with people from another culture. There are bound to be communication problems, including differences in the ways people experience and describe illness. Medical schools do not prepare doctors well for these kinds of *cross-cultural* encounters. As a result, both doctors and patients are uncomfortable.

So there is good evidence that too little income—not too little education or information—is the main cause of poor people's health problems. However, what remains uncertain is the link between poor health and social position, whether measured by income or socio-economic class. Consider two studies that illustrate the complexity of this linkage.

TWO PROVOCATIVE PIECES OF RESEARCH

The British Civil Service Study   All health researchers and epidemiologists know that people's life chances vary with their position in the social order, but they disagree about the reasons why.

A British study tried to find the reason by collecting carefully detailed information over a ten-year period. To make the research manageable, researchers studied 10,000 British male civil servants, aged 40–64 at the time the study began. They limited themselves to men since women's health risks and experiences are different in many respects. And they limited themselves to British civil servants because good records are available on their health and they all have free access to health care. (Moreover, the researchers were British.)

The researchers asked these questions: (1) What proportion of the sample survives for ten years (or more) from the start of the study? (2) How does a man's chance of survival vary with his position in the organization? They found that survival chances do vary with a man's rank in the hierarchy. At every age, the risks of dying during the ten-year study period were three-and-a-half times higher among the (bottom ranking) clerical and manual workers than among the (top ranking)

senior administrators. Researchers ruled out the possibility that good health leads to a higher rank. Instead, high rank produces better health.

It is easier to say what does *not* explain this finding than to say what does. First, higher mortality is not due to unemployment: All of the men sampled were employed. Second, it is not due to absolute poverty: None of those sampled were destitute. Third, it is not due to differences in lifestyle—such as smoking or fatty-food intake. Researchers found the same gradient for causes of death that are unaffected by smoking. And, they found the same gradient after controlling statistically for smoking, cholesterol level, and blood pressure.

These data lead to two conclusions. First, there is an unmistakeable health gradient that varies according to people's socioeconomic position. Being lower down the ladder shortens your life! This applies to the general population, too: Poorer people live shorter lives. British data show that the socio-economic death gradient hasn't changed since 1911. Despite changes to society and medicine and an overall improvement in people's life chances, rich people today are just as far ahead of poor people in the struggle to stay alive as they were 85 years ago. Second, there is no single chain of events from low rank, through illness, to death. Diseases are merely pathways—not causes—of death. Everybody dies of something and highly stressed people can die of almost anything.

What the British study tells us first is that, in studying life chances, we have to focus our attention on social inequality, not poverty *per se*. Second, we have to look for generally (not specifically) harmful effects connected with inequality. What Sennett and Cobb called the "hidden injuries of class" show up in any number of ways.

The "Healthy Work" Study   In their book on "healthy work," researchers Karasek and Theorell bring together evidence from a large variety of studies. The research they compile is from all over the world—some by the authors themselves, some by other researchers.

To make their work more manageable, Karasek and Theorell limit their investigation of the relationship between social inequality and health. The book's argument runs as follows: Heart disease is a major health problem deserving close attention and public concern. The psychological condition *stress* is a known major contributor to heart disease.

In turn, *job strain* is a major cause of stress and, therefore, a major cause of heart disease. Job strain is caused by the interaction of (1) an excessive psychological *job demand*—too much work to do, too little time to do it, and/or conflicting job demands; and (2) low *job control*—few or unvarying skills required by the job and little autonomy in decision making. Jobs that cause the most strain combine a high level of job demand and a low level of job control. Such jobs are found at the bottom of the socioeconomic hierarchy. Thus, according to this theory, people at the bottom of the social ladder, with the most stress-producing jobs, run the highest risk of heart disease.

This theory and its predictions are supported by data from many studies of coronary heart disease. Low level service workers—waitresses, for example—do indeed have higher than average risks of heart disease. Why? Because in any restaurant, waitresses hold the lowest status—well below the manager, chef, (male) waiters, and customers. Often, they have to wear demeaning uniforms and suffer sexual harassment. Always, waitresses are expected to be quick and accurate, yet pleasant and patient. At peak hours, the job demands are nearly impossible. Yet the job is also repetitive and leaves little room for personal creativity or discretion.

Symphony musicians, compared with other kinds of artists, also have a higher than average risk of heart disease. And here, too, the explanation is similar. Symphonic musicians have more skills and a higher income than most waitresses. But they also suffer from heavy job demands: often, a gruelling practice, rehearsal, and travel schedule, for example. And, compared to other artists, they have little control over their own performance. Symphony musicians are merely instruments of the conductor. It is the conductor who has job autonomy, deciding how the work is to be performed.

SUMMING UP

Do people everywhere have the same chance of good health? Certainly not. Poor people suffer from higher rates of illness and have a lower life expectancy than rich people. This section has focused on the factors that may explain these differences. We have considered whether the causal link is to be found in differential, class-based access to good health, or in different life-styles and attitudes that make the poor more prone to getting sick and to dying (relatively) young.

On one side of the debate are those who argue that poor people have higher rates of illness and die younger because of class barriers to adequate health care. On the other side are those who argue that access to good health care is equal (or at least equal enough). By this account, it is because poor people engage in risky or negligent behaviors that they run higher chances of sickness and early death.

But good health is far more complex than just a question of diseases and death. Likewise, important as poverty may be, social inequality means more than wealth or the lack of it: It also means control over one's work and one's life. In its various forms, social inequality stresses the mind, the spirit, and the immune system, resulting in any number of health problems. As we have noted, stresses on people at the bottom of the social ladder can show up in many forms.

A recent book edited by David Leon and Gill Walt points to many of these issues. For instance, the overall health of a population seems related not only to the level of wealth or poverty of its people (and their access to healthcare) but the range of variation between rich and poor extremes. An article by Stephen Kunitz in this volume explores this issue. Societies that have more equality have better health, and their people are longer-lived.

What is clear is that bad health is not a matter of "bad choice" or "incomplete information." The nation's health problem cannot be solved simply by providing more public health education. Society and a great many of its members would therefore be better off with less inequality.

REVIEW EXERCISES

For Discussion and Debate

1. Why would some people appear to choose poor health over good health?
2. What kind of health insurance is likely to provide good health care for the largest number of people?
3. What is it about low rank or low social status that might cause poor health?
4. How might a job like waitressing be changed to make it less of a health risk, and how likely is this to happen?

Writing Exercises

Write a brief (500-word) essay on one of the following topics:

1. "Why I'd rather be a symphony musician than rock musician."
2. "Here's how I would cope with the pressures of high job demand and low autonomy."
3. "Taking health concerns too seriously lets you live longer but worse."
4. "The unhealthiest job I ever had was . . ."

Research Activities

1. Devise a brief questionnaire to find out what information people actually have about real health risks. Then administer this questionnaire to six students at your college and report the results.
2. Choose one disease or health condition and find out whether its prevalence or seriousness varies among people of different social classes in your own community.
3. Choose one disease or health condition and find out whether its prevalence or seriousness varies among people in your own country and one other country (your choice).
4. Study health problems in your college to find out whether lower-ranking (i.e., first-year) students have more or different problems than higher-ranking (i.e., fourth-year) students.

SELECTED REFERENCES

Alegría, Margarita, Glorisa Canino, Ruth Ríos, Mildred Vera, José Calderón, Dana Rusch and Alexander N. Ortega. 2002. "Mental Health Care for Latinos: Inequalities in Use of Specialty Mental Health Services among Latinos, African Americans, and Non-Latino Whites." *Psychiatr. Serv* 53, 12:1547–1555.

Bartley, Mel. 1988. "Unemployment and Health: Selection or Causation—a False Antithesis?" *Sociology of Health and Illness* 10, 1 (Mar.): 41–67.

Blank, Michael B., Marcus Mahmood, Jeanne C. Fox and Thomas Guterbock. 2002. "Alternative Mental Health Services: The Role of the Black Church in the South." *American Journal of Public Health* 92, 10:1668–1672.

Carr-Hill, Roy A. 1988. "Time Trends in Inequalities in Health." *Journal of Biosocial Science* 20, 3 (July): 265–273.

Chow, Julian Chun-Chung, Kim Jaffee and Lonnie Snowden. 2003. "Racial/Ethnic Disparities in the Use of Mental Health Services in Poverty Areas." *American Journal of Public Health* 93, 5:792–797.

Coburn, David. 2004. "Beyond the Income Inequality Hypothesis: Class, Neo-Liberalism, and Health Inequalities." *Social Science and Medicine* 58, 1 (Jan.): 41–56.

Cockerham, William C., Guenther Lueschen, Gerhard Kunz and Joe L. Spaeth. 1986. "Social Stratification and Self-Management of Health." *Journal of Health and Social Behavior* 27, 1 (Mar.): 1–14.

Davis, Karen. 1991. "Inequality and Access to Health Care." *Milbank Quarterly* 69, 2:253–273.

Denton, Margaret, Steven Prus and Vivienne Walters. 2004. "Gender Differences in Health: A Canadian Study of the Psychosocial, Structural and Behavioural Determinants of Health." *Social Science and Medicine* 58, 12 (June): 2585–2600.

Eibner, Christine E. and Williams N. Evans. 2004. "The Income-Health Relationship and the Role of Relative Deprivation." Pp 545–568 in *Social Inequality,* edited by Kathryn M. Neckerman. New York: Russell Sage.

Ford, Graeme, Russell Ecob, Kate Hunt, Sally MacIntyre and Patrick West. 1994. "Patterns of Class Inequality in Health through the Lifespan: Class Gradients at 15, 35, and 55 Years in the West of Scotland." *Social Science and Medicine* 39, 8 (Oct.): 1037–1050.

Fossett, James W., Janet D. Perloff, Philip R. Kletke and John A. Peterson. 1992. "Medicaid and Access to Child Health Care in Chicago." *Journal of Health Politics Policy and Law* 17, 2 (Summer): 273–298.

Halfon, N. and P. W. Newacheck. 1993. "Childhood Asthma and Poverty: Differential Impacts and Utilization of Health Services." *Pediatrics* 91, 1:56–61.

Krieger, Nancy and Elizabeth Fee. 1994. "Social Class: The Missing Link in U.S. Health Data." *International Journal of the Health Services* 24, 1:25–44.

Laveist, Thomas A. 1993. "Segregation, Poverty and Empowerment: Health Consequences for African Americans." *Milbank Quarterly* 71, 1:41–64.

Leon, David and Gill Walt. 2000. *Poverty, Inequality and Health: An International Perspective.* Oxford: Oxford University Press.

Lia-Hoagberg, Betty, Peter Rode, Catherine J. Skovholt, Charles N. Oberg, Cynthia Berg, Sara Mullett and Thomas Choi. 1990. "Barriers and Motivators to Prenatal Care among Low-Income Women." *Social Science and Medicine* 30, 4:487–495.

Lundberg, Olle. 1991. "Causal Explanation for Class Inequality in Health—an Empirical Analysis." *Social Science and Medicine* 32, 4:385–393.

Lynch, John, George Davey Smith, Sam Harper, Marianne Hillemeier, Nancy Ross, George A. Kaplan and Michael Wolfson. 2004. "Is Income Inequality a Determinant of Population Health? Part 1. A Systematic Review." *The Milbank Quarterly* 82, 1:5–99.

Malmgren, J. A., M. L. Martin and R. M. Nicola. 1996. "Health Care Access of Poverty-Level Older Adults in Subsidized Public Housing. *Public Health Reports* 111, 3 (May–June): 260–263.

McCord, Colin and Harold P. Freeman. 1990. "Excess Mortality in Harlem." *New England Journal of Medicine* 322, 3, 18 (Jan.): 173–177.

———, Rosemary Aird, William Bor, Michael O'Callaghan, Gail M. Williams and Gregory J. Shuttlewood. 2004. "The Generational Transmission of Socioeconomic Inequalities in Child Cognitive Development and Emotional Health." *Social Science and Medicine* 58, 6 (Mar.): 1147–1158.

Navarro, Vicente. 1991. "Class and Race: Life and Death Situations." *Monthly Review* 43, 4 (Sept.): 1–13.

———. 2004. "The World Health Situation." *International Journal of Health Services* 34, 1:1–10.

O'Campo, Patricia, William W. Eaton and Carles Muntaner. 2004. "Labor Market Experiences, Work Organization, Gender Inequalities and Health Status: Results from a Prospective Analysis of U.S. Employed Women." *Social Science and Medicine* 58, 3 (Feb.): 585–594.

Patrick, Donald L., Jane Stein, Miguel Porta, Carol Q. Porter and Thomas C. Ricketts. 1988. "Poverty, Health Services, and Health Status in Rural America." *Milbank Quarterly* 66, 1:105–136.

Pereira, Joao. 1990. "The Economics of Inequality in Health: A Bibliography." *Social Science and Medicine* 31, 3:413–420.

Power, Chris. 1991. "Social and Economic Background and Class Inequalities in Health among Young Adults." *Social Science and Medicine* 32, 4:411–417.

Reich, Michael R. 1988. "Technical Fixes and Other Problems in Saving Lives in the World's Poorest Countries." *Journal of Public Health Policy* 9, 1 (Spring): 92–103.

Townsend, Peter. 1990. "Individual or Social Responsibility for Premature Death? Current Controversies in the British Debate about Health." *International Journal of Health Services* 20, 3:373–392.

Wennemo, Irene. 1993. "Infant Mortality, Public Policy and Inequality—A Comparison of 18 Industrialised Countries." *Sociology of Health and Illness* 15, 4 (Sept.): 429–446.

Wilkinson, Richard G. 1989. "Class Mortality, Income Distribution and Trends in Poverty 1921–1981." *Journal of Social Policy* 18, 3 (July): 307–335.

———. 1990. "Income Distribution and Mortality: A 'Natural' Experiment." *Sociology of Health and Illness* 12, 4 (Dec.): 391–412.

Williams, David D. 1993. "Barriers to Achieving Health." *Child and Adolescent Social Work Journal* 10, 5 (Oct.): 355–363.

Wright, James D. 1990. "Poor People, Poor Health: The Health Status of the Homeless." *Journal of Social Issues* 46, 4 (Winter): 49–64.

Zhang, Qi and Youfa Wang. 2004. "Socioeconomic Inequality of Obesity in the United States: Do Gender, Age, and Ethnicity Matter?" *Social Science and Medicine* 58, 6 (Mar.): 1171–1180.

13.3   Should Mentally Ill People Be De-Institutionalized?

The issue: What is the proper way to deal with a group with a chronic health problem: institutionalize them, treat them in the community, or simply let them deal with the problem on their own? Historically, North American societies have tried all of these options; each has its own shortcomings.

Question: What do mental patients have in common with AIDS victims, homosexuals, recreational drug users, heavy drinkers and ex-convicts? Answer: They are all socially stigmatized. Research shows that many people do not want to have them as neighbors, for example.

Today people are less unwilling to have members of racial minorities, recent immigrants, or people with large families as neighbors. The social rejection and exclusion of ethnic and racial minorities has diminished, but the rejection and exclusion of social minorities—including mental patients—continues.

As we noted earlier, applying the "illness" label typically excuses deviant behavior, rendering it blameless. However, for many people the mentally ill remain an exception to this rule. They have been declared ill, their deviance has been medicalized, and they are receiving treatment. Yet many fear or blame the mentally ill for their deviance and don't want them as neighbors.

In light of this, should the care for mental illness be de-institutionalized and mental patients released to community-based care? De-institutionalization of mental patients has become common in the last few decades. The release of mental patients into the community has increased with the reduction

and privatization of social services discussed earlier. But given the widespread stigmatization of mental patients, is de-institutionalization a good idea? And if it is, how should we deal with the problem of social stigma?

As with the other issues discussed in this book, people hold different opinions about the answer to these questions.

CARE FOR MENTAL PATIENTS SHOULD BE DE-INSTITUTIONALIZED

Early Support for De-Institutionalization   The argument in favor of de-institutionalization goes back at least to the early 1960s. It represents the convergence of many trends in social thought, which, themselves, reflect major changes in American society. Thus views on the mentally ill are a good indication of changes in the larger society that occurred from the 1960s onward.

One major support for de-institutionalization was the liberal revolt against *total institutions,* signified by interest in sociologist Erving Goffman's book *Asylums.* We discussed Goffman's views on total institutions in the section on prisons. Essentially, Goffman viewed total institutions, including mental hospitals, as fundamentally antitherapeutic and ineffective in helping the patients. Instead of making inmates healthy and better adjusted to life in the outside world, total institutions made inmates worse and/or less well-adjusted.

A second support for de-institutionalization was provided by social scientists and social workers. They opposed a growing *medicalization* of social problems. For sociology's labeling theorists, the problem posed by mental illness was often a problem of labeling and secondary deviation. Left alone, many "mentally ill" people could function effectively in society. By labeling them and treating them as sick people, doctors (especially psychiatrists) worsened the problem.

The fact that doctors were able to medicalize growing numbers of deviants indicated the growing popular acceptance of psychiatry and professional power of psychiatrists. Social scientists and social workers, holding different views of mental illness and professional goals of their own, challenged this medicalization process. Thus, in part, the fight against de-institutionalization was a fight over the right to define the boundaries of mental illness and ways of dealing with it.

A third support for de-institutionalization came from the legal community. From the 1950s onward, lawyers grew more and more active in fights for the civil liberties of minority groups. In the 1950s and afterward, lawyers fought for equal rights for American blacks. In the 1960s, lawyers entered the fight for the rights of draft dodgers and protesters against the Vietnam War. Increasingly, lawyers fought for the rights of prisoners and against capital punishment. Then they turned their attention to the rights of other dependent or vulnerable people: children, women, the terminally ill, and the mentally ill.

Though a fight for civil liberties, lawyers' actions on behalf of the mentally ill were also part of the war against the medicalization of social problems. From the 1960s onward, lawyers and doctors clashed often over people's rights, needs, and competencies.

A fourth support for de-institutionalization came from community mental health professionals. With encouragement from less traditional physicians,

psychiatrists, and social workers, their numbers had been growing since the 1950s. As their numbers grew even more rapidly in the decades that followed, it became possible to treat more mentally ill people released into the community.

A fifth support for de-institutionalization came from the pharmaceutical manufacturers. By 1960, traditional treatments of depression and schizophrenia such as electro-convulsive therapy (known as ECT or *shock treatment*) had acquired a bad name. Most people viewed them as harsh, excessive and—except as a means of pacifying violent patients—ineffective.

Increasingly, pharmaceutical drugs (especially tranquilizers, antidepressants, and lithium for schizophrenia) were substituted. They had the same pacifying effects but were less visible, cheaper, safer, and did less permanent damage than shock treatment. As these drugs came into general use and momentum gathered to release patients into community care, it became clear that chemical treatment worked just as well outside mental hospitals as it did inside them.

Finally, a sixth source of support came in the 1980s and 1990s with the so-called taxpayers revolt. More and more citizens wanted lower taxes and less public spending, even if that meant fewer social services and more risk for vulnerable groups in society. Taxpayers wanted cheaper alternatives to institutional care for a variety of social deviants, including mentally ill people.

What Supporters Expected Generally, the fight to de-institutionalize mental patients had a negative goal—the release of mental patients—but no positive goal. There was no clear plan about what to do with mental patients once they were in the community.

However, there was widespread agreement about the likely benefits of releasing mental patients. First, supporters believed that de-institutionalization would avoid the disruption of social ties and social roles that came with induction into total institutions—whether mental hospitals, prisons, convents, or military camps. Second, it would permit patients to exercise initiative and learn skills associated with independent living.

Third, in both these ways de-institutionalization would prevent the worsening of patients' original symptoms. In particular, it would prevent the development of institutional behaviors and attitudes connected with *prisonization,* which we discussed in an earlier section. It would also allow mental patients to escape the dangers (like physical and sexual assault) associated with life in total institutions. Hence, outpatient care would be health-preserving and health-enhancing.

Fourth, though there was no standard plan for outpatient care, many felt that community-based professionals (in clinics and half-way houses) would provide better care than mental patients received in institutions. In addition, outpatient care would reduce the stigmatization of mental illness and foster the outpatients' integration back into society.

The supporters of de-institutionalization hoped these things would happen and felt they had good reasons for supporting the plan. But things did not work out precisely as planned.

CARE FOR MENTAL PATIENTS SHOULD NOT BE DE-INSTITUTIONALIZED

Unfortunately, the fine ideals and high hopes of de-institutionalization were rarely achieved. Mental patients without friends or family to care for them had to live in rundown, unregulated rooming houses in poor parts of the city. Thus, the most immediate result of de-institutionalization was to deprive many ex-patients of the community life available within the mental hospital. Whatever its faults, the mental hospital had provided patients with familiar faces and people to talk to. By contrast, life on the outside was often isolated and lonely.

The problem was largely economic: The move to de-institutionalize mental patients coincided with major cuts in spending on health care and social services. Though community-based health care is cheaper than institutional care, it still costs more than many governments were prepared to pay. So, many mental patients released into the community were given less professional care than supporters of de-institutionalization had expected. The results were predictably harmful.

A shortage of funds meant too few resources for outpatient care, including too few professional therapists and support groups. Too few day programs were provided in the community. And there was not enough adequate, affordable housing, whether in halfway houses or through subsidies to private landlords.

Now just imagine what would happen if troubled, vulnerable people left a sheltered environment and came to live in the middle of a big city in poor housing, with little professional help, little to do, and little money to spend. Many (you predict) would become street people, spending most of their time in public, highly visible places. Some would get into trouble, or at least attract the attention of the police.

As a result (you predict), homelessness and public deviance by ex-mental patients would increase. With no one else to handle it, the police would step in. With nowhere else to go, many ex-patients would end up in jail. There, they would get even less treatment than they did in the mental hospital.

And, with more ex-patients on the streets and less treatment provided them, public attitudes would harden against the mentally ill. Middle-class people in particular would oppose the location of shelters, clinics, or group homes for the mentally ill in their neighborhoods. The resulting sentiment toward mental patients would be captured in the acronym N.I.M.B.Y.: "I have nothing against 'them' but, please, Not In My Back Yard."

Did you predict all of these things? Yes, they did all happen and they were perfectly predictable. Governments (and taxpayers) did not want to spend enough to make the programs work. Spending enough is a key. We can solve most of the problems associated with de-institutionalization by spending more money to care for released patients. But what about the N.I.M.B.Y. problem that's been created: Can it be solved, too, and if so, how?

THE NIMBY PROBLEM CAN BE SOLVED

In the last ten years, there has been enough sociological research on the NIMBY problem to give us the answer.

Where mental patients are concerned, researchers find that few people oppose nonresidential facilities. Few people mind outpatients coming into their community for treatment or day programs. However, some do oppose residential facilities (shelters or half-way houses) for the mentally ill in their "backyard." Fortunately, people who oppose a residence in their neighborhood prove to be less politically active than people who support the location. In the end, they are incapable of mounting effective opposition.

Liberal, nontraditional neighborhoods—often working-class neighborhoods—are the most likely to accept and even welcome residential facilities. Opposition is least if people are informed individually about the plan to locate a shelter or halfway-house in their neighborhood. (A community meeting on the topic is likely to mobilize opposition.) Surprisingly, for the best integration of patients, a moderate community reaction is better than none at all. Once established, a facility for mental patients poses no problems for the neighborhood. Research shows that, if uninformed of its presence, most residents do not even know the facility is there. Since no problems arise, opposition to the residence declines in time. There is no adverse effect on property values and no effect—positive or negative—on attitudes to mental illness.

Summing Up

Should mentally ill people be de-institutionalized? Yes, but not if it's only to ignore them more effectively. The de-institutionalization of mental patients was one of many civil liberties fights that gained momentum in the 1960s. Then, like other progressive movements of the 1960s, it ran out of steam.

In the 1990s, de-institutionalized mental patients made up a large share of the homeless and jail population, since there was nowhere else for them to go. It is hard to say whether these mentally ill people were worse off than residents of total institutions had been in the 1950s. Many would say they were better off in some ways but worse off in others.

The plan to de-institutionalize the mentally ill faltered because of tax cuts and insufficient spending. As homeless people, the mentally ill were even more stigmatized than they had been before. In an age of middle-class backlash, N.I.M.B.Y. was a predictable response to the needs of the mentally ill. And it had its effects directly—and again, predictably—on the well-being of the former psychiatric patients themselves.

A study published in 2000 by Eric Wright and his colleagues showed some of the effect. It followed a cohort of 88 people, first in an institution and then for two years after their de-institutionalization, and used a form of labeling theory to interpret findings. The authors concluded that in many ways, it *did not matter* where the people received care (in the community or in an institution) as long as there *was* care—but what did matter was rejection and stigmatizing of the people, and its effects on their self-esteem. Social rejection was a long-running source of social stress for the formerly institutionalized people. Being in a good—that is, a companionable—neighborhood is best. Being in a neighborhood where they are stigmatized, avoided on the street, and where problems routinely arise, is not much good for anybody concerned.

However, the basic thinking behind de-institutionalization was right—and the N.I.M.B.Y. problem is surmountable. With enough public spending and commitment to finding good locations for outpatient facilities, de-institutionalized mental patients will make the best possible recovery. We will not likely return to large-scale institutionalization of the mentally ill in the future. To a greater degree than in the past, our approach will depend on the type of mental illness and its severity.

We ended the last section by noting that in our society, bad health is not a matter of bad choice or incomplete information. The nation's health problem cannot be solved by providing more public health education. Nor, in the case of mental health, can it be solved just by removing people from health-worsening custodial institutions. A more positive input is needed. Mentally ill people need programs of treatment and professionally trained people to provide them.

We also noted that social inequality may be inevitable yet, in some societies, too much social inequality is unnecessary and harmful. Inequality hurts people's health in countless ways—for example, making them sick and shortening their lives.

As we have seen at other points in this book, strains associated with poverty, unemployment, and economic uncertainty, disrupt social relations. For example, they raise the risk of domestic violence and negligent parenting. More relevant to this present debate, social strains hurt people's mental health. No one can deny the importance of genetically-determined influences. At one level, mental illness is nothing more than a chemical imbalance. However, this imbalance is often associated with, and triggered by, traumatic or stressful social conditions.

So, even something as chemical and "psychological" as mental illness is well within the realm of sociological interest. Mental illness is socially defined, and that people defined as mentally ill are socially stigmatized. Social strains increase the risk of mental illness. Competing social groups (usually competing professions) dispute the best treatments for mental illness. Competing social groups also determine the availability of funds to treat mental illness. The failure to treat mental illness adequately produces new social problems (like homelessness). A socially sensible approach to neighbors leads to acceptance of treatment facilities in the neighborhood.

REVIEW EXERCISES

For Discussion and Debate

1. Why are mentally ill people so often stigmatized and excluded?
2. In your opinion, what is the best single argument in favor of de-institutionalizing mental patients? Why do you think so?
3. Would your neighbors object to having a half-way house for former mental patients on your own street? If so, why?
4. What is the best way to ensure acceptance of a half-way house for former mental patents in a middle-class neighborhood?

Writing Exercises

Write a brief (500-word) essay on one of the following topics:

1. "Fears of mental illness reflect nothing more than prejudice and ignorance."
2. "Cost aside, it would be better to have mental patients back in mental hospitals."
3. "Here's how I would re-integrate a former mental patient into the community."
4. "The legal rights of mental patients are still being ignored. For example . . ."

Research Activities

1. Collect some information on mental hospitals and prisons that would allow you to compare them, to determine whether mental hospitals also *prisonize* their inmates.
2. Develop a questionnaire that measures people's attitudes toward, and beliefs about, mental illness. Administer this questionnaire to six people and report on the results.
3. Using published material, find out the degree of connection between homelessness and de-institutionalization. What proportion of the homeless are mentally ill? What proportion of the mentally ill are homeless?
4. Find out about the pharmaceutical control of symptoms of medical illness. Focusing on one commonly used drug, what are its advantages over hospitalization? What are its side effects or other disadvantages?

SELECTED REFERENCES

Arens, D. A. 1993. "What Do the Neighbors Think Now? Community Residences on Long Island, New York." *Community Mental Health Journal* 29, 3:235–245.

Aubrey, T. D., B. Tefft and R. F. Currie. 1995. "Public Attitudes and Intentions Regarding Tenants of Community Mental Health Residences Who Are Neighbours." *Community Mental Health Journal* 31, 1:39–52.

Borinstein, A. B. 1992. "Public Attitudes toward Persons with Mental Illness." *Health Affairs* 11, 3:186–196.

Brokington, I. F. et al. 1993. "Tolerance of the Mentally Ill." *British Journal of Psychiatry* 162:93–99.

Bungener, Martine. 2001. "Living Outside the Walls of the Psychiatric Hospital: The Unavoidable Role of the Family at the Beginning of the Century." *Sciences Sociales et Sante* 19, 1 (Mar.): 107–111.

Carpenter, Mick. 2000. "It's a Small World: Mental Health Policy under Welfare Capitalism since 1945." *Sociology of Health and Illness* 22, 5 (Sept.): 602–620.

Currie, R. R. et al. 1989. "Maybe on My Street: The Politics of Community Placement of the Mentally Disabled." *Urban Affairs Quarterly* 25, 2:298–321.

Davidson, Larry, Connie M. Nickou, Peter Lynch, Silvia Moscariello, Rajita Sinha, Jeanne Steiner, Selby Jacobs and Michael A. Hoge. 2001. "Beyond Babel: Establishing System-Wide Principles of Collaborative Care for Adults with Serious and Persistent Mental Illness." *Research in Social Problems and Public Policy* 8:17–41.

Dodder, Richard A., Dawn L. Stephens and Barbara Murray. *The Impact of Employment on Integration of People with Developmental Disabilities: A Longitudinal Assessment,* Southern Sociological Society (SSS).

Fisher, Gene, Paul R. Benson and Richard C. Tessler. 1990. "Family Response to Mental Illness: Developments since Deinstitutionalization." *Research in Community and Mental Health* 6:203–236.

Goldman, H. H., J. P. Morrissey and L. L. Bachrach. 1983. "Deinstitutionalization in International Perspective: Variations on a Theme." *International Journal of Mental Health* 11, 4:153–165.

Gronfein, William. 1985. "Psychotropic Drugs and the Origins of Deinstitutionalization." *Social Problems* 32, 5 (June): 437–454.

Herman, Nancy J. 1987. "Mixed 'Nutters' and 'Looney Tuners': The Emergence, Development, Nature and Function of Two Informal Deviant Subcultures of Chronic Ex-Psychiatric Patients." *Deviant Behavior* 8, 3:235–258.

Isaac, Rael Jean and Virginia C. Armat. 1990. *Madness in the Streets: How Psychiatry and the Law Abandoned the Mentally Ill.* New York: Free Press.

Malla, A. and T. Shaw. 1987. "Attitudes toward Mental Illness: The Influence of Education and Experience." *International Journal of Social Psychiatry* 33, 1:33–41.

Mechanic, D. and J. Rochefort. 1990. "Deinstitutionalization: An Appraisal of Reform." *Annual Review of Sociology* 16:301–327.

Metraux, Stephen. 2002. "Taking Different Ways Home: The Intersection of Mental Illness, Homelessness and Housing in New York City." *Dissertation Abstracts International, A: The Humanities and Social Sciences* 63, 2 (Aug.): 777-A.

Monohan, J. 1992. "A Terror to Their Neighbours: Beliefs about Mental Disorder and Violence in Historical and Cultural Perspective." *Bulletin of the American Academy of Psychiatry and the Law* 20, 2:191–195.

Morrissey, Joseph P. and Howard H. Goldman. 1986. "Care and Treatment of the Mentally Ill in the United States: Historical Development and Reforms." *Annals of the American Academy of Political and Social Science* 484 (Mar.): 12–27.

Newton, Liz. 2001. "Self and Illness: Changing Relationships in Response to Life in the Community Following Prolonged Institutionalisation." *The Australian Journal of Anthropology* 12, 2 (Aug.): 166–181.

Noh, Samuel and William R. Avison. 1988. "Spouses of Discharged Psychiatric Patients: Factors Associated with Their Experience." *Journal of Marriage and the Family* 50, 2 (May): 377–389.

Parr, Hester. 2000. "Interpreting the 'Hidden Social Geographies' of Mental Health: Ethnographies of Inclusion and Exclusion in Semi-Institutional Places. *Health and Place* 6, 3 (Sept.): 225–237.

Rizzo, A. M. et al. 1992. "Strategies for Responding to Community Opposition to an Existing Group Home." *Psychosocial Rehabilitation Journal* 15, 3:85–95.

Scheper-Hughes, Nancy. 1987. "'Mental' in 'Southie': Individual, Family, and Community Responses to Psychosis in South Boston." *Culture, Medicine and Psychiatry* 11, 1 (Mar.): 53–78.

Scull, Andrew. 1985. "Deinstitutionalization and Public Policy." *Social Science and Medicine* 20, 5:545–552.

Tefft, B., A. Segall and B. Trute. 1987. "Neighbourhood Response to Community Mental Health Facilities for the Chronically Mentally Disabled." *Canadian Journal of Community Mental Health* 6, 2:37–49.

Wahl, O. F. 1993. "Community Impact of Group Homes for Mentally Ill Adults." *Community Mental Health Journal* 29, 3:247–259.

Warner, Richard. 1989. "Deinstitutionalization: How Did We Get Where We Are?" *Journal of Social Issues* 45, 3 (Fall): 17–30.

Wegner, E. L. 1990. "Deinstitutionalization and Community-Based Care for the Chronic Mentally Ill." *Research in Community and Mental Health* 6:295–324.

Wilmoth, G. H., S. Silver and L. J. Severy. 1987. "Receptivity and Planned Change: Community Attitudes and Deinstitutionalization." *Journal of Applied Psychology* 72, 1:138–145.

Wolch, Jennifer and Chris Philo. 2000. "From Distributions of Deviance to Definitions of Difference: Past and Future Mental Health Geographies." *Health and Place* 6, 3 (Sept.): 137–157.

Wright, Eric R. 1999. "Fiscal Outcomes of the Closing of Central State Hospital: An Analysis of the Costs to State Government." *Journal of Behavioral Health Services and Research* 26, 3 (Aug.): 262–275.

Wright, Eric R., George Avirappattu and Joan E. Lafuze. 1999. "The Family Experience of Deinstitutionalization: Insights from the Closing of Central State Hospital." *Journal of Behavioral Health Services and Research* 26, 3 (Aug.): 289–304.

CHAPTER 14

POPULATION

A population can be defined as "the stock of a species with throughput"—which is to say, a set of people (or animals or even inanimate objects) that changes in size as members are added to or subtracted from the set. And the social science that provides sociologists with materials for the study of population is *demography*.

Sociology and demography are two separate disciplines, but they are intimately linked. Demography is the scientific study of the size, structure, distribution, and growth of the world's population. *Social demography*, the topic of this chapter, is concerned with the effects of population on the organization of societies, and vice versa. Demographers play a central role in collecting and analyzing population data such as census data. And sociologists rely on demographers for this information to help us understand population problems.

In this chapter, we focus on three population problems that are causing concern in different parts of the world. First, we consider whether the world as a whole is becoming overpopulated—in effect, a population time bomb that will eventually use up the planetary resources we rely on to survive. Second, we ask whether states—not diseases—are the world's biggest cause of death. Third, we focus on North America (and other economically developed societies) and ask whether it is time to limit immigration to prevent overcrowding, unemployment, or intercultural conflict.

14.1 Are There Too Many People Around?

The issue: Whether we are about to be swamped by too many humans. Some ignore the rapid population growth and, in ignoring it, see no problem. Others hunt for and find dire predictions of ecological disaster, famine, and war over scarce resources. Is there any way we can foresee the likely future consequences of our current population trends?

The answer to this question begins with a theory proposed two centuries ago by Thomas Malthus. His slender and influential book, *An Essay on Population*, argued that populations grow *exponentially*, or *geometrically*. A population growing exponentially at a constant rate adds more people every year than the year before.

Consider a population of 1,000 women and 1,000 men. Each woman marries and has four children. If all survive, in the next generation there are roughly 2,000 women and 2,000 men. If all of those women have four children each, in the next generation there are roughly 4,000 women and 4,000 men, and in the generation after that, 8,000 women and 8,000 men. So, with a constant pattern of four births per woman, the population doubles every generation (roughly 30 years). In 300 years, the original population of two thousand exceeds a million people! This is the power of exponential growth.

On the other hand, increases in the food supply are only *additive* or *arithmetic*. The growth in food supplies is limited by available land, soil quality, and the level of technology. Malthus believed that there is a real risk of populations outgrowing increases in the food supply. The chance of running out of food thus poses a real threat to humanity. For that reason, checks (or limits) are needed to keep population growth in line with the food supply. Welfare schemes to help the poor are futile, said Malthus. If we feed the hungry, they will increase their numbers until they are hungry again.

The only sure solutions are positive checks and preventive checks. *Positive checks* prevent overpopulation by increasing the death rate. They include war, famine, pestilence, and disease. *Preventive checks* prevent overpopulation by limiting the number of live births. They include abortion, infanticide, sexual abstinence, delayed marriage, and contraceptive use.

As you can see, Malthus painted a grim picture of the world's future. But was he right? Is the world a "population time bomb," as Malthus believed? As usual, views on this matter vary.

THE WORLD IS STILL A POPULATION TIME BOMB

Those who argue today that there is still a population problem, that the world is becoming overpopulated, or that the world is a population time bomb, make some of the same arguments Malthus did nearly two centuries ago.

World Population Is Still Growing   Today, in central Africa, women average six children or more—not the four we cited in the example above. However, even the more modest four children per mother is common in southeast Asia, the Islamic world, parts of Africa, and Latin America. In short, hundreds of millions of mothers are still producing children at this rate. As we have seen, with four children per mother a population doubles every thirty years or so. Even allowing for slower growth, experts predict that in twenty years the current world population of roughly 6.4 billion people will be three billion larger. Will the world be able to feed 50 percent more people, let alone 100 percent more, in 20 years?

Population Growing Faster Than Food   Here, expert estimates vary. However, statistics collected by Worldwatch indicate that the world's grain production is falling. The store of available food is only enough to last for a short time, in the event of widespread crop failures. Other ecologists conclude that the number of people on earth will have to drop to at least one-third the current level by 2100 in order to survive in relative prosperity. Though an optimum population is between one and two billion people, the current population is over six billion, and predictions using current growth rates put it at between 12 billion and 15 billion people in 2100.

At the current growth rate of 1.1 percent a year, the population of the United States in 2100 could be 1.2 billion people, the current population of China. Today, each American consumes about 23 times more goods and services than the average person in the Third World and 53 times more than someone in China. A future America, with as many people as China today, might have to settle for something close to a Chinese standard of living.

Population Growth Strains Resources   One of the problems hinted at above is a growing shortage of nonrenewable resources that include land, fresh water, petroleum fuel, and minerals needed for manufacturing. It is not always clear which problems are caused by overpopulation. However, some observers link growing shortages of nonrenewable resources—even shortages of water—in the developed world to the problem of overpopulation.

In recent decades, humans have dramatically transformed the environment. The entire global ecology is affected, especially the equilibrium of the biosphere and the interdependence between living systems. This raises doubts about the survival chances of humanity. The ultimate source of concern for environmental change is its potential effect on the *livability* of the globe and its ability to support the variety and complexity of ongoing human activities.

Too-rapid population growth threatens human self-regulating systems as well as natural ecosystems. Even if rapid population growth does not cause all these problems, it makes them harder to solve.

Population Growth Slows Economic Development One major consequence of rapid growth is a population in which a large proportion is school-aged or younger. And since people need an education, rapidly growing societies must spend a large portion of their budget on schools and schooling. In such societies, child-bearing women are also less likely to be economically active. Along with old people, children, and the infirm, they require much public spending on health and welfare. So in a rapidly growing society, health, education, and welfare spending consume a large part of the national budget. The expense has to be paid by relatively few economically active adults.

Several consequences flow from this. First, high-fertility societies are often unable to afford good health, education, and welfare programs. Money spent on these programs takes money away from programs to develop manufacturing or export industries. This limits the country's ability to develop economically: At best, it slows the process dramatically.

Technology Cannot Solve the Problem In nineteenth-century England, the population problem Malthus had predicted seemed to solve itself. Mortality began to fall and, soon, so did childbearing. Food production increased and people's standard of living began to improve. All of these changes were due, in one way or another, to the development of new technology. Will technology come to our rescue again in the twenty-first century?

Not necessarily, for several reasons. There are limits to what we can expect technology to do. Given present levels of technology, the entire world's people cannot possibly enjoy the level of affluence North Americans enjoy today. There is just not enough wealth to go around. Beyond that, technology is costly and uncertain. As well as population size and consumption (or lifestyle) patterns, technology determines the amount of pollution generated, so it plays a part in destroying the ecosystem. It depletes natural resources, contributing to environmental problems and (even) perpetuating social inequality. Evidence suggests that technology will continue to improve, yet technology also has harmful side effects. Also, if our consumer culture is not checked it will offset gains from technology.

Positive Checks Replace Preventive Checks Malthus noted that in a population that failed to take preventive measures, positive checks would come into play. Plagues, famines, epidemics, wars, and other causes of death would increase. Eventually, a rise in the death rate would bring the population down to a manageable level.

Malthus did not realize that technological advances in agriculture would make it possible to vastly increase the food supply. Today, even in less-developed countries, most people have *some* food to eat. However, famines and epidemics continue to rage throughout the world—especially in the countries where the population is growing most rapidly.

Note also that the twentieth century is remarkable for two major shifts in human experience. One is an explosion of population growth that is still continuing. The other is an explosion of *mega-murders*—deaths by war, civil war, and internal terror—that (by one estimate) have consumed 188 million lives. (Some scholars have estimated that more people have died from genocide than from all wars combined in the twentieth century!) Malthus would not be surprised by these facts. Probably, rapid population growth increases conflict, brings pressure for rapid solutions, and reduces our ability to solve problems peacefully.

THE WORLD IS NOT A POPULATION TIME BOMB

Those who take the opposing view challenge Malthusians on many points of evidence.

Famines Are Political, Not Agricultural Today, few demographers support all of Malthus's gloomy views. They realize that claims of overpopulation are sometimes used to mask issues of powerlessness and social inequality.

For example, the famines that have plagued Ethiopia and Somalia in recent years are not a result of overpopulation. The World Bank has pushed for cash crops there, destroying local means of sustenance. Further, protectionism in agriculture by First World nations has closed markets to Third World nations, thus hurting their economies. Famines are also a result of improper land use, civil wars, and other social and political factors, such as low prices set on foods by the state. For strategic reasons, governments sometimes put a low priority on shipping food to regions of the country where rebel supporters are most numerous, thus trying to starve the rebels into submission. This use of strategic famine has a long history. So we cannot take famines, in themselves, as proof of overpopulation.

Beyond that, many developed societies pay their farmers not to grow crops, even if this means a shortage somewhere else in the world. So we cannot take low rates of food production to indicate the maximum amount of food that can be produced in the world today.

World Food Production Is Growing   Some estimates show food production falling behind population growth. Other estimates however show food production growing faster than world population—that is to say, at more than 4 percent per year.

It is hard to account for the discrepancy between these estimates. Perhaps experts assess the trustworthiness of data sources differently, or count different kinds of foods into their calculation.

Population Growth Not to Blame for Slow Development   It is likely that rapid population growth slows down economic development. However, at issue is *how much* it slows development, compared with other factors.

Note for example that economic growth has been extremely slow in the United States—indeed, in much of the Western world—for the last decade or so. That cannot be blamed on rapid population growth.

There are many possible reasons for slow economic growth: global competition, a shortage of capital, competing economic or social goals, poor corporate planning, poor economic planning, poor political leadership, exploitation by foreign investors, internal strife—even a low level of commitment to economic growth. How much each of these factors contributes to slow growth in a developing country is an empirical question. To answer it we need to study countries carefully, one at a time. We cannot assume that rapid population growth is the most important influence in each, or any, case.

Population Growth Not to Blame for Conflict, Stress   Likewise, we cannot assume that rapid population growth is the most important influence on social conflict or environmental stress.

It is true that social conflict, rapid population growth, and environmental stress are often found together. But showing a correlation is not the same as establishing causation. All three may be caused by yet another factor and at least two possible candidates suggest themselves: national poverty and global inequality.

National poverty and a low position in the global hierarchy of nations are correlated with each other. Both promote social conflict, rapid population growth, and environmental stress. Take poverty: Compared to rich people, poor people are more likely to invest heavily in children (their only insurance against impoverished old age). They are also more likely to overuse their land to get the maximum short-term productivity. And they are more likely to engage in violent conflict with members of other groups or tribes against whom they compete for scarce land, jobs, or housing.

To repeat, rapid population growth is part of each scenario, but it does not necessarily cause the other problems. Poverty and inequality often cause problems that are similar to those caused by overpopulation, and may contribute to overpopulation too.

Technology Will Triumph Again   Taking a long view of human history, you have to put your money on humanity coming through once again. Many civilizations have fallen in the past—Babylonian, Egyptian, Greek, Roman, and so on—yet here we are today, still alive and able to talk about it.

History is full of wars, plagues, epidemics, challenges, and crises. Yet the human race is still here—larger and more prosperous than ever. The human ability to hatch new ideas and technologies—to be creative—has carried us through, and it can do so again. So we may not be able to say precisely which technology will help us out of our present difficulty, nor who will invent it, or when. But we can feel certain that it will happen sooner or later.

Economic Growth Will Slow Population Growth

With the arrival of new ideas and new technology, economic development will explode once again.

When that happens, we can expect rapidly growing populations to enter the demographic transition toward lower death and birth rates. History shows that people have much to gain by doing so, and too much to lose by failing to do so. With low death rates, they will have little need for many children—especially once old age security and middle-class lifestyles become available.

SUMMING UP

Are there too many people around? Well, that really depends on what you mean by "too many." More than that, the issue is how quickly people are increasing, not simply how many heads there are to count.

In his book, *How Many People Can the Earth Support?* population expert Joel Cohen recognizes that our "population time bomb" question cannot be answered as posed. The earth can support many more people than currently live on it, but it supports them with more or less ease under different conditions. Cohen notes a number of factors that determine when more or fewer people are feasible:

Equality of well-being   With more equal global resources, earth can support many more people than it does today.

Technological development   With more time to prepare technologically for their arrival, earth can support many more people.

Political institutions   With governments that are more honest, effective, and peaceful, earth can support many more people. (But more people might limit our liberty and political participation.)

Economic institutions   With safer, better-organized work, and healthier, better-educated workers, earth can support many more people.

Demographic arrangements   With a higher death rate and shorter life span, earth can support many more people. (Also, with better child care arrangements, to allow more women to work.)

Level of well-being   If we can tolerate a lower level of material well-being, earth can support many more people than today.

Environmental conditions   If we can tolerate more physical and biological degradation of the environment, the earth can support many more people.

What range of variation?   If we can tolerate more fluctuation in death rates and material conditions, earth can support many more people.

What risk of catastrophe?   If we can tolerate more uncertainty about the occurrence and outcome of disasters—famines, epidemics, wars, and so on—earth can support many more people.

Two things are to be noted about this list of questions and answers. First, we cannot bank on the occurrence of changes—for example, more equality, better government, or new technology—that will make earth able to support many more people. Second, most of us would be unwilling to give up many "goods"—like material prosperity, long life, political liberty, and a low-risk future—merely to have more people on earth.

Putting these two observations together, Cohen is telling us the world *is not* a population time bomb if we can adjust the earth to accommodating more people, and adjust ourselves to doing without things we like and value. If we cannot or will not make these changes, then there are limits to how many people the earth can support and the world *is* a population time bomb.

REVIEW EXERCISES

For Discussion and Debate

1. Would it be fair to say that the world's population problem is just as Malthus described it two centuries ago?
2. Hasn't the continuing invention of new materials and new technologies shown that it is unnecessary to worry about nonrenewable resources?
3. Would Malthus likely view twentieth-century wars and genocides as "positive checks"?
4. "The problem is not population *size* so much as it is rate of population *growth*."

Writing Exercises

Write a brief (500-word) essay on one of the following topics:

1. "The most important thing I would be unwilling to give up to have more people on earth."
2. "Technology cannot come to the rescue this time."
3. "The real problem is not that there are too many people but that our political institutions cannot take care of the people who already exist."
4. "How I would try to persuade people in less-developed countries to have fewer children."

Research Activities

1. Find out how long it takes the population to double in three countries of your choosing: one highly developed, one moderately developed, one largely undeveloped.
2. For the three countries mentioned above, find out how the "doubling time" has changed in the last fifty years. What accounts for these changes?
3. For the same three countries, collect data on the age distribution of each population and draw an age-sex pyramid to depict each one. What is the (observable) connection between doubling time and the shape of the age distribution?
4. For any of the three age-sex pyramids you just drew, examine irregularities in the shape (i.e., indentations or bulges at various points). What historical events account for these irregularities?

SELECTED REFERENCES

Amalric, Franck and Tariq Banuri. 1994. "Population: Malady or Symptom?" *Third World Quarterly* 15, 4 (Dec.): 691–706.

Aufhauser, Elisabeth and Rosa Diketmuller. 2001. "Overpopulation Poverty Creates Population Politics Wealth? What Families Plan for the Fight against Poverty." *Journal fur Entwicklungspolitik* 17, 1: 47–67.

Barter, Joseph. 2000. "Global War and the Human Population Problem." *Journal of Social, Political and Economic Studies* 25, 2 (Summer): 241–250.

Bartlett, Albert A. 2000. "Democracy Cannot Survive Overpopulation." *Population and Environment* 22, 1 (Sept.): 63–71.

Beckerman, Wilfred. 1994. "'Sustainable Development': Is It a Useful Concept?" *Environmental Values* 3, 3 (Autumn): 191–209.

Bilsborrow, Richard E. 1992. "Population Growth, Internal Migration, and Environmental Degradation in Rural Areas of Developing Countries." *European Journal of Population* 8, 2:125–148.

Boer, Leen and Ad Koekkoek. 1994. "Development and Human Security." *Third World Quarterly* 15 (Sept.): 519–522.

Catton, William R., Jr. 1993. "Carrying Capacity and the Death of a Culture: A Tale of Two Autopsies." *Sociological Enquiry* 63, 2 (Spring): 202–223.

Chapman, Robert. 1999. "No Room at the Inn, or Why Population Problems Are Not All Economic." *Population and Environment* 21, 1 (Sept.): 81–97.

Conelly, W. Thomas and Miriam S. Chaiken. 2000. "Intensive Farming, Agro-Diversity, and Food Security under Conditions of Extreme Population Pressure in Western Kenya." *Human Ecology* 28, 1 (Mar.): 19–51.

Donohoe, Martin. 2003. "Causes and Health Consequences of Environmental Degradation and Social Injustice." *Social Science and Medicine* 56, 3 (Feb.): 573–587.

Dyson, Tim. 1994. "World Population Growth and Food Supplies." *International Social Science Journal* 46, 3 (141) (Sept.): 361–385.

Ehrlich, Paul R. and Anne H. Ehrlich. 1990. *The Population Explosion*. New York: Simon and Schuster.

Gilland, Bernard. 1983. "Considerations on World Population and Food Supply." *Population and Development Review* 9, 2 (June): 203–211.

Grebenik, E. 1989. "Demography, Democracy, and Demonology." *Population and Development Review* 15, 1 (Mar.): 1–22.

Henderson, Conway W. 1993. "Population Pressures and Political Repression." *Social Science Quarterly* 74, 2 (June): 322–333.

Hern, Warren M. 1993. "Has the Human Species Become a Cancer on the Planet? A Theoretical View of Population Growth as a Sign of Pathology." *Current World Leaders* 36, 6 (Dec.): 1089–1124.

Keyfitz, Nathan. 1992. "Seven Ways of Causing the Less Developed Countries' Population Problem to Disappear—in Theory." *European Journal of Population* 8, 2:149–167.

Keyfitz, Nathan. 1989. "The Growing Human Population." *Scientific American* 261, 3 (Sept.): 119–126.

Keyfitz, Nathan. 1994. "Tomorrow's Cold War." *Queen's Quarterly* 101, 1 (Spring): 15–23.

Kirk, Dudley. 2000. "Dudley Kirk on Population Changes and Prospective Power Relations after World War II: A View from 1943." *Population and Development Review* 26, 3 (Sept.): 583–596.

Kumar, G. Stanley Jaya. 2000. "Population and Environment by 2000 AD—A Social Manifesto." *The International Journal of Sociology and Social Policy* 20, 8:55–68.

Livi-Bacci, Massimo. 1994. "Population Policies: A Comparative Perspective." *International Social Science Journal* 46, 3 (141) (Sept.): 317–330.

McNicoll, Geoffrey. 1994. "Population and Institutional Change." *International Social Science Journal* 46, 3 (141) (Sept.): 307–315.

Mohanty, Aliva. 2002. "Women Empowerment: Antidote to Population Explosion and Conducive to Development." *Journal of Social Sciences* 6, 1 (Jan.): 53–57.

Petersen, William. 1982. "The Social Roots of Hunger and Overpopulation." *Public Interest* 68 (Summer): 37–52.

Pimentel, David. 1991. "Global Warming, Population Growth, and Natural Resources for Food Production." *Society and Natural Resources* 4, 4 (Oct.–Dec.): 347–363.

Rivers, Theodore John. 2003. "Technology and the Use of Nature." *Technology in Society* 25, 3 (Aug.): 403–416.

Russell, Claire and W. M. S. Russell. 2000. "Population Crises and Population Cycles." *Medicine, Conflict and Survival* 16, 4 (Oct.–Dec.): 383–410.

Sen, Amartya. 1994. "Population: Delusion and Reality." *New York Review of Books* 41, 15 (Sept. 22): 62–71.

Shandra, John M., Bruce London and John B. Williamson. 2003. "Environmental Degradation, Environmental Sustainability, and Overurbanization in the Developing World: A Quantitative, Cross-National Analysis." *Sociological Perspectives* 46, 3 (Fall): 309–329.

Simon, Julian L. 1990. "Population Growth Is Not Bad for Humanity." *National Forum* 70, 1 (Winter): 12–16.

Skinner, Curtis. 1988. "Population Myth and the Third World." *Social Policy* 19, 1 (Summer): 57–62.

Smith, Richard M. 2001. "Welfare of the Individual and the Group: Malthus and Externalities." *Proceedings of the American Philosophical Society* 145, 4 (Dec.): 402–414.

Waddell, Craig et al. 1994. "Perils of a Modern Cassandra: Rhetorical Aspects of Public Indifference to the Population Explosion." *Social Epistemology* 8, 3 (July–Sept.): 221–237.

Wilmoth, John R. and Patrick Ball. 1992. "The Population Debate in American Popular Magazines, 1946–90." *Population and Development Review* 18, 4 (Dec.): 631–668.

14.2   Are States the Biggest Cause of Death?

The issue: Each person dies his or her own death, yet death—like life—is a social phenomenon. With the rise of both genocide and public health in the twentieth century, has death now become mainly a political issue? Or does death remain individual—a matter of your life and your responsibility?

Death is a universal issue for humans, since death faces everyone. Yet our understanding of death is changing. People are leading longer lives than ever, and we have the ability—as individuals and as societies—to make our lives longer and healthier. As individuals, we can prolong our own lives by giving up smoking, exercising regularly, eating well, and avoiding unnecessary risks (e.g., dangerous driving, excessive alcohol use). As a society we can prolong American lives by improving public sanitation and health education, ensuring that poor people have enough to eat and a clean place to live, and providing medical care for everyone.

But where should we start: with the individual or the state? Who is most responsible for American deaths: the individual or the state? Today, the issue of death often shows itself in debates about public-health versus private-health initiatives. These debates question whether or not the government has central responsibility for the well-being of its citizens. They raise questions like the following: How much public money should be spent on health? What is the public responsibility for personal well-being? And, on an international scale, who is responsible for the fight against HIV/AIDS? Are AIDS-related deaths a result of individual fate or political inaction?

What about deaths that are more directly related to government actions, such as a declaration of war? War may have been the single most important cause of death in the century just passed. Between 1900 and 1999, scores of millions died in wars, directly and indirectly. Statistics readily measure the direct casualties of war; however, civilian casualties are harder to measure—especially deaths that result indirectly from war, due to famine, epidemics, or interpersonal violence. Civil wars and their indirect effects can be even more deadly than world wars, but our death statistics are less reliable for these wars.

War, death, and politics are closely linked, since governments often use wars and death to further their goals. Throughout the twentieth century, governments repeatedly used wars to further their political agendas—often to build international empires. Additionally, many governments have used death, the threat of death, rape, torture, imprisonment, and enslavement in work camps to eliminate political foes or stifle dissenters. Who knows how many people perished in Chinese prisons, Russian gulags, and waves of repression in Africa and South America? Over the century, the numbers would have run into the millions. And that's not counting the deaths caused by German genocide between 1935 and 1945—6 million is a conservative estimate here.

Those who view death as an individual event may recognize the organized, premeditated death around us, but argue that governments are not killing people—people are killing people. They also assert that people must take responsibility for their own lives. This view is especially strong in countries like the United States, where individualism is a central part of the national identity.

The issue of whether death is individual or political is a debate with more than two sides. It is up to you to find the political dimensions in death and then to decide how death ought to be treated—whether as an individual problem, or a societal problem with social solutions.

DEATH IS INDIVIDUAL

"Cause of Death" Is Theoretical   Some people would say that the concept of *cause of death* is theoretical. What constitutes cause of death depends on societal definitions. Most people see the death of a soldier as different from the death of a civilian, for example. Killing a soldier in battle is acceptable—even heroic; but killing a civilian is typically not. In times of war, we change our definition of what constitutes an acceptable death, and return to old definitions once the war is over. Violence in war is kept distinct, since it produces deaths that serve a stated social purpose. These needed war deaths are depersonalized; the killers are rarely identified or identifiable. Sometimes the victims remain "unknown soldiers."

Even in civil society, cause of death is a difficult concept. Since Durkheim wrote his classic work on the topic of suicide, it has been difficult to know who is responsible when people take their own lives: the individual, society, or the individual's attachment to society. Certainly, suicide rates reflect social variations, so society plays a part. Equally evident is the social influence on rates of homicide, mental illness, and physical violence—all of which can result in death.

Individual Responsibility   Under war conditions, dead soldiers are rarely held responsible for their own death, nor are their killers held personally responsible. Rarely is the soldier's government held responsible for a death, though war protesters sometimes try to shift the blame in this way. How different this is from most deaths in civilian life! There, every death has a knowable (if not known) perpetrator: Someone is always to blame.

In the Middle Ages, the ultimate fear was not death but dying alone, unseen, untended, and unloved. Today, many people die in hospital rooms, sometimes alone but rarely untended. Approximately 80 percent of Swedes, 60 percent of Americans, and 20 percent of Romanians die in hospital beds, for example. Modern societies have institutionalized death, just like other key human experiences, by creating large organizations to oversee the event: hospitals to oversee birth, schools to oversee learning, churches to oversee praying, and welfare agencies to oversee unemployment.

Though the place where people die may have changed over the centuries, death remains a deeply personal occurrence. The dying person is still the one most aware of when he or she is going to die and, often, most able to take control of his or her death. This is seen in the increase of palliative and

at-home care, both of which allow people to make their own choices about death. As a result, death remains an individual experience and an individual responsibility, not a political one. Governments fund programs that help lives, but it is up to the individual whether or not to use them. Of course, many people are not even aware of all the programs available through the government and hospice organizations that provide assistance to terminally ill patients. A lack of awareness of options by the patient results from too many choices and insufficient idea of what organizations do what and who to call for help. Many services offer identical help and can run into problems of redundancy. Self-reliance remains a cherished value. Individuals make the critical choices about health care that may result in life or death. In the end, patients are in charge of their own treatment. They sign consent forms and can decline treatments, if they wish.

Saying individuals have "choices" over their illness is a very loaded term. There is a blatant lack of choice available when one is sick or dying. People cannot choose the severity of their disease, the prognosis, the level of pain and discomfort, and people ultimately can't choose to prolong life. Once mental capacities are afflicted, people no longer have any choice over anything that happens to them. Everything revolves around the sickness/disease therefore choice becomes null and void.

As another example of individual responsibility, look at the case of accidents. Departments of health worldwide tell us that "most accidents are preventable"; therefore, with such a warning, responsibility should be on individuals to prevent them. After all, accidents do not happen to a population, they happen to individuals. As such, accidents are individual problems that arise from carelessness—right? If someone decides to be careless and ends up spilling coffee on him or herself, then the resulting burn is that individual's fault. The individual, having been careless, faces the health consequences—just as any sports enthusiast accepts responsibility for injury while playing a sport.

Such a *voluntaristic* point of view is a key part of American culture. Freedom and choice mean that individuals do what suits them best; accordingly, we expect them to choose wisely, in their best interests. If we want people to have the maximum freedom, they, not government, must be prepared to take the maximum risk and responsibility.

Risk-Taking   As we have said, throughout life individuals make choices. People choose whether to cook and eat a healthy meal at home or pick up a less-healthy fast food meal at McDonalds, for example. If someone wants to eat unhealthy food—food that is fattening and salty, for example—shouldn't they be allowed to? Of course they should, so long as they also accept the health risk—that is, the death risk—of doing so over a long period of time.

Smoking provides an excellent example of such individual risk-taking. Most—perhaps all—smokers in North America know the side effects of smoking. If people make an informed decision to start smoking, it is their right to do so. The health consequences are a cost that people accept for the satisfaction they receive from smoking. Some smokers even acknowledge they would rather live a shorter, smoke-filled life than a longer life without smoking. But if people freely choose to smoke, then why do governments spend public money to stop people from smoking, and why do they make life increasingly difficult for smokers? By engaging in campaigns, the government limits the individual's right to smoke. The right to life and hence to death is thus curtailed by the government.

These and other government initiatives in the health area are becoming more and more common. We hear on the news that obesity can lead to premature death or that drinking red wine and eating dark chocolate is good for your circulatory system. We are battered with messages about health from government and the media. Some would say that government and other public agencies are interfering with people's right to choose their own health.

Private Sector Health Care   Unlike the public health-care system, the private health-care system continues to hold the individual responsible for him or herself. From the standpoint of individual responsibility, private health plans are best because they allow individuals to pay for what they use. If people lead riskier lives, they pay higher insurance

premiums, for example, because they will likely make more use of doctors and hospitals. In short, these health providers assign individuals responsibility for their own lives.

By assigning individuals the greatest possible freedom, the American system seems to work best for its citizens. No wonder organizations like the World Bank support private health care worldwide. They do so because private health care reduces government spending on middle-class people and allows governments to target the poor for care. Also, the World Bank notes that private sector health care is available to everyone and people actually find it more equitable than public systems.

That's one side of the debate: the view that health is a private, individual concern, just like death. Governments can't improve on that formula, and even if governments don't cause health problems that result in death, neither do they complicate access to health care in a way that results in death. However, as always, there are two sides to this argument.

DEATH IS POLITICAL

On the other side of the debate, some argue that governments play two roles in increasing or decreasing the death rate. They increase it, for example, by making wars and carrying out genocidal actions against their own citizens. They decrease the death rate by providing health care and public health legislation that help citizens lead longer, healthier lives; and they increase the death rate by failing to do so. Consider these points one at a time.

Capital Punishment   Governments kill people when they legislate and carry out the death penalty. Currently, America is among a very few developed societies—indeed, among a very few societies of the world—that still execute criminals. Most industrial nations have abolished capital punishment and believe that governments should not be in the business of killing people, except in wars. Because some of the United States do use the death penalty, the country effectively maintains a *killing state*. The public may support this activity because they are kept from seeing the full consequence of these actions. Some may imagine that capital punishment deters future crimes; but research shows that it doesn't. Others feel that capital punishment is needed to express their moral outrage, whatever the consequence.

Genocide and Democide Large-scale death by government, sometimes called *democide*, was part of the legacy of totalitarianism in the twentieth century. Mid-range estimates put the toll of death by government at between 167 and 175 million dead in that hundred-year span. Although most of us in North America think of Hitler as the virtuoso in using death as a political instrument, he was not alone. Stalin, Mao Tse-tung, and Lenin all used death as a central part of their political agenda, as did numerous petty dictators in Africa, Asia, and South America over the course of the century.

The Soviet Communist Party alone is responsible for killing over 62 million people; the reasons why are not entirely clear. Generally, the killing was designed to bring dissidents under control, as with the intentional Ukrainian famine of the 1930s. (This, in turn, may not have been unlike the British use of famine against the Irish during the mid-nineteenth-century potato famine.) Death was used as a political tool by the ruling Bolsheviks, just as it was used by other totalitarian regimes, Fascist and Communist, in Germany, Italy, China, Japan, and elsewhere. However, in the Russian case, the activity was based on a theoretical model. In trying to build a new nation modeled on the Marxist utopia, Soviet rulers were willing to sacrifice lives now in hopes of attaining the perfection later.

When talking about democide and genocide, many people take the view that lessons have been learned and genocide will never again happen. Yet organized death has been used repeatedly as a political instrument, and continues to be so used. The terrorist attacks on New York and Washington on September 11, 2001, had a political goal and used death as an instrument to further that goal. The subsequent military attacks on Afghanistan and Iraq by U.S. forces also had a political goal and used death as an instrument. There is no end to this in sight, given the current government's foreign policy.

Other wars have been even worse. Consider the former Yugoslavia. In the case of Bosnia, 200,000 were killed, 750,000 went missing, and an estimated 60,000 women were raped, to further the Serbian goal of ethnic cleansing. Why does this kind of killing happen over and over? In the Bosnian case, what began as a small issue developed into genocide because powerful outside nations refused to get involved. The European Union classified the matter as a civil dispute, as did NATO, the UN, and the United States—though all of these groups knew what was going on in Bosnia. Such systematic ignorance sends a message to the world that, often, it is all right to use genocide—war more generally—to attain political goals.

A more recent crisis showed that death is political in Africa too. Though the *New York Times* began reporting on the Rwandan massacre a mere four days after it began, no Western nation intervened. The lack of foreign assistance allowed 800,000 deaths in three months. A genocidal action, the Rwandan crisis was an attempt by Hutus to get rid of the Tutsis. The Hutu government identified all the Tutsis as enemies of the state and called on Hutus to exterminate them. Even Hutus fleeing the violence were forced to kill at least one Tutsi before they were allowed past roadblocks.

The examples of Bosnia and Rwanda show that, by making ethnic cleansing a political goal, death becomes a tool by which governments carry out their policies. Governments are fully capable of using death as a political instrument. But why are we, ordinary citizens, willing to comply with their killing ways? Why are most of us willing to look on in silence when a government kills people? Or feign ignorance when a government (through its inaction) fails to prevent people from dying? Perhaps the answer is that most of us don't want to know the facts. We want government and its agents to attend to the "dirty work" that keeps us safe and comfortable, but don't want to examine their work in detail. Perhaps, too, we comply because we feel unable to challenge authority.

In a famous experiment to determine whether Americans could behave like Nazis, psychologist Stanley Milgram explored how people can inflict pain and even kill others when they do not feel responsible. Modeled as a learning experiment, a person behind a plate glass—call him the "word learner" (W)—was asked to memorize and recall pairs of words. On the other side of the glass, the experimental subject (S) was supposed to administer an electric shock whenever the W failed to recall the right word. The Experimenter (E), dressed in a scientific white laboratory jacket, told S that he—the Experimenter—would accept full responsibility for any harm done to W. As the intensity of shocks increased, W would scream and show signs of great pain, but E told S to keep administering the shocks. Some Ss continued to do so until W appeared to be dead.

This experiment shows how authorities can influence people to kill others. Governments, as authorities, may tell us that killing is heroic, or that it accepts responsibility for your actions. As the Milgram experiment suggests, people will kill others under these conditions. Killing is not limited to fascist and communist regimes, but also has history in the American Civil War and, some would say, the American war in Vietnam. Americans have often had to grapple with the rights and wrongs of military action ordered by the government, most recently in connection with the war in Iraq.

Public Health Some government killing is through inaction—that is, a failure to provide public health measures that would save American lives. Some argue that one of the greatest achievements in the twentieth century has been the reduction in mortality rates throughout much of the developing world. And in the developed societies, such as America, people have attained a long life expectancy and—for many—a high level of healthy activity over the life span. Yet many Americans have a shorter than average life span and suffer from poor health conditions—whether depression, addiction, diabetes, asthma, cancer, or high blood pressure—that result at least in part from their social class and living conditions.

Currently, no nation spends as much as the United States (per capita) on health care, yet 40 million Americans are without proper health-care coverage. These individuals cannot afford to be

responsible for their health, yet we hold them responsible by not making the government responsible. Many Americans believe that what is needed is a public health-care system that ensures equity, so that everyone is looked after. Public health care also is a cheaper alternative to private care, since no profits are made. Moreover, public health care shifts some of the costs away from increasingly expensive remedial treatment to less expensive preventive treatment, yielding lower costs to the system. People are more likely to seek out preventive care when they don't have to pay for it, thereby reducing the long-term costs through early detection.

Nowhere is the death-defying potential role of government more evident than in the case of epidemics, such as HIV/AIDS.

AIDS Consider the African AIDS epidemic as an illustration of what happens when governments cannot or will not take systematic action. To date, at least 50 million Africans have died or have been infected, yet few African nations have a solid plan to deal with AIDS. Instead, the AIDS situation has given rise to political inaction. In turn, political inaction is directly correlated to rising AIDS infection and death rates. Throughout Africa, the infection rates have not changed, except in Uganda. Efforts by Uganda's government have markedly reduced HIV infection in the 25 and younger group. Most of the inaction in other countries has resulted from the government's unwillingness to discuss sex and its connection to AIDS. This means that governments ignore the problems of AIDS, and NGOs are forced to do all the work of combating the disease in Africa.

The AIDS epidemic provides two interesting insights. First, death and politics are related because government inaction in the health area generally causes death. Secondly, they are particularly related in the case of epidemics. Combating an epidemic cannot be an individual effort, since the disease does not only affect the individual but society as a whole. A public health plan would both help individuals to combat the illness and educate the populace about ways to prevent further infection.

SUMMING UP

As you can see, death and politics are related on many levels. Politics and death are most obviously related when it comes to wars and government-sanctioned killing, such as capital punishment or genocide. No other century has seen as much political killing as the twentieth century. People may be killing other people, but ultimately governments orchestrate these actions. By breaking down the tasks and responsibilities, involving as many citizens as possible, and using propaganda in the service of their actions, governments make killing seem less like killing and more like a civic duty—even an honor.

As we have seen, governments also kill when they fail to save lives by legislating good health care. A public health approach benefits society by allowing everyone to choose good health. All of the nations with top-notch living standards for its citizens have strong public health agencies. However excellent and widespread private health care may be in the United States, it is unattainable for many.

Some might say that a strong public health system takes away freedom and choice, though collectively we are all better off. In fact, private health care fails many people and as such fails to give them any options. In all, death and politics are intertwined and we will continue to think more about this fact as the populations of industrialized nations continue to live longer and health-care systems struggle to deal with their demands. In a large complex society, life and death cannot be left to individual responsibility. When a person dies, the state is never blameless, nor is the individual wholly to blame.

REVIEW EXERCISES

For Discussion and Debate

1. Do people really have free choice about how long and how well they will live?
2. Have states become more or less violent in the last 40 years?
3. "There's no connection between how states provide health care and how they handle war."
4. "Torture is perfectly justifiable when a country is in a life-and-death struggle with terrorists."

Writing Exercises

Write a brief (500-word) essay on one of the following topics:

1. "If America had African-levels of AIDS, research funds for AIDS would be unlimited."
2. "*Ethnic cleansing* has gone on for millennia: It draws on a people's sense of tribal loyalty and will never disappear from human life."
3. "Capital punishment is the most honest, healthiest expression of a nation's morality."
4. "Since people can never live as long or well as they would like, the job of the state is to allocate life and death as fairly and efficiently as possible."

Research Activities

1. How are people's attitudes toward war affected by their experience of war as soldiers or as refugees? Interview at least four people who have first-hand experience of war and find out their views.
2. Investigate the research literature on HIV-AIDS to find out the social circumstances that make people more or less tolerant of AIDS sufferers. For example, are they more likely to be tolerant if they know AIDS sufferers personally, through family or friendship?

3. How do researchers evaluate the merits of different nations' health-care systems? Using the most believable of these evaluative techniques, and examining appropriate statistics, which are the best and which are the worst health-care systems in the world today?

4. What are the main causes of death in your age and sex group, where you live? Examine some recent statistics on this question. Then find equivalent statistics from 100 years ago, describe what has changed, and explain why.

SELECTED REFERENCES

Aries, Philippe and Helen Weaver. 1982. "The Tame Death." Pp. 5–28 in *The Hour of Our Death*. New York: Vintage.

Baines, E. K. 2003. "Body Politics and the Rwandan Crisis." *Third World Quarterly* 24, 3:479–493.

Benson, John M., Charles E. Denk, John C. Fletcher and Tina M. Reigel. 1997. "How Do Americans Want to Die? A Factorial Vignette Survey of Public Attitudes about End-of-Life Medical Decision-Making." *Social Science Research* 26, 1:95–120.

Blank, Robert H. 2001. "Technology and Death Policy: Redefining Death." *Mortality* 6, 2:191–202.

Caldwell, John C. 2000. "Rethinking the African AIDS Epidemic." *Population and Development Review* 26, 1:117–135.

Chalk, Frank and Kurt Jonassohn. 1990. *The History and Sociology of Genocide: Analyses and Case Studies*. New Haven, CT: Yale University Press.

Davey, Judith. 2000. "From Birth to Death: A Social Monitoring Framework from New Zealand." *Social Indicators Research* 49, 1:51–67.

Denton, Margaret and Candace L. Kemp. 2003. "The Allocation of Responsibility for Later Life: Canadian Reflections on the Roles of Individuals, Government, Employers, and Families." *Aging & Society* 23, 6:737–760.

Garland, David. 2002. "The Cultural Uses of Capital Punishment." *Punishment and Society* 4, 4:459–487.

Green, Judith. 1999. "From Accidents to Risk: Public Health and Preventable Injury." *Health, Risk, & Society* 1, 1:25–39.

Gwatkin, Davidson R., Michel Guillot and Patrick Heuveline. 2002. "The Uneven Tides of the Health Transition." *Social Science & Medicine* 55, 2:313–322.

Hionidou, Violetta. 2002. "Why Do People Die in Famines? Evidence from Three Island Populations." *Population Studies* 56, 1:65–80.

Hirsch, Herbert. 1995. *Genocide and the Politics of Memory: Studying Death to Preserve Life*. Chapel Hill, NC: The University of North Carolina Press.

Kimenyi, Alexandre and Tois L. Scott, eds. 2001. *Anatomy of Genocide: State Sponsored Mass-Killings in the Twentieth Century*. Lewiston, NY: The Edwin Mellen Press.

Nahoum-Grappe, Véronique. 2002. "The Anthropology of Extreme Violence: The Crime of Desecration." *International Social Sciences Journal* 54, 174:549–557.

Power, Samantha. 2002. *A Problem from Hell: America and the Age of Genocide*. New York: Basic Books.

Rummel, R. J. 1994. *Death by Government*. New Brunswick, NJ: Transaction Publishers.

Seale, Clive. 2000. "Changing Patterns of Death and Dying." *Social Science & Medicine* 51, 6:917–930.

Seymour, Jane Elizabeth. 2000. "Negotiating Natural Death in Intensive Care." *Social Science & Medicine* 51, 8:1241–1252.

Uplekar, Mukund W. 2002. "Private Health Care." *Social Science & Medicine* 51, 2:897–904.

Wikler, Daniel. 2002. "Personal and Social Responsibility for Health." *Ethics & International Affairs* 16, 2:47–55.

Yoder, Scot D. 2002. "Individual Responsibility for Health: Decision, Not Discovery." *Hastings Center Report* 32, 2:22–31.

14.3   Is It Time to Raise the Drawbridge on Immigration?

The issue: Throughout the West, high rates of unemployment combined with high rates of immigration have resulted in a backlash against immigrants (especially ethnic or racial minorities among them). Is there any way to decide how many, and which kinds, of immigrants are needed—if any?

The United States does not have a "Malthusian" population problem. By any standard, there are not too many people for the land to support. Nor is the American population growing too quickly through high rates of fertility. Yet some people view high rates of immigration as a population problem and a social problem.

Recently, immigration has become an explosive political issue. Many people inside the country want the chance to bring their relatives over to the United States. Many outside the country want a chance to get in. But a weak economy makes many native-born Americans resist the push for an increased number of immigrants. Some even want the immigration rate cut back.

Postwar immigrants have been drawn to America primarily from southern Europe, Latin America, Asia, and Africa. These types of immigrants settled mainly in large metropolitan centers. In this respect they follow the general trend: More and more Americans live near large cities. And in the largest cities, immigrants form a large and growing part of the total population. But even though they follow the general pattern of settlement (westward, and to large cities), immigrants are often singled out for criticism and exclusion. Many are easily identified by their speech, skin color, or manner of dress; this makes them easy targets.

Is immigration becoming a problem in America? If so, should immigration be more limited? As usual, there are conflicting views on this question.

IMMIGRATION SHOULD BE MORE LIMITED

People who argue that immigration should be more limited make four main points, which focus on economic, cultural, political, and social issues respectively. First, they claim that immigration poses an economic problem in a slow-growing economy. Second, they say that immigrants pose a problem of assimilation and cultural unity—an issue we discussed in an earlier section. Third, ideological and cultural divergence debilitates the political culture and system. Fourth, they raise the concern that high rates of immigration produce problems of social cohesion and conflict.

Immigrants Are an Economic Problem   People who want to limit or reduce immigration on economic grounds argue that immigrants use too many public services without making adequate economic or social contributions of their own. Health care is particularly important for older immigrants, educational services for younger immigrants, and welfare for unemployed immigrants. Young and adult newcomers need language instruction, which also places a burden on the school systems, as their budgets are already inadequate. For example, native-born children have to give up extracurricular activities in order to make room for such programs. Thus reducing immigration would grant a better future for generations to come.

On the one hand, critics complain that too many immigrants fail to get (or keep) jobs, so they increase the unemployment rate, thus exerting more pressure on the social system. On the other hand, they complain that too many immigrants take jobs away from native-born Americans in a tight job market. This increases unemployment and the welfare needs of native-borns. Given that the economy is already weak, it seems foolish to import people who put new demands on public spending.

Moreover, it is widely known that in many cases immigrants send large portions of their incomes back to their native countries to help sustain family members left behind. The market needs individual consumption to remain stable, yet these funds sent abroad are not going to stimulate the American economy but that of other countries.

Immigrants Are a Cultural Problem   Increasingly, immigrants come from countries and cultures that are different from the dominant, white American culture. This poses the problem of cultural assimilation.

In an earlier section we discussed the pros and cons of multiculturalism. Whatever your view on this issue, a high rate of immigration puts more pressure on the society to come up with a solution. As with rapid population change due to high rates of fertility, rapid change due to high rates of immigration strains a society's capacity to adapt. Quick solutions to pressing social problems are rarely good or long-lasting. By increasing immigration and the pressure for solutions, we increase the risk of making mistakes.

Political Instability   The more diverse a society, the more political fragmentation there is in the political culture, and this could be dangerous for the stability of democracy and government. Immigrants spend their formative and most crucial years in a different society, and this shapes what they will consider to be their priorities throughout life. Thus their interests are very different from those of the native-born population, and this translates into patterns of opposition and conflicting structuration of policy making and bargaining. This harms democracy, as many start feeling disenfranchised and lose trust in the governments and institutions.

Many immigrants may not commit to the American political system and institutions because they are very different from what they know, or they are distrustful of them. This could be problematic if these feelings are transmitted to their native-born or naturalized children, who may as a result not exercise their right to vote to sustain democracy.

Immigrants Pose a Social Problem   High rates of immigration require society to assimilate and incorporate immigrants or to adopt multicultural policies. Official multicultural policies, by which the system would not place much emphasis on assimilation of the American culture but would promote the expression of the diversity of ethnic groups, can be problematic because many would disagree with them. In Canada, as an example, the adoption of official multicultural policies has not relieved the tensions between the groups, as was initially intended, and the "public acceptance of diversity appears to decline as the visibility of minorities increases" (Brooks 2004).

The type of problem posed will vary with the kind of immigrant. Thus, highly educated immigrants from Hong Kong and other parts of Southeast Asia may place different demands on the system than less-educated immigrants from Latin America or the Mediterranean region. In either case, the possibility of conflict is increased by what some people consider the protective self-segregation strategy that the sociologist Raymond Breton has called "institutional completeness."

Institutional completeness is a measure of the degree to which an immigrant ethnic group provides its own members with the services they need, through their own institutions. These institutions include churches, schools, banks, and media that are separate from those of the larger society. Often it accompanies residential segregation. In a group with strong institutional (or community) completeness, members do not need to depend on the host society.

Living in a community with institutional completeness protects immigrants from a hostile social environment. However, the institutionally complete community is self-perpetuating: Institutions formed within it create a demand for the services they provide. Often, ethnic groups keep to themselves in separate communities even after the discrimination has diminished or disappeared. It also maintains group cohesion by creating institutions, gaining control of resources, and providing a variety of cultural and social services.

This pattern of self-segregation, aided by institutional completeness, is particularly typical of America's recent immigrants. In many cases groups immigrate to escape poverty or oppression. On arriving in their new homeland, these culturally and racially distinct people experience discrimination and exploitation by the local people. Seeing themselves as strangers in the country, they settle in particular parts of towns and cities, among others of their own kind. They become self-employed—often merchants—and keep apart from other groups socially.

For self-protection, they form strong intra-ethnic organizations. They compete with local businesses and, by taking advantage of family and community ties, their businesses prosper. Gradually, a large proportion achieves a middle-class standard of living. The most successful even form business alliances with rich and powerful members of the dominant community.

The problem with institutional completeness is that, from the perspective of the whole society, the population becomes fractured along ethnic, cultural, and political lines. The ultimate goal of multiculturalism is not simply to foster the co-existence of different ethnic groups, but to create ties between those groups—to create communities within communities. The adoption of institutional completeness is an understandable strategy for immigrants greeted in the past with discrimination and hostility from native-borns. However, when institutional completeness remains intact even after prejudices have been overcome, it becomes a source of social tension rather than an instrument for cultural survival. Groups who refuse to participate in their larger communities (e.g., by learning the native language, observing local customs) serve only to maintain a dangerous *us versus them* mentality within society.

IMMIGRATION SHOULD NOT BE MORE LIMITED

People who argue against a limitation on immigrants, or even favor higher rates of immigration, counter each of the arguments we have already examined with opposing evidence.

Immigrants Are Not an Economic Problem Those opposing the view that immigrants are an economic problem note that immigrants generally help the economy grow. In the United States, the agricultural lobby is strongly in favor of immigration, since it supplies cheap labor to pick crops. But because of selective immigration policies, many are highly skilled or highly educated; they provide a cheap source of talented people, which this country has not had to pay a cent to train. Many are also ambitious; just think how much courage and energy it takes to travel to another country and culture, and start life all over again.

Since many (even most) are young and skilled, immigrants tend to enter the work-force and remain in it. They do not increase the general unemployment rate; they often take jobs that native-born people are unwilling to do. (There is evidence of local or sectoral unemployment due to migrant workers, but the effect is limited.) On balance, the evidence shows that immigrants pay more in taxes than they draw in public services and benefits.

Immigrants Are Not a Cultural Problem It is true that high rates of immigration increase cultural diversity and put pressure on the country to come to terms with the multiculturalism issue. However, as we concluded earlier, multiculturalism is both inevitable and desirable. Furthermore, it may be the best way for a country to participate in today's globalized economy.

It is also widely known that most immigrant groups in America come from societies that place high value in the family. With increasing rates of divorce and broken homes, and a consumer-oriented society that displaces family values, immigrants are a constant reminder of the importance of the family. The family is the key socializing agent for children. It provides them with the stability and affection needed for their proper development. Thus having more individuals that place a higher value on the family can only be beneficial to the American society.

Immigrants Are Not a Social Problem We have discussed the self-protective immigrant strategies that lead to institutional completeness and an appearance of clannishness.

However, these boundaries and barriers break down whenever the dominant population behaves in a cordial, hospitable manner. This is evident in soaring rates of intermarriage. Increasing numbers of young people cross ethnic, religious, and racial lines to date and marry. And the sociological evidence shows that intermarriage poses no difficulty for the couples concerned.

In general, measures of ethnic (and race) relations in use since the 1920s show that social distance between groups is shrinking. More people accept "different" kinds of people as neighbors, workmates, and friends (as well as spouses) than ever before. Research shows that the presence of multiple groups acts as a reducing factor of antipathy and segregation, which is not the case when only two groups are present. Ethnic diversity does not become a problem unless we let it.

Research shows that familiarity reduces fear and hostility between groups, especially when interactions between different kinds of people are (1) gradual, relaxed, and repeated; (2) cooperative, not competitive; (3) guided by norms of friendliness; (4) between people of equal status; and (5) supported by legitimate authorities (e.g., government officials, teachers, ministers). Such interactions are particularly beneficial when they contradict the stereotyped notions groups hold about each other.

The worst inter-group problems are likely to arise in fundamentally competitive situations, for example, work settings. Problems are more easily avoided among young people in social or educational settings. This puts a special onus on teachers and others in contact with young people to create the best possible conditions for inter-group understanding and cooperation.

It is important to remember that a century ago immigrants from Eastern European countries were seen as a threat to the American economy and native labor force. However, those immigrants are now part what Americans proudly regard as their history. American immigration history has been one of assimilation, therefore one hundred years from now this new set of "different" immigrants will be regarded as having contributed to American greatness.

Immigrants Are a Demographic Benefit We have saved one of the most important benefits of a high immigration rate for last. This is the demographic benefit.

In America and the rest of the Western world, fertility rates are near or below replacement. That means there is no danger of too many people. In fact, even with the 5.8 unemployment rate registered in 2002, there may be a danger of too few people. Among other things, a shrinking population means a shrinking workforce and thus a shrinking economic base. Immigration provides more people to consume as well as to make the economy's goods and services.

More important still, a population with fertility near or below replacement is an aging population. Low fertility, not increased longevity, is mainly what increases the average (or median) age of the population. Currently, the median American is nearly forty years old (half the population is older, half younger.) While fertility remains low or even shrinks, the median age rises even more. This means a large and growing fraction of old and retired people, and a shortage of young people.

A society can have too many young people, but it can also have too few. Population aging can be a bad thing. First, older people are less productive economically than younger people. Many of them are retired and require costly services, especially health care. The need for these resources and their specialization increases with age. We want to be able to care effectively for those who provided for us in the past. We need young workers to pay for these pensions and other services. The fewer the young people, the more each one has to pay to cover the costs of our old people.

As well, there is evidence that older people are more rigid in their ways and less innovative than younger people. This is bound to affect the economic, social, and cultural life of the country. Increasingly, as we have noted throughout, the country, especially in a globalized context, needs flexibility and adaptiveness, new ideas, new technologies, new ways of relating to other kinds of people, and so on. Young people can adapt in these ways more easily than older people.

High rates of immigration supply the needed young people in two ways. First, as we have noted, a high proportion of immigrants are young—often in their teens or twenties. Second, immigrants from less developed societies tend to have higher rates of fertility than native-born Americans (or other Western peoples). This means the immigrants will supply more babies per capita, and this too will keep the country's median age from rising at a rapid rate (though it is likely to rise nonetheless).

SUMMING UP

Is it time to raise the drawbridge on immigrants? Definitely not.

By this we mean that there should be no fewer immigrants than there are at present. We do not necessarily mean immigration should be unlimited. Nor do we mean that immigration should be set arbitrarily at some particular level (e.g., at a level twice as high, three times as high, or ten times as high as it is at present).

Remember what we learned earlier about the population time bomb. There are no absolute answers to any population question. There is no absolute level at which a country is overpopulated or underpopulated—nor a point at which there are too many immigrants or too few immigrants.

Partly, there are too many unknowns: How many immigrants want to come, and with what skills? What is the state of language training, social services, and local school systems that must receive immigrants? What is the likely state of the economy when they arrive? Five years later? What is the state of public thinking toward immigration, multiculturalism, and intergroup cooperation today? (Usually, public opinion mainly opposes immigration at current or higher levels.) In five years? And so on.

More important still, as Joel Cohen showed us, all answers to population questions are conditional on the kind of society we want to have, and the effort we are willing to make to have it. What changes are needed to accommodate twice as many immigrants, or ten times as many each year; and what would it take to make those changes? Can we afford to make those changes? Can we afford not to make those changes? How long could we put off making those changes before something bad happened? How bad would it be?

All our actions carry a danger and a cost. All inaction also carries a danger and a cost. The job of the sociologist is not to obscure that fact with pat answers; unfortunately, this is what politicians often do. Instead, the sociologist must uncover and dissect the question(s) so that we know exactly what is involved.

Then, the sociologist must supply evidence relevant to the debate: evidence that is timely and untainted by political interest. Ultimately it is not sociologists who make the important decision, and often decision makers do not take into consideration sociological evidence. But we will have done our job, as sociologists and citizens, if we have treated the debate and the evidence fairly and with respect.

REVIEW EXERCISES

For Discussion and Debate

1. Why do people believe that immigrants take more out of the economy than they put into it?
2. How is the "immigration debate" different from the "multiculturalism debate" we examined earlier in this book?
3. "Through immigration, North America gains the talents of the most capable, educated, and dynamic people of the Third World."
4. Are "middleman minorities" a benefit to American society or a problem?

Writing Exercises

Write a brief (500-word) essay on one of the following topics:

1. "Only young, highly educated immigrants should be admitted to the country."
2. "A preference should be given to applicants for immigration who are wealthy."

3. "Immigrants should be told what part of the country they must live in for the first five years."
4. "Only countries that are large importers of American products should be permitted to send large numbers of immigrants."

Research Activities

1. Collect some basic information about immigrants living in your local community: how many there are, where they came from, when they came, what kinds of jobs they do, and what resources are available to them.
2. Prepare a brief questionnaire on the "experience of immigration" that includes questions on why people left their home country, why they came to America and to this community, and how well they feel they have been accepted. Administer it to two immigrant members of your community and report your findings.
3. Sample issues of your local newspaper to see how it has discussed immigration and immigrants over the last 50 years. Do you detect a trend?
4. Consult with governmental agencies to find out what multicultural policies are in place, and try to locate data that could help you assess the effectiveness (or lack of it) of these policies.

SELECTED REFERENCES

Archdeacon, Thomas J. 1992. "Reflections of Immigration to Europe in Light of U.S. Immigration History." *International Migration Review* 26, 2 (98) (Summer): 525–548.

Asuma, Seth N. and Matthew Bradley Todd. 2001. "Making Sense Out of U.S. Immigration Policy and Multiculturalism." *The Western Journal of Black Studies* 25, 2 (Summer): 82–92.

Birmingham, John R. 2001. "Immigration: Not a Solution to Problems of Population Decline and Aging." *Population and Environment: Journal of Interdisciplinary Studies* 22, 4 (Mar.): 365–363.

Bonacich, Edna. 1973. "A Theory of Middleman Minorities." *American Sociological Review* 38, 5 (Oct.): 583–594.

Brooks, Stephen. 2004. "Political Culture in Canada Issues and Directions." P. 70 in *Canadian Politics*. 4th ed. Edited by James Bickerton and Alain-G. Gagnon. Toronto, ON: Broadview Press.

Card, David. 1990. "The Impact of the Mariel Boatlift on the Miami Labor Market." *Industrial and Labor Relations Review* 43, 2 (Jan.): 245–257.

Donato, Katharine M., Thomas J. Espenshade and Ricardo Romo. 1994. "U.S. Policy and Mexican Migration to the United States, 1942–92." *Social Science Quarterly* 75, 4 (Dec.): 705–729.

Durand, Jorge and Douglas S. Massey. 2003. "The Costs of Contradiction: U.S. Border Policy 1986–2000." *Latino Studies* 1, 2 (July): 233–234.

Espenshade, Thomas J. 2001. "'Replacement Migration' from the Perspective of Equilibrium Stationary Populations." *Population and Environment: Journal of Interdisciplinary Studies* 22, 4 (Mar.): 383–389.

Feliciano, Cynthia. 2003. "Selective Immigration and National-Origin Group Characteristics: Explaining Variation in Educational Success among Children of U.S. Immigrants." *Dissertation Abstracts International, A: The Humanities and Social Sciences* 64, 6 (Dec.): 2267-A.

Fix, Michael and Jeffrey S. Passel. 1994. "Setting the Record Straight: What Are the Costs to the Public?" *Public Welfare* 52, 2 (Spring): 6–15.

Foner, Nancy. 2001. "Immigrant Commitment to America, Then and Now: Myths and Realities." *Citizenship Studies* 5, 1 (Feb.): 27–40.

Freeman, Gary P. 1992. "Migration Policy and Politics in the Receiving States." *International Migration Review* 26, 4 (100) (Winter): 1144–1167.

Goldstein, Amy and Robert Suro. 2001. "A Journey in Stages: The Many Faces of Assimilation." *The Responsive Community* 11, 4 (Fall): 55–64.

Habermas, Jurgen. 1992. "Citizenship and National Identity: Some Reflections on the Future of Europe." *Praxis International* 12, 1 (Apr.): 1–19.

Heisler, Barbara Schmitter. 1992. "The Future of Immigrant Incorporation: Which Models? Which Concepts?" *International Migration Review* 26, 2 (98) (Summer): 623–645.

Husbands, Christopher T. 1991. "The Mainstream Right and the Politics of Immigration in France: Major Developments." *Ethnic and Racial Studies* 14, 2 (Apr.): 170–198.

Iceland, John. 2004. "Beyond Black and White Metropolitan Segregation." *Social Science Research* 33, 21 (June): 248–271.

Jones-Correa, Michael. 2001. "Institutional and Contextual Factors in Immigrant Naturalization and Voting." *Citizenship Studies* 5, 1:41–56.

Keely, Charles B. 1993. "The Politics of Immigration Policy in the United States." *Migration World Magazine* 21, 1:20–23.

Kessler, Alan. "Immigration, Politics and the American Labor Market: An Historical Perspective." *Migration News, Research and Seminars.* Available online at http://migration.ucdavis.edu/rs/more.php?id=75_0_3_0.

Kleniewski, Nancy. 1994. "Immigration and Urban Transformations." *Urban Affairs Quarterly* 30, 2 (Dec.): 307–316.

Kposowa, Augustine J. 1993. "The Impact of Immigration on Native Earnings in the United States, 1940 to 1980." *Applied Behavioral Science Review* 1, 1:1–25.

Lee, Yueh-Ting and Victor Ottati. 2002. "Attitude toward U.S. Immigration Policy: The Roles of In-Group/Out-of-Group Bias, Economic Concern, and Obedience to Law." *Journal of Social Psychology* 142, 5 (Oct.): 617–634.

Lutz, Wolfgang and Christopher Prinz. 1992. "What Difference Do Alternative Immigration and Integration Levels Make to Western Europe?" *European Journal of Population* 8, 4:341–361.

Martin, Philip L. 1994. "Immigration and Integration: Challenges for the 1990s." *Asian Migrant* 7, 2 (Apr.–June): 46–51.

Massey, Douglas S. 1990. "The Social and Economic Origins of Immigration." *Annals of the American Academy of Political and Social Science* 510 (July): 60–72.

Min, Pyong Gap. 1990. "Problems of Korean Immigrant Entrepreneurs." *International Migration Review* 24, 3 (91) (Fall): 436–455.

Moore, Stephen. 1990. "Who Should America Welcome?" *Society* 27, 5 (187) (July–Aug.): 55–62.

Murphy, Dwight D. 1994. "The World Population Explosion and the Cost of Uncontrolled Immigration." *Journal of Social, Political and Economic Studies* 4 (Winter): 481–510.

Nevitte, Neil and Mebs Kanji. 2004. "New Cleavages, Value Diversity, and Democratic Governance." Pp. 92–95 in *Canadian Politics.* 4th ed. Edited by James Bickerton and Alain G. Gagnon. Toronto, ON: Broadview Press.

Pedraza-Bailey, Silvia. 1990. "Immigration Research: A Conceptual Map." *Social Science History* 14, 1 (Spring): 43–67.

Pugliese, Enrico. 1992. "The New International Migrations and the Changes in the Labour Market." *Labour* 6, 1 (Spring): 165–179.

Richmond, Anthony H. 1990. "Race Relations and Immigration: A Comparative Perspective." *International Journal of Comparative Sociology* 31, 3–4 (Sept.–Dec.): 156–176.

Ryder, Norman B. 1993. "Reflections on Replacement." *Family Planning Perspectives* 25, 6 (Nov.–Dec.): 273–277.

Rystad, Goran. 1992. "Immigration History and the Future of International Migration." *International Migration Review* 26, 4 (100) (Winter): 1168–1199.

Satzewich, Vic. 1993. "Migrant and Immigrant Families in Canada: State Coercion and Legal Control in the Formation of Ethnic Families." *Journal of Comparative Family Studies* 24, 3 (Autumn): 315–338.

Sciortino, Giuseppe. 1991. "Immigration into Europe and Public Policy: Do Stops Really Work?" *New Community* 18, 1 (Oct.): 89–99.

Simmons, Alan B. and Kieran Keohane. 1992. "Canadian Immigration Policy: State Strategies and the Quest for Legitimacy." *Canadian Review of Sociology and Anthropology* 29, 4 (Nov.): 421–452.

Tarn, Cho W. 1999. "Naturalization, Socialization, Participation: Immigrants and (Non-) Voting." *Journal of Politics* 61, 4:1140–1155.

UN Statistics Division. 2004. "Indicators of Unemployment." *Social Indicators.* Accessed on October 8, 2004 at http://millenniumindicators.un.org/unsd/demographic/products/socind/unempl.htm.

CHAPTER 15

BUILDING A BETTER FUTURE

As we shall see, social change may begin at either a macro or micro level of society, but eventually its effects show up at both levels. Take the growth of high-tech industries. Automated manufacturing is gradually replacing human workers with machines and computers. In this way, it is changing the lives of thousands of workers and their families. Or consider people's decisions to delay childbearing, to have no children, or only one child. These are micro-level choices that people are making one couple at a time, and their impact builds slowly. Yet taken together, these choices are changing the whole world.

Contrary to popular belief, social change is rarely a result of great men and women having great ideas. Social change is happening all the time, a result of the actions of ordinary people. The difference between micro-change and macro-change does not lie in the number of people affected or the importance of the change. It lies in the change's point of origin, with individuals and small groups, or with the political or economic establishment. But whether a change begins at the macro or micro level, understanding it demands a macro level of explanation.

In this chapter we look at three types of social change that have both macro- and micro-aspects. First, we consider whether the natural environment is getting better or worse, and with what social effects—and how this connects with the effects of rapid, often externally funded development on the global environment, and attempts to deal with perceived problems. Second, we look at the information society, in particular the spread of the Internet, and its effects on people. Should the Internet be censored? Third, we ask whether the individualism that is stressed in Western (and especially North American) culture has become excessive and socially disruptive, and ask readers to think of global implications.

15.1   Do We Need the Kyoto Accord?

The issue: A growing fear that humanity may be destroying the planet earth and, with that, humanity's only chance at survival as a species. Some are optimistic that solutions will be found, but is the optimism justified?

We hear a lot of talk these days about the environment. We debate issues of pollution, landfills, water supplies, air quality. We are increasingly aware that we live on a planet of finite resources. For a long time, people believed that we could always find more resources, and always find a place to dump our unwanted products and by-products. Now, most people are aware that this is not the case. Environmental pollution and depletion have taken their toll on the health of plants, people, and animals.

There are new concerns about the future course of world history and many of these have to do with the environment and ecology. We hear that the depletion of the ozone layer and the *greenhouse effect* are making it hazardous just to be out in the sun. The destruction of the Amazon rain forest and the emission of industrial pollutants threaten air quality and the lifestyles of individual people. Oil spills and the dumping of industrial wastes threaten life in the rivers, lakes, and oceans. These new social problems face us *all,* regardless of class or political system. The former Soviet Union had its Chernobyl nuclear mishap, just as the United States had its accident at Three Mile Island (although the former cost a great many lives while the latter did not). The developing world of the South suffers as much from such mishaps, and usually more, than the developed world. In Russia in the 1990s, despite dramatic changes in social organization, economic and health conditions worsened significantly. Are they improving now?

In this section we review, first, the concerns about environment, then pose the question: Is the environment improving? If not, have we caught the problem in time?

Why the Concern for Environment? People live in an environment and they modify this environment as they live in it. Think of your home, with paint, wallpaper, pictures on the walls, and rugs on the floor. What was the last modification you or your family made to your home? Building a deck, perhaps, or painting the walls?

Your environment, however, goes beyond the house you live in: It is the street you bicycle or drive through, the park you jog in, the college whose rooms you sit in, the restaurants and shops you frequent—all of these constitute "environment." Air circulates through this environment, water runs through it, people and other animals move in and out of it. We depend on our environment for what we need to live as biological organisms: air, water, food, warmth, protection from elements, and shielding from harmful rays; and the provision of these needs may result in problems in other areas.

"Is the environment improving" may not be the most appropriate question to ask: It is neither accurate nor precise. Improving for what, and compared with what? Whose environment? However it is a question often asked, or, even more often, a statement that represents a belief that is often taken for granted: Yes, there are environmental problems, but now that we are on to them, we can fix whatever is wrong. This section will explore beliefs about the environment and whether it is improving, focus in particular on the Kyoto Accord, and attempt to summarize the situation as we perceive it.

THE ENVIRONMENT IS IMPROVING

In 1962, Rachel Carson's book *Silent Spring* was first published. Carson pointed to the dangers of a buildup of toxins—derived from pesticides commonly used in agriculture—in the soil and in plants and animals, resulting in the destruction of many species, and great reductions in others. The ghostly "silent spring" of her title would be one in which no birds sang; in some areas this had already occurred. Moreover, in the future she feared people would not be immune to the effects of these toxins.

This work and many others have influenced our awareness of the environment and what may be happening to it. But recognize that not all the effects on environment are caused by people.

Three Kinds of Environmental Problems In fact, there are three categories of environmental problems, which Cylke terms the Ecosystem Problem, the Ecosystem Crisis, and the Biosphere Crisis.

Ecosystem Problems can arise in many ways and some are created by people. They include disruptions to the biosphere that threaten individual members of species—or, as in the case of human-created disasters, large numbers of people and other creatures. They do not, however, threaten the existence of an entire species. The Bhopal explosion was an example of a sudden Ecosystem Problem. Examples of chronic problems, resulting from massive dumping of pollutants, can be found in the toxic soils of Love Canal and Akwesasne.

An Ecosystem Crisis stems from disruptions that threaten or eradicate entire species. These have occurred throughout the earth's history. However, the rate of species extinction has increased significantly due to ecosystem crises resulting from human activities such as logging and dam building.

The third category, Biosphere Crisis, includes events that render the biosphere unable to sustain life for most complex species, including humanity. Few human activities, other than a full-scale nuclear war resulting in nuclear winter, could cause damage on this scale. However, a Biosphere Crisis could be triggered by the occurrence of multiple Ecosystems Crises.

Little attention is commonly given to Biosphere Crisis, possibly because it is unclear to environmental scientists what factors would lead to such an event. Hence, it is not clear what would prevent it. Both scientific and popular concern currently focuses on Ecosystem Problems and Crises.

Environment in the News   One after another, environmental problems have hit the headlines. Oil spills and chemical spills grab our attention. The ozone layer is discussed each year. Cities continue to search for landfill space to solve their garbage problems. Global warming has become a household term.

The extent to which these problems appear in the popular press indicates the extent of public awareness. Towns and cities commence recycling programs. Children's environmental clubs spring up in countless elementary and secondary schools, and many adults say that they have begun recycling as a response to pressure from the students living in their homes. The environmental movement has worked hard to bring problems to people's attention, and people are becoming aware that not all is well, and controls over emissions and other pollution issues have become much more standard. An extreme example was the Kyoto conference in 1997. At the Kyoto conference, thirty-nine industrialized countries pledged a reduction of 5.2 percent in emissions, based on 1990 values,

by the year 2012. Now that sufficient countries have ratified the agreement, this program is going ahead. Rather than ratifying Kyoto, the United States has its own national program emphasizing "Clear Skies," and control of emissions is a strong priority.

The environment has suffered many problems, but many researchers believe it is not too late to deal with them. With warning and through education programs we are able to curb pollution, restrict emissions, and recycle material (thus saving both energy and landfill space). An official statement on U.S. environmental policy in 2003 emphasized that though in the past three decades the U.S. economy has grown 164 percent, population 39 percent, and consumption 42 percent, air pollution from six major pollutants had not grown but indeed decreased by 48 percent. Pesticide use has been greatly reduced in the 40 years since Carson's warning of a coming "silent spring." And the big success story of the last decade has been the ozone layer. Following a worldwide ban on chloroflourocarbons (CFCs), scientists report that we are winning—with the rate of ozone degradation decreasing, and "compelling evidence that we are seeing the very first stages of ozone recovery in the upper atmosphere," according to atmospheric chemist Michael Newchurch. With forethought and planning, we can ensure that the worst excesses are never repeated, and that we can work together, citizens of many countries, toward creating sustainable environments. Or, at least, some believe.

THE ENVIRONMENT IS NOT IMPROVING

The counter view is that, while recycling programs and other initiatives are beneficial, environmental improvement is illusory. It is true that an increasing number of people in North America, and elsewhere, are becoming aware of environmental problems. However this awareness does not necessarily translate into action, and while action may target some problems, other problems go without remedy. And the environmental crisis has arisen at the same time as the emphasis on "catch-up" development, which we looked at in Chapter 5 on global inequality.

There is no doubt the world is finite. There are obvious limits to its resources and its regenerative capacities. With the kind of development we have in the North—and with a model that assumes there can always be more growth—we are pushing the limits of what is possible. We are affecting our environment in ways that in turn affect us. The model of unlimited growth in all areas (notably GDP, capital accumulation, and sheer numbers of goods) has led to a deterioration in our environment. Clean air and water are not "free" resources. The air in our cities is not clean, and our water is polluted. These have led to a deterioration in the quality of our lives here in the North, and indeed everywhere on earth.

When we factor in these environmental concerns, the picture changes. It is the nations of the North, the "developed" nations, who chiefly contribute to global pollution and chiefly use nonrenewable global resources. Twenty percent of the world's population who live in the North are using 80 percent of the world's resources. In the long run, this pattern of consumption may destroy the natural foundations of life worldwide. However, many are reluctant to criticize and relinquish the North's consumption patterns, and to warn the South against imitating the North. From a moral—if not ecological—standpoint, people in the South have the right to the same living standard as those in the North.

The nations of the North are also the chief consumers of renewable resources and of *biomass.* Research in the Netherlands has studied how much land every Dutch person uses on average within the Netherlands and outside it. It concludes that for every one hectare of land that a Dutch person uses within the Netherlands, he or she uses about five hectares outside it, in the third world. Given the limited purchasing power of people in less developed countries, how can they compete with this? They cannot import much of what they need and must rely largely on their own resources, but many of these are being exported to the people of Europe and North America. At the same time, for a variety of reasons—increased soil salinity due to constant irrigation, erosion of forest cover, stress on the ecosystem—the biomass production of land in many less developed countries (e.g., India) is decreasing.

Let's, however, look at another dimension of the global environment problem—the idea of *sustainable development.*

The Paradigm of Sustainable Development
This phrase was popularized by the Brundtland Report, published as *Our Common Future* in 1987. "Sustainable development" is continued economic growth of a kind that does not further compromise the environment and, in this way, "meets the needs of the present without compromising the ability of future generations to meet their own needs." The concept of sustainable development implies limits on the rate and type of growth. However, these limits are bound to change over time. They are imposed by the present state of technology and social organizations on environmental resources and by the ability of the biosphere to absorb the effects of human activities. Technology and social organization, the Brundtland Report argues, can be both managed and improved to make way for a new era of economic growth.

Action Paradigms: Approaches to the Environment   There are two main approaches to problems in the environment and we may need to choose between them. The first, commonly termed the Dominant Western World View, is based on the assumption that humans are fundamentally different from all other forms of life on earth: that we choose our actions, act within a world of vast resources, and have the ability to find solutions to the problems we face. Every problem will have its solution: The only difficulty is in finding it.

The second paradigm, termed the New Ecological Paradigm (NEP), is based on different assumptions. In this way of thinking, humans are only one among many interdependent species. Human actions, as part of an intricate web of global cause and effect, may have unintended consequences. The world's resources available for human use are finite and impose restrictions on human possibilities, and humans do not have the infinite potential to provide solutions to all problems. In the end, ecological laws cannot be repealed.

Popular attitudes therefore, are changing, and this change in beliefs has enormous importance. Humans have acknowledged their role in the depletion of the earth's resources and they worry about global warming. People realize that they need to change their practices in order to avoid major environmental problems. However, we can raise questions about this supposed transformation. Are people acting on their belief—that is, does changed belief actually result in changed practice? And if so, what are the visible results of these changes in practice? Are the people whose beliefs are changing the same people who are directly responsible for environmental pollution?

Species Extinctions   Many species are now threatened, or disappearing. In 1992, Cylke found that three-fourths of the world's bird species are declining in numbers or threatened with extinction; one-third of North America's freshwater fish are rare, threatened, or endangered; one-third of U.S. coastal fish have declined in population since 1975; 100 species of invertebrates are lost to deforestation each day; and of the world's 270 turtle species, 42 percent are rare or threatened with extinction.

Going further afield, more than half of all the known species are to be found in the Central and South American forests. However, their habitats are threatened by land-clearing activities to create farmlands or grazing lands, mining activities, and felling of tropical hardwood trees for exports. Based on such data, we can see that the environment is not "improving." Far from it—diversity in both animal and plant species is being reduced, and when a species is gone, it is gone for good. Humanity is not making progress on this problem. And rain forest reduction is also a contributor to the phenomenon of global warning.

Global Warming and the Kyoto Accord   It will be no surprise to learn that the North countries are the chief producers of greenhouse gases—the United States alone being responsible for around one quarter of the world's carbon dioxide emissions with only 4 to 5 percent of the world's population—hence the idea behind Kyoto, that developed countries should show their commitment to cutting greenhouse gas emissions. But the Kyoto Accord was itself a compromise: The European Union called for 15 percent reduction in emissions; the United States called for stabilizing emissions only; the resultant 5.2 percent (since reduced further) was a compromise, and since then, the United States has refused to ratify the accord.

Global warming that results from a build-up of greenhouse gases in the atmosphere has the potential to produce a Biosphere Crisis. Scientists disagree about the extent and results of this warming, some predicting a meltdown of polar ice with an associated rise in sea level, others a thickening of the Antarctic icecap. There is general agreement, however, that the past decade has been the warmest recorded by modern methods—indeed that the years since 1980 have been warmer than any equivalent period for a thousand years! In 1997, scientists noted that changes in temperature in Antarctica had resulted in increased snowfall on coastal iceflows. In turn, this resulted in breeding-site problems for Adelie penguins and a subsequent reduction in numbers.

Differences in Theory and Practice   We can question to what extent changes in attitude are translated into practice. If more than half the population of North America favors an Ecological Social Paradigm, what changes in behavior are resulting from this? In fact, very few—traffic congestion is increasing, and some household chemicals, such as common bleaches, continue to cause problems of disposal. And while there may be improvement in the ozone layer, Michael Newchurch emphasized to National Geographic News that "It is absolutely essential that we continue not producing these [ozone-depleting] substances for the rest of the time we want to live on this planet." In supermarkets, products claiming to be "environmentally friendly" are generally priced above comparable products. This is odd, since truly "environmentally friendly" products should have received less processing and hence been less costly to produce.

If environmental concerns are being taken up by producers, it is for business reasons. No wonder environmental movements have recognized the need to convince business people that environmentalism is in their interests because it is more efficient and hence more profitable. Environmentalism harnessed to the service of economic growth is likely to strike a responsive chord with Western producers and consumers; otherwise, it remains empty words.

People who favor the Ecological Social Paradigm are not, for the most part, the same people who shape social or business policy. At best, we are offered more environmentally friendly materials and services at a higher price, and with no guarantees that the materials are indeed more environmentally friendly.

A basic problem with the currently popular concept of sustainable development is the idea of focusing attention on means of achieving development (or capital accumulation) so that such means do not cause irredeemable damage. Maintaining development in this way implies that societies such as those of North America can have their cake and eat it too: that by changing some practices, engaging in recycling, becoming more resource-efficient, North Americans can maintain and even expand their current standard of living.

But the truth is otherwise: An increase in resource efficiency alone leads to nothing unless it goes hand in hand with an intelligent restraint of growth. Instead of asking how many supermarkets or how many bathrooms are enough, one focuses on how all these—and more—can be obtained with a lower input of resources. Today's cars are far more energy-efficient than their predecessors. However, there are many more of them on the roads, so that the total amount of energy use and pollution—not only in transit but in car manufacture—is increasing.

And there are many instances where environmentalism has been coopted in the service of capitalist production. However, capitalism is based on the concept of expansion, requiring an increasing demand for products, a growing market for which producers can compete. This tells us that the incompatibility between capitalism and environmentalism may be fundamental, not a matter of informing the public and making small gradual changes.

The environment is polluted and, despite an increasing public discourse of environmentalism, there is little indication that it is becoming less so. Instead of seeing a true improvement, we are seeing the emergence of new areas in which capitalist businesses compete: the creation of an environmental market going hand in hand with a concept of infinitely sustainable development. We are unlikely to see true improvement until we can ask where decisions are made, where power is located, and what level of material resources is enough.

Summing Up

Is the environment improving? That's a problematic question, for many reasons. The definition of environment is, to say the least, imprecise: environment for what, or whom? Living beings constantly modify their environment. We exist on this planet because early plants produced oxygen and so caused change. Today's people, however, change their environment rapidly, and in ways that can threaten both their own well-being and that of other species.

Scientists have not reached a clear consensus about the nature of today's environmental changes, or how to avoid biosphere crisis. What will be the effects of global warming? In North America, people watch the news, express concern, engage to a greater or lesser extent in recycling programs, and put extra-strong sun-screen on their children. As individuals, there is little else we can do.

Sociologists have a different part to play. Sociology has no cure for environmental ills—not even a way of deciding who is *really* right among the wildly differing environmental forecasts. What sociology can do is help us understand how these forecasts are constructed, and who are the interest groups involved in forecasting; how knowledge of environmental issues is communicated to the general public; and how social relations of production and power are implicated in the problems that ecologists debate.

In the case of the Kyoto controversy, sociologists can point to how our thinking about environment is both political and economic, and, indeed, how reports and statistics are manipulated in the public eye. Careful readers will have spotted a major inconsistency—while the U.S. administration claimed, in 2003, that air pollutants had been reduced by an astounding 48 percent, the United States initially (in 1997) campaigned for emissions to be stabilized but not reduced, and since 2001 the administration has refused to ratify the Kyoto Accord, saying that a 7 percent reduction in emissions by 2012 was too much. (Each signatory to the Kyoto Accord was given its own target, the EU 8 percent, the United States 7 percent, and some others less, to achieve the overall target of 5.2 percent.) In setting its own internal *Clear Skies* target—18 percent, which looks better on the face of it than a mere 7 or 5.2 percent—the U.S. administration is using a different method of counting: greenhouse gas *intensity* rather than greenhouse

gas volume. This *intensity* is gas *volume* divided by the country's *Gross Domestic Product* (GDP). U.S. GDP is very high, and is further forecast to grow around 30 percent in the next decade. The apparent "reduction" in intensity may actually be an increase in actual emission, says Paul Krugman, writing in the *New York Times* in 2002. Others point to proposals for a voluntary target of a 4.5 percent reduction, and note that some U.S. states have themselves set targets in line with the Kyoto plans. But currently the withdrawal of the United States from the Kyoto Protocol has global political implications—while it is scheduled to become international law on February 16, 2005, developing countries are showing reluctance to engage in similar procedures. And the atmosphere does not recognize borders or boundaries.

If we need to change the ways we are modifying our environment—and we do—we need to understand how these ways come about, and why some forms of social organization are more environmentally destructive than others. In short, we need to think sociologically about people and their environment, on a global basis, and in the context of their economic, political, and cultural organization.

REVIEW EXERCISES

For Discussion and Debate

1. "The major environmental problem is not that we're going to run out of resources, but that we're going to cover everywhere with our garbage." Discuss.
2. "Business is only interested in the environment if they think they can make money out of people's interest." Discuss.
3. "The Kyoto Accord—should the United States ratify it?" Debate for and against.
4. "What use are wetlands to the average person?"

Writing Exercises

Write a brief (500-word) essay on one of the following topics:

1. "How I could simplify my lifestyle to be more environmentally conscious—and what are the pressures on me to *not* do this."
2. "Think globally, act locally" (a common slogan of the environmental movement).
3. "Can we have environment and jobs too?"
4. "Reduce, reuse, recycle—does it make a difference?"

Research Activities

1. Investigate some of the pronouncements on either "how we can supply our energy needs," or "global warming," up to the end of the twenty-first century. Examine statements by environmentalists, politicians, and power companies. Analyze these for how people's views connect with their jobs or social positions.
2. Conduct a search of the World Wide Web looking for statements by members of the *Deep Ecology* and *Ecofeminist* movements. What similarities and differences do you find in their statements?
3. Examine media coverage of an environmental issue in your area. How is the information presented? Whose views predominate in the media items you collect or hear? Discuss this with other students in your class.
4. Survey at least eight neighbors on their *attitudes* to the environmental movement, and to recycling, and on their *practices*. Do they recycle? Do they commute by car? Do their practices match their views?

SELECTED REFERENCES

Blowers, Andrew. 1993. "Environmental Policy: The Quest for Sustainable Development." *Urban Studies* 30, 4–5:775–796.

Brulle, Robert J. 1996. "Environmental Discourse and Social Movement Organizations: A Historical and Rhetorical Perspective on the Development of U.S. Environmental Organizations." *Sociological Inquiry* 66, 1:58–83.

Carson, Rachel. 1962. *Silent Spring.* Boston, MA: Houghton Mifflin.

Commission on Sustainable Development, 12th Session. 2004. New York, 14–30 April. *Natural Resources Forum* 28, 2 (May): 157–159.

Cylke, F. Kurt, Jr. 1993. *The Environment.* New York: HarperCollins.

Freudenberg, Nicholas and Carol Steinsapir. 1991. "Not in Our Backyards: The Grassroots Environmental Movement." *Society and Natural Resources* 4, 3:235–245.

Gibson, Donald E. 1992. "The Environmental Movement: Grass-Roots or Establishment?" *Sociological Viewpoints* 8:92–124.

Gordon, Cynthia and James M. Jasper. 1996. "Overcoming the 'Nimby' Label: Rhetorical and Organizational Links for Local Protesters." *Research in Social Movements, Conflicts and Change* 19:159–181.

Hardin, Jesse Wolf. 1995. "Deep Ecology: A Quarter Century of Earth Minstrelsy." *Humboldt Journal of Social Relations* 21, 1:95–109.

Kjellen, Bo. 2004. "Pathways to the Future: The New Diplomacy for Sustainable Development." Institute for Development Studies. *IDS Bulletin,* 35, 3 (July): 107–113.

Krugman, Paul. 2002. "Ersatz Climate Policy." *New York Times,* February 15.

Krutilla, Kerry and Clare Breidenich. 1993. "The GATT and Environmental Policy: An Analysis of Potential Conflicts and Policy Reforms." *Policy Studies Review* 12, 3–4:211–225.

Manning, Robert E. and Robert Gottlieb. 1996. "Forcing the Spring: The Transformation of the American Environmental Movement." *Forum for Applied Research and Public Policy* 11, 1:145–146.

Meadows, Donella H. and Dennis Meadows. 1972. *The Limits to Growth: A Report of the Club of Rome's Project on the Predicament of Mankind.* New York: Universe Books.

Merchant, Carolyn. 1992. *Radical Ecology: The Search for a Livable World.* New York: Routledge.

Mies, Maria and Vandana Shiva. 1993. *Ecofeminism.* London: Zed Books.

Peterson, Abby and Carolyn Merchant. 1986. "Peace with the Earth: Women and the Environmental Movement in Sweden." *Women's Studies International Forum* 9, 5–6:465–479.

Pickrell, John. 2003. "Ozone Layer May Be on the Mend, New Data Suggest." *National Geographic News.* August 5. Available online at http://news.nationalgeographic.com/news/2003/08/0805_030805_ozone.html.

Pulido, Laura. 1996. *Environmentalism and Economic Justice: Two Chicano Struggles in the Southwest.* Tucson, AZ: University of Arizona Press.

Redon, R., B. J. Ferhat Richou, G. Azzone, U. Bertele and G. Noci. 1997. "At Last We Are Creating Environmental Strategies That Work." *Long Range Planning* 30, 4:478–479.

Rogers, Raymond A. 1995. "Doing the Dirty Work of Globalization." *Capitalism, Nature, Socialism* 6, 3, 23:117–134.

Rycroft, Robert W. 1991. "Environmentalism and Science: Politics and the Pursuit of Knowledge." *Knowledge* 13, 2:150–169.

Schrepfer, Susan R. and Kirkpatrick Sale. 1995. "The Green Revolution: The American Environmental Movement, 1962–1992." *Journal of American History* 81, 4: 1832–1833.

Schwartz, Peter and Doug Randall. 2003. "An Abrupt Climate Change Scenario and Its Implications for United States National Security." Available online at http://gristmagazine.com/pdf/AbruptClimateChange2003.pdf. Accessed November 15, 2004.

Shah, Anup. 2002. "Kyoto Conference and Global Warming." *Global Issues* Web site. Available online at http://www.globalissues.org/EnvIssues/GlobalWarming.asp. Accessed 15 November 2004.

Shiva, Vandana. 1988. *Staying Alive: Women, Ecology and Development.* London: Zed Books.

Simmons, James and Nancy Stark. 1993. "Backyard Protest: Emergence, Expansion, and Persistence of a Local Hazardous Waste Controversy." *Policy Studies Journal* 21, 3:470–491.

Streeter, Calvin L. and Jacqueline Gonsalvez. 1994. "Social Justice Issues and the Environmental Movement in America: A New Challenge for Social Workers." *Journal of Applied Social Sciences* 18, 2:209–216.

UNFCCC. United Nations Convention on Climate Change—Official Web site of the Third Conference of the Parties (Kyoto Accord). Available online at http://unfccc.int/cop3/. Accessed 15 November 2004.

U.S. Climate Change Technology Program. Available online at http://www.climate technology.gov. Accessed 4 November 2004.

Van der Heijden, Hein Anton, Ruud Koopmans and Marco G. Giugni. 1992. "The West European Environmental Movement." *Research in Social Movements, Conflicts and Change* 2:1–40.

Wolf, Martin. 2004. "Globalization and Global Economic Governance." *Oxford Review of Economic Policy* 20, 1:72–84.

Yearley, Steven. 1989. "Environmentalism: Science and a Social Movement." *Social Studies of Science* 19, 2:343–355.

Zimmerman, Michael E. 1995. "The Threat of Ecofascism." *Social Theory and Practice* 21, 2:207–238.

15.2   Should the Internet Be Censored?

The issue: The Internet has had a profound difference in the way many people engage with society and indeed with people's everyday life and social behavior. But increasingly the Internet is besieged with problems: computer viruses, or the sheer number of unwanted messages we all receive. What should we do? And what are the implications for democracy and freedom?

Within North American and European society, many people make daily use of rapid access to information through the Internet and other means of swift electronic communication. While many other people do not, access to computer technology and the Internet is rapidly spreading around the world. The Internet has been heralded as providing not only a new means of accessing information, but of changing the ways we communicate and even the ways we think about ourselves in relation to other people and communities, and how society is structured.

But the Internet has its problems. As dependence on computerized communication increases, so, too, does the magnitude of what may happen if something goes wrong. And things do go wrong. Despite *patches* and virus-prevention programs, viruses (pieces of programmer code designed, often, with malicious intent) can cripple not only personal computers, but whole systems. And the use of e-mails, often linking to Internet Web pages, to convey unsolicited sales information is increasing to the point where a recent study found that 60 percent of e-mail communication was actually *spam*. Further, employees can spend hours of their work time accessing non-work Web sites, and there are issues about what children may read or view.

What should we do about this? Here we explore two views about the need to censor Internet content and restrict access. What solutions are there? And how might these affect other areas of our lives?

THE INTERNET NEEDS CENSORING

Instant computer communication has been in development at least since the 1960s. The Internet was initially for military use; then in the 1980s it started catching on as a means of exchange of information among academics and government users—through file transfers and, increasingly, e-mail. In the 1990s it really took off, with the development of the World Wide Web, and increasing access from homes, schools, and libraries as well as places of work. Yet, for many people it is still very new—and not everybody has Internet access. Like all new technologies, it requires some adjustment on the part of those who use it—and the technology itself is progressing, becoming increasingly complex.

Let's explain some terms: *Internet* and *World Wide Web* (or simply *the Web*) are often conflated. But essentially, *Internet* is the network connecting millions of computers around the world; *World Wide Web* is the system of *servers* connected through the Internet, which host and support files that are mostly written in a simple programming language, *HTML* (HyperText Markup Language). I have a Web site. It is on a server, and is part of the Web. You use the Internet to read the file on my Web host's server, and to read it you need to have

a *browser* (software) installed on your computer. Most e-mails today are also Web-based—and are sent from a Web server to your computer when you connect via the Internet and call in your e-mail.

The Web enables tools, such as search engines that can find things for you—indeed *to google* has become a common phrase. Some Web sites are organized as *portals,* and viewers can start from these in order to pursue their interests on the Web. Another term often used is *cyberspace.* If we see the Internet as the physical (cable or optic fibre or radio/microwave) linkages, and the Web as the servers and electronic documents that are inked, *cyberspace* refers to the social dimension—the people, the relationships, and the ways they use the Web. Some researchers prefer to talk about *cyberculture* or *cybersociety.*

But how do people use the Internet and the Web? On the one hand, it's not only instant information, but the ability to manipulate and display that information, which is growing all the time. On the other hand, while huge numbers of people around the world have access to computerized information, not all of us produce it. Increasingly, though, people are able to have some input, for instance through *blogs* (Web-logs) informing acquaintances of their thoughts or events in their lives. And, as with any technology, people use the same technology differently in different organizations, societies, or cultures. The precise effect of a new technology depends on the context into which it is introduced. The motives and attitudes of people who control the technology, and the prevailing culture—the beliefs, cultural practices, and existing technology—all make a difference. Cybercultures are complex.

The Web, for example, can be used for good or ill depending on the kind of information it carries and the way that information is organized and used. In turn, the organization and use of Web-based information is a social product; like all social products, it is shaped by culture, political power, class interest, and the value placed on efficiency. Computer use varies from one society to another and from one organization to another within the same society. People determine computer use, not *vice versa.* But some of the most influential of these people are the ones who design computers and computer software, like Microsoft's Bill Gates.

We are in the midst of a microelectronics revolution that is transforming many aspects of our society. With proper use, computers can become instruments of human betterment. What happens with wrong use?

Well, the mistakes that people make have vast potential for damage. Computer systems run our health-care system, our transport systems, our financial systems. Human error can cause immense problems. We have to train people carefully to guard against this, and we have to set fail-safe procedures in place. But what happens when messages, over the Internet, come into these systems?

Internet Problems   There are three kinds of problems that we'll deal with here—problems caused by misguided or malicious use. These include so-called computer viruses, various kinds of *spam,* and the potential content of Web sites and e-mails. Viruses—and *worms* and *trojans*—are a problem for everybody. Some are downloaded from the Internet by people trying to download software or music files or images; however, some kinds of Internet software (including e-mail readers) have loopholes that allow the mailer to be targeted by various virus-type pieces of code. Technically, a virus is a piece of program code that does something you don't expect. While some viruses (particularly those in the early days of computing) were made by people to show off their computing skills, and often did no more than put up an interesting message on the screen, very often today's viruses cause major problems, for instance erasing portions of hard drives. A computer worm is a virus that's able to replicate itself, remaining active in the memory of the computer and often using e-mailers to send copies of itself to other unsuspecting people. A trojan, short for *trojan horse,* is a piece of code that appears to be an application, but that when activated (by clicking on it) is not merely the interesting screen-saver (for instance) that you expected, but does something else, such as destroying or modifying some data. Many of the more prevalent viruses are both worms and trojans—if activated they

cause havoc, and they replicate themselves and send out copies to everybody in your e-mail address book. Most viruses target MicroSoft Windows operating systems, but some are conveyed as *macros* in word-processing software. (See McAfee or Symantec Web pages for up-to-date virus information.)

A virus in a personal computer is bad news: A virus in the computer system of a business, school, or hospital is a major problem and can cause serious financial losses. More than that, it can bring systems to a halt. Universities are particularly susceptible to viruses, as faculty and students are constantly transferring material between home and school systems, and vast floods of e-mail enter the system—not surprisingly, as universities are about creating and exchanging information, and e-mails are an ideal mechanism for this exchange. So universities—and many other organizations—have IT personnel constantly screening the system for viruses, using the latest screening techniques. They encourage people to make sure that any Windows-based home computers have up-to-date virus protection, often provided free by the organization.

Virus screening, therefore, is a necessity for everybody. What of the other problems?

Spam is the name for unsolicited e-mail messages that permeate cyberspace. How many do you receive each day in e-mail? Bill Gates, apparently, gets four million e-mails, mostly spam. Of course, he has people and programs to screen his e-mail. But spam—named for the Monty Python sketch where people could have anything to eat as long as it was tinned meat brand-named "Spam"—is increasingly a problem, for several reasons. It slows down people who want to deal with their actual e-mail; some of it is highly offensive to many people; some of it has serious financial implications if you respond; and it clogs servers and computers and in transit takes up *bandwidth* Spam includes commercial e-mail, often broadcast indiscriminantly to everybody. You get spam if a spammer has your address. A spammer gets your address if that is on a Web site somewhere, or has been on a Web site. Some spam is trying to sell lists of addresses, on CDs, to other spammers! Spam includes the computer worms discussed above, and it includes various scams—such as the "Nigerian scam" (named for its first examples, which pretended to come from people in Nigeria), which promises you lots of money but needs personal information.

Major problems with spam include not only that it wastes time, blocks servers, and can cost money, but that vulnerable people, including children, may read it. Some people have been taken in by the scams. And a lot of people worry about the extent of pornographic material that is available on the Web generally—and is promoted by spam e-mails.

This leads to the third problem: generally, the quality of material available on the Web, and specifically, issues with *cyberporn* and with other sites that promote dangerous or illegal practices. Would you want your niece learning how to build a bomb? Or would you want her reading material on a porn site? Another danger, however, lurks on the Internet: so-called Internet stalkers, who track people through their Web sites and can keep sending them unwanted e-mails, and, in particular, adults who frequent chat rooms and may pose as minors, sometimes enticing children to meet them. On the Web, people can easily disguise their identities. Countries are putting in place regulations to help deal with *cybercrimes,* which may include *grooming* and *enticement* of minors, in addition to the more obvious money scams. But to protect our children and other vulnerable members of society, we need regulation of the Web—not only rules about what can be displayed or discussed, but screening of material so that people aren't offended by things that they don't want to see.

Many Internet service providers have the ability to screen the material that gets sent to your computer. This is a particularly good thing if there are children in the household. They may also be able to screen out viruses—an excellent idea. Bill Gates is now promising software to get rid of all spam, within two years. "Net-nanny" software can screen the Web pages that your children—or you—try to access. And public libraries—where many people go to use the Internet if they don't have personal computers—often use such programs. Finally, there is the issue of people at work either getting spam e-mails, or using their work computers to access non-work sites—perhaps cyberporn sites. This is a waste of employees work-time, and may also be highly offensive to other workers sharing an office.

Many workplaces screen their employees e-mails and monitor their Web-browsing, and one can clearly see why—not only because they might find cyberporn, but because the quality of information on the Web is highly variable. The Web is a good place to find documents of government agencies or nonprofit organizations, or online academic journals. But much of the other material available is of poor quality, often outdated or produced by school students as part of their reports. We cannot rely on all, or even most, Internet information, and we know that employees will often misuse their work time. So a measure of screening is a necessity, both at home and at work. It can come from individual businesses and ISPs, or more centrally from government directives, but either way, we need it. Or, so some believe.

CENSORING THE WEB LEADS TO MORE PROBLEMS THAN IT RESOLVES

Cyberspace is not only about how information is transferred from place to place and person to person. The technology of the Web and the materials made available transform information and the uses to which it is put.

Knowledge as a Commodity in the Modern World   We are now living in what has been called the Information Age. We as a species have more information about more concepts than at any time in history. We make use of this, exchange it. Information is a commodity, to be bought and sold.

Five centuries ago, scholars could decide on what constituted the appropriate body of knowledge within any one literate society: Even fifty years ago, scholars could still demarcate the boundaries of knowledge, what was known and knowable. However, by this time the demarcated body of knowledge was far beyond the reach of a single person, so that we required specialization even within fields (e.g., within chemistry, anthropology, or literature).

This concept of the demarcated body of knowledge—of what educated people should know—was produced by the technology of the day, along with the question of whose was the "knowledge." Until the invention of the printing press, people did not have a concept of *authorship* in the modern sense. In Europe, monks spent time copying manuscripts (deemed to be the word of God). However, most knowledge, or information—information about growing crops or doing blacksmith work, or weaving—was transmitted orally from person to person. The printing press changed this by making possible the rapid copying of what had previously taken months or years. Knowledge was now a *thing* that could be disseminated among strangers, and printers became seekers after material to print. Still, the concept of authorship took several centuries before it gained its modern form.

With the concept of authorship, or of ownership of knowledge, came ideas about standards for knowledge. Eventually the standard, in the popular mind, became what was printed. Mirroring this, we currently distinguish between knowledge producers and knowledge consumers. *Producers* are people who, for whatever reason, are viewed as "experts" and who can get their works into print: whether as academics through peer-reviewed journals and monographs, or as "hands-on" experts through the medium of popular books, or as reporters in far-off places who tell us through newspapers and magazines what is happening in the world.

Consumers, by contrast, are people who use the knowledge so produced, who buy the thousands of *how-to* books. They go to school and college to gain knowledge and skills from their teachers, and then into the world of work, in theory at least, to use this knowledge and these skills, only to find, today, that they require *more*. Producers are themselves consumers, and as such must make clear distinction, in academic publications, between what is "their" knowledge and what has come from other people. The ownership of knowledge is important, both for its own sake and for its market value. Knowledge is a commodity, to be owned and sold.

The Web changes this relationship between consumers, producers, and knowledge. Indeed it may change the whole way we view information and also change the relations of its production. But before exploring these ideas, let us first examine who uses the Internet, and how and where they do so.

The Growth of Cybersociety   In late 1995, an American Internet Survey showed that only 6.4 percent of all U.S. households had one or more Internet users. (These figures did not include people who used only e-mail.) Yet while the figures were small they showed a dramatic growth—half of surveyed users had begun using the Internet during 1995. This was the take-off of the Internet. By August 1996, 23 percent of the combined populations of the United States and Canada had Internet access. By 2000, there were ten countries in which over 10 percent of the population were Internet users. Also in 2000, the number of Web pages exceeded 2 billion—and was estimated to be growing at 7 million per day. By 2004, 68.8 percent of the U.S. population and 64.2 percent of the Canadian population were Internet users. The Netherlands and Iceland scored over 66 percent, Britain over 58 percent—but the highest uptake went to Sweden, with 74.6 percent of the population defined as Internet users.

It seems unlikely that all people will ever have Internet access, and at least in the foreseeable future the majority of the world's population will not. But many now do. What are the implications of this growth—and how do they relate to the questions of censorship or screening that we've raised?

First, there are implications for business organization, with increasing numbers of people working on computers for much of the day—making contacts, tracking orders, and so on—and some of these are able to work from home. And Internet sales are taking off. But some researchers have pointed to deeper implications. The point of the Internet revolution, they say, is neither that it leads to adjustments in employment, nor that consumers use the World Wide Web directly to purchase products.

Instead, the revolutionary potential of the Internet is that it recreates information as something that is commonly shared and exchanged, not a commodity that is to be owned. The Internet is described in phrases such as the Commons of Information and the *Agora* (in Howard Reingold's phrase)—the market-place of ancient Greek cities where people walked and talked.

Another fascinating aspect of the electronic agora is that it is made up of people who have probably never physically met each other, but share beliefs and ideologies, give mutual support, and exchange ideas on a regular basis. The result is a creation of worldwide virtual communities— communities of interest and shared viewpoint that are unhampered by distance and many of the social factors (age, race, gender, class) that often keep otherwise similar people from meeting or interacting with one another.

The Control Issue   Currently the Internet is anarchic. There is no centralized control, and from some points of view, this is a good and healthy thing. What happens when there is censorship?

This question of the type of information available is a difficult one to deal with. If access to the Internet is free and open, anyone can post what they want. This leaves scope for new ideas to surface—and also for hate literature and obscenities. How can the Internet community control the latter without removing the ability of people to speak freely on issues that matter deeply to them?

Many Internet providers have attempted voluntary controls, asking people not to post "offensive" material on their sites. To an extent this does work. However there are campaigns to censor whole categories of material, and some countries have gone beyond this. It is clear that any censorship of the Internet can prevent important ideas from being openly debated. Let's look briefly at some examples.

First, while everybody wants to stop viruses, even antivirus screening can have its problems— if genuine but nonstandard messages are caught in the net. One of the authors sent a message to a colleague containing an important electronic form for a research grant competition. It was blocked as a nonstandard attachment and the colleague was unable to reclaim it from his university server.

Numerous commercial "net nanny" programs are designed to prevent children or adolescents from finding material that parents do not wish them to read. These may be in use not only in homes (where parents can switch them off) but in libraries and other public Internet facilities. They work by screening out sites containing certain words. Screening all messages for the word *rape* will prevent reception of violent pornographic messages that contain this word, but will also remove, or prevent, feminist discussion of problems of date rape among adolescents. A 2001 study testing three nanny programs found that the results of searches on standard women's studies topics were much reduced or indeed completely blocked. However, these programs give purchasers a choice, to use or not to use them. State censorship gives no choice, and mandatory censoring of library material is not much better.

Screening of e-mail messages to filter spam or abusive messages has been tried. Many people use their own *spam filters*. They can "train" them and some of the filters are very good—and they enable people to check, periodically, to see if *false positives* have been screened out by the filter. But when these are applied by an ISP or by an employer, the end user has much less opportunity to set their own parameters for the filter. And people who have sent real messages have no warning that their messages have not been received. A study of messages sent to the British House of Commons found, in 2003, that a high proportion of messages were blocked for "offensive" content—mostly for words that might in some contexts be sexually offensive, but in others were not. (For instance, s-e-x occurs in the name Sexton, and in any discussion of "sexuality" as a source of potential discrimination.) Furthermore, it was discovered that the software was blocking all messages sent in Welsh—yet regular spam was still getting through!

We have assumed, in the above examples, that people might want to block material because it contains offensive language. But state censorship, such as that in place in China from the mid 1990s through 2004, targets political ideas. Researcher

John Tkacik says that in China "the Internet is now a tool of police surveillance and official disinformation." And this brings up yet another problem with censoring, whether by state or library or employer—the ability to find out what people are viewing or contributing to. Issues such as the right to privacy are central to the concerns of many researchers. Browsing can be monitored with cookies and Web bugs. What personal information is being gathered on each of us, and by whom—and how will this be used?

Summing Up

Without vigilance on the part of users, the Internet could go from being a fairly anarchic network of information providers and communicators, to a means of surveillance. Already there is potential to track the messages and Web-site accesses of individual users. The threat here is of the Internet becoming the *panopticon*—the all-seeing eye that allows people in authority to monitor people's thoughts and communications. Some Internet users are campaigning on issues of privacy and security of information, including the information they transmit when they connect to any site.

Internet communication is changing society. Increasing numbers of people can share their information and their experiences. But the final form of that change is not yet clear. Will it be the free "Agora" that Howard Reingold discussed? Or will it be a forum that is highly controlled, where startling or sensitive material is excluded in the name of protecting vulnerable members of society? The Internet issue throws into clear relief the somewhat abstract issues of rights to information property, liberty versus authority, geographic community versus constructed community, and technology-in-theory versus technology-in-social-use. Much of the twenty-first century will be taken up with democratically resolving issues that—before this century and the rise of Internet—were of only theoretical interest.

Review Exercises

For Discussion and Debate

1. "The Internet is just a big waste of time for most people. More work-hours are lost on the Internet than through sick-days or people sleeping on the job."
2. Free, rapid exchange of information—will it change your life?
3. "The Internet has revolutionary potential as great as that of the printing press."
4. Censorship of the Internet—pros and cons.

Writing Exercises

Write a brief (500-word) essay on one of the following topics:

1. "Women and the Internet: Are women still a numerical minority online?"
2. "My own experience. How I use the Internet, and why."
3. "Why members of minorities should (or should not) invest time in the Internet."
4. "The Internet as an Agora."

Research Activities

1. Find current statistics on the growth of the Internet, and examine these. How has the Internet grown since you left high school? Since this book was written? (Hint: Find these statistics on the Internet. Some possible sites are http://www.clickz.com/stats/; http://www.glreach.com/globstats/; and http://www.internetworldstats.com.)

2. Search for the use of the Internet by members of any small-scale group who share a common goal or orientation to the world, such as environmental groups or non-mainstream religions (or even fans of a TV show or a music band). How do group members use the Internet to create community?
3. Survey ten students on their Internet use. What are the most common uses (e.g., e-mail, MUD, news, WWW surfing) and how much time do they spend on Internet use? How many are information producers via the Internet in addition to being information consumers?
4. Conduct a study of a *Usenet Newsgroup*. Sort the messages according to whether they fall into the categories of NOISE (extraneous comments, hellos or "me too" messages, insults or "flames," or "spams" attempting to sell products across a wide range of newsgroups) or SIGNAL (messages that actually attempt to convey information or add material to a discussion). Share your findings with friends who have studied different newsgroups. What would you recommend to a sociologist seeking information about people's opinions or behavior, about using newsgroups as a source of material?

SELECTED REFERENCES

Anderson, John W. 2003. "New Media, New Publics: Reconfiguring the Public Sphere of Islam." *Social Research,* 70, 3:887–906.

Blais, Pamela. 1996. "How the Information Revolution Is Shaping Our Communities." *Planning Commissioners Journal.* Available online at http://www.plannersweb.com/articles/bla118.html.

Cyberlaw Research Unit. "Cyber-Rights and Cyber Liberties." Available online at http://www.cyber-rights.org/. Accessed 22 November 2004.

Electronic Frontier Foundation. 2001. "Public Interest Position on Junk E-Mail: Protect Innocent Users." EFF Statement Regarding Anti-Spam Measures. Available online at http://www.eff.org/Spam_cybersquatting_abuse/Spam/position_on_junk_email.php. Accessed 25 November 2004.

Escobar, Arturo, David Hess, Isabel Licha and Will Sibley. 1994. "Welcome to Cyberia: Notes on the Anthropology of Cyberculture." *Current Anthropology* 35, 3 (June): 211–223.

Forester, Tom. 1992. "Megatrends or Megamistakes: What Ever Happened to the Information Society?" *Information Society* 8, 3 (July–Sept.): 133–146.

Gumpert, Gary and Susan J. Drucker. 1992. "From the Agora to the Electronic Shopping Mall." *Critical Studies in Mass Communication* 9, 2 (June): 186–200.

Heins, Marjorie. 2001. "Criminalising Online Speech to 'Protect' the Young: What Are the Benefits and Costs?" In *Crime and the Internet,* edited by David Wall. London and New York: Routledge.

Hines, Andy. 1994. "Jobs and Infotech: Work in the Information Society." *Futurist* 28, 1 (Jan.–Feb.): 9–13.

Kroker, Arthur and Michael A. Weinstein. 1994. "The Political Economy of Virtual Reality." *Canadian Journal of Political and Social Theory* 17, 1–2:1–31.

Lyon, David. 1993. "An Electronic Panopticon? A Sociological Critique of Surveillance Theory." *Sociological Review* 41, 4 (Nov.): 653–678.

Mantovani, Giuseppe. 1994. "Is Computer-Mediated Communication Intrinsically Apt to Enhance Democracy in Organizations?" *Human Relations* 47, 1 (Jan.): 45–62.

Markus, M. Lynne, Tora K. Bikson and Maha El-Shinnawy. 1992. "Fragments of Your Communication: E-Mail, V-Mail, and Fax." *Information Society* 8, 4 (Oct.–Dec.): 207–226.

Marx, Gary T. 1991. "The New Surveillance." *National Forum* 71, 3 (Summer): 32–36.

Menzies, Heather. 1996. *Whose Brave New World? The Information Highway and the New Economy.* Toronto: Between the Lines.

Mitchell, William J. 1995. *City of Bits: Space, Place, and the Infobahn.* Boston, MA: MIT Press.

Myers, Daniel J. 1994. "Communication Technology and Social Movements: Contributions of Computer Networks to Activism." *Social Science Computer Review* 12, 2 (Summer): 250–260.

Rakow, Lana F. and Vija Navarro. 1993. "Remote Mothering and the Parallel Shift: Women Meet the Cellular Telephone." *Critical Studies in Mass Communication* 10, 2 (June): 144–157.

Rheingold, Howard. 1993. *Virtual Reality.* London: Secker and Warburg.

———. 1996. *The Virtual Community.* Available online at http://www.well.com/user/hlr/vcbook/vcbookintro.html. Accessed 24 November 2004.

———. "Rheingold's Brainstorms." Available online at http://www.rheingold.com/index.html. Accessed 24 November 2004.

Sachs, Hiram. 1995. "Computer Networks and the Formation of Public Opinion: An Ethnographic Study." *Media, Culture and Society* 17, 1 (Jan.): 81–99.

Sampaio, Anna and Janni Aragon. 2001. "Filtered Feminisms: Cybersex, E-Commerce and the Construction of Women's Bodies in Cyberspace." *Women's Studies Quarterly* 29, 3–4:126–147.

Schroeder, Ralph. 1993. "Virtual Reality in the Real World: History, Applications and Projections." *Futures* 25, 9 (Nov.): 963–973.

Sewell, Graham and Barry Wilkinson. 1992. "'Someone to Watch Over Me': Surveillance, Discipline and the Just-in-Time Process." *Sociology* 26, 2 (May): 271–289.

Snider, James H. 1994. "Democracy Online: Tomorrow's Electronic Electorate." *Futurist* 28, 5 (Sept.–Oct.): 15–19.

Spender, Dale. 1995. *Nattering on the Net: Women, Power and Cyberspace.* Toronto: Garamond.

Thurlow, Crispin, Laura Lengel and Alice Tomic. 2003. *Computer Mediated Communication: Social Interaction and the Internet.* London, Thousand Oaks and Toronto: Sage.

Tkacik, John J., Jr. 2004. "China's Orwellian Internet: October 8." *The Heritage Foundation: Policy, Research and Analysis.* Available online at http://www.heritage.org/Research/AsiaandthePacific/bg1806.cfm. Accessed 24 November 2004.

Tribe, Lawrence. 1991. "The Constitution in Cyberspace: Law and Liberty beyond the Electronic Frontier." *Humanist* 51, 5 (Sept.–Oct.): 15–21.

Turkle, Sherry. 1994. "Constructions and Reconstructions of Self in Virtual Reality." *Mind, Culture, and Activity: An International Journal* 1, 3 (Summer): 158–167.

Walther, Joseph B., Jeffrey F. Anderson and David W. Park. 1994. "Interpersonal Effects in Computer-Mediated Interaction: A Meta-Analysis of Social and Antisocial Communication." *Communication Research* 21, 4 (Aug.): 460–487.

Webster, Frank. 1994. "What Information Society?" *Information Society* 10, 1 (Jan.–Mar.): 1–23.

15.3   Has Individualism Become Excessive?

The issue: Life, liberty, and the pursuit of happiness: People have flocked to America from around the world to follow their own individual dreams. But is it actually possible to build a society on energetic individualism? The loneliness and anxiety of many Americans suggests something else is needed.

The question of individualism ties in with both that of the Internet—currently a vehicle for individual expression—and that of environmental change, discussed earlier. *Individualism* has different meanings to different people. To some it means an emphasis on self-actualization, which in turn can be viewed as either a search for personal fulfillment or the selfishness attributed to the "Me-generation" of the 1980s. That is not where we will be going in this discussion.

Instead, we will outline the development of "the individual" in Western society, and point to differences between Western and non-Western interpretations of relations between individuals and society. We examine the view, first, that there is too much emphasis on "the individual," that it indeed has become excessive. Then we turn to an examination of how this concept has benefited people in society, and how it is used today. Finally, we weigh both problems and benefits, and ask if there is any route society can take that emphasizes both the individual and community.

The concept of "the individual" has grown up over time, and varies from one culture to another. This notion seems strange to many Westerners, for whom the idea of "being an individual" is natural and self-evident. Society is made up of people and each person feels herself or himself to be an individual, right? Well, not exactly.

If we look around the world, we can see societies in which this concept of the individual does not exist. People are first and foremost members of clans, lineages, kin groups, or families. Instead of acting in the world as individuals, they act as representatives of these groups, indeed as extensions of them, and think about themselves in these terms. This view has sometimes been described as *familism* and disparaged by advocates of Western-style modernity, as we saw earlier.

Consider a few differences between the Western individualistic perspective and the community-based orientation described by ethnopsychologists. For instance, among the Ifaluk, a people who live on a Pacific atoll, it is the community, not the individual, that has rights, and the community, not the individual, that owns property. Even cigarettes are viewed as community property, and a failure to share them will arouse anger within the community.

Within Western society today, individualism is both an orientation of people toward their everyday world and an orientation of social scientists who study that world and these people. In the sections that follow, we first discuss the popular conception of individualism, then look at individualist versus sociohistoric paradigms of understanding society.

CONSTRUCTING INDIVIDUALISM?

What Is an Individual?   Interest in and concern with "the individual" has a long history within Western thought, but it has rarely been as prevalent as it is today. In the literature of the Middle Ages

we can find narratives of people whose behavior, though related to society and based on social concepts of proper conduct, is that of individuals, with unique properties and feelings.

Examples come from the poetry and prose of Northern Europe, in the old English epic of Beowulf, or sagas such as that of Grettir the Strong. At this time the dominant ideology was that of every person with their place in society; but there was room for individualism of a type we might recognize today. It was later that the concept of the individual became central to Western Society. The American and French revolutions had their philosophical bases in Liberalism—a reaction against the old order of the feudal system. Liberal individualism suggested people acted on rational self-interest, to pursue and achieve goals that seemed good to them. Society came to be seen as composed of interacting, goal-directed people.

In the nineteenth century, the philosopher John Stuart Mill wrote that we could understand society by understanding the motivations, actions, and goals of its individual people:

> Men . . . in a state of society are still men: Their actions and passions are obedient to the laws of individual human nature. . . . Human beings in society have no properties but those which are derived from, and may be resolved into, the laws of the nature of individual man.

Today, following Mill, the philosophical concepts of *freedom, the individual,* and *individual rights*—the basis of philosophical liberalism—are everywhere mentioned in political, constitutional, and everyday discourse. However, some fear we have lost too much through this emphasis on the individual—and some sociologists point out that preserving individual rights requires both individual and collective responsibility.

INDIVIDUALISM HAS BECOME EXCESSIVE

In North America, there is a strong emphasis on the individual, and his or her thoughts, freedom, and rights. Each person is urged to "be an individual."

The focus, in popular thought, is on seeing each person apart from all others. In this view, a community is a collection of individuals who have chosen to live together for their mutual benefit. Each one of us has the right to further our own interest as best we can, to succeed to the best of our ability.

This easily leads to a view that each person is in competition with all others for resources. In the discussion about environment, we saw the results of this. The Tragedy of the Commons occurs when individual people are motivated—even obligated—to maximize their interests at the eventual expense of the community through the destruction of resources previously available to all.

Further, the search for individual success or individual expression can be detrimental to relationships within communities and families. Communities "work" because people cooperate within them, to their mutual advantage. But if each person stands for her or his own interests, the community does not automatically thrive; often, it disintegrates.

Some people think of this in the context of the smallest human community—the family. Half a century ago, in the 1950s, Betty Friedan wrote of "the problem that has no name" in her book *The Feminine Mystique.* A generation of women were feeling themselves to be trapped as homemakers in a world that did not value their domestically based work. For many of these women and their present-day descendants, the solution was to seek fulfillment as individuals in the public world of work and politics. The result, some say, has been a generation of children growing up within households in which their care has been relegated to paid assistants, because both parents (in the case of a two-parent family) are heavily involved with outside interests, and where pressure on these parents—to appear successful and self-reliant, economically, emotionally, and spiritually—is still increasing.

The intense focus on the individual results in the high level of stress displayed by many people today. Workplace health programs advertise stress-reduction courses, in which people are told to engage in recreation activities and within the workplace to delegate responsibilities. The programs do not examine the source of stress in the extreme levels of performance required of people as individuals. Within the workplace, all people have to perform to the same standards and show themselves willing to put in the same long hours, regardless of the other responsibilities that lie on their shoulders. Here, individualism has gone too far. Indeed, are they behaving as "individuals"?

Politically, an extreme individualist position suggests that individuals, and by extension the society that is composed of many individuals, does best when individuals are free to act as they wish. In the words of a classic movie, "we don't need no damn organizations" to run our lives or make decisions for us. This position takes the stance of *rugged individualism,* or self-sufficiency. (It goes along with a dictum to "think for yourself" and "not be politically correct.") Yet a little sociological reflection indicates that for people today, self-sufficiency can never be total, but must go hand-in-hand with the ability to exchange the produce of one household with that of another.

The organizations of society may be in need of reform, but they represent the sum of people coming together to create a community in which all can benefit. In the United States and Canada, the government is accountable to the electorate. Abolition of governmental organizations does not result in greater freedom for all. In fact, governmental regulations have reduced the *freedom* of some—to oppress, to use racial slurs, to pay wages so low that people cannot live on them—in the interests of increasing the freedom of the many people who make up our society. To reduce the role of government may be to revert to what Thomas Hobbes described as "the war of all against all." Philosophical liberalism did not take such a Hobbesian position, but argued that the rights of some must be weighed against the rights of all—for example, the rights of some people to breathe smoke against the rights of all to breathe clean air.

Political parties, including those in government, often take positions that many people disagree with. This is the nature of politics within a democracy: Different groups propose their solutions and then the electorate can decide. Within a pluralist state, groups cannot merely count the weight of numbers of their own supporters, but must show how their policies are beneficial for all within the state. In this area, the extreme individualist position may too easily lead to the horrors of ethnic nationalism discussed in Chapter 6. When all are out for themselves, each is likely to distrust and fear people whose goals are most opposed to their own. Not all people are natural leaders, and they will seek leaders to follow. They are easy prey for demagogues, who seek to further their own interests through attracting a following that does not question their motives but accepts a simple-minded rhetoric.

The extreme popular individualism of the present day is attracting increasing numbers of supporters. It forms part of the ideology of North America—each person for her- or himself, self-reliant, self-sufficient, and with the rights of the individual in opposition to the rights of the entire community. This is a philosophy profoundly attractive to many people holding high positions in large corporations. In recent years we have seen the development of a technique used to prevent people from banding together and making use of state agencies on, in particular, environmental issues: the SLAPP, or Strategic Lawsuit Against Public Participation.

This works as follows. A developer (for instance) has purchased land and plans to start building on it. Local residents are concerned about the effect on wetlands. They debate the issue and petition the Department of Environmental Protection, asking for a review of the environmental impact. They receive notification that they, each as an individual, are being sued for character defamation and for interfering with the developer's right to use his or her property. The result of such SLAPP actions has been to silence some activists and make others cautious about what they do.

In this situation, people's collective rights to assembly and to approach government by peaceful means are being seriously eroded. The government agencies that should assist them are also being targeted. The call for less government (and lower taxes) in people's lives results in decreased funding for many government agencies and programs, with environmental agencies, education, and social programs high on the list for cutbacks. The doctrine of individualism holds that people must achieve on their own merits, and so welfare programs and Head Start programs lose funding.

Individualism has also been attacked from the *right* or conservative tradition by social theorists who promote what is called *communitarianism.* Their idea is that individual lives are lived—and can only be lived—within the context of communities; it is only within communities that individual rights and opportunities become available. Thus, defense of the community is properly seen as a form of enlightened self-interest for everyone. Seen in this way, traditional virtues such as commitment, loyalty, faithfulness, sociability, and even conformity to social standards are strategies for self-preservation and personal development. They also make people better spouses, parents, workers, and friends. Conversely, without these personal traits and healthy relationships, human life is isolated, rapacious, and unfulfilling.

Thus, the communitarians (among others) have put an increasing emphasis on the role of *civil society* as the source of social organization and personal development. This is that portion of social life that exists in neither the economy nor the state, but includes families, clubs, churches—indeed, all voluntary associations. The claim is that just as we cannot expect to get everything we need through our isolated individual pursuits, neither can we expect to get it in the marketplace or through a government program. Not only does civil society make available what other social structures do not; the very process of creating and maintaining a civil society is essential to a meaningful human existence.

INDIVIDUALISM IS NOT THE PROBLEM, AND CAN BE HELPFUL

But now, let us try to imagine the same situation without a concept of individualism; for example, if we had modern technology but no private property.

What would be the pressures on the community to develop, regardless of environmental concerns? Who would control the decision-making? Who would have the final say?

It is not clear what the outcome would be. Many traditional communities around the world do not share our western concept of the individual. Many communities attempt to control and resist the influx of developers who seek to "improve" and modernize land use, such as the determined protests of the tribal people of Gandmardhan against Bauxite mining. These people seek to defend their lifestyle and their land, where their identity as a tribal people is inextricably linked to the land and its use.

And what about the SLAPP lawsuits? We viewed these earlier, as the manifestation of extreme individualism, preventing the communal responses of community-minded, and environmentally minded citizen groups. However there are other ways they can be viewed. Dominant ideology in North America has tended to distance people from their environment conceptually. We can indeed say that the idealization of "the individual" has formed part of this distancing. Yet, within North America we now see people from many different backgrounds uniting, because of the beliefs and values they have chosen as individuals to adopt, in order to resist threats to their common well-being.

The concept of the individual, arising along with Western capitalism, was initially that of the rational person (envisaged as male), acting to maximize self-interest or profit within the opportunities offered by the economic, social, and physical environment. From this followed the concept of individual rights and freedoms. One result of this has been the acknowledgment that people as individuals must be free to choose lifestyles and beliefs, and that these choices are shaped by culture and education. The environmental protests are brought by people who have a right as individuals to protest, and a right to join with others to make the protest communal. Looked at this way, SLAPP lawsuits are as much an attack on individual rights as they are on community rights.

Within North America and across the world, people are contacting others, listening to their stories, and making common cause with them. The individualism of North America leads to innovation not only of technology but of ideas. With today's methods of communication, people are able to exchange news and views through the Internet. Rather than eroding community values, today's individualism permits people to create their communities and feel that they have a say in how these communities develop.

There are excesses of individualism, and abuses of power resulting from these. However, on balance Western individualism has the potential for great good within the societies in which it presently flourishes, so long as it is tempered with a recognition that responsibilities go along with rights, and that other people, as individuals and societies, have rights also.

What Is Missing in the Argument   Our view of individualism lies between the pessimism of the first argument and the optimism of the second. Both are views that are commonly expressed. Something, however, is missing from both of them. Let us examine what it may be.

With the Tragedy of the Commons, the problem is not that individualism drives each farmer to compete until resources are extinguished. Rather, the structure of the economy is such that continuous expansion is the only way for enterprises to remain in business. Individual competition is not the problem; instead, it is a symptom of particular kinds of economic pressures. Competition between villages, or regions, or nations can be just as devastating. The state communism—or state capitalism—of the former Soviet Union provides an example.

The two perspectives above both result from an idealist philosophical approach to the world: the notion that people's actions are driven by their ideas and conceptions. Although this is a popular viewpoint, many sociologists reject it. People plan their actions and base their behavior on what they know, surely, but they act within the real constraints of the resources available to them, and, within a materialist perspective of history and society, it is the concepts of what people are that track the practicalities of what people do, not the other way around.

Thus, instead of seeing individualism as the factor causing social changes of one type or another, we can see its spread as a result of western capitalism. An individualist outlook is beneficial to certain kinds of capitalist development. The concept of individual property ownership facilitates capitalist development. It is in the interests of developers, therefore, to encourage ideas that are individualist rather than communalist. (This gives another slant on the concept of "everyone as an individual" taught in schools.) Yet it must be said here that some studies from formerly communist countries don't necessarily show that capitalism brings an individualist orientation. For instance, a study of capitalism in a Siberian city found a strong collectivist approach by people working and living in strong community groups, along traditional patterns. The relationship of capitalism to individualism is not a simple one.

Yet individualism, in maintaining that each person has potentially the same rights, holds that each person has the right to self-expression, to have their case heard. In practice, some people find that these rights are easier to exercise if they band together with others, and so new communities of ideas and association are born.

Individualism has developed over time in the Western world, along with capitalism. Today it is part of the dominant North American culture, and as such it is implicated in both the excesses of development and resistance to these, as we saw in earlier chapters. Individualism can be exceptionally problematic for many in North America—particularly people who do not form part of the dominant culture and who do not necessarily place the same emphasis on it. However, as mentioned, that same individualism has alerted many people within the dominant culture to the fact that they must, to be true to their principles, support the rights of other people to find their own identities within their cultures. Increasingly, the issue of human rights is seen to predominate in global and national issues, but human rights include those of cultural liberty as well as individual freedoms.

Summing Up

This section concludes with questions instead of answers, and with two further examples. At times, it does seem that individualism may hinder the search to solve social problems. An example comes in looking at prison populations in the United States and Japan, countries that have diametrically opposed views of how to deal with criminals. American prison populations are large and expanding, and offenders generally re-offend. Those in Japan are small and declining, with the proportion who re-offend being small. Dominant ideologies of who has responsibility for crime are very different in the two countries. In Japan, crime is seen as an offense against society. Criminals are expected to admit that they have offended, accept responsibility for the offense, apologize, and try to make good the offense by serving society through a form of community service. The attitude is that to separate the offender from society only prevents him or her from taking appropriate action. In return, the community of neighbors and kin accepts the responsibility of helping to keep the offender from re-offending; if he or she does, this brings great shame on that community.

In North America, an offender is separated from the community, which takes no official responsibility for his or her actions. Instead the offender is sent to live with other offenders. This the Japanese see as merely giving him or her the opportunity to learn how to be a better offender. Meanwhile, vast sums in Western economies go to the building, maintenance, and staffing of prisons that remain full to overflowing, as we saw in an earlier section on prisons.

Japan has perhaps struck a better balance—a culture that places importance on both the individual and community, and sees both as having responsibilities and rights. Each society, ours included, has to find its own balance; but now the pendulum has swung very sharply away from community interests.

In this book, we have seen many examples of both individualism and collectivism. One thing that you, as readers, might do now is to return to some of the disputes we have indicated, for instance, about culture and poverty, or about appropriations of religious and spiritual heritage, or about the environment and the U.S. refusal to ratify the Kyoto Accord. How are ideas of individualism versus collectivism implicated in these? How do different strands of society adhere to one or other side in these issues? And how can we, as citizens of a global as well as national community, help our communities to find that balance?

REVIEW EXERCISES

For Discussion and Debate

1. "It takes a whole village to raise a child," some people say. Who should have responsibility for child care—individuals or the community?
2. "There is no individualism today because we're all expected to behave just like everybody else."
3. "What will give the best care for the environment, an individualistic or a collectivistic approach?"
4. The cult of individualism actively promotes conformity in North America today.

Writing Exercises

Write a brief (500-word) essay on one of the following topics:

1. "How can I be myself, and not a part of my community?"
2. The philosophy of Western Liberalism is based on a concept of the individual as a white, male European who acts out of rational self-interest. What relevance does this have for the present day?
3. How can we achieve true community that at the same time acknowledges people as individuals?
4. "My family and how they form part of who I am today."

Research Activities

1. Work with a group of four to six others. List which of your attributes seem to you to be most "individualistic" and most "communalistic." Discuss.
2. Media research: Watch three hours of TV, noting down commercials you see in this time. Analyze how people are portrayed: as individuals or as members of an (ethnic, religious, or gender) group.
3. What is "individualism"? Devise a questionnaire on characteristics and prevalence of individualism, and use it to interview 15–20 people. Tabulate results for presentation to the class.
4. Interview three people who are as different as possible from each other (e.g., members of different ethnic groups or age groups). Ask them to explain who they are and to tell you something of their backgrounds and life history. Analyze their interviews to show how history and community form part of their identities.

SELECTED REFERENCES

Alexander, Jeffrey C. and Philip Smith. 1993. "The Discourse of American Civil Society: A New Proposal for Cultural Studies." *Theory and Society* 22, 2 (Apr.): 151–207.

Allik, J. and A. Realo. 2004. "Individualism-Collectivism and Social Capital." *Journal of Cross-Cultural Psychology* 35, 1:29–49.

Arato, Andrew. 1990. "Revolution, Civil Society and Democracy." *Praxis International* 10, 1–2 (Apr.–July): 24–38.

Bell, Daniel. 1989. "'American Exceptionalism' Revisited: The Role of Civil Society." *Public Interest* 95 (Spring): 38–56.

Bendix, Reinhard. 1990–1991. "State, Legitimation and 'Civil Society.'" *Telos* 86 (Winter): 143–152.

Bianchin, M. 2003. "Reciprocity, Individuals and Community: Remarks on Phenomenology, Social Theory and Politics." *Philosophy & Social Criticism* 9, 6:631–654.

Calhoun, Craig. 1993. "Civil Society and the Public Sphere." *Public Culture* 5, 2 (Winter): 267–280.

Cohen, Jean L. and Andrew Arato. 1992. *Civil Society and Political Theory.* Cambridge, MA: MIT Press.

Dold, Catherine. 1995. "SLAPP Back!" In *Social Problems: The Search for Solutions,* edited by Frank R. Scarpitti and F. Kurt Cylke. Los Angeles, CA: Roxbury.

Etzioni, Amitai. 1992. "Too Many Rights, Too Few Responsibilities." *National Forum* 72, 1 (Winter): 4–6.

———, Timothy Willard and Daniel M. Fields. 1991. "The Community in an Age of Individualism." *Futurist* 25, 3 (May–June): 35–39.

Friedan, Betty. 1963. *The Feminine Mystique.* New York: Norton.

Gellner, Ernest. 1991. "Civil Society in Historical Context." *International Social Science Journal* 43, 3 (129) (Aug.): 495–510.

Gitlin, Todd. 1995. "After the Failed Faiths: Beyond Individualism, Marxism, and Multiculturalism." *World Policy Journal* 12, 1 (Spring): 61–68.

Hall, John A. 1994. "After the Fall: An Analysis of Postcommunism." *British Journal of Sociology* 45, 4 (Dec.): 525–542.

Hayes, Jeffrey W. and Seymour Martin Lipset. 1993–1994. "Individualism: A Double-Edged Sword." *Responsive Community* 4, 1 (Winter): 69–80.

Healy, Geraldine, Harriet Bradley and Nupur Mukherjee. 2004. "Individualism and Collectivism Revisited: A Study of Black and Minority Ethnic Women." *Industrial Relations Journal* 35, 5 (Sept.): 451–466.

Jensen, Lene Arnett. 1995. "Habits of the Heart Revisited: Autonomy, Community, and Divinity in Adults' Moral Language." *Qualitative Sociology* 1 (Spring): 71–86.

Kateb, George. 1989. "Individualism, Communitarianism, and Docility." *Social Research* 56, 4 (Winter): 921–942.

Kumar, Krishnan and Christopher G. A. Bryant. 1993. "Civil Society: An Inquiry into the Usefulness of an Historical Term." *British Journal of Sociology* 44, 3 (Sept.): 375–395.

Leys, Colin. 1996. "Rational Choice or Hobson's Choice?" *Studies in Political Economy* 49:37–79.

Lodge, George C. 1992. "Ideology and National Competitiveness." *Journal of Managerial Issues* 4, 3 (Fall): 321–338.

Mulhall, Stephen and Adam Swift. 1992. *Liberals and Communitarians.* Cambridge, MA: Blackwell.

Mundy, Liza. 1995. "The Success Story of the War on Poverty." In *Social Problems: The Search for Solutions,* edited by Frank R. Scarpitti and F. Kurt Cylke, Jr. Los Angeles, CA: Roxbury.

Okosun, T. Y. 2003. "And Now Justice for Me Too." *Online Journal of Justice Studies* 1, 2.

Phillips, Derek L. 1993. *Looking Backward: A Critical Appraisal of Communitarian Thought.* Princeton, NJ: Princeton University Press.

Sampson, Edward E. 1991. *Social Worlds, Personal Lives.* San Diego, CA: Harcourt Brace Jovanovich.

Selznick, Philip. 1992. *The Moral Commonwealth: Social Theory and the Promise of Community.* Berkeley, CA: University of California Press.

Shils, Edward. 1991. "The Virtue of Civil Society." *Government and Opposition* 26, 1 (Winter): 3–20.

Shiva, Andana. 1993. "Homeless in the 'Global Village.'" In *Ecofeminism,* edited by Maria Mies and Vandana Shiva. London: Zed Books.

Short, J. R. 2001. "Civic Engagement and Urban America." *City: Analysis of Urban Trends, Culture, Theory, Policy, Action* 5, 3 (Nov.): 271–280.

Spencer, Sara Busse. 2004. "Social Relations in Post-Soviet Society: Russian Capitalism Embedded." *Dissertation Abstracts International, A: The Humanities and Social Sciences* 64, 7 (June).

Taylor, Charles and Partha Chatterjee. 1990. "Modes of Civil Society." *Public Culture* 3, 1 (Fall): 95–118.

Triandis, Harry C. 1993. "Collectivism and Individualism as Cultural Syndromes." *Cross Cultural Research* 27, 3–4 (Aug.–Mar.): 155–180.

Walzer, Michael. 1994. "Multiculturalism and Individualism." *Dissent* 41, 2 (175) (Spring): 185–191.

Werbach, Adam. 2004. "A Dangerous Legacy: Bush's 'Ownership Society' Champions a Hyper-Individualism That Threatens the Commons." *In These Times*. Available online at http://www.commondreams.org/views04/1029-35.htm.

Wildavsky, Aaron. 1994. "Why Self-Interest Means Less Outside of a Social Context: Cultural Contributions to a Theory of Rational Choices." *Journal of Theoretical Politics* 6, 2 (Apr.): 131–159.

Wiley, Norbert. 1994. "History of the Self: From Primates to Present." *Sociological Perspectives* 37, 4 (Winter): 527–545.